KV-193-666

The Techniques of Production Management

Holt U.K. Management Books

Consultant Editor: Ray Wild
Administrative Staff College, Henley

The Techniques of
Production Management

Ray Wild

Administrative Staff College, Henley

Holt, Rinehart and Winston Ltd

London · New York · Sydney · Toronto

To my wife, without whom this would have
been impossible, and to the future without
which it would have been unnecessary.

First printed in Great Britain in 1971
Reprinted 1974
Reprinted 1975
Reprinted 1976
Reprinted 1977
Reprinted 1978

Copyright © 1971 by Holt, Rinehart and Winston Ltd
All rights reserved
SBN 03 910153 3

Reproduced Photolitho in Great Britain by
J. W. Arrowsmith Ltd., Bristol

Preface

This is a book about Production Management. The production function in business is concerned with the conversion or transformation processes, and such processes are technologically diverse, embracing both manufacture (i.e. the conversion of inputs into goods) and the provision of services. In this book production is identified with the processes by which goods are produced. Production management is therefore identified with manufacture, but much of what is discussed is pertinent to other types of transformation process since, whilst such processes may differ technologically, their associated managerial problems are remarkably alike.

This is a book concerned principally with the techniques of production management. It is intended as a teaching text, but this does not of course mean that courses in production management should necessarily be technique oriented. The nature, uses and limitations of available techniques must necessarily form a part of any comprehensive production management course, but whether they constitute the foundations or the superstructure will depend upon the opinions of the lecturer and upon the objectives of the course. Whatever the approach, it is intended that this text should be used in conjunction with other teaching material.

I am grateful to several companies and publishers for their permission to reproduce certain of the tables and figures in either their original or modified forms, and to the universities and colleges who permitted me to reproduce questions from certain of their examination papers. My thanks are also due to colleagues and friends, too numerous to mention, who made useful comments on several of the chapters, to the typists (paid and unpaid) who prepared the manuscript, and to the people who read and corrected the manuscript.

Contents

Part One   Production Management in Context

Part Two   The Design of Production Systems

Part Three   The Operation of Production Systems

Appendices

Introduction

This book was written in order to fill a gap, an objective which determined its content, volume, and presentation.

As regards content, books currently available on this subject appear to be of three basic types. Those of the first type adopt a rather traditional approach and concentrate on the clerical procedures of production management. They lean heavily upon work study, value analysis, standardization, the organization of stores, production control, etc. Theirs is the 'grass roots' practitioner's approach, emphasizing the qualitative rather than the quantitative aspects of management. They adopt a rather 'engineering' approach to production, which concentrates on synthesis rather than analysis. A second and quite opposite approach depends almost exclusively upon mathematics. Such books, usually relatively thin volumes, describe the application of operational research and other disciplines in production and are therefore, by definition, limited to an incomplete treatment of the problems of production function. There has been a tendency over the past twenty years to believe that with the increasing sophistication and application of operational research (OR) and statistical techniques the problems of production management have declined rapidly. This, unfortunately, is untrue. Certainly OR has found application in production (and has also borrowed extensively from production) but, because of the complexities of management in the function, few general solutions have been developed. The third type of book attempts, sensibly, to obtain a compromise between these two types of approach. Standard and traditional practice is discussed alongside more ambitious mathematical treatments, and analysis is blended with synthesis. Such books, however, tend to be rather voluminous, and many, because of rapid progress in the subject, are now rather out of date.

This book was conceived and written with the following specific objectives in mind:

1. to be thoroughly 'up to date'
2. to deal effectively with both quantitative and qualitative aspects of production management
3. to be of value to both student and practitioner

It has not been our intention to explore those quantitative techniques whose application in production has not yet been proved; rather we have concentrated upon techniques and procedures which are of proven value and/or of accepted potential. Nor have we found it necessary to devote a large part of the text to a straightforward description of rudimentary OR and statistical techniques. The Appendices deal with certain of these—those that are a prerequisite to an understanding of the text—otherwise we have assumed that the reader anxious for a better appreciation of these techniques, will study one of the numerous specialist books quoted in the references.

In order to cover an extensive and important subject in the space available, we have adopted a very direct approach. We have assumed that the reader is both interested in the subject and motivated to follow his interest, hence our text is intended to be neither messianic nor persuasive. Little of the text is designed to illustrate the position or importance of the production function, nor are we primarily concerned to emphasize the importance of the various problems and decisions which will be discussed. Ours has been a direct, problem-oriented approach, intended to maximize the value of both the space at our disposal and the time at the disposal of the reader.

The book is arranged in three parts, the second and third—'The design of production systems' and 'The operation of production systems'—being the most important. Our definition of a 'production system' embraces men, materials, machines and procedures; hence, in 'The design of production systems' we deal with all decisions necessary to establish a production facility to manufacture certain products at the desired quantity, quality and time. In the last section, 'The operation of production systems', we are concerned primarily with the control of such a facility. The first section (Chapter 1, 2 and 3), deals with the place of the production function in business and with the two fundamental pre-production problems, namely, the location of the plant and the design of the product. Since neither of these two problems is entirely or even largely the responsibility of production management, our treatment of them is brief.

Test questions are given after most chapters. These are almost exclusively numerical or analytical and several of them are taken from university examination papers. The use of entirely or largely descriptive questions has been minimized since, in our experience, both the student and the teacher seek, and use, only analytical questions, as these are more difficult to devise and need to be more closely fitted to the text than essay or descriptive type questions, which are more easily set.

Perhaps the greatest problem experienced in writing this book lay in deciding what to omit, both in terms of subject-matter, and also in relation to the various aspects covered. The subjects dealt with are, in our opinion, the principal areas of production management. (The terminology used to describe these areas is by no means exclusive, some writers, for example, preferring the use of titles such as 'operations planning', 'materials management', etc.). It would be a mistake to assume that what is discussed in the chapters of this book represents all or even a majority of the knowledge or techniques relating to a particular area, since a great deal has necessarily been omitted.

Since this is an introductory book it has been our policy to include extensive references throughout. A large bibliography is provided which covers both books and papers, hence readers should experience little difficulty in pursuing these topics beyond the scope of the present text.

We have not been concerned with the generality of the techniques discussed, but clearly many of both the qualitative and quantitative techniques and procedures presented find extensive application beyond the production function.

The book is expected to be of value to post-graduate and undergraduate students studying not only management but also engineering, particularly production and industrial engineering. It is also intended to be of value to practising managers seeking to expand their knowledge of technique and procedure in the production function.

I

Production Management in Context

The Techniques of Production Management

1

The Production Function in Business

The purpose of production is to satisfy people's *wants*. Primitive man no doubt spent a great proportion of his time attempting to satisfy his own fundamental wants. Want of food, clothing, accommodation, etc., were important then, as they are now, but the means by which they are satisfied have changed substantially. Initially, individuals worked entirely for their own purposes to ensure their own survival. Later, families, tribes and larger groups became the dominant social units, people's wants multiplied and the procedure which attempted to ensure their satisfaction changed. The role of the worker began to evolve and groups of such workers were involved in hunting, farming, building, etc., to satisfy certain of the community's needs.

With the continued development of civilization, people's wants became even greater and, furthermore, the wants of individuals and of groups, since they were no longer restricted to the necessities of life, began to differ. This development necessitated more complex methods of production and eventually it was virtually impossible for individuals themselves to satisfy all or even a majority of their own wants.

The use of a monetary system facilitated this development since it enabled people to concentrate on those activities for which they were best equipped. They were able to produce goods far in excess of their own demand, to sell these to others, and use the money obtained to satisfy their other wants. The monetary system also enabled people to be paid for working, with money which they then used for purchases. In other words, they were engaged in production in order to satisfy the wants of others, and to earn money by which their own wants, and those of their family, might be satisfied—they were both producers and consumers.

Wants need not be restricted to the acquisition and use of goods but will also extend to the use of services. The services currently in demand are varied and extensive, ranging from professional services, such as those of lawyers, architects, entertainers, to the use of libraries, distribution systems, transport, etc. Accordingly, therefore, the definition of production must also be concerned with the provision of services.

Production in a transport organization, such as British Railways, could be described as the conversion of certain 'inputs', such as rolling stock, railway track, staff, etc., into a distribution or transport service. One of the production functions of a bank might be described as the conversion of deposits into loans, and retailers too might be said to be involved in production as they convert their bulk orders from wholesalers into the single commodities wanted by their customers.

This description of the production function will be familiar to any reader who has studied or read economics, but at the same time it is unlikely to meet with the approval of many readers who see production as being concerned primarily with creating or manufacturing goods rather than services. The economists' definition of production implies a far broader function than we shall consider in this book, where we shall be concerned almost entirely with manufacture. For our purposes *production is the fabrication or assembly of a physical object by means of equipment, men and materials.*

THE GROWTH OF MANUFACTURING INDUSTRIES

The word 'manufacture' is derived from the Latin *factum* meaning making and *manus* meaning hand, but, of course, the term is no longer confined solely to manual operations, and is now used to cover both manual and machine work, or any combination of both.

1776 is often quoted as the year in which the Industrial Revolution began. Certainly this was an important date, as it was during this year that James Watt was able to produce a practical, working version of the steam engine, and also the year in which Adam Smith's famous work *The Wealth of Nations* was first published. It would be true to say, however, that the genesis of modern industry was even earlier than this date.

James Watt was by no means the 'father' of the steam engine; Newcomen and Cowley had developed the 'atmospheric' engine in 1705 and, at an even earlier date (1698), Thomas Savery had installed his first steam engine to raise water from a mine. The textile industry of Lancashire and the West Riding of Yorkshire had begun to evolve prior to 1776. James Kay invented the Flying Shuttle in 1733, the Spinning Jenny was patented by James Hargreaves in 1770, and a roller spinning frame powered by water was first patented by Richard Arkwright in 1769.

The 'Industrial Revolution' was the transformation of a society from peasant and local occupations into a society with world-wide connections which made great use of machinery and conducted commercial operations on a large scale. It was the demise of artisan and domestic manufacture and the growth of an extensive factory system, a transformation which occurred over a considerable period of time.

Adam Smith (1723–1790) said in *The Wealth of Nations*, '. . . the annual labour of every nation is the fund which originally supplies it with all the necessities and conveniences of life'. He went on to expound the idea that to increase productivity a system of specialization or 'division' of this labour is necessary, and that such a principle is the key to economic progress. The division of labour was a radical concept in 1776 but it was quickly accepted and its adoption was one of the principal factors which enabled the Industrial Revolution to occur and the present system of manufacturing to evolve.

Prior to discoveries by Abraham Darby and Henry Cort, the production of iron depended upon the supply of charcoal. The supply of wood was becoming exhausted by the end of the 18th century, but the discoveries of methods of using coal ensured the abundant supply of pig iron for an expanding British industry.[1]

The use of a growing canal network and the rapidly developing railway system,[2] pioneered by Stephenson and Brunel, facilitated industrial development, and the growth of sea transport, although slower than the growth of domestic transport, enabled British industrialists to export their products, and helped establish Britain as the world's leading manufacturing nation.

Steam power, the crucial development of the Industrial Revolution, and later electrical power, enabled adequate machine tools to be designed and made. In 1776 John Wilkinson made a boring machine to produce cylinders for Watt's steam engines, about which Watt wrote[3] 'Wilkinson has bored us several cylinders almost without error, that of 50 inches diameter for Bentley & Co.,

---

[1] The production of pig iron in 1788 was 68 000 tons, and in 1839 was 1 347 000 tons.
[2] By 1848 5 000 miles of railway line had been laid in Great Britain.

doth not err the thickness of an old shilling in no part . . .'. In 1794 Henry Maudsley developed the first all metal lathe, and in 1818 Eli Whitney built the world's first successful milling machine which was subsequently developed by many other engineers.

These were just a few of the developments, which, over 150 years ago, enabled the manufacturing industries, as we know them today, to develop.

For the purpose of publishing statistics and indices the Central Statistical Office of the government divides the manufacturing industries in Great Britain into fourteen groups, as shown in Table 1.1. In October 1968 the total number of people working in those industries was 8·7 million,

TABLE 1.1. Employment in manufacturing industries in Great Britain

Manufacturing industry	No. of employees (Oct. 1968)[a] ('000)
Food, drink and tobacco	832·8
Chemicals and allied industries	515·5
Metal manufacture	587·2
Engineering and electrical goods	2 310·3
Shipbuilding and marine engineering	189·4
Vehicles	817·3
Metal goods	567·2
Textiles	704·8
Leather and fur	56·1
Clothing and footwear	488·7
Brick, pottery, glass and concrete	349·5
Timber, furniture, etc.	304·6
Paper, printing and publishing	634·2
Other manufacturing industries— rubber, brushes, toys, etc.	344·9
	8 702·500

[a] Source: *Employment and Productivity Gazette*, HMSO, Dec. 1968.

which is 15·5 per cent of the population and 38·5 per cent of the total number of employees in Great Britain. By far the largest employer in the manufacturing industries is, of course, the engineering and electrical goods industry, which is almost three times the size of the largest of the remaining manufacturing industries, and which employs a total of 2 310 300 people, of whom 27 per cent are women. These manufacturing industries account for about 85 per cent of Great Britain's exports, and for 13·2 per cent[4] of the total world exports. The manufacturing industries in the United States of America employ 19 million people[5] which is almost 10 per cent of the total population.

---

[3] T. S. Ashton, *Iron and Steel in the Industrial Revolution*, University of Manchester Press, Manchester, 1963, quoted in E. H. Bowman and R. B. Fetter, *Analysis for Production Management*, Irwin, Ill., 1961.
[4] Figure for 1966.
[5] Figure for 1967.

THE TYPES OF MANUFACTURE

Not only are there numerous types of manufacture, there are also many ways of classifying or grouping them for descriptive purposes. A certain amount of description of the various types of manufacture is necessary at this stage in order to 'set the scene' for subsequent discussions, but there is little benefit in attempting either precise classification or elaborate descriptions. We shall divide manufacturing in two traditional, not very subtle, ways which will nevertheless suffice for our purposes.

Firstly, we can identify continuous, repetitive and intermittent manufacture (see Fig. 1.1).

A *continuous* process will theoretically run for 24 hours per day, seven days per week and 52 weeks per year and, whilst this is often the objective, it is rarely achieved. Examples of this type of manufacture are steelmaking, petrochemicals, etc.

A *repetitive* process is one in which the product or products are processed in lots, each item of production passing through the same sequence of operations as, for example, in the assembly of motor vehicles.

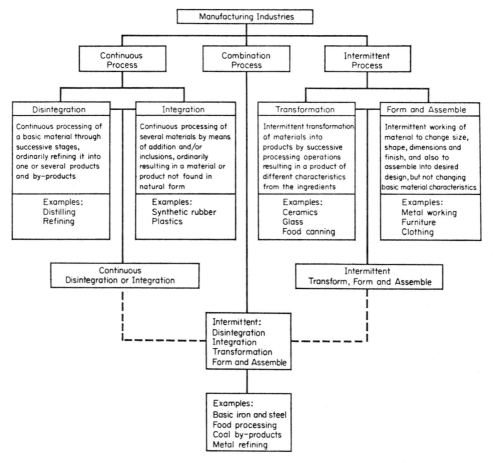

FIGURE 1.1. Classification of manufacturing processes [Reproduced by permission, R. W. Mallick and A. T. Gaudreau, *Plant Layout*, Wiley, New York, 1951]

An *intermittent* process is one in which very small lots, or even single products, are made in response to separate customer orders.

The second and similar classification divides manufacturing processes into process or mass, batch, and jobbing.

Process manufacture involves the *continuous* production of a commodity in bulk, often by chemical rather than mechanical means.

Mass production (or manufacture) is conceptually similar to process manufacture, except that discrete items such as motor cars and domestic appliances are usually involved. A single or a very small range of similar items is manufactured in very large numbers.

Batch production occurs where the number of discrete items to be manufactured in a period is insufficient to enable mass production to be used. Similar items are, wherever possible, manufactured together in batches.

Finally *jobbing* manufacture, although strictly consisting of the manufacture of different products in unit quantities, in practice corresponds to the *intermittent* process mentioned above.

Each of these three or four (depending on which classification is adopted) types of manufacture is characteristic of several different industries, but nevertheless no industry consists exclusively of any one type of manufacture. Increasing demand for products presently manufactured by means of a jobbing-type arrangement may enable a form of *batch* production to be introduced, and similarly increased demand for products presently manufactured in batches may indicate the desirability of mass production. It is, however, quite unrealistic to consider these types of manufacture in a strict or absolute sense since they are only parts of a production continuum, whose ends do not, except in theory, exist (Fig. 1.2).

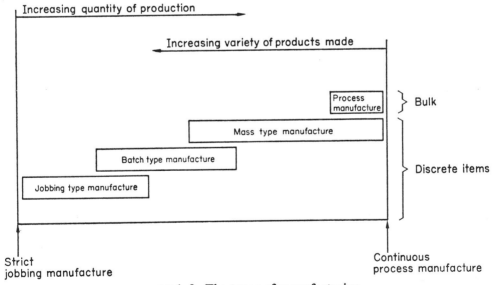

FIGURE 1.2. The types of manufacturing

THE PRODUCTION FUNCTION WITHIN THE FIRM

Production and marketing are the principal functional areas of business. It is true that there exist firms and even industries in which either one assumes a position of overriding importance, but generally speaking we can regard them both as the twin foundations of modern industry.

Production is concerned with the *supply* aspect, and marketing with *demand*, but whilst this provides us with a neat conceptualization of the situation, it is unwise to try to compartmentalize functions in this way, since in practice a considerable amount of interaction and interdependence must exist.

In Figure 1.3 we have shown the usual areas of responsibility of production management, but here again the now familiar disclaimer must be included, since practice in one firm may be undesirable or even impractical elsewhere. For example, the responsibility for purchasing may be attached to either production or marketing, or alternatively it may exist as a separate function, as shown

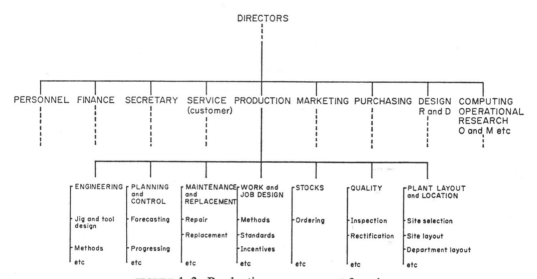

FIGURE 1.3. Production management functions

here. Stock control, whilst normally forming part of the production function, could equally belong to marketing as is the case in retailing and distribution, but in either case stock policy is influenced by both production and marketing policy. In Fig. 1.4 we have outlined the nature of the production function as it might exist in a jobbing or a batch manufacturing firm in the engineering industry, but quite a different diagram would be necessary to depict the equivalent situation in, for example, the process industries where greater emphasis is attached to planning and less to control.

PRODUCTION MANAGEMENT PROBLEMS

Problems of management in the production function basically concern two types of decision: firstly, those relating to the design or establishment of the production system; and, secondly, those relating to the operation, performance and running of the production system. We are regarding the 'production system' as consisting not only of an arrangement of physical facilities, machine tools, etc., but also the predetermined manner in which items or products are to be manufactured. Decisions relating to system design, therefore, include such things as the acquisition and arrangement of plant, determination of manufacturing methods, and establishing of schedules for the production of each item. Decisions relating to the operation of the production system are

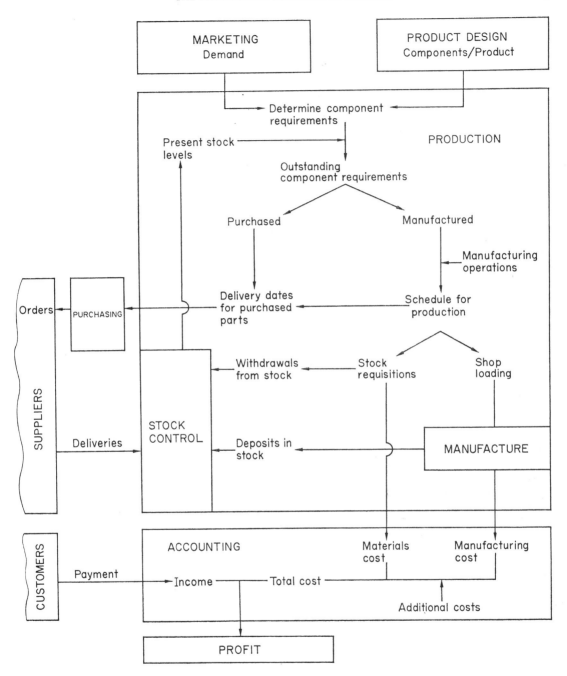

FIGURE 1.4. The production function within a jobbing or batch manufacturing firm

generally of a short-term nature and concern the control of production, quality and stocks, and the maintenance of equipment, etc.

This simple classification of problems enables us, rather belatedly perhaps, to offer a definition of production management as follows:[6] *the design and operation of production systems*.

Problems in the Design of Production Systems

Product Design

On no occasion will the production function of a business be entirely responsible for the design of the product(s) to be manufactured, but on every occasion the design of the product will be influenced by production considerations. There is little economic merit in developing and designing a product, however original or advanced, which can only be manufactured at several times the cost of equivalent products produced by rival firms.

The design of products will normally be the responsibility of a separate function within the company or even of a separate company. A major contribution will often be made by both production and marketing, since theirs is the responsibility for producing and selling it. Some aspect of the marketing function may even be entirely responsible for the design of some feature of the product, e.g. the packaging.

Production Engineering

Production engineering decisions include the selection and/or design of production equipment and processing, the development, manufacture and test of tools, jigs and equipment, and the design and installation of services such as power supplies.

As we have already indicated in this chapter, production engineering as both a science and a profession is a good deal older than production management. This may partly account for the fact that production engineering often exists as a function or department separate from production management. Perhaps for the same reasons, none of the courses in management education offered in this country, other than those organized by engineering departments of faculties, include production engineering as an aspect of the study of production management. Frequently the production manager or director of a factory is responsible for both production engineering and management, a situation which reflects the interdependence and necessary cooperation of the two functions.

Plant Layout and Materials Handling

Decisions relating to the arrangement of departments, and of the equipment within these departments, must be made with the object of enabling given products, or unknown products of a given nature, to be manufactured at minimum cost. The nature of the layout of the factory and the layout within the factory will determine the extent of movement and handling of materials, products, etc.

---

[6] The difference between production management and operations management should be noted. Operations management is concerned with the design and operation of *operating systems* whose purpose is the provision of goods or services. Production using our definition of the term, is the principal type of operating system, hence production management has a great deal in common with operations management.

The Design of Work and of Jobs

The design of jobs has always been largely the responsibility of the production function.[7] Effective methods of doing work are essential for the efficient design of production systems, and some control of workers is necessary in order that adequate utilization of equipment is achieved, and in order that management may accurately determine, and subsequently predict, the times necessary for all production operations.

The development and implementation of 'optimum' work methods frequently necessitates the study and design of work places and of equipment, and the training of workers, all of which will be regarded as the responsibility of production management.

Control is achieved by way of performance standards, which are obtained after exhaustive investigation of work methods, and are subsequently used for the planning of production and as the basis of incentive payment schemes.

Certain aspects of the job, for instance payment systems and supervision, will be the joint responsibility of production and other functions, such as personnel.

Production Planning

Production planning, as the name implies, is undertaken to ensure that items are produced in the correct numbers and of the desired quality at the correct times.

The planning function frequently includes the forecasting of demand, although where this is necessary on a large scale it may be undertaken by, or in conjunction with, the marketing department. The items to be produced must be accurately *scheduled* not only to ensure completion by the desired time, but also to obtain maximum utilization of available capacity, and to minimize the amount of work in progress and the stock of finished items. Strictly speaking, production planning also includes, where necessary, the acquisition of facilities, plant, labour, etc., and their installation, but these are often treated as separate responsibilities, i.e. plant layout (production) and manpower planning (production, marketing and personnel departments).

Problems in the Operation of Production Systems

Production Control

Production control is the complementary activity to production planning and, stated simply, involves the implementation of the production plans. The problem is most severe in jobbing and small batch production, where, because of the variety of jobs, accurate production planning is frequently impossible. Consequently a good deal of 'slack' (i.e. underloading of equipment, work in progress, etc.) normally exists in the system, whose operating efficiency then depends upon short-term, day to day, control procedures.

Stock Control

No manufacturing organization can exist entirely without stocks of raw materials, work in progress, or finished goods. At the end of 1967 the total value of stocks in all manufacturing industries in Great Britain equalled £6 484 million of which £2 248 million was raw material and fuel, £2 444 million was work in progress and £1 791 million was finished goods. In the United States

---

[7] Job design is discussed in Chapter 8, where the consequences and desirability of the dominant influence of production on the design of jobs is examined.

of America total stocks held by the manufacturing industries were valued at $82·56 billion at the end of 1967 which was over 10 per cent of the Gross National Product for that year.

Maintenance of stocks is expensive but necessary. Cost is incurred through depreciation, damage, insurance, use of space and notional loss of interest on the capital tied up, but the necessity occurs because of variations in demand, because of the nature of the manufacturing process and because of the financial benefits of bulk purchase and batch processing.

Quality Control

Rarely, if ever, is production equipment capable of continually producing items to a specified absolute level of accuracy. Variations in quality, i.e. changes in dimension, content, appearance, performance, and so on, will result either because of assignable causes, such as wear in tools, or for reasons of pure chance. The ability of equipment to produce items to the desired level of accuracy must be established and procedures installed to minimize the number of faulty items produced and to ensure that faulty or defective items, once produced, are not accepted or passed to the customers.

Rectification and/or reprocessing procedures must be installed, and inspection procedures used to examine the quality of the raw materials and parts supplied *to* the company.

Maintenance and Replacement

None of the facilities used within industry—whether human or inanimate—can work continually and effectively without maintenance and repair. Some of the problems and decisions involved in the maintenance and repair of equipment are as follows:

(a) Will maintenance consist of servicing or repair, or both?
(b) What shall be the timing of service or preventive work in order to involve minimum effort and cost yet minimize the probability of breakdowns of equipment?
(c) How shall repair work be conducted—in situ; using replacement units; using replacement equipment, etc.?
(d) What will be the size of stocks of spare parts?
(e) What will be the size of maintenance teams?
(f) How will information be gathered and used to enable the above questions to be answered accurately?

Every manufacturing organization will embrace these problems areas to a greater or lesser extent. The relative emphasis will differ between companies and industries, and also over a period of time. Certain problems, particularly those in the second section, will be of a recurring nature, whereas some of those in the first section, being primarily 'long term' will assume considerable importance at only infrequent intervals.

Parts II and III of this book give a detailed analysis of the classification of problems made above.

THE GROWTH OF PRODUCTION MANAGEMENT AS A SCIENCE AND A PROFESSION

The Industrial Revolution occurred in this country largely because of the activities of many fine engineers, such as Watt, Kay, Arkwright, and later, Brunel, Stephenson and many others. They had been responsible for conceiving and often manufacturing the equipment and services which enabled significant progress to be made towards the modern system of manufacture. Having prompted and initiated this change, it was not surprising that it was also engineers who began to examine and develop methods of organizing or managing this new 'industrial' system.

The pioneers of this new science of management adopted what would now be called a 'mechanistic' approach to the problem. 'They accepted without question the engineering approach that had already proved itself in the design of physical objects, and they extended it to the analysis and control of the activities of people.'[8]

Engineers were undoubtedly responsible for initiating the study of management, but, of course, at that time management problems were mainly concerned with production, and the principal objective of many of the early 'management' processes was to establish methods of organization and control which were capable of dealing efficiently with the comparatively new problems caused by the birth of new and elaborate systems of manufacture. The dominance of engineers, both practising and studying management, lasted until the First World War when people from other disciplines became interested in these problems. Emphasis passed to the problems of the individual, the problems of fatigue and health, and the concepts and principles of management began to be modified by psychologists who were interested in environmental conditions; heat, light, humidity, and so on. Later behavioural scientists further modified the principles of 'scientific management' by emphasizing the importance of social relations within industry, the nature of supervision and the influence of workers' needs, etc., on factors such as the design of work and jobs.

The Second World War was also a great stimulus to industry and management, the principal feature of this, and the post-war period, being the birth, growth and adoption of mathematical principles of management, now known as management science and operational research.

All of these, and many other influences, led eventually to the present situation in which management is regarded as a multidisciplinary subject—and furthermore, a subject of crucial importance meriting continued substantial research and considerable educational effort.

At no time throughout this development, and certainly not at the present time, has a stable state existed. The prime cause of the development was the inadequacy of the knowledge of management in comparison to the knowledge of those areas for which management is responsible. A similar state continues to exist. There is now, as there was two hundred years ago, a far greater body of knowledge associated with, say, production engineering, than with production management. Knowledge in certain disciplines is now thought to be nearing saturation point, but knowledge of management has not yet begun to approach this state, consequently potential improvements in industrial efficiency through the improvement of methods of organization and management far outweigh those which might result from improvements in basic processes.

A great deal of progress has yet to be made to improve our knowledge of the subject, but at the same time it should not be assumed that what little is currently known is used to best advantage in industry!

SELECTED READINGS

There are no books which deal exclusively with the subjects dealt with in this chapter, but many production management text-books cover the same ground, often adopting a slightly different approach, and frequently dealing in more detail with some of the topics which are briefly discussed here.

---

[8] H. G. J. Aitkin, *Taylorism at Watertown Arsenal: Scientific Management in Action.* 1908–1915, Oxford University Press, London, 1960.

The reader may find the introductory chapters of the following books of interest:

H. L. TIMMS, *The Production Function in Business*, revised ed., Irwin, Ill., 1966.

H. L. TIMMS, *Introduction to Operations Management*, Irwin, Ill., 1967.

J. E. ULLMAN and S. E. GLUCK, *Manufacturing Management—An Overview*, Holt, Rinehart and Winston, New York, 1968.

The following papers are also well worth reading:

P. H. THURSTON, 'The concept of a production system', *Harvard Business Review*, Nov/Dec, 70–75, 1963.

M. K. STARR, 'Evolving concepts in production management', conference paper, reprinted in G. K. GROFF and J. F. MUTH, *Operations Management—Selected Readings*, Irwin, Ill., 1969.

The paper by Starr defines the production function as relating to the provision of both goods and services. We have referred to such systems as operating systems and consider production to relate only to the provision of goods.

The following book of readings by Starr is well worth examination and is a particularly good treatment of Production Management from a conceptual or methodological point of view.

M. K. STARR, *Management of Production*, Penguin, Harmondsworth, Middx., 1970.

QUESTIONS

1.1. How far is it possible for the production function within the firm to operate independently of the other main functional areas? Which functions, in particular, experience interlocking problems?

[Univ. of Bradford, Management Centre, B.Sc. Business and Admin. Studies, final year,—*Production Management*, May, 1968—45 minutes.]

1.2. Describe the principal types or classes of manufacture. What are the prerequisites for each of these types of manufacture and what are the principal production management problems associated with each type?

Illustrate your answers by describing actual industrial situations with which you are familiar.

2

The Design of the Product

The responsibility for product design is neither exclusively nor largely the responsibility of production management, but since the nature of the product is a major factor influencing the nature, and hence the problems, of production, the subject of product design deserves a brief examination.

Basically two factors influence design: the need to sell or market the product, and the prior need to make or produce it. Unless the product design satisfies both production and marketing requirements, it is unlikely to be commercially successful.

Figure 2.1 outlines the various steps involved in product design and the following brief discussion relates to certain of these steps and certain other important considerations and constraints.

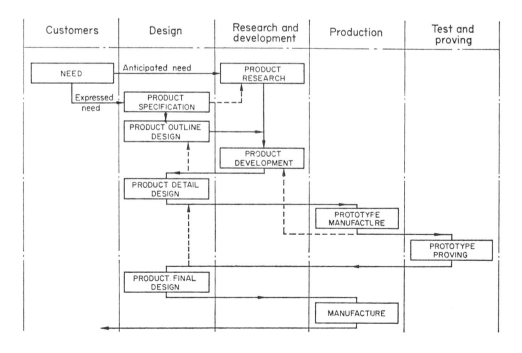

FIGURE 2.1. Product design, development and manufacture

RESEARCH AND DEVELOPMENT

Product research is seldom begun only in response to consumer demand. Indeed a great deal of research is conducted in most industries, the purpose of which is to make discoveries, establish new applications and interpret new findings, in the hope or anticipation that these will lead eventually to commercial application. *Pure* or *fundamental* research is not specifically oriented to commercial application or product design, but is encouraged by companies in anticipation of its future commercial worth. The same justification and motivation applies, but to a lesser extent, to fundamental research conducted on behalf of companies by cooperative research establishments or universities. *Applied* research is of more immediate worth and is often undertaken in order to provide answers to specific problems relating to either existing or proposed products.

It is often difficult to distinguish clearly between research and development; however, development is concerned with either a prototype pre-production product, or a specified design for a product or part of a product.

DESIGN QUALITY

In a later chapter we shall show that quality, and hence reliability, is invested in a product during two stages, namely design and manufacture. During the design stage quality is determined by the specification of appropriate standards and tolerances on dimensions, content, etc.

The quality level obtained is, of course, a function of cost. Whilst no product can be designed to have perfect quality or perfect serviceability and reliability, the expenditure of more money on materials, testing, manufacture and control will naturally improve quality levels. In practice, product quality will be determined not by the availability of suitable materials or production equipment, but by the quality of competitors' products, the elasticity of demand, and the planned product price. In many cases the use of standards, such as those formulated by the British Standards Institute or the American Society for the Testing of Materials, is obligatory or advisable.

PURCHASING

Since no manufacturer is completely independent of suppliers, either for direct materials, indirect materials, components, or sub-assemblies, the purchasing function will influence product design. Not only will the design of a new product depend on the ready availability of certain purchased items, but in the redesign, i.e. modification, replacement or improvement, of existing products the purchasing department will play an important part because of their knowledge of such factors as the development of new materials and improved components.

MARKETING

The extent of the marketing department's influence over product design is dependent upon the relative importance of product function and product appearance. In the manufacture of consumer goods, product aesthetic design and package design are often of paramount importance, unlike the manufacture of capital goods where function is still paramount, despite the valuable contributions made by industrial designers. Often, particularly in the former case, the marketing department will be responsible for prototype testing and proving, particularly when this involves the test launching of products onto the market, prototype evaluation by selected consumers, and so on.

Perhaps the most important thing to notice is that product design is not the sole responsibility of the designer or design draughtsman. Every function in the firm is interested in the nature of the products, and consequently the design adopted should reflect each of their points of view, rather than being a reflection of one man's conception of the customer's need. This joint approach to product design is inherent in value analysis which, whilst not a high-powered analytical technique, is nevertheless of considerable interest.

VALUE ANALYSIS

Value analysis has been defined as follows:

'. . . an organized approach to get the same performance at lower cost without affecting quality.'[1]
'. . . an organized and systematic effort to provide the required function at the lowest cost consistent with specified performance and reliability.'[2]
'. . . a functionally oriented scientific method for improving product value by relating the elements of product worth to their corresponding elements of product cost in order to accomplish the required function at least cost in resources.'[3]

Often the title value engineering is used synonymously with value analysis. We shall use the latter title only, but it is perhaps worth noting that value engineering is normally used in relation to the design of new products and value analysis in relation to existing products.

Value analysis was originated by Lawrence D. Miles of the American General Electric Company around 1947. He was engaged upon cost reduction exercises on a number of the company's products, which led him to consider the nature of value. He developed a series of tests or questions which could be used to establish the value of any product or part. Between 1947 and 1952 Miles developed a set of techniques which later became known as value analysis. Their first application is said to have saved the company $500 000 during the first year.

Value analysis was first introduced into Great Britain by an American management consultancy firm in 1957, since when it has found widespread use in many industries.

How does value analysis differ from conventional cost reduction techniques? Cost reduction generally relates to existing products and is concerned with attempts to manufacture them at lower cost by minimizing the material used, changing the design to facilitate manufacture, changing tolerances, methods, and so on. Value analysis, however, is more comprehensive since it begins with an examination of the purpose or functions of the product and is concerned to establish the means by which such a purpose or function can best be fulfilled.

The principal objective of value analysis is to increase profit by means of a critical examination of areas of high cost, with the purpose of eliminating unnecessary costs. Such an objective can, of course, be pursued retrospectively by an examination of existing products and parts, or currently by involvement in the design of future products or parts. We shall see later that the objective of value analysis, indeed the methods of value analysis, are conceptually similar to those of method study. Whereas the latter is concerned solely with the minimization of labour costs, value analysis

---

[1] J. Burnside, *Value Analysis*, British Productivity Council Seminar, London, 1964.
[2] J. F. A. Gibson, *Value Analysis—A Rewarding Infection*, Pergamon Press, Oxford, 1968.
[3] C. Fallon in *Value Analysis, Value Engineering* (Ed. W. D. Falcon), American Management Association, New York, 1964.

is concerned primarily with material costs which usually contribute substantially to the total manufacturing cost of any product. Although the cost breakdown varies between industries, it is common for direct materials to represent about 50 per cent of total product cost (Fig. 2.2).

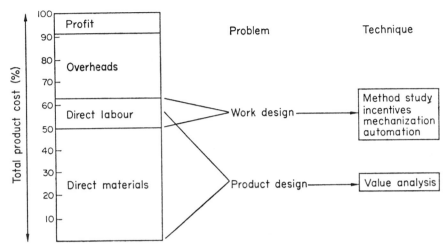

FIGURE 2.2. Methods of reducing product cost

Hence value is maximized when the cost associated with achieving the necessary function is minimized. Alternatively 'value' can be defined as the 'lowest cost reliably to accomplish the essential function'.[4]

Two types of value can be identified, firstly *esteem* value and secondly, *use* value. *Use* value is related entirely to function, i.e. the ability of an item to perform its specific purpose. *Esteem* value is not directly concerned with function but with the status or regard associated with ownership. Value, for our purpose, is the sum of these two, use value normally being the principal component.

The result of properly applied value analysis is not, as is sometimes claimed, an inferior product but rather a product whose value/cost relationship is improved, a product which provides the necessary function with the essential qualities, at a minimum cost.

Although other methods of conducting value analysis are available, it is usually found that the team approach is most appropriate and successful. Value analysis teams should consist of members with complementary skills drawn from the following departments within a company.

Design
Purchasing
Marketing
Production
Accounts

Such an approach is desirable, since value can be determined at any or all of the stages between initial conception and final delivery. Furthermore, since maximum cost savings are often associated with purchased items, it is usual to draw upon the specialized knowledge of the supplier.

---

[4] J. F. A. Gibson, *Value Analysis—A Rewarding Infection.*

Value analysis is therefore a common-sense approach to product design or redesign, which involves the following steps:

1. Determine the function of the product
2. Develop alternative designs
3. Ascertain the costs
4. Evaluate alternatives

The relative importance placed by the customer upon the following will determine design or redesign objectives:

1. Function
2. Appearance
3. Esteem associated with possession
4. Intrinsic cost of materials or labour
5. Replacement, exchange or disposal value

As regards existing products the following questions will help to identify potential value improvements:

1. Which areas appear to offer largest savings?
2. What percentage of total cost is associated with bought out items?
3. What percentage of total cost is associated with labour?
4. What percentage of total cost is associated with materials?

Often the maximum cost saving associated with existing products relates to bought out parts or materials. The value of purchased parts and material can be investigated with a view to material or design changes by asking questions such as the following:

1. How does it contribute to the value of the product?
2. How much does it contribute to the total cost of the product?
3. Are all its features and its specification necessary?
4. It is similar to any other part?
5. Can a standard part be used?
6. Will an alternative design provide the same function?

Generally six main steps are involved in a value analysis investigation, whether in relation to a new or an existing product.

The first step involves the collection of information. Information should be collected about costs, function, customer requirements; the history and possible future development of the product design; the manufacturing methods, and so on.

The second stage covers the development of alternative designs, i.e. alternative methods of achieving the required function. This is the creative, speculative stage during which use may be made of 'brainstorming' sessions, etc.

No reasonable alternative or suggestion should be rejected during this stage, irrespective of apparent cost or practical disadvantages.

It should be the objective during this stage to:

1. Eliminate parts or operations
2. Simplify parts or operations

3. Substitute alternative materials
4. Use standard parts or materials
5. Relax manufacturing tolerances
6. Utilize standard manufacturing methods
7. Eliminate unnecessary design features
8. Change design to facilitate manufacture
9. Buy rather than manufacture parts if cheaper
10. Use prefinished materials
11. Use prefabricated parts
12. Rationalize product ranges
13. Substitute low cost manufacturing processes
14. Nationalize range of purchased parts
15. Eliminate material waste

Use of check lists such as that shown in Table 2.1 may be of value during this stage.

The third stage involves the *evaluation of alternatives*. Alternative design must be compared on a cost basis, cost information relating to all aspects of the designs being obtained from the purchasing, production and accounts departments. The temptation to perfunctorily dismiss alternatives should be resisted. Furthermore, whenever possible, ideas should be salvaged from eliminated alternatives.

The final stage involves *recommendation and implementation*.

Value analysis certainly cannot claim to be a glamorous or esoteric management technique, indeed, it can be criticized as mere application of common sense. It is certainly lacking in the ingredients which appeal to contemporary qualitative management, but nevertheless should not be lightly dismissed. Value analysis is a product-oriented management technique concerned with both optimization and innovation. In appropriate circumstances, particularly where production involves large quantities of low to medium price items, the potential benefits of value analysis are considerable. For example, in the year ending June 1965 the use of value analysis is claimed to have saved the US government $329 000 000 or $1\frac{1}{4}$ per cent of expenditure on military stores.[5] Reductions in the cost of manufactured items of 40 per cent are frequently obtained and a return on investment in value analysis as high as 75·1 has been reported.

CLASSIFICATION, CODING AND COMPANY STANDARDIZATION

There is a certain amount of confusion as to the meaning of the two words, *standard* and *specification*. Specifications provide details of product or component requirements in terms of materials, composition, dimensions, performance, and so on, whilst a standard can be defined as any accepted or established rule, model or criterion against which comparisons can be made. *Standardization* is therefore concerned with the concept of variety, and more specifically with the control of *necessary* variety. Company standardization begins to operate once unnecessary variety has been eliminated. The elimination of unnecessary variety—variety reduction—can be defined[6] as 'the process of eliminating the unnecessary diversity which frequently exists in the various stages from design

---

[5] L. R. Beesly, 'Some aspects of military aircraft production', *Production Engineer*, Aug. 1966, 419–435.
[6] A. S. McInery and R. S. Geoghegan, *Variety Reduction*, British Productivity Council Seminar, London, 1959.

TABLE 2.1. Value analysis check list

Area	Questions
Product function	1. What are basic functions?
	2. What are secondary functions?
	3. Are all the functions necessary?
	4. What else will perform the same function?
	5. Can any of the functions be incorporated in other components?
Materials	1. What material is used?
	2. What is the material specification?
	3. Can any other material be used?
	4. Can any other specification of the same material be used?
	5. Can waste material be reduced?
	6. Can raw material be standardized?
	7. Can raw material be obtained in a different form?
	8. What is the price of the material?
	9. What indirect materials are used? (e.g. packing, lubrication, etc.)
	10. Can pre-finished materials be used?
Size and specification	1. Can dimensions be reduced?
	2. Is the part oversize?
	3. If less expensive material is used can size be increased?
	4. What tolerances are specified?
	5. Which tolerances are not critical?
	6. Can tolerances be increased?
	7. Can a standard part be used?
	8. What finish is required?
	9. Are the finish standards essential?
	10. Can an alternative method of applying the finish be used?
Manufacture	1. Can any operations be eliminated?
	2. Can any operations be combined?
	3. Can any operations be simplified?
	4. Would a different material simplify manufacture?
	5. Can standard processes be used?
	6. Can standard tools and jigs be used?
	7. Can assembly operations be reduced?
	8. Can prefabricated parts be used?
	9. Would it be cheaper to buy the parts?

to manufacture or selling' and is undertaken in anticipation of obtaining some or all of the following advantages:

1. Increased interchangeability of parts, simpler stock-keeping and improved customer service.
2. Production of parts in larger quantities enables better machine utilization.
3. Production planning and control are facilitated.
4. Operator training is simplified.
5. Drawing office records, sales and service records are simplified.
6. Lower stocks of raw materials, work in progress, and finished products.
7. Fewer jigs, tools and fixtures.
8. Fewer set-ups and changeovers of machinery.

B

The principal prerequisite for successful standardization is an effective system of coding and classification which will enable component or part variety to be identified and controlled. An appropriate classification and coding method is invaluable during variety reduction, as well as during the design of new products, and such a coding and classification method should satisfy the following requirements:

1. It should enable items identical, or similar, to others to be identified and located.
2. It should enable existing items to be used in new designs where possible.
3. It should facilitate the reduction of necessary variety.
4. It should enable substitutes for 'out of stock' items to be identified.
5. It should enable groups of similar items to be located for production planning and production purposes.

Clearly an adequate coding and classification system is beneficial to many departments in the company (see Table 2.2), indeed, one of the principal benefits of such a system is contained in requirement (5) above. The manufacture of parts in groups or families rather than in small quantities makes increased machine utilization possible and often results in an entirely different plant layout. This method of manufacture, normally called *group technology*, depends entirely upon effective coding and classification methods and will be discussed in more detail in Chapter 12.

In this chapter we are concerned primarily with the design of products, and hence the principal benefit of an effective coding system is that it enables similar items to be classified together and thus facilitates the control of variety during design. In many cases, because of the lack of such a system, a great deal of time is wasted in designing items similar (often identical) to designs already in existence.

TABLE 2.2. Use and benefits of parts coding and classification in certain departments

Department	Design	Stores	Production
Use	Code similar parts under similar code numbers	Code similar parts under similar code numbers	Code similar parts, tools, jigs, etc., under similar code numbers
	Classify parts by shape and size	Classify parts according to type	Classify parts, tools, jigs, etc., by type
	Locate similar past designs	Layout stores according to code numbers	Layout facilities for group production
	Ensure use of existing designs when possible	Control variety by examining records	Ensure use of existing jigs, tools, etc.
Benefits	Control and reduce number of designs by variety reduction	Code together all purchase documents	Control variety of jigs, tools, fixtures, etc.
	Collect data for family formation	Provide for bulk buying of a smaller variety	Control variety of sub-assemblies
	Establish a preferred range of items		

Methods of Coding

Parts or components are frequently coded by one of the following methods (see Table 2.3):

Sequential coding

When drawings for new parts are coded sequentially, with numbers taken from a register, no useful classification results. Occasionally code letters are used in conjunction with sequential numbering, but even so little useful classification is obtained.

Product Coding

Parts are often coded in such a way as to indicate the product for which the part was originally designed. Alpha/numerical codes are often used, the numerical portion giving a unique identity to the part, whilst the alphabetical part identifies the original product or even the original contract or customer.

Production process code

Less frequently parts are coded according to their method of manufacture or their sequence of operations. For example, differing codes will be used for cast, forged and welded items, for items produced from stock bar, plate, etc.

Design code

Often, where an effort to maintain variety control and standardization is adopted, parts coding is mainly on a design basis. Products of similar appearance or purpose are coded in a similar manner, hence facilitating the selection and adoption of suitable existing parts rather than the design of new ones.

Clearly, if any useful classification of products or components is to result some form of design coding must be adopted. The problem of devising such a method of coding has engaged the attention of research workers for about ten years, the initial research being conducted in Russia.[7]

There have been basically two approaches to the problem, the *overall* or *macro* approach and the *specific* or *micro* approach.

Several research workers, adopting the macro approach, have attempted to develop Universal Component Classification Systems, as a result of studies of statistics of the components most commonly found in certain industries. The first of these research projects was begun at the Aachen Machine Tool Laboratory in Germany in the early 1950's, and resulted in the Opitz method of coding and classification. The object of this research was to determine the statistics of the components commonly manufactured in the engineering industries.

The Opitz method of classification,[8] which is used for machined parts only, utilizes a five-digit form code to describe the shape of the component, and a four-digit supplementary code to specify the component size, material, raw material and accuracy (Fig. 2.3).

---

[7] S. P. Mitrofanov, *Scientific Principles of Group Technology* (Translated from Russian), National Lending Library for Science and Technology, 1966.

[8] E. A. Howarth, 'Group technology—using the Opitz system', *Production Engineer*. Jan. 1968, p. 25; H. Opitz, *Werkstückbeschreibenches Klassifizierungssystem*, Essen, 1946.

TABLE 2.3. Types of part coding

Method of part coding	Nature and example	Extent of classification	Usefulness for:			
			Variety reduction	Standard-ization	Group technology	Production planning
Sequential	Drawing or part numbers taken from register e.g. 12345	None	None	None	None	None
Product	Usually two part. First to identify product Second-unique number e.g. HD4–12345[a]	Little	None	None	None	Very little
Production	Usually two part. First to identify product method of material. Second-unique No. e.g. F.MS–12345[b]	Some Useless after changes in production methods	None	Very little	Useful	Useful
Design	Often identifies nature and principal character-of product e.g. S.14. 12345[c]	Useful	Useful	Useful	Some	Some

[a] e.g. Product type HD. Model 4.
[b] e.g. Forging (F) in Mild Steel (MS).
[c] e.g. Stud (S) overall length 14″ (14).

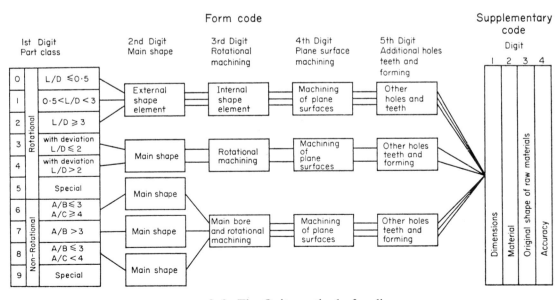

FIGURE 2.3. The Opitz method of coding

TABLE 2.4. Remainder of code for rotational parts 0, 1 and 2

	2nd digit — External shape element	3rd digit — Internal shape element	4th digit — Machining of plane surfaces	5th digit — Other holes and teeth
0	Smooth without shape elements (constant diameter)	Without bore blind hole	No surface machining	Without other holes
1	No shape elements	No shape elements	External plane and/or circular surfaces	Axial only no regular divisions
2	Threads	Threads	External surfaces dividing each other in a given ratio	Axial only regular divisions
3	Functional grooves	Functional grooves	External groove and/or slot	Radial only no regular divisions
4	No shape elements	No shape elements	External spline (polygon)	Axial, radial, others, without regular divisions
5	Threads	Threads	External spline groove and/or slot	Axial, radial, others, with regular divisions
6	Functional grooves	Functional grooves	Internal plane surface and/or groove	Spur gear teeth
7	Functional cone	Functional cone	Internal spline (polygon)	Bevel gear teeth
8	Operating (moving) threads	Operating (moving) threads	External and internal splines and grooves	Other gear teeth
9	Others >10 functional diameters	Others >10 functional diameters	Others	Others

(2nd and 3rd digit: codes 1–3 "One side increasing or smooth"; codes 4–6 "Several sides increasing". 5th digit: codes 1–5 "Without gear teeth"; codes 6–8 "With gear teeth".)

The first digit of the code form divides parts into two groups—rotational and non-rotational, the former being described by their length/diameter ratio, and the latter by the ratio of their three edge lengths (A, B and C in descending size). Two codes for special parts are available (5 and 9).

The second, third, fourth and fifth digits describe the main shape, rotational machining, plane surface machining, and additional holes, teeth and forming of the part.

Rotational parts with a first-digit code of 0, 1 and 2 have the same classification system for the remaining four digits, the coding for which is shown in Table 2.4. Rotational parts with a first-digit code 3 and 4 have the same classification system for the remaining digits, but non-rotational parts 6, 7 and 8 have different classifications for the second digit (main shape) and the same classification for the last three digits. The complete Opitz code, which was developed at the Machine Tool Institute, Aachen Technical University, is contained on only eight sheets of paper. Notice that for each of the five digits larger numbers indicate more complex parts.

The 'Vuoso' method of coding was developed at the Prague Machine Tool Research Institute and represents a more recent attempt to develop a universal system. The coding method is simpler than the Opitz method and is contained on only one piece of paper. The four-digit code is naturally less detailed than the Opitz code, but it offers a simple method of coding adequate for most small companies or manufacturing units. The Vuoso coding method is depicted in Fig. 2.4. This chart is read from top to bottom for the first three digits—'Kind'; 'Class'; 'Group'; and the last digit— 'Material' is obtained from the right-hand side. An example of a class number is given in the figure, whilst Fig. 2.5 shows two parts coded by both the Opitz and the Vuoso methods.

Despite the relative popularity of universal classification systems, particularly the Opitz System, macro systems have recently been subject to a good deal of criticism. It is argued that the proportion

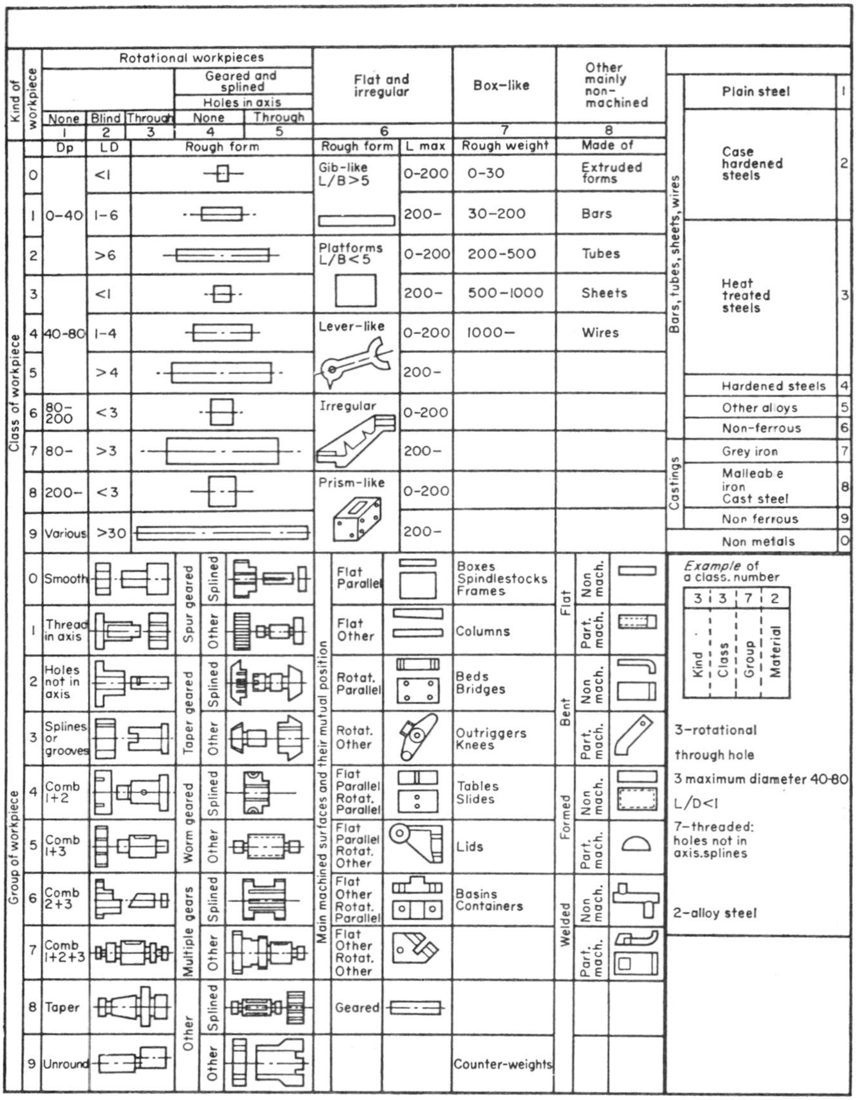

FIGURE 2.4. The Vuoso method of coding [Figs. 2.3, 2.4 and Table 2.4 reproduced by permission, C. C. Gallagher, 'Small firms benefit from group technology', *Metalworking Production*, 19 March, 1969]

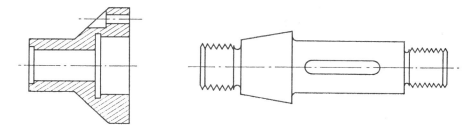

Opitz: 11402–2301   Opitz: 27030–3301
Vuoso: 3321   Vuoso: 1781

FIGURE 2.5. Comparison of Opitz and Vuoso code systems

of certain types of component, e.g. rotational components found in industry, is likely to vary with the nature of the industry concerned;[9] and that the statistics or features of a particular class of components are likely to vary according to the type of industry concerned.

Several researchers have concluded, therefore, that there is no fixed pattern of components throughout industry and that the concept of a universal classification system is at worst mistaken and at best of very limited value.

In contrast to the overall or macro approach, the micro approach concentrates on the particular requirements and characteristics of an individual company. Perhaps the best example of this approach is the Brisch classification system.[10]

The Brisch system is designed for the needs of each particular company, needs which can be established only after a survey of the types of components and methods of production. The method of coding is mainly design-oriented, but additional 'production' information can be added by means of a second code. The design information is contained in a *monocode*, e.g. shape, design, size, features, etc., whilst a *polycode* contains information relevant to during-production planning. The micro system can therefore be designed specifically according to the requirement of the drawing office concerned and is therefore considered by many to be a superior approach to company standardization.

SUMMARY

Product design is essentially a multi-functional problem, involving functions such as production, marketing, purchasing, accounts, etc. This team approach is inherent in value analysis, a technique applicable both to the design of new products (sometimes called value engineering) and to the redesign or modification of existing products.

The economic benefit of minimizing the variety of products made, derives from increased

---

[9] Research at the University of Manchester Institute of Science and Technology has shown that the average percentage of rotational components found in samples from 12 firms was 39·5 but that the percentage varied from 14·5 to 89.
A. T. Fatheldin, *Ph.D. Diss.* Unpublished, Department of Management Sciences, Univ. of Manchester, Institute of Science and Technology, 1969.
Even within a specific industry, different research workers have found different proportions of rotational parts e.g. in the machine industry: 'Vuoso' (Prague)—67 per cent; 'Production Engineering Research Association', research project conducted in Britain—30 per cent; Fatheldin—48 per cent.
[10] J. Gombinski, 'Component classification—Why and How', *Machinery and Production Engineering*, March, 1968.

facility utilization, lower stock levels, simpler production planning and control, and so on. Product variety might be minimized either by examining the existing range with the objective of rationalization and/or by standardizing materials and parts during initial design. An essential prerequisite for both variety reduction and standardization is an effective method of component coding and classification. Basically, two approaches to this problem exist—the macro approach, aimed to provide a universal method, and the micro approach, tailored to the requirements of individual situations.

SELECTED READINGS

Whilst there are no books which deal exclusively with the design of products in a manner relevant to the production manager, the reader may find the following of value:

J. R. BRIGHT, *Research Development and Technological Innovation*, Irwin, Ill., 1964.

J. BURNSIDE, *Value Analysis*, British Productivity Council Seminar, London, 1964.

J. F. A. GIBSON, *Value Analysis—A Rewarding Infection*, Pergamon Press, Oxford, 1968.

J. PILDITCH and D. SCOTT, *The Business of Product Design*, Business Publications, 1965. This book deals with industrial design.

A. S. McINERY and R. S. GEOHEGAN, *Variety Reduction*, British Productivity Council Seminar, London, 1959.

L. D. MILES, *Techniques of Value Analysis and Engineering*, McGraw-Hill, London, 1961.

M. K. STARR, *Product Design and Decision Theory*, Prentice-Hall, London, 1963.
   This book is concerned largely with decision theory, and decision-making processes.

E. A. PESSEMIER, *New-Product Decisions*, McGraw-Hill, New York, 1966. This is an excellent book written from a marketing strategy point of view.

The following articles describe workpiece coding and classification in design and production.

J. GOMBINSKI, 'Group technology—an introduction', *Production Engineer*, **46**, No. 9. 557–564 (1967). (The Brisch System.)

E. A. HOWARTH, 'Group technology—using the Opitz system', *Production Engineer*, **47**, No. 1, 25–35 (1968).

H. OPITZ, W., W. EVERSHEIM and H. P. WIENDAHL, 'Workpiece Classification and its Industrial Application', *Int. J. Machine Tool Res.*, **9**, 39–50 (1969).

QUESTIONS

2.1.

(a) What is value analysis?

(b) What is value engineering?

(c) How does value analysis differ from conventional cost reduction?

(d) 'Value Analysis is merely the application of the techniques of method study (see chapter 5) to the problems of product design'—Discuss.

(e) 'There is no need for the existence of a value analysis department in a company which employs competent product designers'—Discuss.

2.2. You are required to conduct a value analysis exercise on the product shown below which is a domestic 5 amp electrical plug. Enumerate the principal steps involved in such an exercise and at each step provide the appropriate information or answers from your knowledge of this particular product, its use and specification. You are required as a result of this exercise to suggest an alternative design if possible.

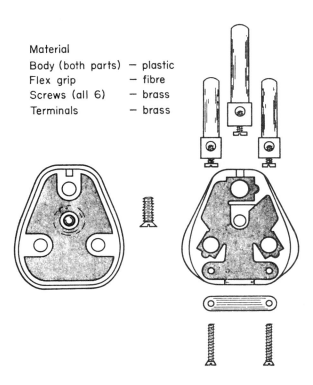

Material
Body (both parts) — plastic
Flex grip   — fibre
Screws (all 6)   — brass
Terminals   — brass

2.3. Discuss the advantages and disadvantages of employing a value analysis engineer working on his own against the use of an organized value analysis team. What would you consider to be the best composition of the value analysis team, and to whom should the team leader report?

2.4. What are the requirements of an effective method of coding and classification? What are the benefits to a small jobbing engineering company of adopting such a method of coding and classification?

2.5. Use the Opitz coding method to determine a five-digit part code for the rotational components shown in the diagram.

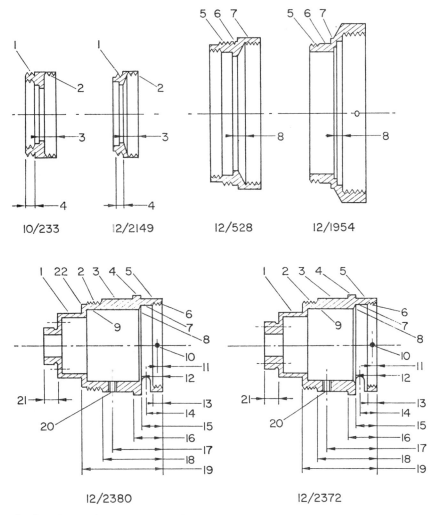

Q 2.5. Scale drawings of components with similar features. Identical features are indicated by the same number on each

3

Plant Location

Having decided the nature and specification of the product to be manufactured, the location of the manufacturing facility is the next problem to be considered. In most cases this will be the logical order of decisions, i.e. 'What?' and then 'Where?', since often the nature of the product will suggest suitable manufacturing locations and preclude others. At times, however, these decisions may occur in the reverse order or the two decisions may even be quite unconnected. For example, a company intending to manufacture ships will be restricted to comparatively few locations, unlike a company intending to manufacture scientific electronic instruments.

We can consider the plant location problem as applying in two basic situations, i.e. the case of the entirely new firm, and the case of the existing firm.

The choice of location is a vital decision for any new firm, indeed numerous examples exist of new firms which have enjoyed brief and troubled lives, solely because of their disadvantageous location. Theoretically the new firm has a vast choice of possible locations from which to choose. The problem will involve not only the selection of an appropriate part of the country, but also the selection of an appropriate site within a locality. In practice the company is not entirely free to take an open decision since the government, anxious that the choice of location shall be to the national benefit, will often seek to influence the decision.

The existing firm will seek plant locations either in order to expand capacity, or to replace existing plant. An increase in demand, if it is to be satisfied by the producer, gives rise to one or more of three decisions:

1. Whether to expand the present capacity and facilities
2. Whether to seek locations for additional plant
3. Whether to close down existing plant in favour of larger premises elsewhere

Replacement of existing facilities may be occasioned by one or more of the following occurrences:

(a) The movement of markets, i.e. changes in the location of demand
(b) Changes in the cost or availability of local labour
(c) Changes in the availability of materials
(d) Demolition or compulsory purchase of premises
(e) Changes in the availability or effectiveness of transport
(f) Relocation of associated industries or plants
(g) National legislation

For our purposes, in discussing the plant location problem, it makes little difference whether we consider the problem as applying to a new firm or to an existing one. However, since the latter tends to be the more complex case our discussion will largely relate to the problems of the existing company. An increase in demand will, unless associated with increased productivity, inevitably result in pressure for additional capacity; the only alternatives to an expansion of the existing facilities, or the acquisition of additional facilities, are a reduced share of the market or an increased amount of sub-contracting. On the other hand, a reduction in demand will often result in the underutilization of existing capacity and encourage a move to smaller premises. Figure 3.1 describes the forces within a company which give rise to the pressure for either an increase or decrease in the amount of space available. Whilst the main forces are associated with demand, and hence with the production and marketing functions, it is worth noting that both finance and labour management might also be instrumental. Changes in interest rates may affect the cost of holding stock and cause a change in stock-holding policy, which in turn may affect space

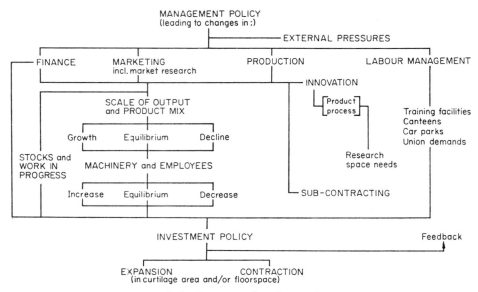

FIGURE 3.1. Pressures for change in space

requirements. Legislation relating to investment allowances, employment tax, depreciation, etc., may influence company financial policy sufficiently to affect the scale or the nature of the undertaking; similarly legislation relating to labour may necessitate a change in the nature or extent of facilities, e.g. the addition of extensive training facilities, welfare facilities.

Scientific discoveries or developments, new fields of technology, increasing competition, licensing or patent arrangements, all may affect company research and development effort, which in turn will influence space requirements. Likewise, changes in production technology, the obsolescence of equipment, etc., will influence space requirements.

A change in space requirements is only one of several possible reasons for the need to conside the acquisition of an additional plant location. Figure 3.2 summarizes the forces which may give rise to such a decision.

The need to seek smaller or larger premises may arise without the occurrence of a change in demand and output. For example, the costs associated with the present location may change through increases in the cost of labour caused, perhaps, by increased employment opportunities in the area. The price of raw materials or indirect materials may change through changes in the

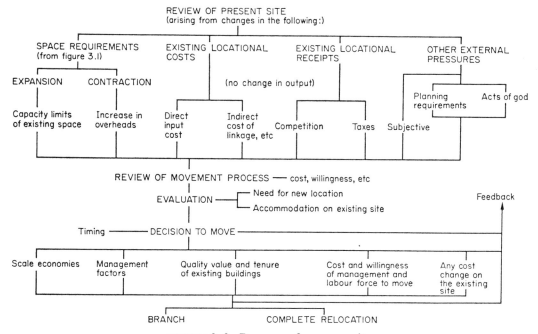

FIGURE 3.2. Pressures for a new site

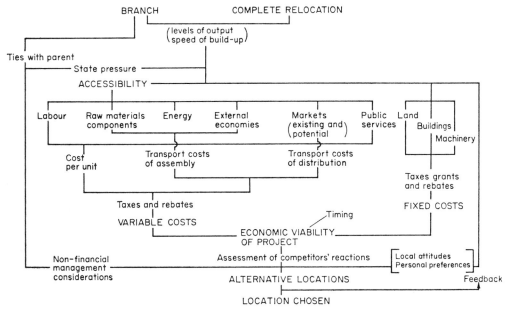

FIGURE 3.3. The choice of a new site [Figs. 3.1, 3.2 and 3.3 reproduced in modified form by permission, P. M. Townroe, 'Locational choice and the individual firm', *Regional Studies*, **3**, No. 1, 15–24 (1969)]

cost of transport or changes within associated industries. Indirect costs such as those associated with communications, education, housing, etc., may change, also new competition or changes in local taxation may prompt the decision to seek alternative premises as may other external pressures such as labour disputes. Such forces may prompt the consideration of a complete move or the acquisition of an additional site(s).

Now let us consider the actual choice of plant location or site. Three general considerations will influence the location decision, namely the variable costs involved, the fixed costs involved and, finally, subjective assessments (see Fig. 3.3).

Consider first the *variable costs*. Perhaps the main factor here is the 'accessibility' of the proposed location in terms of both inputs and outputs. As regards input, accessibility to labour is important, not merely sufficient labour, of course, but labour of the correct type, and at a correct price. Accessibility of raw materials, sub-assemblies and components is important, the cost of such input being mainly a function of transport. Accessibility to energy is less important now than was the case 50 years ago, but nevertheless, in certain industries, such a consideration may be crucial. Access to technical advice and to other services such as warehousing, maintenance, etc., is often essential.

With regard to output, a location must clearly be within easy access of adequate markets, as well as public services and associated industries.

The principal *fixed costs* are associated with the provision and maintenance of facilities. The design of buildings and the layout of facilities will influence such costs. The cost of erecting and maintaining buildings, the cost of access roads, transportation of machinery, rates, rent, and so on, will all influence the choice of location. As fixed costs, we should also consider the cost of inventories of materials and finished items which may depend upon the plant location.

A further factor which will influence the choice of location is the time factor, i.e. the urgency of acquiring the facility compared to the time required to make it available, the latter being influenced by the necessity for planning permission, construction of plans, purchase of land, availability of building labour, provision of services, electricity, water, roads, etc.

Finally it must be admitted that certain *subjective* or *non-quantitative* assessments may influence the decision, namely individual preferences, congeniality of the district, attitudes of present employees, etc.

National and regional data relating to the various factors influencing the plant location decision are available from a variety of sources. Figures 3.4 and 3.5 are examples of such data taken from two regional studies.

Before leaving the subject of locational choice, we should emphasize the role of central governments and the influence of legislation and incentive. Initially there were three basic reasons for government concern with the location of companies and industry in Great Britain, namely the high regional unemployment of the 1930's, the high costs associated with the congestion of the major industrial conurbations and, finally, the strategic disadvantage of industrial concentrations in time of war.

Because of the undesirability of permitting a continued concentration of industry and population in the South West and the Midlands, governmental legislation was recommended to ensure urban redevelopment, the decentralization of industry and the better balancing of regional industrial structures.

Over the past 30 years the government has been increasingly active, in terms of legislation and through both positive inducement and negative prohibitions, to ensure that these objectives are attained. Legislation such as the Special Areas (Development and Improvement) Acts (1934 and 1937), the Distribution of Industry Act (1945), the Town and Country Planning Acts (1947 ards), the Distribution of Industry (Industrial Finance) Act (1958) and the Local Employ-

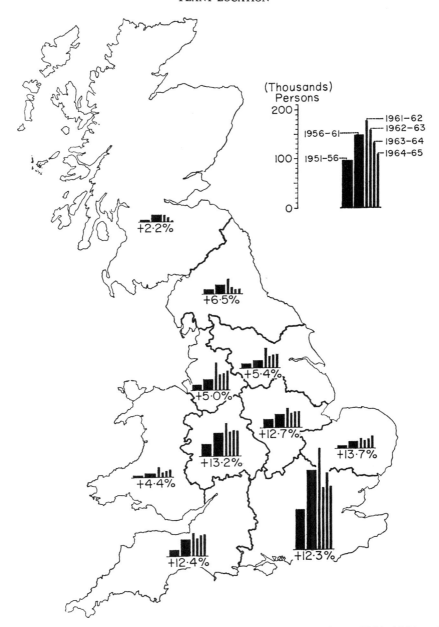

FIGURE 3.4. Civilian population: Total change, Great Britain by regions, 1951–1956 to 1964–1965

The heights and widths of the columns are proportional to the mean annual total change and to the length of the period respectively. Thus, volume of change is represented by the area of the columns. Percentage growth over the period 1951–1965 as a whole is given in figures. The total increase 1951–1965 in Great Britain was 4 357 600 or 9·0 per cent

ment Act (1960) were but the forerunners of a great deal of direct and indirect effort by the government to influence the location of manufacturing industry, offices, etc.

In the present situation, very substantial incentives exist to encourage companies to establish

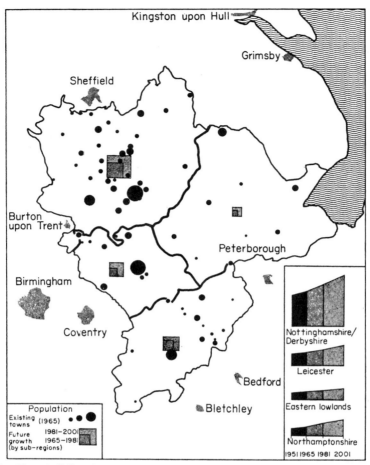

FIGURE 3.5. The East Midlands: Existing urban population distribution: possible future sub-regional growth [Figs. 3.4 and 3.5 reproduced by permission of Controller of Her Majesty's Stationery Office, *The East Midlands Study*, H.M.S.O., 1966]

The populations of existing urban areas, 1965, are shown by proportional circles. The forecasts take account of estimates of current planned movements of population to Northamptonshire (Daventry, Corby, Northampton and Wellingborough) and Sheffield 'overspill' to Chesterfield RD

plants in certain parts of the country, designated for industrial and economic development, all of which has tended to reduce but not, of course, to eliminate the influence of the factors discussed in the previous section.

LEAST COST CENTRE ANALYSIS

This simple type of analysis is appropriate where the location problem concerns the placement of a single plant. Least Cost Centre Analysis[1] is a useful technique despite the fact that it suffers from two rather severe limitations, namely:

---

[1] For a comprehensive description of the method see E. E. Smykay, D. J. Bowersox and F. H. Mossman, *Physical Distribution Management*, Collier-Macmillan, London, 1961.

1. The choice of plant location is assumed to be dependent entirely upon the minimization of transport costs.
2. Transport costs are assumed to be linearly related to the distances involved.

It is clear from our previous discussion that many factors other than transport costs are likely to affect locational choice. Nevertheless, this simple technique is of value in that it provides a rapid means of obtaining an initial solution to the single plant location problem, a solution which might subsequently form a basis for further discussion, analysis and modification. The technique is best described by means of a simple example.

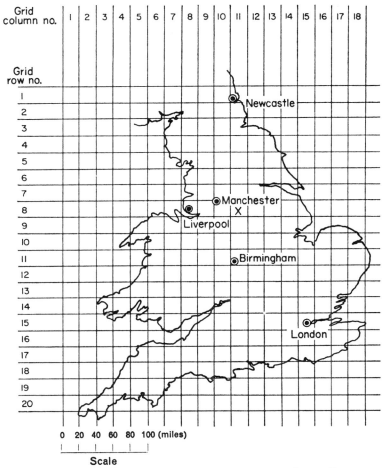

FIGURE 3.6. Hydromatics Ltd—customers and suppliers

Hydromatics Ltd. is a small company presently situated in Manchester, engaged in the manufacture of hydraulic equipment which it is contracted to supply to two companies situated in Newcastle and London. The manufacture of the equipment is largely an assembly process, depending upon the supply of electric motors from a company in Liverpool and pumps from a company in Birmingham. Figure 3.6 is a scale map showing the location of the manufacturer, its two suppliers and two customers, whilst Table 3.1 provides the relevant transport cost information.

TABLE 3.1. Calculation of 'location cost factors'

Sub-assembly or product (a)	Annual quantities involved (b)	Transport cost per item per 20 miles (c)	Location cost factor (d) = (b × c)	Location grid references	
				Row (e)	Column (f)
Motor	7 000	£0·5	3 500	8	8
Pump	7 000	£0·4	2 800	11	11
Product*a*	4 000	£0·8	3 200	1	11
Product*b*	3 000	£0·8	2 400	15	15

a Delivered to Newcastle.
b Delivered to London.

Column (c) in this table gives the transport cost per item per 20 miles (the 'grid' size on the map). This cost multiplied by the quantity of items, i.e. motors, pumps or finished products, provides the 'location cost factor' given in column (d).

The 'least cost' location for the manufacture of the products can be determined by the weighting procedure shown in Table 3.2. The map grid *row* number of the 'least cost' location is obtained by:

1. Multiplying each 'location cost factor' by the grid row number
2. Summing the four figures so produced
3. Dividing this total by the sum of the four location cost factors

The map grid *column* number for the 'least cost' centre is obtained in a similar manner.

These weighting calculations indicate that the present location of Hydromatics Ltd. is quite close to the least cost centre (row 8, column 11; shown by the cross on Fig. 3.11). The annual transportation cost of remaining in Manchester rather than transferring manufacture to the new location can be calculated in the manner shown in Table 3.3. In this case the cost is relatively

TABLE 3.2. Calculation of plant location grid numbers

Location cost factor	Grid row no.	Weight	Least cost grid row and column no.
3 500	8	28 000	
2 800	11	30 800	
3 200	1	3 200	
2 400	15	36 000	
———		———	$\dfrac{98\,000}{11\,900} = 8 \cdot 25 \equiv$ ROW 8
11 900		98 000	
	Grid column no.		
3 500	8	28 000	
2 800	11	30 800	
3 200	11	35 200	
2 400	15	36 000	
———		———	$\dfrac{130\,000}{11\,900} = 10 \cdot 9 \equiv$ COLUMN 11
11 900		130 000	

TABLE 3.3 Comparison of present and proposed locations

Sub-assembly or product	From	To	Quantity per year	Actual distance (miles)	Transport cost/20 ml /item	Annual transport cost
Present Location						
Motor	Liverpool	Manchester	7 000	38	£0·5	6 650
Pump	Birmingham	Manchester	7 000	80	£0·4	11 200
Product	Manchester	Newcastle	4 000	135	£0·8	21 600
Product	Manchester	London	3 000	190	£0·8	22 800
					Total =	62 250
Proposed location						
Motor	Liverpool	×	7 000	55	£0·5	9 600
Pump	Birmingham	×	7 000	65	£0·4	9 100
Product	×	Newcastle	4 000	130	£0·8	20 800
Product	×	London	3 000	160	£0·8	19 200
					Total =	58 700
					Saving	£ 3 550

small; consequently, it seems unlikely that a change in location is justified unless there are other more important factors influencing the decision.

Clearly this technique is of limited value only, not only because of the basic assumptions mentioned earlier but also because of the inaccuracies included in the method of calculation. Unless a very small map grid is used the weighting procedure introduces significant distance errors which will, of course, be reflected in the accuracy of the solution. Nevertheless, despite its limitations the 'least cost centre' technique is a valuable means of obtaining a first solution or of comparing alternative locations.

DIMENSIONAL ANALYSIS

Even if we are able to identify the various factors influencing locational choice the problem of quantification remains. How, for example, do we determine, for various potential locations, the cost of moving or the cost of labour? Furthermore, having quantified such factors, what weight or importance do we attach to each? Do we, for example, consider the subjective factors as being of equal importance to the fixed cost factors? Do we consider the cost of labour as being of more or less importance than transportation costs? Indeed we may even find that we are unable to attach actual cost figures to some of the important factors. For example, regarding the cost of moving, we may be able to rank the potential locations or evaluate them only in terms of 'high', 'medium' or 'low' cost.

Consider a simple example in which we are faced with two possible locations. We have decided that the selection of the best of these locations will be made on a basis of the following factors:

1. The cost of land
2. The cost of buildings
3. The cost of labour (total required labour force)

We have further found that the cost associated with each of those three factors for each of the possible locations, is as shown in Table 3.4.

TABLE 3.4

Factor	Location A	Location B
1. Land	£10 000	£15 000
2. Buildings	£25 000	£30 000
3. Labour	£15 000	£10 000

We might compare the relative merits of the two locations merely by summing the relevant costs, i.e.

$$\text{Total for A} = £50\ 000$$
$$\text{Total for B} = £55\ 000$$

Using this method of comparison we would, presumably, choose location A since it is the cheaper of the two. This method assumes that each of the factors is of equal importance, a situation which may be far from the truth. For example, suppose we decide that whilst the costs of land and buildings are equally important to our decision, the cost associated with labour is of more importance—say twice as important as the two other costs. Then we may assess the alternatives by introducing this weighting factor.

$$
\begin{array}{ll}
\text{Location A:} & \begin{array}{r} 10\ 000 \\ 25\ 000 \\ +2(15\ 000) \\ \hline = £65\ 000 \\ \hline \end{array}
\end{array}
$$

$$
\begin{array}{ll}
\text{Location B:} & \begin{array}{r} 15\ 000 \\ 30\ 000 \\ +2(10\ 000) \\ \hline = £65\ 000 \\ \hline \end{array}
\end{array}
$$

Now it appears that each location is equally attractive.

Let us take this type of argument a little further by introducing two more factors into our examination of the two locations, A and B. Now, as well as the costs associated with land, buildings and labour, we need to consider the influence of community relations and the cost of moving. Because of the subjective nature of the former and the rather complex nature of the latter, we find it extremely difficult to place an accurate cost on either of these factors for the two locations concerned; consequently we settle for a system of rating using a scale of 1 to 100. A rating of 1 indicates that a location scores very highly, i.e. it is the best possible result, whereas a rating of 100 is the worst possible result. In other words, in terms of costs 1 is equivalent to a low cost whereas 100 is equivalent to a high cost.

Because we are no longer dealing with cost, we have a dimensional problem. In fact in this case we are dealing with two separate dimensions, a fact which should influence our analysis.

Suppose that the five factors for the two locations are quantified as shown in Table 3.5, then we might again compare locations by adding together the figures to obtain the totals shown in Table 3.5. This comparison would lead us presumably to select location A.

TABLE 3.5

	Location A	Location B
Land (cost)	10 000	15 000
Buildings (cost)	25 000	30 000
Labour (cost)	15 000	10 000
Community relations (score)	60	30
Cost of moving (score)	80	40
Total	50 140	55 070

However, this type of analysis is quite wrong, because we have quite indiscriminately mixed together two dimensions. To illustrate the inadequacies of the procedure, suppose that we alter the scale of factors 1, 2 and 3, and perform our calculations in £' 000's rather than £'s, i.e.

Location A	10'	Location B	15'
	25'		30'
	15'		10'
	60		30
	80		40
	190		125

Such an analysis would lead us to select location B. In other words, the change of scale has distorted our analysis.

In order that such an anomaly should not occur, we must take care to treat multidimensional analysis such as this in a more satisfactory manner. Such a method was developed almost 50 years ago by Bridgeman,[2] and is referred to as dimensional analysis.

Using the following notation:

$$O_{i_1}, O_{i_2}, O_{i_3}, \ldots, O_{i_n} = \text{costs, scores etc. associated with factors}$$
$$1, 2, 3, \ldots, n \text{ for location } i$$
$$W_1, W_2, W_3, \ldots, W_n = \text{the weight to be attached to factors}$$
$$1, 2, 3, \ldots, n$$

the merit of the various locations should be assessed as follows:

$$\text{For location } i, \text{ merit} = (O_{i_1})^{W_1} \times (O_{i_2})^{W_2} \times (O_{i_3})^{W_3} \times \ldots \times (O_{i_n})^{W_n}$$

In the case of two possible locations the merit might be compared as follows:

$$\frac{\text{Merit of A}}{\text{Merit of B}} = \left(\frac{O_{A_1}}{O_{B_1}}\right)^{W_1} \times \left(\frac{O_{A_2}}{O_{B_2}}\right)^{W_2} \times \ldots \times \left(\frac{O_{A_n}}{O_{B_n}}\right)^{W_n}$$

Example

Several factors are identified as being important in choosing one of two available locations for a new factory. Wherever possible the factors have been costed; otherwise, a score from 1 to 10

[2] P. W. Bridgeman, *Dimensional Analysis*, Yale University Press, New Haven, Conn., 1922 (later edition 1963).

has been given, 1 representing the best possible result and 10 the worst possible. The several factors are considered as being of varying importance consequently they have been weighted from 1 to 10, weight of 1 indicating least importance, and 10, most importance.
The data are as follows:

Factor	Location A	Location B	Weight
1. Cost =	£10 000	£15 000	1
2. Score =	3	7	2
3. Score =	6	2	3
4. Cost =	£1 500 000	£1 000 000	4
5. Score =	4	7	4
6. Score =	5	5	3

The merit of Location A is represented by:

$$(10\ 000)^1 \times (3)^2 \times (6)^3 \times (1\ 500\ 000)^4 \times (4)^4 \times (5)^3$$

and that of location B by:

$$(15\ 000)^1 \times (7)^2 \times (2)^3 \times (1\ 000\ 000)^4 \times (5)^3$$

To assist the calculations we can change the scales as and where convenient, i.e. changing the scale of the cost dimension gives:

$$A : (1) \times (3)^2 \times (6)^3 \times (150)^4 \times (4)^4 \times (5)^3$$
$$B : (1 \cdot 5) \times (7)^2 \times (2)^3 \times (100)^4 \times (7)^4 \times (5)^3$$

$$\therefore \quad \frac{\text{Merit of A}}{\text{Merit of B}} = 1 \cdot 79$$

Such an analysis indicates that location B is superior on a basis of the six factors considered.

In this example we have considered only factors which should be minimized, i.e. costs. Such an analysis might also be undertaken even where some factors are to be maximized (e.g. profits, revenue, etc.), whilst others are to be minimized. In such a case the powers would be positive for factors to be minimized and negative for factors to be maximized.

Example

Compare the merit of two locations X and Y on the basis of factors having different weights, i.e.

	Location X	Location Y	Weight
Costs (£)	10 000	12 000	4
Benefits (score)	8	6	3

$$\frac{\text{Merit of X}}{\text{Merit of Y}} = \frac{(10\ 000)^4\ (8)^{-3}}{(12\ 000)^4\ (6)^{-3}}$$

$$= \frac{(10)^4\ (8)^{-3}}{(12)^4\ (6)^{-3}}$$

$$= 0 \cdot 203$$

$$\therefore \text{Select location X}$$

THE MULTI-PLANT LOCATION PROBLEM

Whereas in the case of the single-plant location problem we have been concerned to select the minimum cost location, in the multi-plant location problem we must select the location which, *when added to existing locations*, minimizes the cost of the *entire system*. Each of the potential locations must be assessed not on its *own* merits alone as was the case previously, but in the context of a multi-plant situation.

Let us examine the problem by way of the following examples:

A company presently has two plants both manufacturing the same range of goods. These plants are located at Cambridge and Bradford. Both distribute goods to five major centres, i.e. London, Bristol, Birmingham, Manchester and Hull. Because of an increase in demand the company is anxious to establish one further plant. The choice has been narrowed to two possible locations, Nottingham and Crewe, both of which are within easy access of all major distribution centres (Fig. 3.7).

The unit production and distribution costs and the capacity of the existing plants are shown in Fig. 3.8. The forecast unit production and distribution costs, and the capacity of plants at the

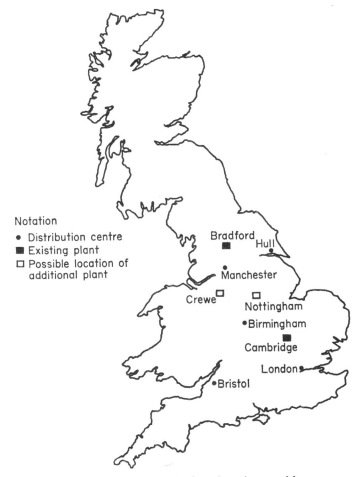

FIGURE 3.7. The multi-plant location problem

Plant \ Distribution centre	London	Bristol	Birmingham	Manchester	Hull	Unit production cost	Monthly production capacity
Cambridge	0·3	0·4	0·4	0·5	0·6	1·3	10 000
Bradford	0·5	0·5	0·4	0·2	0·3	1·2	15 000

FIGURE 3.8. Production and distribution cost data, existing plants (£)

Location \ Distribution centre	London	Bristol	Birmingham	Manchester	Hull	Unit production cost	Monthly production capacity
Nottingham	0·3	0·3	0·2	0·2	0·3	1·4	12 000
Crewe	0·4	0·3	0·2	0·2	0·4	1·3	12 000
Forecast monthly demand	9000	7000	8000	7000	6000		

FIGURE 3.9. Forecast demand, production and distribution cost data (£) for each of possible plants

two possible new locations, together with forecast demand for the five distribution centres, are shown in Fig. 3.9.

Clearly we are faced with the problem of selecting one of two possible situations:

    1. Plants at Cambridge   2. Plants at Cambridge
                  Bradford   Bradford
                  Nottingham   Crewe

In order to make this choice we must investigate the costs associated with each of the two situations. Considering first of all situation (1), we can rearrange our data in the manner shown in Fig. 3.10. This figure shows the production plus distribution costs associated with the delivery of goods from each of the plants to each of the distribution centres. The total output of the three plants is sufficient to satisfy the total demand, but in order to be able to evaluate the merit of this situation we must find the minimum cost allocation of goods between plants and distribution centres.

This is now a straightforward linear programming problem which can be solved quite easily using the transportation method, or algorithm.[3]

Plant \ Distribution centre	London	Bristol	Birmingham	Manchester	Hull	Capacity
Cambridge	1·6	1·7	1·7	1·8	1·9	10 000
Bradford	1·7	1·7	1·7	1·4	1·5	15 000
Nottingham	1·7	1·7	1·6	1·6	1·7	12 000
Requirements	9000	7000	8000	7000	6000	

FIGURE 3.10. Total unit costs (production and distribution) associated with situation (1)

Plant \ Distribution centre	London	Bristol	Birmingham	Manchester	Hull	Capacity
Cambridge	9000	1000				10 000
Bradford		2000		7000	6000	15 000
Nottingham		4000	8000			12 000
Requirements	9000	7000	8000	7000	6000	

FIGURE 3.11. Minimum cost allocation of goods for situation (1)

[3] An algorithm is an iterative solution procedure, i.e. a procedure which by means of a defined sequence of steps or calculations converges on a solution.

This method of obtaining an optimal solution to allocation problems such as this is described in detail in Appendix I. Using this technique, the minimum cost allocation of goods from plant to destination shown in Fig. 3.11 can quite easily be found.[4]

The total production and distribution cost associated with this situation and with the choice of this location is found as follows (referring to Fig. 3.11):

$$9\,000 \times 1 \cdot 6$$
$$1\,000 \times 1 \cdot 7$$
$$2\,000 \times 1 \cdot 7$$
$$4\,000 \times 1 \cdot 7$$
$$8\,000 \times 1 \cdot 6$$
$$7\,000 \times 1 \cdot 4$$
$$6\,000 \times 1 \cdot 5$$

$$\therefore \text{Total} = £57\,900$$

Now consider the alternative situation (2).

Figure 3.12 shows the total unit costs associated with the delivery of goods from each of the plants to each of the distribution centres. (Only the third line, the costs associated with the additional location, differs from Fig. 3.10. We can again use the transportation method of linear programming to obtain the optimum allocation of goods shown in Fig. 3.13. The quantities allocated from the three plants to the five distribution centres is the same as in the previous case, but for this situation the total cost is as follows:

$$9\,000 \times 1 \cdot 6$$
$$1\,000 \times 1 \cdot 7$$
$$2\,000 \times 1 \cdot 7$$
$$4\,000 \times 1 \cdot 6$$
$$8\,000 \times 1 \cdot 5$$
$$7\,000 \times 1 \cdot 4$$
$$6\,000 \times 1 \cdot 5$$

$$\text{Total} = £56\,700$$

Plant \ Distribution centre	London	Bristol	Birmingham	Manchester	Hull	Capacity
Cambridge	1·6	1·7	1·7	1·8	1·9	10 000
Bradford	1·7	1·7	1·7	1·4	1·5	15 000
Crewe	1·7	1·6	1·5	1·5	1·7	12 000
Requirements	9000	7000	8000	7000	6000	

FIGURE 3.12. Total unit costs (production and distribution) associated with situation (2)

Plant \ Distribution centre	London	Bristol	Birmingham	Manchester	Hull	Capacity
Cambridge	9000	1000				10 000
Bradford		2000		7000	6000	15 000
Crewe		4000	8000			12 000
Requirements	9000	7000	8000	7000	6000	

FIG 3.13. Minimum cost allocation of goods for situation (2)

[4] The reader may wish to read Appendix I at this point. Having familiarized himself with the transportation method, he will be able to solve the problem shown in Fig. 3.10.

Since this cost is less than the minimum obtained for situation (1), then on a basis of the criteria considered here, i.e. cost of distribution and production, we would select situation (2), i.e. Crewe, as the location of our additional plant. It should of course be remembered that distribution costs are rarely the sole criteria considered during the determination of plant locations; however this type of analysis is often useful if only as a means of providing a first solution.

The final least cost location and distribution pattern is shown in Fig. 3.14.

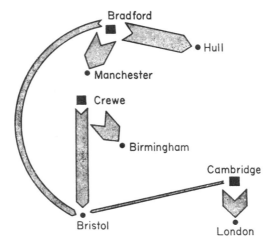

FIGURE 3.14. Solution to example

It should also be noted that the factors influencing location decisions are liable to change. The logical location at the present time may, at a later date, appear quite inferior because of change in one of the many factors which influenced the original choice.

Conceptually, the problem of the location of plants abroad does not differ from the problems discussed in this chapter. In practice, such a problem will often be more complex and will assume greater proportions, if only because more investment may be involved. In such situations the identification and quantification of factors may be more difficult; nevertheless the decision is amenable to the type of technique discussed earlier.

SUMMARY

The problem of plant location is rarely the entire responsibility of the production manager; consequently our discussion of this topic has been rather brief.

Conceptually there is little difference between the problem of plant location as it relates to either the entirely new firm or the existing firm. In practice, in the former case, the problem will often concern the location of a single plant, whereas in the case of the existing firm, unless the existing premises are being replaced, the problem will concern the location of several plants.

Numerous factors will influence the plant location decision, not least of which is the pressure brought to bear by the government in terms of legislation and incentive. Other factors may be categorized as follows: firstly fixed costs, such as the cost of buildings, land, etc.; variable costs, such as the cost of labour, materials, transport, power; and finally, subjective factors, such attitudes of management, and so on.

Dimensional analysis is a useful technique for comparing the merits of several available locations where an assessment of factors may involve a comparison of figures other than those relating to cost.

The transportation method of linear programming (Appendix 1) is a useful technique, applicable to the multi-plant layout problem.

SELECTED READINGS

The only textbooks devoted solely to this subject treat the problem from an economist's point of view; the following book reviews economic location theory as well as plant location practice (it is now rather dated, however):

M. GREENHUT, *Plant Location in Theory and Practice*, University of North Carolina Press, Chapel Hill, N.C., 1956.

The following papers also deal with the plant location problem:

J. D. DILLON, 'The geographical distribution of production in multiple plant operation', *Management Sci.*, 2, No. 4, 353–365 (1956).

R. L. FRANCIS, 'On the location of multiple new facilities with respect to existing facilities', *J. Ind. Eng.*, 15, No. 2, 106 (1964).

P. M. TOWNROE, 'Locational choice and the individual firm', *Regional Studies*, 3, No. 1, 15–24 (1969).

Dimensional analysis is described in:

P. W. BRIDGEMAN, *Dimensional Analysis*, Yale University Press, New Haven, 1922. (Later ed. 1963).

QUESTIONS

3.1. Briefly, what changes might result in the need for additional space to manufacture products? Under what circumstances might such changes lead to the need for an entirely new site, and what would influence the choice of such a site?

3.2. Galvanated Decorations Ltd. is a family business, situated in the heart of the industrial midlands, i.e. at Birmingham. The company make ornamental lamp-posts which are sold exclusively through agents in London, Newcastle and Manchester. All the material for the product is obtained from Liverpool. The tables below show the annual quantities involved, the distances and

Material or product	Annual quantity	Transportation cost per unit per 20 miles
Raw materials (per lamp-post)	13 000	£0·4
Lamp-post for London	7 000	£0·8
Lamp-post for Newcastle	3 000	£0·65
Lamp-post for Manchester	2 400	£0·65

Mileage chart

	London	Manchester	Birmingham	Liverpool	Newcastle
London	—				
Manchester	190	—			
Birmingham	110	80	—		
Liverpool	200	38	90	—	
Newcastle	295	135	180	150	—

the transport cost per item per 20 miles travelled. What maximum total transportation cost benefit would Galvanated Decorations Ltd. obtain by relinquishing their Birmingham premises for a factory elsewhere, and where should this new factory be located? (Use the grid given in Fig. 3.6.)

3.3. Incredible Chemicals Ltd. intend to establish a plant solely for the blending of Formula X14 which is a composite of X9 and X5 and is used by the company in the manufacture of agricultural fertilizer.

X9 is imported by Incredible Chemicals and is to be transported from London docks, whilst X5 is obtained from a subsidiary company at Hull.

Formula X14 is to be used at three other Incredible Chemicals works at Manchester, Bristol and Newcastle where the requirements are 40, 30 and 50 tons per week respectively. Equal quantities of X9 and X5 are required to blend Formula X14, but because of atmospheric contamination 15 per cent of the tonnage of Formula X14 is wasted and has to be burnt.

Incredible Chemicals transport all products and materials by road, the cost per ton per mile being £0·025. There is, however, an additional charge associated with imported items which effectively increases transportation costs to £0·029 per ton per mile. Considering only transportation costs, where should the new Incredible Chemical blending plant be situated?

3.4. In the interests of public health Incredible Chemicals Ltd. decide not to burn the 15 per cent of Formula X14 which is wasted by atmospheric contamination during blending. (See previous question.) After careful consideration and research they decide to sell this 'waste' product to a company in London who intend to use it in their patent weed killer.

How does this decision affect the choice of site for the new Formula X14 blending plant, and what is the total weekly transportation cost difference between the previous choice of site and the new choice of site?

Mileage chart

	Manchester	Bristol	Newcastle	London	Hull
Manchester	—				
Bristol	160	—			
Newcastle	135	300	—		
London	190	120	295	—	
Hull	75	180	120	200	—

3.5. The British Confectionery Corporation are anxious to build a new factory for the manufacture of a range of export goods. Although in theory the choice of location for this factory is wide, in practice, the choice is limited to two government-designated development areas centred on Sunderland and Birkenhead. One of the economists employed by the B.C.C. has evaluated both of these locations and has compiled the following information. Which location should the company choose?

Factor	Sunderland	Birkenhead	Weighting Factor[b]
Cost of land	£10 000	£12 500	4
Cost of buildings	30 000	35 000	4
Cost of labour	7 500	10 000	3
Transport cost p.a.	6 000	2 000	3
Industrial relations[a]	50	80	5
Labour training needs[a]	75	60	2
Community benefiits[a]	70	30	1

[a] Because of the difficulty of costing these factors a score, 1–100, has been given where 1 is equivalent to a low cost and 100 to a high cost.
[b] This weighting factor indicates the importance of each factor. 1 is of least importance, and 10 is of most importance.

3.6. Space-age Transport Ltd. is a British company, and the world's only successful manufacturer of highspeed, three-wheeled, electrical automobiles. After several years successful trading in Europe the company has decided to establish a subsidiary company in North America. The possible locations for the American company have been reduced to three, i.e. Chicago, Seattle and Michigan.

The following information has been provided by the company's accountants and marketing people. All other things being equal, which location should the company adopt for its American operations?

	Chicago	Seattle	Michigan
1. Cost of buildings	$50 000	$45 000	$38 000
Cost of land	$10 000	$ 8 000	$ 7 000
Distribution costs	$ 7 000	$10 000	$12 000
2. Initial labour training and recruitment costs	$ 4 000	$ 6 000	$ 7 000
3. Percentage annual labour turnover expected[a]	10%	20%	35%
4. Recreational attractions[a]	1	2	3
Availability of housing[a]	2	1	3
5. Suitability of site for subsequent expansion[b]	5	7	10

[a] Ranking 1 = most attractive; 3 = least attractive
[b] Rating on ten point scale provided by managing director 1 = most attractive; 10 = least attractive

As a means of evaluating the alternatives, the managing director considers that factors under 1. and 3. above have twice the importance of the factors under 2. and 4. and three times the importance of factor 5.

3.7. Company Z manufactures the same product at two existing factories located at A and B, and distributes them to three retail outlets at L, M and O. Because of an expected increase in demand for the product the company is considering opening an additional factory at *either* C or D.

The tables below show:

1. The unit production costs, the unit distribution costs and the monthly production capacity associated with the present situation, i.e. factories at A and B distributing to L, M and O.
2. The unit production costs, the unit distribution costs and the monthly production capacities associated with each of the possible additional factories.
3. The forecasted monthly product demands for each of the three retail outlets.
Where should the additional factory be established?

1	Outlet L	Outlet M	Outlet O	Unit production cost	Monthly production capacity
Factory A	0·2	0·4	0·3	1·0	4 000
Factory B	0·3	0·3	0·2	1·2	6 000

2	Outlet L	Outlet M	Outlet O	Unit production cost	Monthly production capacity
Factory C	0·3	0·2	0·4	1·2	3 500
Factory D	0·2	0·3	0·5	1·0	3 000

3	Outlet	Forecasted monthly demand
	L	3 800
	M	4 500
	O	4 500

3.8. Referring to the previous question, how does the inclusion of *both* of the following modifications affect the choice of location?

(a) The cost per unit associated with the underutilization of production capacity is 0·1 for factories A and C and 0·12 for factories B and D. (For example, if the required output from factory A is 3 500 units per month compared to its production capacity of 4 000 units per month, a cost of (4 000–3 500) × 0·1 is incurred.)

(b) The forecasted monthly demand for outlet L is 4 000 units.

3.9. A company rents three warehouses at A, B, and C from which they supply timber to two builders P and Q. The profit (£) per ton of timber supplied, the annual demands of the builders and the supplies available from the warehouses are shown below.

	P	Q	Supply ('000 tons)
A	3	4	4
B	2	3	4
C	5	4	3
Demand ('000 tons)	6	6	

The company is unhappy at not being able to meet the total annual demand of the builders and for this reason is considering replacing warehouse C with a warehouse rented at D whose annual supply capacity would be 5 000 tons, the use of which would give a profit of £6 and £5 per ton of timber distributed to P and Q respectively. The additional annual cost of renting warehouse D in place of C would be £5 000.

(a) Should the company replace warehouse C?
(b) If warehouse C were replaced, at which warehouse would the excess supply capacity be stored, assuming that storage is possible at A, B, or D at negligible cost?

II

The Design of Production Systems

We consider a production system to comprise men (labour), machines, materials and procedures; consequently, in the design of production systems we are concerned with the acquisition and arrangement of physical facilities, the design of work methods, work places and jobs, and also the planning and scheduling of production.

4

Plant Layout and the Movement of Materials

The layout problem is common to every type of enterprise. The housewife must arrange her kitchen, not only the cupboards, shelves and appliances, but also the utensils, crockery, food, etc. The retailer must arrange his counters, shelves, cashdesk to utilize available space, facilitate movement and attract custom. Manufacturers must arrange their facilities, not only the departments within the factory, but the plant, stores and services within those departments as well. The problems of layout are fundamental to every type of undertaking, and the adequacy of the layout affects the efficiency of subsequent operations, perhaps more than any other single decision.

The question is not, 'Shall we have a layout?', but, 'What sort of layout shall we have?' and, 'How shall we attempt to solve the layout problem?' Some form of layout will always be necessary and, good or bad, we will be forced to live with it—a fact which is only too evident in many of Britain's cities. Wren was prevented from arranging London's facilities after the great fire—a decision which still affects us all 350 years later.

It is appropriate that we should consider this problem at the beginning of the book because it is an important prerequisite for efficient operations, and it also has a great deal in common with many of the problems we shall be discussing later. Here we have an absolutely fundamental and common problem but, unfortunately, there is no single meaningful goal since objectives will vary from one situation to the next. Furthermore, there is no single acceptable and rigorous procedure by which to achieve our objectives. The housewife in arranging her kitchen will aim to minimize the amount of walking, bending and reaching she has to do, but since she will be dealing with a comparatively small problem she may achieve these objectives quite quickly by trial and error. Objectives in one industrial situation may differ substantially from those in another. In a steel mill dealing with hot metal the speed of movements will be of paramount importance, whereas in a small engineering shop, utilization of equipment and labour may be the primary concerns. Even in seemingly straightforward situations, where comparatively few items are to be arranged, a vast number of alternative acceptable solutions are available. For example, arranging six different departments in two adjacent rows of three produces 720 possible answers. Not surprisingly, such an apparently intractable problem has, in the past, proved discouraging and people have relied heavily on intuition, experience and improvization. Recently some progress has been made in the more scientific treatment of this type of problem. We must, therefore, in this chapter, discuss traditional methods, which have proved valuable and which are widely adopted, together with recent developments in the treatment of the same problems which are either of value now or promise well for the future.

Industry annually invests a great deal of money in new plant and machinery. Fixed capital expenditure by the British manufacturing industries in plant and machinery during 1967 was £1 038 million, an increase of 30 per cent over the last five years (even allowing for inflation).

Expenditure in the distributive and service industries on plant and machinery in 1967 was £393 million. During 1967 American manufacturing industries spend 26·69 billion dollars on plant and equipment. Only a portion of such new equipment will become part of new or modified layouts; nevertheless, the return obtained on a large proportion of this investment will depend to some extent on the efficiency with which the facilities are arranged.

Although we are confining ourselves to the terminology of the manufacturing industries, the problems, and particularly the solutions that we shall discuss, are not exclusive to any industry; in fact, some of the early and most important work conducted in this area concerned hospitals. Conceptually the nature of most layout problems is the same and examples exist of the successful application of the same procedures and techniques in many diverse situations.

Compared to a decade ago the proportion of direct and indirect employees in industry has changed remarkably. Indirect and staff workers now often outnumber direct or production workers, whereas a short while ago the reverse invariably applied. Consequently, even within industry the emphasis of layout problems has changed. The major part of many factories is devoted to service functions and, whilst the objectives and characteristics of such departments differ from those of production departments, many of the same layout considerations apply and the treatment is frequently similar.

PLANT LAYOUT PROBLEMS

Plant layout begins with plant location and continues through three further levels:

1. The layout of departments within the site
2. The layout of items within the departments
3. The layout of individual work places

Chapters 5, 6 and 7 relate to work-place layout, and the other two levels will be considered in this chapter.

In this chapter we are explicitly concerned with level (1), but implicitly the discussion relates to level (2) also, since they are the large- and small-scale levels of the same problem. Level (3), the layout of the work-place, being concerned with ergonomics and work study, is dealt with in chapters 5, 6 and 7.

Why do layout problems occur in industry? The need to produce a new or redesigned product may result in a need to reorganize existing plant or to provide additional plant. Changes in the level of demand or the location of markets for existing products may have similar results. Obsolescence or failure of existing equipment may result in the decision to install equipment whose characteristics provoke some rearrangements. The need for cost reductions may promote a reappraisal of layouts, as may factory legislation, accidents, and so on. We often tend to think in terms of planning complete layouts, designing entirely new factories, but although such occasions undoubtedly do arise the following are the types of problems we are much more likely to encounter.

Enlarging or reducing existing departments The addition or removal of machines, the trading of areas between departments, or a complete re-layout may be necessary because of increases or decreases in demand for a product, or changes in the scope or capability of production processes. For example, over the last ten years in medium and heavy engineering, there has been a steady increase in the use of steel fabrications where iron castings previously predominated.

Movement of a department The need to move a department because of a change in the design of the product, the demand, or method of production may constitute a simple exercise; alternatively, if the existing layout is inadequate, it may present the opportunity for a major reshuffle, the extent of which bears little relationship to the primary cause.

Adding a department This may result from the desire to undertake work never before done in the plant, or the desire to centralize work previously undertaken in several separate departments.

Replacing equipment and adding new equipment Frequently, even equipment designed to perform exactly the same function as its predecessors is physically different and its installation necessitates a certain amount of reorganization. Occasionally new machines may be installed to replace or supplement existing machines: a numerically controlled machining centre may be installed to replace existing milling and drilling machines, or an electron beam welder installed, in addition to existing welding equipment, to undertake work previously done with difficulty on conventional machines.

What are the objectives of plant layout, and what criteria should be adopted to assess and compare the various alternative layouts which undoubtedly will be suggested? A general definition of plant layout is, 'the arrangement of the physical production facilities to provide efficient production'. Operationally 'efficient production' is too general a concept and more specific objectives are necessary. Some of the advantages of good plant layouts and hence some possible objectives whilst planning layouts are as follows.

Minimum cost of materials handling and movement The handling and movement of materials, components and the finished product, as well as the movement of labour, is primarily dependent upon the location of the production and service facilities. Adequate layout will result in a reduction in the distance moved, the time consumed and, hence, in the cost of materials handling and movement.

Low work in progress and high turnover The objective of any manufacturing company is to add to the value of its raw materials. This is achieved by subjecting the raw materials to some form of processing. No value is added, and nothing is contributed to profits by delays or storage during production. Although the extent of work in progress is also determined by the effectiveness of production control and the nature of the production process, poor plant layout may necessitate high work in progress and hence increase through-put time.

Effective utilization of space, facilities and labour A small percentage of the total floor area of any plant is occupied by production equipment; the remainder is necessary for movement and services. The cost of factory floor area is high, but wasted floor area may be eliminated and the area necessary for movement minimized by adequate plant layout. Effective arrangement of plant may reduce idle time and cut down investment in both production and materials handling equipment. Adequate layout also facilitates operation, maintenance, service and supervision, and therefore enables a better utilization of labour.

THE MAIN SYSTEMS OF PLANT LAYOUT

There are, classically, three main systems of plant layout, each with individual characteristics and each appropriate to some form of production, depending upon the output rate and the range of products involved. Although each system is normally associated with a particular type of production, none is exclusive to any one industry. We will examine each of these basic systems in turn, identifying the nature of production and the characteristics of each.

Layout by Process or Functional Layout

In a process or functional layout all operations of a similar nature are grouped together in the same department or part of the factory. For example, separate areas may exist for drilling operations, milling, grinding, fitting and so on.

Layout by process is appropriate where small quantities of a large range of products are to be manufactured, perhaps the best example being jobbing production. The nature of the layout permits flexibility in production, i.e. complex products, requiring processing in every one of the functional departments, may be made alongside simple products requiring processing in only a few departments. Such a situation would be difficult to accommodate in either of the other two systems of layout. This same flexibility, however, brings disadvantages. Process layouts normally operate with a comparatively high level of work in progress and through-put time is high.

Specialist supervision is possible, and the grouping of operatives of a similar type and skill within the same department promotes cohesiveness and enables individual bonus schemes to be used. The provision of services, e.g. water, power, removal of scrap, is simpler than in other forms of layout, but the cost of materials handling is high.

Layout by Product

In contrast to the flexible but somewhat inefficient production system inherent in process layout, layout by product, appropriate for the production of a small range of products in very large quantities, is a comparatively rigid and certainly efficient production system. Ideally, only one standardized product is involved and production should be continuous, as in mass production industries such as the motor industry. The equipment is arranged according to the needs of the product and in the same sequence as the operations necessary for manufacture (Fig. 4.1). Because this is a specialized production layout, designed solely for the production of large quantities of one or at least a very small range of standardized products, it is relatively inflexible. Sufficient and stable demand to ensure a high utilization of equipment is absolutely essential, as is a regular supply of the right quantities of raw materials and components. Failure in the supply of a piece of equipment results in the entire production line stopping, and apparently quite remote failures can result in disproportionately high losses, e.g. the British motor industry.

The provision of services is difficult, since where particularly elaborate machinery is used quite different pieces of equipment with different characteristics and requirements may be located adjacent to one another. A mixture of skills and operations frequently occurs resulting in difficulties as to payment and supervision; but usually little specialized supervision is required since the work performed is often highly rationalized. Minimum floor space is required, work in progress is minimized and through-put is high. The requirements for handling materials are small and machine utilization is high.

Layout by Fixed Position

In the two previous layout systems the product moves past stationary production equipment. In this case the reverse applies. In the extreme case, e.g. civil engineering, neither the partly completed nor the finished product moves. Alternatively, as in ship building, the product remains stationary only until it is completed.

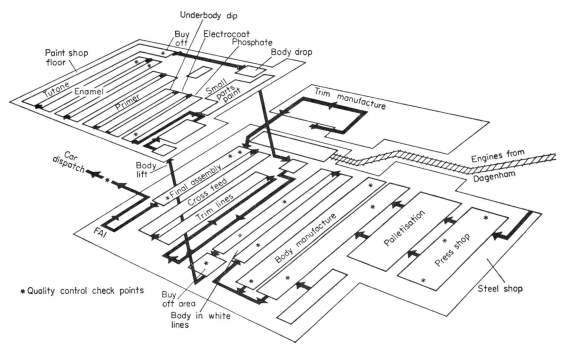

FIGURE 4.1. Product-type layout—general arrangement of facilities at the Halewood plant of the Ford Motor Company [Reproduced by permission, Ford Motor Co. Ltd.]

TABLE 4.1. Comparison of process and product layouts

	Layout by process	Layout by product
Nature	All similar facilities grouped together	Sequence of facilities derived from needs of product
Application	Low quantity production	Large quantity production
	Large range of products	Only a few products
Characteristics	Permits specialist supervision	Little specialized supervision required
	High work in progress	Minimum work in progress
	High material handling cost	Minimum material handling cost
	Ease of provision of services	Difficult to provide services
		Minimum space required
	Can tolerate breakdowns	Single breakdown stops all machines
	Easy to incorporate inspection	Difficult to incorporate inspection
	Individual bonus possible	Group bonus
	Flexibility, variety and product changes possible	Little variety possible
	Possibility for loss or neglect of some jobs/items	
	Maintenance easy	Maintenance out of production hours
	Production control complex	Production control simple
	Production planning simple	Production planning complex
		Accurate work measurement essential
	Long production time	Low production time

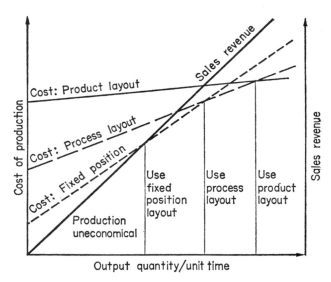

FIGURE 4.2. Break-even analysis showing economic advantage of various types of layout for same product at different output levels

Unlike the period prior to the Industrial Revolution, when a large proportion of production was undertaken by artisans in their own homes, layout by fixed position is now comparatively unimportant, except where civil engineering or large items such as ships and aircraft are concerned.

The characteristics of layout by product and by process are listed and contrasted in Table 4.1. Figure 4.2 shows a break-even point analysis of three types of production, indicating the relative cost benefits firstly of process layout, then of product layout as output increases.

Most practical layouts are combinations of process and product layout. Rarely are companies in the enviable situation where they are able to produce continuously large quantities of an absolutely standard product. Similarly, even the largest range of products normally utilizes certain common components, and firms obliged to concentrate on process layouts are normally able to support some product layouts as well. (See the discussion of group technology in Chapter 11.)

PLANT LAYOUT PROCEDURE

The planning of an entirely new layout is *the* most comprehensive problem and although such occasions are compararively rare we shall consider this case in detail in order to cover the subject adequately.

Figure 4.3 attempts to show the various sources from which information is obtained and the sequence in which the data are used in planning the layout. In practice, plant layout procedure tends to be elaborate and complex, and any attempt to represent all the variables and decisions diagrammatically inevitably results in complex figures. Nevertheless, beneath this elaborate facade a comparatively straightforward procedure exists and this is what we shall consider, despite a risk of oversimplification.

We are proposing to build our new factory with the intention of producing one or more products for which an adequate demand is known to exist. It is assumed that the precise nature

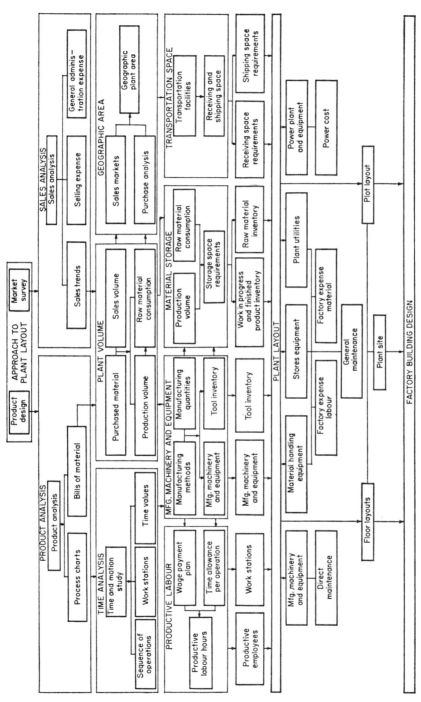

FIGURE 4.3. Sources and uses of information in layout planning [Reproduced by permission, R. W. Mallick and A. T. Gaudreau, *Plant Layout*, Wiley, New York, 1951]

of our product, i.e. its design, specification, performance, etc., and the output required are either known or may be determined by appropriate market research. The product consists of components, which we shall either manufacture or purchase. Given a list of operations, their durations and the output for each component, and knowing the total working hours available, machine requirements can be calculated.

Type of products to be manufactured + Output required = Machinery required

Machines are normally only part of the total plant required in a factory. Storage space will be required, depending upon such factors as fluctuations in demand for the product and the supply of materials. Service departments, such as goods receiving, tool-room, canteen and medical, may also be required. Furthermore, the nature and extent of movement, the need for maintenance, the possibility of expansion, etc., will all influence the layout design.

Machinery required + Other factors affecting layout = Plant layout

Plant layout procedure involves the following stages:

1. Product Demand

Normally, the reason for production is the existence of demand. If we are building a new factory to increase the output of an existing product, then the extent of demand of the nature of the product will be known. Otherwise we will rely upon market research to establish the following:

> specification of the product required
> selling price
> demand for each product
> expected fluctuations in demand, i.e. the life of the product

This information gives rise to production requirements.

2. Production Requirements

As well as the output of each product for a given period, the approximate total manufacturing costs should be known in order to achieve a suitable profit; also the stock levels necessary to accommodate demand fluctuations whilst maintaining a level production rate. These are the basic data with which we shall plan the layout.

3. Components and Parts Analysis

Each product will consist of manufactured or purchased components, many of which may be common to more than one product. Parts lists will normally be available, which enumerate all sub-assemblies, components and parts, together with raw materials specifications, quantities required, drawing number, stock number, etc.

4. Work Methods and Measurement

Work study data should exist or be generated for each component. Method study (see Chapter 5) will establish the sequence of operations to be performed during the manufacture of the component and the type of equipment to be used. Given a standard work method, work measurement (see

Chapter 6) will establish time standards for production. Such information, which is a prerequisite for all production planning, is often summarized on standard practice sheets.

5. Machine Requirements

Given the available work hours, i.e. the number and duration of work shifts, the total machinery and total direct labour requirements can be calculated for a known production rate. Minimum total requirements may be calculated from the data, but it is usually necessary to provide additional capacity to allow for breakdown and maintenance of machinery, labour absenteeism, scrap, etc.

6. Handling and Movement

The routing of each product through the necessary machines is obtained from the method study documents, such as flow process charts (see Chapter 5). In the case of high quantity production of a few products, movement, handling and work-in-progress storage is minimal. In the case of batch or jobbing production of a range of items, movement and handling will be extensive and complex. Routing data from the flow process charts may be summarized and such information used when planning the actual layout.

7. Space Requirements

In addition to the space necessary to accommodate machinery, allowances must be made for the movement of workers around and about machinery, for service and repair and, in the case of process-type layouts where queues of components invariably exist, for the storage of components immediately prior to and after processing.

8. Other Factors Affecting Layout

(a) A company making instruments was experiencing a quality problem due to the failure of a delicate spring mechanism. On investigation it was found that failure resulted from corrosion by moisture deposits left on the springs during handling in assembly. The installation of an extensive air-conditioning system was necessary.
(b) In order to conduct routine maintenance on a coalmine conveyor system, it was found, because of the nature of the conveyor and because of the layout of equipment, to be necessary to remove the unit completely.
(c) The management of a timber mill were concerned about their storage problems. Wood was stacked in lots on the floor, but often when a particular lot was required it was found buried beneath several others. In order to help overcome this problem and convert their essentially two-dimensional storage system to three dimensions, they resorted to storing some lots by hanging them from the hook of a redundant gantry crane!

Normally, as in these three cases, additional and often obscure factors affect layout. For example, the removal, reprocessing or use of scrap and waste materials; characteristics of the materials used, e.g. stability, value, etc; noise; safety legislation; anticipated developments, and the necessity for change may all be important.

Consequently, stages (1) to (7) above can be considered only as a general procedure for the generation and collection of basic data which, along with other considerations peculiar to the particular circumstances, enable us to begin to plan the layout.

PLANNING THE LAYOUT—1

New Layouts

In many fields of management current practice is far removed from current theory and research. Present practice is a reflection of previous research, and current research results from the inadequancies of present practice. Progress is continually being made in both practice and research, but the variance between the two levels rarely decreases. Nowhere is this more apparant than in plant layout. The conventional layout procedures appear quite mundane beside current theory, but nevertheless these procedures are proven, accepted and valuable.

Visual aids play an important part in layout planning. Some form of scale representation is invariably used, e.g. scale drawings, templates, three-dimensional models, etc. Frequently movement patterns are shown on the drawings or models, but one often wonders whether this information has been used in developing the layout or merely to justify it! String diagrams are a familiar method of showing movement, coloured cord being attached to diagrams or models to indicate the paths taken by different products.

The main criticism of these methods, about which little more need be said here, is that they are completely unstructured and depend entirely upon the knowledge, experience and insight of the planner. This same fact can, however, be interpreted as their main advantage. If they are completely unstructured it is theoretically possible, whilst planning the layout, to take into account all relevant constraints. Their merit, therefore, is the breadth of their approach rather than their rigour.

If we are to attempt to develop analytical methods of layout planning, we must determine precisely what our objective function shall be. For example, whether we shall attempt to maximize machine utilization, minimize movement, work in progress, etc. Undoubtedly, the lowest common denominator of all plant layouts is the need for movement. Even in visual planning procedures the need to minimize movement is usually the first consideration, and only after an initial layout has been obtained are additional objectives allowed to intervene. In manufacturing, movement consists mainly of materials handling, and the type of handling equipment used, the distance travelled and the time involved will all affect the total cost. However, in planning layouts, particularly new layouts which exist only on paper, it is frequently possible to measure only the distance involved in movement. Each handling operation normally involves pick-up, movement, put-down; but movement is the only variable factor.

It is not unreasonable, therefore, to adopt as our primary objective the minimization of the total materials handling cost, and as our main criterion the total distance moved.

Cross and Relationship Charts

The pattern and extent of movement or handling which is known to take place, or expected to exist, within a factory is often summarized on some form of chart, which can then be used to assist in layout planning.

The cross chart, shown in Fig. 4.4 indicates the amount and pattern of movement of items between ten departments in a small factory. In the case of a new layout the routing will have been obtained from routing instructions, e.g. flow process charts, and the quantities from production requirements. The figures in the matrix are the number of items or loads of items which in a given period of time must move from department i to department j. In the case of the existing layouts this information may be obtained by actual sampling of the activity taking place within the factory.

Notice that the row and the column totals are not necessarily equal. Where some of the items

FROM \ TO	Receiving 1	Stores 2	Planning 3	Milling 4	Turning 5	Assembly 6	Test 7	Paint 8	Pack 9	Dispatch 10	TOTAL
Receiving 1		15				12	8	5			40
Stores 2			10	5							15
Planning 3				10							10
Milling 4					5	7		3			15
Turning 5						5					5
Assembly 6							12				12
Test 7								12	8		20
Paint 8									12	8	20
Packing 9										20	20
Dispatch 10											
TOTAL		15	10	15	5	24	20	20	20	28	

FIGURE 4.4. Cross chart showing the nature and extent of the movement of items amongst departments over a given period of time

are consumed, or assembled to other items during production, row totals may be less than column totals. For example, in this particular case twelve items were sent from the receiving department directly to the asssembly department; the assembly department also received seven items from the milling and five from the turning department, i.e. in total, twenty-four items were sent to assembly. However, only twelve items left assembly for the test department, since the two groups of twelve had been assembled in pairs.

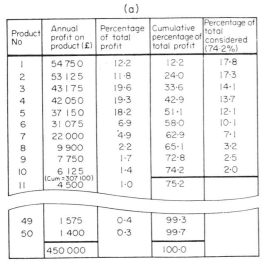

(a)

Product No	Annual profit on product (£)	Percentage of total profit	Cumulative percentage of total profit	Percentage of total considered (74.2%)
1	54 750	12.2	12.2	17.8
2	53 125	11.8	24.0	17.3
3	43 175	9.6	33.6	14.1
4	42 050	9.3	42.9	13.7
5	37 150	8.2	51.1	12.1
6	31 075	6.9	58.0	10.1
7	22 000	4.9	62.9	7.1
8	9 900	2.2	65.1	3.2
9	7 750	1.7	72.8	2.5
10	6 125 (Cum = 307 100)	1.4	74.2	2.0
11	4 500	1.0	75.2	
49	1 575	0.4	99.3	
50	1 400	0.3	99.7	
	450 000		100.0	

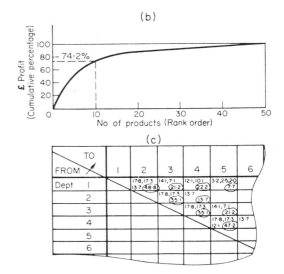

(b)

(c)

FIGURE 4.5. A weighted cross chart—method of construction. (a) Profit per product; (b) Cumulative profit; (c) Weighted cross chart (principal parts only)

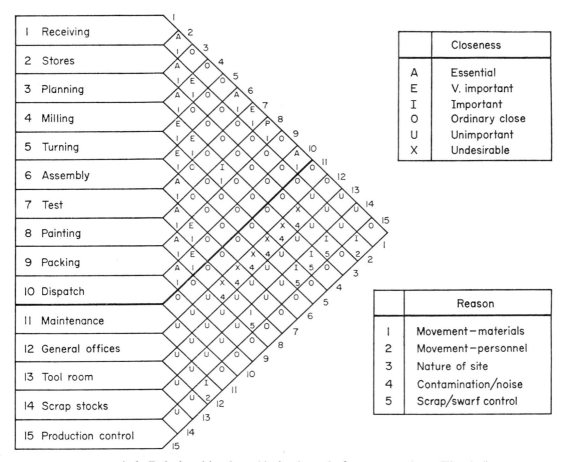

	Receiving
2	Stores
3	Planning
4	Milling
5	Turning
6	Assembly
7	Test
8	Painting
9	Packing
10	Dispatch
11	Maintenance
12	General offices
13	Tool room
14	Scrap stocks
15	Production control

	Closeness
A	Essential
E	V. important
I	Important
O	Ordinary close
U	Unimportant
X	Undesirable

	Reason
1	Movement – materials
2	Movement – personnel
3	Nature of site
4	Contamination/noise
5	Scrap/swarf control

FIGURE 4.6. Relationship chart (derived partly from cross chart, Fig. 4.4)

Notation based on Muther and Wheeler (see Selected Readings)

The movement pattern shown in this chart is associated with a process-type layout. Absence of any figures below the diagonal means that none of the items backtrack between departments, but the scatter above the diagonal indicates a varied movement pattern characteristic of the production of several products. A proportion of the items follow the path—straight through from department (1) to department (10), but judging from this data alone, a 'product layout' seems impractical.

Various elaborations on the cross chart have been suggested from time to time, but the simple principle remains the same. For example, a weighted cross chart may on occasions offer sufficient advantages to justify the extra effort. Fig. 4.5 shows the method of constructing a weighted cross chart, the weighting in this case being related to the product's contribution to total profits. Instead of placing a mark on the cross chart to represent one item's journey between two departments, the figures from either column three or five in the first table are used. So far throughout this chapter we have assumed that all the products to be made, and hence all the parts passing through the factory, are to be considered in planning the layout. An alternative is to consider only the principal parts. In Fig. 4.5(c) the figures from column five of Fig. 4.5(a) are used to compile the cross chart, as only the ten principal products and their associated parts are being used. These ten products account for 74·2 per cent of the total annual profits.

Cross charts are a means of collecting and presenting information from which preferable departmental relationships can be obtained. This information can then be summarized on a relationship chart. For example the relationship chart shown in Fig. 4.6 is partly derived from the previous cross chart (Fig. 4.4). Most of the preferable relationships between departments (1) to (10) result from a desire to minimize the materials movement given on the cross chart. The relationships between departments (11) to (15) and between these and the other departments have been obtained from elsewhere.

Before discussing quantitative methods and planning layouts, we will look briefly at a method of layout planning developed in the late 1950s. This will not only indicate the shortcomings of the methods we have discussed so far, but also help us to enumerate the features which are desirable in any rigorous planning procedure.

Sequence Analysis

Figure 4.7(a) summarizes the routing necessary for the production of five parts, i.e. part A must pass through departments 1, 4, 7, 9 and 10 in that order, and part B through departments 1, 2, 4, 5, 6, 8, 9 and 10. The production quantities in terms of the units of each part to be moved (whether each load consists of one item or a batch of ten) are given in Fig. 4.7(b).

Figure 4.7(c) is derived from the previous two figures and is a summary of the load and movement data. For example, in a given period of time 450 unit loads must move from department 1 to department 2, i.e. the parts moving from department 1 to 2 are, from Fig. 4.7(a), B, C and D, for which the unit loads per period are 100, 200 and 150 respectively—a total of 450.

Given this information it is now possible to start planning the layout. By representing each department by a circle, and assuming each department to be of equal area, an initial diagrammatic solution can be obtained by arranging the circles in the form of a grid, following the logic of the pattern indicated by Fig. 4.7(c). Connecting lines and figures indicate the extent of the inter-departmental movement (Fig. 4.7(d)). The initial diagrammatic solution can be simplified and the layout modified until the best solution is achieved (Fig. 4.7(e)). This can then be changed into an actual layout by substituting the required departmental areas for the circles in the diagrammatic representation (Fig. 4.7(f)).

The shortcomings of this procedure are immediately obvious. How, for instance, does one get from Fig. 4.7(c) to Fig. 4.7(e)? What method is used to convert the *data* into the *solution*? As with the above methods, the solution depends entirely upon individual insight and manipulation. Sequence analysis is, in this respect, directly analogous to the cross chart/relationship chart method of layout planning; in fact Fig. 4.7(c) is equivalent to a relationship chart. This is not to say that sequence analysis does not have some advantages over the visual procedure. At least a routine method is used, but it is nevertheless far short of the ideal procedure which we would like to be able to offer, since too much reliance is placed on the skill and patience of the planner. It may be relatively easy in this particular example to devise alternative layouts for evaluation, many of which may be as good as, or even superior to, that shown, but in a practical situation where many more departments are likely to exist the procedure has very severe shortcomings. In fact, as the size of the problem increases so does the number of apparently satisfactory solutions, but the individual's ability to visualize and evaluate the increasing number of alternative solutions decreases and hence the probability of adopting an inferior or sub-optimum solution is greater.

To overcome this difficulty we require a systematic procedure which, although capable of taking into account only a few criteria, or even just one, will reliably eliminate all the inferior

(a)   Operation sequences

PART \ DEPT	A	B	C	D	E	AREA REQD (Sq.ft)
1	4	2	2	2	3	450
2		4	4	5	4	300
3					2	150
4	7	5	5		7	300
5		6	6	6		400
6		8	9	7		250
7	9			9	10	300
8		9				150
9	10	10	10	10		300
10						600

(c)   Load/movement summary

FROM \ TO	1	2	3	4	5	6	7	8	9	10
1		450	50	50						
2				350	150					
3	50									
4					300		100			
5						450				
6							150	100	200	
7									200	50
8									100	
9										500
10										

(b)   Load (per period time)

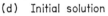

50	100	200	150	50

(d)   Initial solution

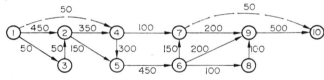
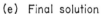

(e)   Final solution

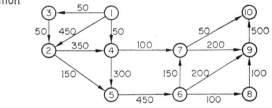

(f)   Actual layout

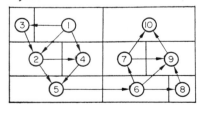

FIGURE 4.7. Sequence analysis

solutions and present a selection of good solutions from which we can select one for use or further modification. What we require, in the absence of a completely rigorous procedure capable of producing an optimum solution, is a method of reducing the problem to a manageable size.

To be of any value our procedure must:

1. Take as its objective something that we believe to be of overriding importance, if not of sole importance.
2. Be capable of producing several good layouts from which we can choose the best, or which we can modify, depending upon other additional objectives and constraints.

We have previously agreed that our primary objective will be the minimization of total materials handling cost. We also require a procedure which has the ability to accommodate:

(a) different floor areas for departments
(b) the wide variety of material flow patterns amongst departments typical in process-type layouts
(c) different costs of material handling
(d) the fact that certain departments may need to remain in a given position
(e) the fact that in certain circumstances certain departments must bear a given relationship to one another
(f) utilizing more than one floor.

Not until after 1960 were procedures developed which began to comply with these requirements. Since 1963 several quite different computer programs have been written and tested, and several other quantitative methods of layout planning suggested.

Computer Programs

In 1963 a computer program called CRAFT (Computerized Relative Allocation of Facilities Technique)[1] was first published. It was developed in order to satisfy many of the requirements listed above and takes as its objective minimization of total materials handling costs.

Let n = number of departments

v_{ij} = number of unit loads moving between departments i and j in direction $i \to j$ in a given time.

u_{ij} = cost per unit distance to move one unit load between i and j in direction $i \to j$.

l_{ij} = Distance between i and j.

v, u and l, can be represented as matrices (V, U and L), for example matrix L below shows the distances between all pairs of departments in a layout.

$$\text{Matrix } L = \begin{bmatrix} l_{11} & l_{12} & . & . & . & l_{1n} \\ l_{21} & l_{22} & . & . & . & l_{2n} \\ . & . & . & . & . & . \\ . & . & . & . & . & . \\ l_{n1} & l_{n2} & . & . & . & l_{nn} \end{bmatrix}$$

The number of loads moving between departments does not vary with changes in department location. For simplicity we can also assume that the unit cost of the movement does not vary with

___

[1] See 'Selected Readings' for this chapter.

the changes in location and consequently v_{ij} and u_{ij} can be combined and represented as a single matrix Y.

$$\text{Matrix } Y = \begin{bmatrix} y_{11} & y_{12} & . & . & . & y_{1n} \\ y_{21} & y_{22} & . & . & . & y_{2n} \\ . & . & . & . & . & . \\ . & . & . & . & . & . \\ y_{n1} & y_{n2} & . & . & . & y_{nn} \end{bmatrix}$$

Total material handling cost for a layout
$$E = \sum_{i=1}^{n} \sum_{j=1}^{n} y_{ij} l_{ij}$$

Unfortunately, there is no practical mathematical method of minimizing E, consequently we must rely upon a heuristic[2] method such as the one provided by the CRAFT program. A

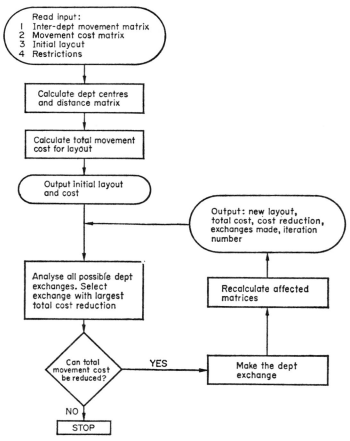

FIGURE 4.8. (a) Simplified flow chart for CRAFT program

[2] A heuristic procedure is an intuitively designed procedure capable of providing a good, but not necessarily optimum, solution to a problem. Because of the complexity of many situations facing the production manager, rigorous methods providing optimum solutions are rarely available, hence heuristic procedures are of considerable importance.

simplified flow diagram for the program, whose objective is the minimization of total materials handling cost (E), is shown in Fig. 4.8(a).

CRAFT takes as part of its input an initial layout of the departments. This may be either an arbitrary initial layout or an existing layout, whichever is appropriate. The input must also include a matrix giving the material load flows between departments, and a cost matrix giving the cost of materials movement between all pairs of departments. The program then attempts to improve on the initial layout by interchanging pairs of departments. Every pair of departments is examined and the effect of their interchange upon the total materials handling cost for the layout is calculated. The pair change giving the greatest reduction in total materials handling cost is effected and the process is repeated until no further interchange of departments will provide any further reduction in the total materials handling cost associated with the layout.

The necessary input is:

1. Interdepartmental flow matrix (V) which gives the number of unit loads moving between all departments over a given period of time (Fig. 4.8(b)). This matrix need not be symmetrical.

	A	B	C	D	E	F	G	H	J	K	L	M	N	P	R	S	T	U	V	W
A	-0.	120.0	80.0	-0.	-0.	-0.	-0.	-0.	-0.	40.0	80.0	-0.	-0.	80.0	-0.	-0.	-0.	-0.	-0.	-0.
B	120.0	-0.	80.0	1630.0	30.0	-0.	930.0	-0.	80.0	90.0	-0.	-0.	-0.	-0.	-0.	-0.	-0.	-0.	460.0	-0.
C	80.0	80.0	-0.	-0.	-0.	130.0	-0.	-0.	210.0	260.0	-0.	-0.	-0.	870.0	-0.	-0.	-0.	-0.	910.0	-0.
D	-0.	1630.0	-0.	-0.	60.0	380.0	500.0	-0.	130.0	-0.	-0.	70.0	-0.	-0.	-0.	-0.	-0.	100.0	1050.0	-0
E	-0.	30.0	-0.	60.0	-0.	-0.	150.0	90.0	-0.	60.0	-0.	-0.	-0.	-0.	90.0	-0.	-0.	-0.	-0.	-0.
F	-0.	-0.	130.0	380.0	-0.	-0.	410.0	-0.	-0.	-0.	-0.	30.0	-0.	-0.	-0.'	-0.	-0.	70.0	-0.	-0.
G	-0.	930.0	-0.	500.0	150.0	410.0	-0.	1600.0	-0.	110.0	-0.	-0.	-0.	60.0	-0.	-0.	-0.	110.0	-0.	250.0
H	-0.	-0.	-0.	-0.	90.0	-0.	1600.0	-0.	-0.	-0.	-0.	-0.	40.0	-0.	-0.	-0.	-0.	-0.	500.0	2230.0
J	-0.	80.0	210.0	130.0	-0.	-0.	-0.	-0.	-0.	-0.	-0.	-0.	-0.	500.0	-0.	-0.	500.0	-0.	-0.	-0.
K	40.0	90.0	260.0	-0.	60.0	-0.	110.0	-0.	-0.	-0.	30.0	800.0	-0.	1240.0	160.0	-0.	-0.	-0.	350.0	-0.
L	80.0	-0.	-0.	-0.	-0.	-0.	-0.	-0.	-0.	30.0	-0.	150.0	-0.	200.0	80.0	1500.0	350.0	90.0	-0.	-0.
M	-0.	-0.	-0.	70.0	-0.	30.0	-0.	-0.	-0.	800.0	150.0	-0.	-0.	-0.	110.0	-0.	1000.0	-0.	560.0	-0.
N	-0.	-0.	-0.	-0.	-0.	-0.	-0.	40.0	-0.	-0.	-0.	-0.	-0.	500.0	40.0	500.0	-0.	40.0	-0.	-0.
P	80.0	-0.	870.0	-0.	-0.	-0.	60.0	-0.	500.0	1240.0	200.0	-0.	500.0	-0.	650.0	-0.	-0.	60.0	-0.	-0.
R	-0.	-0.	-0.	-0.	90.0	-0.	-0.	-0.	-0.	160.0	80.0	110.0	40.0	650.0	-0.	-0.	350.0	-0.	-0.	-0.
S	-0.	-0.	-0.	-0.	-0.	-0.	-0.	-0.	-0.	-0.	1500.0	-0.	500.0	-0.	-0.	-0.	1000.0	-0.	-0.	-0.
T	-0.	-0.	-0.	-0.	-0.	-0.	-0.	-0.	500.0	-0.	350.0	100.0	-0.	-0.	350.0	1000.0	-0.	-0.	500.0	-0.
U	-0.	-0.	-0.	100.0	-0.	70.0	110.0	-0.	-0.	-0.	90.0	-0.	-0.	60.0	-0.	-0.	-0.	-0.	310.0	-0.
V	-0.	460.0	910.0	1050.0	-0.	-0.	-0.	500.0	-0.	350.0	-0.	560.0	-0.	-0.	-0.	-0.	500.0	310.0	-0.	-0.
W	-0.	-0.	-0.	-0.	-0.	-0.	250.0	2230.0	-0.	-0..	-0.	-0.	-0.	-0.	-0.	-0.	-0.	-0.	-0.	-0.

FIGURE 4.8. (b) Interdepartmental unit load movement (per period of time)

2. Interdepartmental materials handling cost matrix (U) giving the cost per unit distance of movement between all departments (Fig. 4.8(c)). This matrix need not be symmetrical, so that with matrix V volumes in different directions can be given different costs.
3. Initial layout configuration showing size of departments, arranged so that one line can be represented by an 80 column punch card (Fig. 4.8(d)). It may be an arbitrary or an existing layout.
4. Any restrictions, i.e. fixed departments which cannot be moved.

	A	B	C	D	E	F	G	H	J	K	L	M	N	P	R	S	T	U	V	W
A	-0.	0.015	0.015	-0.	-0.	-0.	-0.	-0.	-0.	0.026	0.014	-0.	-0.	0.015	-0.	-0.	-0.	-0.	-0.	-0.
B	0.015	-0.	0.012	0.015	0.026	-0.	0.015	-0.	0.015	0.015	-0.	-0.	-0.	-0.	-0.	-0.	-0.	-0.	0.015	-0.
C	0.015	0.012	-0.	-0.	-0.	0.017	-0.	-0.	0.015	0.015	-0.	-0.	-0.	0.015	-0.	-0.	-0.	-0.	0.015	-0.
D	-0.	0.015	-0.	-0.	0.018	0.015	0.015	-0.	0.015	-0.	-0.	0.020	-0.	-0.	-0.	-0.	-0.	0.015	0.015	-0.
E	-0.	0.026	-0.	0.018	-0.	-0.	0.015	0.015	-0.	0.026	-0.	-0.	-0.	-0.	0.015	-0.	-0.	-0.	-0.	-0.
F	-0.	-0.	0.017	0.015	-0.	-0.	0.015	-0.	-0.	-0.	-0.	0.015	-0.	-0.	-0.	-0.	0.015	-0.	-0.	-0.
G	-0.	0.015	-0.	0.015	0.015	0.015	-0.	0.015	-0.	0.017	-0.	-0.	-0.	0.016	-0.	-0.	-0.	0.015	-0.	0.01
H	-0.	-0.	-0.	-0.	0.015	-0.	0.015	-0.	-0.	-0.	-0.	0.015	-0.	-0.	-0.	-0.	-0.	-0.	0.015	0.01
J	-0.	0.015	0.015	0.018	-0.	-0.	-0.	-0.	-0.	-0.	-0.	-0.	0.015	-0.	-0.	0.015	-0.	-0.	-0.	-0.
K	0.026	0.015	0.015	-0.	0.026	-0.	0.017	-0.	-0.	-0.	0.012	0.015	-0.	0.015	0.012	-0.	-0.	-0.	0.015	-0.
L	0.014	-0.	-0.	-0.	-0.	-0.	-0.	-0.	-0.	0.012	-0.	0.015	-0.	0.015	0.012	0.015	-0.	-0.	0.015	-0.
M	-0.	-0.	-0.	0.020	-0.	0.015	-0.	-0.	-0.	0.015	0.015	-0.	-0.	0.015	-0.	0.015	-0.	0.015	-0.	-0.
N	-0.	-0.	-0.	-0.	-0.	-0.	-0.	0.015	-0.	-0.	-0.	-0.	-0.	0.016	0.026	0.012	-0.	-0.	-0.	-0.
P	0.015	-0.	0.015	-0.	-0.	-0.	0.016	-0.	0.015	0.015	0.015	-0.	0.016	-0.	0.015	-0.	-0.	0.015	-0.	-0.
R	-0.	-0.	-0.	-0.	0.015	-0.	-0.	-0.	-0.	0.012	0.012	0.015	0.026	0.015	-0.	-0.	0.015	-0.	-0.	-0.
S	-0.	-0.	-0.	-0.	-0.	-0.	-0.	-0.	-0.	-0.	-0.	-0.	0.012	-0.	-0.	-0.	0.012	-0.	-0.	-0.
T	-0.	-0.	-0.	-0.	-0.	-0.	-0.	-0.	0.015	-0.	-0.	0.015	-0.	-0.	0.015	0.012	-0.	-0.	0.015	-0.
U	-0.	-0.	-0.	0.015	-0.	0.015	0.015	-0.	-0.	-0.	-0.	-0.	-0.	0.015	-0.	-0.	-0.	-0.	0.015	-0.
V	-0.	0.015	0.015	0.015	-0.	-0.	-0.	0.015	-0.	0.015	0.015	0.015	-0.	-0.	-0.	-0.	0.015	0.015	-0.	-0.
W	-0.	-0.	-0.	-0.	-0.	-0.	0.015	0.015	-0.	-0.	-0.	-0.	-0.	-0.	-0.	-0.	-0.	-0.	-0.	-0.

FIGURE 4.8. (c) Interdepartmental movement cost (per unit load, per unit distance)

LOCATION PATTERN   ITERATION O

	1	2	3	4	5	6	7	8	9	10	11	12	13	14	15	16	17	18	19	20	21	22	23	24	25	26	27	28	29	30
1	A	A	A	A	A	A	B	B	B	L	L	L	L	L	L	L	S	S	S	S	S	S	S	S	S	W	W	W	W	W
2	A	A	A	A	A	A	B	B	B	L	L	L	L	L	L	L	S	S	S	S	S	S	S	S	S	W	W	W	W	W
3	A	A	A	A	A	B	B	B	B	L	L	L	L	L	L	L	S	S	S	S	S	S	S	S	S	W	W	W	W	W
4	A	A	A	A	A	B	B	B	B	L	L	L	L	L	L	L	S	S	S	S	S	S	S	S	S	W	W	W	W	W
5	A	A	A	A	A	B	B	B	B	L	L	L	L	L	L	L	S	S	S	S	S	S	S	S	S	W	W	W	W	W
6	C	C	C	C	C	C	D	D	D	L	L	L	L	L	L	L	S	S	S	S	S	S	S	S	S	W	W	W	W	W
7	C	C	C	C	C	C	D	D	D	L	L	L	L	L	L	L	G	G	G	S	S	S	S	S	S	W	W	W	W	W
8	C	C	C	C	C	D	D	D	D	L	L	L	L	L	L	L	G	G	G	S	S	S	S	S	S	W	W	W	W	W
9	C	C	C	C	C	D	D	D	D	L	L	L	L	L	L	L	G	G	G	S	S	S	S	S	S	W	W	W	W	W
10	C	C	C	C	C	D	D	D	D	N	N	N	N	N	N	H	H	H	T	T	T	T	T	T	T	T	T	T	T	T
11	E	E	E	E	E	E	F	F	F	N	N	N	N	N	N	H	H	H	T	T	T	T	T	T	T	T	T	T	T	T
12	E	E	E	E	E	E	F	F	F	N	N	N	N	N	N	H	H	H	T	T	T	T	T	T	T	T	T	T	T	T
13	E	E	E	E	E	E	F	F	F	P	P	P	P	P	P	J	J	J	T	T	T	T	T	T	T	T	T	T	T	T
14	K	K	K	K	K	K	F	F	F	P	P	P	P	P	P	J	J	J	T	T	T	T	T	T	T	T	T	T	T	T
15	K	K	K	K	K	K	F	F	F	P	P	P	P	P	P	J	J	J	U	U	U	U	U	U	T	T	T	T	V	V
16	K	K	K	K	K	K	F	F	F	P	P	P	P	P	P	R	R	R	U	U	U	U	U	U	U	V	V	V	V	V
17	K	K	K	K	K	K	K	M	M	M	M	M	M	R	R	R	R	R	U	U	U	U	U	U	U	V	V	V	V	V
18	M	M	M	M	M	M	M	M	M	M	M	M	M	R	R	R	R	R	U	U	U	U	U	U	U	V	V	V	V	V
19	M	M	M	M	M	M	M	M	M	M	M	M	M	R	R	R	R	R	U	U	U	U	U	U	U	V	V	V	V	V
20	M	M	M	M	M	M	M	M	M	M	M	M	M	R	R	R	R	R	U	U	U	U	U	U	U	V	V	V	V	V

TOTAL COST   10164.34   EST. COST REDUCTION   O.   MOVE A   MOVE B

FIGURE 4.8. (d) Initial layout configuration

The algorithm by which the program operates is as follows:

(a) Determine which pairs of departments may be interchanged. Departments are considered for interchange when they are either adjacent, of equal area, or bordering upon a common third department.
(b) Calculate the distance between departments (l), the distances being taken as those between the centres of the departments.
(c) Calculate the reduction in total materials handling costs resulting from the interchange of all possible pairs of departments.
(d) Interchange the two departments which provide the greatest saving in total materials handling costs.
(e) Calculate the total materials handling cost and print out the revised layout (Fig. 4.8(e)).

This procedure is repeated until no further cost saving is possible, whereupon the final layout is printed (Fig. 4.8(f)).

LOCATION PATTERN   ITERATION 1

	1	2	3	4	5	6	7	8	9	10	11	12	13	14	15	16	17	18	19	20	21	22	23	24	25	26	27	28	29	30
1	V	V	V	V	V	V	B	B	B	L	L	L	L	L	L	L	S	S	S	S	S	S	S	S	S	W	W	W	W	W
2	V	V	V	V	V	V	B	B	B	L	L	L	L	L	L	L	S	S	S	S	S	S	S	S	S	W	W	W	W	W
3	V	V	V	V	V	B	B	B	B	L	L	L	L	L	L	L	S	S	S	S	S	S	S	S	S	W	W	W	W	W
4	V	V	V	V	V	B	B	B	B	L	L	L	L	L.	L	L	S	S	S	S	S	S	S	S	S	W	W	W	W	W
5	V	V	V	V	V	B.	B	B	B	L	L	L	L	L	L	L	S	S	S	S	S	S	S	S	S	W	W	W	W	W
6	C	C	C	C	C	C	D	D	D	L	L	L	L	L	L	L	S	S	S	S	S	S	S	S	S	W	W	W	W	W
7	C	C	C	C	C	C	D	D	D	L	L	L	L	L	L	L	G	G	G	S	S	S	S	S	S	W	W	W	W	W
8	C	C	C	C	C	D	D	D	D	L	L	L	L	L	L	L	G	G	G	S	S	S	S	S	S	W	W	W	W	W
9	C	C	C	C	C	D	D	D	D	L	L	L	L	L	L	L	G	G	G	S	S	S	S	S	S	W	W	W	W	W
10	C	C	C	C	C	D	D	D	D	N	N	N	N	N	N	H	H	H	T	T	T	T	T	T	T	T	T	T	T	T
11	E	E	E	E	E	E	F	F	N	N	N	N	N	N	N	H	H	H	T	T	T	T	T	T	T	T	T	T	T	T
12	E	E	E	E	E	E	F	F	F	N	N	N	N	N	N	H	H	H	T	T	T	T	T	T	T	T	T	T	T	T
13	E	E	E	E	E	E	F	F	F	P	P	P	P	P	P	J	J	J	T	T	T	T	T	T	T	T	T	T	T	T
14	K	K	K	K	K	K	F	F	F	P	P	P	P	P	P	J	J	J	T	T	T	T	T	T	T	T	T	T	T	T
15	K	K	K	K	K	K	F	F	F	P	P	P	P	P	P	J	J	J	U	U	U	U	U	U	T	T	T	T	A	A
16	K	K	K	K	K	K	F	F	F	F	F	P	P	P	P	R	R	R	U	U	U	U	U	U	A	A	A	A	A	A
17	K	K	K	K	K	K	M	M	M	M	M	M	R	R	R	R	R	R	U	U	U	U	U	U	A	A	A	A	A	A
18	M	M	M	M	M	M	M	M	M	M	M	M	R	R	R	R	R	R	U	U	U	U	U	U	A	A	A	A	A	A
19	M	M	M	M	M	M	M	M	M	M	M	M	R	R	R	R	R	R	U	U	U	U	U	U	A	A	A	A	A	A
20	M	M	M	M	M	M	M	M	M	M	M	M	R	R	R	R	R	R	U	U	U	U	U	U	A	A	A	A	A	A

TOTAL COST 8979.26   EST. COST REDUCTION 1185.08   MOVEA A MOVEB V

FIGURE 4.8. (e) First iteration (departments A and V changed)

The program can deal with up to 40 departments and since 1965 it has been available through the IBM 'Share Programme Service'. Ostensibly only coplanar departments can be used; but, for example where two floors are used and where material moves between them by means of a lift, the bottom of the lift may be treated as a fixed department on the lower floor and the top of the lift as a fixed department on the upper floor. Material flow between the floors can be described and each floor treated as a separate layout problem. Fixed departments may be specified in the input and consequently obstacles, such as staircases, etc., can be accommodated by describing them as fixed departments.

LOCATION PATTERN   ITERATION 7

	1	2	3	4	5	6	7	8	9	10	11	12	13	14	15	16	17	18	19	20	21	22	23	24	25	26	27	28	29	30
1	E	E	E	E	E	E	F	F	F	L	L	L	L	L	L	L	S	S	S	S	S	S	S	S	S	U	U	U	U	U
2	E	E	E	E	E	E	F	F	F	L	L	L	L	L	L	L	S	S	S	S	S	S	S	S	S	U	U	U	U	U
3	E	E	E	E	E	F	F	F	F	L	L	L	L	L	L	L	S	S	S	S	S	S	S	S	S	U	U	U	U	U
4	E	C	C	C	C	F	F	F	F	L	L	L	L	L	L	L	S	S	S	S	S	S	S	S	S	U	U	U	U	U
5	C	C	C	C	C	F	F	F	F	L	L	L	L	L	L	L	S	S	S	S	S	S	S	S	S	U	U	U	U	U
6	C	C	C	C	C	C	D	D	D	L	L	L	L	L	L	L	S	S	S	S	S	S	S	S	S	U	U	U	U	U
7	C	C	C	C	C	C	D	D	D	L	L	L	L	L	L	L	G	G	G	S	S	S	S	S	S	U	U	U	U	U
8	C	C	C	C	C	D	D	D	D	L	L	L	L	L	L	L	G	G	G	S	S	S	S	S	S	U	U	U	U	U
9	C	V	V	V	V	D	D	D	D	L	L	L	L	L	L	L	G	G	G	S	S	S	S	W	W	W	W	W	W	W
10	V	V	V	V	V	D	D	D	D	N	N	N	N	N	N	H	H	H	T	T	T	T	W	W	W	W	W	W	W	W
11	V	V	V	V	V	V	B	B	B	N	N	N	N	N	N	H	H	H	T	T	T	T	W	W	W	W	W	W	W	W
12	V	V	V	V	V	V	B	B	B	N	N	N	N	N	N	H	H	H	T	T	T	T	W	W	W	W	W	W	W	W
13	V	V	V	V	V	V	B	B	B	P	P	P	P	P	P	J	J	J	T	T	T	T	W	W	W	W	W	W	W	W
14	K	K	K	K	K	K	B	B	B	P	P	P	P	P	P	J	J	J	T	T	T	T	T	W	W	W	W	W	W	W
15	K	K	K	K	K	K	B	B	B	P	P	P	P	P	P	J	J	J	T	T	T	T	T	W	W	W	W	W	A	A
16	K	K	K	K	K	K	B	B	B	P	P	P	P	P	P	R	R	R	T	T	T	T	T	T	A	A	A	A	A	A
17	K	K	K	K	K	K	M	M	M	M	M	M	M	R	R	R	R	R	T	T	T	T	T	T	A	A	A	A	A	A
18	M	M	M	M	M	M	M	M	M	M	M	M	M	R	R	R	R	R	T	T	T	T	T	T	A	A	A	A	A	A
19	M	M	M	M	M	M	M	M	M	M	M	M	M	R	R	R	R	R	T	T	T	T	T	T	A	A	A	A	A	A
20	M	M	M	M	M	M	M	M	M	M	M	M	M	R	R	R	R	R	T	T	T	T	T	T	A	A	A	A	A	A

TOTAL COST 7862.09   EST. COST REDUCTION 213.54   MOVE A E MOVE B C

FIGURE 4.8. (f) Final arrangement [Figures 4.8(b)–4.8(f) reproduced by permission, G. C. Armour and E. S. Buffa, 'A heuristic algorithm and simulation approach to the relative location of facilities', *Management Sci.*, 9, No. 2 (1963)]

The major disadvantages of CRAFT are:

1. Since minimizing the cost of materials handling is adopted as the objective function, only production departments may be considered; service departments are excluded because of the absence of any production flow to or from them.
2. Since an initial layout is required the programme only applies to either the modification of existing layouts, or the planning of new layouts where the outline shape of the layout is known.
3. The distance between the departments is taken as a straight line between department centres, whereas movement is often rectangular along orthogonal aisles.

CORELAP (Computerized Relationship Layout Planning)[3] was developed about 1967 and adopts quite a different approach to layout planning. Unlike CRAFT, CORELAP concerns itself only with the latter part of the layout problem, i.e. developing an acceptable layout from given preferable departmental relationships. In fact a relationship chart of the type described previously (Fig. 4.6) forms part of the input to this program, the rest of the input being (1) departments and their required areas, and (2) a maximum building length to width ratio.

Lee and Moore, who developed this program, adopted the following rather unusual terminology:

Victor: a department which has earned the privilege of being next to be placed in the layout.
Winner: a Victor which has been placed earlier in the layout.

---

[3] R. C. Lee and J. M. Moore, 'CORELAP Computerized Relationship Layout Planning', *J. Ind. Eng.*, XVIII, No. 3, 195–200 (1967).

Each of the closeness ratings used in the relationship chart, i.e. A, E, I, O, U, is given a numerical value, and the total closeness rating (TCR) for each department is calculated by adding together the value for that department's relationships with all other departments. Departments are listed in descending order of TCR, and the department with the highest TCR is the first to be placed in the layout, i.e. it becomes the first Winner. This department is placed in the middle of the layout and the programme then asks, 'Which department is to be placed next?' and, 'Where is this Victor to be placed in the layout?'. The programme searches the relationship chart to determine if any departments have an A relationship (the highest relationship) with the first Winner. If there are any departments with A relationships then the one with the highest TCR becomes the first Victor

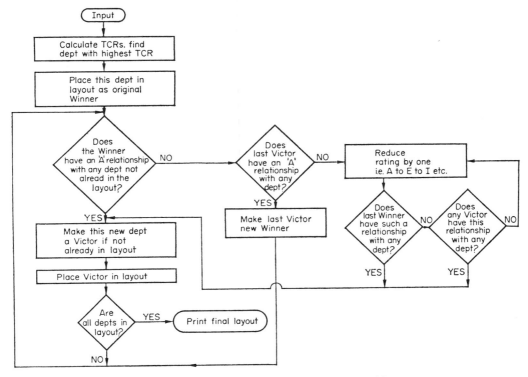

FIGURE 4.9. Simplified flow diagram for CORELAP program

and it is positioned in the layout as close as possible to the Winner. Other departments with A relationships with the Winner are placed in the layout, those with the highest TCR first. They are placed as close as possible to the Winner, and also as close as possible to any other departments already in the layout with which they have a desired relationship. When all departments with an A relationship with the first Winner have been placed, the first Victor becomes the second Winner and the procedure is repeated until all departments with an A relationship with this second Winner have been placed. When all departments with an A relationship with the first and subsequent Winners have been placed the complete procedure is repeated for E, I, O and finally U relationships. A simplified flow diagram for the programme is shown in Fig. 4.9.

The advantage of this approach is that since layouts are developed from stated, preferred relationships, all the necessary reasons for a desired relationship between departments can be taken into account in developing the layouts, unlike CRAFT, which depends solely upon product flow.

A further advantage of CORELAP is that an initial layout is not required, the only constraint being the maximum building length to width ratio. This ratio is necessary to ensure that the programme does not develop unrealistic layout configurations, e.g. very long, thin layouts.

At least three other computer programmes have been written for developing plant layouts,[4] but these two are the best known and indicate the alternative approaches to this problem. In the first case, CRAFT tackled the whole layout problem, and in the second case, CORELAP tackled the single but important steps of developing layouts from given desired relationships. Both programmes have been shown to be capable of quickly developing good layouts for subsequent appraisal and perhaps modification by the planner.

PLANNING THE LAYOUT—2

Additions to or Extension of Existing Layouts

By concentrating on the planning of entirely new layouts we have been prevented from mentioning the interesting Level Curve concept, since it is primarily concerned with the positioning of equipment amongst existing plant.

Supposing we wish to position one additional machine in an existing single floor layout. Adopting the same materials handling cost objective, and knowing the machines to and from which the new machine will send or receive material, we can calculate for every point in the layout a numerical value which represents the total cost of materials handling to and from that point. For example, if we assume that movement is a straight line and that cost is proportionate to distance then, for an existing layout consisting of one machine, a position ten feet away will be twice as attractive as one twenty feet away, and vice versa. Where we can calculate the cost of several points in the layout and then join up these points of equal cost we can produce an *isocost* curve. These curves we shall call Level Curves, since they can be considered analogous to contour lines on maps. For the single machine, straight line movement example, the level curves are shown in Fig. 4.10.

Where L equals the cost value of a point, and x, y = ordinates of existing machines.[5]:

$$L = |\sqrt{x^2+y^2}|$$

In the case of n machines existing at positions $x_1 y_1$; $x_2 y_2$; $x_3 y_3$; ... $x_n y_n$, the L value for any point x, y is given by:

$$L = \sum_{i=1}^{n} |\sqrt{(x-x_i)^2+(y-y_i)^2}|$$

For example, Fig. 4.11 shows the level curves for a layout with four existing machines.

Two disadvantages of this method are evident. Firstly, where the problem involves the positioning of several machines in an extensive layout the construction of level curves becomes rather lengthy and tedious. However, in practice a limited number of possible locations are usually available, which reduces the extent of the calculations. Secondly, we have so far assumed that movement between machines is via the shortest direct route. Whilst this may well be the case

[4] B. Whitehead and M. Z. Eldars, 'The planning of single storey layouts', Building Sci., 1, 127–139 (1965).
R. Muther and K. McPherson, 'Four approaches to computerized layout planning', Industrial Eng., Feb. 39–42 (1970).
J. M. Seehof and W. O. Evans, 'Automated layout design programme', J. Ind. Eng., Dec., 690–695 (1967).
[5] | | indicates that the value contained is taken to be a positive value only.

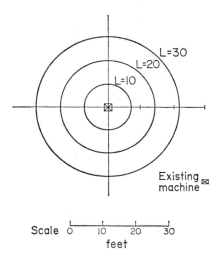

Scale

feet

FIGURE 4.10. Level curves for a single existing machine layout, assuming straight line movement

where overhead cranes are used, it is unlikely to apply where ground transport is relied upon. At the expense of greater calculations a case of indirect movement can be accommodated. For example, if we assume movement to be rectangular, as would be the case where trucks, etc., are confined to a series of orthogonal aisles, the formula for L becomes:

$$L^l = \sum_{i=1}^{n} |x - x_i| + \sum_{i=1}^{n} |y - y_i|$$

We have further assumed throughout this section that movement between all machines is equally important, whereas in the previous sections we have used a product of distance and the

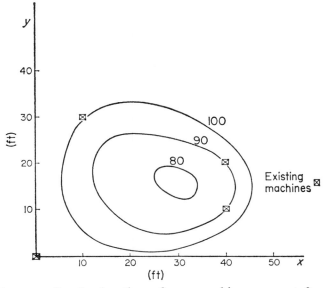

FIGURE 4.11. Level curves for the location of one machine amongst four existing machines

amount of materials moving as our criterion. We must therefore apply some weighting to the distances in these two equations, which then become:

$$L = \sum_{i=1}^{n} w_i \left| \sqrt{(x-x_i)^2+(y-y_i)^2} \right|$$

and

$$L^l = \sum_{i=1}^{n} w_i \left(|x-x_i| + |y-y_i| \right)$$

where w_i = weighting factor for movement to and from machine i.

EVALUATION OF ALTERNATIVE LAYOUTS

Determining which of many alternative layouts to adopt is often a very difficult problem. If we consider all the possible features and characteristics then our list is likely to be very long indeed. If, on the other hand, we consider only the problem of movement and evaluate the alternative layouts only in this light then we shall very probably neglect certain quite important considerations and be guilty of sub-optimization. One factor should be common to whatever considerations we adopt—cost. We must, as a rule, aim to minimize the total cost involved in establishing and using the layout. Muther (see Selected Readings) has suggested that layouts should be evaluated on the basis of the following costs.

Investment

Initial cost of new facilities of all kinds:

* Buildings
* Construction
* Machinery
* Equipment

Accessory costs:

   Tools, jigs, fixtures
* Handling equipment
* Containers
   Benches and chairs
   Timeclocks, water coolers, etc.
   Shelves, bins, racks
   Wiring and lighting
   Piping and ducting

Installation costs:
* Building changes
* Machinery and equipment
* Services and supporting facilities
* Auxiliary service lines

Depreciation and obsolescence costs

Operating costs

Material:

> Production
> Scrap and waste
> Supplies and packing
> Maintenance parts and materials

Labour:

> Direct
> Overtime or extra-shift premium
> Idle or waiting time
> Efficiency variation
> Clerical
> Maintenance
> Inspection
> *Handling and storerooms
> Other indirect labour
> Supervision

General:

> *Floor space
> Power
> Fuel
> Taxes
> Insurance
> Rentals
> Interest on investment

This is not the most comprehensive list that could be suggested, but even so it is a little difficult to appreciate how certain of these items will vary with different layouts, or to understand how some depend upon layout at all. We would suggest that cost items marked with an asterisk will be, in the majority of cases, the most important. Nevertheless, in certain circumstances many of the other costs will merit consideration. The comparison and evaluation of designs for completely new layouts is a difficult problem and whilst such factors as movement, cost of equipment, space required, etc., are normally the principal components of comparison, they are by no means the only components.

The evaluation or rearrangement of parts of factories or departments constitutes an easier problem only because of the relative lack of size of the layouts and not because fewer factors need be considered.

SUMMARY

The plant layout problem was shown to be not only one of the most important problems facing the production manager, but also one of the most difficult. The sheer size of the problem, the number of alternative solutions available, the different objectives of layout planning in different situations, and the difficulty of establishing generally acceptable and applicable criteria all combine to make conventional plant layout a rather subjective procedure.

Three classical layouts exist, i.e. layout by process, by product and by fixed position, although practical layouts are usually combinations of process and product.

Although plant layout planning is normally regarded and treated as a rather elaborate routine, fundamentally a simple procedure exists:

1. determine which are the products to be produced and the quantities required
2. determine the number of different parts to be made for these products
3. determine machine requirements to produce these parts
4. determine which departments (production and service) are required
5. plan the layout

Given the necessary data, planning methods usually depend upon a visual procedure often using cross charts to collect data and relationship charts to summarize them.

Various promising quantitative methods are available for developing layouts, normally by attempting to minimize total materials handling costs. Perhaps the most important of these are the computer programmes CRAFT and CORELAP, although the layouts that they produce can only be taken as a suggestion for further consideration.

SELECTED READINGS

R. MUTHER, *Practical Plant Layout*, McGraw-Hill, New York, 1956. This book is an extensively illustrated traditional treatment of the subject.

R. REED, *Plant Layout*, Irwin, Ill. 1961.

J. M. APPLE, *Plant Layout and Materials Handling*, 2nd ed., Ronald Press, New York, 1963.

R. W. MALICK and A. T. GAUDREAU, *Plant Layout, Planning and Practice*, Wiley, New York, 1951.

W. G. IRESON, *Factory Planning and Plant Layout*, Prentice-Hall, New Jersey, 1952.

J. M. MOORE, *Plant Layout and Design*, Collier-Macmillan, London, 1962. This is perhaps the best available book on the subject, but now somewhat out of date, it contains a description of the level curve concept.

E. S. BUFFA, 'Sequencing analysis for functional layout', *J. Ind. Eng.*, **6**, No. 2, 12–15 (1965).

R. MUTHER and K. MCPHERSON 'Four Approaches to Computerized Layout Planning' *Industrial Eng J.*, Feb., 39–42 (1970).

G. C. ARMOUR and E. S. BUFFA, 'A heuristic algorithm and computer simulation approach to the relative location of facilities', *Management Sci.*, **9**, No. 2, 294–309. This description of CRAFT appears in a similar form in the Harvard Business Review, March and April, 136–168 (1964).

B. WHITEHEAD and M. Z. ELDARS, 'The planning of single storey layouts', *Building Sci.*, **1**, 127–139 (1965).

R. C. LEE and J. M. MOORE, 'CORELAP—computerized relationship layout planning', *J. Ind. Eng.*, **18**, No. 3, 195–200 (1967).

J. M. SEEHOP and W. O. EVANS, 'Automated layout design programme', *J. Ind. Eng.*, **18**, No. 12, 690–695 (1967).

F. S. HILLIER, 'Quantitative tools for plant and layout analysis', *J. Ind. Eng.*, **14**, No. 1, 33–40 (1963).

R. MUTHER and J. D. WHEELER, 'Simplified systematic layout planning', *Factory*, **120**, No. 8, 68–77, No. 9, 111–119, No. 10, 101–113 (1962).

QUESTIONS

4.1. The following cross chart has been constructed by means of actual observations of all movement between the seven production departments of a factory over a typical one month period.

In addition to these seven production departments, three other departments exist, namely the general office, drawing office and personnel department. The general office should preferably be close to the assembly department but not close to the test department. The drawing office should preferably be close to assembly, stores and the general office, but must not be close to the test area. The location of the personnel department is comparatively unimportant; however, it should not be too far away from any of the production departments. The relative location of the production departments depends upon materials flow only, as shown in the table below.

	R	S	T	M	G	A	T
Receiving		40				3	3
Stores			20	20			
Turning				18	2		
Milling					18	20	
Grinding						10	10
Assembly							38
Testing						5	

Construct a relationship chart showing the desirable relative location of each of these ten departments. Use an appropriate notation to indicate the desired proximities.

4.2. 'Visual or graphical minimization is the only satisfactory and practical method of designing plant layouts, and the minimization of total materials handling costs is the most appropriate objective function during layout planning'—discuss.

4.3. Use sequence analysis to determine a rectangular plant layout consisting of the eleven departments included in the table on the following page.

4.4. What are the fundamental differences between the methods of layout planning adopted in the two computer programmes—CRAFT (Computerized Relative Allocation of Facilities Technique) and CORELAP (Computerized Relationship Layout Planning)?

Make a comparative evaluation of each of these programmes with respect to each of the following:

1. input requirements
2. limitations as regards departments and factory shape, size and configuration
3. the heuristic procedures used and the 'objective functions'
4. the value of the programme for planning layouts of non-industrial facilities

4.5. What factors, other than the cost of the movement of materials, need to be considered during the planning of a new layout, and how is the consideration of these factors included in the whole layout planning procedure.

Dept.	Part A	B	C	D	E	Dept. area (ft²)
1	2	2	2	2	2	500
2	3	7	3	4	3	400
3	5		4		4	200
4			7	6	7, 7	600
5	7					200
6	9	9		10	4	500
7	6	8	8		8, 9	1 000
8		6	9			500
9	10	10	10		10	800
10	11	11	11	11	11	500
11						

	A	B	C	D	E
Loads/month	50	100	250	100	100

Table for Question 4.3

4.6. Evaluate the comparative merits of locating an additional machine at points A, B and C in the four existing machine layout shown below. You may assume that all movement between the new machine and each existing machine is equally costly, and that movement is by the shortest direct route.

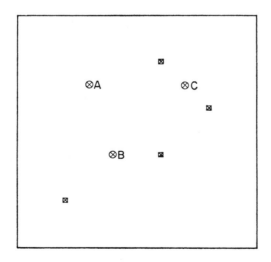

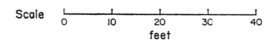

Scale

⊠ Existing machines

4.7. Calculate the cost value (L) for each of points 1, 2, 3, 4 and 5 in the two existing machine layouts shown below, assuming:

(a) rectangular movement between machines and a weighting of 2 for all movement between the upper existing machine and the point under consideration.
(b) direct movement by shortest route between machines and a weighting of 2 for all movement between the lower existing machine and the point under consideration.

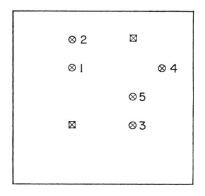

Scale

⊠Existing machines

5

Work Study I—Work Methods

In a book concerned with management there are many very good reasons for discussing work study. In this book, we shall concentrate on the uses of work study, and particularly its value in designing work methods and establishing work standards. Nevertheless, in order to place the subject in perspective, and in order to explain the nature and principles of work study, it will be valuable initially to examine the birth and growth of the subject.

Work Study is concerned primarily with human manual work, more specifically with the efficient design of such work, and with the establishment of standards of performance. Of course there is nothing new or radical in this, people have always been concerned about the way in which jobs are done and the time required, because they are anxious to minimize their own or other people's efforts and consequently provide time for doing other jobs.

Over 150 years ago industralists, such as Robert Owen, were concerned not only with the effici. ent design of plant and machinery, but also with the work methods used by their operatives- Charles Babbage, as well as being a professor of mathematics and one of the 'inventors' of the computer, was also concerned with manufacturing methods and organization. He was an advocate of specialization in work, arguing that this resulted in production at lower cost. His concern with establishing proper manufacturing costs led him to conduct many exercises in which the time necessary for certain jobs was established. Perhaps most important was his belief that manufacturing could be treated analytically and that there existed optimum methods of operation both at the shop floor level and in management.

This belief had previously been expressed by Robert Owen, who said in 1825[1]:

> From the commencement of my management I viewed the population, with the mechanism and every other part of the establishment, as a system composed of many parts, and which it was my duty and interest so to combine, so that every hand, as well as every spring, lever, and wheel, should effectually cooperate to produce the greatest pecuniary gain to the proprietors.

There are many other examples, particularly during the Industrial Revolution, of people being concerned with what has since become known as work study, but the most important contributions were undoubtedly made by three Americans, namely Taylor, Gilbreth and Bedeaux.[2]

F. W. Taylor was concerned principally with the time factor in work. He realized that the overall times for jobs were of little value as standards of performance, and that times for 'elements' of jobs were more appropriate if methods were to be examined. Taylor believed that management

---

[1] R. Owen, *New View of Society*, Everyman Series, Dent, London.
[2] The work of Taylor and Gilbreth is described briefly in L. Urwick *The Golden Book of Management*, Newman Neame, London 1956. Little has been written about Bedeaux, however R. L. Currie (See Selected Readings for this chapter) devotes a little space to him.

should accept the responsibility for planning and organizing work, and that the planning function should be separated from the execution function. His main objective was to treat work and management in a 'scientific' manner and to replace the rather inexact and subjective procedures which had hitherto predominated. He was responsible for introducing the production planning function and for developing a bonus system based on time studies of jobs.

The work of the Gilbreths (Frank and Lilian) was contemporary with, and complementary to, that of Taylor. Gilbreth was concerned with the method by which jobs were done, and believed that once optimium methods were established the time factor would look after itself. His initial, now famous, work was undertaken in the building industry where, after intensive study, he developed improved methods of bricklaying which resulted in far greater productivity. He was responsible for defining the 17 fundamental movements by which all manual work could be described, and together the Gilbreths developed the 'principles of motion economy' by which optimum work methods could be developed. They coined the term 'motion study' for their work and described it as the breaking down of work into the fundamental movements and, by analysing and studying these, developing the *best* method of working.

Taylor was concerned only with the observed or actual times for elements and jobs, and not with the time that should be required. Charles Bedeaux was responsible for introducing the concept of rating, to determine how actual observed times differ from the times which should be required. He attempted to construct an objective system of time study by which work methods could be compared and on which incentive schemes could be based. In Bedeaux's system a common unit was used to describe work on any particular job; furthermore, the time unit included rest and re-laxation allowances.

From the work of these pioneers developed what was later known as the Scientific Management movement, the first comprehensive theory of management. The object of this movement was to achieve efficiency in organization but, unlike subsequent management theories, scientific manage-ment was concerned primarily with the 'bottom' of the organization, with the efficient use of men and machines in routine tasks. Using precision measurement and detailed analysis, optimum work methods could be developed and resources used to the full, this benefiting both the organization and the individual. The concept of the *best* way of doing a job was fundamental to this approach, and although workers tended to be regarded merely as additional facilities, as extensions to machines, their increased earnings were regarded as adequate compensation for the repetitive work life they had to lead. Rationalization in work has been a continuing trend since the birth of scientific management movement, firstly in manual work, and later in clerical and white collar work. From time to time people have expressed concern about this, but there is little doubt that highly rationalized work of this type has, to a large extent, made possible the tremendous economic growth and increase in the standard of living that has occurred in industrialized countries during this century.

In a later chapter we will look at the human problems associated with repetitive work, but for the time being it is sufficient to say that there has been little change in the philosophy of work study in the last 50 years. Work study, or time and motion study as it is sometimes called, is still prim-arily concerned with discovering the *best* ways of doing jobs and with establishing standards based upon such methods.

THE STRUCTURE AND PURPOSES OF WORK STUDY

'Work Study is a term used to embrace the techniques of Method Study and Work Measurement which are employed to ensure the best possible use of human and material resources in carrying out a specified activity.' This is the definition of work study given by the International Labour

D

Office (see Selected Readings). Work study is a predominantly British title, time and motion study being preferred in America. Throughout these two chapters we will use the British terminology and, where possible, the British Standard definitions (*Glossary of Terms in Work Study*, B.S. 3138, 1959). The British Standards Institution defines work study as 'a generic term for those techniques, particularly Method Study and Work Measurement, which are used in the examination of human work in all its contexts, and which lead systematically to the investigation of all the factors which affect the efficiency and economy of the situations being reviewed, in order to effect improvements'.

Neither work study nor time and motion study are directly equivalent to industrial engineering. Industrial engineering, a term which is gaining wider adoption in this country, has greater scope than work study and is concerned with the design of man, machine and material systems, whether these be production control systems, stock control, quality control or whatever.

The aims of work study are, by analysis of work methods and the materials and equipment used, to:

1. Establish the most economical way of doing the work.
2. Standardize this method, and the materials and equipment involved.
3. Establish the time required by a qualified and adequately trained worker to do the job, whilst working at a defined level of performance.
4. Install this work method as standard practice.

Work study then is a comparatively low cost way of either designing work for high productivity, or of improving productivity in existing work by improving current work methods and by reducing ineffective or wasted time. In each case the design or improvements are sought within the context of existing resources and equipment; consequently work study is an immediate tool and is not dependent upon redesign of products, research and development of production processes, or extensive rearrangement of plant.

As with any other procedure it is particularly important that it should be applied in circumstances where it is likely to achieve maximum benefit. There is little point in conducting an extensive work study investigation of jobs in which there is little manual work, since production will be dependent largely upon the design of the machines; and basic redesign of machinery is neither a short-term nor an inexpensive method of improving productivity. Similarly there is little benefit in applying work study to manual work which is temporary or which, for some other reason, is expected to be short-lived. We must apply the technique in circumstances from which we expect maximum returns. The economic results of the study, whether they are increases in output, reduction in scrap, improved safety, reduction in training time, better use of equipment or labour, etc., should always outweigh the cost of the investigation; and to attempt to ensure this we should consider:

1. The anticipated life of the job.
2. Whether manual work is an important part of the job, e.g. (a) the wage rate for the job, (b) the ratio of machine time to manual time in the work cycle.
3. Utilization of equipment, machines, tools, jigs, etc.; the cost of such equipment, and whether the utilization is dependent upon the work method.
4. The importance of the job to the company, e.g. the output quantity, profit margin, and so on.

We should distinguish between work study of existing jobs, and of proposed or anticipated jobs. Whenever new products are to be made or new equipment used, jobs must be designed. Consequently the question is to what extent shall we use work study, and how much effort is justified by the importance of the job? Some investigation may be necessary on existing jobs, not necessarily because they were inadequately designed in the first place, but perhaps because there has been a slight change in the product, new equipment is being used, wage rates or incentives are to be altered. Examination of existing work methods could also result from low machine utilization, excessive labour overtime or idle time, complaints from the workers, inadequate quality, high scrap or wastage rate, etc.

Finally, before describing work study techniques, it should be emphasized that circumstances play a very significant role in work study. Not only are there often severe 'human' repercussions and implications in applying work study, but also the treatment of any job, old or new, will be

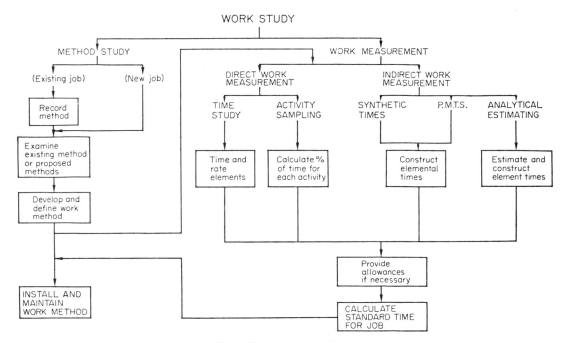

FIGURE 5.1. The structure of work study

influenced by the payment system used, the history of the job, future plans for the product and labour policies. The object of work study is to reduce or eliminate ineffective time, which can of course be attributed either to the direct workers or to management, or both. It should be pointed out that detailed work study and the implementation of improved *working* methods will lead only to confusion and frustration, and will result in comparatively small economic benefits, unless those areas of *management* ineffectiveness are also corrected, e.g. materials availability, equipment maintenance, working instructions, quality control, and so on.

This is certainly one area of management where a cautious, often circumspect, approach is rewarded, where cooperation with all interested parties and experts is essential, and where tact is necessity.

Figure 5.1 shows the structure of work study, and it can be seen that essentially two aspects exist; firstly, method study, concerned with establishing optimum work methods, and secondly, work measurement, concerned with establishing time standards for those methods. It is not exactly true to say that the two are inseparable. One *can* consider methods without considering time, although in practice this rarely occurs. Occasionally the reverse applies, i.e. work measurement is conducted without prior method study.

Method study is normally conducted before work measurement. Apart from the possible need to compare the times for old work methods with the times for new methods, work measurement conducted before method study is poor practice.

METHOD STUDY

'Method Study is the systematic recording and critical examination of existing and proposed ways of doing work, as a means of developing and applying easier and more effective methods and reducing costs' (B.S. 3138).

The unique feature of Gilbreth's work was the detail and objectiveness of his approach to work design. Gilbreth was not responsible for defining new objectives for management, nor does method study today concern itself with unique or novel goals. People have always been concerned with finding the best way of doing a job and method study merely provides a routine, comprehensive and fairly satisfactory procedure for pursuing this objective. This procedure consists of a maximum of six steps:

1. *Select* the work to be studied.
2. *Record* the existing work method and all other relevant facts.
3. *Examine* the record.
4. *Develop* the most efficient or optimum method of doing the work.
5. *Install* this method as standard practice.
6. *Maintain* this practice.

These six steps constitute method study procedure when applied to an *existing* job. Productivity may be increased by eliminating inefficiencies from existing work, but a greater contribution can be made by ensuring that these inefficiencies never arise in the first place. Nevertheless, the case of existing work is the most comprehensive problem, and this is what we shall use as our example throughout the chapter.

Select

The problem of selecting the work to be studied has been mentioned above. Maximum cost benefit is the normal objective, but here we should perhaps define what we mean by cost. We ought to be concerned with the total cost of production, and ostensibly we are. Direct cost of labour, materials and equipment is certainly the main component of total cost, but indirect cost, such as the cost of supervision, training, recruitment, welfare, is also relevant. Although work methods may affect each of these costs there is an understandable tendency to restrict one's consideration to direct costs, and to develop work methods which minimize the cost of labour, machinery and materials. This practice has been the subject recently of a consolidated attack by managers, researchers, theorists and academics who are concerned with the human or behavioural implications of work design. They rightly point out that factors such as labour absenteeism and labour turnover may result from the nature of the work, and that work design should be evaluated in a far broader manner than has hitherto been the practice.

This is undoubtedly true, but there are other complications. One cannot consider, for example, all workers as being alike; consequently the same work may be attractive and unattractive to different people. Similarly, an individual's attitude to work and his behaviour will depend, to some extent, on the situation in which he is working, e.g. the availability of alternative jobs.

In this context, work and job design is really a rather complex business and many variables outside the normal scope of work study must be considered. We will attempt to evaluate the situation in a later chapter, after having considered method study in its traditional, perhaps rather narrow, format.

Record

Numerous techniques exist for recording existing work methods and the main distinction between them is the amount of detail they are able to accommodate. It is usually evident from the circumstances which of the various methods is appropriate; for example, in preliminary investigation it may be sufficient to adopt a rapid method of recording. If subsequent examination is justified, a more detailed but time-consuming recording procedure may be used. Since this is the normal way in which a method study investigation proceeds we will deal first with the less detailed but rapid recording procedures.

Multiple Activity Charts (These are also referred to as *activity analysis* or *man and machine charts*) This type of record is of value where the activities of one or more men and/or machines are to be examined. The activities and their duration are represented by blocks or lines drawn against a time scale. It is not usually possible to include much detail on such charts, but colour or shading is often used to distinguish between:

1. Independent work (man working independently of machine, e.g. reading drawings, preparing material, etc.; or machine working independently of man, e.g. cutting)
2. Combined work, where both man and machine work together, e.g. setting up, adjusting, etc.
3. Waiting time, by either man or machine.

Figure 5.2 shows a multiple activity chart for five drilling machines in a small furniture company. The cycle of work for each machine consists of changing the drill head, locating the job in the machine, and finally drilling. A certain amount of idle or waiting time is also involved.

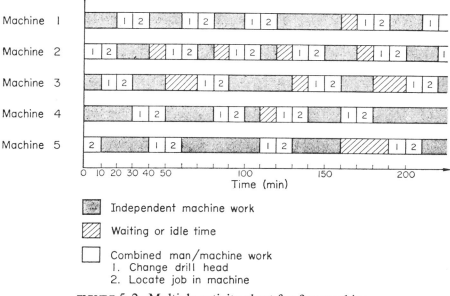

FIGURE 5.2. Multiple activity chart for five machines

Multiple activity charts were used in a study of work methods in post offices. It had previously been the practice to allocate certain jobs to different counters in the post office, stamps and parcels being dealt with at one or more counters, pensions, telegrams, licences, savings, etc., at others. Method study, using multiple activity charts, showed that the load on each of the counters was by no means even. Certain items were dealt with throughout the day and throughout the week, whereas others were confined to particular periods. As a result of the analysis it was possible to reallocate items to counters to provide a more even work load.

Multiple activity charts are also of value in studying maintenance jobs where work loads are varied and uneven, and where several products and machines are to be attended by one operative.

Process Charts

The three types of process charts are certainly the most familiar of the method study recording procedures. The sequence of events is represented by using a series of symbols which are basically the same for each type of chart. The symbols shown in Table 5.1 differ slightly from those originally developed by Gilbreth, but these are the ones currently used. The definitions are based on those suggested by the British Standards Institution.

TABLE 5.1. Process chart symbols

Symbol	Process chart			
	Outline	Flow process chart		Two handed (or operator)
		Man type	Material type	
○	Operation	Operation	Operation	Operation
⇨	Transportation	Transportation	Transportation	Transportation
□	—	Inspection	Inspection	—
▽	—	—	Storage	Hold
D	—	Delay	Delay	Delay

Operation—indicates the main steps in a process, method or procedure. Usually the part, material or product concerned is modified or changed during the operation.
Transportation—indicates the movement of workers, materials or equipment from place to place.
Storage—indicates a controlled storage in which material is received into or issued from a stores under some form of authorization, or an item is retained for reference purposes.
Delay—indicates a delay in the sequence of events, for example work waiting between consecutive operations, or any object laid aside temporarily without record until required.
Inspection—indicates an inspection for quality and/or a check for quantity.
Hold—indicates the retention of an object in one hand, normally so that the other hand may do something to it.

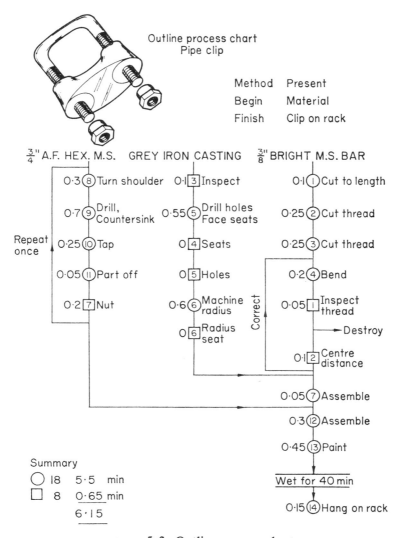

FIGURE 5.3. Outline process chart

An outline process chart. (Fig. 5.3) is a record of the main parts of the process only (i.e. the operations and the inspections). It is frequently used as a preliminary step in a method study investigation, prior to a more detailed study. Alternatively, outline process charts are often used to record basic information for use during the arrangement or layout of plant, during the design of the product, or even during the design of machinery for manufacturing that product. It is a simple record of the important 'constructive' and essential steps in a process, omiting all ancillary activities.

A flow process chart may be concerned with either materials (material flow process chart), or men (man flow process chart), or both. It is an amplification of the outline process chart and shows, in addition, the *transportations*, *storages* and *delays* which occur. In material flow process charts, *operations* occur when an object is intentionally changed in any way; *transportations* when an

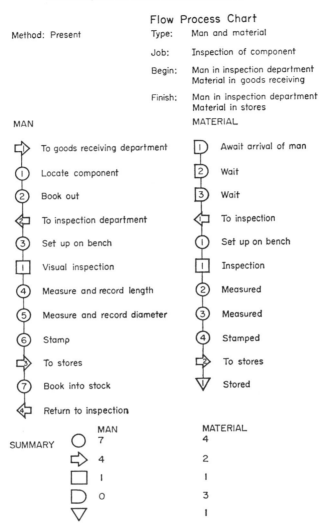

FIGURE 5.4. Man and material flow process chart

object is moved, except where such movement forms part of the operation; *inspections* when an object is examined; *storage* when an object is deliberately kept or protected against unauthorized removal, and *delay* when conditions do not permit the performance of the next activity. There is no storage symbol for man flow process charts since it is assumed that the operator will never have cause to deliberately place himself in confinement, otherwise the symbols for the two types of chart are the same. Figure 5.4 shows a simple man and material type flow process chart.

A two handed or operator process chart is the most detailed type of flow process chart, in which the activities of the worker's hands are recorded in relation to one another. Unlike the previous recording methods, the two handed process chart is normally confined to work carried out at a single place. The ordinary symbols are used except that *inspection* is omitted since this can be represented by movements of the hands, and the *storage* symbol is now taken to mean *hold*.

Pre-printed charts are normally used, and the necessary comments, descriptions and explanations of activities are usually included in the record. The value of the chart is restricted by the rather broad meaning of the symbols, which prevent detailed descriptions of the movement of hands

Date: 14·4·70

Charted by: RW

Proposed
Present   } Method

Operation: Assemble bolt and nut

Summary per 1 pieces	Present		Proposed	
	L.H.	R.H.	L.H.	R.H.
○	2	5		
⇨	2	4		
▽	2	0		
D	3	0		
Total	9	9		
Distance	36"	56"		

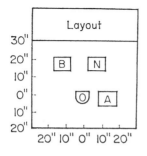

B—Bolts
N—Nuts
O—Operator
A—Assembly

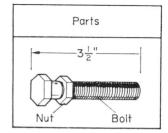

Left hand		Right hand	
Reach for bolt 18"	○⇨▽D ○⇨▽D	Reach for nut	18"
Grasp bolt head		Grasp nut	
Carry to central position 18"		Carry to central position	18"
Hold bolt		Place nut on bolt	
Hold bolt		Screw nut onto bolt	
Release assembly to right hand		Grasp assembly	
Idle		Carry to box	10"
Idle		Release	
Idle		Return hand to central position	10"

FIGURE 5.5. Two-handed process chart

and arms from being shown. Furthermore, the paths and directions of movement are not shown on the chart. Nevertheless, this is certainly the most popular chart used to record movement when studying methods at a single location, and whilst even more detailed recording methods are available, the occasions when the extra work involved is justified are infrequent. A two handed process chart for a simple job is shown in Fig. 5.5.

SIMO (Simultaneous Motion Cycle) Charts

On the infrequent occasions when it is necessary to study work in more detail than is possible using two handed or flow process charts, a different notation is required. Frank Gilbreth was responsible for identifying and defining the seventeen elementary or fundamental movements which together constitute all types of manual work. These Gilbreth called Therbligs (almost the reverse of his own name). Since Gilbreth's work (about 1924), one additional element has been added to the original list of seventeen, and the symbols have been altered. It is now conventional to use the symbols given in Table 5.2.

TABLE 5.2. Therbligs

Symbol	Name	Colour code
⬭	Search	Black
⬮	Find	Grey
→	Select	Light grey
⌒	Grasp	Red
* ⌓	Hold	Gold ochre
⌣	Transport loaded	Green
9	Position	Blue
⚹	Assemble	Violet
∪	Use	Purple
⚹	Disassemble	Light violet
()	Inspect	Burnt ochre
△	Pre-position	Pale blue
⌢	Release load	Carmine red
⌣	Transport empty	Olive green
⚲	Rest for overcoming fatigue	Orange
⌂	Unavoidable delay	Yellow
⌐o	Avoidable delay	Lemon yellow
℘	Plan	Brown

* Omitted from Gilbreth's original list

This classification of elementary movements is based on an analysis of the purpose of the movement and not on physiological definitions. Because of the precise nature of Therbligs, their use facilitates a very detailed study of movements, and Therbligs are normally used in conjunction with SIMO charts, this technique being referred to as micromotion study (Fig. 5.6).

Operation Sharpening pencil			Method	By	R.W.		Page	'I of I	
Department	I		present ~~proposed~~	Film number	015		Date	5.12.69.	
Operator	W.R.			Study number	007				

Left hand						Right hand			
Description	Time	Therblig		Frame number ($\frac{1}{1000}$ min)	Therblig		Time	Description	
		Sym	Code		Code	Sym			
Reach for pencil	10	TE				TE	10	Reach to sharpener	
Grasp from desk	6	G		10		G	5	Grasp handle	
Carry to sharpener	8	TL		20					
Position	6	P		30		(H)	21	Idle/Hold	
Insert	6	A							
				40					
				50					
Hold pencil	34	H		60		U	34	Use i.e. turn handle	
				70					
Withdraw	6	DA				RL	4	Release	
Take pencil to initial position	10	TL		80		TE	10	Take hand to initial position	
Release	4	RL		90			16	Idle	
Return hand to initial position	10	R		100					
				110					
				120					
				130					
								Form number 000 AI	

FIGURE 5.6. SIMO (simultaneous motion) chart

In the methods of recording we have referred to previously, visual observation has been sufficient to obtain the data necessary to construct the charts. By contrast, in micromotion study visual observation is quite inadequate for identifying the detail required, and consequently photography is normally used. By using a suitable camera and projector, work methods can be filmed and played back at various speeds, or even frame by frame, and from this the SIMO chart can be constructed.

Cyclegraphs and Chronocyclegraphs

The Gilbreths were also responsible for developing another interesting and valuable technique for recording movement at the workplace. The cyclegraph is a record of the paths of movement obtained by attaching light sources to the moving objects and exposing them to a photographic plate. Usually small bulbs lit from a battery are attached to the wrists of the operator, who then performs his work cycle in front of a plate camera with an open shutter. The paths of movement are shown as continuous white lines on the photograph. The overall time for the cycle can be obtained using a stop watch, otherwise no time scale is included on the record. The main defect of the cyclegraph is that it does not indicate either the speed of movement or the direction of movement. A further development of this technique therefore was to arrange for the power to the bulbs to be pulsed at a known frequency, one which could be adjusted according to the speed of movement. The record then appears as a dotted line, the spacing of the dots corresponding to the speed of movement, and the pointed end of the pear-shaped dots indicating the direction of movement.

The two photographs shown as Figs 5.7 and 5.8 are chronocyclegraph records of the original and the improved method of folding a towel.

FIGURE 5.7. Chronocyclegraph—old method of folding a towel

FIGURE 5.8. Chronocyclegraph—new method of folding a towel [Figs. 5.7 and 5.8 supplied by and reproduced by permission of the Anne Shaw Organisation Ltd.]

Memomotion Photography and Work Sampling

Memomotion photography is a technique for recording movements using a cine-camera designed to take pictures at longer than normal intervals. A normal 16 mm cine-camera exposes film at a speed of 16 frames per second whereas a camera designed for memomotion photography can film at from 1 frame per second to 2 frames per minute. Memomotion photography is a method of sampling, of observing activities at regular intervals rather than continuously and it is, therefore, particularly suitable where long or irregular work cycle times occur, or where method studies of groups of workers are to be undertaken. Frame by frame analysis of a memomotion film will indicate the nature of movement about an area, the utilization of equipment and space, the extent of idle time, presence of bottle-necks, etc.

To the best of our knowledge no one has devised a memomotion camera to sample activities at irregular periods. Where work cycle times are regular, it is inadvisable to adopt a sampling routine which also uses regular sampling intervals, since this may cause certain activities during the work cycle to be missed altogether. In such cases, work sampling at irregular intervals is essential and this must be conducted manually without the assistance of a camera.

In addition to the recording methods outlined above, reference should also be made to **the** use of travel or cross charts (described in Chapter 4), flow diagrams and string diagrams.

A flow diagram shows the location and sequence of the activities carried out by workers, **and** the routes followed by materials, components, etc. It is, in other words, a spacial version of **the** flow process chart, as can be seen in Fig. 5.9. A string diagram is a scale diagram (or model) **on** which coloured thread wrapped around pins or pegs is used to indicate the paths taken by **workers,**

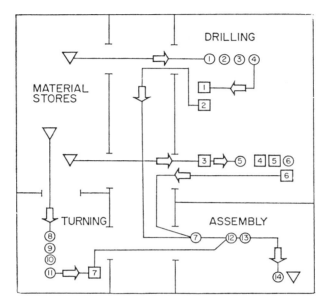

FIGURE 5.9. Flow diagram for the process shown in Fig. 5.4

materials or equipment during a sequence of activities. String diagrams are a useful means of recording when complex movement patterns are involved and/or when the objective is to record and illustrate the movement of numerous items or workers. They can, like flow diagrams, be used to record movements throughout large areas, such as entire departments or buildings, or movement throughout smaller areas, such as individual work-places.

Examine

The third stage of method study begins the constructive procedure. The purpose of recording the existing method is to enable subsequent examination and criticism. The recording method used should be sufficient to show all the relevant information but, of course, not until we examine the record are we likely to know exactly how much information is needed. Therefore, it may be necessary on occasions to repeat the second stage, either to obtain more detail of the entire work method or to enlarge upon certain areas.

The whole purpose and procedure of this stage of methods study was summed up (unknowingly) by Kipling who wrote:

> I have six good serving men.
> They serve me good and true.
> Their names are Why and What, and How
> And When, and Where and Who.

This, perhaps, partly explains the rather inferior image that work study has gained amongst the new generation of quantitative management scientists. It is not their fear of the literary but their scorn of the subjective. It is futile to deny the allegation—method study is a subjective procedure, and the synthesis of work methods depends very largely upon the individual's skill and his application of a set of rather general rules or guidelines. On many occasions procedures for examining and criticizing existing work methods have been suggested and adopted, but in the final analysis they only involve asking six basic questions, which ensure that a sufficiently close and comprehensive examination is made.

We have avoided the temptation to reproduce in this section the extensive charts and check lists which appear in some books on the subject, and will confine ourselves to the following basic procedure:

Examine the Process as a whole

The purpose of this is to define what is accomplished, how and why.

> Why was the process undertaken?
> What purpose does it serve?
> Where is it accomplished and why?
> When is it accomplished and why?
> Who are involved and why?
> How is it accomplished and why?

The answer to these primary questions will serve as a means of determining the effectiveness of the process as a whole, and should indicate whether or not any of the following major changes would be beneficial:

> Changes in material used.
> Changes in design of product.
> Changes in nature or design of process.

Examine Aspects and Parts of the Process

The various activities in the process belong in one of two categories. First are those in which something is actually happening to the material or the product, i.e. it is being moved, inspected or worked. Second are those in which nothing constructive is happening to the material or the product, i.e. it is being delayed or stored. Opinions differ as to which of these two categories should be examined first. It is argued that the second class, since these activities are in no way productive, should be the first to be examined. Alternatively, by examining and, perhaps, changing productive activities, non-productive activities may be eliminated or reduced. Either way (and we believe that there can be no useful categorical rule about which to tackle first) the purpose of this stage of the examination is to eliminate or establish suitable alternatives to existing methods.

The first category can be further divided into *make ready*, *do*, and *put away*. *Make ready* activities are required to prepare the material or workpiece and set it in position ready to be worked upon; *do* activities occur whenever the material or product is changed in shape, condition, or composition; and *put away* activities occur when the material or product is moved away from the machine or workshop. (This may also constitute the subsequent *make ready* activity.) It is obviously beneficial to have a high proportion of *do* activities during the process and a low proportion of the others, since it is only *do* activities which carry the product towards completion; and it is only during these activities that value is added to the raw material.

Whatever the detail of the procedure, a well-conducted examination will question the purpose, place and sequence of activities, the person undertaking the activity and the means by which it is performed in order to establish useful alternatives, which subsequently can be examined and perhaps incorporated in an improved work method.

Develop an Improved Work Method

In Fig. 5.2 it appears that the idle time on the five machines occurs because the drill heads can only be changed on one machine at a time, perhaps as a result of the shortage of tools. Unfortunately, we cannot rely on improvements in work methods being so obvious and, consequently, a rather more exhaustive and time-consuming examination is normally required. The device specifically designed for improving work methods is known as the *process improvement formula*. The formula, which consists of four steps—eliminate, combine, sequence, simplify—is applied to each separate activity in the job, i.e. each meaningful group of work elements.

Complete *elimination* of unnecessary activities is clearly the most important step that can be taken in developing an improved work method. An activity may have been retained because of custom, history, inertia, inadequate communications, or even ignorance. Changes in materials, product design, process design, tools, or the work-place may facilitate the elimination of activities. If elimination is not possible, then *combination* of activities should be considered. In many processes two or more activities may be usefully combined, e.g. drilling and facing holes, or drilling and countersinking holes. Changes in the *sequence* of activities is the next possibility, and this may then facilitate elimination or combination. Should none of these three steps succeed in eliminating or combining the activity then the last, most expensive, step should be considered, i.e. attempt to *simplify* the activity by reducing the number of operations, reducing or eliminating delays and storage, or minimizing transportation. It may become necessary to conduct a more detailed motion study to obtain sufficient information to enable activities to be simplified, and again consideration should be given to changes in materials and to product and process design. The object of simplifying the activity is to permit the worker to complete the job more quickly and easily. Here again Gilbreth made a valuable contribution to the subject by devising *the principles of motion economy*, a list or set of rules which improve efficiency and reduce fatigue in manual work. In the last 50 years these principles have been supplemented by many people, notably Barnes (see Selected Readings), so that the list shown in Fig. 5.10 is longer than that given by Gilbreth. In addition, principles relating to the design of the workplace, tools and equipment have been compiled. We shall briefly consider the use of ergonomic principles in work design in Chapter 7, and a great deal of what will be said there relates to workplace, tool and equipment design. The principles listed in Fig. 5.11 cover most of the areas normally considered to be important. (In many cases, design standards and recommendations are available, e.g. lighting—*American Standards Practice for Industrial Lighting*.)

Finally, having determined the work method to be adopted, a certain amount of experimental development work will usually be necessary in order to locate and eliminate snags or 'teething problems'.

Install and Maintain

The only remaining problem now is to have the new work method adopted and used. But in many respects this is both the most difficult problem and the most important step.

The ease with which a work method is installed and the enthusiasm with which it is received, are often unconnected with its merit as a method of undertaking work. Success at this stage may

Use of the Worker's Body

1. It is easier and more natural to work with two hands rather than one.
2. The two hands should begin and complete their movements at the same time.
3. The motion of the arms should be in opposite directions and should be made simultaneously and symmetrically.
4. Hands and arms naturally move smoothly in arcs, and this is preferable to straight line movement.
5. Hand, arm, and body movements should be confined to the lowest classification with which it is possible satisfactorily to perform the work:
   e.g. Gilbreth's classification of hand movements—
   (a) fingers
   (b) fingers and wrists
   (c) fingers, wrists and forearm
   (d) fingers, wrists, forearm and upper arm
   (e) fingers, wrists, forearm, upper arm and shoulder
6. Work should be arranged to permit natural and habitual movements.
7. Movements should be continuous and smooth with no sharp changes in direction or speed.
8. The two hands should not, except during rest periods, be idle at the same time.
9. Whenever possible, momentum should be employed to assist the work, and minimized if it must be overcome by the worker.
10. Ballistic movements are faster, easier and more accurate than controlled (fixation) movements.
11. The need to fix and focus the eyes on an object should be minimized, and when this is necessary, the occasions should occur as close together as possible.

FIGURE 5.10. *Principles of motion economy*: use of the worker's body.

Arrangement of the Workplace

1. There should be a definite and fixed position for all tools, equipment and materials.
2. All tools, equipment and materials should be located as near as possible to the workplace.
3. Drop deliveries of materials (and even tools and equipment) should be used whenever possible.
4. Tools, equipment and materials should be conveniently located, in order to provide the best sequence of operations.
5. Illumination levels and brightness ratios between objects and surroundings should be arranged to avoid or alleviate visual fatigue.
6. The height of the workplace and the seating should enable comfortable sitting or standing during work.
7. Seating should permit a good posture and adequate 'coverage' of the work area.
8. The workplace should be clean and adequately ventilated and heated.
9. Noise and vibration, both local and general, should be minimized.

Design of Tools and Equipment

1. Wherever possible, clamps, jigs or fixtures should be used to hold work, rather than hands.
2. Wherever possible, two or more tools should be combined.
3. Wherever possible, tools and equipment should be pre-positioned.
4. The loads should be distributed amongst the limbs according to their capacities.
5. Wheels, levers, switches, etc., should be positioned to enable manipulation with the minimum movement of the body.

FIGURE 5.11. *Principles of motion economy*: design of workplace, tools and equipment.

depend entirely upon care and attention during installation. Often the work study practitioner, who has previously exhibited considerable insight, care and attention in conducting the method study, exhibits a marked lack of such qualities whilst trying to install the method. There is little benefit in installing work methods against the resistance of the operatives.

Work study is neither an exact nor a comprehensive science. Work methods, however well contrived, are not usually beyond criticism of details and it is invariably possible to think of factors in the work situation, other than those considered in developing the work method, which will affect performance.

Clearly the first stage is to gain acceptance of the method from management, supervision, and workers. Acceptance by management will depend principally upon the cost benefit of the work method, i.e. the relative cost of materials, labour, equipment and overheads, the cost of installation, and the expected cost savings. Management and supervision are also likely to be concerned with the likely effects of the adoption and use of the method; the training, recruitment, redundancy or reallocation requirement; the effects upon quality and the utilization of equipment.

The workers, and hence the trades unions, are likely to be concerned with the effect of the work method upon wage levels, work hours, work pace, security, fluctuations, interpersonal relations amongst workers, and the interest and variety of the work.

A programme for the installation of the method should be used, showing the main steps, those responsible for carrying them out, and the timetable and dates involved.

Assuming general acceptance, the two remaining steps in installation are training, and the arrangement of equipment, tools, workplaces, etc. Training either newly-recruited operatives, or retraining operatives previously engaged upon the old work method, is an essential, difficult and often lengthy procedure and is best carried out by, or at least in cooperation with, skilled and experienced trainers. The training programme will depend entirely upon the nature of the work and of the trainees. Extensive off the job training, using perhaps films or programmed learning, may be necessary where high skill content, dexterity, discretion, etc., are involved. Alternatively, a short period of instruction followed by a period of learning on the job may be required where the job differs little from the previous method. In either case, and particularly where a high work speed is required, a learning period is necessary. In addition to training direct production workers, it may also be necessary for inspection workers and supervisors to be trained.

Where product changes are involved, stocks of obsolete items and materials should be depleted while stocks of new materials, tools, etc., are accumulated. The availability of the necessary tools, equipment and services should be checked and clerical procedures may need to be modified. Invariably some rearrangement or change of workplaces and layouts is necessary, but this can usually be accommodated outside normal working hours during evenings, week-ends or holidays.

Actual installation of the method may be preceded by a rehearsal, and certainly, unless the alterations are of a very minor nature, care in supervision, immediate attention to snags and a temporary reduction in output will be a necessary result.

Finally, once the method is installed, a period of maintenance will be required. Unless necessary or beneficial, deliberate or accidental alterations in the new work method should not be allowed, and periodic reviews should be conducted to ensure that the work method is satisfactory; that disputes do not arise; that earnings are maintained; and that complications in associated departments or with suppliers do not jeopardize the benefits of the new work method.

SUMMARY

Work study is concerned with the design of efficient work methods and with establishing standards of work performance.

It has been the subject of some criticism, mainly resulting from the fact that it is an inexact science whose results tend to be taken and applied rigidly. In this chapter we have examined method study, which consists of six steps as follows:

1. *Select* the job to be examined.
2. *Record* the work method.
3. *Examine* the method.
4. *Develop* an improved method.
5. *Define* the improved method.
6. *Install* and *maintain* the improved work method.

Throughout the chapter we have concentrated on the use of method study, but not on the criticisms and weaknesses which will be discussed later. We have considered also the case of an existing job rather than an entirely new job, and the application of method study to manual and productive work. In connection with the last point, this is still the greatest application of work study; but the principles we have discussed in this chapter are entirely suitable for, and are often used in relation to, clerical work and in connection with non-industrial work.

SELECTED READINGS

R. M. CURRIE, *Work Study*, Pitman, London, 1968. This is a good, well-organized introductory book on work study.

INTERNATIONAL LABOUR OFFICE, *Introduction to Work Study*, ILO, Geneva, 1960. This is a good simple introduction, concentrating on the economic justification and benefits of work study.

R. M. BARNES, *Motion and Time Study* 6th ed., Wiley, New York, 1969. This is still one of the best books on work study; though slightly confusingly arranged.

B.S. 3138, *Glossary of Terms in Work Study*, British Standards Institute, London, 1959.

J. A. LARKIN, *Work Study Theory and Practice*, McGraw-Hill, New York, 1969. This is an introductory book in the style of Currie (above):

QUESTIONS

5.1. Describe, with examples, the method study techniques you would use to investigate the work of:

(a) a team of six operators in a foundry
(b) a single operator on a short cycle repetitive assembly task

5.2. The Gobust Co. packs 'nignogs'. They are imported and weighed out in lots of one pound. There are 12 'nignogs' to the pound, on average. The 'nignogs' must be inserted in a jar, to which a portion of 'nignog' juice is added. The jar is then sealed with a twist cap.

(a) Analyse the job. Develop a 'good' sequence of work elements
(b) Sketch the process flow and layout
(c) Use an operation chart to detail the work involved

[Univ. of Lancaster, M.A. Operational Research, June 1967—part of question only.]

5.3. The electrical plug shown in Chapter 2, question 2, is to be assembled manually in large quantities.

Develop a method of assembling the *nine* components of the plug and sketch the workplace layout. Use a two handed process chart to indicate your method. You may approximate the element times.

5.4. Develop a method for manually assembling the pipe clip shown in Fig. **5.3.** Sketch the workplace layout and approximate the element times.

5.5. Draw up a micromotion analysis of the two handed operation shown in Fig. **5.5**, using a SIMO chart and Therbligs.

5.6. What are the six important steps involved in performing a method study? Describe very briefly the principal techniques available for the execution of the second of these steps, and describe also the logical sequence or 'formula' which constitutes step 4.

5.7. Discuss the problems in human relations which are likely to occur during a method study exercise, and indicate how they might be minimized. In your answer show how the problems differ at various stages of the investigation.

6

Work Study II—Work Measurement

Attempts to measure work and to establish work standards have always aroused reactions, promoted criticisms and generally been the subject of considerable controversy. F. W. Taylor's work was by no means uncritically received and he met with a great deal of opposition both from managements and from the workers themselves. The workers were understandably apprehensive about the control that might be exercised using work standards and were afraid that the net result would be the need to work harder for less pay. This was not usually the case, since where Taylor's principles were used to establish standards of performance, output was usually increased and workers were able to earn higher wages. This, however, was the cause of Taylor's unpopularity with management who were reluctant to meet the higher wage bills. The father of time study became known as 'speedy Taylor', and was very unpopular for some considerable time before the principles and rationale of 'scientific' management were eventually accepted.

Charles Bedeaux was another unpopular pioneer. He was responsible for adding the concept of rating to Taylor's time study. Previously the 'correct' time for a job, or portion of a job, had been obtained by timing with a stopwatch on a sufficient number of occasions, and then averaging the readings. Bedeaux refined this method by introducing the concept of a standard rate of work. Each observed time was adjusted by a factor depending upon whether the worker had been working below or above the standard rate. Not surprisingly, this rather subjective procedure aroused a great deal of opposition, and 'Bedeaux men', as time study men became known, were very unpopular: nor was their image improved by the surreptitious and secretive way in which many of them went about their jobs, the time study often bearing a close resemblance to spying, or so the workers thought.

A great many of these malpractices and the resultant suspicions have since been removed, and time study, together with method study, is now sympathetically received, in principle at least. Nevertheless, many disputes, both national and local, arise from attempts to establish and implement standards. Furthermore, time study, like other aspects of work study, can be criticized on fundamental grounds as basically inaccurate, ill-conceived, or even unnecessary. So why do we persist, and what precisely are we trying to achieve with time study?

First of all let us define our terms. In the title to this chapter we used the phrase Work Measurement, but subsequently referred to time study. Work measurement is defined in British Standard 3138 as 'the application of techniques designed to establish the time for a qualified worker to carry out a specified job at a defined level of performance', and time study as 'a work measurement technique for recording the times and rates of working for the elements of a specified job carried out under specified conditions, and for analysing the data so as to obtain the time necessary for carrying out the job at a defined level of performance'. Time study is considered then as that part of work measurement concerned with the direct timing of job elements by means of a suitable device, such as a stopwatch. This is not the only method of obtaining times for jobs, as we shall see later. In fact, there are two classes of work measurement; firstly, direct time study and secondly, indirect time study which does not rely upon the use of a stopwatch.

Attempts to establish times for jobs or operations may cause some resistance or dispute, but it is surely a necessary exercise. How, for example, are we to determine what is the best method of doing a job unless there is some basis by which we can compare methods? Certainly in designing work methods there are many important criteria but, all other things being equal, the method which takes the least time will normally be regarded as the best. Times are necessary before production schedules can be established, and before labour and machine requirements can be determined, and the proper coordination of operations depends upon the availability of accurate time estimates for manufacture.

In many situations workers are responsible for the operation of several machines, or, alternatively, teams of workers are jointly responsible for certain jobs or operations. The allocation of machines to a single worker and the even distribution of work amongst members of a team cannot be accomplished without estimates of the duration of all operations. The output of assembly or flow lines depends, to a large extent, on the output of the workers with the longest work cycle; consequently the balanced allocation of work to each worker is essential.

Standard times for jobs, once established, may be used to set labour standards for payment purposes, to determine the operating effectiveness of equipment, workers, groups of workers, departments or factories, and to determine standard costs of manufacture for pricing or estimating purposes.

It seems that work measurement is not just necessary but absolutely essential for both the planning and control of production. Without work measurement data we cannot determine what output can be achieved from our equipment, nor will we be able to quote delivery dates or costs; we cannot determine what extra facilities are required to achieve a certain output, nor can we measure the efficiency with which the existing equipment or labour is being used; we cannot operate incentive schemes, or use standard costs for budget control. In fact, we may not even be able to determine which manufacturing methods to adopt.

It is almost always necessary to obtain some assessment of the time required for jobs, so again the question is not 'whether' but 'how?'. It is hardly necessary to say that one method of obtaining any information is to guess. We are not anxious to encourage the use of this somewhat unreliable method; but at the same time, in all honesty, one must admit that guesswork is not entirely absent from work measurement. It is not usually referred to as such but nevertheless some of the estimating procedures do bear a close resemblance to guesswork. A second procedure for which there is also precious little to be said is assumption, i.e. assuming that whatever is, is right! If a job takes 30 minutes to complete, then it could be assumed that 30 minutes was and is the correct time for that particular job. No doubt this reasoning could lead to a fascinating discussion of logic, but for our purposes there is little justification for basing work standards on free occurrence.

This leaves us with only one alternative, namely to apply some systematic measuring technique. Few people would claim that any contemporary method of work measurement is entirely accurate or consistent, consequently we must attempt either to compensate for, or to avoid, the shortcomings, and not to apply work measurement methods or results in situations where either the basic assumptions are infringed or where acceptable accuracy levels are exceeded.

MEASUREMENT OF WHAT?

Work study is concerned primarily with manual work; to a smaller extent it is concerned with work performed by machines, but it is hardly ever concerned with mental work.

Concern with machine work cannot be avoided since most production results from man–machine systems. There is normally little difficulty in measuring machine work since machine times are usually a function of rotational speeds, tool feed rates, etc.

Even in modern industry, where human manual work is often highly rationalized and repetitive, there still remains a need for most workers to exercise their mental ability in some perhaps small, but nevertheless important, way. In fact it is probably this very requirement that has necessitated the use of human beings rather than more machinery. The human being possesses an inherent capacity to think, reason and decide, and although it is doubtless possible to construct electro-mechanical or hydraulic devices to 'think' in a similar but limited way, the tremendous expense is rarely justified. Consequently, human beings are likely to remain as important parts of the production process until the production technology itself is improved sufficiently to eliminate the need for mental work.

As far as work study and work measurement are concerned, mental work is considered to be of obvious importance, but it is thought to be too difficult to measure directly. Part of the process of establishing standard times for a job involves the adoption of allowances, i.e. provision of additional time to compensate for atmospheric conditions, contingencies, etc. Mental effort is dealt with in precisely the same way, i.e.

1. *Physical* human work is *measured*
2. *Machine* work is *calculated*
3. *Mental* human work is *allowed for*

PROCEDURE

There are two categories of work measurement procedure (see Figure 5.1 Chapter 5). Time study is the traditional stopwatch procedure and this accounts for the majority of the exercises conducted.

Indirect methods are, on occasions, either desirable or necessary. In the case of a new job it is impossible to conduct direct studies, and, where jobs are to be undertaken for a comparatively short period of time, there may be insufficient time to conduct direct work measurement. With the exception of analytical estimating, the indirect methods are of more recent origin. They have many advantages in terms of consistency and accuracy, and possibly additional developments may well increase their future scope and value. But before we can look at these techniques we must first appreciate traditional direct time study, its benefits and limitations.

DIRECT WORK MEASUREMENT—TIME STUDY

There is a great deal to be done before we can even begin our time study. Let us assume, to begin with, that the time study follows a previous method study and that, consequently, there is no 'selection' problem. In theory it is reasonable to assume that the need to establish a time for a job has arisen either because there has been some change in the nature of the job, or because the job is entirely new. There are few occasions when it is necessary or reasonable to time a job which is unchanged but, unfortunately, this happens not infrequently. For example, time studies are sometimes conducted where previous studies have resulted in either very 'loose' times and high earnings, or 'tight' times, low earning and complaints. Time study without previous method study is poor practice. There is little point in establishing times for inferior methods of doing work since, in the first place, this is not fulfilling the objective of work study, which is to increase productivity by eliminating wasted time. Secondly, if an inadequate method is in use, workers may well improve the methods themselves and invalidate the time study (and who can blame them?). Finally the inferior work method may be changed at a later date, thus necessitating a further time study exercise.

Very many work measurement exercises have been doomed before they have begun, consequently time spent in the preparatory stages is a valuable investment. Fortunately, in most firms, suspicion between workers and work study engineers is a thing of the past and the purpose and benefits of work study are generally accepted; but nevertheless it is understandable that people will be suspicious and apprehensive of things about which they are ill informed, and every effort should be made to ensure that workers, particularly those to be studied, are aware of, and sympathetic to, the nature and purpose of any work measurement exercise.

As with method study, we can break down time study procedure into a series of simple, logical and important steps.

Obtain All Necessary Information

Our objective in conducting a work measurement exercise is to determine the time required for a job carried out under specified conditions. It is necessary, therefore, to have a record of these conditions in case the exercise is referred to or used at a later date. There is usually provision for recording information about the worker, machine, material, layout, product, method, quality, standard, etc., on one of the forms used during the study or, alternatively, it may be sufficient to refer to the appropriate method study for all of this information.

Divide the job into Elements

Taylor was the first to realize that overall times for jobs were of litle value, and that in order to obtain useful data it was necessary to break down the job into its constituent elements. A detailed breakdown into elements is necessary for the following reasons:

(a) To provide a better understanding of the nature of the job and to attract attention to the work method.
(b) To break a time study exercise up into manageably sized pieces. For example, it may be inconvenient or even impossible to study, as a whole, a large and complex job, but if the job is divided into its components then accurate study is possible.
(c) To permit a more accurate study. Both timing and rating are likely to be more accurate for small elements than for large jobs. Furthermore, a worker may not work at the same pace throughout a job, and overall rating may therefore be misleading.
(d) To distinguish different types of work, so that elements causing worker fatigue, for example, may be isolated and appropriate allowances provided.
(e) To enable 'machine' elements, i.e. machine-paced work, to be isolated from 'man' elements.
(f) To enable detailed job descriptions to be produced.
(g) To enable time standards to be checked or modified at a later date, and omissions and errors to be rectified.
(h) To enable times for certain common or important elements to be extracted and compared with other studies, or used in place of, or as part of, subsequent time studies.

Jobs may consist of constant or variable elements, manual or machine elements, repetitive, occasional or even 'foreign' elements. Constant elements are of identical specification and have the same duration whenever performed, unlike variable elements whose times vary according to characteristics such as weight, size, distance, etc. Machine elements are often constant whilst man elements are often variable. Occasional elements do not occur in every cycle but are nevertheless an essential part of the job, whereas foreign elements are unnecessary.

The ease with which the study is conducted, as well as the value of the data obtained, is very much dependent upon the definition of the job elements; fortunately, there are some general and well-tried rules which can be used at this stage.

1. The elements selected will be timed separately and repeatedly; consequently it is essential that a clearly defined beginning and ending point should be available to identify the element. Elements beginning or ending with some unmistakable manoeuvre or occurrence, such as dropping a part into a tray, switching a tool on or off, picking up or putting down an item, etc., are superior to those of indistinguishable beginning or termination which the observer may well miss. Some means of anticipating the beginning or ending of an element is also of value if accurate times are to be obtained.

2. Elements should be as short as possible yet not too short to be conveniently timed. It is generally considered that 0·04 minutes (2·4 seconds) is the shortest period that can be timed accurately by a manually operated stopwatch, and that 0·33 minutes (20 seconds) should be regarded as the maximum.

3. Elements should be as unified as possible. Whenever possible, elements consisting of a logical sequence of basic motions should be used, e.g. motions such as, reach for, take hold, move, place (TE, G, TL, P, A, RL). It would be illogical to divide such sequences because these represent both functional and rhythmic movements.

4. Man and machine elements should be separated. Unlike times for machine elements, which can often be calculated or extracted from manuals, times for man or hand elements are determined by the operator.

5. Regular and irregular elements should be separated. Elements that do not occur in every cycle should be kept separate so that time allowances to cover these intermittent tasks can be provided.

6. Elements involving heavy or fatiguing work should be separated so that appropriate allowances can be calculated and provided.

7. Finally, constant elements should be separated from variable elements. Starting a machine, adjusting a tool, etc., are examples of elements whose duration is likely to be constant and not influenced by either preceding or subsequent elements, or by the nature of the job. The separation of these two types of element assists in the development of data which may be used in subsequent studies, and facilitates cross-checking between studies.

Time the Elements

Although there are other types of instrument, the stopwatch is the conventional means for timing elements. Work study stopwatches are calibrated in seconds, milli-minutes, centi-minutes or centi-hours. Calibration in centi-hours (1/100 h), milli-minutes (1/1000 min) or centi-minutes (1/100 min) is preferable to using seconds since, although the second is an established unit of time, its use in this context makes both recording and subsequent calculations slightly more difficult. Stopwatches calibrated in milli- or centi-minutes are the most popular, although the choice of either hours or minutes depends, to a large extent, upon the length of the job and the length of the elements. There are also alternative methods of using the stopwatch, i.e. using 'continuous' or 'flyback' timing, and again the choice is dependent upon circumstances and personal preference. In continuous timing the watch runs throughout the study, times are read off, and element durations are obtained by subtraction. No time is lost in stopping the watch, and every element must be recorded. Flyback timing records the duration of each element separately, the watch is zeroed after every element, and element times are known immediately; consequently it is easy to spot errors and irregularities.

A more sophisticated system of flyback timing uses two watches mounted close together on a special board. A press button operates a lever mechanism to stop one of the watches and start the other at the end of each work element. The advantage of this method, sometimes known as accumulative timing[1], is that the ease and accuracy of reading a stopped watch is combined with the principal advantage of continuous timing, namely that minimum time is wasted during element timing.

A pre-printed form is normally used to record the observations and the stopwatch is usually mounted above this sheet (Fig. 6.1). Nevertheless, it requires considerable concentration, dexterity

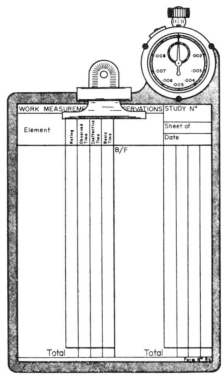

FIGURE 6.1. Time study observation sheet; board and watch

and practice to watch the worker, manipulate the watch and record the time, and of course the ease with which this is done is principally dependent upon the ease with which the observer can identify the element, or elements, he is timing.

There are references in certain books to timing devices such as the kynograph and other electro/mechanical or electronic devices, and many such devices have been used where extreme accuracy is necessary, or some other condition prevails. Nevertheless, the stopwatch, in one form or another, remains the principal direct method along with photography. Movie films may have been taken of the work method during or at the termination of the method study and, provided these are

---

[1] For a clear description see R. M. Barnes, *Motion and Time Study*, 6th Ed., Wiley, New York, 1969.

records of the correct method and conditions of work, they can be used for timing. In such cases it may not be necessary to use a stopwatch since, knowing the speed at which the film was taken, the time interval between each frame can be calculated. Alternatively, when films are taken, an accurate clock is often included in the picture or even built into the camera lens. Chronocyclegraphs may be used in the same way.

There is, however, one snag to the use of films for establishing time standards. Normally a film or chronocyclegraph record only covers a few cycles of the job, and unless we can be absolutely sure that these work cycles were conducted at a known (or rated) pace our record times may well be biased.

The Number of Cycles to be Timed

We must take sufficient readings to be reasonably confident of an accurate result. Direct time study is a sampling process, and the accuracy of the sample as a measure of the elements themselves is determined by the variability of the elements and the size of the samples.

The number of observations to be taken depends upon:

1. the variation in the times of the element
2. the degree of accuracy required
3. the confidence level we require

A 95 per cent confidence level and an accuracy of ± 5 per cent or ± 10 per cent are usually adopted. This means that the chances are at least 95 out of 100 that the mean or average we obtain from the observations will be in error by ± 5 per cent or ± 10 per cent, or less, of the true element time.

Before the number of observations necessary to fulfil this requirement can be calculated we must establish the variability of the actual element time by conducting a brief 'pilot' study. We can then use one of the following formulae to calculate the required number of observations. 95 per cent confidence ± 5 per cent accuracy:

$$N^1 = \left(\frac{40\sqrt{N\sum x^2 - (\sum x)^2}}{\sum x}\right)^2$$

95 per cent confidence ± 10 per cent accuracy:

$$N^1 = \left(\frac{20\sqrt{N\sum x^2 - (\sum x)^2}}{\sum x}\right)^2$$

Where N^1 = required number of observations for given confidence and accuracy.
N = actual number of observations taken in pilot study.
x = each observed element time from the pilot study.

Calculation using one of those formulae is a simple exercise, but alternatively we can use graphs or nomographs, such as the one shown in Fig. 6.2 to obtain the same result.

Rating the Operator

So far in this section we have been concerned only with the observed or actual times required by our operative to perform elements of work; but the object of work measurement and time study is to determine not how long it *did* take to perform a job or elements of a job, but how long it *should* take. It is necessary, therefore, to compare the actual rate of working of the operator

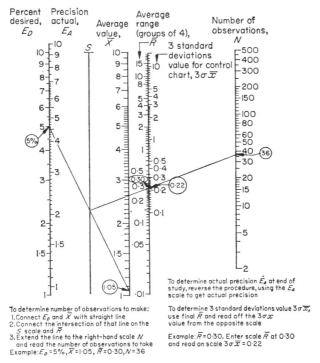

Percent desired, E_D | Precision actual, E_A | S | Average value, $\bar{X}$ | Average range (groups of 4), $\bar{R}$ | 3 standard deviations value for control chart, $3\sigma\bar{x}$ | Number of observations, N

To determine number of observations to make:
1. Connect E_D and $\bar{X}$ with straight line
2. Connect the intersection of that line on the S scale and $\bar{R}$
3. Extend the line to the right-hand scale N and read the number of observations to take

Example: $E_D = 5\%$, $\bar{X} = 1 \cdot 05$, $\bar{R} = 0 \cdot 30$, $N = 36$

To determine 3 standard deviations value $3\sigma\bar{x}$, use final $\bar{R}$ and read off the $3\sigma\bar{x}$ value from the opposite scale

Example: $\bar{R} = 0 \cdot 30$. Enter scale $\bar{R}$ at $0 \cdot 30$ and read on scale $3\sigma\bar{x} = 0 \cdot 22$

To determine actual precision E_A at end of study, reverse the procedure, using the E_A scale to get actual precision

FIGURE 6.2. Nomograph for determining the number of observations required for 95 per cent confidence level and 15 per cent precision [Reproduced by permission, R. H. Barnes, *Motion and Time Study*, 6th ed., Wiley, New York, 1969]

Skill			Effort		
+0·15	A1	Superskill	+0·13	A1	Excessive
+0·13	A2		+0·12	A2	
+0·11	B1	Excellent	+0·10	B1	Excellent
+0·08	B2		+0·08	B2	
+0·06	C1	Good	+0·05	C1	Good
+0·03	C2		+0·02	C2	
0·00	D	Average	0·00	D	Average
−0·05	E1	Fair	−0·04	E1	Fair
−0·10	E2		−0·08	E2	
−0·16	F1	Poor	−0·12	F1	Poor
−0·22	F2		−0·17	F2	

Conditions			Consistency		
+0·06	A	Ideal	+0·04	A	Perfect
+0·04	B	Excellent	+0·03	B	Excellent
+0·02	C	Good	+0·01	C	Good
0·00	D	Average	0·00	D	Average
−0·03	E	Fair	−0·02	E	Fair
−0·07	F	Poor	−0·04	F	Poor

FIGURE 6.3. Factors and point values in the Westinghouse system of performance rating or levelling

with a standard rate of working so that the observed times can be converted to basic times, i.e. the time required to carry out an element of work at standard performance. In fact, every observation we make must be rated and the appropriate rating factor recorded on the record chart *before* the observed time is recorded (Fig. 6.3).

Performance rating is the comparison of an actual rate of working against a defined concept of a standard rate of working. This is fine in theory, but how in practice do we establish what the standard rate is and how do we make the comparison?

The standard rate corresponds to, 'the average rate at which qualified workers will naturally work at a job, provided they know and adhere to the specified method, and provided they are motivated to apply themselves to their work' (BS 3138). Various methods of rating have been evolved, but at best they only assist in what remains essentially a subjective procedure. On the British Standard performance scale (which we shall use throughout this chapter), standard rating is equal to 100, i.e. a rating of 50 is equal to half the standard rate of working.[2]

Although standard rate is defined above, it is really only a concept; in practice the standard rate of working is a function of the situation, e.g. the physical conditions, the type of labour, company policy, and may differ greatly between companies. British Standard 100 is considered to be equivalent to a walking speed of a constant 4 mile/h, or to dealing a pack of cards into 4 hands in 22½ seconds, but unfortunately neither of these jobs occurs very frequently in industry! Consequently, the company must train the time study analyst to recognize what the company or industry regards as standard performance. This normally involves the use of films depicting the same operation performed at different speeds, which the observer is then asked to rate. In fact, in rating films in this way the observer is only assessing the speed of the filmed sequences of operations against a given standard speed, but the judgement he is using is equivalent to that which he would use in performance rating of jobs on the shop floor.

Thus it is obvious that performance rating is a subjective procedure which is wide open to criticism. In fact this is one of the most controversial aspects of work study. Various attempts have been made to place it on a more scientific and indisputable basis, but little improvement has been made, and performance rating remains as a weak but necessary link in an otherwise comparatively strong chain. Because of this inevitable subjectivity it is important that work study analysts should be given as thorough a training as possible in this area. It should, of course, be fully emphasized that speed of operation is *not* the only factor measured, and that comprehensive work measurement depends upon the simultaneous assessment of speed, effort and effectiveness.

---

[2] Several other scales are in common use but these differ from the BS Scale in one important respect. Only one point is defined on the BS Scale, namely 100, which is equal to standard performance, in comparison the other scale defined two points, a lower one corresponding to the rating and performance of time-workers, and a higher one corresponding to the rating and performance of piece-workers.

The four most popular scales are compared in the diagram below:

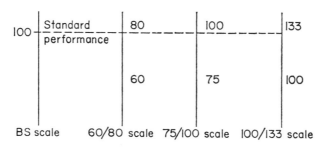

Several systems or rating have been developed. *Effort rating*[3] is concerned primarily with work speed, the operator being rated according to the speed of his movement, adjustments being made to the rating according to the perceived difficulty of the job being done. *Objective Rating*[4] is a somewhat similar method depending upon the consideration of two factors—speed and difficulty. The operator is rated firstly according to the speed of his movement, irrespective of the nature of the job. After this speed rating an adjustment is made depending upon the nature of the job being performed and particularly:

1. The amount of the body used
2. The use of footpedals
3. The need for bimanualness
4. Eye-hand coordination
5. The handling requirements
6. The weight of objects handled.

Tables of adjustment factors are available for various categories of each of these six factors.[4]

The Westinghouse Company devised a system about 1927 in which four characteristics were considered; the skill used, the effort required, the conditions prevailing and the consistency required. A numerical scale is attached to each of these characteristics (Fig. 6.3). Unlike the two systems mentioned above, the Westinghouse system is used to rate a job, rather than the separate elements of the job. For this reason it is sometimes referred to as a *Levelling System* rather than a rating system. A separate rating for each element is made for each area and the sum of the four figures represents the final rating factor for each element. e.g.

$$\begin{aligned}
\text{Observed (actual) element time} &= \quad 0\cdot45 \text{ minutes} \\
\text{Element rating} &= +0\cdot06 \text{ (skill)} \\
&\quad +0\cdot12 \text{ (effort)} \\
&\quad +0\cdot00 \text{ (conditions)} \\
&\quad +0\cdot01 \text{ (consistency)} \\[4pt]
\hline
&\quad +0\cdot19 \\
\text{Basic time for element} \quad &= 0\cdot45 \times (1\cdot00 + 0\cdot19) \\
&= 0\cdot54 \text{ minutes}
\end{aligned}$$

Whichever one of these or other methods of rating or levelling is used the basic time corresponds to the observed time after rating, i.e.

$$\text{basic time for element or job} = \text{observed time} \times \frac{\text{rating}}{100}$$

Allowances

Even after rating, we have not yet obtained the standard time for the elements or the job, since it may be necessary to provide allowances to compensate for fatigue, personal needs, contingencies, etc. The basic time does not contain any allowances and is merely the time required by

[3] R. Presgrave, *The Dynamics of Time Study*, McGraw-Hill, New York, 1945.
[4] M. E. Mundel, *Motion and Time Study*, Prentice-Hall, Englewood Cliffs, New Jersey, 1960.

the worker to perform the task at a standard rate without any interruptions or delays. Allowances are normally given as a percentage of the basic element times and usually include:
(a) Relaxation allowances

    1. Fatigue allowances to give the workers time to recover from the effort (physiological and psychological) required by the job.
    2. Personal needs—to visit toilets, washrooms, etc.

(b) Contingency allowances given to compensate for the time required by the workers to perform all necessary additional and periodic activities which were not included in the basic time because of infrequent or irregular occurrence and the difficulty of establishing the times, e.g. reading drawings, cleaning machinery.
(c) Tool and machinery allowance to compensate the worker for the time necessary for adjusting and sharpening tools, setting up equipment, and so on.
(d) Reject allowance, necessary where a proportion of defective items must necessarily be produced.
(e) Interference allowance to compensate for time unavoidably lost because of the stoppage of two or more machines, attended by one worker; at the same time.
(f) Excess work allowance to compensate for the extra work necessary because of unforeseen or temporary changes in the standard conditions.

Problems of fatigue in industry and the effect of environmental conditions were popular and important research subjects before and during the Second World War, when these were considered to be the main factors which affected output. More recently, as a result of the development of ergonomics and man/machine engineering as a discipline (see Chapter 7), these subjects have again received attention. Despite all this activity, however, comparatively little of direct importance to work measurement has evolved; consequently the provision of appropriate allowances still constitutes the second subjective area of work measurement, and is both the centre of justifiable controversy and the target for sceptics.

Total allowances are often of the order of 15–20 per cent, so inaccuracies are of some consequence. Nevertheless, practice is again very much a function of the situation. Allowances intolerable in one company may be perfectly acceptable elsewhere, consequently the time study analyst should be trained in this area as carefully as in performance rating.

Table 6.1 gives representative figures for some of the allowances mentioned above.

Work Units

The standard time for an element or a job is calculated as follows:

$$\text{standard time} = \left(\text{observed time} \times \frac{\text{rating}}{100}\right) \times \text{ per cent total allowance}$$

For example, where the worker was observed to be working at greater than the standard rate the three element times may bear a relationship to one another as shown in Fig. 6.4.

The *standard minute* is the unit of measurement of work consisting partly of work and partly of relaxation. It represents the output in one minute if the work is performed at the standard rate. By means of work measurement we can express the work content of jobs in terms of single units—standard minutes (SM's)—irrespective of the differences between the jobs themselves.

Notice that an SM is a measure of *work* and not a measure of time. It is connected with time only in that one SM of work will take one minute of time at 100 performance.

TABLE 6.1. *Typical allowance factors*—Personal, Rest and fatigue—expressed as percentage of basic times

			Men (%)	Women (%)
1. Normal Personal Needs			2–5	2–7
				(%)
2. Physical Effort	(a) very light	1 lb		0
	(b) light	1–10 lb		3
	(c) medium	10–25 lb		6
	(d) heavy	25–60 lb		9
	(e) very heavy	60–112 lb		12
3. Visual Concentration	(a) normal attention to plain work			0
	(b) normal attention to intricate work			2
	(c) constant attention to plain work			4
	(d) constant attention to intricate work			10
4. Posture	(a) can vary sitting with standing or walking			0
	(b) constant sitting			1
	(c) constant standing			5
	(d) body crouching or bent			8
	(e) hands raised above shoulders			15
5. Working Conditions	(i) Atmosphere	(a) fresh air, good ventilation		0
		(b) harmless but unpleasant odours		1– 5
		(c) harmful dust or fumes		6–10
	(ii) Heat	(a) cold (35°F–50°F)		1– 5
		(b) normal (50°F–80°F)		0
		(c) hot (>80°F)		1–20
	(iii) Noise	(a) normal bench work noise		0
		(b) normal machine noise		1
		(c) loud constant noise		5
		(d) loud frequent noise		6–10
	(iv) General	(a) dirt		1– 5
		(b) wet floors		1– 5
		(c) vibration		1– 5
		(d) monotony		0– 4
		(e) mental strain		1– 8
	(v) Protective clothing	(a) overalls, aprons		0
		(b) gloves		1– 3
		(c) heavy, special suits		10–20
		(d) masks		10–20

SM's can therefore be used in calculating wages and performance. For example, performance can be measured by:

$$\frac{\text{output of work in SM's}}{\text{total labour time in minutes}}$$

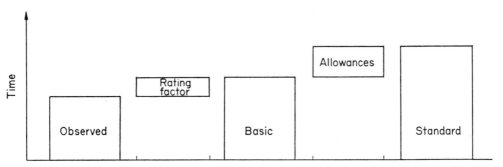

FIGURE 6.4. Breakdown of Standard Minute

INDIRECT WORK MEASUREMENT

Synthetic Timing (Elemental, Standard or Basic Data)

Data obtained from direct time studies are likely to be filed away, after use, in some safe and convenient place. After even a comparatively short period a very substantial amount of data may well have been accumulated and, providing this information is accurately filed and readily accessible, it may, on occasions, prove quite valuable.

Should the need arise to manufacture an item which differs only marginally from one produced at present or previously, there is no necessity for a complete work measurement exercise to be carried out, since much of the information we require is already available. It may not even be necessary to study that portion of the job which differs, since this may also resemble part of a previous job for which work measurement data is available. On occasions, therefore, the times for a new job may be constructed entirely from existing data. Work measurement data is often classified and stored with this possible use in mind, and the process of reconstruction is usually referred to as *synthesizing*.

As time studies are completed the 'elemental' data is coded and stored. Periodically this data is examined to determine whether any consistency exists amongst times for similar elements and, when sufficient, consistent data has been gathered, the information can be condensed as tables, graphs or equations for easy future application. If elemental times are being collected for this purpose the definitions of work elements should be more precise than would normally be required. Furthermore, because of the slow accumulation of data suitable for synthesizing, it is often preferable to plan the entire work measurement activity with the object of obtaining accurate data.

The generation of data for machine elements normally involves comparatively little trouble, since such times are often either constant or the functions of known variables. For example, the graph shown in Fig. 6.5 gives the times required for cutting square, rectangular and channel section steel, the times being a function of the saw speed and the distance travelled. Similarly, constant 'man' elements provide little difficulty since an equal time will be required whenever the job or element is performed.

It is more difficult to deal with variable elements. Firstly, we must examine the variations in time which occur in our accumulated data to establish whether this variation results from a difference in the nature of the element itself, or whether it results from the action of one or more variables. If the variations are particularly large there may be fundamental differences in the nature of the elements, in which case the data cannot be assembled together. The remaining variation can usually be attributed to variables such as distance, size and weight, and graphs or tables can then be constructed.

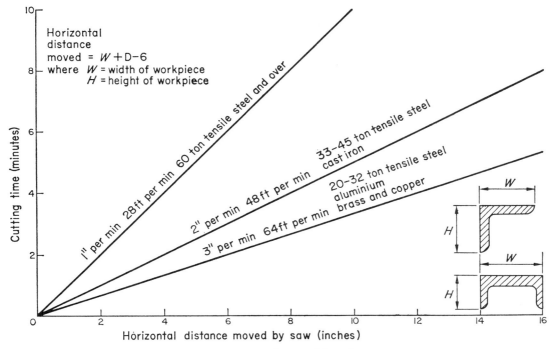

FIGURE 6.5. Data for machine elements

Figure 6.6 is an extract from a manual of synthetic data developed by a company for bricklaying and building jobs.

Synthetic data is reliable and consistent since it has normally resulted from many studies over a period of time. It can be used to establish time standards for short run work on which there would be insufficient time to conduct a direct Time Study, and to construct time standards for jobs not yet begun.

A practical advantage is that there is no need for the use of a stopwatch, but it can be expensive and time consuming to develop synthetic data. It is normal to synthesize Basic times to which allowances must be added. The need to rate the job under consideration is avoided and since the synthetic data will probably have been derived from numerous studies, the consequence of inaccuracies in the original studies is reduced.

Predetermined Motion Time System (PMTS)

In BS 3138 PMTS is defined as 'A work measurement technique whereby times established for basic human motions (classified according to the nature of the motion and the conditions under which it is made) are used to build up the time for a job at a defined level of performance'. A PMT system therefore consists of a list of all motions that a worker can utilize in doing a task together with time values for these motions at a specified level of performance and in specified circumstances.

The concept of a Predetermined Motion Time System originated with F. W. Taylor, who around 1880 attempted to develop elemental time data for groups of motions. Since that time

Building with partition blocks

		BM's per square yard				
		2"	2½"	3"	4"	6"
	Hollow Blocks					
B13.1	Clinker Concrete			32·00	35·20	44·80
B13.2	Ballast Concrete			54·40	67·20	83·20
B13.3	Clay Blocks		32·00	38·40	44·80	54·40
	Solid Blocks					
B13.4	Clinker and lightweight	28·80	32·00	38·40	44·80	54·40
B13.5	Extra allowances for the above items when building circular work on plan:					

        (A) up to 5' 0" radius BM's × 2·00
        (B) up to 20' 0" radius BM's × 1·50

Additional operations to the above

		BM's per linear yard				
		2"	2½"	3"	4"	6"
B13.6	Cut, tooth and bond to brickwork	6·40	9·60	9·60	12·80	12·80
B13.7	Raking or angular cutting	3·20	3·20	3·20	3·20	6·40
B13.8	Circular cutting	6·40	6·40	6·40	9·60	12·80
B13.9	Cutting, wedging and pinning	6·40	9·60	9·60	12·80	12·80
B13.10	Cutting around openings	3·20	3·20	3·20	3·20	3·20
B13.11	Cutting hole for small pipe (2")	6·40	6·40	9·60	9·60	12·80
B13.12	Cutting hole for large pipe (4")	6·40	9·60	9·60	12·80	16·00

Taking down partition walls

		BM's per square yard				
		2"	2½"	3"	4"	19·20
B14.1	Take down partition walls	12·80	12·80	16·00	6"	19·20

FIGURE 6.6. *Synthetic data for bricklaying operations.* (Reproduced by permission of G.E.C. Power Engineering Ltd.)

many successful PMT systems have been developed, the first of which was called *Motion Time Analysis* (MTA) and was developed by A. B. Segur around 1925. MTA was exceedingly detailed, remained very much a proprietary system, and consequently was never widely adopted.

A second system, known as *Work Factor*, was developed independently by a group headed by J. H. Quick, around 1934. Again the system remained essentially proprietary and details were not published in book form until 1962.[5]

Methods Time Measurement (MTM) was developed by Maynard, Stegemerten and Schwab during the latter part of the Second World War, and was first published in book form in 1946.[6]

Like the two previously mentioned systems MTM provided times for basic motions, the argument being that because such motions approximated to the 'lowest common denominators' of all work, it was possible, theoretically at least, to construct time standards for all jobs from a set of tabular data. In addition to this assumption, that all work can be divided into basic units,

[5] J. H. Quick, Duncan, Malcolm, *Work Factor Time Standards*, McGraw-Hill, London, 1962.
[6] H. B. Maynard, G. T. Stegemerton, J. L. Schwab, *Methods-time Measurement*, McGraw Hill, London, 1946.

i.e. given a qualitative description, a further assumption was made, i.e. that for each of these qualitative units a universal time value can be obtained. It was assumed, for example, that the time required for a particular elemental motion is not influenced unduly by preceding or succeding motions.

To establish times of each motion under various conditions was a tremendous job, and was usually accomplished by analysing motion films. The problem of rating still remained but at least all times were derived from ratings by small groups of observers working under carefully controlled conditions.

Many of the better PMT systems are extremely comprehensive and attempt to take into account as many variables as possible. Nevertheless, factors such as the influence of the sequence of units, the overall complexity of the task, the repetitiveness of the sequence of units, the direction of movement etc. must necessarily be omitted from even the better systems.

MTM quickly became the most widely used PMT System, largely because unlike the others at that time, it was non-proprietary and was backed up by a widespread Association which provided both momentum to the system and training for practitioners.

MTM classifies all hand motions into basic units as follows:

Reach (R)   the basic element employed when the predominant purpose is to move the hand to a destination or general location.

Move (M)   the basic element employed when the predominant purpose is to transport an object to a destination.

Turn (T)   a movement which rotates the hand, wrist and forearms.

Apply Pressure (AP)   the element employed whenever pressure is applied.

Grasp (G)   a hand or fingers element employed when an object is required for further operation.

Position (P)   the basic element employed to align, orient or engage one object with another, when motions used are minor and do not justify classification as other basic elements.

Release (RL)   the basic element employed to relinquish control of an object by the fingers or hand.

Disengage (D)   the basic element employed to break contact between objects.

Eye Travel and Eye Focus (ET EF)
Body Leg and Foot Motions

The times for various sub-groups of each of these units, and under various conditions are shown in Table 6.2. In addition Table 6.3 shows how the MTM notation is constructed, and Fig. 6.7 indicates the ease or difficulty with which simultaneous motions are achieved.

The time units used in MTM are 'Time Measurement Units' where

$$1 \text{ TMU} = 0 \cdot 0006 \text{ mins.}$$

It should be noted that because MTM was developed in America, TMU values do not necessarily correspond to 100 on the BS rating scale. There has been a good deal of controversy over the relationship of the ratings included in the TMU values and the BS scale, but recently it has been suggested that for all practical purposes job times derived using MTM values should be accepted as equivalent to a BSI rating of 83.[7]

---

[7] P. M. Burman and others, MTM and the BSI rating scale, *Work Study and Management Services*, **13**, No. 2, 97, 1969.

TABLE I—REACH—R

Distance Moved Inches	Time TMU A	B	C or D	E	Hand In Motion A	B	CASE AND DESCRIPTION
3/4 or less	2.0	2.0	2.0	2.0	1.6	1.6	A Reach to object in fixed location, or to object in other hand or on which other hand rests.
1	2.5	2.5	3.6	2.4	2.3	2.3	
2	4.0	4.0	5.9	3.8	3.5	2.7	
3	5.3	5.3	7.3	5.3	4.5	3.6	B Reach to single object in location which may vary slightly from cycle to cycle.
4	6.1	6.4	8.4	6.8	4.9	4.3	
5	6.5	7.8	9.4	7.4	5.3	5.0	
6	7.0	8.6	10.1	8.0	5.7	5.7	
7	7.4	9.3	10.8	8.7	6.1	6.5	C Reach to object jumbled with other objects in a group so that search and select occur.
8	7.9	10.1	11.5	9.3	6.5	7.2	
9	8.3	10.8	12.2	9.9	6.9	7.9	
10	8.7	11.5	12.9	10.5	7.3	8.6	
12	9.6	12.9	14.2	11.8	8.1	10.1	D Reach to a very small object or where accurate grasp is required.
14	10.5	14.4	15.6	13.0	8.9	11.5	
16	11.4	15.8	17.0	14.2	9.7	12.9	
18	12.3	17.2	18.4	15.5	10.5	14.4	
20	13.1	18.6	19.8	16.7	11.3	15.8	E Reach to indefinite location to get hand in position for body balance or next motion or out of way.
22	14.0	20.1	21.2	18.0	12.1	17.3	
24	14.9	21.5	22.5	19.2	12.9	18.8	
26	15.8	22.9	23.9	20.4	13.7	20.2	
28	16.7	24.4	25.3	21.7	14.5	21.7	
30	17.5	25.8	26.7	22.9	15.3	23.2	

TABLE II—MOVE—M

Distance Moved Inches	Time TMU A	B	C	Hand In Motion B	Wt. (lb.) Up to	Factor	Constant TMU	CASE AND DESCRIPTION
3/4 or less	2.0	2.0	2.0	1.7	2.5	1.00	0	A Move object to other hand or against stop.
1	2.5	2.9	3.4	2.3	7.5	1.06	2.2	
2	3.6	4.6	5.2	2.9	12.5	1.11	3.9	
3	4.9	5.7	6.7	3.6	17.5	1.17	5.6	
4	6.1	6.9	8.0	4.3	22.5	1.22	7.4	B Move object to approximate or indefinite location.
5	7.3	8.0	9.2	5.0	27.5	1.28	9.1	
6	8.1	8.9	10.3	5.7	32.5	1.33	10.8	
7	8.9	9.7	11.1	6.5	37.5	1.39	12.5	
8	9.7	10.6	11.8	7.2	42.5	1.44	14.3	C Move object to exact location.
9	10.5	11.5	12.7	7.9	47.5	1.50	16.0	
10	11.3	12.2	13.5	8.6				
12	12.9	13.4	15.2	10.0				
14	14.4	14.6	16.9	11.4				
16	16.0	15.8	18.7	12.8				
18	17.6	17.0	20.4	14.2				
20	19.2	18.2	22.1	15.6				
22	20.8	19.4	23.8	17.0				
24	22.4	20.6	25.5	18.4				
26	24.0	21.8	27.3	19.8				
28	25.5	23.1	29.0	21.2				
30	27.1	24.3	30.7	22.7				

TABLE III—TURN AND APPLY PRESSURE—T AND AP

Weight	Time TMU for Degrees Turned 30°	45°	60°	75°	90°	105°	120°	135°	150°	165°	180°
Small—0 to 2 Pounds	2.8	3.5	4.1	4.8	5.4	6.1	6.8	7.4	8.1	8.7	9.4
Medium—2.1 to 10 Pounds	4.4	5.5	6.5	7.5	8.5	9.6	10.6	11.6	12.7	13.7	14.8
Large—10.1 to 35 Pounds	8.4	10.5	12.3	14.4	16.2	18.3	20.4	22.2	24.3	26.1	28.2

APPLY PRESSURE CASE 1—16.2 TMU. APPLY PRESSURE CASE 2—10.6 TMU.

TABLE IV—GRASP—G

Case	Time TMU	DESCRIPTION
1A	2.0	Pick Up Grasp—Small, medium or large object by itself, easily grasped.
1B	3.5	Very small object or object lying close against a flat surface.
1C1	7.3	Interference with grasp on bottom and one side of nearly cylindrical object. Diameter larger than 1/2".
1C2	8.7	Interference with grasp on bottom and one side of nearly cylindrical object. Diameter 1/4" to 1/2".
1C3	10.8	Interference with grasp on bottom and one side of nearly cylindrical object. Diameter less than 1/4"
2	5.6	Regrasp.
3	5.6	Transfer Grasp.
4A	7.3	Object jumbled with other objects so search and select occur. Larger than 1" x 1" x 1".
4B	9.1	Object jumbled with other objects so search and select occur. 1/4" x 1/4" x 1/8" to 1" x 1" x 1".
4C	12.9	Object jumbled with other objects so search and select occur. Smaller than 1/4" x 1/4" x 1/8".
5	0	Contact, sliding or hook grasp.

TABLE V—POSITION*—P

Class of Fit	Symmetry	Easy To Handle	Difficult To Handle
1—Loose No pressure required	S	5.6	11.2
	SS	9.1	14.7
	NS	10.4	16.0
2—Close Light pressure required	S	16.2	21.8
	SS	19.7	25.3
	NS	21.0	26.6
3—Exact Heavy pressure required	S	43.0	48.6
	SS	46.5	52.1
	NS	47.8	53.4

*Distance moved to engage—1" or less.

TABLE VI—RELEASE—RL

Case	Time TMU	DESCRIPTION
1	2.0	Normal release performed by opening fingers as independent motion.
2	0	Contact Release.

TABLE VII—DISENGAGE—D

CLASS OF FIT	Easy to Handle	Difficult to Handle
1—Loose—Very slight effort, blends with subsequent move.	4.0	5.7
2—Close—Normal effort, slight recoil.	7.5	11.8
3—Tight—Considerable effort, hand recoils markedly.	22.9	34.7

TABLE VIII—EYE TRAVEL TIME AND EYE FOCUS—ET AND EF

Eye Travel Time=15.2 x $\frac{T}{D}$ TMU, with a maximum value of 20 TMU.

where T=the distance between points from and to which the eye travels.
D=the perpendicular distance from the eye to the line of travel T.

Eye Focus Time=7.3 TMU.

TABLE 6.2. Methods-time measurement application data in TMU

TABLE 6.2. Continued

TABLE IX—BODY, LEG AND FOOT MOTIONS

DESCRIPTION	SYMBOL	DISTANCE	TIME TMU
Foot Motion—Hinged at Ankle.	FM	Up to 4″	8.5
With heavy pressure.	FMP		19.1
Leg or Foreleg Motion.	LM —	Up to 6″	7.1
		Each add'l. inch	1.2
Sidestep—Case 1—Complete when leading leg contacts floor.	SS-C1	Less than 12″	Use REACH or MOVE Time
		12″	17.0
		Each add'l. inch	.6
Case 2—Lagging leg must contact floor before next motion can be made.	SS-C2	12″	34.1
		Each add'l. inch	1.1
Bend, Stoop, or Kneel on One Knee.	B,S,KOK		29.0
Arise.	AB,AS,AKOK		31.9
Kneel on Floor—Both Knees.	KBK		69.4
Arise.	AKBK		76.7
Sit.	SIT		34.7
Stand from Sitting Position.	STD		43.4
Turn Body 45 to 90 degrees—			
Case 1—Complete when leading leg contacts floor.	TBC1		18.6
Case 2—Lagging leg must contact floor before next motion can be made.	TBC2		37.2
Walk.	W-FT.	Per Foot	5.3
Walk.	W-P	Per Pace	15.0
Walk.	W-PO.	Per Pace	17.0

The advantages of a PMTS are much the same as the advantages of synthetic standards, but the main disadvantage of the use of such systems is the considerable amount of time normally needed to construct element and job times from such detailed information. This was perhaps the main reason why PMTS systems were slow to be accepted in many companies, particularly in the UK, and as a result, certain 'second generation' systems were developed which relied on the use of elements rather than basic motions. MTM–2 is such a system. It was developed in Europe with the purpose of fulfilling several objectives, one of which was that the data should be easily and rapidly handled in practice.

TABLE 6.3. Examples of MTM notation

Motion	Code	Meaning and TMU Value
Reach	R7A	Reach, path of movement 7″, class A. Hand not in motion at beginning or end. (7·4 TMU)
Move	M6A	Move, 6″, class A, object weighs less than 2·5 lb. (8·9 TMU)
Turn	T90M	Turn, 90° object weighing 2·1 to 10 lb. (8·5 TMU)
Grasp	G1C1	Grasp, case 1C1. (7·3 TMU)
Position	P2NSE	Position, close fit, non-symmetrical part, Easy to handle. (21·0 TMU)
Release	RL1	Release, case 1. (2·0 TMU)
Disengage	D1D	Disengage, loose fit, difficult to handle. (5·7 TMU)
Eye Travel	ET10/12	Eye travel, between points 10″ apart, line of travel 12″ from eye. (12·7 TMU)

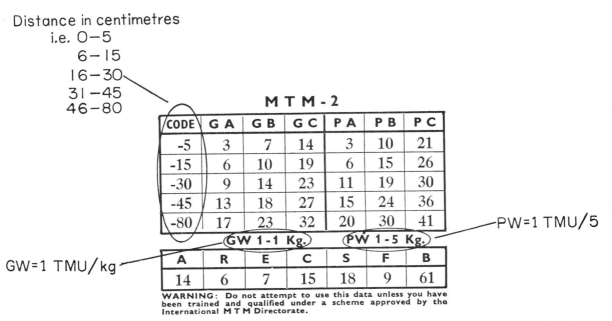

TABLE X—SIMULTANEOUS MOTIONS

FIGURE 6.7. Simultaneous motions [Table 6.2 and Fig. 6.7 reproduced by permission, MTM Association of UK]

MTM–2 was synthesized from MTM data and consists of nine motions—Get; Put; Apply Pressure; Regrasp; Eye Action; Crank; Step; Foot Motion; Bend and Arise. Only Get and Put have variable categories, consequently the MTM–2 data card has only 39 time standards. As with MTM, the motions and their various sub-categories are closely defined and precise rules cover their use.

Distance in centimetres
i.e. 0–5
6–15
16–30
31–45
46–80

MTM-2

CODE	G A	G B	G C	P A	P B	P C
-5	3	7	14	3	10	21
-15	6	10	19	6	15	26
-30	9	14	23	11	19	30
-45	13	18	27	15	24	36
-80	17	23	32	20	30	41

GW 1-1 Kg.   PW 1-5 Kg.

PW=1 TMU/5

GW=1 TMU/kg

A	R	E	C	S	F	B
14	6	7	15	18	9	61

WARNING: Do not attempt to use this data unless you have been trained and qualified under a scheme approved by the International M T M Directorate.

FIGURE 6.8. The MTM-2 data card [Reproduced by permission, MTM Association of UK]

Get (G)—a motion with the predominant purpose of reaching with the hand or fingers to an object, grasping the object, and subsequently releasing it.

Class A—no grasping motion required

Class B—grasping involving closing of the hand or fingers with one motion

Class C—complex grasping motion

Class W—*get weight*, the action required for the muscles of the hand or arm to take up the weight of an object.

Put (P)—a motion with the predominant purpose of moving an object to a destination with the hand or fingers.

Class A—continuous smooth motion

Class B—discontinuous motion, but without obvious correcting motion (i.e. unintentional stop, hesitation or change in direction)

Class C—discontinuous motion with obvious correcting motions

Class W—*put weight*, is an addition to a put action depending on the weight of the object moved.

Apply Pressure (A)—an action with the purpose of exerting muscular force on an object.

Regrasp (R)—the hand action performed with the purpose of changing the grasp of an object.

Eye Action (E)—the action with the purpose of either (a) recognizing a readily distinguishable characteristic of an object, or (b) shifting vision to a new viewing area.

Crank (C)—a motion with the purpose of moving an object in a circular path more than 180° with hand or fingers.

Step (S)—either (a) a leg motion with the purpose of moving the body or (b) a leg motion longer than 30 centimetres.

Foot Motion (F)—a short foot or leg motion the purpose of which is *not* to move the body.

Bend and Arise (B)—bend, stoop or kneel on one knee and subsequently arise.

The time standard, in TM units, for each of the motions is easily obtained from the MTM–2 data card (Fig. 6.8). The values for the seven motions without variable categories are given at the bottom of the card, whilst the remaining figures on the card relate to Get and Put. The time standard for both of these is determined by the category of the motion and the distance involved. The left hand column gives distance in centimetres.

The time standards for GW and PW are shown on the card, in the case of the former, a time value of 1 TMU per Kilogramme applies and in the case of the latter 1 TMU per 5 Kilogrammes, i.e. the TMU associated with 'Getting' an object of effective net weight 10 Kg (GW 10) is 10 TMU whereas the time standard for PW 10 is 2 TMU.

Figure 6.9 is an example of the use of MTM–2 data. For comparison the same operation is analysed with MTM data in Fig. 6.9(b).

Several other second generation systems have been synthesized from original MTM data, for example *Primary Standard Data* was developed by the British management consultants, Urwick-Orr and Partners in the early 1960's. It is a simple system, the use of which does not depend upon a knowledge of the basic system from which it was developed. A further feature of this British PMT system is that no correction is necessary to equate times to standard performance on the BS scale. Motion definitions, the principles of the system etc. can be found in the book published in 1967.[8]

---

[8] F. J. Neale, *Primary Standard Data*, McGraw-Hill, London, 1967.

Methods Analysis Chart

Operation: Assemble damper brackets on washing machine container   Page 1 of 2

MTM–1

Description—Left Hand	f	L.H.	T.M.U.	R.H.	f	Description–Right Hand
1. Assemble rubber to damper bracket						
To bracket		R24C	22.5			
		G4A	7.3			
			8.4	R4C		To rubber
			7.3	G4A		Grasp rubber
Bracket to support		M20B	18.2			
			10.3	M6C		Rubber onto bracket
			5.6	PISE		Position rubber in bracket
			64.8	API	4	Push in rubber
			5.7	M3B		Turn rubber
			5.6	G2		Regrasp rubber
			15.8	MI6B		Aside bracket
			2.0	RLI		Release rubber
			172.5	x4	=	690.0 T.M.U.'s per container
2. Assemble screws and damper brackets to container						
			22.5	R24C		To bracket
			7.3	G4A		Grasp bracket
To bracket		R4C	8.4			
Grasp bracket		G4A	7.3			
To bracket in other hand		(R-A)	9.7	M8A		Move bracket to other hand
		G2				
Grasp bracket		G3	5.6			
			45.0	R24C	2	To bolt
			18.2	G4B	2	Grasp bolt
			51.0	M24C	2	Bolt to container bracket
			11.2	PISE	2	
Position 2nd bracket		M4C	8.0			
		PISE	5.6			
To container		MIOC	13.5			
Position bracket		PISSE	9.1			
			4.0	RLI	2	
			226.4	x2	=	452.8 T.M.U.'s per container

Methods Analysis Chart

Operation: assemble damper brackets on washing machine container   Page 1 of 2

MTM–2

Description—Left Hand	f	L.H.	T.M.U.	R.H.	f	Description–Right Hand
1. Assemble rubber to damper bracket						
Obtain bracket		GC80	32			
			19	GCI5		Obtain rubber
Bracket to support		PA80	20			
			15	PBI5		Rubber to bracket
			56	A	4	Push in rubber
			6	PAI5		Turn rubber
			6	R		Regrasp rubber
			15	PA45		Aside bracket
			69x	4	=	676 T.M.U.'s per container
2. Assemble screws and damper brackets to container						
			32	GC80		Obtain bracket
Obtain bracket		GCI5	19			
			11	PA30		Bracket to other hand
Grasp bracket		GB5	7			
			64	GC80	2	Obtain bolt
			60	PB80	2	Bolt to bracket container
Position 2nd bracket		PBI5	15			
Position 2nd bracket		PC30	30			
			238x	2	=	476 T.M.U.'s per container
3. Position nuts onto bolts						
		GB	32	GC80		To nut
			41	PC80		Nut to bolt
			3	PA5		Engage nut
			15	PA5	5	Run nut with fingers
			28	GB5	4	
			119x	4	=	476 T.M.U.'s per container

(a)

FIGURE 6.9. (a) Comparison of operation analysed by MTM-2 and MTM-1 data

Four different types of *Work Factor* system have been developed, each appropriate for certain applications, depending upon the amount of detail and/or the speed of the analysis required. These four systems are known as 'Detailed Work factor', 'Simplified Work Factor', 'Abbreviated Work Factor', and 'Ready Work Factor'. Other 'second generation systems' include 'Unified Standard Data', 'Integrated Standard Data', 'General Purpose Data', 'Master Standard Data', 'Basic Work Data', etc.

Analytical Estimating

Analytical Estimating is described as 'A Work Measurement technique, whereby the time required to carry out elements of a job at a defined level of performance is established from knowledge and practical experience of the elements concerned'. (BS 3138).

Analytical Estimating is intended to replace a procedure known as *rate-fixing* which was, and regrettably still is occasionally, used to establish time standards for non-repetitive work such as maintenance. In such circumstances there is often insufficient synthetic data available to allow time standards to be established, consequently standards must be constructed using whatever data is available, plus estimates of the basic times for the remaining elements. Clearly a requirement in Analytical Estimating is that the estimator is completely familiar with, and preferably skilled and experienced in the work concerned.

The procedure used is much the same as before, in that jobs are firstly divided into appropriate

Methods Analysis Chart

Operation: Assemble damper brackets on washing machine container   Page 2 of 2

MTM-1

Description—Left Hand	f	L.H.	T.M.U.	R.H.	f	Description—Right Hand
3. Position nuts onto bolts						
Slide hand down to hold bolt	R–B	22·5	R24C			To nut
	G5	9·1	G4B			Grasp nut
Hold		25·5	M24C			Nut onto bolt
Hold		5·6	PISE			Position nut
Hold		2·9	MIB			Engage nut
Hold		14·5	MIB		5	Run nut with fingers
Hold	RLI	10·0	RLI		5	Run nut with fingers
Hold		10·0	RIA		4	Run nut with fingers
Hold		8·0	GIA		4	Run nut with fingers
		108·1	x4	=		432·4 T.M.U.'s per container
						container
4. Tighten up nuts on damper brackets						
To box spanner		R24B	21·5	(R–B)		To nut runner
Grasp box spanner		GIA	2·0	GIA		Grasp nut runner
Spanner to nut	2	M24C	51·0	(M–B)		Nut runner to work area
Ensure to hold	4	G2	—			
Onto nut	2	PISSE	18·2			
			13·6	MIC	4	Nut runner to bolt
			22·4	PISE	4	Position runner
			464·0		4	Process time
To brackets	2	R8B	20·2	(M–B)		Gun clear
		G2				
Grasp bracket	2	GIA	4·0			
Straighten bracket	2	MfA	4·0			
	2	API	32·4			
Spanner to nut	2	M6C	20·6			
Onto nut	2	PISSE	18·2			
Spanner aside		M24B	20·6	M24B		Nut runner aside
		RLI	2·0	RLI		
			714·7			T.M.U.'s per container

Methods Analysis Chart

Operation: _____ Page 2 of 2

Description—Left Hand	f	L.H.	T.M.U.	R.H.	f	Description—Right Hand
4. Tighten up nuts on damper bracket						
Obtain spanner		GB80	23	(GB)		Obtain nut runner
Spanner to nut	2	PC80	82			
			40	PB5	4	Nut runner to bolt
			464			Process time
Obtain brackets	2	GB30	28			
Straighten bracket	2	PA5	6			
	2	A	28			
Spanner to nut	2	PCI5	52			
Aside spanner		PA80	20	PA80		Aside nut runner
			743			T.M.U.'s per container

(b)

	Summary of Operation		
Element number	By MTM		By MTM-2
1	690·0		676
2	452·8		476
3	432·4		476
4	714·7		743
Total	2289·9		2371

(c)

FIGURE 6.9. (b) and (c) Comparison of operation analysed by MTM-2 and MTM-1 data [Figs. 6.9. (a), (b) and (c) reproduced by permission, B. W. Jones, 'MTM-2 appreciation', *Work Study and Management Services*, November 1967)]

elements, synthetic data is used for as many of those elements as possible, whilst basic times are estimated for the remainder. Rather than applying allowances to individual elements, relaxation and contingency allowances are applied as overall or blanket figures for the whole job.

ACTIVITY SAMPLING

The work measurement techniques we have described so far are appropriate where we are concerned with short cycle repetitive work. If, however, it is necessary to establish work standards in situations where long irregular cycle work is conducted, or where many different jobs are performed, these techniques may well be quite inappropriate.

It may be necessary to study the activities of several workers on several machines in order to establish the proportion of time each worker spends on various activities, or to determine the utilization of resources, space etc. and in such cases some form of sampling procedure is invaluable.

Memomotion photography, discussed in the previous chapter, was a sampling technique by which, in particular circumstances, we are able to obtain sufficient information about jobs or activities without conducting a continuous study. In memomotion study the sampling interval was constant, but in certain cases we may wish to sample at irregular intervals in order to avoid any chance of our observations regularly coinciding with some particular feature of the activity being studied.

The accuracy of our sample as a measure of the actual activity is clearly dependent upon the number of observations we take. If we are willing to take very many observations our confidence in the result can be high, but this will have been obtained only at higher cost.

Again we must decide what confidence level and accuracy we require before we can decide how many observations to take. Furthermore, a pilot study must be conducted to establish the frequency of occurrence of the activity being studied, then for a confidence level of 95 per cent the formula to determine the number of observations required is:

$$N = \frac{4p\,(100-p)}{L^2}$$

Where N = number of observations needed.

p = percentage of total time occupied by the activity with which we are concerned, as obtained from a pilot study.

L = required limits of accuracy (expressed as a percentage).

Rated Activity Sampling

Activity sampling is normally used to determine the percentage of the total time that a person or machine spends on certain activities. In the simplest case, the requisite number of random observations are taken to determine the percentage of total time spent by either a man or a machine in working or not working.

Occasionally it is practical to sample activities at regular rather than random intervals because of the random nature of the activities concerned. In such circumstances it is possible to use an extension of activity sampling, known *rated activity sampling* or *rated systematic sampling*.

Example 1

A simple machine is either working or not working. A series of observations are made at regular one minute intervals to determine the proportion of the total time devoted to each of these activities. The table below gives the results of the survey; each of the marks in the table has resulted from an observation.

Observation number (one minute intervals)	Machine running	Machine not running
1	1	
2	1	
3	1	
4		1
5	1	
6	1	
7		1
8	1	
9	1	
10	1	
Total	8	2

If the production of items from this machine during the period observed was 25, and if we assume standard performance, then the *basic minutes*[9] for each product is given as follows:

$$BM/product = \frac{8}{25} = 0.32$$

Example 2

A man is performing a job which has an irregular cycle and consists of a maximum of three elements of work. Observations are made at regular intervals of 0·1 minutes; the number of items produced during the period of the study is determined; and the operator is rated at each observation. Determine the *basic minutes* for each element and for each item produced.

The table below shows the results of the sampling. The figures in the columns indicate not only which element was being performed on each observation, but indicate also the performance rating for that element at that time.

The output during this two minute study was 10 items.

The basic minutes for each element per product can be calculated using the following formula:

$$BM/element = \frac{\text{sum of all ratings}}{100} \times \frac{\text{observation interval}}{\text{output}}$$

i.e. For element 1:
$$BM = 7.9 \times 0.1/10$$
$$= 0.079$$

For element 2:
$$BM = 6.1 \times 0.1/10$$
$$= 0.061$$

For element 3:
$$BM = 3.1 \times 0.1/10$$
$$= 0.031$$

The total basic minutes for each item are of course the sum of the above figures, i.e. 0·171.

[9] i.e. after rating but before the addition of allowances.

Observation number (0·1 min intervals)	Man			
	Element 1	Element 2	Element 3	Idle
1	100			
2		100		
3	95			
4			110	
5	95			
6				100
7		100		
8	95			
9	100			
10			105	
11		100		
12				100
13		100		
14	95			
15		100		
16	110			
17		110		
18			95	
19				100
20	100			
Total ('00)	7·9	6·1	3·1	3·0

INCENTIVE PAYMENT SYSTEMS

Although the use of incentive payment systems is not a necessary corollary of a work measurement exercise, it is a fact that the installation or use of an incentive payment scheme is one of the usual reasons for work measurement.

It is also a fact that there is a great deal of confused thinking about the merits, design and use of methods of incentive payment. Consequently, whilst we do not wish to comment directly upon the merits of such schemes, it is perhaps worthwhile to describe some of the more popular schemes.

100 per cent Participation or One for One Schemes

This is one of the simplest and most widely used incentive payment systems. Under this system, increases in production efficiency above a certain level lead to directly proportional increases in wages. In its simplest form, incentive payment is provided for outputs above 100 performance, there being a guaranteed payment of base rate for performances at 100 or less (see Fig. 6.10). In other words, earnings are calculated on a time basis as follows:

$$E = RH + R(S-H)$$

where E = earnings for a given period
R = base pay rate
H = hours worked
S = standard hours allowed for job
= standard hours for each piece (s) × number of pieces (N)

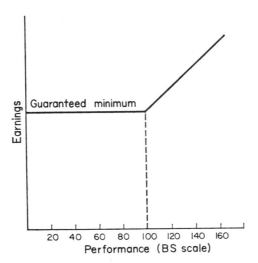

FIGURE 6.10. 100 per cent participation incentive payment scheme beginning at 100 performance

Example 1

Base pay rate   = 25 new pence/hour
Hours worked   = 8
Standard minutes/piece = 20
Output   = 30 pieces

$$E = 25(8) + 25\left[\left(\frac{20}{60} \times 30\right) - 8\right]$$

$$= 200 + 25(10 - 8)$$

$$= \quad 200 \quad + \quad 50$$
$$\text{(base pay)} \quad \text{(incentive pay)}$$

$$= 250 \text{ p. (total pay)}$$

Often 100 per cent participation or one for one schemes begin at a level less than 100 performance, i.e. incentive payment is offered to workers who exceed a performance of say 75 or 80. As with the previous scheme, it is usual to guarantee minimum base rate earnings. In this case earnings are calculated as follows:

$$E = RH + R\left(\frac{100S}{X} - H\right)$$

where X = the performance at which participation begins, e.g. 75 or 80.

Example 2

Base pay rate   = 25 new pence/hour
Hours worked   = 8
Standard minutes/pieces = 20
Output   = 30 pieces

Participation from 80 performance

$$E = 25(8) + 25 \left(\frac{100 \times 20 \times 30}{60 \times 80} - 8 \right)$$

$$= 200 + 25\,(12{\cdot}5 - 8)$$

$$= \quad 200 \quad + \quad 112{\cdot}5$$
$$\text{(base pay)} \quad \text{(incentive pay)}$$

$$= 312{\cdot}5 \text{ p. (total pay)}$$

Less than 100 per cent Participation or Geared Schemes

A large number of schemes have been developed which differ from those described previously in that they do not offer 100 per cent increases in payment for 100 per cent increases in performance.[10] Such schemes differ mainly in the extent to which workers participate as a result of increased performance. Figure 6.11 illustrates a 50/50 scheme in which increased earnings increase by a

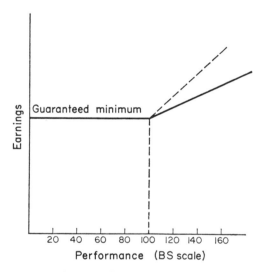

FIGURE 6.11. 50/50 geared incentive scheme

half per cent for every 1 per cent increase in performance beyond 100. The main benefit of such incentive payment schemes is that they provide some measure of safeguard for management in circumstances where allowed times may have been inaccurately estimated. An additional safeguard can, of course, be provided by applying an upper limit to incentive earnings.

The formula for calculating earnings for geared schemes without an upper earnings limit, and starting at a performance level of 100 is as follows:

$$E = RH + YR\,(S - H)$$

where Y = the extent of the gearing, e.g. 0·5 for a 50/50 plan.

---

[10] See for example the 'Halsey' and 'Rowan' incentive payment plans described in the book by Avery (see **Selected Readings** for this Chapter).

Example 3

Base pay rate $= 25$ new pence/hour
Hours worked $= 8$
SM/piece $\quad = 20$
Output $\qquad = 30$ pieces
Gearing $\qquad = 50/50$

$$E = 25(8) + 0\cdot5(25)\left(\frac{20 \times 30}{60} - 8\right)$$

$$= 200 + 12\cdot5\ (10 - 8)$$

$$= \quad 200 \quad + \quad 25$$
$$\text{(base pay)} \quad \text{(incentive pay)}$$

$$= 225 \text{ p. (total pay)}$$

As before, participation may begin at a level below 100, in which case earnings are calculated by the following formula:

$$E = RH + YR\left(\frac{100S}{X} - H\right)$$

Piece-work

This is one of the oldest methods of incentive payment, under which workers are paid a fixed amount for each piece produced. In fact the piece-work system is very similar to the 100 per cent participation or one for one system previously described, the principal difference being that in piece-work the standard is described in terms of money and not time. As with the previous systems, it is usual to operate the incentive payment system in conjunction with a guaranteed minimum payment level.

The piece-rate (P) is defined as follows:

$$P = Rs$$

consequently earnings (E) over a period of time are calculated by means of the following simple equations:

$$E = RsN$$

where performance is above 100.

$$E = RH$$

where performance is below 100.

Example 4

Base pay rate $\ = 25$ new pence/hour
Hours worked $= 8$
SM/piece $\quad = 20$
Output $\qquad = 30$

$$\text{Piece-rate} = Rs$$

$$= 25 \times \frac{20}{60}$$

$$\text{Performance} = \frac{\text{standard hours produced}}{\text{hours worked}} \times 100$$

$$= \frac{\frac{20}{60} \times 30}{8} \times 100$$

$$= 125$$

$$\therefore \text{Earning (E)} = RsN$$

$$= 25 \times \frac{20}{60} \times 30$$

$$= 250 \text{ p. (as in Example 1)}$$

Finally, it should be noted that certain practical complexities must be accommodated during the operation of any incentive payment method. For example, a certain amount of waiting time will be incurred throughout most working periods and, in addition, unmeasured work may be undertaken. It is usual to pay both of these at base rate or at day-work rate and, consequently, care must be taken to include these in the wage calculations.

Example 5

Base pay rate	= 25 new pence/hour
Total hours worked	= $9\frac{1}{2}$
Hours worked on unmeasured work	= $\frac{1}{2}$
Waiting hours	= 1
Standard minutes/piece for measured work	= 20
Output of measured work	= 30 pieces

Using a 100 per cent participation system above a 100 performance.

$$E = 25\left(9\tfrac{1}{2}\right) + 25\left[\left(\frac{20}{60} \times 30\right) - \left(9\tfrac{1}{2} - 1\tfrac{1}{2}\right)\right]$$

$$= 237\tfrac{1}{2} + 50 \text{ (incentive pay)}$$

$$= 287\tfrac{1}{2} \text{ p. (total pay)}$$

COMPUTERS IN WORK STUDY

Electronic computers have been used by work study analysts for many years. Numerous programmes have been written, these being basically of two types:

(a) programmes for analysing data, for example in treating time study data[11]
(b) programmes for applying standard data[12]

---

[11] e.g. K. K. Kopp, 'A computer program for time study analysis', *J. Ind. Eng.*, **XVIII**, No. 2, 147–152 (1967).
[12] M. F. Mobach, *AUTORATE—Computer Aid in Industrial Engineering*, Proc. 16th Ind. Eng. Inst. of California, Berkeley, 1963.

In the former case data are punched on cards or paper tape, or input directly into the computer for subsequent analysis.

In the latter case the input consists of a sequence of motions, for which the programme gives the correct PMTS symbols and times, and calculates the basic time for the movement sequence.

Recently there have been attempts to render the computer a more constructive and useful tool in work study; in particular, a computer programme has been written the purpose of which is to actually synthesize work methods,[13] i.e. given an initial workplace layout and other information to generate a motion pattern, it will list the movements involved and their elemental times, and calculate the basic time for the sequence.

						ASSEMBLE PHIL SCR	II
REACH TO PHIL SCR		RI7B	16·5				
GRASP PHIL SCR		GIA	2·0				
MOVE PHIL SCR TO ASSEM		MI7B	16·4	M 4B	MOVE SCRDR PH TO ASSEM		
POSITION PHIL SCR		PISD	11·2				
			6·7	M3C	MOVE SCRDR PH		
			14·7	PISSD	POSITION SCRDR PH		
			5·6	G2	REGRASP SCRDR PH		
			142·5	M3B	25 MOVE SCRDR PH		
			50·0	RLI	25 RELEASE SCRDR PH		
			132·5	R3B	25 REACH TO SCRDR PH		
			50·0	GIA	25 GRASP SCRDR PH		
OFF PHIL SCR		RL2	16·2	APL	AP. PRES SCRDR PH		
					464·3 SUBTOTAL		

						REMOVE EL.TUBE	
			24·9	M3IB	MOVE SCRDR PH ASIDE		
REACH TO EL.TUBE		R26D	23·9				
GRASP EL.TUBE		GIA	2·0	RLI	RELEASE SCRDR PH		
AP. PRES EL.TUBE		API	16·2				
MOVE EL.TUBE		MFC	2·0				
DISENGGE EL.TUBE		D2D	11·8				
					80·8 SUBTOTAL		

						REMOVE ADAPT	
			5·3	R 3A	REACH TO ADAPT		
			2·0	GIA	GRASP ADAPT		
			16·2	API	AP. PRES ADAPT		
			2·0	MFC	MOVE ADAPT		
			11·8	D2D	DISENGGE ADAPT		
					37·3 SUBTOTAL		

FIGURE 6.12. ARMAN computer output [Reproduced by permission, A. K. Mason and D. M. Towne, 'Towards synthetic methods analysis, *J. Ind. Eng.*, **XVIII**, No. 1, 52 (1967)]

The input to the ARMAN (ARtificial Methods ANalyst) programme consists of a description of all parts to be manipulated, the initial location of objects, the operations and the sequence in which they are to occur. The programme constructs a motion pattern, establishes a sequence of motions and performs a micro-motion analysis.

The output is in the form of a two handed process chart of the conventional type. Fig. 6.12 is a sample of the output, which in this case uses MTM notation and relates to the assembly of a piece of electronic equipment.

---

[13] A. K. Mason and D. M. Towne, 'Toward synthetic methods analysis', *J. Ind. Eng.*, **XVIII**, No. 1, 52–56 (1967).
D. M. Towne, *Computerized Work Factor*, Work Factor Assoc. Conf., London, 10th October, 1968.

This programme is not completely satisfactory in its present form, the main disadvantage being its inability to deal adequately with manipulative motions. Nevertheless, development is proceeding, and it is perhaps a good example of the type of computer application which could be available in the near future.

SUMMARY

Time standards for operations or jobs are essential for production scheduling, wage incentives, cost control and budgeting, comparison of work methods, etc.

There are basically two methods of work measurement. In direct time study, which is the conventional stopwatch technique, the job to be timed is first broken down into its constituent elements which are each timed for a sufficient number of occasions. Since the objective of the exercise is to determine the time required by a qualified worker using a given method at a defined level of performance, it is necessary, whilst timing, to assess or rate the operator's performance so that the observed time can be converted. Then the addition of allowances is necessary in order to provide time to compensate for contingencies, delays, etc. These two steps are justifiably the most controversial and subjective aspects of work study.

Synthesis and predetermined motion time systems are the two main methods of indirect time study. In both cases, the time required for a job, less allowances, is synthesized from available data.

In certain unfortunate circumstances none of these three methods may be suitable, in which case we are forced to use even less precise and more subjective procedures for estimating time standards, such as analytical estimating.

Activity sampling is appropriate for long cycle and/or non-repetitive work, or for studies involving several workers and several machines.

Work measurement studies are often conducted to provide data on which incentive payment schemes may be based. The most widely used scheme relates earnings directly to output, as measured in work units.

SELECTED READINGS

The first three books given as readings for the previous chapter cover the techniques and uses of work measurement. In addition to these, the following may be of interest to readers.

M. F. AVERY, *Time Study, Incentives and Budgetary Control*, Business Publications, Illinois, 1964. This covers much of the same ground covered in this chapter, but in no great depth.

H. B. MAYNARD, G. T. STEGEMERTON and J. L. SCHWAB, *Methods-time Measurement*, McGraw-Hill, 1948. This was the first detailed presentation of MTM.

D. W. KARGER and F. H. BAYHA, *Engineered Work Measurement*, 2nd ed., Industrial Press, New York, 1955. This, more recent, book also deals with MTM.

R. MARRIOTT, *Incentive Payment Systems*, Staples Press, London, 1961. This is a well-written and comprehensive review of the various methods of incentive payment, which will be of value to readers interested in pursuing the subject further.

R. E. HEILAND, and W. J. RICHARDSON, *Work Sampling*, McGraw-Hill, New York, 1957. This covers what has been described as activity sampling in this chapter.

C. F. GRAHAM, *Work Measurement and Cost Control*, Pergamon Press, London, 1965. This is a good introductory book, with effective coverage of incentive schemes and labour cost control.

N. A. DUDLEY, *Work Measurement—Some Research Studies*, Macmillan, London, 1968. This book will be of interest to readers anxious to pursue the subject to greater depth, since it contains descriptions of some of the more important British research studies in work measurement.

W. GOMBERG, *A Trade Union Analysis of Time Study*, Prentice Hall, Englewood Cliffs, New Jersey, 1954 (2nd edition). This book is a well-known and somewhat critical examination of work measurement.

QUESTIONS

6.1. The figures below are the observed times obtained by stopwatch, during 25 observations of a single element of a manual task. Have sufficient observations of this element been made to provide an accuracy of ± 5 per cent with a confidence interval of 95 per cent?

Observation number	Time for element (in 1/100 min)
1	40
2	45
3	43
4	42
5	45
6	47
7	40
8	48
9	47
10	42
11	40
12	39
13	42
14	41
15	43
16	44
17	46
18	43
19	42
20	42
21	44
22	43
23	40
24	42
25	45

6.2. The Westinghouse method of rating (see Fig. 6.3) was used to rate the performance of the element for which the observed times given in the previous question were also obtained. The rating is to be made on a basis of the following:

Skill	C1
Effort	B2
Conditions	E
Consistency	D

Calculate the standard time for the element if a personal allowance of 5 per cent is given.

6.3. (a) Using the data given on the sheet shown below and the following information, calculate the output of an operator at standard performance for an 8-hour shift.

Study	Operator	Times	Date	Sheet
	MALE	1/10 mins		1

Element number	Rating	Observed time	Ineffective time	Basic time	Element number	Rating	Observed time	Ineffective time	Basic time
1	110	0·45			1	105	0·45		
2	100	0·70			2	110	0·70		
3	110	0·35			3	115	0·40		
1	105	0·50			1	100	0·45		
2	110	0·65			2	100	0·80		
3	105	0·40			3	90	0·50		
1	100	0·45			1	95	0·52		
2	100	0·72			2	100	0·75		
3	100	0·42			3	110	0·45		
					1	100	0·45		
*			3·80		2	100	0·75		
					3	100	0·40		
1	110	0·47			1	110	0·52		
2	90	0·85			2	100	0·75		
3	110	0·50			3	100	0·38		
1	100	0·45							
2	100	0·75			*		Adjust jig—every 25 cycles		
3	110	0·48							

Allowances: Fatigue 5 per cent
Personal 10 per cent
Delay 2 per cent

(b) The operator working on this job produces 2 600 pieces during an eight hour working shift. He is working on a 10 per cent participation incentive scheme, in which the base pay rate is 30 new pence per hour, and in which incentive payment is given for outputs in excess of 75. What are the operator's total gross earnings for the shift?

6.4. The following task relates to a series of four time studies which were taken of an operative assembling an electric plug which had two identical terminal pins.

Description of Operation

The operative removes a completed plug from a jig and sets it aside; he takes a base for a new plug and fits this in the jig. He then takes two terminal pins and inserts these through the base and a lid is placed on top of the base. By exerting pressure on the lid a mechanical screwing device, situated under the jig, automatically fastens the base and the lid together. The cycle then starts again.

After every 1 000 plugs assembled the screwdriver blade in the mechanical screwing device has to be resharpened.

Four studies were made of this operation and the results tabulated.

Study number	1	2	3	4
Repetitive elements				
A Remove complete plug and fit new base in jig (BM)	1·61	3·31	2·55	1·72
Number of occurrences	20	40	30	20
B Insert one terminal pin through base (BM)	2·11	4·06	3·31	2·05
Number of occurrences	40	80	60	40
C Locate lid on base and fix with mechanical device (BM)	1·96	3·92	3·05	2·04
Number of occurrences	20	40	30	20
Occasional elements				
D Remove, sharpen and refit Screwdriver blade (BM)	7·60	—	—	7·30
Number of occurrences	1	—	—	1
Contingencies				
E (BM)	1·3	—	0·9	—
Number of occurrences	2	—	1	—

Note: (i) BM in each case are the total basic minutes (i.e. the observed time adjusted for rating) spent on that element during the study.
(ii) A relaxation allowance of 10 per cent is appropriate for all the elements except the occasional element. For this latter element a relaxation allowance of 15 per cent should be given.

Determine the standard time for assembling one plug.
[Univ. of Salford, Dip. for Advanced Studies in Management, 1st year, *Production Management*, July 1968—35 minutes.]

6.5. Assume that after the application of appropriate work simplification techniques, you have taken a direct time study and, after subtraction, you get the following results (time in minutes):

Cycle number	Element number				
	1	2	3	4	5
1	0·15	0·62	0·33	0·51	0·23
2	0·14	0·58	0·20	0·50	0·26
3	0·13	0·59	0·36	0·55	0·24
4	0·18	0·61	0·37	0·49	0·25
5	0·22	0·60	0·34	0·45	0·27

(a) Elements 2 and 4 are machine paced.
(b) You have a decision rule which states that any reading which varies by more than 25 per cent from the average of all readings for an element will be considered 'abnormal'.
(c) The operator is rated at 120 per cent.
(d) Allowances have been set at (for an eight hour shift):
    personal time: 30 minutes
    unavoidable delay: 36 minutes
    fatigue: 5 per cent
(e) The operator, who is paid on a straight time rate, receives 50 p per hour.
(f) Material costs are 3 p per piece.
(g) Overhead costs are calculated at 80 per cent of the sum of direct labour and material costs.

How many pieces per shift should each operator produce and what is the production cost per piece? Discuss the appropriateness of these estimates for planning purposes.
[Univ. of London Faculty of Economics, M.Sc. Business Studies, *Production Management*, June 1968—35 minutes (modified)]

6.6. 'The principal benefit in using predetermined motion time systems to develop work standards is the avoidance of performance rating, and hence the avoidance of undue dispute over the resultant standards'—Discuss.

6.7. Discuss the function of performance rating in the determination of production standards. Compare stopwatch study and work sampling in the determination of production standards.
    You have obtained the following work sample from a study during a 40 hour work week:

idle time: 20 per cent
performance rating: 135 per cent
total parts produced: 280

The allowance for this particular type of work is 10 per cent. Determine the standard time per part.
[Univ. of London, Faculty of Economics, M.Sc. Business Studies, *Production Management*, June 1968—35 minutes]

6.8. Activity sampling has been used as a convenient means of studying the activities of an operator tending a wood-planing machine on which batches of planks are grooved and chamfered.
    The following figures have been calculated from the results of such a survey in which the sampling interval was a constant five minutes, and in which the total non-stop duration of the survey was three hours,

% of total time	operator idle	30%
,,	operator adjusting machine	40
,,	operator cleaning workplace	10
,,	stacking wood	20

What is the percentage accuracy of each of these figures at 95 per cent confidence interval?

6.9. A worker is capable of giving a regular 125 performance over a working week of 40 hours. If he is employed on assembly work and if the SH per piece assembled is 0·75, what would be the gross total pay per week on a base rate of 27 new pence per hour under the following systems of payment?

(a) 100 per cent participation with incentive payment for performances over 100.
(b) 100 per cent participation with incentive payment for performances over 75.
(c) 50/50 scheme with incentive payment for performances over 100.
(d) 50/50 scheme with incentive payment for performances over 75.

What piece-rate must be paid to the worker if his gross total weekly earnings under a piece-work system are to equal the largest gross total weekly earnings provided by one of the above incentive schemes.

6.10. The table below gives details of the data obtained during a rated activity sampling or rated systematic sampling exercise. The observations were made at 0·4 minute regular intervals, and the figures in the columns are the performance rating (on the BS scale) for each of the elements during particular observations. (Notice that each element does not necessarily occur during each work cycle.)

If a total allowance of 15 per cent of the basic time is to be provided, what is the standard time in SM for the assembly of one product?

Observation Number	Assembly Element Numbers				Idle
	1	2	3	4	
1	100				
2		100			
3	105				
4		95			
5					100
6				100	
7			95		
8	90				
9		105			
10	95				
11			90		
12				105	
13	100				
14					100
15		110			
16			105		
17	110				
18				105	
19	95				
20		90			

Number of assemblies produced during this eight minute exercise = 12.

6.11. The technique of rated activity sampling is used to study the activities of three workers employed on an assembly line. The first two workers on the line have two elements to perform on each item, whereas the third worker has one element of work for each item.

At the beginning of the study the line is empty. Sufficient parts to enable the assembly of ten items are then provided, and observations are taken at 0·1 minute intervals as follows:

Time	Observed Worker
0·1	A
0·2	B
0·3	C
0·1	A
0·2	B
0·3	C
etc.	etc.

These observations result in the ratings shown in the table below.

What are the basic times for each of the five work elements and for each of the three workers?

Observation number			Worker A			Worker B			Worker C	
A	B	C	El 1	El 2	Idle	El 3	El 4	Idle	El 5	Idle
1	2	3	80					100		100
4	5	6		110		90				100
7	8	9		100				100	75	
10	11	12		90			80		85	
13	14	15			100			100	90	
16	17	18	110					100		100
19	20	21		100		100				100
22	23	24			100	100			100	
25	26	27		75			85		110	
28	29	30	120			110			100	
31	32	33			100	85			120	
34	35	36			100			100		100

6.12. What are the basic objectives of work measurement?

Describe briefly the main techniques and give in detail the situations suitable for one particular technique.

Measured work standards are frequently used as a basis for production planning and control. Comment briefly on the requisite accuracy of the work standards.

[Univ. of Lancaster, Supp. exam, M.A. Operational Research, September 1965—35 minutes]

7

Ergonomics and Job Design

ERGONOMICS

Ergonomics is the study of man in his working environment; consequently, in this section we shall be concerned with man at work, and particularly with the design of workplaces and equipment with man (or woman) in mind. The design of equipment, etc., has already been mentioned at the end of Chapter 5 and, without attempting a close study of ergonomics, in this section we shall look further at the nature of the man/machine system.

Conditions in factories and offices have improved immeasurably over the last 50 years. Whereas even quite recently workers were committed to spending a great deal of their waking hours in intolerable conditions, most contemporary factories offer clean, hygienic and comfortable accommodation. Conditions are likely to continue to improve, both as a result of continued legislation, and also because attractive working conditions are essential to attract labour in an employment situation where many alternative jobs exist.

Fifty years ago or more, it would have been readily apparent to any observer which aspects of the work situation needed improvement, but now this is less apparent and the study and design of the working environment has consequently become a detailed science.

The period between the two world wars saw the beginning of the large-scale study of working conditions and their influence on the worker's behaviour. Many psychologists were concerned during this period with the causes of fatigue, and bodies such as the Industrial Fatigue Research Board (later the Industrial Health Research Board) were established. The famous Hawthorne studies conducted by Elton Mayo at the Hawthorne plant of the Western Electric Company at Chicago began with a study of the working environment, lighting levels, etc.

The Second World War stimulated this type of research work, but by this time the emphasis had, of necessity, changed. Complex military equipment placed new demands on workers and operators who were required to exercise considerable dexterity and concentration in using radar and other equipment. In fact, the success or failure of the British defence system depended almost entirely upon the ability of individuals to work consistently and reliably at high speed. This new demand gave rise to extensive programmes of research designed to improve the performance of such workers.

It was during this period that the term *ergonomics* was coined in Britain, whilst in America the phrases *human engineering* or *human factors engineering* were in use to describe basically the same activities.

---

[1] The Hawthorne Studies are described in detail in F. J. ROETHLISBERGER and W. J. DICKSON, *Management and the Worker*, Harv. Univ. Press, Cambridge, Mass., 1939. They are also described adequately in S. W. GELLERMAN, *Motivation and Productivity*, American Management Assn., New York, 1963.

Ergonomics has progressed further in the last 20 years. The emphasis now is frequently upon what, to the 'man in the street', might seem highly esoteric research in applied cybernetics, control, learning theory, and so on.

This presents us with a problem. In an introductory book of this type we are not justified in attempting to describe such theories and research, both because this would consume a considerable amount of space, and because at present its value to the production manager is largely unproven. We must, therefore, confine ourselves to a more prosaic level which is of immediate application. This section will, therefore, consist of a very brief introduction to ergonomics and its use in industry, particularly to the industrial engineer and designer. Those readers who are dissatisfied with this approach, or who wish to pursue the subject at a higher level, are referred to the Selected Readings at the end of the chapter.

The Man–Machine System

Despite the ever-increasing mechanization of industry, people are involved in, and are essential to every system of equipment. It is true that the worker's role in modern industry is continually changing; he is being relieved of many of the routine tasks which can be better, or more economically performed by the machines themselves or some appendages of the machines. There is no doubt that this trend will continue and that it is generally regarded as a beneficial movement, but what is equally certain is that there will always be a place for man in systems of machines. Fewer men perhaps, and certainly performing different duties than at present, but nevertheless man will remain an essential component of production systems.

Let us now consider the present situation in which man and machine are interdependent, in which neither can work effectively or continually without the other. When a man uses a machine

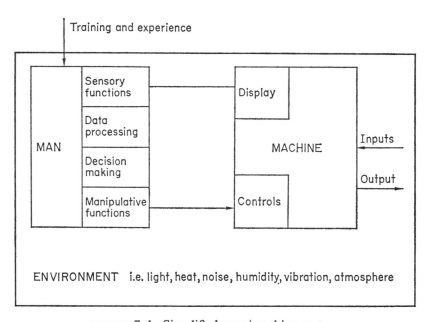

FIGURE 7.1. Simplified man/machine system

a loop or closed system results. The man will receive certain information from the machine, either from dials, displays, etc., designed for that purpose, or by observation of the machine itself. He will process this information and make decisions on what action, if any, to take and may then manipulate machine controls or attend to the machine in some other way so as to affect its behaviour in the desired manner. This man/machine system is depicted diagrammatically in Fig. 7.1. Notice that various aspects of the environment affect the man/machine relationship, and also that both man and machine are the subject of some additional input.

The efficiency with which the man functions depends on environmental factors, on his own characteristics such as age, motivation, training, and experience, as well as on the efficiency with which the machine provides the information feedback and accepts control measures.

If we accept, for our present purposes, the man and his characteristics as being fixed, this leaves us with only three aspects of the man/machine system to discuss, i.e.
1. design of information displays
2. design of controls
3. environmental factors
The first two relate to machine design, and we will consider these first.

Design of Information Displays

The most common means of displaying or communicating information is visual, and perhaps the most common visual display is the graduated scale. In fact we can identify two categories of visual display—analogue and digital. Analogue methods, such as the circular graduated scale, are common in industry and almost everywhere else, but this is mainly due to expediency rather than functional merit. The discovery of the effect of a magnetic field on a conductor carrying an electric current led to the design of the electric motor and, consequently, to the use of clocks, ammeters, voltmeters, etc., working on the same principle. Use of digital displays is a more recent phenomenon which has resulted from the functional advantages of this method rather than design expediency.

We can further classify visual displays as follows:

Displays used without controls:

(a) For quantitative measurement, e.g. clocks, voltmeters. The purpose of these is to determine whether the correct value exists, or whether corrective action is necessary.
(b) For check reading, i.e. to determine the proximity of a characteristic to a desired value, and not for obtaining a precise measurement.
(c) For comparison, e.g. to compare the readings on two dials.
(d) For warning. Although warning systems often include audible devices, lights are also frequently used.

Displays used with controls:

(a) For controlling, i.e. to extract information and measure the effect of corrective action.
(b) For setting, i.e. to use a control and display to ensure that a correct value is obtained; for example, setting the running speed of an engine after starting up.
(c) For tracking, i.e. to use a control continuously to correct movement or to compensate for external factors; for example, keeping two indicators synchronized, or on target by means of a control.
The main types of visual indicators and their uses are shown in Fig. 7.2.
Many of the handbooks and reference works on ergonomics and human engineering present

✓✓ Very good ✓ Fair — Poor	Moving pointer	Moving scale	Digital	Light	Switch
Quantitative	✓	✓	✓✓	—	—
Check reading	✓✓	—	—	—	✓✓
Comparison	✓	—	—	—	—
Warning	—	—	—	✓✓	—
Tracking	✓	✓	—	—	—
Controlling	✓	✓	—	—	—
Setting	✓✓	✓	✓✓	—	—

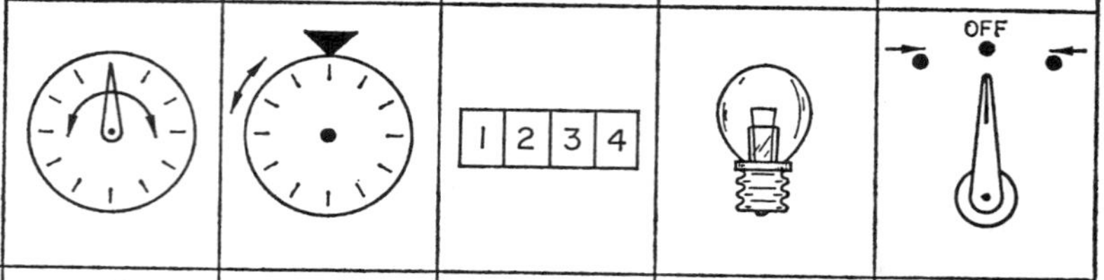

FIGURE 7.2. Visual displays (dials and indicators)

standards and design data for visual displays. They are not identical in their recommendations, but the following list contains most of the important points relating to the design of dials, etc.

1. Instruments should enable the worker to read information as accurately as necessary, but no more so.
2. The scale used should be both simple and logical, using the minimum number of suitable divisions.
3. The scale should provide information in an immediately usable form, and no mental conversions should be necessary.
4. Scales that must be read quantitatively should be designed so that workers need not interpolate between marks.
5. Vertical figures should be used on stationary dials and radial figures used on rotating dials.
6. Scales should not be obscured by the pointer.

Also in the visual category are written or printed information, radar, and television displays.
Visual methods of communication involving permanent copies, such as line output from computers or teletype machines, are particularly valuable where the message must be retained for future reference, where there is no urgency in the transmission of the information and where lengthy or complex messages are involved.

Instruments such as gauges and dials are of value where many sets of information are to be transmitted, and where the worker's job permits him to receive such information when it arrives.

Aural information 'displays', such as telephones, buzzers, bells and speech, are more appropriate where speed of transmission is important, where messages are short and uncomplicated and where a record of the message need not be retained. Often aural communication is essential in industry where visual channels are overloaded or where the environment does not permit visual communication. However, within the context of the man/machine system aural communication is infrequent, except where workers are able to determine the state of equipment from the sound of operation.

Design of Controls

The types of control commonly used and their suitability for various tasks are shown in Table 7.1. The first and most important step is to select the type of control best suited to the requirements. This will involve answering the following questions:

1. What is the control for?
2. What is required, e.g. in terms of precision, force, speed, number of settings?
3. What information must be displayed by the control; i.e. must the control be identified from the others, must it be picked out in the dark and should the worker be able to tell how the control is set?
4. How do environmental conditions affect or limit the use of the control?

TABLE 7.1. Suitability of various controls for different purposes

Type of control	Speed	Accuracy	Force	Range	Loads
Cranks					
Small	Good	Poor	Unsuitable	Good	Up to 40 in/lb
Large	Poor	Unsuitable	Good	Good	Over 40 in/lb
Handwheels	Poor	Good	Fair/Poor	Fair	Up to 150 in/lb
Knobs	Unsuitable	Fair	Unsuitable	Fair	Up to 15 in/lb
Levers					
Horizontal	Good	Poor	Poor	Poor	Up to 25 lb[a]
Vertical (to—from body)	Good	Fair	Short: Poor / Long: Good	Poor	Up to 30 lb[a]
Vertical (across body)	Fair	Fair	Fair	Unsuitable	One hand up to 20 lb[a] / two hands up to 30 lb[a]
Joysticks	Good	Fair	Poor	Poor	5–20 lb
Pedals	Good	Poor	Good	Unsuitable	(30–200 lb depends on leg flexion and body support) (ankle only up to 20 lb)
Push buttons	Good	Unsuitable	Unsuitable	Unsuitable	2 lb
Rotary selector switch	Good	Good	Unsuitable	Unsuitable	Up to 10 in/lb
Joystick selector switch	Good	Good	Poor	Unsuitable	Up to 30 lb

[a] When operated by a standing operator depends on body weight.

Reprinted from 'Ergonomics for Industry No. 7', Min. of Technology, 1965. Reproduced by permission of Controller of H.M.S.O.

Finally, having selected the most appropriate types of control to use, they should be logically arranged, clearly marked and easily accessible. They should suit the capabilities of the operator's limbs and should be positioned to distribute the loads evenly amongst them. Functionally similar controls may be combined as, for example, in the combined sidelights, headlights and flasher switch on many motor cars; also, as far as possible, controls should 'match' the changes they produce in the machine or the system, as in Figs. 7.3(a) and 7.3(b). There should be consistency in the direction of movement of controls and they should be close to, and identifiable with, their associated displays.

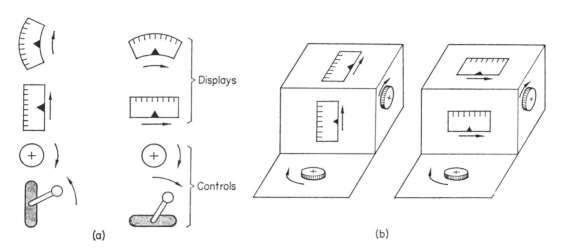

FIGURE 7.3. Relationship between controls and displays (a) Display and control in same plane (b) Display and control in perpendicular planes

Environmental Factors

In the great majority of factories and workshops physical working conditions are quite acceptable. Even in situations traditionally associated with poor working conditions improvements have been made and it unusual now to find situations in which working conditions are intolerable or unnecessarily bad. It is true that many workers must work in factories which are cold in winter and hot in summer, in atmospheres which are stuffy, in poor lighting, etc., but such factors no longer appear to be primary sources of dissatisfaction, the cause of strikes and rapid labour turnover as once was the case.[2] This is not to minimize the importance of adequate environmental conditions, which clearly must be provided. Nevertheless, provision of particularly good lighting, heating and ventilation alone is unlikely either to motivate workers or to prevent job dissatisfaction.

Lighting. Good lighting is necessary for the efficient performance of most tasks by workers, but good lighting is not achieved merely by adding extra lights since the type of lighting system adopted

---

[2] Over the past two years we have been conducting a research project in which it was necessary to interview approximately 3000 women manual workers in about ten different factories in different parts of the country. On very many occasions complaints were received about the working conditions, light, heat, and so on, but on no occasion did such factors appear to contribute significantly to the workers' job satisfaction or dissatisfaction.

will depend upon the type of work being performed, the size of objects, the accuracy, speed and duration of the work, etc. In fact an adequate lighting system should provide

Sufficient brightness
Uniform illumination
A contrast between brightness of job and of background
No direct or reflected glare

Although a considerable amount of research has been conducted to establish optimum levels of illumination for various jobs, there is little agreement on the subject, and American recommendations in particular differ from British in suggesting higher levels of illumination. Illumination levels recommended by the Illumination Engineering Society of Great Britain for various tasks are given in Table 7.2(a). Table 7.2(b) gives the limiting Glare Index for various tasks recommended by the same body. (The Glare Index is a numerical value depending upon the type of light fitting, room size, level of illumination and surface reflection.)

Lighting should also be arranged to avoid 'flicker' and to provide an acceptable amount of shadow. Notice that freedom from shadow is not always desirable since in certain circumstances, e.g. inspection, shadows can be used to improve visibility of details by accentuating or 'modelling' surface details.

TABLE 7.2(a). Examples showing amounts of light required for adequate visual performance (from the IES Code)

Visual task	Recommended illumination (lm/ft^2)
Assembly and inspection shops	
rough work	15
medium work	30
fine work	70
very fine work	150
Weaving (cotton and linen)	
light cloth	30
dark cloth	70
cloth inspection	70
Sheet metal work	20
Plastics and sheet fabrication	20
Woodworking	
rough sawing	15
planing	
medium bench and machine work	20
fine bench and machine work	
finishing	30

TABLE 7.2(b). Some typical examples of limiting Glare Index (from the IES Code)

Visual task	Limiting Glare Index
Assembly and inspection shops	
rough work	28
medium work	25
fine work	22
very fine work	19
Weaving (cotton and linen)	
light cloth	19
dark cloth	19
cloth inspection	19
Sheet metal work	25
Plastics moulding and sheet fabrication	25
Woodworking	
rough sawing	22
planing	
medium bench and machine work	22
fine bench and machine work	
finishing	22

Reprinted from 'Ergonomics for Industry No. 9', Min. of Technology 1966, by permission Controller of H.M.S.O.

Noise. We can at the outset make the obvious distinction between continuous and intermittent noise, both of which are to some extent inevitable in industry; both can have detrimental effects on behaviour and even cause physical damage to the worker.

Noise levels and the effect on workers can be reduced by controlling noise at its source, by putting barriers between the worker and the source of noise, by providing protective devices for the workers or by modifying work processes to reduce workers' exposure to noise. Prolonged exposure to continuous noise levels in excess of 90 dB (decibels) is likely to result in hearing loss: 40 dB is an acceptable maximum level for comfort.

The problem of intermittent noise has received renewed attention with the possibility of overland supersonic flight by the *Concorde* and similar aircraft. Sudden noises greatly in excess of the background noise level can and do produce a reaction, shock, or startling effect which could well have disastrous consequences for workers employed on or close to machinery. Regularly repeated intermittent noises are more readily accepted by people, a fact which has recently been proved by the regular supersonic test flights over Oklahoma. Regular intermittent noise is a common feature in industry where, for example, automatic machines such as presses are involved. There is a real danger of underestimating the effect of such noise by assuming an eventual adjustment by the worker to the prevailing situation.[3]

Temperature and Ventilation. Whilst many experiments have been conducted to discover the extremes of temperature in which human beings can survive or exist with adequate protection comparatively little is known about the effect of temperatures, in the range which we are likely to encounter, on the behaviour and efficiency of human beings.

Figure 7.4 shows that the type of work and its duration determines the individual's tolerance

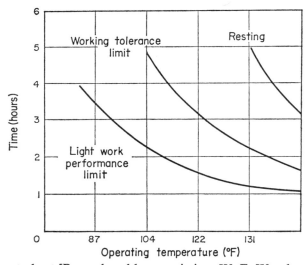

FIGURE 7.4. Tolerance to heat [Reproduced by permission, W. E. Woodson and D. W. Conover, *Human Engineering Guide for Equipment Designers*, University of California Press, Berkeley, 1964]

---

[3] It is of interest to note here that experiments have been conducted for the purpose of testing the possible use of intermittent stimuli, such as noises, to increase the vigilance of workers on simple repetitive work. Such experiments have on occasions shown beneficial results, but of course the stimuli were carefully designed to arouse and not to shock.

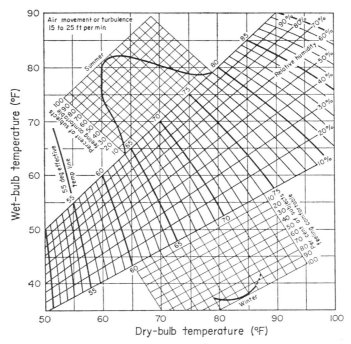

FIGURE 7.5. Scale of effective temperature and comfort chart for still air [Reproduced by permission, *Guide and Data Book, Fundamentals and Equipment*, American Society of Heating, Refrigerating and Air Conditioning Engineers, Inc.]

to heat. Figure 7.5 relates physical comfort to both temperature and humidity,[4] and Table 7.3 indicates the relation of space requirements to ventilation.

Workplace Design. Design of workplaces and equipment was mentioned in Chapter 5, and all of the comments made there would be appropriate under this heading.

Most of the production jobs in industry oblige the worker to remain sitting or standing for long periods of time whilst performing a given series of tasks. It is unreasonable to expect the detailed design of the product or its components to be influenced unduly by the ergonomic requirements of the workers responsible for making it, except of course in such cases as the need for access during assembly, but it is perfectly reasonable to expect any other aspect of workplace design to be influenced by ergonomic considerations. Inadequate design of workplaces will

---

[4] The data given in Fig. 7.5 result from research conducted in the laboratory of the American Society of Heating, Refrigerating and Air Conditioning Engineers. The horizontal scale gives the dry bulb temperature and the vertical scale gives the wet bulb temperature. Dry and wet bulb temperatures are equal only at a relative humidity of 100. Relative humidity is given by the diagonal lines. The lines sloping from top left to bottom right represent effective temperature which the Society defines as 'an arbitrary index which combines into a single value the effect of temperature, humidity, and air movement on the sensation of warmth or cold felt by the human body'. The numerical value of effective temperature is 'that of still, saturated air which would induce an identical sensation'.

The graph is interpreted as showing when, for example, a dry bulb temperature of 60°F at relative humidity 100 gives the same subjective sensation as (a) a wet bulb temperature of 67°F (by definition) or (b) a dry bulb temperature of 65°F at relative humidity 10 per cent and so on.

The two supplementary graphs show the percentage of experimental subjects feeling comfortable at various effective temperatures in both winter and summer.

F

TABLE 7.3. Relation of space requirements to ventilation

$=\dfrac{\text{Rate of air change (minutes)}}{\dfrac{\text{Net volume of space (cubic feet)}}{\text{Fresh air supply (cubic feet per minute)}}}$	Volume of space required per person (cubic feet)
1 000	500
600	450
400	400
200	300
100	200
60	150
35	100
22	65

Source: L. J. Fogel, *Biotechnology: Concepts and Applications*, Prentice-Hall, New Jersey, 1963. Reprinted by permission.

inhibit the ability of the worker to perform his tasks and may result in injuries, strain or fatigue, a reduction in quality or output, etc.

Determination of workplace requirements will involve an examination of the work elements which constitute the work cycle and an examination of the body measurements, reach and movement capacities of the worker.

Anthropometric Data. Figure 7.6 and Table 7.4 give anthropometric data, in terms of mean dimensions in inches for adult males and females. The dimensions for males, given in Table 7.4

TABLE 7.4. Anthropometric data (mean dimensions—adult males and adult females). See Fig. 6.7

Measurement	Adult Male (mean dimension—in)	Adult Female (mean dimension—in)
1	69·0	64·0
2	35·5	33·5
3	19·0	18·0
4	23·2	21·8
5	14·2	13·4
6	21·6	20·0
7	3·6	3·4
8	70·0	64·0
9	42·0	40·0
10	34·2	31·0
11	23·4	22·0
12	18·7	18·3
13	18·5	17·0
14	9·0	—
15	10·4	9·6
16	17·5	15·5
17	13·0	13·5
18	3·6	3·4

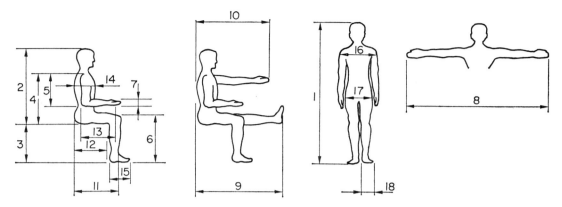

FIGURE 7.6. Anthropometric data (for dimensions see Table 7.4)

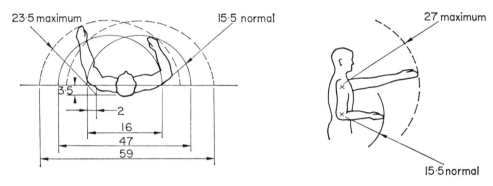

FIGURE 7.7. Normal and maximum working areas in horizontal plane

FIGURE 7.8. Normal and maximum working areas in vertical plane

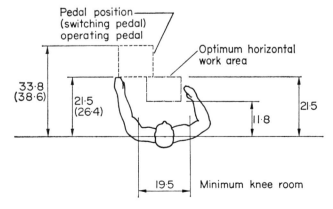

FIGURE 7.9. Optimum working area, pedal positions and knee room

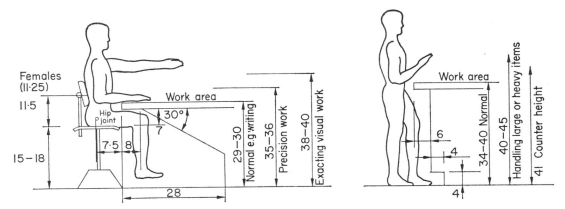

FIGURE 7.10. Space for seated work   FIGURE 7.11. Space for standing work

correspond to a 'nude' height of 5 ft 9 in, and those for women, to a height of 5 ft 4 in. Corrections for different heights can be made by increasing or decreasing the given dimensions in proportion to the differing heights.

Figures 7.7 and 7.8 give the normal and maximum working areas in both the horizontal and vertical planes. The optimum horizontal working area is given in Fig. 7.9.

Figures 7.10 and 7.11 present dimensions for working space and work area height for both sedentary and standing work.

The data given in these figures are offered for guidance purposes only. They have been extracted from several specialist books (see Selected Readings) each of which provides more detailed information, should this be required.

JOB DESIGN—A NOTE ON BOTH THEORY AND PRACTICE

Several of the previous chapters have been concerned with, or have related to, jobs and work (we will distinguish between the two terms shortly). We have already noted several implications for job design, but the importance of the subject is such that it is necessary for us to devote a short section entirely to the subject of job design for manual workers.[5]

Fifty years ago, the design of work and jobs would readily have been acknowledged as the principal function of production management. Nowadays the same problem is considered by many to be of less importance, a belief which is no doubt associated with the comparative decline in the status of work study in industry. Many others, academics included, accord increasing importance to the problem of job design. They argue that the majority of industries are still labour intensive, that the cost of labour is high, that employment opportunities are good and, consequently, that human labour is still the most valuable commodity in industry. Whereas fifty years ago job and work design was influenced almost exclusively by engineers, it is now the province of psychologists, sociologists, anthropologists and a host of other professions; all of which has tended to make the subject somewhat esoteric, leading the average production manager to feel a little out of touch with current thinking and practice.

---

[5] This section is based upon articles by the author published in *Work Study and Management Services*, **13**, No. 8, 1969, and *Chartered Mech. Eng.*, **17**, No. 6, 1970.

In order to place the subject in some perspective, and in order to fully understand current research and practice, it will be beneficial first to briefly examine its history.

The Theories of Job Design

For centuries the nature of work has been a subject which has engaged the attention of philosophers and the like, but the scientific study of work is a comparatively recent phenomenon. It is well known that the two American pioneers, F. W. Taylor and F. B. Gilbreth, were among the first to take a really objective look at the design of work and the relationship of the worker to his job. In the 60 years since the work of Taylor and Gilbreth and the birth of the scientific management movement, many theories of work and job design (we can use the two terms synonymously for the time being) have been advanced, a great deal of research work has been conducted and a great deal learnt, but what progress has been made? Do we today know much more about the efficient design of jobs than we did 60 years ago? Which of the various theories proved valid, and what is yet to be learnt?

Both Taylor and Gilbreth were intent upon finding the best method of working. Taylor's two fundamental objectives were to:

1. Select the *best* man for the job.
2. Instruct him in the *best* method of doing the job.

In 1911 Taylor said, 'Those who have anything to do with Scientific Management realize, however, that *there is a best way in doing everything*, and that the best way can always be formulated into certain rules'.[6]

Similarly Gilbreth was anxious to discover the best way to work although, unlike Taylor, he sought this through the elimination of wasteful and inefficient motions. Both Taylor and Gilbreth, despite their differing emphases, considered the worker rather as any other production facility, as something that could be 'set up' to work continuously and efficiently in a predetermined manner. They assumed that the worker exhibited only financial and security needs, a view of human motivation which would be considered naive today, but which was, of course, more appropriate 60 years ago when employment was scarce, wages meagre and educational levels low. The scientific management movement brought an engineering approach to the study and design of work, but soon such an approach was found to be, if not inappropriate, inadequate.

These concepts of the worker and the principles of work and job design were to be modified firstly by industrial psychologists who, during World War 1, became interested in the problems of monotony, boredom and fatigue. Up until about 1935 the emphasis of research was upon the causes of boredom and fatigue and their consequences. Britain took a lead in this work through bodies such as the Industrial Fatigue Research Board, and although theory was advanced substantially during this period the practical consequences of such research were confined to the design of working environments and working conditions. An ergonomic approach to work and job design evolved in which the emphasis was upon the influences of working conditions (heat, light, rest pauses, etc.) on worker behaviour. Here we must distinguish between work and jobs. Taylor and Gilbreth were concerned principally with work, with work methods and work content, whereas the psychologists were concerned with jobs, the 'job' being something larger than the 'work'—in their case incorporating the work and the working conditions. The limitations of this approach became apparent around 1925 when the first of several experiments was conducted at the Hawthorne works of the Western Electric Co. in Chicago.

---

[6] From a paper presented at the first conference on Scientific Management at the Amos Tuck School, Dartmouth, College, U.S.A., October 1911.

The Hawthorne experiments were begun on the then classical lines in that the objective was to investigate the influence of physical working conditions upon working behaviour, with particular reference to fatigue and output. The first experiment concerned the influence of lighting on worker output. Two groups of workers were observed, one a control group and the other a test group; lighting levels were adjusted for the test group, but irrespective of what change was made, output for both groups increased. Similar results were obtained in the experiment begun in 1927 in which the influence of work hours, particularly rest periods, was examined. Irrespective of the changes made in the hours and the frequency and duration of rest periods, output showed an encouraging upward trend. The conclusion drawn from these experiments was that the worker was not an isolated machine whose performance was influenced only by the type of work he was asked to do and the conditions in which he was asked to do it. The early concepts of work were now seen as grossly oversimplified. It was clear that in order to conduct sensible studies of workers and of their behaviour something other than work and working conditions should be considered.

The Human Relations Theory

In an attempt to come to terms with these new-found complexities the Hawthorne studies were continued for several more years. An approach later known as the Human Relations Theory was to evolve, which placed emphasis upon the social needs of the worker. The famous Bank Wiring Room experiments clearly indicated the importance of social attitudes and informal social control as determinants of worker behaviour.

The human relations theorists investigated factories as social systems rather than as collections of workers and their jobs. In searching for optimum methods of job design these theorists were to place emphasis upon the workers' social and affiliation needs. However, man is no more an exclusively social animal than he is a financial animal, consequently in some respects the human relations theory was as abstract as earlier theories since it was concerned primarily with only one dimension—the social—which was considered to be of overriding importance.

The Human Resources Theory

McGregor in his book *The Human Side of the Enterprise*[1][7] presents two theories relating to the worker and his job. Firstly theory x, the assumptions of which are as follows:

1. The average worker dislikes work and prefers to avoid it.
2. Workers must be coerced and controlled in order to work for organizational objectives.
3. The average worker prefers to be directed, to avoid responsibility; he has little ambition and seeks security foremost.

In contrast to this theory, McGregor suggests a theory y, the basis of which is as follows:
1. The capacity for physical and mental effort are natural abilities of the average worker.
2. External control is not the only means of motivating workers, since the average worker will exercise self-direction and self-control in the service of objectives to which he is committed.
3. Commitment to objectives is a function of the rewards associated with their achievement.
4. The average worker learns under proper conditions not only to accept, but also to seek, responsibility.
5. The capacity to exercise a relatively high degree of imagination, ingenuity and creativity is widely, not narrowly, distributed amongst the population.

---

[7] Numbers in square brackets refer to references in Selected Readings at the end of this chapter.

6. Under the conditions typical of modern industry the intellectual potentials of the average worker are only partially utilized.

This concept of the worker, with its implications for job design, was appealing and reasonable on paper, but did not influence job design practice unduly mainly because of the difficulty of designing work and providing jobs which made adequate use of individual workers' abilities. During the past fifteen years many people have suggested, and several have shown, the benefits of allowing workers more scope for discretion in their jobs. It has been emphasized that workers exhibit achievement needs as well as the needs for security, wages and social relations, but the recognition of this fact has done comparatively little to influence the design of jobs.

The Job Enlargement Philosophy

Throughout this period, despite the various theories and movements that we have discussed, there has been a continuing trend towards the increasing rationalization of work. The principles of work study developed and first applied by Taylor and Gilbreth have been widely and largely unquestioningly adopted. As a consequence, in the majority of cases work, particularly manual work, has become highly rationalized and repetitive.

Fifteen years ago Davis, Cantor and Hoffman [2] conducted an interviewing programme in several American companies from which they concluded that the following were generally considered to be important objectives of job design.

1. Break the job into the smallest components possible to reduce skill requirements.
2. Make the content of the job as repetitive as possible.
3. Minimize internal transportation and handling time.
4. Provide suitable working conditions.
5. Obtain greater specialization.
6. Stabilize production and reduce job shifts to a minimum.
7. Have engineering departments wherever possible take an active part in assigning tasks and jobs.

The comparative unimportance of any human resource objectives was again emphasized by the results of a questionnaire programme conducted in 24 companies, which again showed that the most important consideration in job design was the minimization of the time required to perform operations (Table 7.5). Clearly, despite the research which has been conducted and the theories which have been suggested during the past 40 years, all of which might have been expected to change concepts of job and job design, the principles of job and work design still correspond closely to those evolved during the scientific management movement.

In the last fifteen years the increased rationalization of work has been condemned by many researchers. They [3 and 4] have argued that such work is incapable of fulfilling the basic work needs, i.e. the need for achievement, recognition and so on, and that as a consequence job satisfaction would be minimal. It has been argued that a point of diminishing returns has been reached beyond which further work rationalization will lead to detrimental results, the decreased job satisfaction inevitably leading to reductions in productivity. In defence of the situation industrial engineers have argued that output is known to increase as cycle times are reduced, but of course, output is only one component of productivity. Productivity should also be considered as being influenced by indirect costs such as the cost of defective output, labour absenteeism and labour turnover.

Over the past ten years the philosophy of *job enlargement or enrichment* has evolved, which

TABLE 7.5. Major considerations in choice of particular methods for performing operations (based on 24 operations)

Major considerations ranked in order of weighted aggregate rating	Total number times mentioned order of importance from high to low					Weighted aggregate rating
	5	4	3	2	1	
(a) Minimizing time required to perform operation	14	4	1	—	—	89
(b) Obtaining highest quality possible	4	6	1	3	—	53
(c) Minimizing skill requirements of operation	1	3	4	3	4	39
(d) Utilization of equipment or tools presently on hand	1	4	2	—	—	27
(e) Minimizing floor space requirements	2	2	1	1	—	23
(f) Achieving specialization of skills	—	1	4	1	1	19
(g) Minimizing learning time or training	—	—	4	—	1	13
(h) Minimizing materials handling costs	1	—	—	2	1	10
(i) Equalizing and developing full work load for work crew members	—	1	1	1	—	9
(j) Providing operator satisfaction	—	1	1	1	—	9
(k) Minimizing equipment or tool costs	—	1	—	1	1	7
(l) Controlling materials used in operation	—	—	1	2	—	7
(m) Providing maximum production flexibility	—	1	1	—	—	7
(n) Simplifying supervision of operation	—	—	—	—	3	3
(o) Providing maximum safety in operation	—	—	—	1	1	3

Source: L. E. Davis, R. R. Cantor and J. Hoffman, 'Job Design Criteria', *J. Ind. Eng.*, March/April, 5 (1955). Reproduced by permission.

advocates the enlargement of all rationalized jobs so that they provide for the greater use of workers' abilities and skills, and permit the use of discretion and the exercise of responsibility. Job enlargement, for our purposes, can be defined as the design or redesign of jobs so that they enable the worker to use more of his skills and abilities, determine his own work pace, make decisions regarding work methods, quality, etc. Jobs might be enlarged by the addition of more and different work elements; by giving the worker responsibility for quality, tool set-up, repair, acquisition of materials from stores; by allowing the worker to set his own pace and determine his own work method. Similar objectives might be achieved by permitting a group of workers to organize their own work collectively, or to rotate amongst several available jobs. It should, of course, be noted that job enlargement does not consist merely of giving a worker more of the same task to do but is necessarily concerned with increasing task variety. Furthermore, job enlargement is not restricted to the manipulation or redesign of work method and content, but involves a consideration of social relations, supervision, and so on.

Many such job enlargement exercises have been conducted which have led to beneficial results in terms of increased output, reduced labour turnover and absenteeism, improved quality, etc. For example, Conant and Kilbridge [5] have reported one exercise in which assembly lines were replaced by individual and independent work stations. The product being manufactured was a washing machine pump comprising 27 parts. The assembly was originally done by six men on an assembly line each operator having a work cycle of 0·30 minutes involving six work elements. The job was changed to a one-man operation of cycle time 1·49 minutes, each operator now being responsible for 35 work elements. There was no work pacing and each operator was responsible for the quality of his output. The result of this job enlargement was a reduction in the percentage of defective output from 2·9 per cent to 1·4 per cent, and an increase in the productive labour time. However, the fact that many job enlargement exercises amongst manual workers have been conducted without any such beneficial results, indeed often with detrimental results, is a fact which has tended to be overlooked by many people. Furthermore, despite extensive research in Europe and America, it has been shown that there is no general and positive relationship between employee job satisfaction and output, although there is more evidence to indicate the relationship of job satisfaction and labour turnover [6, 7 and 8]; all of which tends to destroy the generality of the traditional model of employee attitudes and behaviour (Fig. 7.12).

The job enlargement philosophy can be criticized in much the same way as many of the previous concepts of job and work design since, like them, it presumes a rather simple situation. The scientific management theorists assumed the dominance of the financial and the security needs;

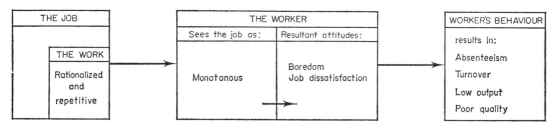

FIGURE 7.12. Traditional model of employee attitudes and behaviour

later it was assumed that the social need was paramount, and later still that the need for achievement was important for all workers. Surely, however, it is quite unreasonable to make such generalizations since workers are not an homogeneous commodity. It is not unreasonable to assume that enlarged jobs would benefit some workers, but belief that all workers would benefit from job enlargement is surely rather an oversimplification. It has been shown by many researchers that only a proportion, often a small proportion, of workers express dissatisfaction when employed on the repetitive jobs typical of modern industry. For example, our own research has shown that only one in five women manual workers employed on repetitive assembly jobs in the electronics industry expresses general job dissatisfaction, whilst the remaining 80 per cent are satisfied with such jobs [9]. Walker and Marriott, in an investigation amongst male workers in two mass production factories and six rolling mills, found that from 59 per cent to 75 per cent of employees expressed satisfaction with the operations they performed [10].

Many authors have suggested that an individual worker's attitude to his or her job is a function of certain individual characteristics. In 1929 Thompson [11] found that intelligence might be a useful predictor of susceptibility to and satisfaction in repetitive work, whilst Smith [12] more recently has found no support for this view. Smith suggested that the worker who is likely to be bored with repetitive work is likely to be 'young, restless in his daily habits and leisure-time activities, and less satisfied with personal, home and plant situations in aspects not directly concerned with . . . repetitiveness'. Our own research has shown the importance of biographical factors, in that amongst women manual workers the dissatisfied worker is typically single and under 21 years of age [9].

Although there is by no means universal agreement about which individual worker characteristics influence job attitudes and behaviour, it is now widely accepted that such characteristics are of some importance, and consequently this is one reason why the simple model shown in Fig. 7.12 is inadequate.

A second factor which has until recently been ignored is the influence of the situation, by which we mean the economic, employment and geographical situation. Clearly, as regards labour turnover, the workers' decision to leave a job must be influenced not only by attitudes to that job but also by the availability of alternative employment. In a situation in which employment is scarce security will assume higher importance; consequently job dissatisfaction may be both less prevalent and less likely to result in turnover. Furthermore, situational factors have been found to be important in job design in a broader sense. Katzell, Barrett and Parker [13] have found that there is a strong relationship between job satisfaction and productivity and certain community characteristics or situational variables. They have found that, other things being equal, warehouse employees working in small towns exhibit greater job satisfaction than those working in urban situations. Kendall [14] and Turner and Lawrence [15] have also shown that job satisfaction and attitudes to repetitive jobs differ in rural and urban situations. In 1968 Hulin and Blood [16] surveyed the results of the majority of the job enlargement exercises which have been conducted and published, and they too concluded that the relationship between job design and satisfaction is dependent upon a third variable which is associated with the situation. They concluded that:

'These studies (surveyed) do not support the hypothesis that job size or job level is positively correlated in general with job satisfaction.—Such hypotheses must be modified to take into account the location of the plant and the cultural backgrounds of the workers.'

The Job Enlargement Technique

It is clear that because of both individual worker characteristics and situational characteristics the efficient design of work and the design of jobs is a matter far more complex than has hitherto been widely believed. Despite this wealth of research evidence there is still widespread advocacy of general job enlargement, but the model which is a prerequisite to this philosophy is clearly an oversimplification of the true situation. The model shown in Fig. 7.13 more closely resembles fact, but even here certain simplifications have been made.

Clearly, as an antidote to job dissatisfaction, job enlargement is justified in certain cases for a proportion of workers. In other words, it appears to have merit as a technique rather than as a philosophy.

Job Design—the Present Situation

You will recall that in discussing work study we showed that the objective of method study was the determination of the most efficient work method, whilst the objective of work measurement was the determination of a standard time for such a method. Quite apart from the fact that work study tends to lead to specialization and work rationalization, these objectives have been criticized For example, how appropriate or reasonable is it to expect a worker to execute any task, large or small, in precisely the same way and in precisely the same time on each repetition? Is it not reasonable to expect the worker's pace to vary, and to expect him to vary his work method in order to achieve more variety in his work? In a later chapter we shall show that work pacing, i.e. imposing a rigid work cycle time, is often detrimental to output. Indeed it can be said that the whole concept of work study, in that it seeks to impose a rigidity of method and duration, is illconceived and inappropriate. Such an argument, however, again assumes the homogeneity of the workforce, as did the job enlargement philosophy. It is undoubtedly true that some workers would prefer to avoid work pacing, method imposition and highly rationalized work, but equally others will willingly tolerate and even prefer such circumstances.

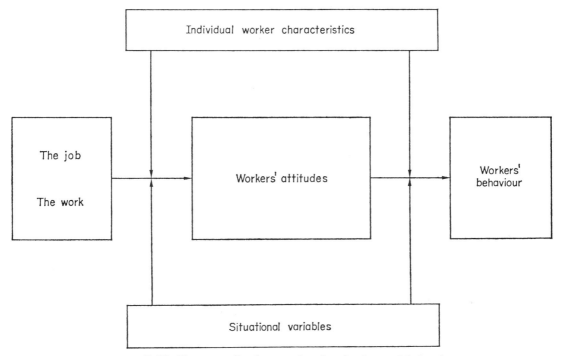

FIGURE 7.13. Factors affecting workers' attitudes and behaviour

There is no doubt that the activities of the industrial engineer or work study practitioner are of prime importance in determining job satisfaction, since despite the importance of aspects of the job such as social relations, supervision and environmental conditions, the nature of the work is the principal determinant of job satisfaction.[8]

The influence of the industrial engineer, the work study practitioner and hence the production manager on job satisfaction is very clear. However, one thing that is immediately apparent from our discussion is the futility of generalization. A frequent mistake of the past has been the belief that the relationship between the worker, his work and his job is a simple one, a belief which has ofted lead to the formulation of oversimplified and abstract theories of job design.

Job satisfaction can be regarded as a function of the extent to which job needs are fulfilled. Workers, however, exhibit different needs and with differing emphases. For some people the need for achievement is particularly important, and for them an interesting, challenging job is essential. For others the achievement need is less important than the financial or social needs.

Clearly, highly rationalized work is not universally detrimental, but equally in the present situation job enlargement could often be beneficial.

Ideally one would wish to design a job appropriate to the requirements of the individual, but

[8] There is a certain amount of disagreement about the precise manner in which the nature of the work affects job satisfaction. Many people believe that the presence or absence of interesting, challenging, varied work is capable of causing job satisfaction and job dissatisfaction respectively. Others believe that the nature of the work acts only as a satisfier, and that the absence of interesting, challenging, varied work does not result in job dissatisfaction. This latter view is by no means generally adopted and is basically the hypothesis presented by F. Herzberg, etc. in *The Motivation to Work*. [18].

even if this were possible it is unreasonable to expect that it would be practical. If we regard the objective of job design as being the design of jobs appropriate to the requirements of the individual so as to maximize job satisfaction and productivity, then we can alternatively consider the problem as being one of labour selection and placement. In the former case, jobs are designed appropriate to the requirements of an available labour force, whereas in the latter case labour is selected and placed into available jobs. Ostensibly, the former is the responsibility of the industrial engineer and the latter the responsibility of the personnel manager, but since neither job design nor labour selection and placement can be performed independent of knowledge of one another, this complete division of responsibilities is perhaps no longer appropriate.

In the short term, neither job design nor labour selection and placement can be fully effective because sufficient knowledge is not yet available. Further research must be conducted to determine the relationships between job design, situational variables and individual characteristics and their influence upon job satisfaction and behaviour, before adequate procedures and principles can be evolved. In the short term, therefore, the responsibility of the industrial engineer must extend to an awareness of this problem, since without sympathy from management and the professions involved the present situation cannot be improved. In practical terms the responsibility of the industrial engineer must at present be to ensure that a variety of jobs is available within any firm, so that job dissatisfaction, once identified, can be remedied by means of internal transfers of workers to jobs more appropriate to their requirements.

SUMMARY

The first part of this chapter dealt with that part of the field of ergonomics or human engineering which is of relevance to the Production Manager. Three important aspects of the man/machine system were distinguished and discussed namely:

1. Design of information displays
2. Design of controls
3. Environmental factors.

Anthropometric data, essential in the design of work places was also provided. In the second part of the chapter we have attempted briefly to place in perspective the problem of job design for manual workers. Through a survey of relevant research we have shown that a certain proportion of the labour force is predisposed to intolerance of repetitive, rationalized jobs of the type common in industry. We have shown that despite continuing controversy the nature of the work is for the majority of people one of the most important aspects of their jobs.

The problem of job design has been equated to the problem of labour selection and placement, since ideally the objective in both cases is to ensure that workers are given jobs which are not only compatible with their skills and abilities but also consistent with their needs and expectations.

In the present situation, the production manager's responsibility is to ensure that a variety of jobs is available within a company so that effective placement may be attempted, and so that internal transfer of workers and/or selective job enlargement may be effected as antidotes to job dissatisfaction.

SELECTED READINGS

A. CHAPANIS, *Man–Machine Engineering*, Tavistock, London, 1966.
K. F. H MURRELL, *Ergonomics: Man in his Working Environment*, Chapman and Hall, London, 1965.

W. E. WOODSON and D. W. CONOVER, *Human Engineering Guide for Equipment Designers*, University of California Press, Berkeley, 1965.

The following comprises 12 booklets, available from the Ministry of Technology, Warren Spring Laboratory, Stevenage, Herts., which are a splendid treatment of the subject in an applied and practical manner.

MINISTRY OF TECHNOLOGY, *Ergonomics in Industry Services*.

T. BEDFORD, 'Researches on Thermal Comfort', *Ergonomics*, **4**, 289–310 (1961).

The following are specialist books which provide more detailed information with reference to the section on Anthropometric data in this chapter:

F. KELLERMAN, P. VAN WELY and P. WILLEMS, *Vade Mecum Ergonomics in Industry*, Macmillan, London, 1963.

E. J. McCORMICK, *Human Factors Engineering*, McGraw-Hill, New York, 2nd ed., 1964.

C. T. MORGAN, J. S. COOK, A. CHAPANIS and M. W. LUND, *Human Engineering Guide to Equipment Design*, McGraw-Hill, New York, 1963.

R. M. BARNES, *Motion and Time Study*, Wiley, New York, 1963.

No textbook deals adequately with the subject of Job Design. Readers are, therefore, referred to the papers and books cited below for expansion of the individual topics involved.

1. D. McGREGOR, *The Human Side of Enterprise*, McGraw-Hill, London, 1960.
2. L. E. DAVIS, R. R. CANTER and J. HOFFMAN, 'Current job design criteria', *J. Ind. Eng.*, March/April, 5 (1955).
3. G. FRIEDMANN, *The Anatomy of Work*, Heinemann, London, 1961.
4. R. LIKERT, *New Patterns of Management*, McGraw-Hill, London, 1961.
5. E. H. CONANT and M. D. KILBRIDGE, 'An interdisciplinary analysis of job enlargement: technology, costs and behavioural implications,' *Indust. and Labour Relat. Rev.*, **18**, No. 3, 377–395 (1965).
6. F. HERZBERG *et al.*, *Job Attitudes: Review of Research and Opinion*, Psychol. Service of Pittsburg, 1957.
7. A. H. BRAYFIELD and W. H. CROCKETT, 'Employee attitudes and employee performance', *Psychol. Bull.*, 396–424 (1955)
8. F. HERZBERG *et al.*, *Motivation to Work*, Wiley, London, 1959.
9. R. WILD, 'Job needs, job satisfaction, and job behaviour of women manual workers', *J. Appl. Psychol.*, **54**, No. 2, 157–162 (1970).
10. J. WALKER and R. MARRIOT, 'A study of some attitudes to work', *Occup. Psychol.*, **25**, 181–191 (1951).
11. L. A. THOMPSON, 'Measuring susceptibility to monotonous work', *Personnel J.*, **8**, No. 3, 172–192 (1929).
12. P. C. SMITH, 'The prediction of individual differences in susceptibility to industrial monotony', *J. appl. Psychol.*, **39**, No. 5, 322–329 (1955).
13. R. A. KATZELL R. S. BARRETT and T. C. PARKER, 'Job satisfaction, job performance and situational characteristics', *J. Appl. Psychol.*, **45**, No. 2, 65–72 (1961).
14. L. M. KENDALL, *Ph.D. Diss.*, 'Canonical analysis of job satisfaction and behavioural, personal background and situational data', Cornell University, 1963 (unpublished).
15. A. N. TURNER and P. R. LAWRENCE, *Industrial Jobs and the Worker*, Harvard University Press, Cambridge, Mass., 1965.
16. C. L. HULIN and M. R. BLOOD, 'Job enlargement: individual differences and worker responses, *Psychol. Bull.*, **69**, No. 1, 41–55 (1968).

8

The Planning of Production

Despite the obvious difference in meaning of the two words planning and control, a good deal of confusion has arisen about their use in production. In this book it is our intention to treat production planning and production control separately. We will regard production planning as dealing entirely with *pre-production* activities, i.e. the determination of which products to make, the equipment required and the construction of a schedule by which products will be made in the correct quantities and in the times available. Production control we consider to be essentially a *during-production* activity, quite simply involving the implementation of the production planning decisions, i.e. an activity to ensure that products are manufactured according to the previously determined production plan. Our definition of the two functions is, therefore, as follows:

Production planning is concerned with the determination, acquisition and arrangement of all facilities necessary for the future production of certain products.

Production control is concerned with the implementation of a predetermined production plan or policy and the control of all aspects of production according to such a plan or policy.

There are good reasons for treating these two subjects in this way, as will become evident later, but for the time being let us consider how this treatment differs from that presented elsewhere.

In many text-books on production and production management, the term production control is used to cover both the planning and the control functions. Chapters on production control often deal with topics such as sales forecasting, the planning of aggregate production, production scheduling, sequencing and the progressing of production, whereas in our presentation only the last two mentioned relate to production control, since the other topics are essentially pre-production activities. In many companies, planning and control of production are the responsibilities of the same department, which might be called production control or, less frequently, production planning.

Such a situation is neither infrequent nor unreasonable since although two identifiable aspects exist, they do not exist independently nor in isolation. Production planning and production control are very closely linked and entirely interdependent. Decisions during planning will determine the problems and often the nature of control, and experiences during control will doubtless influence future planning. To illustrate this relationship consider a simple example. A small company is engaged in the production of special purpose diesel engines. A fairly large range of basic models is produced; manufacture is in response to customers' orders rather than for stock, and customers normally require their engines to have special features, equipment, etc. On receipt of an order from a customer, the marketing (or sales) department will provide details of the required engine to the production planning department, whose job it will be to do the following:

1. Determine what are the parts required for the engine.
2. Compare this requirement to the present available stock levels.
3. Determine which parts must be manufactured or purchased.
4. Using the required delivery date for the engine, the operations planning documents (i.e. the order and duration of all manufacturing operation) and knowing the present load on all resources, construct a schedule for the manufacture and purchase of all items.

It is mainly the last step (4) which influences production control. Production controllers must attempt to ensure that manufacture proceeds according to plan. The accuracy with which such schedules or plans have been constructed clearly determines the difficulty of production control. For example, in situations such as this it is not sufficient to construct manufacturing schedules based solely on operation times, since queues of parts invariably exist, and allowances for queuing/idle/non-processing time must always be made in the construction of the production schedule. Information about such allowances will be obtained from production control.

In cases such as this one the production planning function will be of a routine nature, whereas the production control function, because of the nature of production, will be complex. It is not unreasonable, therefore, that the title production control, since this represents the more important problem, should be used to describe both functions. For other industries the reverse applies. For example, in mass production planning is more complex and important than control which, because of special purpose equipment—assembly lines, etc., is a routine procedure.

These differing characteristics and demands of the various types of manufacture are one of the fascinations of production management, as well as being one of its main challenges. It might be worthwhile to examine the situation a little more closely at this stage, since the differing characteristics are really fundamental to this and several of the following chapters. Joan Woodward has examined the organizational characteristics of about 100 companies in the south-east Essex area, and her findings, presented in her book[1] are of interest to us. She examined the influence of technology on organization in unit (jobbing) or small batch production, large batch or mass production, and process production. We can summarize some of the findings as follows:

1. The number of levels of management is greater in continuous manufacture.
2. The span of control of the chief executive is greater in continuous manufacture.
3. The relative size of the management and supervisory group is greater in continuous manufacture.
4. The span of control of first level supervision is small in both unit and process manufacture.
5. Unit and process manufacturing companies employ more skilled workers than batch manufacturing companies.
6. Production control procedures are more elaborate in large batch or mass production.

From these few points it is fairly clear that although the large investment in equipment in continuous manufacture results in the employment of comparatively few direct production workers it also necessitates a large managerial structure, the main purpose of which is to protect this investment by ensuring adequate and efficient loading. Many of the direct workers in such industries are also employed to protect equipment; they are, for example, concerned with maintenance, replacement, etc. At both ends of the production continuum relatively small work groups exist, hence the span of control of first line supervision is small. The reason for this is quite simple for,

[1] J. Woodward, *Industrial Organization: Theory and Practice*, Oxford Univ. Press, London, 1965.

unlike large batch or mass production, in process production few direct workers are associated with the same part of the process, and in unit production there are few direct workers of a common type because of the large and diverse nature of production facilities. Both unit and process industries employ a greater proportion of skilled workers because, in the case of the former, in order to retain production flexibility and because of the discrete nature of demand, production jobs have not been de-skilled to any significant extent, and in the case of the latter, different yet equally important skills are necessary to ensure the efficient performance of elaborate and expensive equipment. Production control in unit and in process production is less elaborate than in batch or mass production, but the reasons for this simplicity of procedure at both ends of the scale are quite different. In unit production, production control is such a complex function that (apparently) few of the firms investigated wholeheartedly attempted the task, whereas in process production, control is essentially easy and often automatic, hence there was little need for elaborate procedures. The results of this research also indicated that the quality as well as the quantity of management was greater in continuous manufacture—relatively few specialists being employed in the production departments of unit or small batch production companies. Again we can see that the inherent complexity of small-scale production seemingly discourages the application of specialist knowledge and, unlike process production, control depends primarily upon the use of acquired know-how and clinical judgements. The obvious importance of the planning function in continuous manufacture and the risk involved normally results in the employment of a comparatively large number of specialists, but the less evident but equally important problem of control in intermittent manufacture has not, as yet, attracted the same attention.

The remainder of this chapter will be devoted to the common components or rudiments of production planning, whilst in the following three chapters we will deal with planning in different types of production. In Chapter 13 we will deal with production control.

FORECASTING

Clearly the essential prerequisite for any production planning is a statement of demand; whether this is a known, expressed demand, i.e. a reflection of the orders already received from customers, or an estimated, forecasted or expected demand. Here the production function overlaps that of marketing or sales. The extent of the contact between the two functions is not merely the transmission of demand information from the latter to the former, but also communication in the other direction. Frequently a customer's decision to place an order with a manufacturer will depend, partly at least, on the delivery time of that order, which in turn depends on manufacturing capacity and present commitments. The production planning department, therefore, will often be involved with the marketing department in the quotation of delivery dates and schedules. Such collaboration is more likely and more important in small-scale, intermittent manufacture than in large-scale, continuous manufacture. In the latter case the production system will have been designed to manufacture products at a given date in response to an initial demand estimation and, except perhaps for manufacturing models in different proportions, little can be done without major redesign of the facility. The rigidity of this type of production necessitates particularly accurate demand forecasting.

Forecasting of demand is rarely undertaken within the production planning department, hence we are not justified in examining the subject in detail; nevertheless, we must spend a little time on the topic.

Forecasting, for a long time often a rather subjective procedure of questionable accuracy, is a subject which is currently receiving a great deal of attention from mathematicians, statisticians, econometricians and marketing and operational research personnel. It is easy to see why such a great deal of effort is lavished on the subject since accurate forecasting can be, quite simply, the making or breaking of a firm. Many of those involved in forecasting, particularly those at lower levels who are called upon only to supply figures or estimates, tend to adopt a derogatory approach to the subject, as they see their figures apparently manipulated and changed. There are, of course, occasions when such derision is entirely justified; many forecasting procedures are ludicrous in their naivety, many blatantly optimistic in the accuracy claimed for their enlightened guesswork, but this does not detract from the importance of the exercise, and certainly emphasizes the importance of selecting and adopting suitably accurate and appropriate forecasting techniques Some of the more important techniques are described briefly in Appendix II and here we shall confine ourselves to a brief discussion of the problem and a classification of the techniques available.

A company may be involved in the production of two types of product: firstly standard products in large quantities to satisfy a large reasonably stable demand, and secondly the production of fewer products to satisfy specific customer orders. Although sales forecasting is essential in the first case, it is not entirely unimportant in the second case since those products may well make a significant contribution to total profits. The company may set aside facilities for this type of production, in which case they will need to be sure of continuing stable or increasing trade, hence the need for some form of demand forecast. Nevertheless, it is mainly the first type of product with which we shall be concerned.

One further point should be mentioned, namely that forecasting may be undertaken for every single type of product manufactured by the company or, if more appropriate, for groups of products. It is inconceivable to think of companies, those for example in the motor industry, accurately forecasting future demand for every single type of vehicle made; rather it is likely that forecasting will concern groups of existing models, e.g. saloon cars up to 850 cc, 850–1 100 cc and 1 300–1 600 cc, and commercial vehicles of different capacities and types.

Perhaps the most obvious, and incidentally, one of the most frequently used forecasting techniques is the assumption of *persistence*. The technique involves the assumption that what is happening will continue to happen. This is not so unreasonable as it might at first seem and such forecasts are, in certain situations, notably accurate. Many retailers depend upon this forecasting technique, but often secondary factors are allowed to influence the forecast. For example, the effect of local weather conditions, redundancies in local factories and local and national holidays may be assessed by the retailer and used as a factor for modifying the sales of the last period. When the influence of such factors is considered, a more sophisticated forecasting technique is intuitively being used. This we shall mention shortly.

All forecasting depends to some extent upon personal opinion. However, some forecasts might depend entirely upon this and we can, therefore, identify a technique which we shall call *collective opinion*. Consider this actual example. A company manufactures internal telephone systems which are either sold or rented to companies, offices, etc. Regional sales offices exist in about a dozen major areas of the UK and demand (outright sales and rental) forecasting is based upon the collective opinion of the managers of each of these regional offices. Their estimates of annual demand for existing and planned equipment are based on past performance, on the known activities and suspected plans of competitors, on industrial expansion in the area, on the number of enquiries received from existing and potential customers and on advertising and promotion policies. Their individual forecasts, which are rarely questioned by their head office (except where they indicate a fall in demand), are added together, the result with little modification then constituting the manufacturing quantity for the coming period. This is a simple procedure and one which is used with notable success by many organizations. It has the obvious advantage of placing the forecasting decision on those people who supposedly are in possession of most of the relevant information, and furthermore it requires no special mathematical expertise. One disadvantage is that because it depends so much upon individuals, any changes in staff might affect forecasts. The technique has also been criticized because of its unsuitability for long-term or very short-term forecasting. Accurate forecasts are obtained with decreasing probability for periods in excess of one year and for periods of less than about three months.

A very large area of forecasting and many forecasting techniques depend upon a formal analysis of past data for a prediction or forecast of future sales. The objective of such techniques

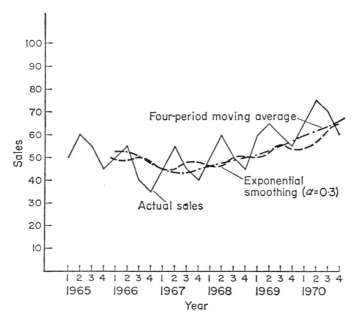

FIGURE 8.1. Sales trends plotted by four-period moving average and exponential smoothing

is to project past performances into the future, to assess past output, sales, demands, and to determine a trend which might then be used to forecast future sales or demand. Such procedures are applied with varying degrees of sophistication. One of the simplest methods of identifying trends in the use of *moving averages*. Figure 8.1 shows how a 4 period moving average has been used to indicate the trend in a series of sales figures. These figures also show the results obtained by an alternative method, *exponential smoothing*, which unlike the previous method places more weight upon recent data:

Forecast for next period $= \alpha$ [sales in last period] $+ (1-\alpha)$ [forecast for last period]

where α is the *smoothing* constant.

The more recently developed *cumulative sum technique* has also found widespread application in short-term forecasting, and is particularly valuable for examining data with the object of detecting significant changes in mean or average values.

The final forecasting technique involves the use of *economic indicators* or *associative predictions*. Many companies have found that there is a close relationship between the sale of their products and certain of the indices of economic conditions produced by the government or by trade associations. Where such relationships exist a change in the index or indices might usefully be regarded as an indication of a likely change in demand. The objective, therefore, is to find one or more indices whose fluctuations are *afterwards* reflected in changes in product demand (without this time lag, the association is useless). For example, the sales of cars might be regarded as a useful prediction for the subsequent sale of accessories; the building of houses as a prediction or index for the sale of furnishings. To develop forecasting techniques based on associative predictions can be a rather lengthy business which usually involves an extensive examination of the statistical relationship of past sales data and various likely indices. The closeness of the statistical association of variables can be measured by calculation of a *correlation coefficient*. Once indices bearing a close correlation with historical data have been found, this relationship can be used for forecasting. The relationship is expressed mathematically by means of a *regression equation*.

Each of these techniques and terms will be discussed more fully in Appendix II.

MAKE OR BUY DECISION

Whilst discussing the prerequisites for production planning we must certainly mention what is perhaps the most fundamental decision of all, i.e. whether to make the item ourselves or whether to buy it. Theoretically, every item which is currently purchased from an outside supplier is always a candidate for internal manufacture. Conversely, every item currently manufactured by ourselves is a potential candidate for purchase. Of course, in reality the problem is not quite so extensive as this, since there will always be a good many items which it would just not be in our interest to make, such as raw materials, specialist parts and indirect items like stationery, ink, etc. Similarly there will always be many items which it would not be in our interest to purchase.

The obvious question to ask is, 'How can we determine whether it is or is not in our interest to buy or to make an item?'; and the obvious but not very helpful answer is, 'by determining which alternative involves least cost'. Inevitably this must be an economic decision, but the problem is how to determine what contributes to total cost.

Let us briefly consider some of the cost benefits which might accrue from our deciding to make an item ourselves rather than purchase it. By making an item we reduce our dependence on other companies and avoid the consequences of their labour disputes; we are able to determine our own quality levels and we preserve our trade secrets. Conversely, to purchase items rather than make them ourselves may enable us to obtain them more quickly, to obtain the benefits from a continual development programme which we ourselves could not sustain. Additionally, purchase instead of self manufacture may reduce costs such as those associated with storage, handling, paperwork, etc., as well as releasing our facilities for jobs on which they might be more suitably and profitably employed. Consequently, we can see that the apparently simple motto, 'if it's cheaper to make than buy—make', and vice versa is a little difficult to put into practice. We can usefully consider the make or buy decision as falling into two categories: firstly, as above, decisions regarding items already being manufactured or purchased, and secondly, decisions regarding new items. As regards current items, neglecting those factors which cannot readily be costed, we must ask ourselves the following questions:

If we choose to manufacture items which are currently purchased, what *additional* costs will necessarily be incurred, and how do these compare to the costs which will be saved?

If we choose to purchase items rather than make them, what costs will necessarily be *avoided* and how do these compare with the costs which will be incurred?

An analysis such as this is frequently referred to as *incremental cost* analysis. At the outset it is important to distinguish between fixed and variable costs. For example, the decision to cease purchasing an item does not necessarily result in a saving of a portion of purchasing department overheads since many of the factors which contribute to overheads are, in the short term, fixed, e.g. purchasing department salaries. Similarly, the decision to cease manufacturing an item does not necessarily result in the saving of such costs as manufacturing overheads or even direct labour unless the released capacity can be immediately devoted to other jobs. It is normally easy to account for the direct cost associated with both manufacture and purchase but more difficult to account for, or even to identify, indirect cost. It should not be forgotten, however, that the cost of purchasing an item is not represented merely by the purchase price, but is also dependent upon the cost of implementing the purchase, such items as inspection, receiving, etc., often contributing significantly to total cost.

As regards projected or new items, the make or buy decision is often simpler but rarely simple. The prospect of making an item on presently underutilized equipment is a far more attractive situation than if the present facilities are fully utilized and capital investment in equipment or recruitment of labour would be necessary. Nevertheless, even in the latter case it may be desirable to make items oneself if the quantity required is likely to increase considerably, or if the present manufacture of another item is due to cease, thus liberating capacity.

It is precisely because of complications such as these that we are unable to offer a definitive formulation of this problem or to define a general procedure for the solution. When concerned with those borderline cases which inevitably arise, nothing short of a comprehensive costing exercise will reveal data sufficient to make a truly objective decision but, except in a few cases, such an extensive and costly exercise is unwarranted. Few companies will continually assess presently manufactured and presently purchased items, and rarely will changes in make/buy strategy be made unless a very clear economic benefit can be shown. A value analysis team may occasionally suggest that it would be beneficial to purchase rather than continue to make an item, particularly when recent developments in technology or product developments result in the item offered by suppliers being either greatly improved or substantially cheaper. It may be beneficial also to sub-contract or purchase items rather than acquire additional facilities when an additional product must be made, but apart from such clear-cut cases decisions will inevitably be contentious. Because of the inability or impracticability of considering all possible incremental costs, many companies make a policy of not reversing previous make/buy decisions unless a direct cost difference of at least 10 per cent can be shown.

OPERATIONS PLANNING

Having decided on a make rather than a buy policy the first step of production planning is to decide how the product or item is to be made—a function commonly known as operations planning. Here again we must preface our brief discussion by saying that this problem and the procedures for its solution overlap production planning and other departments. For example, all of the following will be involved, to a greater or lesser extent, in operations planning:

product design
production engineering
jig and tool department
work study
production planning

Three decisions are involved in Operations Planning:

1. Determine which operations are necessary.
2. Determine at which machine centres such operations will be performed.
3. Determine the order of these operations.

The result of these decisions will be presented on a master operations or routing sheet such as the one shown in Fig. 8.2. This document will be used in the preparation of job tickets, material requisition cards, etc., all of which will be required during manufacture (Fig. 8.3). Such cards are often prepared by spirit duplication methods, and each contains the common or fixed information from the top of the operations sheet, plus one line from the body of the sheet.

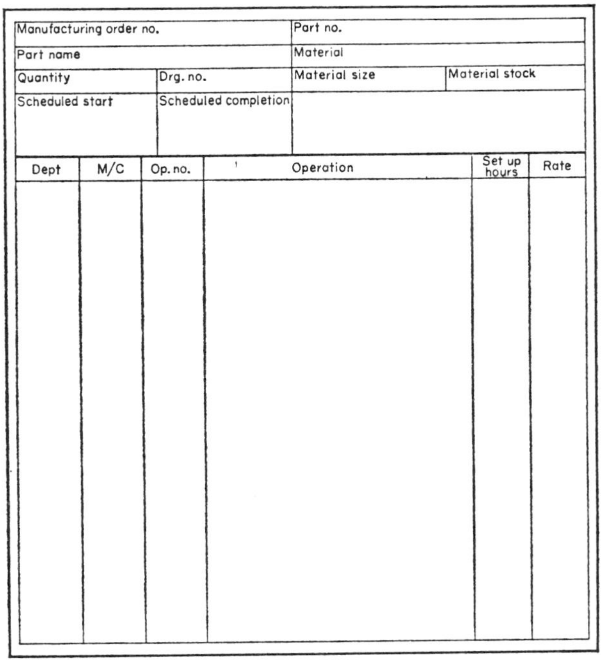

Manufacturing order no.			Part no.		
Part name			Material		
Quantity		Drg. no.	Material size	Material stock	
Scheduled start		Scheduled completion			

Dept	M/C	Op. no.	'	Operation	Set up hours	Rate

FIGURE 8.2. Operations sheet

Production Planning in Mass or Large-scale Production

In continuous production the above sequence of decisions will culminate in the design of a fairly rigid production system such as an assembly line. Once such facilities have been provided, few production planning problems will arise. It will not be necessary to plan the production of each item since the schedule for each item manufactured on the facility will be the same. A principal characteristic of this type of production is that the order or customer lead time (i.e. the length of time between the receipt of the customer order and the delivery of the product to the customer) is less than the production lead time (i.e. the length of time between receipt of the order and delivery of a product to finished stock). In other words, customer orders are satisfied directly from finished stock which is continually replenished according to a production plan based on forecasted demand. This type of situation is shown diagrammatically in Fig. 8.4(a).

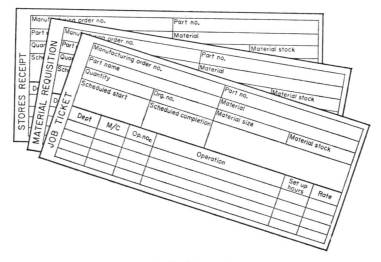

FIGURE 8.3. Job tickets, etc.

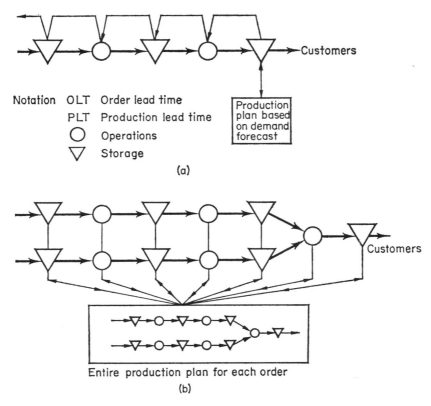

FIGURE 8.4. (a) Production planning when OLT<PLT
(b) Production planning when OLT⩾PLT

The main problems, therefore, are to ensure that sufficient demand exists, to ensure that operations planning is accurate and that during the design of, say, the assembly line an efficient method of production is evolved. Assembly line design will be dealt with in detail in Chapter 11.

Production Planning in Jobbing, Small Batch or Intermittent Production

In this type of production operations planning does not represent this termination of the planning stage since it is still necessary to construct a production schedule for each item or product, or for each batch of items and products, to be made. A principal characteristic of this type of production is that the order or customer lead time is greater than or equal to the production lead time. Consequently, products can often be made to order rather than for stock, and hence planning is concerned with the entire schedule for each individual item or order. This type of situation is shown diagrammatically in Fig. 8.4(b).

It is in this type of production that two-way communications between production planning and marketing are essential, and for the remainder of this chapter we shall be concerned with the purpose of this relationship and with the construction of production schedules.[2]

The relationship between the customer, the marketing/sales department and production planning is shown in the flow diagram in Fig. 8.5.

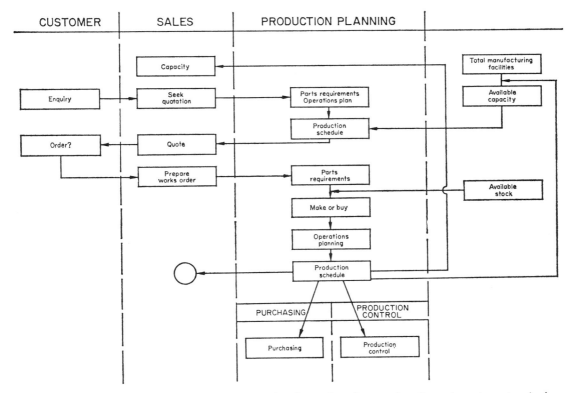

FIGURE 8.5. The relationship between production planning and other departments during pre-production

---

[2] Chapter 10 also deals with production planning in this type of manufacture, but is concerned with one specific technique—network analysis.

PRODUCTION SCHEDULING

Scheduling has been defined as the time coordination of production in advance of performance, or the fitting of new orders into the spaces available in the manufacturing programme. To undertake production scheduling, whether for individual jobs or for batches, we must have the following:

1. Operations planning details
2. Knowledge of the available capacity of equipment
3. Knowledge of the relative priorities of existing jobs
4. Knowledge of available labour, materials, etc.
5. A required delivery or completion date for the job

Almost all production scheduling in intermittent manufacture involves the successive subtraction of operation times from the required completion date. This is known as *due date* or *reverse scheduling*. Unfortunately, production scheduling, if it is to be accurate and worthwhile, is not quite so simple as this description might indicate, for the simple reason that it is not sufficient merely to deal with operation times since this assumes that the total manufacturing time for a product or item is simply the sum of its operation times. Whilst this is almost the case in mass production, it is definitely not so in jobbing or small batch production where a large proportion of total manufacturing time consists of waiting, idle or queueing time.

If we were able to predict accurately all operation times for all jobs; if we could be certain that no machine failures or labour absences would occur; if we could be sure that there would be no mistakes during operations; and if we knew the exact time required to transport items between all machines, then theoretically a schedule could be constructed in which idle time or queueing time was zero. But, of course, we know none of these things, and consequently in this type of production a great deal of work in progress exists, and the throughput or total manufacturing time for jobs is greatly in excess of the sum of individual operation times.

In many respects this is an unfortunate situation, since it means that a great deal of capital is tied up in partially completed jobs, and a great deal of deliberate and incidental storage space is required. But in one important respect it is beneficial. Given the nature of this type of production (i.e. unpredictable operation times, etc.), it is necessary to have a queue of jobs before each machine in order to ensure adequate utilization. We can, in fact, use *queueing theory* to investigate the relationship of queue length to machine utilization. Figure 8.6 shows this relationship.[3] It is quite clear that if the arrival of jobs into the queue can be considered to be random, then a queue of at least two jobs is necessary to ensure adequate machine utilization, and queues longer than this do not substantially increase machine utilization.

The problem with due date scheduling (Fig. 8.7), is to decide what allowances shall be made for idle or waiting time. Operation times are known sufficiently accurately but queueing allow-

---

[3] Using simple, single station queueing theory:

$$\text{Average queue length} \quad Q = \frac{\rho^2}{2(1-\rho)} \qquad \left(\begin{array}{l}\text{random arrival of jobs and} \\ \text{constant service time}\end{array}\right)$$

$$\text{,,} \qquad Q = \frac{\rho^2}{(1-\rho)} \qquad \left(\begin{array}{l}\text{random arrival of jobs and} \\ \text{exponential service time}\end{array}\right)$$

where $\rho = \dfrac{\lambda}{\mu}$

     λ = mean arrival rate (expected number of arrivals per unit time)
     μ = mean service rate (expected number of units completing service/unit time)

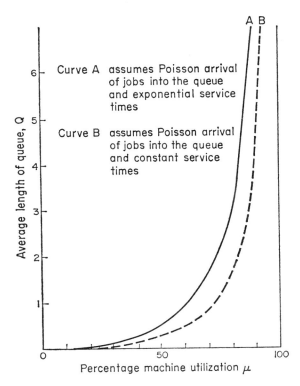

FIGURE 8.6. Theoretical relationship of queue length and utilization of machine (single machine, unlimited queue length)

Operation Planning

Operation no.	Description	Set up time	Processing time	Machine
1	– – – – – – –	2	15	– – – –
2	– – – – – – –	3	6	– – – –
3	– – – – – –	0	10	– – – –
4	– – – – –	0	10	– – –
5	– – – – –	1	8	– – –
6	– – – – – –	3	4	– –
Completion	date: Day	5		

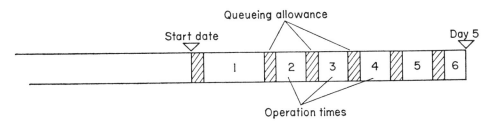

FIGURE 8.7. Due date or reverse scheduling

ances are not initially known. The only realistic way in which queueing allowances can be obtained is by experience. Experienced production planners will schedule operations, making allowances which they know from past performances to be correct. Such allowances may vary from 50 per cent to 2 000 per cent of operation times and can be obtained empirically or by analysis of the progress of previous jobs. It is normally sufficient to obtain and use allowances for groups of similar machines or for particular production departments, since delays are dependent not so

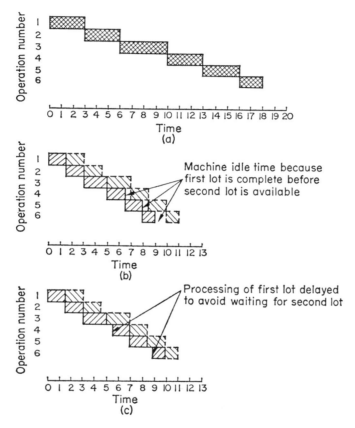

FIGURE 8.8. Gantt charts showing use of 'dovetail' scheduling (a) Schedule for the manufacture of a lot of 200 items through six operations ($T=18$) (b) Schedule for the manufacture of 200 items in two lots of 100 ($T=11$) (c) Alternative schedule for the manufacture of 200 items in two lots ($T=11$)

much on the nature of details of the job, but on the amount of work passing through the departments and the nature of the facilities. Production schedules of this type are usually depicted upon Gantt or bar charts. The advantage of this type of presentation is that the load on any machine or on any department is clear at a glance, and available or spare capacity is easily identified. The major disadvantage is that the dependencies between operations are not shown and, consequently, any readjustment of such schedules necessitates reference back to operation planning documents. Notice that, in scheduling the manufacture of items, total manufacturing or throughput time can be minimized by the batching of similar or identical items to save set-up time, inspection time, etc. In scheduling for batch manufacture, throughput time can be minimized by allowing subsequent operations to start before the entire batch has completed previous operations. A method of dovetail scheduling may be used, as shown in Fig. 8.8.

COMPUTERS AND DATA PROCESSING IN PRODUCTION PLANNING

Looking back over this chapter, we have identified several steps in production planning which can now be summarized as follows:

1. As a result of direct orders or forecasted demand, decide which and how many parts or items will be required.
2. Determine whether parts are available from stock.
3. Determine whether remainder of parts will be purchased or made.
4. For those items which are to be made and are not available from present stock, decide which manufacturing operations are to be performed, on which machines and in which order.
5. Knowing the required completion or delivery date for the product, the operation times, allowances and available capacity (a) schedule production and (b) date purchase orders.
6. Issue master production schedule or plan to departments concerned, i.e.

   Stock control
   Sales
   Production control
   Purchasing

Many production planning procedures exist without the assistance of computers. Nevertheless, even in such cases it is desirable to try to 'routinize' the procedures as far as possible in order to speed up the process yet minimize the possibility of mistakes. Use is frequently made of data processing equipment, and particularly of punched card equipment. Figures 8.9 and 8.10 show flow diagrams for a data processing system using punched cards which determines parts requirements and machine load.

Rarely will either computer or data processing-type production planning procedures exist in isolation. Because this function is so closely linked with production and stock control, procedures are usually designed to cover the whole production and stock planning and control area. We will discuss two such systems in Chapter 13.

AGGREGATE PLANNING—PRODUCTION SMOOTHING AND WORK FORCE BALANCING

In this section we will look briefly at one important medium-term planning problem, the objective of which is to ensure smooth production and to avoid unnecessary fluctuations in the size of the workforce. Basically there are three levels of production planning—the long-term (approximately one to five years, or more) which often depends upon 'technological forecasting' and influences corporate policy; the medium-term (approximately one month to one year); and the short-term dealing with immediate operating plans. Aggregate planning is medium-term production planning, concerned with the setting of production rates and workforce levels and, hence, the determination of the finished inventory levels and overtime or sub-contracting requirements necessary to satisfy a given demand.

For the sake of simplicity let us assume that only one type of production facility is concerned

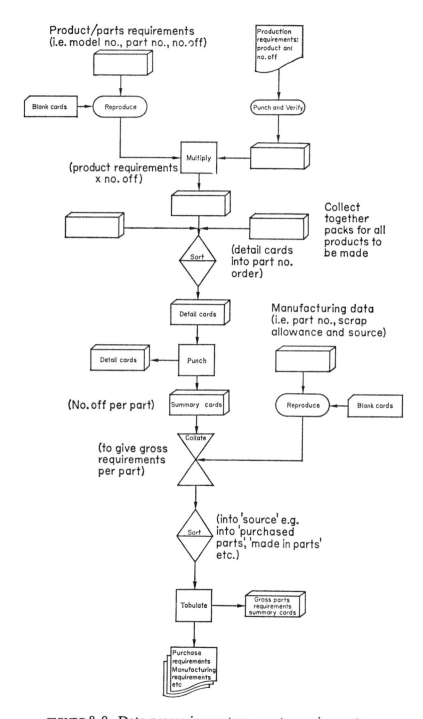

FIGURE 8.9. Data processing system—parts requirements

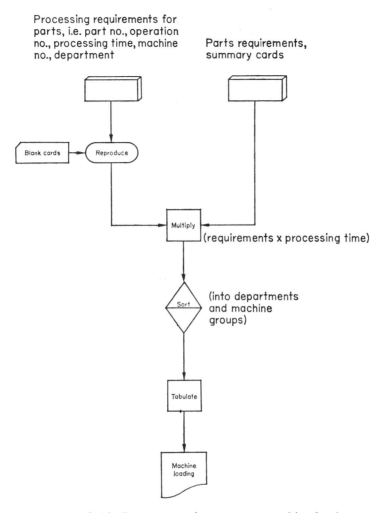

FIGURE 8.10. Data processing system—machine load

(although this is not an essential prerequisite of the method we shall discuss); that the available production capacities are known; and that either an expressed or forecasted demand is also known. If demand is perfectly constant, the same output being required each period, a uniform production rate can be adopted. However, demand frequently fluctuates and this fluctuation can be accommodated only by associated fluctuations in inventory, in production rates, or in both. More specifically, in such a situation one or more of the following solutions might be adopted:

1. Vary the production rate by working overtime where necessary, and accepting idle time where necessary.
2. Vary the size of the labour force by taking on additional labour and/or laying off labour where necessary.
3. Adopt a constant production rate and allow demand fluctuations to be met by changes in stock levels.

Solution of this problem depends first upon our being able to identify, and then to quantify, the various costs involved. The following costs are clearly important:

Production costs: the cost of production of a particular item at a given rate.

Stock-holding costs:

(a) cost of capital tied up in stock
(b) administrative costs of maintaining stocks

Cost of changing production rates.

Shortage costs: associated with an inability to provide customers with goods:

(a) loss of future orders and goodwill
(b) cost of expediting orders

The problem then is to determine the production rates and workforce level that will best (i.e. most economically) satisfy a fluctuating demand pattern. Numerous analytical methods of attempting to solve this aggregate planning problem are available, but in practice in industry, non-optimizing qualitative methods are frequently used. Often aggregate planning decisions are reached by a haggling process in which each department or manager seeks to enforce a decision that benefits their own operations; for example, the sales department will seek large inventories and the accounts department small inventories, and so on. Often, in practice, aggregate planning consists merely of the routine modification of previous medium-term production plans, despite the fact that such a strategy can quite easily result in a series of inferior planning decisions.

Several mathematical optimizing models have been developed for aggregate planning. For example the *linear decision rule* was developed in the late 1950's at the Carnegie Institute of Technology.[4] This model, which depends upon the assumption that all costs involved (regular payroll, hiring and lay-off, overtime and inventory costs) can be approximated by quadratic functions, has achieved considerable prominence in the literature on the subject. It has certainly been used in industry, but even so it, in common with many of the other models, has certainly not been extensively adopted.

Various linear programming methods of aggregate planning have been developed; for example, the *simplex* method has been proposed by at least three writers,[5] and in 1956 the problem was forwarded as a *transportation* problem by Bowman.[6] This latter formulation of the problem is described below.

For the sake of easy illustration let us consider a situation in which planning is necessary for only four sales and production periods ($n = 4$).[7]* The sales demand during each of these periods is represented by S, i.e. S_1, S_2, S_3 and S_4 and this demand may be met from one of the following:

Stock
'Regular' production during the normal shifts
Overtime production

The costs associated with each of these are:

---

[4] C. C. Holt, F. Modigliani, J. F. Mutch and H. A. Simon, 'A linear decision rule for production and employment scheduling', *Management Sci.*, **2**, No. 2, 8, October (1955); *Production Planning Inventories and Work Force*, Prentice-Hall, London, 1960.

[5] F. Hanssmann and S. W. Hess, 'A linear programming approach to production and employment scheduling,' *Management Technol.*, No. 1, (1960).

R. E. McGarrah, *Production and Logistics Management*, Wiley, London, 1963.

[6] E. H. Bowman, 'Production scheduling by the transportation method of linear programming', *Operat. Res.*, **4**, 100–103 (1956).

[7] The following description (between asterisks) should be read after Appendix II and may be omitted at first reading.

Storage—C_I—cost of storage per unit per period
Regular production—C_R—cost of production per unit per period
Overtime production—C_O—cost of production per unit per period

We might further assume that items produced during one period are not available to the customer until the following period; consequently some initial stock must be available to satisfy demand for sales period 1. We can now represent the unit costs as a transportation matrix as shown in Table 8.1.

TABLE 8.1. Matrix of costs associated with production, stock and demand during four periods

PRODUCTION PERIOD		SALES PERIOD				Final stock	Total capacity
		1	2	3	4		
0	Opening stock	0	C_I	$2C_I$	$3C_I$	$4C_I$	I_0
1	Regular production	—	C_R	C_R+C_I	C_R+2C_I	C_R+3C_I	R_1
	Overtime production	—	C_O	C_O+C_I	C_O+2C_I	C_O+3C_I	O_1
2	Regular production	—	—	C_R	C_R+C_I	C_R+2C_I	R_2
	Overtime production	—	—	C_O	C_O+C_I	C_O+2C_I	O_2
3	Regular production	—	—	—	C_R	C_R+C_I	R_3
	Overtime production	—	—	—	C_O	C_O+C_I	O_3
Total demand during period		S_1	S_2	S_3	S_4		

Notation: I_i = Stock level at end of i'th period
R_i = Max. No. of units that can be produced on regular time during i'th period
O_i = Max. No. of units that can be produced on overtime during i'th period

Notice that some certain cells contain 'dashes' since these represent impossible routes (the production from one period cannot be used to satisfy demand for an earlier period). In order to ensure that these cells do not feature as part of the solution, it is conventional to allocate extremely high cost values to them. To indicate how this table has been constructed, consider Period 2. Sales during this period may be satisfied from stock which has incurred cost associated with storage for one period, i.e. C_I, or from production which was undertaken during the previous period at cost C_R, for regular production and C_O for overtime production. The case shown in Table 8.1 deals only with one product; however, this method can easily be extended to cover production planning for two or more products merely by constructing two or more columns for each of the sales periods and for final stock.

Furthermore it is not necessary that the costs of production C_R and C_O or the costs of storage C_I should be the same for each period or each product.

Example

Two very similar products, A and B, are to be manufactured. The total demand for each for three future periods is:

Period 1	A = 100	B = 50
Period 2	A = 70	B = 105
Period 3	A = 50	B = 125

It is estimated that the stock of products at the beginning of period 1 will be:

$$A = 150$$
$$B = 75$$

The cost of stockholding per product per period, C_I, is £2. The costs of production are as follows:
for production during period 1:

Product A	$C_R = £1$ per product
	$C_O = £2$,,
Product B	$C_R = £1$,,
	$C_O = £2$,,

for production during period 2:

Product A	$C_R = £2$ per product
	$C_O = £3$,,
Product B	$C_R = £2$,,
	$C_O = £3$,,

The production capacity per period is as follows:

Period 1	regular production = 125 units (of either type)
	overtime production = 50 units (,, ,, ,,)
Period 2	regular production = 125 units (,, ,, ,,)
	overtime production = 50 units (,, ,, ,,)

What is the optimal production plan and what is the cost associated with satisfying the above demands?

The cost matrix is shown in Table 8.2. Using the transportation methods of linear programming

TABLE 8.2. Costs associated with a three-period production plan for two products

PRODUCTION PERIOD		SALES PERIOD						Final stock		Total capacity (both products)
		1		2		3				
		Product		Product		Product		Product		
		A	B	A	B	A	B	A	B	
0	Opening stock	0	0	2	2	4	4	6	6	225 (150+75)
1	Regular production			1	1	3	3	5	5	125
	Overtime production			2	2	4	4	6	6	50
2	Regular production					2	2	4	4	125
	Overtime production					3	3	5	5	50
Total demand during period		100	50	70	105	50	125	75		(575)

TABLE 8.3. Three-period production plan for two products

PRODUCTION PERIOD		SALES PERIOD						Final stock	Total capacity (both products)
		1		2		3			
		Product		Product		Product		Product	
		A_0	B_0	A_2	B_2	A_4	B_4	$(A+B)_6$	
0	Opening stock $_0$	100 $_0$	50 $_0$	70 $_2$	5 $_2$	$_4$	$_4$	$_6$	225
1	Regular production $_{-1}$			100 $_1$	$_1$	25 $_3$	$_3$	$_5$	125
	Overtime production $_0$			$_2$	$_2$	25 $_4$	25 $_4$	$_6$	50
2	Regular production $_{-2}$					100 $_2$	25 $_2$	25 $_4$	125
	Overtime production $_{-1}$					$_3$	$_3$	50 $_5$	50
	Total demand	100	50	70	105	50	125	75	

described in Appendix II, the solution shown in Table 8.3 can easily be obtained. The cost associated with this production plan is as follows:

$$100(0) + 50(0) + 70(2) + 5(2)$$
$$+ 100(1) + 25(3)$$
$$+ 25(4) + 25(4)$$
$$+ 100(2) + 25(4)$$
$$+ 50(5) \qquad\qquad = \text{£1 075.}$$

Notice that in this solution a proportion of both regular and overtime production during production period 2 is delivered to stock. This is necessary because production capacity during this period is in excess of demand. If, however, the total production capacity in any period need not be used then our solution would have involved the production of 100 of product A during regular production in period 2. This would result in a saving of 25(4)+50(5), i.e. £350 during this period, but of course no opening stock would be available for the next period.*

Most of the early work dealing with methods of solving aggregate planning problems concerned mathematical optimizing techniques, and most of the methods developed suffered from the need for excessive computation and/or the abstract nature of the problems treated. Recently the emphasis of research has changed and considerable effort is now being made to develop non-optimizing, yet satisfactory, methods of solving the same problem.

Bowman[8] developed the *management coefficients* method, which depends upon a statistical analysis of management's past decisions in order to determine the numerical value of certain coefficients which are then used in previously derived equations. Taubert[9] has developed a computer based *search* method for aggregate planning.

[8] E. H. Bowman, 'Consistency and optimality in management decision making', *Management Sci.*, **9**, 310–321 (1963).
[9] E. S. Buffa and W. H. Taubert, 'Evaluation of direct computer search methods for the aggregate planning problem,' *Ind. Management Rev.* Fall (1967).

Other heuristic methods include *parametric planning*, developed by Jones,[10] and the *descriptive model* developed by Gordon.[11]

JOB AND MACHINE ASSIGNMENT

Frequently, when attempting to decide how orders are to be scheduled on to available equipment, one is faced with various alternative solutions. For example, in a general machine shop many different machines may be capable of performing the operations required on one item. Production management must then decide which jobs are to be scheduled on to which machines in order to achieve some objective, such as minimum cost or minimum throughput time. We will look at two methods of tackling this problem; the first a rapid, inexpensive, yet not necessarily optimum method, and the second a mathematically rigorous, but time-consuming technique.

The Index Method

This simple, rapid, but approximate method of machine/job assignment is best described by means of an example.

A company must complete five orders during a particular period. Each order consists of several identical products and each can be made on one of several machines. Table 8.4 gives the operation time for each product on each of the available machines.

TABLE 8.4. Operation time per product on each machine

Order no. (i)	No. of products in order (Q_i)	Operation time per product on machine j (x hours)		
		A	B	C
1	30	5·0	4·0	2·5
2	25	1·5	2·5	4·0
3	45	2·0	4·0	4·5
4	15	3·0	2·5	3·5
5	10	4·0	3·5	2·0

The available capacity for these machines for the period in question is:

$$A = 100 \text{ h}$$
$$B = 80 \text{ h}$$
$$C = 150 \text{ h}$$

The index number for a machine is a measure of the cost disadvantage of using that machine for production, and is obtained by using this formula.

$$I_i = \frac{x_{ij} - x_{i \min}}{x_{i \min}}$$

[10] C. H. Jones, 'Parametric production planning', *Management Sci.*, **15**, 843–866 (1967).
[11] J. R. M. Gordon, 'A multi-model analysis of an aggregate scheduling decision', *Ph.D. Diss.*, Mass. Inst. Technol., 1966.

When 　　　I_j = index number for machine j
　　　　　　x_{ij} = operation time for product i on machine j
　　　　　$x_{i\ min}$ = minimum operation time for product i

For order 1:

$$I_A = \frac{5 \cdot 0 - 2 \cdot 5}{2 \cdot 5} = 1 \cdot 0$$

$$I_B = \frac{4 \cdot 0 - 2 \cdot 5}{2 \cdot 5} = 0 \cdot 6$$

$$I_C = \frac{2 \cdot 5 - 2 \cdot 5}{2 \cdot 5} = 0$$

Table 8.5 shows the index numbers for all machines and orders:

TABLE 8.5.

Order no.	No. of products in order	Machine A		Machine B		Machine C	
		Index no.	Production time for order	Index no.	Production time for order	Index no.	Production time for order
1	30	1·0	150	0·6	120	0	75
2	25	0	37·5	0·67	62·5	1·67	100
3	45	0	90	1·0	180	1·25	202·5
4	15	0·2	45	0	37·5	0·4	52·5
5	10	1·0	40	0·75	35	0	20
Capacity (% utilization)			100 (90)		80 (78)		150 (98)

Using Table 8.5, and remembering that the index number is a measure of the cost disadvantage of using that machine, we can now allocate orders to machines. The best machine for order 1 is C ($I_C = 0$); the production time for that order (75 h) is less than the available capacity. We can, therefore, schedule the production of this order on this machine. Machine A is the best machine for order 2, but also the best for order 3. Both cannot be accommodated because of limitations on available capacity, so we must consider the possibility of allocating one of the orders to another machine. The next best machine for order 2 is machine B ($I_B = 0·67$) and for order 3 the next best machine is also machine B ($I_B = 1$). Because the cost disadvantage on B is less for order 2, allocate order 2 to B and 3 to A as shown in the table. The best machine for order 4 is B but there is now insufficient capacity available on this machine. The alternatives now are to reallocate order 2 to another machine or to allocate order 4 elsewhere. In the circumstances it is better to allocate order 4 to machine C. Finally order 5 can be allocated to its best machine, namely machine C.

The disadvantages of this method are readily apparent. Firstly, with problems involving more orders and machines than the one used here, the allocation and reallocation of orders might be very tedious. Secondly, we have not considered the possibility of splitting an order. For example, rather than reallocate all of order 2 to machine 3, it might have been economically better to allocate 10 hours of work (6 products) to A (the remaining available capacity) and reallocate only the remaining 19 products to machine B. Assuming that it is possible to split batches in this way, the benefits of doing so depend upon the costs of setting up the machines. These costs, being fixed and not varying with order quantity, are not considered in the index method.

Linear Programming[12]

The problem of assigning jobs to available machines, discussed above, can also be solved by *linear programming*. The objective and the constraints can be formulated as a set of linear inequalities, which might then be solved using, say, the simplex method described in Appendix I. Let us assume, for the sake of simplicity, that the operating costs of the machines are not dependent upon the type of job assigned to them and that, unlike previously, individual orders may be assigned to more than one machine. Consider our previous 3-machine 5-order problem.

TABLE 8.6

Order No. (i)	Quantity in order (Q_i)	Output per hour per machine		
		A	B	C
1	30	0·20	0·25	0·40
2	25	0·67	0·40	0·25
3	45	0·50	0·25	0·22
4	15	0·33	0·40	0·29
5	10	0·25	0·29	0·50
Capacity available (h)		100	80	150
Operating cost (£/hr) C_j		1·0	0·75	0·85

We can represent the assignment of products to machines by the following notation:

$$Q_{i, j} \quad \text{where} \quad i = \text{order no.}$$
$$j = \text{machine}$$

i.e. $Q_{1, A}$ = Quantity of order 1 assigned to machine A
$Q_{1, B}$ =   „   „   „   „   „   B

Our objective is to obtain the least cost assignment of jobs to machines; we must, therefore, minimize the following objective function:

$$\text{Total cost} = C = 1 \cdot 0 \left(\frac{Q_{1, A}}{0 \cdot 20} + \frac{Q_{2, A}}{0 \cdot 67} + \frac{Q_{3, A}}{0 \cdot 50} + \frac{Q_{4, A}}{0 \cdot 33} + \frac{Q_{5, A}}{0 \cdot 25} \right)$$

$$+ 0 \cdot 75 \left(\frac{Q_{1, B}}{0 \cdot 25} + \frac{Q_{2, B}}{0 \cdot 40} + \frac{Q_{3, B}}{0 \cdot 25} + \frac{Q_{4, B}}{0 \cdot 40} + \frac{Q_{5, B}}{0 \cdot 29} \right)$$

$$+ 0 \cdot 85 \left(\frac{Q_{1, C}}{0 \cdot 40} + \frac{Q_{2, C}}{0 \cdot 25} + \frac{Q_{3, C}}{0 \cdot 22} + \frac{Q_{4, C}}{0 \cdot 29} + \frac{Q_{5, C}}{0 \cdot 50} \right)$$

[12] This section should be read after Appendix I and may be omitted at first reading.

Since the number of jobs allocated to machines must not exceed the quantity in the order, the following constraints must be observed:

$$Q_{1, A} + Q_{1, B} + Q_{1, C} = 30$$
$$Q_{2, A} + Q_{2, B} + Q_{2, C} = 25$$
$$Q_{3, A} + Q_{3, B} + Q_{3, C} = 45$$
$$Q_{4, A} + Q_{4, B} + Q_{4, C} = 15$$
$$Q_{5, A} + Q_{5, B} + Q_{5, C} = 10$$

Also:

$$Q_{i, j} \begin{pmatrix} i = 1, 2, 3, 4, 5 \\ j = A, B, C \end{pmatrix} \geqslant 0$$

These inequalities may be solved simultaneously and the objective function minimized by using the simplex method of linear programming. The situation in which machine operating cost is dependent upon the type of product being manufactured may be formulated in the same manner.

Machine Interference

When more than one machine is assigned to a single operator a phenomenon known as *machine interference* may occur. For example, if one operator attends three weaving machines, when one stops—either at the end of its production cycle or for any other reason (e.g. breakdown)—then the operator will attend to it. If, however, while he is attending to it one of the other machines stops, then since he is unable to attend to both a certain amount of machine idle time must result. This is known as machine interference.

The assignment of two or more machines to one operator is a common feature in many industries, and, of course, the nature of the work being done on such machines will determine the amount of attention required from the operator. This will, in turn, determine the optimum number of machines to assign to the operator. This man/machine assignment, since it determines the production capacity, is of considerable importance during production planning.

The mathematical treatment of multi–machine assignments has been attempted by many authors but the problem is a particularly complex one, especially when the operators have duties other than simply attending to the machines, and when the characteristics of the machines differ. In this section we will confine ourselves to a simple deterministic case, in which machines, all of which are the same behave in some predictable manner.

We can identify three types of activity, thus:

Independent activities performed by either machine or operator without the need for the services or attention of the other.

(a) Machine independent running time per cycle $= t$
(b) Operator independent time per cycle $= b$

Concurrent activities which must be performed by operator *and* machine together $= a$
Idle time, when either operator or machine is waiting for the other.

(a) Operator idle time per cycle $= i_o$
(b) Machine idle time per cycle $= i_m$

For example, if an operator attended only one machine, the situation in Fig. 8.11 might result.

Unless the operator is able to perform other duties during the period in which the machine operates independently, a great deal of operator idle time must result. In such a case the operator might reasonably be asked to attend to more than one of these machines. (In the example in Fig. 8.11 he could attend to at least 2 machines.)

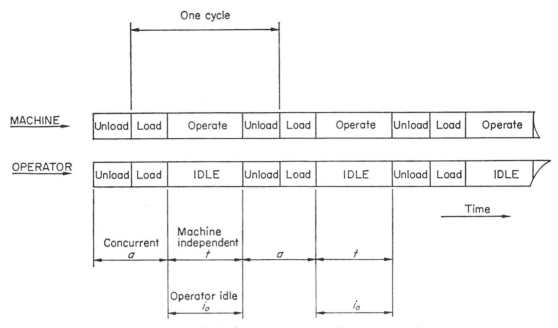

FIGURE 8.11. Cycle for operator attending one machine

The ideal number of machines to allocate to one operator (n^1) can be calculated using this formula:

$$n^1 = \frac{a+t}{a+b}$$

Unless we are particularly fortunate n^1 will not be a whole number; but as it is usually only possible to assign whole machines to operators, we must decide whether to allocate the next whole number smaller than n^1 and hence incur operator idle time, or the next whole number larger than n^1 and incur machine idle time, i.e.

$$(n) < n^1 < (n+1)$$

This decision will, of course, depend upon the relative cost of operator and machine idle time.

If

$$C_o = \text{Cost of operator/h}$$
$$C_m = \text{Cost of machine/h}$$

and

$$E = \frac{C_o}{C_m}$$

then the best multi-machine assignment can be found by using the formula[13]:

$$\frac{Y_n}{Y_{(n+1)}} = \frac{E+n}{E+n+1} \times \frac{n^1}{n}$$

---

[13] The derivations of this and subsequent formulae in this section may be found in Eilon's book, for which the reference is given in Selected Readings at the end of the chapter.

Y_n is the cost per unit of production with an assignment of n machines and $Y_{(n+1)}$ likewise for an assignment of $n+1$ machines.

If $Y_n/Y_{(n+1)}$ is greater than 1, then $n+1$ machines should be used, and if $Y_n/Y_{(n+1)}$ is less than 1, then n machines should be used.

When the machine independent time (t) and the concurrent activity time (a) per cycle are constant, then we can calculate, as above, the assignment arrangement to avoid interference; but when either or both of those times vary the problem is considerably more difficult.

One of the best-known treatments of this complex, queueing-type situation was presented by Ashcroft almost twenty years ago. He made the following assumptions:

1. The probability of a machine requiring service by the operator is independent of the time it has been running hitherto.
2. All service times (a) are constant.
3. No priority system of servicing operates.
4. All machines have similar operational characteristics.

Such assumptions are seldom completely justified in practice, but often the situation does not differ too much and, in such cases, the Ashcroft treatment has been found to provide good results. Using a statistical queueing theory approach, Ashcroft derived a table of numbers which give the average number of machine running hours per clock hour. The Ashcroft number, therefore, is a measure of the expected output from machines when these are all assigned to one operator. Consequently, they are of value during production planning for determining the machine output in multi-machine assignments.

Table 8.7 gives Ashcroft numbers for one to ten machines and for ratios of concurrent (service) time (a) to machine independent running time (t) from 0·01 to 1·00.

Example

If:
$$\text{Service time/cycle} \quad = \quad 5 \text{ min}$$
$$\text{Machine running time/cycle} = 10 \text{ min}$$

$$p = \frac{a}{t} = 0.5$$

i.e.

No. of machines n	Ashcroft no. A_n	Efficiency (%) $\dfrac{A_n}{n} \times 100$
1	0·67	67
2	1·24	62
3	1·67	56
4	1·90	48
5	1·98	40

To determine the best assignment, operator and machine costs must again be taken into account. The cost per clock hour is the cost of one operator per hour, plus n times the cost of a machine per hour:

$$Y = C_0 + nC_m$$

TABLE 8.7. Ashcroft numbers

p	$n=1$	$n=2$	$n=3$	$n=4$	$n=5$	$n=6$	$n=7$	$n=8$	$n=9$	$n=10$
0·00	1·00	2·00	3·00	4·00	5·00	6·00	7·00	8·00	9·00	10·00
0·01	0·99	1·98	2·97	3·96	4·95	5·94	6·93	7·92	8·91	9·90
0·02	0·98	1·96	2·94	3·92	4·90	5·88	6·85	7·83	8·81	9·78
0·03	0·97	1·94	2·91	3·88	4·84	5·81	6·77	7·74	8·70	9·66
0·04	0·96	1·92	2·88	3·84	4·79	5·74	6·69	7·64	8·58	9·52
0·05	0·95	1·90	2·85	3·79	4·74	5·67	6·61	7·53	8·45	9·37
0·06	0·94	1·88	2·82	3·75	4·68	5·60	6·51	7·42	8·31	9·19
0·07	0·93	1·86	2·79	3·71	4·62	5·52	6·42	7·29	8·15	8·99
0·08	0·93	1·85	2·76	3·67	4·56	5·44	6·31	7·16	7·98	8·76
0·09	0·92	1·83	2·73	3·62	4·50	5·36	6·20	7·01	7·78	8·50
0·10	0·91	1·81	2·70	3·58	4·44	5·28	6·08	6·85	7·57	8·21
0·11	0·90	1·79	2·67	3·53	4·38	5·19	5·96	6·68	7·33	7·89
0·12	0·89	1·77	2·64	3·49	4·31	5·10	5·83	6·50	7·08	7·55
0·13	0·88	1·76	2·61	3·44	4·24	5·00	5·69	6·31	6·81	7·19
0·14	0·88	1·74	2·58	3·40	4·18	4·90	5·55	6·10	6·53	6·83
0·15	0·87	1·72	2·55	3·35	4·11	4·80	5·40	5·90	6·25	6·48
0·16	0·86	1·71	2·52	3·31	4·04	4·70	5·25	5·68	5·97	6·14
0·17	0·85	1·69	2·50	3·26	3·97	4·59	5·10	5·47	5·70	5·82
0·18	0·85	1·67	2·48	3·22	3·90	4·48	4·94	5·26	5·44	5·52
0·19	0·84	1·66	2·44	3·17	3·83	4·37	4·79	5·05	5·19	5·24
0·20	0·83	1·64	2·41	3·12	3·75	4·26	4·63	4·85	4·95	4·99
0·21	0·83	1·62	2·38	3·08	3·68	4·15	4·48	4·66	4·73	4·75
0·22	0·82	1·61	2·35	3·03	3·61	4·04	4·33	4·47	4·53	4·54
0·23	0·81	1·59	2·33	2·98	3·53	3·94	4·18	4·30	4·34	4·34
0·24	0·81	1·58	2·30	2·94	3·46	3·83	4·04	4·13	4·16	4·16
0·25	0·80	1·56	2·27	2·89	3·39	3·72	3·90	3·98	4·00	4·00
0·26	0·79	1·55	2·24	2·85	3·31	3·62	3·77	3·83	3·84	3·84
0·27	0·79	1·53	2·22	2·80	3·24	3·52	3·65	3·69	3·70	3·70
0·28	0·78	1·52	2·19	2·75	3·17	3·42	3·53	3·56	3·57	3·57
0·29	0·77	1·51	2·16	2·71	3·10	3·33	3·42	3·44	3·45	3·45
0·30	0·77	1·49	2·14	2·67	3·03	3·23	3·31	3·33	3·33	3·33
0·31	0·76	1·48	2·11	2·62	2·97	3·14	3·21	3·22	3·22	3·22
0·32	0·76	1·46	2·09	2·58	2·90	3·06	3·11	3·12	3·12	3·12
0·33	0·75	1·45	2·06	2·53	2·84	2·98	3·02	3·03	3·03	3·03
0·34	0·75	1·44	2·03	2·49	2·77	2·90	2·93	2·94	2·94	2·94
0·35	0·74	1·42	2·01	2·45	2·71	2·82	2·85	2·86	2·86	2·86
0·40	0·71	1·36	1·89	2·25	2·43	2·49	2·50	2·50	2·50	2·50
0·45	0·69	1·30	1·78	2·07	2·19	2·22	2·22	2·22	2·22	2·22
0·50	0·67	1·24	1·67	1·90	1·98	2·00	2·00	2·00	2·00	2·00
0·55	0·64	1·19	1·57	1·76	1·81	1·82				
0·60	0·62	1·14	1·48	1·63	1·66	1·67				
0·65	0·61	1·10	1·40	1·51	1·54	1·54				
0·70	0·59	1·05	1·32	1·41	1·43	1·43				
0·75	0·57	1·01	1·25	1·32	1·33	1·33				
0·80	0·55	0·97	1·19	1·24	1·25	1·25				
0·85	0·54	0·94	1·13	1·17	1·17	1·18				
0·90	0·53	0·91	1·07	1·11	1·11	1·11				
0·95	0·51	0·87	1·02	1·05	1·05	1·05				
1·00	0·50	0·84	0·98	1·00	1·00	1·00				

Reproduced by permission from *Productivity and Probability* by T. F. O'Connor, published by Emmott & Co. Ltd., Manchester, 1952.

The best assignment is that which minimizes the ratio:

$$\frac{Y}{A_n C_o}$$

which can also be expressed as:

$$\frac{1 + (n C_m / C_0)}{A_n}$$

Example 1

$$p = 0 \cdot 1$$
$$C_0 = £2$$
$$C_m = £6$$

n	A_n	$\dfrac{Y}{A_n C_o}$	
1	0·91	4·44	
2	1·81	3·87	
3	2·70	3·71	
4	3·58	3·63	
5	4·44	3·61	
6	5·28	3·60	← best assignment
7	6·08	3·62	
8	6·85	3·65	

Example 2

$$p = 0 \cdot 25$$

$$\frac{C_m}{C_o} = 2 \cdot 0$$

n	A_n	$\dfrac{1 + (n C_m / C_o)}{A_n}$	
1	0·80	3·75	
2	1·56	3·21	
3	2·27	3·08	← best assignment
4	2·89	3·11	
5	3·39	3·24	
6	3·72	3·50	

SUMMARY

Semantic problems surround the area and functions of production planning and control. In this chapter production planning was defined as the pre-production activity which embraces the following objectives:

To decide whether an item shall be made or bought (the make or buy problem).
To decide how an item will be made (operations planning).
To decide when the various operations will be performed (scheduling).

Production planning was defined as being concerned mainly with scheduling, unlike production control which was said to be concerned mainly with sequencing. These definitions are logical since they distinguish two aspects or problems, each of which is at its most complex in one type of production; i.e. in continuous production the problem is one of planning and hence the main function is scheduling, whereas in intermittent production the problem is one of control and hence the main function is sequencing. Because the following chapters deal at length with planning by *network analysis*, and with planning for batch and mass production, this chapter has dealt mainly with planning and scheduling for intermittent production. In this type of production accurate scheduling is impossible and consequently, in practice, a great deal of work in progress and lengthy queues of jobs result. Because of the inevitability of this situation, production schedules must take into account not only the actual operation time but also the anticipated idle or waiting time. The method usually adopted is reverse scheduling from a due date. Gantt charts are frequently used as visual presentations of the production schedules calculated in this manner.

Two special problems were dealt with: firstly the assigning of jobs to machines, which was formulated as a linear programming problem, and secondly the multi-machine assignment problem in which one operator attends to two or more machines. In such a situation a phenomenon known as *machine interference* can occur if two or more machines each require the attention of the operator at the same time. Treatment of the situation, based on the queuing theory and developed by Ashcroft, was briefly described.

SELECTED READINGS

This book is a good, analytically biased treatment of the planning and control of production. Multi-machine assignment and interference using the Ashcroft treatment is dealt with in Chapter 12:

S. EILON, *Elements of Production Planning and Control*, Collier-Macmillan, London, 1966.

The following books deal with production planning from a practitioner's point of view:

J. L. BURBIDGE, *The Principles of Production Control*, Macdonald & Evans, London, 1968.
F. G. MOORE, *Production Control*, 2nd ed., McGraw Hill, London, 1959.

The Index Method of job/machine assignment is described in:

L. J. GARRETT and M. SILVER, *Production Management Analysis*, Harcourt, Brace, & World, New York, 1966.

The transportation formulation of the same problem is described in:

E. H. BOWMAN, 'Production scheduling by the transportation method of linear programming', *Operations Res.*, **4**, 100–103 (1956).

The following excellent paper surveys many methods of production smoothing and workforce balancing, including the techniques discussed in this chapter:

E. A. SILVER, 'A tutorial on production smoothing and workforce balancing', *Operations Res.*, **5**, No. 6, 985–1010 (1967).

The linear decision rule is described in:

C. C. HOLT, F. MODIGLIANI, J. F. MUTH and H. A. SIMON, *Planning Production, Inventories and Work Force*, Prentice-Hall, London, 1960.

and more simply in Chapter 15 of:

E. C. BURSK and J. F. CHAPMAN (Ed.), *New Decision-making Tools for Managers*, Mentor, London, 1965.

QUESTIONS

8·1· A small company is engaged in the manufacture of automatic gigglecocks for three principal customers, Messrs. Smith, Brown and Jones. These three customers are in the habit of placing their orders for a four week period three weeks in advance; indeed a set of orders has just been received by the company and is shown below:

	Quantity to be delivered during week number:			
Customer	26	27	28	29
Smith	10	14	20	15
Brown	14	20	25	17
Jones	7	9	10	7
Total	31	43	55	39

Given the following information, determine the optimal production plan and the cost associated with the satisfaction of these orders for automatic gigglecocks according to such a plan.

Stockholding cost per gigglecock per week   = £1
Production cost per gigglecock   = £10 during normal shift work
   = £15 during night shift work
'Free' stock of gigglecocks at end of week 25 = 35
Production capacity each week   = 35 gigglecocks per normal shift
   = 15 gigglecocks per night shift

8.2. The acceptance of an order for a particular product is followed by a sequence of events necessary to get the goods manufactured. Explain this sequence of events, discuss the necessary documents and orders needed to link the departments involved, and explain the functions of these departments and their contribution to the final fulfilment of the order.

[Univ. of Salford, Dip. for Advanced Studies in Management, 1st Year, *Production Management*, July 1968—35 minutes]

8.3. Products A and B can be produced at factories I and II. The production time required per product unit is one hour for A and two hours for B—the same at both factories.

The demand for A and B, the time available at each factory and production costs and inventory holding costs per product unit are given for the forthcoming two months in the table below.

	Demand (product units)	
Product	May	June
A	100	110
B	150	190

	Time available (hours)		Cost per product unit (mu)*	
	May	June	Product A	Product B
Factory I				
Normal time	200	200	3·0	6·2
Overtime	40	10	3·6	6·8
Factory II				
Normal time	250	200	3·1	6·4
Overtime	60	40	3·9	7·2
	Inventory holding costs			
	(mu* per product unit per month)			
Factory I	0·6			
Factory II	0·4			

* mu = money units.

Determine an optimum production plan that will meet demand at minimum cost. What is the total cost of this optimum programme?

[Univ. of London, Imperial College, M.Sc. Operational Research and Management Studies, *Production Planning and Control*, 1968—45 minutes]

8.4. A finished product is assembled from one sub-assembly and two other components—A, which is manufactured within the factory and B, which is bought out. The sub-assembly requires three components—C and D, which are manufactured within the factory and E, which is bought out.

Part	Production dept. no.	Production time required	Delivery time
Assembly	200	20 m/c hours	
Sub-assembly	190	30 m/c hours	
Component A	180	15 m/c hours	
Component C	170	35 m/c hours	
Component D	180	40 m/c hours	
Component B			4 weeks
Component E			2 weeks

All necessary raw materials are in stock. No overtime working is allowed. All orders have equal priority.

An order for one assembly is received at the end of week 7, when the factory load is as shown in the following table:

Dept. no.	Total weekly available capacity	Machine hours already allocated in week							
		8	9	10	11	12	13	14	15
170	80 man hours	75	80	70	55	50	30	20	10
180	160 man hours	130	140	100	90	20	10	10	20
190	80 man hours	80	80	80	80	70	30	10	0
200	120 man hours	100	120	110	100	60	80	40	15

(a) What is the earliest delivery date which can be promised?
(b) In which weeks should the various components be loaded for manufacture?
(c) When should the orders for bought out components be placed, and what special instructions should be given to the suppliers?

[Cranfield Inst. Tech. School of Management, Dept. of Prod. Eng., Dip. Industrial Eng. and Admin., Part II, *Production Management*, 1968—30 minutes]

8.5. Table 1 below shows the number of each of two products, A and B, which have recently been ordered from company X for delivery to customers during the four months May to August.

Each of the two products consists of two sub-assemblies (I and II or II and III) as shown in Table 2. Table 2 also gives the man hours of production required for each sub-assembly.

The company works a three shift system. The production capacity in man hours per shift is shown in Table 3.

The company is in the habit of planning production for several months ahead, each additional customer order being included in the production plan when it is received. The production plan, prior to the receipt of the recent orders, is shown in terms of man hours of production capacity required in Table 4.

Table 5 shows the unit production costs for each sub-assembly for each shift, whilst Table 6 gives the unit storage cost per sub-assembly per month.

Assume (1) that the details of the existing production plan cannot be altered; (2) that sub-assemblies manufactured during one month enable the products of which they are part to be delivered to customers no later than the last day of the same month; (3) that there will be no sub-assemblies in stock at the end of April.

Formulate this planning problem as a linear programming problem, arrange the data in a manner which permits a linear programming algorithm to be used, but do not solve the problem. Comment upon any important characteristic of the solution which is evident from the initial formulation.

TABLE 1. Demand from new orders

Product	May	June	July	August
A	20	40	25	40
B	30	25	50	32

TABLE 2. Sub-assemblies product, and man hours/sub-assembly

Product	No. of sub-assemblies per product		
	I	II	III
A	1	1	
B		1	1
Man hours production	5	7	5

TABLE 3. Production capacity (man hours)/month

	March to July inc.	August
Shift 1	400	400
Shift 2	400	300
Shift 3	400	300

TABLE 4. Man hours committed to previous orders

	March	April	May	June	July	August
Shift 1	300	250	250	200	150	100
Shift 2	300	200	200	100	100	50
Shift 3	300	200	200	50	100	50

TABLE 5. Unit production cost (£)/sub-assembly

	Sub-assembly I		Sub-assembly II		Sub-assembly III	
	March–July	August	March–July	August	March–July	August
Shift 1	5	6	6	7	4	5
Shift 2	7	8	8	9	6	7
Shift 3	7	8	8	9	6	7

TABLE 6. Unit storage cost/month

Sub-assembly	£/month
I	0·5
II	0·6
III	0·5

[Univ. of Bradford, Management Centre, Dip. Management Studies, *Production Management*, 1970—45 minutes]

8.6. What are the organizational characteristics of jobbing, mass and process production, and how do the production planning problems differ in these three basic types of production?

8.7. Holdtight Company Ltd. have just received orders from four customers for quantities of different 'expanderbolts'. Each order is to be manufactured over the same very short period of time, during which three machines are available for the manufacture of the bolts.

The table below shows the manufacturing time in hours/bolt for each of the three machines and the total available hours capacity on each for the period in question.

Assuming that each order is to be manufactured on one machine only, how should orders be allocated to machines?

Order	Number of expanderbolts	Manufacturing time (hours/bolt)		
		M/c A	M/c B	M/c C
1	50	4	5	3
2	75	3	2	4
3	25	5	4	3
4	80	2	5	4
Total capacity (hours)		175	275	175

8.8. Five orders are received by a company, each order being for a quantity of one type of agricultural bucket. Each type of bucket can be made on any of the five machines which happen to have available production capacity. The table below gives details of the numbers of buckets in each order, the manufacturing time (in hours/bucket) for each machine, and the total hours of production capacity available on each machine.

Using the index method described in this chapter, determine the optimum allocation of orders to machines, assuming (1) that orders cannot be split between several machines, and (2) that individual orders can be manufactured on a maximum of two machines.

Order no.	No. of products	Machine				
		A	B	C	D	E
1	30	2·0	2·5	3·0	4·0	3·5
2	25	3·0	3·0	3·5	4·0	2·5
3	40	4·0	5·0	2·0	3·0	2·5
4	25	3·5	2·0	3·5	2·5	3·0
5	30	4·0	2·0	2·5	3·0	4·0
Total hours available		175	150	130	120	120

8.9. If the hourly operating costs of each of the three machines described in question 8.7 are as follows:

Machine	Operating cost/hour
	£
A	2·0
B	3·0
C	2·5

express the allocation problem given in question 8.7 as a set of equations or inequalities suitable for solution using the Simplex method of linear programming.

8.10. An operator is required to attend to one or more semi-automatic injection moulding machines. The cycle of operations for each machine is as follows:

Man loads/unloads machine—5 min
Machine operates without requiring attention of man—12 min
Repeat

During this cycle the man must stack up the items which he has unloaded from the machine. This takes him 2 minutes.

     What is the ideal number of such identical machines to allocate to one worker, given the following additional information?
Total cost associated with each machine = £50/h
Total cost associated with each worker = £5/h

8.11. A skilled worker is required to attend 4 injection moulding machines. After being unloaded/loaded by the operator, which takes 3 min., each machine runs for 10 min. (average) before requiring to be unloaded and loaded again. During this period the operator is not required to perform any work. The total hourly cost associated with each machine, which is independent of the proportion of time the machine is idle, is five times the total hourly cost associated with each man.

(a) What is the efficiency of each machine in terms of the percentage of total time devoted to operation?
(b) How many machines should be allocated to each operator?
(c) What assumptions have you made in arriving at your answer?

9

Network Planning

One of the intriguing characteristics of this so-called technological age is the need to produce very complex items in very small numbers. For example, many companies, particularly in America, are involved in some aspect of the space programme and are concerned with producing large and elaborate space vehicles. In Europe, airframe and electronics companies are building satellites for international communications and the European space effort proceeds in the shadow of the American and Russian efforts. Likewise in civil engineering, the construction of motorways, dams, etc., are complex single projects. The construction of the Polaris submarine fleet presented much the same problems; complex items needed to be manufactured in comparatively small quantities and in the minimum possible time.

It was this last example which gave rise to *network analysis*, a planning technique which has, in the last ten years, generated a great deal of interest and become almost standard practice in planning the manufacture of large items, as well as in planning maintenance, research and development. In fact, many government departments and other main contractors now often insist that sub-contractors use network analysis in planning operations.

Since we have chosen to use the term network analysis in this chapter rather than one of the other numerous alternatives, we will no doubt already have incurred the wrath of many readers. The fact is that since this has been such a popular management technique many people have contributed to both its theory and practice, and scores of different titles have been used to describe techniques which differ only marginally one from another.[1] It has also been fashionable to describe techniques by the initial letter of the words in their titles; consequently something of a mnemonic maze has resulted from the use of descriptions such as the following:

PERT
CPM
APPRAISE
CPPS
RAMPS
PEP
CPS
SCANS
SPERT
RPSM

---

[1] The need for a name to embrace all of these variants was recognised by the Operational Research Society (London), whose Study Group came up with RETROMETRY (L. *rete*, net; Gr. *metron*, a measure). It remains to be seen whether this title is adopted, and if so, whether or not it serves to clarify or add further confusion to the situation!

LESS
PERT CO.
SUPER PERT CO.

PERT (Programme Evaluation Review Technique) was developed in 1958 by the Programme Evaluation Branch of the U.S. Navy Special Projects office with the assistance of Booz-Allen and Hamilton, the management consultants, and the Lockheed Missile Systems Division. The technique of representing projects by an arrow diagram was developed, and by the time the first report of this group was published the name PERT had been adopted. It was decided to apply this technique to the Polaris missile programme late in 1958, where it was subsequently said to have saved two years during the engineering and development stage. PERT took no account of costs but was capable of accommodating uncertainty in job and project durations.

Morgan R. Walker of the E. I. du Pont de Nemours Co. and James E. Kelly of Remington Rand introduced the Critical Path Method (CPM) to the E. I. du Pont de Nemours Co. in 1957. The technique was first used in 1958 when it was compared with conventional planning procedures for the construction of a new plant. In 1959 CPM was used on a maintenance project at the Louisville works where it is said to have reduced the plant 'down time' from an expected 125 hours to 78 hours. It is credited with saving this company $1 million during its first full year of use.

Ten years ago the main difference between these two techniques was the ability of PERT to accommodate probabilistic job durations, i.e. jobs of uncertain duration; but since that time a considerable amount of work has been undertaken so that now there is comparatively little difference between the various approaches. Most computer companies and consultants offer a network analysis service, often coining different names to describe their programmes: for example, APPRAISE—Atlas Project Planning, Resourse Allocation and Integrated Schedule Evaluation—was devised by ICT Computers for use on Atlas 1 and 2 machines, and RAMPS—Resource Allocation and Multi-Project Scheduling—by CEIR Ltd.

We prefer the title network analysis both because it is an adequate description of the procedure involved and also because it is one of the few non-mnemonic titles.

The rudimentary steps in production planning by network analysis are as follows:

1. Construct an arrow or network diagram to represent the project to be undertaken, indicating the sequence and interdependence of all necessary jobs in the project.
2. Determine how long each of the jobs will last and insert those times on the network.
3. Perform network calculations to determine the overall duration of the project and the criticality of the various jobs.
4. If the project completion date is later than required, consider modifying either the network and/or the individual job durations in order that the project may be completed within the required time.

This is the extent of the planning phase of simple network analysis; there are, however, subsequent steps concerned with the control of production and these will be dealt with in Chapter 13. Furthermore, this simple description of the procedure has omitted all considerations of costs and resources, and these will be dealt with later in this chapter.

THE CONSTRUCTION OF NETWORKS

Any project may be represented by means of an arrow diagram in which the arrangement of arrows indicates the sequence of individual jobs and their dependence on other jobs. Arrow diagrams consist of two basic elements—*activities* and *events*.

An *activity* is a time-consuming task and is represented by an arrow or line.

An *event* is considered as instantaneous, i.e. a point in time. An event may represent the completion or the commencement of an activity and is represented by a circle. A sequence of events is referred to as a path.

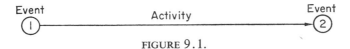

FIGURE 9.1.

Unlike bar charts, the scale to which activities are drawn has no significance. The length of an activity arrow on a network diagram is unrelated to the duration of that activity. It is normal to number events as in Fig. 9.1 in order that paths within the network can be easily described but, other than for identification, event numbers have no significance.

The network diagram is constructed by assembling all activities in a logical order. For example, the networks shown in Fig. 9.2 and 9.3 relate to a decorating job.

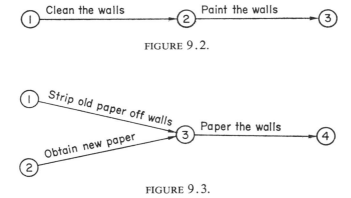

FIGURE 9.2.

FIGURE 9.3.

No activity may begin until all the activities leading to it are completed. In Fig. 9.2, only after the walls have been cleaned can they be painted. In Fig. 9.3, starting to paper the walls is dependent not only on the old paper having been removed but also on the new paper being available.

Activities occurring on the same path are *sequential* and are dependent directly upon each other. *Parallel* activities on different paths are independent of one another (Fig. 9.4).

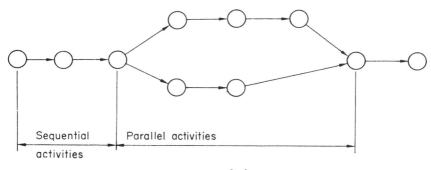

FIGURE 9.4.

The convention in drawing networks is to allow time to flow from left to right, and to number events in this direction so that events on the left of the diagram have smaller numbers than, and occur before, events on the right of the diagram.

It is not usually possible to use network diagrams in which 'loops' or 'dangles' occur; a loop such as that in Fig. 9.5 may be a perfectly legitimate sequence of operations where, for example, a certain amount of reprocessing of materials or rectification takes place but, because of the calculations which must later be performed on the diagram, it cannot be accepted in network analysis.

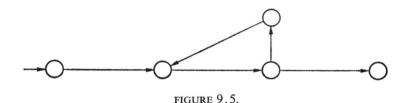

FIGURE 9.5.

Whilst there are certain computer programmes which will accept multiple-finish and -start events on networks, it is not normally possible to leave events 'dangling' as in Fig. 9.6.

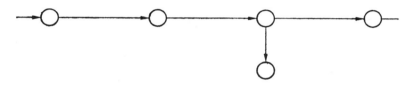

FIGURE 9.6.

Dummy Activities

The activities discussed above represent some time-consuming operation or job to be performed during the project. Dummy activities consume no time; they are of zero duration and are used solely for convenience in network construction. Dummy activities, represented by dotted lines, may be necessary on the following occasions:
1. To provide the correct logic in the diagram.
   In Fig. 9.7 the completion of activities C and D is necessary before either E or F may begin.

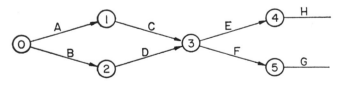

FIGURE 9.7.

In practice, only activity E needs to depend on the completion of both activities C and D: activity F depends on D alone. To represent this logic a dummy activity is required (Fig. 9.8).
2. To avoid having more than one activity with the same beginning and end event (Fig. 9.9).

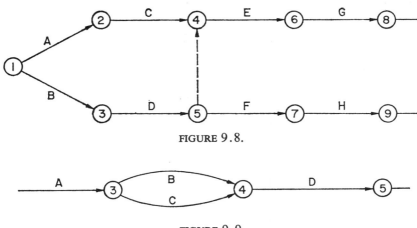

FIGURE 9.8.

FIGURE 9.9.

It is not usually possible to represent activities in this manner since activities B and C would be described from their event numbers as 3–4, so a dummy activity is necessary (Fig. 9.10).

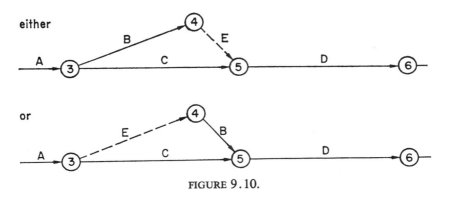

either

or

FIGURE 9.10.

3. For convenience in drawing.

The two networks in Fig. 9.11 are equivalent, but the use of dummy activities facilitates representation. This is often necessary in complex networks.

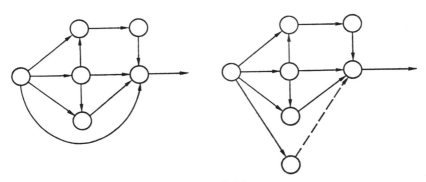

FIGURE 9.11.

It may be necessary to use dummy activities when initially constructing networks to avoid complicated and untidy diagrams. Nevertheless, since the amount of subsequent analysis is dependent upon the number of activities in a diagram, the redundant dummies should be eliminated in order to save calculation time.

In drawing large networks for projects with many activities we have often found it to be easier to begin from the end of the project and work backwards. It is often helpful to consider large projects in separate parts, i.e. certain sections of the project or, if more appropriate, certain periods during the manufacture of the project, and then to piece together several smaller networks rather than try to construct the complete network from scratch. For example, the manufacture of a large water turbine could be divided into rotating parts (impeller, shafts, etc.) and stationary parts (housing, ducting, etc.). Alternatively it may be considered in terms of two time periods, the first covering the cutting, forming and welding of the parts and the second, the machining and assembling.

Except in the case of simple projects it is usually beneficial to construct the network around the important activities. Identify the important or major parts, locate the important activities on the diagram, then attach all the other secondary activities to construct the complete network.

NETWORK CALCULATIONS

Dates

The objective of initial network calculations is to determine the overall duration of the project so that either a delivery date can be given to the customer, or so that we can consider what are the alterations necessary for the project to be completed on or before a date to which we are already committed.

To perform the network calculations two things are required: firstly an *activity network* representing the project, and secondly the durations of all the activities in that network. Network analysis is only a tool; its value depends entirely on the way in which it is used and the information upon which it is based. Consequently, the collection of activity durations from records, or the estimation of durations, is an important part of the exercise.

If the activities have been performed previously then, assuming the use of the same resources and procedures, the durations may be obtained from records. On the many occasions where the activities have no direct precedent some form of estimation is necessary. For the time being we shall ignore the possibility of using multiple estimates of activity durations and consider only the case in which each activity is given one duration.

Earliest Start Date for Activities (ES)

The earliest start date for each activity is calculated from the *beginning* of the network by totalling all preceding activity durations (d).

Where two (or more) activities lead into one event the following activity cannot begin until both of the preceding activities are completed. Consequently, the last of these activities to finish determines the start date for the subsequent activity.

In Fig. 9.12 the earliest start date for activity I is day 17 (assuming the project starts at day 0), since the start date of activity I will depend on the completion of the latter of the two activities G and H, which is H.

Therefore, when calculating *ES* dates work from the *beginning* of the network and use the *largest* numbers at junctions.

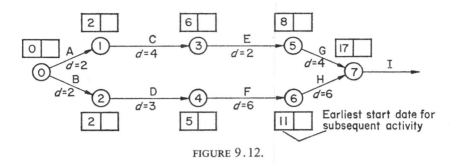

FIGURE 9.12.

Latest Finish Dates for Activities (LF)

This is calculated from the *end* of the project by successively subtracting activity durations (*d*) from the project finish date.

Where two (or more) activities stem from one event the earliest of the dates will determine the latest finish date for previous activities.

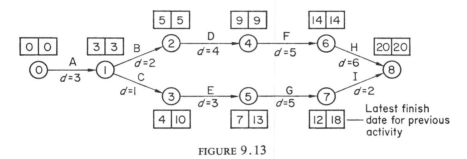

FIGURE 9.13

In Fig. 9.13 the latest finish date for activity A is day 3 since activity B must start at day 3 if the project is not to be delayed.

Therefore, when calculating *LF* dates begin from the *end* of the network and use the *smallest* numbers at junctions.

Earliest Finish Date for Activities (EF)

The earliest finish date for any activity is determined by that activity's earliest start date and its duration, i.e. for any activity: $EF = ES + d$.

Latest Start Date for Activities (LS)

The latest start date for any activity is determined by that activity's latest finish date and its duration, i.e. for any activity: $LS = LF - d$.

Float

In the previous example the earliest completion date for the project, i.e. the date of event 8, is determined by the *EF* dates for activities H and I. Activity I could finish at day 14 (the *EF* date for activity I is $ES+d = 12+2$), but activity H cannot finish until day 20 and it is this activity which determines the finish date for the project. In fact, it is the path consisting of activities A B D F H which determines the project earliest finish date rather than path A C E G I.

The earliest finish date for any project is determined by the longest path through the network; consequently, it follows that the shorter paths will have more time available than they require. The difference between the time available for any activity and the time required, is called the *total float* (*TF*).

In Fig. 9.13 the time required for Activity I is 2 but the time available is 8 and hence the *TF* on Activity I is 6.

Time available $= LF - ES$
Time required $= d$
Total float $= LF - ES - d$

i.e. for any activity (say G) using our notation the *TF* can be expressed as in Fig. 9.14.

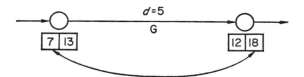

$TF=$ Difference between these two figures less the duration
$\quad = (18-7)-5$
$\quad = 6$

FIGURE 9.14.

Total float is a characteristic of a path and not a characteristic of a single activity. For example, in Fig. 9.13 the total float on activities A C E G and I is 6. If the total float is used up at any time by delays or lateness in one of the activities then it is no longer available to any of the other activities on that path.

The Critical Path

The *critical path* is the longest path through the network and is, therefore, the path with minimum total float (zero *TF* in the above example). Any delay in the activities on the critical path will delay the completion of the project, whereas delay in activities not on the critical path will initially use up some of the total float on that path and not affect the project completion date.

Slack and Other Types of Float

This is perhaps an appropriate point at which to mention two additional items. The term *slack* is sometimes used with reference to network analysis. It is often taken as equivalent to float but, strictly speaking, whereas float relates to activities, slack relates to events. So far we have only mentioned total float but two further types of float exist, i.e. *free float* and *independent float*. In this chapter we shall be concerned only with total float but, for the sake of completeness, free float is the difference between the time required for an activity and the time available for that activity if both preceding and succeeding activities occur either as early or as late as possible (free float early and free float late respectively). Independent float is the difference between the time required for an activity and the time available for that activity without effecting any other activities, i.e. it is the spare time available when the preceding activity occurs as late as possible and the succeeding activity as early as possible.

Example 1

The table below lists all the activities which together constitute a small engineering project. The table also shows the necessary immediate predecessors for each activity and the activity durations.
(a) Construct an activity network to represent the project.
(b) Determine the earliest finish date for the entire project, assuming the project begins at day 0.

Activity	Immediate predecessors	Activity duration (days)
A	—	2
B	A	3
C	A	4
D	A	5
E	B	6
F	C D	3
G	D	4
H	B	7
I	E F G	2
J	G	3

Answer:

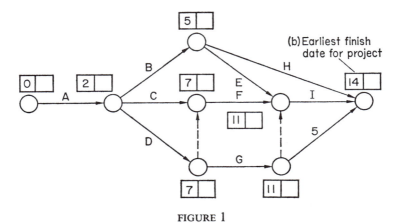

FIGURE 1

Example 2

For the project described in Example 1 determine:
(a) the total float on each activity
(b) the critical path
(c) the latest start date for activity B
(d) the earliest finish date for activity F
(e) the effect on the project duration if activity I were to take 3 days
(f) the effect on the project duration if activity F were to take 6 days

Answer:

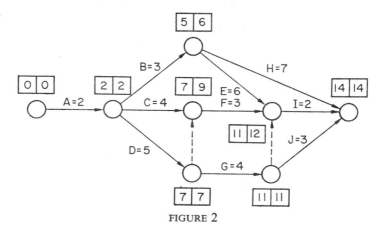

FIGURE 2

(a) *Activity* A B C D E F G H I J
    TF   0 1 3 0 1 2 0 2 1 0
(b) Critical path = A D G J
(c) Latest start date for B = *LF* − duration
                            = 6 − 3
                            = Day 3
(d) Earliest finish date for *F* = *ES* + duration
                                 = 7 + 3
                                 = Day 10
(e) No effect, but since increase in duration is equal to total float on activity, this activity would become critical
(f) Project would be delayed by one day since only 2 days *TF* are available on activity

Schedule Dates

At the beginning of this section we indicated that one objective of network calculations was to calculate the earliest completion date for the project and to compare this with the desired completion date. We may be committed to deliver a product by a certain date and, if the calculated earliest finish date for the project occurs after this scheduled finish date, it will be desirable to try to reduce the project duration. If we had used the schedule completion date in the calculations then we would have obtained negative total float values, the greatest negative values occurring on the critical path and indicating the minimum amount by which the project would be late unless some alterations were made. Schedule dates may be placed on intermediate events also. If it is necessary to complete one of the intermediate activities by a given date, e.g. so that the customer or the main contractor may inspect or test the partly completed product, then an *intermediate schedule date/late* may be used. If this date is earlier than the *LF* date for that activity it would be used in the network calculations instead of the calculated *LF* date. If one of the intermediate activities cannot be started until a given date for some reason, e.g. because of the delivery of materials, then an *intermediate schedule date/early* may be used. If this data is later than the *ES* date for that activity it would be used instead of the calculated *ES* figure.

In the example in Fig. 9.15 the final schedule date, day 20, is earlier than the calculated finish date for the project and therefore replaces the calculated *LF* date. The same applies to the intermediate schedule date/late for the completion of activity C. The intermediate schedule date/early

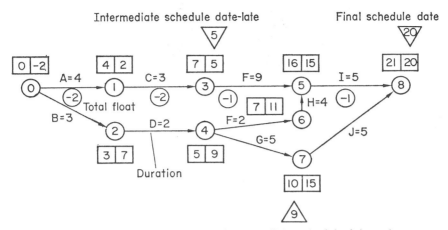

FIGURE 9.15.

for the start of activity J has no effect since this date is earlier than the calculated *ES* date for that activity.

Using schedule dates it is possible to obtain not only negative values of total float but also different values along the critical path. In the example in Fig. 9.15 the *TF* on activities A and C is −2, and on E and I it is −1, but all four activities form a critical path.

Alternative Methods

The two figures which are written at each event on the network are sometimes called *event dates*. The first figure, which we have obtained by considering the earliest finish date for the activities, is referred to as the earliest event date or time, whilst the second one is referred to as the latest event date or time.

To facilitate network calculations the *matrix* method is sometimes preferred. Any network diagram can be represented as a matrix; for example, the matrix shown in Fig. 9.16 represents the network diagram in Fig. 9.17. The event numbers are listed across the top of the matrix and also down the left-hand side. The figures in the cells are the durations of the activities connecting pairs of events. For example, event 1 is connected to event 2 by an activity of duration 4, i.e. event 1 is the initial event for activity A, and 2 is the ending event for that activity. Similarly, event 2 is connected to event 3 by an activity of duration zero, i.e. a dummy. Because the network shown in Fig. 9.17 has events numbered sequentially, all the entries in the matrix are above the diagonal; however this situation will not always occur, for example, if the direction of the arrow for activity E had been reversed, then an entry would have occurred below the diagonal in the matrix.

The earliest times (*E*) for each of the events are calculated as follows. The earliest time—zero—for initial event 1 is entered opposite 1 in the column on the right of the matrix. Now referring to initial event 2, move along the second row of the matrix until the diagonal is reached. Read the figure(s) from above the diagonal in this column (i.e. 4) add them to the E values for their rows (i.e. 0) and enter the largest answer as E for initial event no. 2. Similarly, for initial event no. 3 move along the third row to the diagonal, read the figures from above the diagonal in this column (3 and 0), add them to the E values for their rows (0 and 4) and enter the largest answer as E for initial event no. 3 (i.e. 4).

		Ending event number								
j / i	1	2	3	4	5	6	7	8	9	EARLIEST TIME (E)
1		4	3							0
2			0	7						4
3					6					4
4					3	2	4			11
5							5			14
6							0	7		13
7								2		15
8									4	19
9										23
LATEST TIME (L)	0	4	8	11	14	16	21	19	23	

FIGURE 9.16. Matrix equivalent of network, Fig. 9.17

For initial event 4 there is only one figure above the diagonal (7); add this to the E values for that row (4) and enter the answer (11) as the earliest time for initial event no. 4.

The latest times are calculated in the reverse manner. Firstly the latest time for the last event is entered. In this case the last event is 9 and the latest time, L, is the same as E; hence 23 is entered under ending event no. 9 in the L row. Now move to ending event no. 8; move up the column to the diagonal, read the figure(s) to the right of the diagonal in this row (i.e. 4), subtract them from the L values for those columns (23) and enter the smallest answer as the latest time for ending event no. 8. Similarly, the calculation of the latest time for ending event no. 7 is as follows:

$$L = 23 - 2 = 21$$

For ending event no. 6 there are two figures to the right of the diagonal, hence the calculation of L is as follows:

$$L = 21 - 0 \text{ or } 23 - 7$$
$$\therefore L \text{ for ending event no. 6 is } 16$$

The matrix method of calculating dates gives precisely the same result as the method used previously. It is perhaps preferable in that it is a simple, routine procedure but of course, unlike the

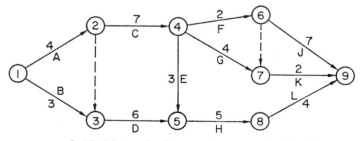

FIGURE 9.17. Network diagram from matrix, Fig. 9.16

previous method, it gives no indication of the reasons for or the logic of the calculations. For this reason it is preferable first to master the original method. In this example calculations by either method reveal that the critical path for the network passes through events 1 2 4 5 8 9.

MULTIPLE TIME ESTIMATES

We have previously assumed that a single time can be given for the duration of every activity. There are many occasions, however, when the duration of activities is not certain or when some amount of variation from the average duration is expected. For example, in maintenance work unexpected snags may occur to increase the activity duration, or failures may be found to be less serious than had been expected and the activity duration reduced. In construction work jobs may be delayed because of unfavourable weather, etc.

In such cases it is desirable to be able to use a time distribution rather than a single time for activity durations to represent the uncertainty that exists.

In network analysis uncertainty in durations can be accommodated and the following notation is usually used:

m = the most likely duration of the activity
a = the optimistic estimate of the activity duration
b = the pessimistic estimate of the activity duration

These three estimates can be used to describe the distribution for the activity duration. It is assumed that the times are distributed as a 'beta' distribution (Fig. 9.18).

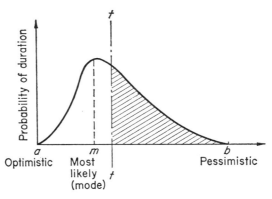

FIGURE 9.18.

where t = the expected time, the mean of the distribution.

σ = the standard deviation (which is a measure of the spread of the curve).

$\equiv$ the range between the extreme values divided by 6.

$$\equiv \frac{b-a}{6}.$$

If certain assumptions are made about the distribution, the mean (t) and the variance (σ^2) can be expressed as follows:[2]

$$\text{Mean (the expected time) } t = \frac{a+b+4m}{6}$$

$$\text{Variance} \qquad \sigma^2 = \frac{(b-a)^2}{36}$$

Probability of Achieving Scheduled Dates

Suppose we have two sequential activities, A and B, for which the durations are:

$$a_A = 0\cdot5 \text{ days} \qquad a_B = 4 \text{ days}$$
$$b_A = 3\cdot5 \text{ days} \qquad b_B = 12 \text{ days}$$
$$m_A = 2 \text{ days} \qquad m_B = 8 \text{ days}$$

Using these formulae, for activity A the expected duration t_A is 2 days and the variance $\sigma^2 = 0\cdot25$ days, and for activity B the expected duration t_B is 8 days and variance $\sigma_B^2 = 1\cdot75$ days. Assuming activity durations to be independent the expected duration for the pair of activities is 10 days and, since the variances may be added together, the variance for the pair is 2 days. It is usually assumed that the distribution for the duration of a series of activities corresponds to the 'normal' probability curve; consequently, in this case, the probability that the two activities will be completed in a minimum of 10 days is 50 per cent, since the normal distribution is symmetrical about the mean (Fig. 9.19) and consequently the probability is given by the proportion of the area to the left of the mean of 10 days (50 per cent).

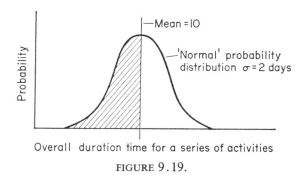

Overall duration time for a series of activities

FIGURE 9.19.

Suppose we have 3 activities which represent the critical path in a network, as in Fig. 9.20.

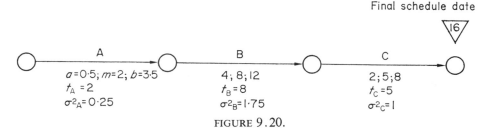

FIGURE 9.20.

---

[2] For the derivation of these formulae see the Appendix to A. Battersby, *Network Analysis for Planning and Scheduling*, 3rd ed., Macmillan, London, 1970.

If we assume that these durations are independent, i.e. that the duration of activity A does not affect that of B, and so on, and that the normal distribution applies for the project duration, then we can calculate the probability that the project will be completed on or before the required schedule date.

Expected project duration $(t) = 2+8+5 = 15$

$$\sigma^2 = 3$$

In the distribution shown in Fig. 9.21 the probability of meeting the schedule date is represented by that portion of the area under the curve to the left of the 16-day ordinate. This area can be obtained from normal distribution tables if the diagram is first converted to a standardized scale. In this case the probability of completing the project by day 16 is 0·72 since the area to the left of the 16-day ordinate is 72 per cent of the total area[3].

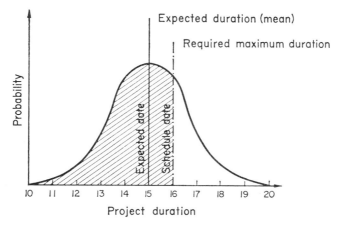

FIGURE 9.21.

---

[3] The standardized scale is used solely for convenience. The standardized normal distribution has a total area of 1·00, a mean value of 0, and variance σ^2 of 1:

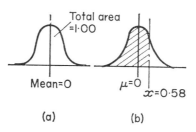

(a)   (b)

FIGURE 9.21. (a) and (b)

where s = schedule date
$\quad t$ = expected date
$\quad \sigma$ = standard deviation
$\quad x$ = standardized value for the ordinate required, i.e. the schedule date

$$x = \frac{s-t}{\sigma} = \frac{16-15}{\sqrt 3} = 0.58$$

This value can then be located in normal distribution tables and the area to the left of the value found.

The assumptions underlying the use of probabilities in this way in network analysis are, to say the least, of doubtful validity. The assumptions that the distribution for each activity duration corresponds to a 'beta' distribution and that the distribution of the duration of a sequence of activities can be regarded as 'normal', are not based on thorough research and should only be regarded as empirical rules which, over a period of time, have been found to work. Furthermore, in calculating the probability on project end dates only the critical path is used, but where the duration of each activity in the network is uncertain any path through the network has a certain probability of being critical and we should perhaps examine more than one path.

Suppose that in a network in which most of the activities' durations are uncertain the critical path has an expected duration of 16 days and a standard deviation of 1 day. In the same network

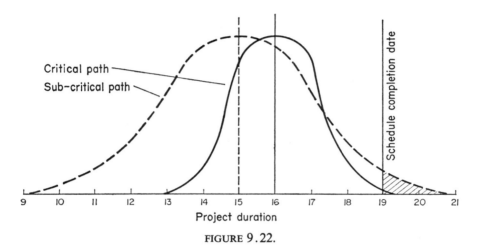

FIGURE 9.22.

there is a path of expected duration 15 days with a standard deviation of 3 days. According to the usual practice we ought to consider only the critical path in calculating our probabilities, but to do so in this case would mislead us since there is a possibility that it will be the second path which will determine the project duration (Fig. 9.22).

Had our scheduled completion date been day 19 then, considering the critical path only, we would be almost certain of meeting it, but the probability would be less if we considered the sub-critical path since, although the expected duration of this path is shorter, it is subject to greater variance.

Example

The three time estimates (optimistic; likely; pessimistic) for the duration of the individual activities which form a small project are shown on the network diagram below.

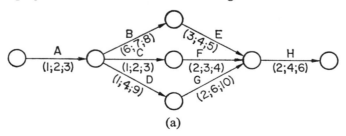

(a)

(a) Calculate the expected project duration.

(b) Determine the probability of finishing the project by day 18 or earlier.

Answer:

(a)

Activity	t (days)	σ^2
A	2	4/36
B	7	4/36
C	2	4/36
D	4·33	64/36
E	4	4/36
F	3	4/36
G	6	64/36
H	4	16/36

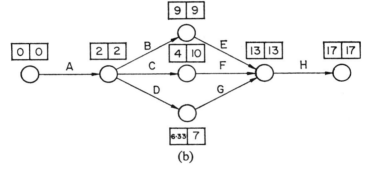

(b)

Expected project duration—17 days.

(b) Considering critical path A B E H:

$$t = 17$$

$$\sigma^2 = 4/36 + 4/36 + 4/36 + 16/36$$

$$= 0.776$$

$$x = \frac{s-t}{\sigma} = \frac{18-17}{\sqrt{0.776}}$$

$$x = 1.14$$

From normal probability tables $x \equiv 87.3\%$.

Considering sub-critical path A D G H:

$$t = 2 + 4.33 + 6 + 4$$

$$= 16.33$$

$$\sigma^2 = 4/36 + 64/36 + 64/36 + 16/36$$

$$= 4.1$$

$$x = \frac{s-t}{\sigma} = \frac{18-16.33}{\sqrt{4.1}}$$

$$x = 0.825$$

From normal probability tables $x = 79.6\%$.

H

In using three activity duration estimates to calculate probabilities of completing projects or parts of projects on or before given scheduled completion dates, it is important to consider sub-critical paths. This is particularly important when the length of such paths approaches the length of the critical path, and also where the duration of the activities on such paths is subject to comparatively large variance.

Unless jobs have been done before it is often difficult to obtain accurate estimates of activity durations. One advantage of using multiple estimates is that it encourages people to commit themselves to estimates when they might be reluctant to give a single estimate. But if this method is used principally for this reason, then there is little to be said for using these figures and subsequently calculating project durations and probabilities to several places of decimals. In such cases it may be sufficient merely to take the average of the three estimates—in fact many computer programmes provide this facility.

RESOURCES

Our treatment of network analysis so far has assumed that only time is important in executing tasks. There are certainly many situations where time is indeed the only or the most important factor, but in the majority of cases other factors effect our ability to do the job. We have assumed, for example, that the correct facilities have been available and in the correct quantities. The availability of such facilities as manpower, plant, etc., determines not only our ability to do the job but also the time required to do it. Estimates of activity duration will rely implicitly upon our capability to undertake those activities, consequently it is a little unrealistic to speak of activity durations in the abstract. An estimate of the duration of an activity may differ substantially depending on the time at which the activity is undertaken. When very little other work is being undertaken an activity duration is likely to be shorter than when facilities are already heavily loaded or committed.

Each estimate of durations is based upon the assumed use of a certain amount of resources and consequently, when the project duration is initially calculated, we may also calculate the forward resource utilization, e.g. Fig. 9.23.

In this example an overload occurs from day 5 to day 8; consequently, unless we arrange to either subcontract this work or obtain additional resources, we cannot expect to meet our project completion date. The only remaining alternative is to reschedule some of the jobs which constitute this overload. We can delay, for example, 3 man/days of work from this period until days 8–11 and avoid overloading the resources.

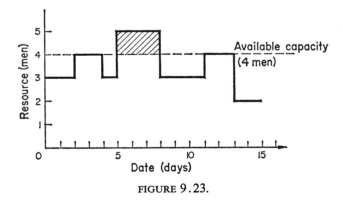

FIGURE 9.23.

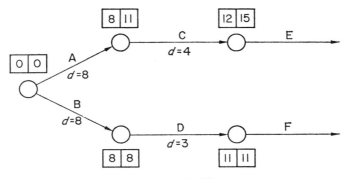

FIGURE 9.24.

Consider the part of a network shown in Fig. 9.24. To be completed in 4 days activity C requires 6 men and 4 machines; activity D requires 8 men and 5 machines for 3 days. The total resources available are 8 men and 6 machines, therefore activities C and D cannot occur together. The solution is to:

1. Subcontract one of the activities.
2. Obtain additional resources.
3. Reschedule one or both of the activities.

Solutions (1) and (2) are particularly suitable where large overloads would occur and where this occurance can be predicted well in advance. Often rescheduling is undertaken, and certainly where the overload is small and has occurred unexpectedly this is perhaps the only solution. The question is how can we reschedule the project to avoid overloading the resources and yet incur a minimum delay in completion? Activity D is on the critical path (it has a total float of 0) and the total float of activity C is 3 days, consequently activity D should be undertaken before C and this results in no additional project delay (Fig. 9.25).

Resource aggregation, i.e. calculating the total resources necessary in any period to complete the project as in Fig. 9.23, is a straightforward job, but resource allocation, as in Fig. 9.25, can involve extensive computation for a large project. Networks involving more than a few hundred activities are normally processed on a computer, but the use of one of the numerous computer/network analysis programmes is still economic for networks for fewer activities if resource allocation is to be undertaken. Although methods of resource allocation suitable for manual

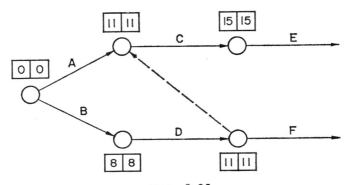

FIGURE 9.25.

processing are available (see Schaffer, Ritter and Meyer, Selected Readings), in practice almost all resource allocation in network analysis occurs during computer processing. We shall describe one such procedure later in this chapter.

COSTS

The duration of an activity depends upon the quantity of resources allocated to it. At additional cost more resources can usually be required and the activity duration decreased. In many cases this additional expenditure can be justified by the earlier completion of the activity and of the project. If a heavy penalty clause applies for late completion of the project, or if the project must be completed by a given date so that it can begin earning revenue (e.g. a hotel or holiday camp ready for the beginning of the holiday season), then additional expenditure during manufacture may be economically justifiable. In network analysis it is assumed that cost is linearly related to activity duration, and that as duration decreases the cost increases (Fig. 9.26).

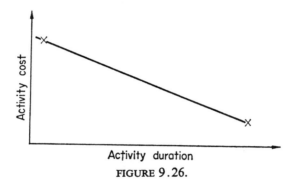

FIGURE 9.26.

When it is possible to reduce an activity duration by engaging extra resources at additional cost, two extreme cases are assumed to exist:

Normal activity duration at normal cost utilizing the normal quantity of resources.
A shorter *crash* activity duration at crash cost utilizing additional resources.

Where the difference between normal and crash durations results from the use of a different method of manufacture, no intermediate duration may be possible. For example, an estate of houses built by conventional techniques may require 50 days and cost £20 000 but an estate of industrialized buildings may require 25 days and cost £33 000. Since two entirely different resources are used no compromise state exists on the same cost/duration function; whereas where the difference between normal and crash duration results from the use of additional similar resources, the two extremes may be interpolated, as in Fig. 9.26.

The total cost of a project is determined not only by variable costs such as production resources, but also by fixed or overhead costs such as rent for buildings, insurance, power, administration, etc. Consequently the project duration involving minimum total cost is not necessarily the duration with minimum cost of resources.

The network diagram for a small construction project, activity cost data and network dates are shown in Fig. 9.27(a). Only the activities on the critical path affect the project duration, therefore reduction in project duration must be sought on the critical path and from those activities

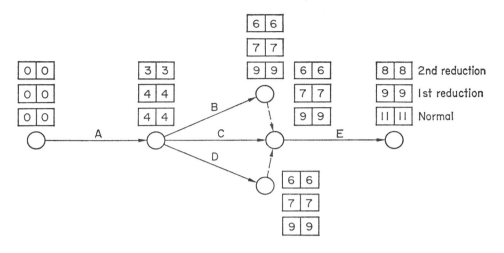

	Normal		Crash	
Activity	Duration (days)	Cost (£)	Duration (days)	Cost (£)
A	4	30	3	40
B	5	12	2	18
C	3	10	2	20
D	5	10	3	12
E	2	15	1	30
		Total 77		

N.B. Indirect fixed cost—£5/day.

FIGURE 9.27. (a) Network diagram and comparison between cost of Normal and Crash activities

offering time savings at least cost. Initially there are two critical paths—A B E and A D E, and the least cost time saving is 2 days from both activities B and D. After activities B and D have been reduced from 5 to 3 days all three paths are critical and, since no further reduction is possible on activity D, savings must be obtained from activities A and E. Activity A can be reduced by 1 day at a cost of £10, then activity E by 1 day at a cost of £15. This procedure for reducing the project duration is given in the table in Fig. 9.27(b), which also shows the construction of the total cost/project duration curve. The least cost project duration is 9 days.

Before terminating our discussion of costs we must draw attention to a rather interesting 'twist' or variation of the procedure followed in the preceding example. Again we will consider a simple example in order to explain the variation. Consider the simple project represented by Fig. 9.28. Let us calculate the total cost associated with the completion of this project in firstly one, and secondly two days less than the normal duration.

The normal duration of the project is 32 days at a normal cost of £1 620. Under those conditions the critical path is 0 1 4 3 5 6 (see Fig. 9.28 and Table 9.1). To reduce this duration by one day, one of the jobs on the critical path must be reduced by one day. The cheapest reduction is available on job 1–4 (£15), consequently a project duration of 31 days is achieved at a cost of £1 635.

Normal duration—11 days
Normal cost—£77

Job	Cost/day saved	Reduction	Total reduction	Addl. cost	Duration
Initial critical paths = $\begin{cases} A\,B\,E \\ A\,D\,E \end{cases}$					
Least cost saving occurs on B and D					
$\left.\begin{matrix} B \\ D \end{matrix}\right\}$	2+1	2	2	6	9
Now three critical paths = $\begin{cases} A\,B\,E \\ A\,C\,E \\ A\,D\,E \end{cases}$					
Least cost saving on A					
A	10	1	3	16	8
Least cost saving on E					
E	15	1	4	31	7

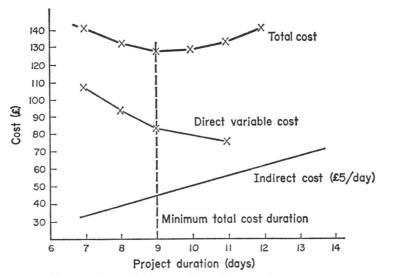

FIGURE 9.27. (b) Activity variable cost/duration relationships for Fig. 9.27. (a)

There are now three critical paths (0 1 4 3 5 6, 0 2 4 3 5 6 and 0 1 3 5 6), consequently a reduction of the project duration by a further day is achieved by reducing each of these paths by one day. Job 1–4 cannot be reduced any further, hence the cheapest direct method of reducing the project duration from 31 to 30 days is by reducing, by one day, the duration of job 1–3 (thereby reducing critical path 0 1 3 5 6) and the duration of job 4–3 (thereby reducing the duration of *both* paths 0 1 4 3 5 6 and 0 2 4 3 5 6). Thus the additional cost incurred is £40 and the total cost for a project duration of 30 days is £1 675. Notice that although three critical paths were involved, job 4–3 was common to two of those and it was necessary only to alter the duration of two jobs.

Job 0–1 is also common to two critical paths and we could therefore have reduced the duration

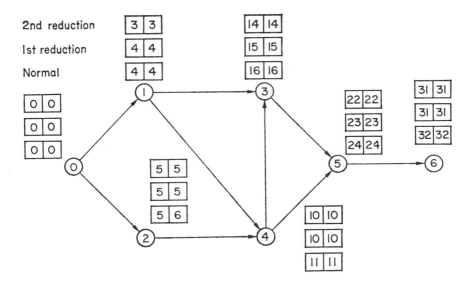

Activity	Normal		Crash	
	Duration (days)	Cost (£)	Duration (days)	Cost (£)
0–1	4	200	3	230
0–2	5	180	4	200
1–3	11	200	9	240
1–4	7	150	6	165
2–4	5	150	4	170
4–3	5	170	4	190
3–5	8	170	7	265
4–5	8	200	8	200
5–6	8	200	8	200

Total 1620

N.B. Indirect fixed cost considered to be zero.

FIGURE 9.28.

of this job and that of either job 0–2 or 2–4 to reduce the duration of the project; but such a solution would have been more expensive than that outlined previously. One further means of reducing the duration of the project would have been to reduce the duration of jobs 0–1 and 4–3. This again would have been a more expensive solution than the original. Notice, however, that both jobs 0–1 and 4–3 are common to two paths. Reduction of job 0–1 would reduce both path 0 1 3 5 6 and path 0 1 4 3 5 6, whilst reduction of job 4–3 would reduce path 0 1 4 3 5 6 and path 0 2 4 3 5 6. The reduction of both of these jobs by one day would reduce path 0 1 4 3 5 6 by two days, hence an alternative method of obtaining a project duration is to reduce, by one day, jobs 0–4 and 4–3, and to *increase* by one day job 1–4. In fact this alternative is cheaper than the previous one, the cost of the reduction being 30 + 20 − 15, i.e. £35 compared to the £40 cost of the previous method.

TABLE 9.1.

Job or activity	Cost/day saved	Reduction	Total reduction	Additional cost	Duration
Normal duration =					32
Normal cost = £1 620					
Critical path 0 1 4 3 5 6					
Least cost reduction occurs on path 1–4					
1–4	15	1	1	15	31
Critical paths $\begin{cases} 0\ 1\ 4\ 3\ 5\ 6 \\ 0\ 2\ 4\ 3\ 5\ 6 \\ 0\ 1\ 3\ 5\ 6 \end{cases}$					
Method 1					
$\left.\begin{array}{l} 1\text{–}3 \\ 4\text{–}3 \end{array}\right\}$	20 + 20	1	2	55	30
Alternative method					
$\left.\begin{array}{l} 0\text{–}1 \\ 4\text{–}5 \end{array}\right\}$	30 + 20	1	2	50	30
1–4	− 15 (increase duration)				

This interesting twist occurs only infrequently, nevertheless it is worthwhile keeping a lookout for this type of solution when the analysis involves more than one critical path—when two or more reducible activities are common to these paths which themselves contain previously reduced activities.[4]

PRODUCTION PLANNING WITH NETWORK ANALYSIS

Production planning using network analysis is normally undertaken with the assistance of an electronic computer; for the remainder of this chapter we will concentrate on this approach. Numerous programmes are available but we shall use, as an example, the PERT Bureaux procedure offered by International Computers Limited (previously English Electric Computers Ltd.). We are concerned primarily with the nature and value of computer-based network analysis and this programme can be regarded as typical although it has certain minor peculiarities.

When more than 200 or 300 activities are involved the use of a computer is advisable, particularly if regular updating of the network is envisaged for production control purposes (Chapter 14), or if resource allocation is necessary.

The important stages during network analysis based production planning are:

1. Construct the network.
2. Estimate the duration of each activity and the resources required.
3. Define any necessary schedule dates.
4. Define the maximum amount of resources available and the working hours available.
5. Perform network calculations.
6. Compare schedule dates and calculated dates.
7. Modify network and/or activity durations if necessary.

---

[4] Unfortunately a description of the circumstances under which this 'twist' occurs makes the recognition of the situation seem more difficult than in fact it is!

8. Recalculate network.
9. Repeat 6, 7 and 8 as necessary.
10. Issue production plan to all necessary departments.

The input for the network analysis programme will normally include the following:

List of activities, described by the beginning and ending event number.
The duration(s) for each activity.
Schedule dates on intermediate and/or finish events.
The description of each activity. This is not necessary for the programme but forms part of the output so that the information is meaningful and activities can be easily recognised.
The *responsibility code* for each activity, i.e. whether it is performed in the drawing office, foundry, and so on, so that, if desired, the output can be broken down into separate lists showing the production plan for each department or area.
Description of the work week and the holidays, etc., so that the work will not be scheduled during holidays and so that activity durations in hours or days can be used to calculate project durations in weeks or months.
The resource levels normally available, i.e. normal man and machine hours per week.
Additional resources available due to overtime, etc.
Maximum activity delay which, if necessary, can be tolerated because of the rescheduling of activities to conform to resource availability.
Computer run parameters, e.g. customer's name, name of project.
Output parameters to determine the type of output required, etc.

PROJECT ..MOTOR YACHT 39...... RUN NO . !..........
DATE ....PAGE.............OF .!......

TRAN CODE	BEGIN EVENT	END EVENT	DURATION/ DATE	OPTIONAL FIELDS* (MAX 16 SPACES/3 FIELDS)			DESCRIPTION		
AB		1	05 - APR - 65		MY39				→
AA	1	2	- 30 -	office			Draw plans		→
AA	2	9	- 60 -	office			Order and await engine		→
AA	9	10	- 20 -	yard			Prepare engine		→
AA	10	11	- 10 -	yard			Install engine		→
AA	11	12	- 30 -	yard			Construct deck & clean off		→
AA	12	13	- 40 -	yard			Paint & varnish		→
AA	13	14	- 20 -	yard			Final fit-out		→
AA	2	3	- 40 -	office			Order and await timber		→
AA	3	11	- 40 -	yard			Cut timber for deck		→
AA	2	4	- 60 -	office			Order and await joinery fittings		→
AA	4	8	- 30 -	yard			Assemble joinery units & fittings		→
AA	8	11	- 20 -	yard			Install joinery		→
AA	2	5	- 20 -	yard			Make hull templates		→
AA	5	6	- 40 -	yard			Cut hull timber		→
AA	6	7	- 40 -	yard			Construct hull		→
AA	7	12	- 10 -	yard			Clean off hull		→
AA	2	12	- 40 -	office			Order and await paint & varnish		→
AA	3	4	- 30 -	yard			Make joinery units		→
AA	3	5	- 0 -				Dummy		→
AA	7	8	- 0 -				Dummy		→
AA	7	10	- 0 -		↓		Dummy		→
AF		14	08 - OCT - 65		MY39				→
			- -						→
			- -						→

*PLEASE MARK OFF COLUMNS REQUIRED WITH DOUBLE LINE SEPARATORS

FIGURE 9.29. Part of input for small project—building a motor yacht

Figure 9.29 shows part of the input for a small project—building a motor yacht. Single time estimates are being used and no resources are defined. The beginning and the scheduled end dates are given, as are the departments responsible for each activity. The network for the project is shown in Fig. 9.30. Most programmes provide for output in several different forms suitable, for example, for the customer, production planning dept., production control, etc., and some of the input will consist of instructions to specify the type and format of output required. It is usual in the output to have the definitions (event numbers, descriptions, etc.) on the left-hand side of the page and the results on the right of the page. Each line of output represents one activity, and each activity is identified by its event numbers and, for convenience, by its description.

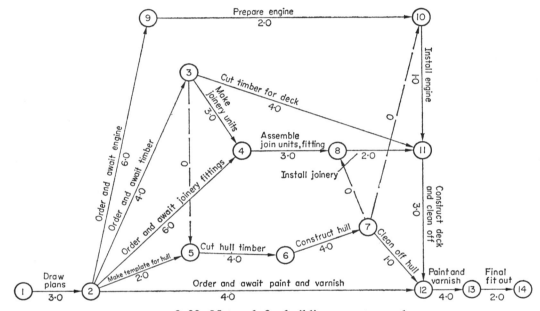

FIGURE 9.30. Network for building a motor yacht

In this example the output from the first run is shown in Fig. 9.31, which gives the results in the format specified by the output parameters. The activities are listed in order of increasing total float. The last total float is −1·8 weeks and the critical path is 1 2 3 5 6 7 8 11 12 13 14. The project cannot be completed by the scheduled end date and consequently either activity durations and/or the network itself must be modified.

The second network shows the modified arrangement and duration of activities designed to reduce the project duration by at least 1·8 weeks and meet the scheduled finish date of 8th October (Fig. 9.32).

The output from the second run is shown in the sequences from Fig. 9.33 to Fig. 9.39. Fig. 9.33 is a complete list of results suitable for use by the production planning department. The activities are listed in order of increasing total float, hence the most critical activities appear at the top of the page. There is now a positive total float of 0·2 weeks, the critical path being through event numbers 1 30 31 5 6 7 8 11 12 13 14. Dummies are still included in this output, but since they are of little practical value they can be, and are, omitted from the other outputs.

Fig. 9.34 contains precisely the same information as the previous output, but in this case the

CONSTRUCTION OF A MOTOR YACHT   FLOATSHIP + CO. LTD   ORDER: TOTAL FLOAT   PAGE 1
           RUN NUMBER: 1   ACTIVITY PERT   BY SEQUENCE ORDER
           REPORT DATE: 08MAR65

BEGIN EVENT	ENDING EVENT	DEPT.	PROJECT	DESCRIPTION	ACT DUR	EARL FINISH	LATEST FINISH	TOTAL FLOAT
*1	2	OFFICE	MY039	DRAW PLANS	3.0	28APR65	13APR65	- 1.8
2	3	OFFICE	MY039	ORDER AND AWAIT TIMBER	4.0	26MAY65	13MAY65	- 1.8
3	5		MY039	D	.0	26MAY65	13MAY65	- 1.8
5	6	YARD	MY039	CUT TIMBER FOR HULL	4.0	24JUN65	11JUN65	- 1.8
6	7	YARD	MY039	CONSTRUCT HULL	4.0	22JUL65	09JUL65	- 1.8
7	8		MY039	D	.0	22JUL65	09JUL65	- 1.8
8	11	YARD	MY039	INSTALL FITTINGS + JOINERY	2.0	05AUG65	23JUL65	- 1.8
11	12	YARD	MY039	CONSTRUCT DECK + CLEAN OFF	3.0	26AUG65	13AUG65	- 1.8
12	13	YARD	MY039	PAINT + VARNISH	4.0	07OCT65	24SEP65	- 1.8
13	14*	YARD	MY039	FINAL FIT OUT	2.0	21OCT65	08OCT65	- 1.8
7	10		MY039	D	.0	22JUL65	16JUL65	- .8
10	11	YARD	MY039	INSTALL ENGINE	1.0	29JUL65	23JUL65	- .8
2	5	YARD	MY039	MAKE TEMPLATE FOR HULL	2.0	12MAY65	13MAY65	.2
3	4	YARD	MY039	MAKE JOINERY UNITS	3.0	17JUN65	18JUN65	.2
4	8	YARD	MY039	ASSEMBLE JOINERY UNITS + FITTINGS	3.0	08JUL65	09JUL65	.2
2	4	OFFICE	MY039	ORDER AND AWAIT JOINERY FITTINGS	6.0	10JUN65	18JUN65	1.2
7	12	YARD	MY039	CLEAN OFF HULL	1.0	29JUL65	13AUG65	2.2
2	9	OFFICE	MY039	ORDER AND AWAIT ENGINE	6.0	10JUN65	02JUL65	3.2
9	10	YARD	MY039	PREPARE ENGINE	2.0	24JUN65	16JUL65	3.2
3	11	YARD	MY039	CUT TIMBER FOR DECK	4.0	24JUN65	23JUL65	4.2
2	12	OFFICE	MY039	ORDER AND AWAIT PAINT + VARNISH	4.0	26MAY65	13AUG65	11.2

FIGURE 9.31. Output from first run on construction of motor yacht

activities are ordered by the earliest finish date. This type of output would be of value to the customer who could use it to evaluate the progress of the project. If the project is running according to plan, the activities above the current date in the earliest finish date column should have been completed.

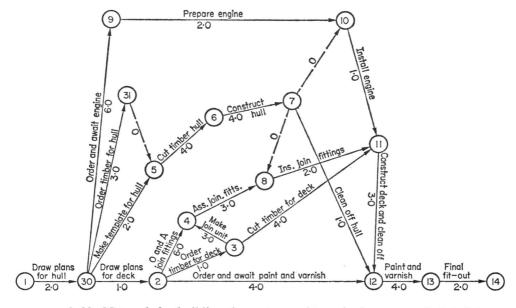

FIGURE 9.32. Network for building the motor yacht, revised to meet scheduled date

BEGIN EVENT	ENDING EVENT	DEPT	PROJECT	DESCRIPTION	ACT DUR	EARL FINISH	LATEST FINISH	TOTAL FLOAT
1*	30	OFFICE	MYO39	DRAW PLANS FOR HULL	2.0	21APR65	22APR65	.2
30	31	OFFICE	MYO39	ORDER TIMBER FOR HULL	3.0	12MAY65	13MAY65	.2
31	5		MYO39	D	.0	12MAY65	13MAY65	.2
5	6	YARD	MYO39	CUT TIMBER FOR HULL	4.0	10JUN65	11JUN65	.2
6	7	YARD	MYO39	CONSTRUCT HULL	4.0	08JUL65	09JUL65	.2
7	8		MYO39	D	.0	08JUL65	09JUL65	.2
8	11	YARD	MYO39	INSTALL FITTINGS + JOINERY	2.0	22JUL65	23JUL65	.2
11	12	YARD	MYO39	CONSTRUCT DECK + CLEAN OFF	3.0	12AUG65	13AUG65	.2
12	13	YARD	MYO39	PAINT + VARNISH	4.0	23SEP65	24SEP65	.2
13	14*	YARD	MYO39	FINAL FIT OUT	2.0	07OCT65	08OCT65	.2
30	2	OFFICE	MYO39	DRAW PLANS FOR DECK	1.0	28APR65	06MAY65	1.2
30	5	YARD	MYO39	MAKE TEMPLATE FOR HULL	2.0	05MAY65	13MAY65	1.2
2	4	OFFICE	MYO39	ORDER AND AWAIT JOINERY FITTINGS	6.0	10JUN65	18JUN65	1.2
4	8	YARD	MYO39	ASSEMBLE JOINERY UNITS + FITTINGS	3.0	01JUL65	09JUL65	1.2
7	10		MYO39	D	.0	08JUL65	16JUL65	1.2
10	11	YARD	MYO39	INSTALL ENGINE	1.0	15JUL65	23JUL65	1.2
2	3	OFFICE	MYO39	ORDER TIMBER FOR DECK	1.0	05MAY65	27MAY65	3.2
3	4	YARD	MYO39	MAKE JOINERY UNITS	3.0	26MAY65	18JUN65	3.2
30	9	OFFICE	MYO39	ORDER AND AWAIT ENGINE	6.0	02JUL65	02JUL65	4.2
9	10	YARD	MYO39	PREPARE ENGINE	2.0	17JUN65	16JUL65	4.2
7	12	YARD	MYO39	CLEAN OFF HULL	1.0	15JUL65	13AUG65	4.2
3	11	YARD	MYO39	CUT TIMBER FOR DECK	4.0	02JUN65	23JUL65	7.2
2	12	OFFICE	MYO39	ORDER AND AWAIT PAINT + VARNISH	4.0	26MAY65	13AUG65	11.2

FIGURE 9.33. Output from second run giving complete list of results suitable for production planning department

DEPT	PROJECT	DESCRIPTION	ACT DUR	EARL FINISH	LATEST FINISH	TOTAL FLOAT
OFFICE	MYO39	DRAW PLANS FOR HULL	2.0	21APR65	22APR65	.2
OFFICE	MYO39	DRAW PLANS FOR DECK	1.0	28APR65	06MAY65	1.2
YARD	MYO39	MAKE TEMPLATE FOR HULL	2.0	05MAY65	13MAY65	1.2
OFFICE	MYO39	ORDER TIMBER FOR DECK	1.0	05MAY65	27MAY65	3.2
OFFICE	MYO39	ORDER TIMBER FOR HULL	3.0	12MAY65	13MAY65	.2
YARD	MYO39	MAKE JOINERY UNITS	3.0	26MAY65	18JUN65	3.2
OFFICE	MYO39	ORDER AND AWAIT PAINT + VARNISH	4.0	26MAY65	13AUG65	11.2
OFFICE	MYO39	ORDER AND AWAIT ENGINE	6.0	02JUN65	02JUL65	4.2
YARD	MYO39	CUT TIMBER FOR DECK	4.0	02JUN65	23JUL65	7.2
YARD	MYO39	CUT TIMBER FOR HULL	4.0	10JUN65	11JUN65	.2
OFFICE	MYO39	ORDER AND AWAIT JOINERY FITTINGS	6.0	10JUN65	18JUN65	1.2
YARD	MYO39	PREPARE ENGINE	2.0	17JUN65	16JUL65	4.2
YARD	MYO39	ASSEMBLE JOINERY UNITS + FITTINGS	3.0	01JUL65	09JUL65	1.2
YARD	MYO39	CONSTRUCT HULL	4.0	08JUL65	09JUL65	.2
YARD	MYO39	INSTALL ENGINE	1.0	15JUL65	23JUL65	1.2
YARD	MYO39	CLEAN OFF HULL	1.0	15JUL65	13AUG65	4.2
YARD	MYO39	INSTALL FITTINGS + JOINERY	2.0	22JUL65	23JUL65	.2
YARD	MYO39	CONSTRUCT DECK + CLEAN OFF	3.0	12AUG65	13AUG65	.2
YARD	MYO39	PAINT + VARNISH	4.0	23SEP65	24SEP65	.2
YARD	MYO39	FINAL FIT OUT	2.0	07OCT65	08OCT65	.2

FIGURE 9.34. Output from second run with activities ordered by earliest finish date

FLOATSHIP + CO. LTD
CONSTRUCTION OF A MOTOR YACHT · ACTIVITY PERT · ORDER: DEPT · PAGE 1
RUN NUMBER: 2 · BY PLANNED START
REPORT DATE: 15MAR65 · BY TOTAL FLOAT

DEPT	PROJECT	DESCRIPTION	ACT DUR	PLANNED START	PLANNED FINISH	ACTUAL FINISH	REMARKS
YARD	MYO39	MAKE TEMPLATE FOR HULL	2.0	21APR65	05MAY65		
YARD	MYO39	MAKE JOINERY UNITS	3.0	05MAY65	26MAY65		
YARD	MYO39	CUT TIMBER FOR DECK	4.0	05MAY65	02JUN65		
YARD	MYO39	CUT TIMBER FOR HULL	4.0	12MAY65	10JUN65		
YARD	MYO39	PREPARE ENGINE	2.0	02JUN65	17JUN65		
YARD	MYO39	CONSTRUCT HULL	4.0	10JUN65	08JUL65		
YARD	MYO39	ASSEMBLE JOINERY UNITS + FITTINGS	3.0	10JUN65	01JUL65		
YARD	MYO39	INSTALL FITTINGS + JOINERY	2.0	08JUL65	22JUL65		
YARD	MYO39	INSTALL ENGINE	1.0	08JUL65	15JUL65		
YARD	MYO39	CLEAN OFF HULL	1.0	08JUL65	15JUL65		
YARD	MYO39	CONSTRUCT DECK + CLEAN OFF	3.0	22JUL65	12AUG65		
YARD	MYO39	PAINT + VARNISH	4.0	12AUG65	23SEP65		
YARD	MYO39	FINAL FIT OUT	2.0	23SEP65	07OCT65		

FIGURE 9.35. Departmental printout with activities listed in order of planned start dates

Figures 9.35 and 9.36 are departmental printouts with the activities listed in order of planned start (earliest start) dates. All the activities for that department are listed and this document, therefore, is the production plan for the department. Notice that no finish dates are included but a blank column is provided in which the actual finish date may be entered. This information can be

FLOATSHIP + CO. LTD
CONSTRUCTION OF A MOTOR YACHT · ACTIVITY PERT · ORDER: DEPT · PAGE 1
RUN NUMBER: 2 · BY PLANNED START
REPORT DATE: 15MAR65 · BY TOTAL FLOAT

DEPT	PROJECT	DESCRIPTION	ACT DUR	PLANNED START	PLANNED FINISH	ACTUAL FINISH	REMARKS
OFFICE	MYO39	DRAW PLANS FOR HULL	2.0	05APR65	21APR65		
OFFICE	MYO39	ORDER TIMBER FOR HULL	3.0	21APR65	12MAY65		
OFFICE	MYO39	DRAW PLANS FOR DECK	1.0	21APR65	28APR65		
OFFICE	MYO39	ORDER AND AWAIT ENGINE	6.0	21APR65	02JUN65		
OFFICE	MYO39	ORDER AND AWAIT JOINERY FITTINGS	6.0	28APR65	10JUN65		
OFFICE	MYO39	ORDER TIMBER FOR DECK	1.0	28APR65	05MAY65		
OFFICE	MYO39	ORDER AND AWAIT PAINT + VARNISH	4.0	28APR65	26MAY65		

FIGURE 9.36. Departmental printout with activities listed in order of planned start dates

fed back to the production control department and used for updating the network (Chapter 13). The use of *planned start* date rather than *earliest start* date has obvious psychological advantages!

Figures 9.37 and 9.38 are the bar chart equivalents of the previous two figures, showing earliest start and finish dates. (Latest dates—either start or finish—have been excluded from all outputs intended for use on the shop floor, lest they should provide encouragement for delays!).

Finally Fig. 9.39, unlike all the previous outputs, is concerned with events and not activities. In the input certain key events were specified corresponding to major landmarks in the project. This output lists the key events in order of their planned (earliest) start dates. The slack on each event is given. This type of output is designed for the project manager or company executive who, whilst concerned with the overall progress of the project, is normally unconcerned with the details.

```
                                      FLOATSHIP + CO. LTD
CONSTRUCTION OF A MOTOR YACHT           ACTIVITY PERT          ORDER: DEPT                    ·PAGE 1
         RUN NUMBER:  2                                               BY PLANNED START
         REPORT DATE: 15MAR65                                         BY TOTAL FLOAT


DEPT     PROJECT                             05APR    21APR    05MAY    19MAY    02JUN    17JUN
                        DESCRIPTION            1        1        1        1        1        1

YARD     MY039    MAKE TEMPLATE FOR HULL          XXXXXXXXXX
YARD     MY039    MAKE JOINERY UNITS                        XXXXXXXXXXXXXXX
YARD     MY039    CUT TIMBER FOR DECK                       XXXXXXXXXXXXXXXXXX
YARD     MY039    CUT TIMBER FOR HULL                              XXXXXXXXXXXXXXXXXXX
YARD     MY039    PREPARE ENGINE                                           XXXXXXXXXX

YARD     MY039    CONSTRUCT HULL                                                 XXXXXXXXXXXXX
YARD     MY039    ASSEMBLE JOINERY UNITS + FITTINGS                              XXXXXXXXXXXXX
YARD     MY039    INSTALL FITTINGS + JOINERY
YARD     MY039    INSTALL ENGINE
YARD     MY039    CLEAN OFF HULL

YARD     MY039    CONSTRUCT DECK + CLEAN OFF
YARD     MY039    PAINT + VARNISH
YARD     MY039    FINAL FIT OUT
```

FIGURE 9.37. Bar chart equivalent of Fig. 9.35 showing earliest start and finish dates

```
                                      FLOATSHIP + CO. LTD
CONSTRUCTION OF A MOTOR YACHT           ACTIVITY PERT          ORDER: DEPT                    PAGE 1
         RUN NUMBER:  2                                               BY PLANNED START
         REPORT DATE: 15MAR65                                         BY TOTAL FLOAT


DEPT     PROJECT                             05APR    21APR    05MAY    19MAY    02JUN    17JUN
                        DESCRIPTION            1        1        1        1        1        1

OFFICE   MY039    DRAW PLANS FOR HULL           XXXXXXXXXX
OFFICE   MY039    ORDER TIMBER FOR HULL                     XXXXXXXXXXXXXX
OFFICE   MY039    DRAW PLANS FOR DECK                       XXXXX
OFFICE   MY039    ORDER AND AWAIT ENGINE                    XXXXXXXXXXXXXXXXXXXXXXXXXXXXX
OFFICE   MY039    ORDER AND AWAIT JOINERY FITTINGS                 XXXXXXXXXXXXXXXXXXXXXXXXXXXXXX

OFFICE   MY039    ORDER TIMBER FOR DECK                     XXXXX
OFFICE   MY039    ORDER AND AWAIT PAINT + VARNISH           XXXXXXXXXXXXXXXXXXX
```

FIGURE 9.38. Bar chart equivalent of Fig. 9.36 showing earliest start and finish dates

```
                                      FLOATSHIP + .CO. LTD
CONSTRUCTION OF A MOTOR YACHT             EVENT PERT          ORDER: PLANNED DATE            PAGE 1
         RUN NUMBER:  2                                               BY SLACK
         REPORT DATE: 15MAR65


                    EVENT      REP                          PLANNED   SLACK
                    NUMBER     CODE    DESCRIPTION           DATE

                      30        MD    PLANS FOR HULL COMPLETED    21APR65    .2
                       2        MD    PLANS FOR DECK COMPLETED    28APR65   1.2
                       7        MD    HULL CONSTRUCTED            08JUL65    .2
                      11        MD    INSTALLATIONS COMPLETED     22JUL65    .2
                      12        MD    DECK LAID                   12AUG65    .2

                      14*       MD    READY FOR SEA TRIALS        07OCT65    .2
```

FIGURE 9.39. Output showing key events in order of planned start dates [Figs. 9.29—9.39 reproduced by permission, International Computing Services Ltd.]

Resources—Aggregation and Allocation

Resource aggregation is a comparatively simple procedure and the output consists of either lists or histogrammes showing the total requirements per resource per period. There are occasions where such information might be of value. When the computer programme does not provide for resource allocation an aggregation of resources will indicate which periods and which resources are over-loaded. It is then possible either to manually reschedule the activities using these resources during the overload periods to obtain extra resources, or to subcontract some of the work.

Unless the factory is working considerably under capacity, some form of resource allocation is normally necessary, and a procedure often adopted in computer-based network analysis is as follows[5]:

1. Aggregate resources.
2. Identify periods of overload.
3. Reschedule activities during these periods as follows:
   (a) Delay activities in order of decreasing total float by a period up to the allowed maximum delay.
   (b) If overload still occurs use additional resources available.
   (c) If overload still occurs allow overload to stand.

This is far from perfect procedure. No attempt has been made to overcome resource overloads by moving activities forward, nor is any attempt made to compare the cost of extra resources with either the cost of project delay or the cost of subcontracting work. The difficulty of dealing with resource allocation in a routine manner is illustrated by the fact that only recently has resource allocation become a feature of network analysis computer programmes. Allocation is often a time-consuming routine by computer standards and, whilst it is no doubt possible to devise more exhaustive routines, it is doubtful whether the extra cost in computing time is worth the marginal extra benefits. The procedure outlined above has been available for several years and is regarded by many users as sufficiently accurate and exhaustive for all practical purposes.

Multi-Project Production Planning

Network analysis was originally developed for use on large single projects of the type mentioned at the beginning of this chapter, and this still remains the most important application of the technique. Recently, however, greater use has been made of network planning procedures for the simultaneous manufacture of several items. This type of application is best dealt with on a computer, and contemporary network analysis programmes, which have provision for up to 15 000 activities, are easily capable of dealing with several quite large projects.

Perhaps the main thing to avoid is compromise. Network analysis is such an effective planning procedure that, unless all the projects in any particular situation are planned in this way, there is a very real danger that those to which network analysis is applied will progress at the expense of the remainder. One of the important advantages of this procedure is that it highlights critical activities and encourages those responsible to make a real effort, not only to meet the required finish dates but also to 'get off the critical path!' Under this sort of influence there is little incentive to worry unduly about other projects which do not appear in the limelight.

To use network analysis on several projects the following additional information is required:

1. The activities in each network must be separately identifiable, either by using different event numbers or by the use of a prefix letter to identify the project.
2. In addition to responsibility codes to identify which department is responsible for the activities, a further code must be used to identify the project so that the output for each project and each department can be collected together if necessary.

---

[5] An alternative procedure in which activities are scheduled, in each period, up to the resource limit is described in: J. D. Weist, 'A heuristic model for scheduling large projects with limited resources', *Management Sci.*, Feb., 359–377 (1967).

One of the difficulties in using this method for multi-project planning is to define the relative importance of each project. For example, if three projects are running concurrently and at any time one department is responsible for processing an item from each and each item has the same total float and start date, which is the most important? To some extent this problem can be overcome by deciding upon the order of priority of the projects and communicating this to all concerned; alternatively schedule dates may be used to indicate priorities. Nevertheless, this assumes firstly that priorities remain constant and that decisions about activities will necessarily be resolved in relation to the priority of the overall projects, whereas there may be occasions when it is preferable to do jobs from less important projects first (when, for example, the set-up cost of a machine is substantially less if two or more jobs are done in this order rather than in order of project priority).

VARIATIONS ON CONVENTIONAL NETWORK ANALYSIS

Throughout this chapter we have concentrated on one particular method of constructing network diagrams, namely the method in which activities or jobs are represented by arrows, i.e. the *arrow diagram* or *activity on arrow* method. An alternative approach represents activities or jobs by circles or nodes, and is known variously as the *activity on node, precedence,* or *circle and link* method.[6] For example, the two arrow diagrams shown in Fig. 9.40 can be redrawn as the activity on node diagrams shown in Fig. 9.41.

The advantages of this type of network construction which, nevertheless, is not generally adopted are:

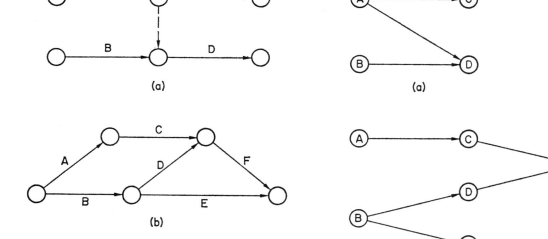

FIGURE 9.40. Arrow diagrams   FIGURE 9.41. Activity on node diagrams

[6] For a lengthier description of this method see J. J. Moder and C. R. Phillips, *Project Management with CPM and PERT*, Reinhold, New York, 1964.

R. A. Milligan and D. F. Brooks, 'Precedence diagrams for critical path analysis', *The Engineer*, 5th April, 556–557; 12th April, 594–595; 19th April, 636–637 (1968).

1. The diagrams are simpler both to construct and interpret, mainly because there is no necessity to use dummies.
2. The diagrams are easy to modify.
3. Description of activities by a single number rather than a pair of numbers is possible.

Network calculations are performed in much the same manner as before. For example, consider the simple network shown previously in Fig. 9.41(a). Given the duration of each of the activities the earliest and latest start and finish dates can be calculated (see Fig. 9.42).

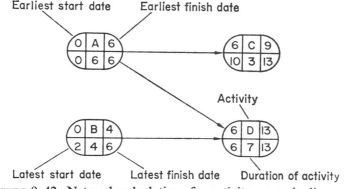

FIGURE 9.42. Network calculations for activity on node diagrams

In the past network analysis has been criticized because of the difficulty of altering the network construction in the light of experience or circumstance, during the actual performance of jobs. In other words it has been suggested that there is inadequate connection between the planning stage, during which the network is constructed, and the usage stage, during which the network and the activity start and finish dates are used to schedule and control the overall project.

In some cases, particularly when concerned with new or novel projects never before undertaken, the initial network drawn up during the project planning stage proves either impractical or disadvantageous in use. In many cases, because for example of a delay in certain parts of the project, or because of unforeseen snags and circumstances, it becomes necessary to modify part of the network in order to undertake part of the project in a different manner to that initially envisaged. Often during the planning stage alternative methods of undertaking the project are evident, but because such alternatives cannot be included in conventional network analysis, one of these alternatives is chosen in the hope that in practice this will prove to be the best method.

Network analysis, as defined by Crowston and Thompson,

is commonly considered to be a technique for planning and scheduling projects—the planning phase is usually identified with the construction of the project graph, during which time specific decisions are made on the method of performing jobs as well as their technological ordering. At the same time standard times are assigned to these jobs. At the completion of the planning stage it is possible, using the conventional . . . calculations, to schedule the start time of each job in the project. Unless several different plans are evaluated in this way, or unless the technique of job crashing is used, there is no interaction between the planning and the scheduling phase . . .[7]

[7] W. Crowston and G. L. Thompson, 'Decision C.P.M.: A method for simultaneous planning, scheduling, and control of projects', *Operations Res.* **15**, No. 3, 407–426 (1967).

In order to ensure that projects are completed in the optimum manner, it would be necessary for:

1. All alternative methods of completing the project, i.e. different job durations and technological orderings, to be included in the network.
2. The effects and the merits of alternative methods to be considered at (a) the planning stage and (b) throughout the usage or control stage of the project.

In this chapter we are concerned primarily with production planning using network analysis, nevertheless it is pertinent to point out that, in order to overcome the discontinuity between planning and control, attempts have been made to devise methods of constructing and using networks which show the several possible ways of completing the project rather than only one method. This type of network can be described as a *generalized* or *probabilistic* network and has the merit of permitting alternative methods to be evaluated during the completion or control of the project.[8]

Several methods of treating this more complex type of network have been suggested and tested but, as yet, the use of this logical extension of conventional network analysis is not sufficiently straightforward to render it a useful management technique.

SUMMARY

In this chapter we have been concerned with the planning uses of network analysis.

Network analysis is one of many titles for planning and control technique in which arrows are used to represent time-consuming jobs, the arrows then being arranged in a diagram to represent the sequence of jobs and their dependence upon one another.

Network analysis is a popular, widely used and powerful planning tool, particularly valuable for large and complex projects. It is, however, only a tool and its value depends entirely upon the manner in which it is used and the data upon which it is based.

Activity and project durations depend upon the resources allocated to them, consequently duration is a function of cost. Resource allocation in network analysis is usually a lengthy procedure and best accomplished by using one of the many computer programmes. Multiple time estimates may also be used for activities, but the assumptions on which the treatment is based necessitate careful use of this technique if misleading and inaccurate results are to be avoided.

For projects with over 200 to 300 activities a computer is necessary, particularly if resource allocation is to be undertaken. Many computer programmes exist which can be used for either single- or multi-project planning. The programmes are usually flexible and provide for the output of the basic results to be designed for specific purposes, i.e. for the customer, manager, shop floor, etc.

SELECTED READINGS

The following is an extremely simple introduction to the subject, adequately covering most of the topics in this chapter, except computers:

K. G. LOCKYER, *An Introduction to Critical Path Analysis*, 2nd ed., Pitman, London, 1967.

The following is a considerably enlarged version of this popular book—perhaps the best British book on the subject; although inferior to the second edition.

A. BATTERSBY, *Network Analysis*, 3rd ed., Macmillan, London, 1970.

K. G. LOCKYER, *Critical Path Analysis: Problems and Solutions*, Pitman, London, 1966.

---

[8] W. Crowston and G. L. Thompson, op. act.

S. E. Elmaghraby, 'On generalized activity networks', *J. Ind. Eng.*, **17**, No. 11 (1966).

A. A. B. Pritsker, 'GERT networks', *Prod. Engr.*, **47**, No. 10, 499–506 (1968).

The following is a good introductory text:

H. S. WOODGATE, *Planning by Network: Project Planning and Control using Network Techniques*, 2nd ed., Business Publications, London, 1967.

The following is an introductory book comparable to, but more comprehensive than, Lockyer's *Introduction to Critical Path Analysis*:

R. I. LEVIN and C. A. KIRKPATRICK, *Planning and Control with PERT/CPM*, McGraw-Hill, London, 1967.

The following book deals with, amongst other things, a method of Resource Allocation:

L. R. SHAFFER, J. B. RITTER and W. L. MEYER, *The Critical Path Method*, McGraw-Hill, London, 1965.

E. W. DAVIS, 'Resource allocation in project network models', *J. Ind. Eng.*, April (1966), 177–188.

This is a survey of methods of resource allocation in network analysis.

QUESTIONS

9.1. Construct a network diagram for the following activities:

Activity	A	B	C	D	E	F	G	H	J	K	L	M	N	O
Necessary preceding activities	—	—	A	A B	C	C	D	D	E	E F	G H	H	L K	L M

9.2. Redraw the following network diagram so that the logic is retained and dummy activities are used correctly.

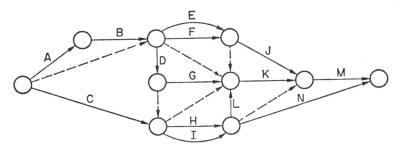

FIGURE Q9.2.

9.3. Draw an activity network for the following activities. Assuming that the project starts at day 0, calculate the earliest start and latest finish dates for all activities, and the project earliest completion date. Calculate also the total float on all activities and identify the critical path.

Activity	A	B	C	D	E	F	G	H	I
Immediate predecessors	—	—	A	A B	B C	C D	C D	E F	E G F
Activity duration (days)	3	5	6	2	4	7	3	4	5

9.4. In the following network, assuming that the project starts at day 0, what is the probability that the project will be completed by day 26?

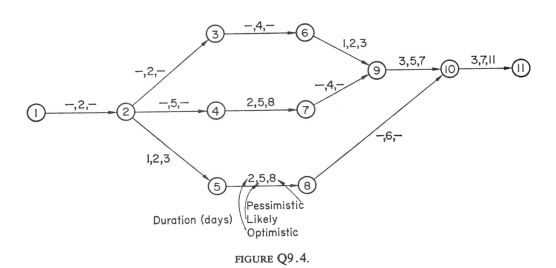

FIGURE Q9.4.

9.5. The following table describes the various activities of a small project. What is the probability that the project will be completed in $22\frac{1}{2}$ days or less?

Activity	Immediate predecessor(s)	Estimates of activity duration (days)		
		Optimistic	Likely	Pessimistic
A	—	2	4	6
B	A	1	5	9
C	A	—	9	—
D	C	5	6	7
E	B	5	7	9
F	B	4	10	16
G	D E	—	7	—
H	F	6	9	12

9.6. The manufacture of a piece of engineering equipment involves twelve separate jobs (A–L inclusive). The table below gives the normal duration of these jobs. The necessary dependencies of the jobs upon one another are also shown in the table. It is possible to reduce the normal duration of many of the jobs if additional money is spent on resources.

The normal total cost of the project would be £1 500, which includes a fixed cost of £200 and indirect costs which are charged at £25 per day.

What is the minimum duration of the project irrespective of cost and what is the least cost duration? Draw a curve of total cost versus project duration.

Notice that because of unavoidable constraints on the delivery of materials job H cannot start before the seventh day, and because of further constraints job B must on no account be finished later than day 14.

Job	Predecessors	Normal duration (days)	Number of days by which job may be reduced	Cost of shortening job duration (£/day)	Increments by which job might be reduced (days)
A	—	4	3	50	1
B	—	8	0	—	—
C	—	3	1	100	1
D	A	6	3	50	2
E	C	5	2	80	1
F	D	8	3	100	½
G	D	2	1	75	1
H	E	6	2	75	1
I	E	2	1	60	1
J	F	1	0	—	—
K	G B H	6	3	50	1
L	I	5	2	35	2

[Univ. of Bradford, Management Centre, Dip. Industrial Admin., *Production Management*, May 1968—45 minutes]

9.7. A small civil engineering project consists of 15 activities and can be represented by the network diagram below:

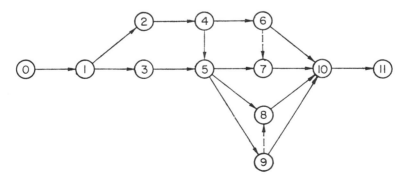

FIGURE Q9.7.

The duration of each of the activities is as follows:

Activity		Duration (days)
Begin event	End event	
0	1	10
1	2	5
1	3	6
2	4	3
3	5	4
4	5	3
4	6	8
5	7	4
5	8	5
5	9	9
6	7	Dummy
6	10	7
7	10	2
8	10	3
9	8	Dummy
9	10	6
10	11	9

(a) If the project is to start at, say, day 0 and is to end as soon as possible, calculate the total float on each activity and identify the critical path.

(b) Activity 3–5 is 'lay 6 inch pipe'.
   Activity 6–10 is 'lay 10 inch pipe'.

   The project is begun on day 0 but the supplier of the pipes informs the company that the 6 inch pipe will be delivered on day 18 and the 10 inch pipe on day 34.

   (i) What effect do these deliveries have on the earliest completion date of the project?
   (ii) What is the new critical path?
   (iii) What is the latest start date for the project to meet the new project completion date?

[Univ. of Bradford, Management Centre, Dip. Management Studies, *Production Management*, 1968—45 minutes]

9.8. If certain multiple time estimates are used for the duration of individual jobs in a project, probabilities may be calculated for the completion of the project or part of the project by certain schedule dates.

   What are the basic assumptions necessary for such calculations, and how justified are such assumptions in practice?

Under what circumstances is this procedure likely to be beneficial, and in what circumstances below the results likely to be either inaccurate or unrealistic?

Wherever possible, construct numerical examples to illustrate your answer.

The network diagram shown above has been drawn up by a project planning engineer. The diagram represents the sequence of jobs which will be undertaken during the manufacture of a large component which must be delivered to the customer by day 35. Using the estimates of the job durations given by the foremen of the various departments, the project planner has calculated event dates which indicate that the project will be completed one day before the scheduled completion date.

9.9.

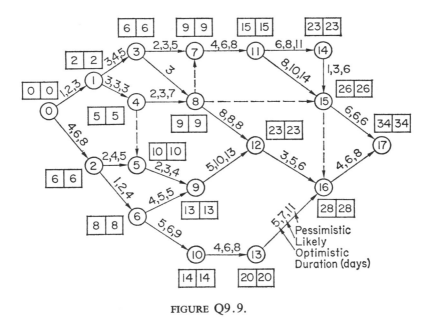

FIGURE Q9.9.

The information given on the diagram has been submitted to you, the project executive, for approval prior to being distributed to the various departments.

9.10. The following table gives the durations of the individual jobs in a complex project and shows the sequential relationship between the jobs. The activities are not listed in order of occurrence and the letters refer to events. It is possible to reduce the duration of some of the jobs to the extent shown in column (4) at an incremental cost per week saved as shown in column (5).

The target time for completing the project is 23 weeks, and the benefits of completion before the target date are estimated at £160 per week saved.

Find the most economical duration for the whole project, and the corresponding durations for individual jobs.

(1) Job designation	(2) Prior job(s)	(3) Duration of job (weeks)	(4) Number of weeks by which job can be shortened	(5) Cost of shortening job by 1 week (£)
P–L	—	5	2	120
P–D	—	10	0	—
P–M	—	9	2	80
L–Z	P–L	7	2	100
Z–D	L–Z	0	0	—
Z–Y	L–Z	5	3	50
D–Y	L–D P–D M–D Z–D	6	3	80/week for first week, thereafter 100/week
Y–R	Z–Y D–Y	3	1	170
M–R	P–M	10	2	30
M–D	P–M	2	0	—
L–D	P–D	4	3	100

[Univ. of London, Faculty of Economics, M.Sc. Business Studies, *Operational Research*, June 1968—45 minutes]

9.11. From the information given below, construct a network diagram.
(a) Neglecting resource considerations, what is the earliest finish date for the project?
(b) Assuming that each activity begins as early as possible, construct a graph showing the amount of resources used during each period.
(c) The maximum number of resources available is 19 men. Again, assuming that activities are begun as soon as possible, redraw the network so that the resources used at any time do not exceed 19 men, and so that a minimum project delay is incurred.
(d) What project delay is incurred through this adherence to the resource limit?

Activity	Immediate predecessor	Duration (days)	No. of men used
A	—	8	4
B	—	7	8
C	A	6	5
D	B	8	4
E	B	4	8
F	B	8	6
G	C D	5	5
H	E	6	4
I	F	6	5
J	G H I	10	6

N.B. Because of the nature of the work, jobs cannot be interrupted and must be finished once begun.

9.12. Unit Construction Ltd. is a small company engaged on the manufacture of high class furniture. About every year a new product is added to the already extensive range. In the past some difficulty has been experienced in coordinating the various activities involved in introducing the new product, hence this year it has been decided to draw up an activity network for the entire job. The managing director of the company has described the entire design and 'launching' process as follows, and this information is to be used in constructing the activity network:

Basic designs are prepared by our furniture design department, following which detailed drawings are produced and several prototypes made. The prototypes are tested in the laboratories, after which it is usually necessary to make minor design modifications.

Preliminary market research is normally begun after the detailed drawings have been produced, but of course full-scale market research cannot be started until after the original prototypes have been made. Incidentally, customer reactions uncovered during the full-scale market research are normally included in the final design along with modifications resulting from prototype laboratory testing. The main purpose of full-scale market research is to establish (1) the likely demand for the product—information which is required before we can begin to tool-up for production or layout the factory for manufacture, and (2) the nature of press adverts and TV commercials (we always do both).

Final design details are required before these two types of advertisement can be designed. Following the preparation of the TV film and the press copy, both sets of advertisements are approved by myself, then released. Copies of the press adverts are sent to the showrooms for point-of-sale advertising.

Once a final design has been established, the prototypes are modified and sent to our showroom where displays are established. When these displays are established and copies of the press adverts have been received, the showroom manager designs his final display. The display material is made by the showroom artists and should, of course, be ready in time for the delivery of the products to the showroom.

9.13. The diagram given below shows the sequence and interdependence of the eleven activities (A–K) which together constitute a small engineering project. Each of the circles represents an

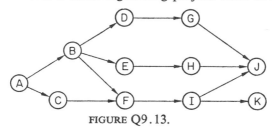

FIGURE Q9.13.

Activity	Duration (days)	Men required
A	2	4
B	4	3
C	3	6
D	5	5
E	6	7
F	3	4
G	4	6
H	7	8
I	6	3
J	8	7
K	4	10

activity and the arrows show the interdependence of these activities. This type of diagram is known variously as an *activity on node, precedence*, or *circle and link* diagram and is sometimes adopted in preference to the more usual *activity on arrow* diagram when using network analysis.

The durations (in days) of each of the activities are given in the table. Also given are the numbers of men required to complete each activity in the given time.

(a) Using either the type of diagram given or by redrawing the diagram in the conventional form, calculate the earliest completion date for the project, identify the critical path and calculate the total float on each activity. (Assume that the project is begun at day 0.)

(b) Assuming (i) that each activity is begun as soon as possible, and (ii) that each activity once begun cannot be interrupted, draw a graph to indicate the manpower requirements for each day during the project.

(c) What are the advantages of the *activity on node* type of network construction over the more conventional method?

[Univ. of Bradford, Post-Grad. Dip. Management Studies, *Production Management*, 1970— 35 minutes]

9.14. This morning the following information collected by the previous company network analyst on the installation of new production facilities was presented to you. Make a full analysis and propose a work schedule for the project. Report on what actions may be necessary to ensure that the facilities are ready for the September/October production peak this year.

The machines were ordered on 1st January, 1969 with a six months delivery promise. The plant manager requires a one or two week pilot production run, extending to at least three weeks if building modification work is in progress. The engineering department is to produce sub-nets for the temporary building modification and their removal, and machine installation. Approximate durations which assume that these three jobs do not overlap are given, together with other durations, on the skeleton network.

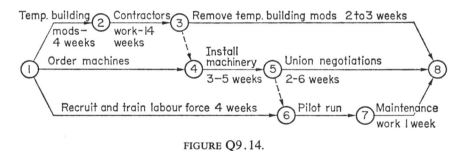

FIGURE Q9.14.

[Univs. of Lancaster and Sussex, M.Sc. Operational Research, *Paper* 4, 1969—35 minutes]

10

Planning for Mass Production—The Design of Assembly Lines

The widespread adoption of mass production techniques in industry is a comparatively recent phenomenon resulting, of course, from the desire to manufacture very large quantities of items cheaply. There has always been the need for individuals, or groups of individuals, to produce or acquire goods or items to satisfy the demands of others, but many of the present day large-scale systems resulted from the growth and demands of an affluent consumer society over the last fifty years.

It is not strictly true to say that the mass production concept is entirely a recent phenomenon; as long ago as 1792 Eli Whitney was making muskets with certain standardized design features and in large quantities. Isambard Brunel set up a plant in 1806 for the manufacture of pulley blocks at a rate of 100 000 per year, and the advantages of large-scale production were understood and used in several other industries, e.g. textiles, over 100 years ago.

Nevertheless, it was not until after Henry Ford began making the Model T Ford at his Highland Park plant in 1913 that mass production techniques were widely adopted in industry. It was at about this time that *making* became *manufacturing* and a new generation of production began.

Henry Ford, in his book *My Life and Work*[1] published in 1922, described this change as follows:

A Ford car contains about five thousand parts—that is counting screws, nuts, and all. Some of the parts are fairly bulky and some are almost the size of watch parts. In our first assembling we simply started to put a car together at a spot on the floor and workmen brought to it the parts as they were needed in exactly the same way that one builds a house. When we started to make parts it was natural to create a single department of the factory to make that part, but usually one workman performed all of the operations necessary on a small part. The rapid press of production made it necessary to devise plans of production that avoid having the workers falling over one another. The undirected worker spends more of his time walking about for materials and tools than he does in working; he gets small pay because pedestrianism is not a highly paid line.

The first step forward in assembly came when we began taking the work to the men instead of the men to the work . . . .

Along about April 1, 1913 we first tried the experiment of an assembly line. We tried it on assembling the flywheel magneto . . . .

I believe that this was the first moving line ever installed. The idea came from the overhead trolley that the Chicago packers use in dressing beef. We had previously assembled the flywheel magneto in the usual method. With one workman doing a complete job he could turn out from thirty-five to forty pieces in a nine hour day, or about twenty minutes to an assembly. What he did alone was then

---

[1] Henry Ford, in collaboration with Samuel Crowther, *My Life and Work*, Heinemann, London, 1922, pp. 79, 80, 81.

spread into twenty-nine operations; that cut down the assembly time to thirteen minutes ten seconds. Then we raised the height of the line eight inches—this was in 1914—and cut the time to seven minutes. Further experimenting with the speed that the work should move at cut the time down to five minutes. In short, the result is this: by aid of scientific study one man is now able to do somewhat more than four did only a comparatively few years ago. That line established the efficiency of the method and we now use it everywhere.

Henry Ford described his principles of assembly as being:

1. Place the tools and the men in the sequence of the operation so that each component part shall travel the least possible distance while in the process of finishing.
2. Use work slides or some other form of carrier so that when a workman completes his operation he drops the part always in the same place—which place must always be the most convenient place to hand—and if possible have gravity carry the part to the next workman for his operation.
3. Use sliding assembly lines by which the parts to be assembled are delivered at convenient distances.

Motor cars had been produced for about twenty years prior to 1913 but they were *made* in very small quantities, to individual requirements, in small factories, garages or stables using general purpose equipment and consequently at high cost. After 1913 they were *manufactured* in very large quantities in large purpose-designed factories, on special purpose equipment, in a small range of standard designs but comparatively cheaply. The first Model T Ford was made in 1908 and sold at $850. During that year 10 607 were made, but during the last year of manufacture—1926—1 800 000 cars were made to sell at about one-third of the original price.

Whilst the advantage of mass production is the ability to produce cheaply with unskilled labour, high machine utilization and low stock levels, the resultant disadvantages are inflexibility and the need for a high and stable demand to justify the large capital investment involved.

Assembly lines, sometimes called flow or production lines, are undoubtedly the principal feature of mass production systems. Whilst the details may differ somewhat, the concept remains the same—the items are manufactured or assembled as they pass through a series of work stations. Raw materials or components are fed in at the beginning of, and at certain points along, the assembly line, and finished goods are delivered from the end of the line. In the assembly of motor vehicles the chassis unit is delivered to the first work station on the line and the workers at subsequent stations add the engine, transmission, suspension, body, trim and so on, until the vehicle is completed. The total work content of the job, i.e. the total standard time for the job, is divided as evenly as possible amongst the stations on the line where a worker, or groups of workers, continually performs this same operation on successive items.

Whilst the motor industry is perhaps the most apparent example of mass production it is untypical in certain respects. Work stations on assembly lines in the motor industry normally consist of more than one worker, as it is often impossible for one man to handle the large parts involved. For example, assembling the engine to a chassis normally requires two workers working from opposite sides of the line. Often in the motor industry the line moves continuously, the workers riding along to complete their operation then walking back to the next vehicle to perform the same operation. In other industries, such as the manufacture of domestic appliances, radios, televisions, etc., assembly lines usually consist of benches or belts along which the work is passed, the workers sitting at stations along one or both sides of the line, passing the work to one another along the line either at specified times or when they have completed their operations.

In many cases this type of production can be achieved without the use of human operators. For example, a *transfer line* consists of a series of work stations at which automatic tools perform operations. The workpieces are fed onto the line, move along and are automatically clamped at each station where one or more tools perform set machining cycles.

The output of assembly lines and transfer lines is determined by the *cycle time* at the stations. The cycle time at each station must be the same since each one must deal with the same number of items. If the cycle time is one minute, then the output from the last station, and consequently from the line, is one item every minute or sixty items per hour. Whilst it is comparatively easy to determine the cycle time in this manner, the allocation of the work to the stations is a somewhat more complex matter, and this aspect of assembly line design is normally referred to as assembly line balancing.

SIMPLE ASSEMBLY LINE BALANCING

Before we deal with this problem let us first clarify some of the terminology we will be using.

Work Elements (sometimes called Minimum Rational Work Elements)

As we have seen in Chapters 5 and 6, work can be divided into elements or even smaller components such as therbligs or basic motions. In the present context an element of work is the minimum feasible or practical subdivision of the total work content of the job. If, for example, part of a job is to drill six holes in a casting, a work study element would be 'drill one hole', but in assembly line balancing, since the objective is to determine which elements of work to allocate to each station, the logical element is 'drill six holes'. It would be pointless and illogical to subdivide this further since there would be no benefit in allocating parts of such a task to different work stations.

Work Stations

A combination of work elements to be performed serially forms a work station. In the type of assembly line we shall be considering, a work station is a physical location on the line normally staffed by a single worker.

Total Work Content

This is the total time required to complete the entire job, that is the total standard time for all the work elements in the job.

Work Station Time

This is the standard time *required* to complete the elements allocated to a particular work station.

Cycle Time

This is the amount of time *available* for the worker at a station to complete his work, which must of course be equal to or greater than the work station time.

The cycle time can be calculated, at least theoretically, from the required output. For example, if N items are to be produced in T minutes, then the cycle time should be equal to T divided by N.

$$C = \frac{T}{N}$$

Furthermore, given these two figures and knowing either the total work content or each of the element times (t), the minimum number of work stations ($n_{\min}$) can be calculated.

$$n_{\min} = \frac{N\Sigma t}{T}$$

In fact, since we must have a whole number of work stations, $n_{\min}$ will be the integer equal to or just greater than $N\Sigma t/T$. The average work station time ($\bar{c}$) is simply the total work content (Σt) divided by the number of stations.

$$\bar{c} = \frac{\Sigma t}{n}$$

But, almost invariably, this figure is less than the cycle time (C), and consequently a certain amount of idle time will exist. This idle time is referred to as balancing loss[2] and it occurs because, in practice, it is usually impossible to allocate elements to work stations so that all work station times are equal and correspond to the desired output rate of the assembly line.

$$\text{Balancing loss } (\%) = \frac{C - \bar{c}}{C} \times 100$$

$$\text{or } (\%) = \frac{n(C) - \Sigma t}{n(C)} \times 100$$

In practice, when designing assembly lines, we cannot normally achieve a situation such as that shown in Fig. 10.1 where perfect line balancing is achieved—work station times being the same

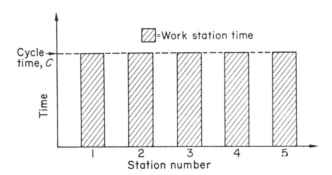

FIGURE 10.1. Perfectly balanced five-station assembly line

and each being equal to the desired cycle time. A situation such as the one shown in Fig. 10.2(a) will result if we are lucky, but often the result will be as shown in Fig. 10.2(b), in which neither the work station times are balanced nor is the maximum work station time equal to the desired cycle time.

Although we have spoken of and depicted idle time resulting from imperfect line balancing, in practice, periods of idleness caused by the difference between cycle times and the work station times rarely exist because a worker will normally be inclined to perform his work operations in the time he has available. In fact, a Parkinson's Law type of situation will exist in which the work will expand to fill the available time. Nevertheless, the consequences are precisely the same because an underutilization of labour will result.

---

[2] M. Kilbridge and L. Wester, 'The balance delay problem', *Management Sci.*, Oct. (1961).

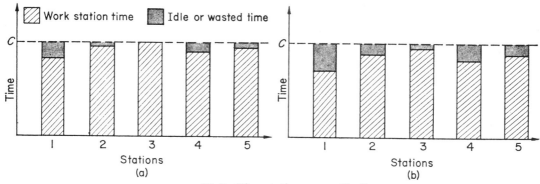

FIGURE 10.2. Five-station assembly line

It has been estimated that the balancing loss occurring in industry today is between 5 and 20 per cent.

The objective of assembly line balancing is that, given a desired cycle time or output rate, the minimum rational work elements and their standard times, and other constraints, one should attempt to assign work elements to work stations in order to:

(a) minimize idle time or balancing loss
(b) minimize the number of work stations
(c) distribute balancing loss evenly between stations
(d) avoid violating any constraints.

Constraints

There will of course be numerous constraints operating to govern or restrict the way in which work elements are allocated to work stations. For example, certain work elements will need to be performed before others (to use the usual example, holes must be drilled before being tapped). *Precedence* constraints such as this are determined by the nature of the product or the method of production. Furthermore, it may be necessary for some reason to allocate certain elements to the same station, or to adjacent stations, e.g. operations which cause a great deal of noise, or which produce dust or toxic gases, or operations which utilize the same piece of equipment. Conversely, it may be desirable or indeed necessary to ensure that certain operations are not allocated to the same or adjacent work stations. For example, elements involving work on opposite sides of a heavy product should not be allocated to the same single-person work station. Such considerations are referred to as *zoning* constraints.

An Analogy[3]

Assembly line balancing can be considered analogous to the following packing problem.

The despatch department of a large department store must pack a large quantity of different-sized blocks into several equal-sized boxes which are to be delivered to various locations by the store's van. The objective, of course, is to pack the blocks into the boxes leaving the minimum

---

[3] This analogy was previously used by M. Kilbridge and L. Wester, 'The balance delay problem', *Management Sci.*, Oct., 69–84 (1961).

amount of empty space. Complications arise because certain of the blocks must be packed together as they are to be delivered to the same customer; furthermore, many of the blocks must be packed into the boxes in a given order to correspond to the delivery order of the blocks and the route of the delivery van. If we regard the blocks in this example as minimum rational work elements and the boxes as station cycle times, then the analogy with the assembly line balancing problem is clear. The difficulty in solving such a problem will depend upon the sizes and the distribution of sizes of the blocks since, other things being equal, the higher the ratio of small to large blocks the easier the solution. Also the relationship of the sizes of the blocks to that of the boxes is important since again, other things being equal, the smaller the blocks are compared to the boxes the easier is the solution. Finally, the complexity of the problem is also dependent upon the number of constraints; the fewer the constraints the easier the solution.

The same considerations apply to the assembly line balancing problem, and consequently examination of this analogy should suggest suitable procedures for balancing assembly lines.

METHODS OF SIMPLE ASSEMBLY LINE BALANCING

As in so many areas of production management there are two methods of solving this problem, namely the analytical, largely objective method and the intuitive, largely subjective method. Analytical methods have been formulated only during the last fifteen years, consequently the alternative approach has been the convention for about forty years. The majority of the mathematical treatments that have been proposed are of academic or developmental value only, and consequently there continues a dependence on the well tried, if mathematically unattractive, methods.

The first analytical treatment of the assembly line balancing problem was developed by Bryton in 1954, whilst Salveson published a linear programming solution in 1955[4], as did Bowman in 1962[5]. Similar rigorous procedures have been suggested by Mitchell[6], Hoffman[7] and Klien[8] but they all suffer from the same disadvantage—they are impractical for large and realistic problems! Because of the nature of the problem and the inadequacy of these treatments, several authors and several organizations have developed heuristic methods of assembly line balancing, those suggested by Helgerson and Birnie (1961), Tonge (1961), Kilbridge and Wester (1961) and Arcus (1966) being perhaps the best known and the most suitable (see Selected Readings). Many of the heuristic treatments bear some resemblance to intuitive procedures and some are little more than formal statements of such procedures, a situation which may be taken as an endorsement of the basic suitability of some traditional practice.

The Kilbridge and Wester Method

This simple heuristic method of assembly line balancing is best described by means of an example.

Assembly of a simple component requires the performance of 21 work elements which are governed by certain precedence constraints, as shown in Fig. 10.3. This precedence diagram has

---

[4] M. E. Salveson, 'The assembly line balancing problem', *Trans. Am. Soc. Mech. Eng.*, **77**, Aug., 939 (1955).
[5] E. H. Bowman, *Operational Res.*, **8**, No. 3, 385 (1962).
[6] J. A. Mitchell, Rept. No. 6—94801-1-R3, *Westinghouse Research Laboratories* (1957).
[7] T. R. Hoffman, *Management Sci.*, **9**, No. 4, 551 (1959).
[8] M. Klien, *Operational Res.*, **11**, No. 2, 274 (1962).

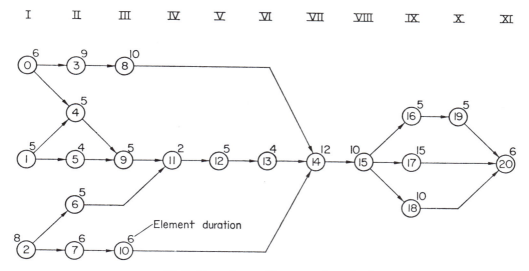

FIGURE 10.3. Precedence diagram of work elements

been constructed according to the procedure described by Jackson[9], namely that circles representing work elements are placed as far to the left as possible, and that all of the arrows joining circles slope to the right and are not vertical. The figures above the diagram are column numbers. Elements appearing in column I can be started immediately, those in column II can be begun only after one or more in column I have been completed, and so on.

The data shown on this diagram can now be represented in tabular form as shown in Table 10.1. Column (c) of this figure describes the lateral transferability of elements amc•gst columns, for example element 6 can be performed in column III as well as in column II without violating precedence constraints. Element 8 can also be performed in any of the columns IV to VI, likewise element 10. Element 3 can also be performed in any of the columns III and V provided element 8 is also transferred, likewise element 7.

Suppose that it is our objective to balance the assembly line for a cycle time of 36, then in this case we would proceed as follows:

1. Is there a duration in column (f) of the table equal to the cycle time of 36? *No.*
2. Select the largest duration in column (f) less than 36 *i.e. 19 for column I.*
3. Subtract 19 from 36 = 17.
4. Does one or more of the elements in the next column (II) equal 17? *No, the nearest is 16 for element nos. 4, 6 and 7 which will give a work station time of 35.*
5. Select the smallest duration from column (f) which is larger than 36 *i.e. 48 for columns I and II.*
6. Can one or more of the elements in columns I and II be transferred beyond column II so as to reduce the duration to 36? *No, but element 3 (with 8) plus 6 can be transferred to give a work station time of 34.*
7. Select the next largest duration from column (f) *i.e. 69 for columns I, II and III.*
8. Can one or more of the elements in columns I, II and III be transferred beyond column III so

[9] J. R. Jackson, 'A computing procedure for a line balancing problem', *Management Sci.*, 2, No. 3 (1956).

I

TABLE 10.1. Tabular presentation of data in Fig. 10.3.

Column no. in precedence diagram (a)	Element no. (b)	Transferability of element (c)	Element duration (d)	Duration for column (e)	Cumulative duration (f)
I	0		6		
	1		5		
	2		8	19	19
II	3	III–V (with 8)	9		
	4		5		
	5		4		
	6	III	5		
	7	III–V (with 10)	6	29	48
III	8	IV–VI	10		
	9		5		
	10	IV–VI	6	21	69
IV	11		2	2	71
V	12		5	5	76
VI	13		4	4	80
VII	14		12	12	92
VIII	15		10	10	102
IX	16		5		
	17	X	15		
	18	X	10	30	132
X	19		5	5	137
XI	20		6	6	143

as to reduce the duration to 36? *No, the nearest is elements* 3, 8, 7 *and* 10 *which would give a duration of* 38, *which is too large.*

9. Will an improved allocation of elements for station no. 1 be obtained by considering a large duration from column (f)? *No.*
10. Adopt the best allocation found previously *i.e. step* 4 *which gave a work station time of* 35.
11. Rewrite the table to show this allocation, and calculate new cumulative figures for column (f) *Table* 10.2.
12. Is there a duration in column (f) of the new table equal to 36? *Yes, for columns III and IV.*
13. Allocate the elements in these columns to the second work station and redraw the table showing new figures for column (f) *Table* 10.3.
14. Is there a duration in column (f) of the new table equal to the cycle time of 36? *No.*
15. Select the largest duration in column (f) which is less than 36 *i.e.* 31 *for columns V, VI, VII and VIII.*
16. Subtract 31 from 36 = 5.
17. Does one or more of the elements in the next column (IX) equal 5? *Yes, element* 16.
18. Allocate the columns concerned and that element to the work station and redraw the table *Table* 10.4.
19. Is there a duration in column (f) of the new table equal to 36? *Yes, for columns IX, X and XI.*
20. Allocate the element in these columns to the work station.

TABLE 10.2

Column no. in precedence diagram (a)	Element no. (b)	Transferability of element (c)	Element duration (d)	Duration of column (e)	Cumulative duration (f)
I	0		6		
	1		5		
	2		8		Station 1
II	4		5		
	6		5		
	7		6		(35)
III	3	IV–V (with 8)	9		
	9		5		
	5		4		
	10	IV–VI	6	24	24
IV	8	V–VI	10		
	11		2	12	36
V	12		5	5	41
VI	13		4	4	45
VII	14		12	12	57
VIII	15		10	10	67
IX	16		5		
	17	X	15		
	18	X	10	30	97
X	19		5	5	102
XI	20		6	6	108

All 21 elements have now been assigned to four work stations in the manner shown in Fig. 10.4, the balancing loss involved being:

$$\frac{n(C) - \Sigma t}{n(C)} \times 100$$

$$= \frac{4(36) - 143}{4(36)} \times 100$$

$$= 0 \cdot 7\%$$

As can readily be seen from the example, this heuristic method is rapid, easy and often quite efficient. The allocation of elements is basically determined by precedence relationships, lateral transferability of elements being used to aid allocation when necessary. The originators of this method offer the following comments to aid in the application of the method.

1. Permutability within columns is used to facilitate the selection of elements (tasks) of the length desired for optimum packing of the work stations. Lateral transferability helps to deploy the work elements (tasks) along the stations of the assembly line so they can be used where they best serve the packing solution.

2. Generally the solutions are not unique. Elements (tasks) assigned to a station which belong, after the assignment is made, in one column of the precedence diagram can generally be permuted within

TABLE 10.3

Column no. in precedence diagram (a)	Element no. (b)	Transferability of element (c)	Element duration (d)	Duration of column (e)	Cumulative duration (f)	
	0					Station 1
	1					
	2					
	4					
	6					
	7			35	(35)	
III	3		9			Station 2
	9		5			
	5		4			
	10		6			
	8		10			
IV	11		2	36	(36)	
V	12		5	5	5	
VI	13		4	4	9	
VII	14		12	12	21	
VIII	15		10	10	31	
IX	16		5			
	17	X	15			
	18	X	10	30	61	
X	19		5	5	66	
XI	20		6	6	72	

the column. This allows the line supervisor some leeway to alter the sequence of work elements (tasks) without disturbing optimum balance.

3. Long-time elements (tasks) are best disposed of first, if possible. Thus, if there is a choice between the assignment of an element of duration, say, 20 and the assignment of two elements of duration, say, 10 each, assign the larger element first. Small elements are saved for ease of manipulation at the end of the line. The situation is analogous to that of a paymaster dispensing the week's earnings in cash. He will count out the largest bills first. Thus, if the amount to be paid a worker is $77, the paymaster will give three $20 bills first, then one $10 bill, one $5 bill and two $1 bills in that order.

4. When moving elements laterally, the move is best made only as far to the right as is necessary to allow a sufficient choice of elements for the work station being considered.

In view of point 3 above, the *ranked positional weight* (RPW) method of assembly line balancing described next, might be considered a logical extension to the present method, in that in the RPW method a heuristic procedure is used which allocates elements to stations according to both their position in the precedence diagram and their duration.

Ranked Positional Weights

The *ranked positional weight* procedure was developed by Helgerson and Birnie of the General Electric Company in the late 1950's. It is a rapid, but approximate, method which has been shown

TABLE 10.4

Column no. in precedence diagram (a)	Element no. (b)	Transferability of element (c)	Element duration (d)	Duration of column (e)	Cumulative duration (f)	
	0					Station 1
	1					
	2					
	4					
	6					
	7			35	(35)	
	3					Station 2
	9					
	5					
	10					
	8					
	11			36	(36)	
V	12		5			Station 3
VI	13		4			
VII	14		12			
VIII	15		10			
IX	16		5	36	(36)	
IX	17		15			
	18		10	25	25	
X	19		5	5	30	
XI	20		6	6	36	

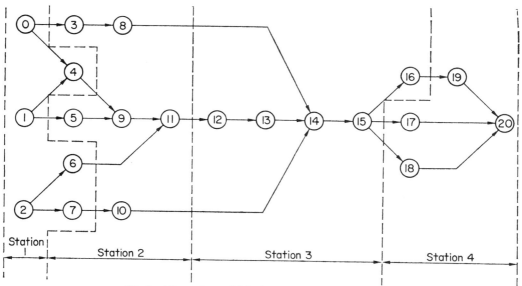

FIGURE 10.4. Allocation of 21 elements to four work stations

to provide acceptably good solutions quicker than many of the alternative methods. It is capable of dealing with both precedence and zoning constraints. The procedure is best illustrated by considering a simple example.

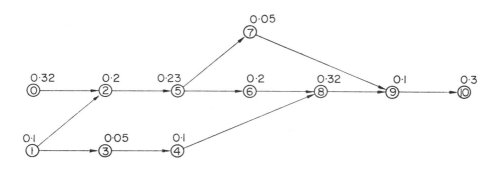

FIGURE 10.5. Element precedence diagram

Assembly of a very simple component involves 11 minimum rational work elements. There are constraints on the order in which these elements are to be undertaken, but there are no zoning constraints. Figure 10.5 is a precedence diagram in which the circles depict work elements. Element 2 must follow elements 0 and 1 and must precede element 5, etc. The standard element times (hours) are also shown in Fig. 10.5. In Fig. 10.6 this same information is listed—in the first column the element number is given, and in the second its standard time. The middle of the table shows the element precedences; for example, element 0 is immediately followed by element 2, which in turn is followed by 5, which is followed by 6 and 7, and so on. A single mark indicates the element which follows immediately, and crosses indicate elements which follow because of their relationship with other elements. The final column of the table gives the *positional weight* (PW) for each element.[10] This is calculated by summing the element's own standard time and the standard time for all following elements. Thus in the case of element 0:

$$
\begin{aligned}
PW = \text{element} \ \ 0 &= 0\cdot32 \\
+ \text{element} \ \ 2 &= 0\cdot20 \\
+ \text{element} \ \ 5 &= 0\cdot23 \\
+ \text{element} \ \ 6 &= 0\cdot20 \\
+ \text{element} \ \ 7 &= 0\cdot05 \\
+ \text{element} \ \ 8 &= 0\cdot32 \\
+ \text{element} \ \ 9 &= 0\cdot10 \\
+ \text{element} \ \ 10 &= 0\cdot30 = 1\cdot72
\end{aligned}
$$

---

[10] This layout, and also that of Tables 10.5 and 10.6 has been adopted for reasons of convenience and clarity. Whilst unnecessary in this very simple example, this presentation has been found valuable in more complex cases.

Element number	Element time (hours)	0	1	2	3	4	5	6	7	8	9	10	Positional weight
0	0.32	\		I			+	+	+	+	+	+	1.72
1	0.1		\	I	I	+	+	+	+	+	+	+	1.65
2	0.2			\			I	+	+	+	+	+	1.40
3	0.05				\	I				+	+	+	0.87
4	0.1					\				I	+	+	0.82
5	0.23						\	I	I	+	+	+	1.20
6	0.2							\		I	+	+	0.92
7	0.05								\		I	+	0.45
8	0.32									\	I	+	0.72
9	0.1										\	I	0.40
10	0.3											\	0.30

FIGURE 10.6. Precedence and positional weights table

The positional weight is, therefore, a measure of the size of an element and its position in the sequence of elements.

In Table 10.5 the elements, their times and immediate predecessors are given in order of decreasing positional weights.

We are required to design an assembly line with the minimum number of stations to provide a cycle time of 0·55 h (i.e. an output of 1·82 per hour). Using Table 10.5, elements are allocated to work stations in order of decreasing positional weights and without violating precedence constraints. Element 0 with the highest PW of 1·72 is allocated first to station 1. This allocation is acceptable because element 0 has no immediate predecessors, and furthermore its element time is less than the spare time available in station 1 (see Table 10.6).

Element 1 is next to be allocated since it has the next highest PW. It is acceptable in station 1 since no precedence constraints are violated and there is sufficient unassigned cycle time left to accommodate it.

The next highest PW belongs to element 2, but this cannot be assigned to station 1, even though its immediate predecessors have been assigned, because the unassigned station time remaining (0·13) is less than the element time (0·2).

Element 5 cannot be allocated because it must follow element 2, nor is there sufficient time available.

Element 6 cannot be allocated to station 2 for the same reasons.

TABLE 10.5. Elements in order of positional weights

Element no.	0	1	2	5	6	3	4	8	7	9	10	Total
Element time	0.32	0.1	0.2	0.23	0.2	0.05	0.1	0.32	0.05	0.1	0.3	1.97
PW	1.72	1.65	1.4	1.2	0.92	.87	.82	.72	.45	.40	.30	
Predecessors (Immediate)	—	—	0,1	2	5	1	3	4,6	5	7,8	9	

TABLE 10.6. Element allocation for cycle time of 0·55 hours

Work station	Element	PW	Immediate predecessor	Element time	Cumulative station time (X)	Unassigned station time $(C-X)$
1	0	1·72	–	0·32	0·32	0·23
	1	1·65	–	0·1	0·42	0·13
	3	0·87	1	0·05	0·47	0·08
2	2	1·4	0,1	0·2	0·2	0·35
	5	1·2	2	0·23	0·43	0·12
	4	0·82	3	0·1	0·53	0·02
3	6	0·92	5	0·2	0·2	0·35
	8	0·72	4,6	0·32	0·52	0·03
4	7	0·45	5	0·05	0·05	0·50
	9	0·4	7,8	0·1	0·15	0·40
	10	0·3	9	0·3	0·45	0·10

$C = 0·55$

Balancing loss $= \dfrac{4(0·55) - 1·97}{4(0·55)} \times 100 = 10·4\%$

Element 3 can be allocated to station 1 since its immediate predecessor is already allocated and there is sufficient time available.

Of the remaining elements only 7 is short enough for accommodation in station 1, but it cannot be allocated here because it must follow element 5.

The same procedure is now repeated for the remaining stations.

Four work stations are required for this assembly line, and the initial allocation gives a balancing loss of 10·4 per cent. Notice that there is unassigned time at each station, the largest work station time of 0·53 h occurring at station 2. In fact we now have a situation similar to the one depicted in Fig. 10.2(b).

For the specified output required (1·82 per hour), there is no better solution than the one given above, but if other considerations permit, the cycle time could be reduced to 0·53 h with a corresponding increase in output to 1·89 per hour and a reduction of balancing loss to 7 per cent. A reduction of the cycle time to less than 0·53 h would necessitate the use of five work stations.

There is really little point in retaining a cycle time of 0·55 h in this case, since to do so is merely to introduce inefficiency into the system for the sake of obtaining a given output. Here, as in many cases of assembly line balancing, it is desirable to modify output in order to minimize balancing loss. In this case therefore the assembly line balancing procedure would be firstly to seek a balance for a given cycle time C, and then to minimize the cycle time for the same number of work stations. A flow diagram for such a procedure using the Ranked Positional Weight technique is shown in Fig. 10.7.

It is not difficult to criticize this simple assembly line balancing procedure or to suggest improvements. Mansoor (1964) has developed an 'Improved Ranked Positional Weight Technique' involving a 'backtracking' procedure which appears to provide better results in certain conditions. We can, of course, criticize the heuristic involved in the RPW method, but like all heuristic methods proof of efficiency can only be obtained empirically or by simulation. The positional weight of an element is a measure of its own size and its precedence position. Elements with high PW occur as the beginning of the job and/or have large standard times, and using the improved ranked positional weight technique we attempt to allocate these first, and those with low PW's last.

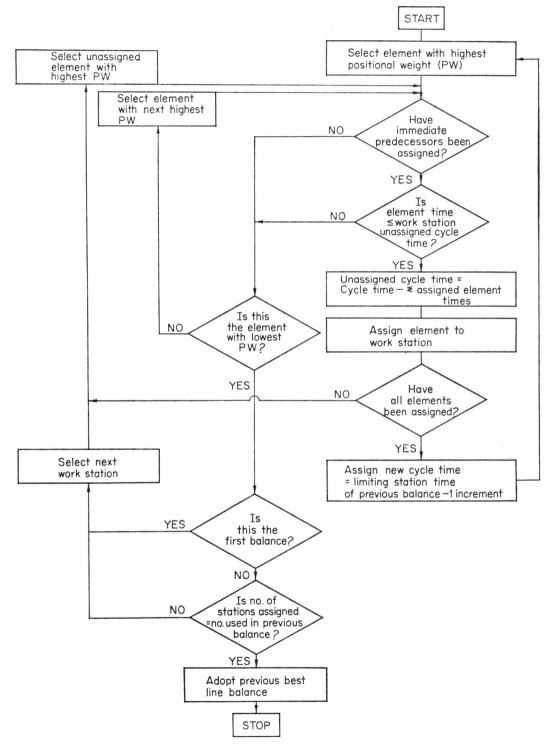

FIGURE 10.7. Assembly line balancing (RPW method) (line first balanced for a given cycle time C and then minimum cycle time obtained for the same number of stations)

Looking back to the packing analogy, we would surely have intuitively adopted the same procedure there. After fulfilling zoning constraints by putting those blocks with a fixed destination into the appropriate boxes, we would probably have packed the large blocks whilst there was ample remaining space in the boxes, and afterwards fitted the smaller blocks into the remaining corners and smaller spaces.

Comsoal

An interesting method of assembly line balancing called COMSOAL (Computer Method of Sequencing Operations for Assembly Lines) was developed around 1965 by Arcus.[11] COMSOAL uses a digital computer to sample data and simulate possible assembly line balances. The simulation follows the following comparatively simple, basic procedure:

1. Consider the job in terms of a precedence diagram of minimum rational work elements, of the type shown in Fig. 10.5. Construct a list (List A) showing, in one column, all work elements and, in an adjacent column, the total number of elements which *immediately precede* them in the precedence diagram. (Such a list based on Fig. 10.5 is shown in Table 10.7.)

TABLE 10.7. List 'A'—COMSOAL

Element no.	No. of immediate predecessors
0	0
1	0
2	2
3	1
4	1
5	1
6	1
7	1
8	2
9	2
10	1

2. Construct a list (List B) showing all elements which have *no* immediate predecessors (i.e. elements having a zero in the second column of List A (Table 10.8).

TABLE 10.8. List 'B'—COMSOAL

Elements without immediate predecessors
0
1

[11] A. L. Arcus, 'COMSOAL—A computer method of sequencing operations for assembly lines', *Intern. J. of Prod. Res.*, **4**, No. 4, 259–277 (1966).

3. Select at random one element from List B, say element 0.
4. Eliminate the selected element from List B and move all elements below the selected element up one position.
5. Eliminate the selected element from the precedence diagram and update List A
6. Add to List B those elements which immediately follow the selected element and now have no immediate predecessors

This simple procedure is then repeated until a sequence containing all elements has been constructed. The elements (in this order) are then assigned to station 1, 2, 3, etc., the cycle time at each station being diminished until no further elements can be accommodated, at which stage the next element is assigned to the next station. The number of stations used in the balance is counted, and compared to the previous best balance. If there is an improvement the new balance is stored in the computer and the previous best discarded, thus by generating a fairly large set of possible solutions a good assembly line balance can be obtained.

Arcus improved this basic procedure by extracting from list B, a further list, C, consisting of those elements whose times did not exceed the time available at the station under consideration, and then selecting elements randomly from this new list. A further improvement was achieved by using a biased or weighted sampling procedure to select elements from list C, in place of purely random selection. Arcus also incorporated a procedure whereby a solution could be aborted before completion, if the total station idle time of the incomplete solution exceeded that of the previous best solution.

HUMAN ASPECTS OF ASSEMBLY LINE DESIGN

Readers familiar with mass production industries or with the behaviour of people on repetitive jobs may object to the fundamental assumption of simple assembly line balancing—namely that elements of work require a given constant time, the Standard Element time. In the chapters on Work Study the validity of the assumption that there was a single best method of doing a job and consequently a single time for the job was criticized, and rightly so. But even assuming this to be the case, or assuming that for some other reason a worker continually adopts the specified work method, it still does not follow that the time required will be constant. There may be occasions when faulty materials or parts are received and consequently more time is required to assemble them. The worker may drop or fumble with the parts or the tools, or his attention may be distracted. He may talk to his neighbour or think about something else and all of these things may well affect the time he requires to complete the operation.

This phenomenon of variability is the fundamental difference between assembly lines involving human operators and those depending exclusively upon machines, i.e. transfer lines. It is not invalid to assume that machines at stations on transfer lines require a constant time for elements of work, but it certainly is quite unrealistic to make the same assumption about human beings. Assembly line balancing procedures are adequate *by themselves* for the design of transfer lines, but inadequate for the design of assembly lines involving human workers.

After a considerable amount of research it has been found that unpaced work time distributions (the time taken by workers to perform elements of work or operations) are usually *unimodal* and *positively skewed*, i.e. the distributions have a single peak, and a long 'tail' to the right of the peak. The distribution shown in Fig. 10.8 is that of work times for a packing task.

Clearly, if we were to design assembly lines in which workers were allowed a fixed *standard* time and neither more nor less, in which to complete an operation, we might find that on some occasions the worker would easily complete his task within this time, whilst on other occasions he

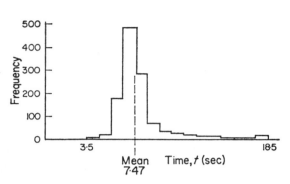

FIGURE 10.8. Work time distribution for an unpaced
packing task [Reproduced by permission, R. Conrad,
'Comparison of paced and unpaced performance
at a packing task', *Occupational Psychol.*, **29**, No.
15, 15]

FIGURE 10.9. Unpaced work time
distribution

would be prevented from doing so. This type of situation is referred to as *rigid pacing*. There is no
'freedom' for the worker, since he is confined to perform each and every operation in a given time.
Consider the time distribution for the unpaced task shown in Fig. 10.9. This is the distribution
which would result, in the absence of any pacing influence or imposed work time. If an assembly line
is designed in which there is rigid pacing and in which the worker is allowed the mean time to
complete the task, then on some occasions he may be unable to complete the task, and the product
would pass on down the line partially completed, later to be rejected. On the remaining occasions
he would have more time available than he requires, and whilst idle time may not necessarily
result, there would certainly be an underutilization of the worker.

This phenomenon is referred to as *System Loss* and often occurs where workers on assembly
lines are subject to some form of pacing. In practice, rigid pacing rarely occurs (except on transfer
lines) but some degree of pacing, involving a tolerance about a given time, often occurs. For
example, in motor vehicle assembly, pacing is not rigid since the workers can ride along on the line
whilst completing their jobs.

System Loss

It has been found that the differences in average operation times of workers on assembly lines are
not primarily a result of differences in standard or work station times, but largely a result of differences in the speed at which workers work. In other words, it appears that the losses resulting
from workers' variable operation times (System Loss) is perhaps more important than the losses
resulting from uneven allocation of work to stations (Balancing Loss). Consequently the problem
of assembly line design is not primarily the equal division of work between stations but the
adaptation of tasks to the speed of the workers.

There are three ways in which we might attempt to overcome the problem of system loss, or at
least reduce it.

One solution that is often suggested involves an increase in the cycle time. If a cycle time longer
than the mean unpaced work cycle time is adopted then fewer occasions will arise on which the
worker has insufficient time to complete his operation. This is, however, quite unsatisfactory, and
is not really a solution at all, since there are now more occasions on which the worker could

complete his operation in less than the time available. There may be some marginal benefit in increasing the cycle time if the cost of faulty or incomplete items is particularly high, but in general such a 'solution' does not reduce total system loss. Nevertheless, there is often the temptation to increase cycle time. For example, if 10 per cent of the output from an assembly line is defective because of incompleted operations, a corresponding increase in cycle time will perhaps reduce the defective output level—but only at the cost of lower utilization of labour.

A second and superior solution is to eliminate or reduce the cause of the problem, i.e. the pacing effect, (we can safely assume that variability in work cycle times cannot easily be reduced by any appreciable amount). There are two ways in which we can attempt to do this, both involve making the items available to the worker for a longer period of time. Take, for example, an assembly line consisting of workers sitting at a bench above which jobs travel by means of conveyor belt with suspended baskets. The worker must take the job off the belt, perform the operation and replace it on the belt, which carries it to the next station. Jobs spaced at 5 ft intervals on a belt moving at 5 ft/min will produce an output of 60 products/h. The same output will result from a spacing of 10 ft and belt speed of 10 ft/min, or a spacing of 2·5 ft and belt speed of 2·5 ft/min. But each of these different arrangements has different consequences for the seated worker who can only reach a certain distance either side of his work station. If he can reach $2\frac{1}{2}$ ft either way then in the first case each job will be within his reach and available to him for one minute only, in the second case for half a minute and the last case two minutes. Clearly the greater the time the job is available to the worker the lower is the pacing effect and system loss is reduced.

On assembly lines where jobs pass *directly* from one worker to the next, every worker, except the one at the first station on the line is dependent upon the previous worker. Under such conditions, the work must be strictly paced in order to avoid excessive labour idle time. If, for example, because of faulty material or a mistake in assembly, a worker at one station takes longer than the cycle time to complete the operation, then the worker at the next station on the line will have to wait for work (unless coincidentally he also has exceeded the cycle time for his operation!). This coupling or interdependence of stations necessitates pacing, but if the stations could be de-coupled in some way the pacing effect, and also system loss, could be reduced.

The way in which this is done is to introduce *buffer stocks* of several jobs between stations, so that temporary hold-ups or delays at stations do not immediately result in idle time at subsequent stations. It is, of course, perfectly true that there are certain disadvantages of using buffer stocks on assembly lines. Work in progress stock and hence tied-up capital will be increased, and additional space will be required. In fact, in many cases, because of the size of the items it may be quite unrealistic to consider using buffer stocks. (Introducing inter-station buffer stocks onto a motor vehicle assembly line would not be a suggestion that the company accountant or the works manager would receive too enthusiastically.) However in many situations buffer stocks are an important feature of assembly line operation.

Van Beek (1964) of the Philips Company, Eindhoven, has conducted an interesting experiment to assess the influence of buffer stocks and the number of stations, on system loss. He used a computer to simulate the performance of perfectly balanced assembly lines of various lengths, and obtained the results shown in Fig. 10.10, from which it is clear that the use of buffer stocks of only one item, had a substantial effect on system loss, and furthermore, that system loss increases as the number of stations increases.

It is possible using statistical queueing theory[12] to calculate the effect of inter-station buffer stocks on assembly line efficiency. In order to be able to use the conventional formulae, one must

[12] For a description of queueing theory see any book on operational research, e.g. R. L. Ackoff and M. W. Sasieni, *Fundamentals of Operations Research*, Wiley, London (1968).

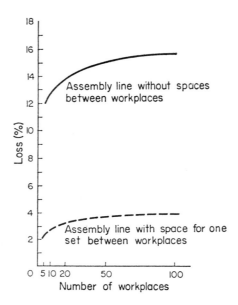

FIGURE 10.10. System losses related to length and layout of assembly line [Reproduced by permission, H. G. Van Beek, 'The influence of assembly line organisation on output, quality and morale', *Occupational Psychol.*, **38**, 161–172 (1964)]

assume that work time distributions conform to the negative exponential distribution. Furthermore using this approach it is difficult to treat lines of more than two stations. Despite this perhaps unjustified assumption, and the highly unlikely number of stations, the results of such calculations merit examination. If we assume that an infinite stock is available before the first station[13] and that no stock is allowed between the stations, then the utilization of the line is only 67 per cent, whereas the introduction of buffer stocks between the stations increases utilization as follows:[14]

Buffer stock	Utilization (%)
2	75
3	80
4	83
8	90

A certain amount of research work has been undertaken in an attempt to determine the optimum inter-station buffer stock capacity (i.e. the maximum amount of buffer stock to allow between stations) under more practical conditions. This research has again depended upon assumptions about the nature of work time distribution and also upon the assumption of a 'steady state' i.e. that

---

[13] This is not such an unreasonable assumption, since it only implies that there are sufficient stocks of raw materials or components to continually maintain the line.

[14] G. C. Hunt, 'Sequential arrays of waiting lines', *Operations Res.*, **4**, 675 (1956).

the assembly line has been operating for a sufficient time to allow a steady or stable condition to arise at each station. Of all the conventional statistical probability distributions it is perhaps most realistic to assume that the work time conforms to the normal distribution. Young[15], using a model previously developed by Barten[16] assuming steady state conditions, and the normal work time distribution, has developed a formula for the optimum buffer stock capacity, as follows:

$$X = \left(\frac{CC_2\sigma}{C_1}\right)^{0.61}$$

where X = Optimum buffer capacity at stages in a balanced production line
C_2 = Idle facilities cost per unit time
C_1 = Unit inventory cost per unit time
σ = Standard deviation of the normally distributed work times
C = A constant which depends on the number of stations, i.e.
C = 0·39 for 4 stages
0·43 for 6 stages
0·47 for 8 stages

Young used a computer to simulate assembly lines (in which no machine maintenance time was required) to test the above formula. He found that the buffer capacities calculated by the formula were very close to the simulated optimum buffer capacities.

More recently computer simulation has been used by Anderson and Moodie[17] to determine optimum buffer stock capacity. Theirs was a somewhat involved piece of research which cannot be described in detail here, but suffice to say that their simulation and analysis, '. . . showed that both the numbers of stages and the in-process inventory buffer capacity have a significant effect on the average delay of the production line and the average in-process inventory'.

COMPLEX ASSEMBLY LINE BALANCING

Our previous description of assembly line balancing concerned the relatively simple situation in which only precedence and zoning constraints were considered and in which standard, fixed work cycle times were assumed to apply. Already we have discovered one additional complexity, namely that work cycle times usually vary, and we should therefore re-examine assembly line balancing in the light of this situation. In practice the previous assumption is usually implicit in assembly line balancing, an approach which although theoretically incorrect, can perhaps be justified in the case where buffer stocks are included to absorb the effect of work cycle time variations. Indeed there is very little alternative to this practice, since as yet there is no completely acceptable, widely adopted method of balancing assembly lines for probabilistic work cycle times. There are two published papers which deal specifically with the problem, but neither is primarily concerned with obtaining line balances[18, 19]. Perhaps the most attractive method of dealing with this complexity was

[15] H. H. Young, 'Optimization models for production lines', *J. of Ind. Eng.*, **XVIII**, No. 1, 70–78 (1967).
[16] K. A. Barten, 'A queueing simulator for determining optimum inventory levels in a sequential process', *J. Ind. Eng.*, **13**, No. 4 (1962).
[17] D. R. Anderson and C. L. Moodie, 'Optimal buffer storage capacity in production lines', *Int. J. Prod. Res.*, **7**, No. 3, 233–240 (1969).
[18] C. L. Moodie and H. H. Young, 'A heuristic method of assembly line balancing for assumptions of constant or variable work element times', *J. Ind. Eng.*, **XVI**, No. 1 (1965).
[19] E. M. Mansoor and S. Ben-Tuvia, 'Optimizing balanced assembly lines', *J. Ind. Eng.*, **XVII**, No. 3 (1966).

developed by Arcus, who extended his COMSOAL method (described previously) to deal with the assembly line balancing problem in its more complex form. As well as probabilistic work cycle times, the COMSOAL method is claimed to be able to balance lines subject to numerous other complexities, such as work elements larger than the cycle time, zoning constraints, work elements requiring more than one operator, etc. Because of this flexibility, the COMSOAL method is undoubtedly an attractive technique, but even so it has not been widely adopted in practice, industry preferring, it seems, to use simpler, more subjective, procedures rather than computationally complex but more comprehensive methods, such as COMSOAL and others[20].

MULTI-MODEL AND MIXED-MODEL ASSEMBLY LINES

In 1909 the Ford company decided to concentrate exclusively on the Model T. The chassis was to be the same for all cars built, and Henry Ford announced, 'Any customer can have a car painted any colour that he wants so long as it is black'. Such were the circumstances in which assembly line technology was born. Sixty years ago cars were luxury items and there were comparatively few companies making them. It was a manufacturers' market and consequently companies were able to make what they wanted, how they wanted, yet still :emain in business—a situation which does not exist today.

The use of assembly or flow line techniques certainly leads to highly efficient production when product variety is small or non-existent, but any increase in the variety of the product not only leads to more complex design and management problems but also results inevitably in reduced production efficiency. The increasing affluence and discretion of consumers and increasing competition from other manufacturers restrict a company's ability to rationalize production and consequently few, if any, motor vehicle assembly lines are now devoted to the continuous production of single uniform products, and a similar situation exists in many other industries.

Consider the case of the Ford Capri, introduced by the Ford Company of England in January 1969 and manufactured at their Halewood plant near Liverpool. Five different engine builds were available (1300, 1300 GT, 1600, 1600 GT and 2000 GT). Additionally five Custom Plans' were available, two of which are offered only on the GT models, so in total there are 26 'basic derivatives' to choose from. If extras such as inertia reel safety belts, rear seat belts, radio, cloth trim and radial ply tyres which are available on each of the 26 basic derivatives are added to this the total range is in excess of 800 and this without consideration of options such as automatic gearbox, electric clock, servo assisted brakes and a range of body shell colours[21]. In fact the company claimed that they could build $1\frac{1}{4}$ million Capris without any two being precisely the same.

The nett result of situations such as this, is that the design of suitable and efficient assembly lines becomes a problem of some complexity. Our discussion of the human problems of assembly line design is still pertinent, even in such situations, but balancing procedures must be reconsidered and in addition several other problems now arise.

Basically two alternatives are available to a company that wishes to use one assembly line to manufacture products of differing types, or differing models of the same product. These two alternative solutions will be referred to as:

1. *Multi-model assembly lines*, on which only one model or product type is manufactured at a time, i.e. the models are manufactured in batches and are not mixed together in anyway.

---

[20] For an example of a recent approach to assembly line balancing in complex situations see: E. M. Mansoor, 'Assembly line balancing—A heuristic algorithm for variable operator performance methods', *J. Ind. Eng.*, XIX, No. 12, 618–629 (1968).

[21] Ford Motor Company publication No. FA 41/748668/691/DOM.

This type of production requires the following major decisions to be made:

(a) How will the line be 'balanced'?
(b) What will be the production batch sizes of the models?
(c) In what order will the *batches* be manufactured? (The *batch sequencing* problem.)
(d) What inter-station buffer stock capacity will be permitted?

2. *Mixed-model assembly lines*, on which at any one time one *or more* different models or product types are being manufactured. Models are not 'batched' together, but mixed together in such proportions as to provide the requisite production quantity of each type over a given production period. (Motor vehicle assembly lines are frequently of this type.)

This type of production requires the following major decisions to be made:

(a) How will the line be balanced?
(b) In what order will the *models* be launched into the line? (The *model sequencing* problem.)
(c) What inter-station buffer stock capacity will be permitted?

Multi-Model Assembly Lines

The design of assembly lines for multi-model operation is a good deal simpler than the design of lines for mixed-model operation. The multiple models may either be different products or different versions of the same product, but in either case the different models or products will have similar though not identical manufacturing requirements, since otherwise there would be little justification in manufacturing them on the same basic assembly line. In practice the line is 'set-up' for one model, then adjustments are made to the line prior to the manufacture of a batch of the second model, and so on. We can therefore consider the problem as being a succession of separate assembly line design problems, hence decisions (a) and (b) above may be treated in the manner outlined previously. Decision (b), production batch sizes, is dealt with in detail in the following chapter, hence we shall only be concerned with decision (c) here, the *batch sequencing* problem.

The optimum manufacturing sequence for the batches of different models is clearly influenced by the cost of setting up the assembly line. The total cost of setting up the line comprises the cost of tool and machine changeovers, tool and machine resetting, machine and labour idle time, etc. and is clearly influenced by the nature of the preceding and succeeding models. The problem therefore is to determine the sequence order of the model batches to minimize the total setting up cost over a given period of time. It is highly unlikely that line 'set-up' costs will be constant, but, of course, if this were the case the sequence order of model batches would be immaterial.

One attractive and simple technique for solving the batch sequencing problem is the *assignment* method of linear programming.[22] The matrix shown in Fig. 10.11 shows the setting up cost associated with pairs of models, i.e. the figures in the matrix are the cost of changing the assembly line from a set-up suitable for production of the preceding model to one suitable for production of the succeeding model. The zeros appear in the diagonal of this matrix, because these batch sequences involve no changes in the line set-up, however, since our objective is to determine the least cost sequence of changes, we must ensure that the diagonal elements do not feature in the solution by attaching very high cost values to them.

The solution to this assignment problem which is shown in Fig. 10.12, indicates that for

---

[22] The *assignment* method of linear programming is described in detail in the latter part of Appendix I. The remainder of this section assumes a knowledge of the technique and should therefore be read only after the Appendix has been studied.

Cost ↗ Preceding model	Succeeding model			
	A	B	C	D
A	0	100	150	80
B	50	0	100	75
C	80	40	0	110
D	115	100	60	0

Cost ↗ Preceding model	Succeeding model			
	A	B	C	D
A	920	20	70	[0]
B	[0]	950	50	25
C	40	[0]	960	70
D	55	40	[0]	940

N.B. A cost of 1000 was allocated to the diagonal elements

FIGURE 10.11. Setting up cost associated with pairs of models

FIGURE 10.12. Least cost solution to the assignment problem in Fig. 10.11

minimum setting up cost, model D must follow model A, model A must follow model B, B must follow C and C must follow D. In other words starting with model A, the model batch sequence would be as follows:

A–D–C–B–A–D–C– and so on[23]

Mixed-Model Assembly Lines

The advantage of this type of production is that, unlike multi-model lines, a steady flow of models is produced in order to meet customer requirements, theoretically without the need for large stocks of finished goods. The major disadvantages arise from the differing work contents of the models, resulting in the uneven flow of work and consequent station idle time and/or congestion of semi-finished products.

This type of assembly line undoubtedly presents the most complex design and operating problems, indeed some of these problems are so complex that adequate analytical solutions have not yet been developed.

A certain amount of research has been undertaken, but a great deal more has yet to be learnt before fully satisfactory management techniques are developed. We can therefore only attempt to summarize the issues involved and describe briefly some of the solutions that have been suggested. We will deal mainly with the line balancing and the model sequencing problems, the latter being the more complex. Some computer programmes have been developed by companies to deal with their own particular balancing and sequencing problems[24] but none of these is available for general use.

Line balancing for mixed-model assembly lines might be considered merely as several single model balancing problems, i.e. each model could be considered separately and the total work content divided as equally as possible between the work stations. Consider a case where a line is built for the assembly of two similar models of a product, A and B. The work elements of model A

[23]A solution by this method is not always possible.

It is possible to extend this technique to cover the situation in which the initial state of the line is important, e.g. in which the initial state of the line is a result of the production of a model now discontinued. See H. H. Young, 'Optimising models for production lines', *J. Ind. Eng.*, **XVIII**, No. 1, 70–78 (1967).

[24] For example, 'This is line balancing', *Factory*, **121**, No. 4, 84–90 (1963).

are allocated to the work stations so that during the periods in which A is being assembled, balancing loss is minimized. Similarly, the work elements of B are allocated to work stations in order to
minimize balancing loss during the assembly of model B. Such a procedure is often adopted and is
fairly satisfactory when the models to be produced are of a similar nature, i.e. when the production
of each model involves similar work elements to be undertaken in a similar order or when the
production of all models merely involves the repetition of similar work elements. When such
circumstances apply the workers at each station will be required to do the same type of work
irrespective of which model is being produced. If, on the other hand, basically dissimilar models
are to be produced then independent line balancing for each will often result in dissimilar work
elements, e.g. work involving different skills, necessitating different training etc., being allocated to

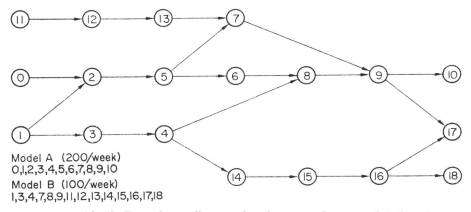

Model A (200/week)
0,1,2,3,4,5,6,7,8,9,10
Model B (100/week)
1,3,4,7,8,9,11,12,13,14,15,16,17,18

FIGURE 10.13. Precedence diagram for elements of two models (A, B)

each station. In circumstances such as these, balancing should be undertaken in such a way as to
ensure that similar work elements are allocated to the same work stations or groups of stations,
irrespective of which model is being produced. A method by which this might be achieved is to
assign elements to stations on a total time rather than cycle time basis.

Consider the case mentioned above. Two models, A and B are to be assembled on the same line.
Model A is the product we have considered previously (Fig. 10.5) and Model B is dissimilar but
nevertheless has several work elements in common with Model A.

The precedence relationship of the elements of both models are shown in Fig. 10.13 (elements 1,
3, 4, 7, 8 and 9 are common to both models). The production requirements are: Model A, 200 per
week; Model B, 100 per week. Table 10.9 gives all the data that we shall require for balancing the
line. Column (b) gives the element duration. Column (e) shows the number of times the work
element must be performed during the week to satisfy the output requirements of both models. The
total time required for each work element per week is given in column (f) (total time/wk = b x e).

The line balance is obtained using the ranked positional weights technique but instead of calculating positional weights by summing element times, they are found by summing total times. All that
now remains is to allocate elements to work stations. The available time per station per week is
considered to be 40 hours (five 8-hour days) and the element allocation is shown in Table 10.10.
Balancing loss is 5·1 per cent but it has been necessary to combine several work stations because the
total time for four elements (0, 5, 8 and 10) is greater than the available 40 hours.

These figures indicate that, in respect of one week's production, we have achieved quite a
respectable line balance—a 5·1 per cent balancing loss is very good. Notice however that such a
method of line balancing is justified *only* when production is truly *mixed*-model. Had there been a

TABLE 10.9. Data for two-model line balancing problem

(a) Element no.	(b) Element duration (hr)	(c) A	(d) B	(e) Total/wk	(f) Total time/wk (hr) Σ = 569	(g) Positional weight (using total times)
		No. of times elements must be performed				
0	0·32	200	0	200	64	411
1	0·10	200	100	300	30	463
2	0·2	200	0	200	40	347
3	0·05	200	100	300	15	292
4	0·1	200	100	300	30	277
5	0·23	200	0	200	46	307
6	0·2	200	0	200	40	246
7	0·05	200	100	300	15	125
8	0·32	200	100	300	96	206
9	0·1	200	100	300	30	110
10	0·3	200	0	200	60	60
11	0·1	0	100	100	10	167
12	0·15	0	100	100	15	157
13	0·17	0	100	100	17	142
14	0·08	0	100	100	8	61
15	0·07	0	100	100	7	53
16	0·13	0	100	100	13	46
17	0·20	0	100	100	20	20
18	0·13	0	100	100	13	13

tendency to send models through the line in batches rather than individually, a quite unsatisfactory situation would have resulted. If a batch of model A is being assembled, stations 1, 8, 9, 10, 11, 13, 14 and 15 will be underutilized and incur a great deal of balancing loss, and whilst the batch of model B is being assembled stations 2, 3, 4, 5, 6, 7, 13 and 14 will be underutilized. Only if model A and model B are produced concurrently on the line and particularly if the line has been designed to include buffer stocks between stations, will a satisfactory situation result from the allocation shown in Table 10.10. In other words this method of 'combined' line balancing for a shift's or a week's production of all models is beneficial where:

(a) Models are to be produced concurrently on the line, and not in batches.
(b) Dissimilar work elements are involved and it is desirable to ensure that work of a similar nature is allocated to separate stations or groups of stations.

The efficient design and operation of mixed-model assembly lines depends on the solution of two problems. Firstly, the line balancing problem just discussed and secondly the model sequencing problem. The latter problem, for which there is yet no satisfactory general solution, is concerned both with the time interval between the 'launching' or starting of models on to the line, and also with the order in which models are launched onto and flow along the line. The objective of such sequencing is to provide for the best utilization of the assembly line, high utilization being associated with minium station idle time and minimum congestion of work along the line (item waiting).

Two systems of launching are used—*Variable Rate* and *Fixed Rate*.

TABLE 10.10. Two-model assembly line balance

Station no.	Element no.	Total time per week for element (hr)	Time remaining from 40 hr week (hr)
1	1	30	10
	11	10	0
2 & 3	0	64	16
	3	15	1
4	2	40	0
5 & 6	5	46	34
	4	30	4
7	6	40	0
8, 9 & 10	8	96	24
	12	15	9
	14	8	1
11	13	17	23
	7	15	8
	15	7	1
12	9	30	10
13 & 14	10	60	20
	16	13	7
15	17	20	20
	18	13	7

In variable rate launching the time interval between the starting of successive models down the line is equal to the station cycle time of the leading model. For example, if three models C, D and E whose station cycle times are 4, 2 and 1 minutes respectively, are to be assembled on a line, a variable rate launching system such as that shown in Fig. 10.14 might be used.

It is quite clear from this figure that the time interval between successive stations starting work on any one model (α) is equal to the largest model cycle time and consequently when models with shorter cycle times are being assembled, a considerable amount of item waiting time results. Notice also that this same idle time results even when none of the models with longer cycle time are present on the line (after the 19th minute there are no model C's on the line, yet the time interval is still 4 minutes).

There is little that can be done by way of model sequencing to minimize this item waiting time since, assuming that for each model the cycle time remains constant, and is equal at each station, the amount of item waiting time will always be determined by the difference in model cycle times. A reduction in item waiting time would be obtained by launching models with shorter cycle times

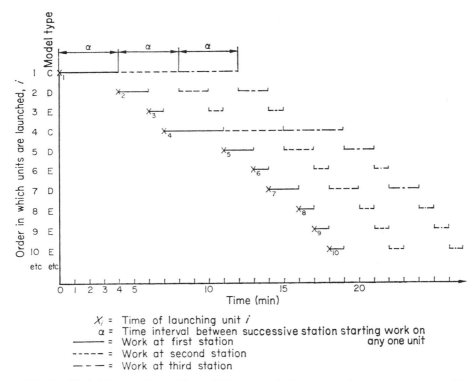

FIGURE 10.14. Variable-rate launching of three models onto a three-station assembly line

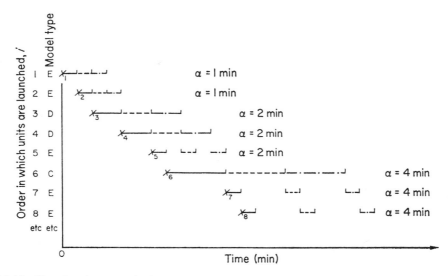

FIGURE 10.15. Showing increase in item waiting time after launch of model (C) with longer cycle time

first, but unless complete batching of models were possible, i.e. assembly of all model E's, then all model D's and finally model C's, the improvement would last only until it was necessary to launch one model C (see Fig. 10.15).

An important practical disadvantage of variable rate launching occurs where there is a need for related activities to be synchronized with the assembly line, e.g. the supply of materials at points along the line or the joining of two or more assembly lines (such as the merging of chassis and body assembly lines in automobile manufacture. In such a case these related activities must be carefully planned and controlled to synchronize with the variable launching on the assembly line. In such circumstances a system of fixed-rate launching may be preferable in which units are launched or started on the line at regular intervals (γ).

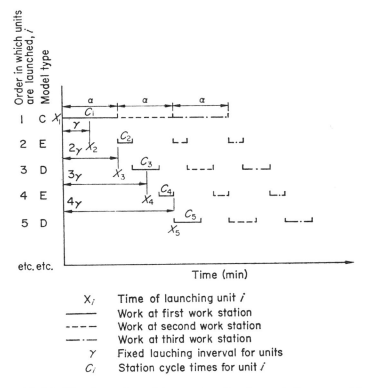

X_i Time of launching unit i
———   Work at first work station
- - - -   Work at second work station
—·—   Work at third work station
γ Fixed lauching inverval for units
C_i Station cycle times for unit i

FIGURE 10.16. Fixed-rate launching system for three-station assembly line

It is clear from Fig. 10.16 that the fixed launching interval must not be greater than the cycle time of the first unit or model launched, otherwise station idle time will result:

$$\gamma \leqslant C_1$$

Similarly:

$$2\gamma \leqslant C_1 + C_2$$

$$3\gamma \leqslant C_1 + C_2 + C_3$$

$$4\gamma \leqslant C_1 + C_2 + C_3 + C_4$$

We can rewrite these requirements as follows:

$$\gamma \leqslant C_1$$

$$\gamma \leqslant \frac{C_1 + C_2}{2}$$

$$\gamma \leqslant \frac{C_1 + C_2 + C_3}{3}$$

$$\gamma \leqslant \frac{C_1 + C_2 + C_3 + C_4}{4}$$

$$\vdots \qquad \vdots$$

$$\gamma \leqslant \frac{C_1 + C_2 + C_3 + C_4 + \cdots + C_m}{m}$$

where m = Total number of units to be produced.

Each of the requirements must be satisfied simultaneously if station idle time is to be eliminated.

From Fig. 10.16 it can also be seen that α, the time interval between successive stations starting work on any one unit, must ideally be equal to the longest station cycle time:

$$\alpha_{\text{optimum}} = \text{Max } C$$

and it can be shown that the optimum value for γ is equal to the average of the station cycle times for all units:

$$\gamma_{\text{optimum}} = \frac{\Sigma N_j C_j}{\Sigma N_j}$$

where N_j = Total number of model j required

$\quad\ \ C_j$ = Cycle time for model j.

In order to avoid both operator idle time and the congestion of work on the line, the following double inequality must be satisfied each time a unit is launched onto the line:[25]

$$0 \leqslant \sum_{h=1}^{i} C_h - i\gamma \leqslant \alpha - \gamma$$

where C_h = Cycle time.

It is usually impossible, unless both models and station times are very carefully chosen, to avoid both station idle time and work congestion, but by careful ordering of the models, both of these inefficiencies can be minimized. To select the correct order, a decision must be made every time a unit is launched onto the line, i.e. every step i. For example in order to avoid station idle time and minimize work congestion, models should be launched onto the line, so that for every launching or step i, the following function is minimized

$$\sum_{h=1}^{i} C_h - i\gamma$$

---

[25] For the derivation of this and the other formulae in this section see L. Wester and M. Kilbridge, 'The assembly line model—mix sequencing problem', *Proc. of 3rd Intern. Conf. on Operations Res.* 1963, Dunod, Paris (1964).

Example

Three models A, B and C of a particular product are assembled concurrently on an assembly line. The quantities required over a given period and the model cycle times are as follows:

Model	No. of units required	Model Cycle time
j	N	C_j
A	60	0·5
B	110	0·6
C	55	0·8

Calculate the fixed interval at which units must be launched onto the line, and show how the sequence of models might be determined in order to avoid station idle time.

$$\gamma = \frac{\Sigma N_j C_j}{\Sigma N} = \frac{30+66+44}{60+110+55}$$

$$= 0{\cdot}62.$$

Units must be launched onto the line in such a way that multiples of the launching interval $(i\gamma)$ are less than but as nearly equal as possible to the sum of the model cycle times

$$\left(\sum_{h=1}^{i} C_h\right).$$

Such a method of launching is illustrated in Table 10.11.

Notice that in this example the optimum sequence of models results from the repeated launching of models in the order:

$$\text{C–A–B–B–B}$$

but notice also that the continual launching of units in this order would not lead to the assembly of the requisite number of each model in the given time period (too many of model B and too few of models A and C would be completed). Consequently in practice it would be necessary to depart from this optimal procedure to some extent in order to satisfy manufacturing requirements. Had the figure in the final column $(\Sigma C_h - i\gamma)$ been greater than $\alpha - \gamma$, (0·18) at any time, this would have indicated that the operator would have been forced out of his work station in order to complete his work on the particular unit, or alternatively that the unit would continue to the next station incomplete.

The only other published treatment of the mixed-model assembly line sequencing problem is by Thomopolous. He deals with the fixed-rate launching system but develops a more comprehensive treatment of the subject than that presented briefly here. He attempts, by means of a simulation procedure (which in cases involving either many models and/or units, would be very lengthy) to determine the ordering of models to minimize total cost of station idle time and work congestion. In many respects both of these treatments are inadequate and a great deal of progress must be made before practical, comprehensive and efficient methods of mixed-model assembly line design are available.

TABLE 10.11. Fixed interval launching of units onto an assembly line

Unit i	$i\gamma$	Model	Model Cycle time C_i	h	$\sum_{h=1}^{i} C_h$	$\sum_{h=1}^{i} C_h - i\gamma$
1	0·62	C	0·8		0·8	0·18
2	1·24	A	0·5		1·3	0·06
3	1·86	B	0·6		1·9	0·04
4	2·48	B	0·6		2·5	0·02
5	3·10	B	0·6		3·1	0·00
6	3·72	C	0·8		3·9	0·18
7	4·34	A	0·5		4·4	0·06
8	4·96	B	0·6		5·0	0·04
9	5·58	B	0·6		5·6	0·02
10	6·20	B	0·6		6·2	0·00
11	6·82	C	0·8		7·0	0·18
12	7·44	A	0·5		7·5	0·06
13	8·06	B	0·6		8·1	0·04
14	8·68	B	0·6		8·7	0·02
15	9·30	B	0·6		9·3	0·00
16	9·92	C	0·8		10·1	0·18
17	10·54	A	0·5		10·6	0·06
18	11·16	B	0·6		11·2	0·04
19	11·78	B	0·6		11·8	0·02
20	12·40	B	0·6		12·4	0·00
21	13·02	C	0·8		13·2	0·18
22	13·64	A	0·5		13·7	0·07
…	…	…	…		…	…
etc.	etc.	etc.	etc.		etc.	etc.

SUMMARY

Although the use of assembly or flow lines can be traced back to the 1700's their use on a large scale only began about 1913 when Henry Ford began producing the legendary Model T Ford.

Many types of assembly line exist but the concept in each is similar—products are assembled or made at a series of work stations, consequently work in progress and space requirements are minimized, but only at the cost of high capital investment and comparative inflexibility.

The object of assembly line balancing is to allocate work as evenly as possible to the work stations on the line, so as to minimize idle time or balancing loss. The analytical treatment of this problem was only begun in the 1950's, and like many other areas of production there has been little success in the various attempts to develop rigorous methods of obtaining optimum solutions. Heuristic procedures are normally adopted, perhaps the best known being the ranked positional weight method, and the Kilbridge and Wester method.

Line balancing alone is insufficient for the design of assembly lines on which people are employed. Because of the inevitable variability of work cycle times certain losses are incurred, known as system loss. This is particularly so when the work is highly paced, i.e. the workers must complete their operation in the specified cycle time. To overcome this problem, which in many respects is more important than the line balancing problem, the pacing effect must be reduced, either by making the jobs available longer to the workers by different spacing of items on conveyors or by providing buffer stocks between stations.

It is frequently necessary to produce more than one model, or product on an assembly line. When the different models are to be produced in separate and large batches (multi-model assembly lines) line balance might be obtained separately for each model, but where different models are to be produced concurrently (mixed-model assembly lines) and where all work of a similar type is to be allocated to the same work stations, combined line balancing for all models for a shift or week may be desirable. The problem of sequencing in mixed-model assembly lines is complex and largely unsolved. There are two general approaches to the problem. The first involves launching or start-units on the assembly line at a variable rate, the time between launching successive units being equal to the cycle time of the leading unit. With this method, random ordering of models on to the line is adequate. The second method involves launching the units on to the line at a fixed interval, and careful ordering of models is necessary to achieve efficient utilization of the line.

SELECTED READINGS

Assembly line balancing is covered in the following papers:

D. R. FREEMAN and J. V. JUCKER, 'The line balancing problem', *J. Ind. Eng.*, **XVIII**, No. 6, 361–364 (1967).

E. J. IGNALL, 'A review of assembly line balancing', *J. Ind. Eng.*, **XVI**, No. 4, 244 (1965).

W. B. HELGERSON and D. P. BIRNIE, 'Assembly line balancing using the ranked positional weight technique', *J. Ind. Eng.*, **XII**, No. 6, 394 (1961).

F. TONGE, 'Summary of heuristic line balancing procedure', *Management Sci.*, **7**, No. 1, 21 (1960).

M. KILBRIDGE and L. WESTER, 'A heuristic method of assembly line balancing', *J. Ind. Eng.*, **XII**, No. 4, 292–298 (1961).

A. L. ARCUS, 'COMSOAL—A computer method of sequencing operations for assembly lines', *Int. J. Prod. Res.*, **4**, No. 4 (1966).

The following references relate to system loss:

L. E. DAVIS, 'Pacing effects on manned assembly lines', *Int. J. Prod. Res.*, **4**, No. 3 (1966).

E. S. BUFFA, 'Pacing effects in production lines', *J. Ind. Eng.*, **XII**, No. 6, 383 (1961).

The following papers deal with the determination of buffer capacity and batch sequencing:

H. H. YOUNG, 'Optimization models for production lines', *J. Ind. Eng.*, **XVIII**, No. 1, 70–78 (1967).

D. R. ANDERSON and C. L. MOODIE, 'Optimal buffer storage capacity in production line systems', *Int. J. Prod. Res.*, **7**, No. 3 (1969).

The remaining three references deal with mix-model assembly lines. The treatment of model sequencing in this chapter is similar to that given in the first reference. Thomopoulos deals with the subject in more detail and presents a particularly useful classification and description of different types of assembly line work station.

L. WESTER and M. KILBRIDGE, 'The assembly line model-mix sequencing problem', *Proc. of 3rd Intern. Conf. on Operations Res.* 1963, Dunod, Paris (1964).

N. THOMOPOULOS, 'Line balancing—Sequencing for mixed model assembly', *Management Sci.*, **14**, No. 2, B.59–B.75 (1967).

N. THOMOPOULOS, 'Some analytical approaches to assembly line problems', *Prod. Engr.*, July, 345–351 (1968).

QUESTIONS

10.1. A multi-station assembly line is to produce a minimum of 6 000 completed items per 40-hour working shift. The assembly of one item consists of 25 elements of work together constituting a total work content of 11 minutes.

What is the minimum number of work stations for this assembly line and what will the cycle time ideally be?

10.2. What will the balancing loss be of the assembly line, the requirements of which are given above?

10.3. The diagram shown below indicates the necessary precedence requirements of twelve work elements which together constitute the total work content of a simple assembly task.

Using the assembly line balancing technique devised by Kilbridge and Wester, design an assembly line (i.e. assign work elements to the requisite number of work stations) to produce as near as possible, and no less than, three items per hour.

What is the balancing loss for the line that you have designed?

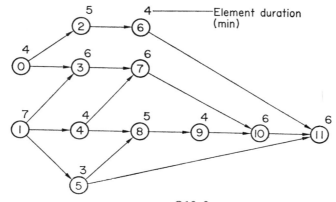

FIGURE Q10.3

10.4. Use the Kilbridge and Wester line balancing technique to balance a simple assembly line, with the minimum number of work stations, to produce a minimum of 60 items per hour. The production of each item consists of 21 work elements, some of which must be performed in a given order as shown by the precedence diagram below.

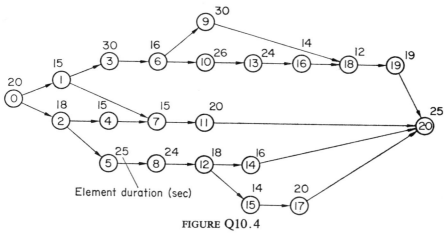

FIGURE Q10.4

10.5. The work involved in assembling a small component can be described in terms of eleven minimum rational work elements whose elemental times are as follows:

Element	Time (min)
0	4
1	3
2	3
3	3
4	7
5	5
6	4·5
7	9·5
8	5
9	7
10	7

Certain precedence constraints apply to the work, these are shown diagrammatically below:

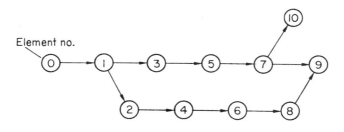

FIGURE Q10.5

Furthermore, because of the nature of the work it is necessary to ensure that elements 0 and 3 *do not* occur at the same work station, elements 3 and 5 *do not* occur at the same work station, and that elements 8 and 10 *do* occur at the same work station. Two assembly lines are to be designed (without buffer stocks), one producing components at a rate of 4·61 per hour and the other at a rate of 5·0 per hour.

Use the ranked positional weight method to assign work elements to work stations in order to minimize the number of work stations and the balancing loss on each line. Calculate the balancing loss in both cases.

Describe the heuristic device you are using to solve this problem and justify its use as a method of assembly line balancing.

[Univ. of Bradford, Management Centre, Post-Grad. Dip. Management, *Production Management*, May 1968—35 minutes]

10.6. The precedence diagram for an assembly operation and the corresponding work element times are given below.

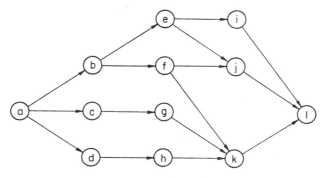

FIGURE Q10.6

Work element	Time (min)	Work element	Time (min)
a	0·20	g	0·30
b	0·65	h	0·45
c	0·40	i	0·65
d	0·10	j	0·40
e	0·30	k	0·35
f	0·15	l	0·25

If there are three operators available for this work, determine the maximum output of completed assemblies that can be achieved by the assembly line.

[Univ. of London, Imperial College, M.Sc. Operational Research and Management Studies, *Industrial Engineering* 1, *Production Planning and Control*, April 1968—45 minutes]

10.7. What is 'system loss', how is it caused, and how can it be reduced?

10.8. Analytical line balancing procedures are sufficient for the successful design of 'transfer lines' but are they adequate themselves for the design of mass production systems in which human operators are involved in executing the work?

What are the 'human' problems associated with the design and operation of mass production systems such as flow lines?

[Univ. of Bradford, Management Centre, Post-Grad. Dip. Industrial Admin., *Production Management*, May 1969—part of question only]

10.9. Determine the 'optimal' inter-station buffer stock capacities for a assembly line consisting of six stations. Assume that the station work times are distributed normally with (a) a variance of 1·6 and (b) a variance of 3·2. The unit inventory cost per hour is £0·005 and the unit cost of the facilities per hour is £0·007.

Which formula have you used in calculating the optimal buffer capacity, and what other assumptions does this treatment of the problem depend upon?

10.10. Describe briefly the following:

(a) A multi-model assembly line
(b) A mixed-model assembly line
(c) Simple assembly line balancing
(d) Complex assembly line balancing
(e) Batch sequencing on assembly lines
(f) Model sequencing on assembly lines.

10.11. The matrix below shows the costs incurred through changing an assembly line from a set-up suitable for the production of one type of item, to a set-up suitable for the production of a different type of item.

During each shift, each of the five types of item must be produced once. A batch of item type A must be produced first. In what order must the batches of the five items be produced, if the cost of setting-up the line is to be minimized?

What is the total line set-up cost per shift?

		Succeeding type				
Cost		A	B	C	D	E
Preceding type	A		150	70	100	65
	B	100		70	80	110
	C	50	100		110	65
	D	75	65	75		90
	E	125	110	80	70	

FIGURE Q10.11

10.12. Two models (A and B) of a simple product are to be produced on a short 'manual' assembly line. Because of the nature of the demand for these items, it is preferable to design the assembly line for mixed production of the two models, rather than for separate production in batches.

The line output for the two types, per 8-hour shift must be:

$$A = 500 \text{ products}$$
$$B = 250 \text{ products}$$

The diagrams below show the precedence relationships of the work elements which constitute both models. Certain of the elements are common to both models, and the remainder are peculiar to each. (Common elements have the same numbers in both diagrams.)

Design an assembly line with the minimum number of stations, and allocate work elements to stations.

What is the average balancing loss of your line over a period of one shift?

Model A

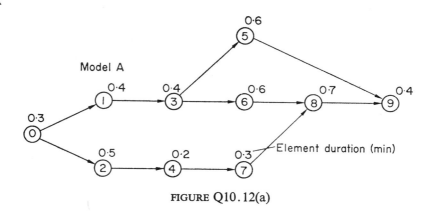

FIGURE Q10.12(a)

Model B

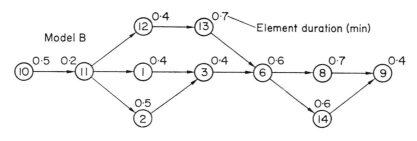

FIGURE Q10.12(b)

10.13. Four models of a product are to be produced on a 'mixed-model' assembly line. The relative proportions of each of the models to be produced over any given period are given below. The model cycle times are also given below (i.e. the cycle times for each model at each station).

Model	Relative production (quantities required)	Model Cycle times (min)
A	0·2	0·6
B	0·3	0·3
C	0·3	0·4
D	0·2	0·7

The models must be launched onto the assembly line at fixed intervals. Determine the sequence in which models must be launched onto the line to minimize congestion on the line.
Comment on this model sequence.

10.14. 'The minimization of balancing loss should be a secondary objective during the design of assembly lines, particularly mixed-model assembly lines.' Discuss.

10.15. The diagrams below indicate the precedence relationships for the work elements of two jobs. Certain of the elements are common to both jobs (i.e. elements 1, 2, 3, 4, 6), whilst the remainder are peculiar to one job.

At the moment product A is made on assembly line A, whilst product B is made on assembly line B.

The allocation of work elements to stations, and the line outputs are also shown below.

Product A

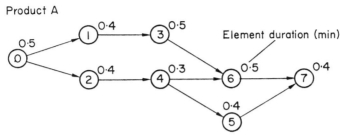

FIGURE Q10.15(a)

Output required = 60 per hour (i.e. Cycle time = 1 min).

Station	Elements	Work station time (min)
1	0, 2	0·9
2	1, 4	0·7
3	3, 5	0·9
4	6, 7	0·9

Product B

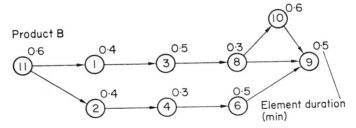

FIGURE Q10.15(b)

Output required = 50 per hour (i.e. Cycle time = 1·2 min).

Station	Elements	Work station time (min)
1	11, 1	1·0
2	2, 3	0·9
3	4, 6, 8	1·1
4	10, 9	1·1

K

The company manufacturing these two products is anxious to evaluate the merits of three possible methods of manufacture:

1. The manufacture of both A and B together on a mixed-model assembly line.
2. The manufacture of A and B separately in batches on an existing larger assembly line which would also be expected to manufacture batches of another product—product C.
3. The present arrangement.

The evaluation of the three methods of manufacture is to be accomplished by comparing the total costs for each alternative, as follows:

Present Situation

$$\text{Total cost} =$$

Indirect costs: associated with line for product A = £100
                : associated with line for product B = £75

+Inefficiency costs: assumed to be incurred at a rate of £5 per 1% balancing loss per line.

Alternative 1

$$\text{Total cost} =$$

Indirect costs: associated with a mixed-model line = £150
+Inefficiency costs: £5 per 1% balancing loss per line.

Alternative 2

$$\text{Total cost} =$$

Indirect costs: addition to indirect costs for existing product C line = £50
+Inefficiency costs: associated with balancing loss and calculated to be £50.
+Change-over costs, incurred when the 'set-up' of the multi-model line is changed between production of batches of two different products. The matrix below details such costs (assume the production of one batch of each model only and three line 'set-ups').

Preceding product \ Succeeding product	A	B	C
A	—	70	45
B	60	—	80
C	70	65	—

FIGURE Q10.15(c)

Which is the most economic method of producing products A and B in the quantities specified?

11

Planning for Batch Production

In the previous two chapters we have discussed production planning in relation to jobbing and mass production. Both of these types of production are comparatively easy to describe since, in both cases, reference can be made to their *pure* forms. For example, we have described *pure* jobbing production as being concerned with unit quantities of differing items, and *pure* mass production as concerned with continuous production of a single item. Although neither of these extreme cases exist in practice it is not difficult to visualize situations differing only slightly from them. Description of batch production is more difficult since no pure form exists. It is by definition the situation which exists between jobbing and mass production. Fewer different items are produced than in jobbing production, yet the quantity required is insufficient to justify continuous or mass production. Unlike jobbing production, items are not produced to individual customer orders but, like mass production, in anticipation of future customer orders. Unlike mass production, the rate of production is not equal to the rate of demand, but in excess of it.

Consider just one item or product. If demand was both low and uncertain then a company would manufacture that item only on receipt of a customer order. If, on the other hand, demand was both high and reasonably stable, they might undertake to produce items continuously knowing that unless the situation were to change, all items produced would be consumed. If, however, demand is limited but nevertheless predictable and reasonably stable, or alternatively if the item can only be manufactured at a rate which is in excess of the demand rate, the item can be manufactured periodically in quantities which are sufficient to satisfy expected demand. The batches of items so produced would be placed in stock, manufacture of another batch being undertaken when stock had fallen to a predetermined level. The interval between production of batches of this item would be occupied by the production of other items.

Notice then that in jobbing production no stock of finished items need exist. In batch production, a stock of items is essential, whilst in mass production finished item stock is maintained to accommodate stoppages in production or fluctuations in demand. Furthermore, in jobbing production, manufacturing equipment is of a general purpose and versatile nature. In batch production equipment must also be capable of dealing with a variety of products, whereas in mass production, special purpose equipment may be utilized.

Figure 11.1 depicts batch production in its simplest, though not practical, form. Production of the item takes place during period T_p, and stock is consequently built up to a level Q. After production of this batch of Q items, production ceases. The consumption period T_c is sufficient to reduce stock to zero, whereupon the cycle is repeated.

From simple trigonometry, if q is taken to be the constant production rate during period T_p and r the constant consumption rate during period T_c, then the maximum stock level Q is equal to $T_p q$ and $T_c r$. Hence the ratio T_p/T_c is equal to q/r. To return to our previous discussion, this ratio is

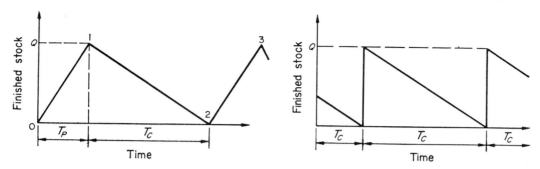

FIGURE 11.1 AND FIGURE 11.2. Simple forms of batch production

unity in mass production, since production and consumption rates are equal, i.e.

$$\frac{q}{r} = 1$$

Likewise when the ratio is zero:

$$\frac{q}{r} = \infty$$

the situation shown in Fig. 11.2 must exist. This is a pure inventory system in which quantities of items Q are delivered to stock instantaneously, rather than being built up over a definite period of time. Such might be the case where goods are purchased rather than manufactured.

The production/inventory system shown in Fig. 11.1 is one which is unlikely to exist in practice, since an unrealistic assumption was made, namely that there is no consumption during production. In practice, consumption will be continuous, consequently for the same production rate q, the finished stock of items will grow more slowly. In fact the rate of increase of stock, s, will be determined by the difference between production and consumption rates, i.e.

$$s = q - r$$

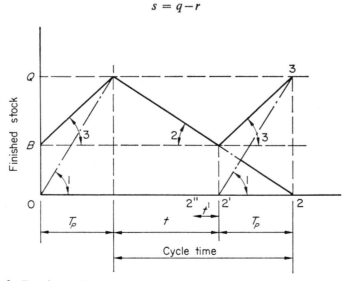

FIGURE 11.3. Batch production showing consumption concurrent with production

Notice also that in order to ensure that a zero stock of finished items does not exist, except momentarily, production may need to begin before stock falls to zero. Furthermore, it may be desirable to avoid allowing stock to fall to zero, even momentarily, and consequently a buffer stock may be maintained. More realistic, therefore, is the situation depicted in Fig. 11.3.

In this situation, because consumption is concurrent with production, the rate of growth of stock is less than the production rate, i.e.

$$\text{angle } 3 < \text{angle } 1$$

In fact,

$$\text{angle } 1 = \tan^{-1} q \qquad \dots \text{ the angle whose tangent is } q$$

and

$$\text{angle } 3 = \tan^{-1} (q-r)$$

$$= \tan^{-1} s.$$

Now instead of arranging for production to begin so that the stock level falls momentarily to zero (point 2), a buffer stock of B is often maintained, hence production is often begun earlier (point 2′). In practice, although actual production is to begin at point 2′, it may be necessary as we have pointed out above, to begin preparations for production even earlier, say point 2″. Consequently the time available for the manufacture of other items on the equipment is:

$$(\text{Cycle time} - T_p - t')$$

where $t' = $ production preparation time (see Fig. 11.3).

It should be reasonably clear from this discussion that the problems of batch production are to a large extent associated with the timing and the length of production runs. The paramount problem is probably the determination of batch sizes and this we shall discuss first.

DETERMINATION OF BATCH SIZES

Batch quantities which are too large will result in high stock levels and cause a large amount of capital to be tied up in stock which might otherwise be invested elsewhere. Additionally, unduly high stock levels will incur other costs, such as the cost of stock-keeping, insurance, depreciation, etc. On the other hand, batch quantities which are too small, will result in both low stock levels, which may be insufficient to meet large fluctuations in demand, and also the frequent production of small batches each time incurring costs associated with set-up, tooling, etc.

The problem then is to determine the batch size which minimizes total costs, consequently we must consider the following:

1. Stock holding
2. Production
3. Set-up and preparation of machines and equipment

Minimum Cost Batch Size

The minimum cost batch size can easily be determined providing, of course, that the assumptions made in deriving the formula are justified in practice, and providing also that the various costs can be determined accurately.

We shall consider firstly a simple, *static* and *deterministic* situation, i.e. one in which both production and consumption rates are *known* and *constant*. Further, let us assume that a buffer stock of B items is required, and that items are delivered into stock, as a complete batch at the end of the production period. In other words we are considering the type of batch production system shown in Fig. 11.2, but with the addition of a buffer stock.

Our notation is as follows:

Q = Production batch quantity
C_s = Set up or preparation cost/batch
C_1 = Stock holding cost/item/unit of time
B = Buffer stock quantity
r = Consumption rate/unit of time
q = Production rate/unit of time
p = Manufacturing cost/unit

Then:

Average stock level $= B + Q/2$
Stock holding cost/unit of time $= C_1[B + Q/2]$
Set up of cost per unit of time $= \dfrac{C_s r}{Q}$

To determine the optimum batch size we need only consider those costs which vary according to batch size thus:

Total cost of set up and holding:

$$C = C_1[B + Q/2] + \frac{C_s r}{Q} \tag{1}$$

Differentiating with respect to Q:

$$\frac{dC}{dQ} = \frac{C_1}{2} - \frac{C_s r}{Q^2}$$

Equating this to zero to obtain a maximum or minimum point gives:

$$\text{Minimum cost batch size} = Q^* = \sqrt{\frac{2C_s r}{C_1}} \tag{2}$$

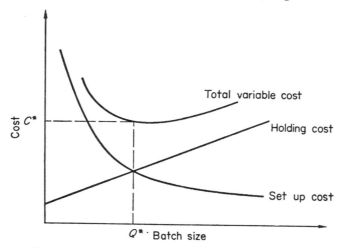

FIGURE 11.4. Minimum cost batch size and associated total cost

Substituting (2) into (1) gives the total cost per unit of time, associated with this production policy, i.e.

$$C^* = \sqrt{2rC_sC_1} + C_1B \qquad (3)$$

Notice also the production cycle time for this product,

$$t = \frac{Q}{r}$$

$$\therefore \quad t^* = \sqrt{\frac{2C_s}{rC_1}} \qquad (4)$$

These formulae are very simple to use but often, to simplify matters even further, nomographs, tables or charts are used.

The minimum cost batch size and its associated total cost is shown on Fig. 11.4.

Example

Watertight Ltd. are the manufacturers of a range of plastic overshoes. The complete range consists of fourteen different types (i.e. sizes and styles). Type BB (Big and Black) is sold in the largest quantities, demand being reasonably stable at 4 500 pairs per month.

All overshoes are manufactured in batches, the production process being such that the entire batch is completed at the same time.

(a) Given the following information, use the formulae above to determine the economic batch production quantity:

  Machine set up cost per production batch = £150
  Stock-holding cost per pair   = 75/- per annum

(b) The present production policy is to manufacture BB overshoes in batch sizes of 3 000 pairs, at regular intervals.

How does the actual production cycle time compare with the optimal production cycle time?

(a)

$$r = 4\ 500 \text{ per month}$$

$$C_s = £150$$

$$C_1 = \frac{75}{20} \times \frac{1}{12} = £0.313 \text{ per month}$$

$$\therefore \quad Q^* = \sqrt{\frac{2C_sr}{C_1}} = \sqrt{\frac{2.150.4\ 500}{0.313}}$$

$$= 2\ 070 \text{ pairs}$$

(b)

$$t^* = \sqrt{\frac{2C_s}{rC_1}}$$

$$= \sqrt{\frac{2.150}{4\ 500.0.313}}$$

$$= 0.46 \text{ months}$$

$$\text{Actual } Q = 3\ 000 \text{ pairs}$$

$$\therefore \quad \text{Actual } t = \frac{Q}{r} = \frac{3\ 000}{4\ 500}$$

$$= 0.67 \text{ months } (45\% \text{ longer interval than optimum policy})$$

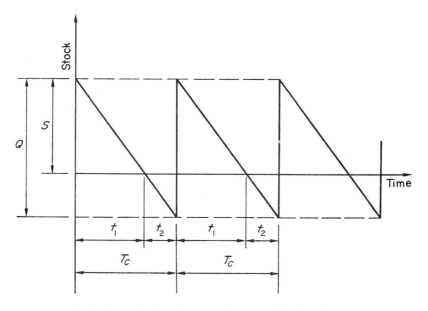

FIGURE 11.5. A stock/batch production model allowing shortages

One might further extend this simple model to include the possibility of stock shortages, or 'stock-outs'. This introduces an additional cost factor, namely the cost of shortages, C_2. The model, which still assumes known and constant demand, is depicted in Fig. 11.5. The areas below the horizontal axis, i.e. periods t_2, represent demand which would have been satisfied had adequate stock been available. The cost of such shortage, in terms of loss of profit, etc., must be introduced into the formula, since they will influence the choice of batch size.

Using the previous notation; plus C_2 = Shortage cost/item/unit of time:

$$\text{Stock holding cost per unit of time} = \frac{S}{2}\left(\frac{t_1}{t_1+t_2}\right) C_1$$

$$= \frac{C_1 S}{2}\left(\frac{S}{Q}\right)$$

$$= \frac{C_1 S^2}{2Q}$$

$$\text{Shortage cost per unit of time} = C_2 \frac{(Q-S)}{2}\left(\frac{t_2}{t_1+t_2}\right)$$

$$= \frac{C_2 (Q-S)^2}{2Q}$$

$$\text{Set up cost per unit of time} = \frac{C_s r}{Q}$$

Total set up, holding, shortage cost/unit time

$$C = \frac{C_1 S^2}{2Q} + \frac{C_2 (Q-S)^2}{2Q} + \frac{C_s r}{Q} \tag{1}$$

Differentiating with respect to S:

$$\frac{dC}{dS} = \frac{SC_1}{2Q} - \frac{(Q-S)\,C_2}{Q}$$

$$= 0 \text{ for maximum or minimum}$$

$$\therefore \quad S^* = \frac{QC_2}{C_1+C_2} \tag{2}$$

Differentiating with respect to Q:

$$\frac{dC}{dQ} = \frac{-S^2C_1}{2Q^2} + \left[\frac{4Q(Q-S)-2(Q-S)^2}{4Q^2}\right] C_2 - \frac{C_s r}{Q^2}$$

$$= 0 \text{ for maximum or minimum}$$

$$Q^* = \sqrt{\frac{2rC_s}{C_1}} \; \sqrt{\frac{C_1+C_2}{C_2}} \tag{3}$$

Substituting (3) into (1)

$$C^* = \sqrt{2rC_1C_s} \; \sqrt{\frac{C_2}{C_1+C_2}} \tag{4}$$

also

$$t^*_s = \frac{Q^*}{r} = \sqrt{\frac{2C_s}{rC_1}} \; \sqrt{\frac{C_1+C_2}{C_2}} \tag{5}$$

Example

$$r = 9\,500 \text{ per month}$$
$$C_1 = \pounds5 \text{ per item per annum}$$
$$C_s = \pounds1\,250$$
$$C_2 = \pounds2 \text{ per item per month}$$

(a) Compare the optimum production quantities for:

    (i) a policy in which stock-outs are permitted and
    (ii) a policy in which stock-outs are not to occur.

(b) What is the maximum set-up cost per batch which can be accepted under policy (ii) if the total cost per month associated with this policy is not to exceed the total cost per month of policy (i)? (Assume all other data above to apply excepting C_s for policy (ii).)

(a) (i)

$$Q^* = \sqrt{\frac{2C_s r}{C_1}} \; \sqrt{\frac{C_1+C_2}{C_2}}$$

$$= \sqrt{\frac{2.1250.9\,500}{5/12}} \; \sqrt{\frac{5/12+2}{2}}$$

$$= 7\,520 \times 1\cdot1$$

$$= 8\,250$$

(ii)

$$Q^* = \sqrt{\frac{2C_s r}{C_1}}$$

$$= 7\,520$$

(b) (i)

$$C^* = \sqrt{2rC_1C_s} \ \sqrt{\frac{C_2}{C_1 + C_2}}$$

$$= \sqrt{\frac{2.9500.5.1250}{12}} \ \sqrt{\frac{2}{5/12 + 2}}$$

$$= 3\,140 \times 0\text{·}905$$

$$= \text{£2 820 per month}$$

(ii)

$$\text{£2 820} = \sqrt{2rC_sC_1}$$

$$C_s = \frac{2\,820^2}{2rC_1}$$

$$= \frac{2\,820^2.12}{2.9500.5}$$

$$\text{Max. } C_s = \text{£1 010}$$

Now instead of considering the total production batch to be delivered into stock at the same time, we will consider a situation in which the items which constitute the batch are delivered into stock continuously throughout the production period. Such a situation is depicted in Fig. 11.6.

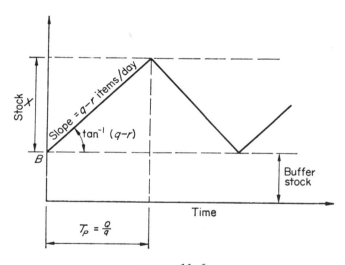

FIGURE 11.6

We can again calculate optimum batch quantities, etc. as follows (adopting the notation used above):

$$\text{Maximum stock level} = B + X$$

$$= B + \frac{Q}{q}(q - r)$$

$$\text{Average inventory} = B + \frac{Q}{2}(1 - r/q)$$

$$\therefore \quad \text{Stock holding cost per unit of time} = C_1\left[B + \frac{Q}{2}(1 - r/q)\right]$$

Total cost of set up and holding per unit of time

$$C = C_1 B + \frac{C_1 Q}{2}(1 - r/q) + \frac{C_s r}{Q} \qquad (1)$$

Differentiating with respect to Q:

$$\frac{dC}{dQ} = \frac{-C_s r}{Q^2} + \frac{C_1}{2}(1 - r/q)$$

Equating this to zero gives the maximum or minimum point of the function hence:

$$\text{Minimum cost} = Q^* = \sqrt{\frac{2 C_s r}{C_1 (1 - r/q)}} \qquad (2)$$

The total cost per unit of time associated with this production policy is given by substituting equation (2) into equation (1)

$$C^* = \sqrt{2 r C_s C_1} \ \sqrt{1 - r/q} + C_1 B \qquad (3)$$

Example

A product is sold at a constant rate of 600 per day, the production rate for the item being 2 000 per day. It is known that set up costs are £10 per batch and that stock holding costs, including notional loss of interest on capital is 10/- per item per year. If a buffer stock of 500 items is maintained, what is the minimum cost production batch quantity?

$$C_s = £10$$
$$B = 500$$
$$q = 2\ 000$$
$$r = 600$$

Assuming that there are 250 working days per year:

$$C_1 = \frac{0 \cdot 5}{250} = £0 \cdot 002 \text{ per item per day}$$

$$Q^* = \sqrt{\frac{2 . 10 . 600}{0.002\ (1 - 6/20)}}$$

$$Q^* = 2\ 920.$$

The Production Range

Because of the frequent difficulty of accurately establishing costs such as C_1 and C_s it is fortunate that the total cost curve (see Fig. 11.4) is fairly flat at the point of minimum cost, since this means that the minimum cost batching policies are not terribly sensitive to deviations from optimal batch size. It is possible, therefore, to adopt a batch size which differs slightly from the optimal without incurring substantially increased costs. This feature of the total cost curve gives rise to the 'Production Range' concept (see Fig. 11.7). Batch quantities within this range are considered as acceptable.

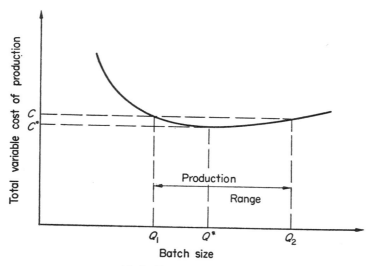

FIGURE 11.7. Economic production range

Eilon has developed a procedure for the determination of acceptable production range (see Selected Readings) which is dependent upon knowing the allowable increase in the total variable costs of production, i.e.

let
$$p = \frac{\text{Actual variable costs per unit}}{\text{Minimum variable costs per unit}}$$

(corresponding to C and C^* on Fig. 11.7)

$$q = \frac{\text{Actual batch size}}{\text{Minimum cost batch size}}$$

then
$$q = p \pm \sqrt{p^2 - 1}$$

and the two limits of production range are:

$$Q_1 = Q^*(p - \sqrt{p^2 - 1}) = Q^* q_1$$
$$Q_2 = Q^*(p + \sqrt{p^2 - 1}) = Q^* q_2$$

The values of q_1 and q_2 can be found from the curve given in Fig. 11.8 and consequently the production range can be calculated.

Example

In our previous example optimal batch size was 2 920 units. A policy of an allowable increase in cost per unit of 10 per cent has been adopted, i.e.

$$p = 1 \cdot 1.$$

From Fig. 11.8

$$q_1 = 0 \cdot 65$$
$$q_2 = 1 \cdot 55$$
$$Q_1 = Q^* q_1 = 2\ 920\ (0 \cdot 65) = \underline{1\ 898}$$
$$Q_2 = Q^* q_2 = 2\ 920\ (1 \cdot 55) = \underline{4\ 526}$$

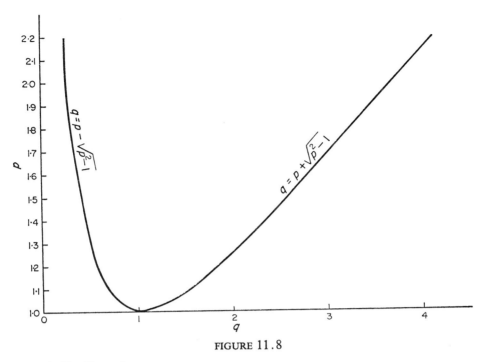

FIGURE 11.8

Further Batch Size Formulae

Throughout our discussion in this section no mention has been made of the selling price of items, this is because the *minimum cost* batch size can be determined without reference to selling cost or profit. One might argue that other criteria for batch size determination should be adopted, and indeed many other treatments of the batch size determination problem exist which depend upon criteria such as profit maximization; maximization of 'return' (i.e. the ratio of profit to cost of production); maximization of rate of return, etc. It is beyond the scope of an introductory book such as this to delve thoroughly into this problem, but readers can find an adequate examination of these further extensions of the problem in the books mentioned in the references.[1]

The batch size models we have discussed have been of a simple, static and deterministic nature, but clearly in practice, such simple and convenient conditions might not exist. Consequently care should be taken in the application of the simple formulae we have presented.

The mathematical treatment of the production batch quantity problem is almost identical to the treatment of the purchase order batch quantity problem. This latter problem we shall discuss more fully in the chapter on stock control. All that has been presented here is relevant to stock control, and much of what will be discussed in the later chapter is relevant to our present topic; therefore we will delay a more extensive treatment of economic batch quantities until later.

SCHEDULING FOR BATCH PRODUCTION

Having now decided the optimal size of the production batch for each item which is to be manufactured, we must consider when these batches are to be manufactured, in other words we must now consider the production scheduling problem. Previously we have considered each item in

---

[1] See particularly S. Eilon, *Elements of Production Planning and Control.*

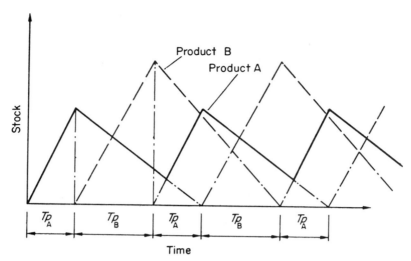

FIGURE 11.9. Successive production of batches of A and B on same equipment—ideal situation

isolation, whereas we must now consider how these batches are to be manufactured on the available equipment, and how they affect one another.

As an illustration of the batch scheduling problem, consider a situation in which only two products (A and B) are to be manufactured successively on the same equipment. The economic (minimum cost) batch quantity for each product has been calculated by use of one of the previous formulae, and the manufacturing schedule is shown in Fig. 11.9. In this case there is no idle time on the equipment nor do the optimum and individually calculated production policies for the two batches clash, consequently we must think ourselves particularly lucky. Quite easily we could have found ourselves in a far from ideal situation in which, for example, the sum of the production times for the batches of products was either greater or less than the time available. Alternatively a situation might have resulted in which production of successive batches of one product was constrained to take place at greater than the desired interval, and consequently stocks of that item would fall to a level below the desirable safety or buffer stock level. Any of these situations are quite likely to arise if, in a multi-product situation, we attempt to calculate batch sizes and production cycles for products individually and without reference to their effect upon one another.

Very often the order or sequence in which the different products are to be manufactured will be determined by either the process itself or by the setting up or preparation requirements for each product. For example, in a paint manufacturing process it is desirable to manufacture lighter colours first and darker colours later.

In the manufacture of engineering components, the order in which batches of items are manufactured is often determined by the changeover costs of jigs and tools. In such cases the only problems to be solved are the desirable length of the complete manufacturing cycle (i.e. the time required to manufacture one batch of all the products) and the frequency of the cycles.

The problem is to find the most economical cycle, i.e. that which minimizes set up and holding or inventory costs. As before, the set up costs increase and the holding costs decrease, as the number of cycles increase.

It is clear from the foregoing discussion that to obtain a satisfactory solution the cycle time for all products must be set simultaneously.

Furthermore, the production and consumption rates for each product in the sequence must be expressed in common units. The unit normally used is 'hours of production', hence consumption is expressed as 'hours of production used per unit of time'. Of course, using this convention the production rate for all products will be the same.

When a number of products are to be manufactured successively, and when production is of the type shown in Fig. 11.6, the total number of complete cycles N is given by the following formula:[2]

$$N = \sqrt{\frac{\sum_i C_{1i} r_i \left(1 - \frac{r_i}{q_i}\right)}{2 \sum_i C_{si}}}$$

where N = Number of complete production cycles, each consisting of the manufacture of a batch of each product

r_i = Consumption rate for product i

q_i = Production rate for product i

C_{1i} = Holding cost/unit of time for product i

C_{si} = Set-up cost for batch of products i

Furthermore since

$$Q_i = \frac{r_i}{N}$$

$$Q_i = \sqrt{\frac{2 r_i^2 \sum_i C_{si}}{\sum_i C_{1i} r_i \left(1 - \frac{r_i}{q_i}\right)}}$$

Example

Four products A, B, C and D are to be manufactured successively in batches on the same equipment. The consumption and production rates, batch set up and item holding costs for each product, are shown in Table 11.1. To use the formula, the production and consumption rates for all products must be expressed in common units. The unit used will be 'days of production per year'. If there are 250 working days per year, then the rates will be as shown in Table 11.2.

TABLE 11.1.

Product	Consumption per year	Production rate per day	Holding cost per item per year (£)	Set-up cost of batch (£)
A	10 000	250	0·005	10
B	5 000	100	0·005	5
C	8 000	200	0·010	8
D	12 000	300	0·008	6

Notice that the holding cost per item must also be related to 'days of production' and that the production rate for each product is the same since in each case it requires one day to produce one unit of each (i.e. one day's production).

---

[2] The derivation of these formulae can be found in Appendix A. J. F. Magee and D. M. Boodman, *Production Planning and Inventory Control*, McGraw-Hill, London, 1967.

TABLE 11.2.

Product	r_i	q_i	C_1	C_s
A	40	250	1·25	10
B	50	250	0·50	5
C	40	250	2·00	8
D	40	250	2·40	6

The consumption rate (r_A) for product A is 40 in the new units because 40 days at 250 per day are necessary to produce 10 000. Similarly:

$$r_B = \frac{5\,000}{100} = 50 \text{ etc.}$$

Referring now to the formula for N:

TABLE 11.3.

Product	$\dfrac{r_i}{q_i}$	$1 - \dfrac{r_i}{q_i}$	$C_1 r_i$	$C_1 r_i\left(1 - \dfrac{r_i}{q_i}\right)$	C_{si}
A	0·16	0·84	50	42	10
B	0·20	0·80	25	20	5
C	0·16	0·84	80	67·2	8
D	0·16	0·84	96	80·6	6
				$\Sigma C_{1_i} r_i\left(1 - \dfrac{r_i}{q_i}\right)$	ΣC_{s_i}
				$= 209·8$	$= 29$

Hence

$$N = \sqrt{\frac{209\cdot8}{2 \times 29}}$$

$$N = 1\text{·}9 \text{ cycles/year.}$$

Consequently for minimum cost 1·9 complete runs per year should be made.
Each complete cycle will consist of four batches as follows:

$$Q_A = \frac{r_A}{N} = \frac{10\,000}{1\text{·}9} = 5\,250 \text{ items}$$

$$Q_B = \frac{r_B}{N} = \frac{5\,000}{1\text{·}9} = 2\,630 \text{ items}$$

$$Q_C = \frac{r_C}{N} = \frac{8\,000}{1\text{·}9} = 4\,220 \text{ items}$$

$$Q_D = \frac{r_D}{N} = \frac{12\,000}{1\text{·}9} = 6\,300 \text{ items}$$

and each complete run lasting

$$t_A = \frac{5\,250}{250} = 21 \cdot 0 \text{ days}$$

$$t_B = \frac{2\,630}{100} = 26 \cdot 3 \text{ days}$$

$$t_C = \frac{4\,220}{200} = 21 \cdot 1 \text{ days}$$

$$t_D = \frac{6\,300}{300} = 21 \cdot 0 \text{ days}$$

$$89 \cdot 4 \text{ days}$$

Since the production rate for each product is such that total annual consumption or demand can be satisfied by substantially less than one year's production, unless consumption is increased or additional products manufactured, equipment will spend some time idle each year.

THE LINE OF BALANCE TECHNIQUE

Our previous discussion has taken for granted the fact that batch production proceeds in a series of steps. For example, we have assumed that in a process consisting of several operations 1, 2, 3, etc. the entire batch is completed on operation 1 before being passed to operation 2 and so on. This type of situation is desirable to some extent since it facilitates production control. On the other hand there are disadvantages in this iterative type of procedure. For example, the through-put time for any batch will be high, the work-in-progress will be high, and consequently a large amount of storage space will be required. Ideally, therefore, we must look for a procedure in which batches of items might be 'split', i.e. processing begun on subsequent operations before the *complete* batch has been processed on previous operations and yet a procedure which enables adequate control of production to be exercised.

When batches are kept complete during production, and when a production schedule for each batch on each operation is available, then it is an easy matter to determine whether production is proceeding according to plan. If the splitting of batches is allowed then the situation is more

TABLE 11.4. Delivery requirements

Week no.	Delivery of finished items required	Cumulative delivery
0	0	0
1	12	12
2	14	26
3	8	34
4	6	40
5	10	50
6	12	62
7	14	76
8	16	92
9	18	110
10	22	132

complex and it is often quite difficult both to establish a production schedule and to determine whether progress is satisfactory or not. It is difficult, for example, to determine whether, at a given time, sufficient items have completed sufficient operations.

For example, consider the delivery schedule shown in Table 11.4.

Twelve finished items must be delivered to the customer at the end of the second week, fourteen at the end of the third, and so on. It is clear from this that at the end of the fifth week, fifty items should have completed the final operation and been delivered to the customer. What is not clear, however, is how many items should have passed through the previous operations at this date so as to ensure delivery of the requisite quantity of items in later weeks.

The 'Line of Balance' technique was developed to deal with precisely this type of situation. It originated at the American Goodyear Company in the early 1940s, was developed during the 1950s at the request of the US Department of Defence, and has been used largely by the American Army and Navy. Its birth and development clearly has something in common with network analysis and PERT, but unlike these techniques, line of balance, which is less sophisticated, has, until recently, attracted little attention in industry. It is, however, an attractive, simple and useful planning and control technique[3] and there are now signs of growing interest in it both in this country and elsewhere.

The line of balance technique is an example of 'management by exception' since it deals only with the important or crucial operations in a job, establishes a schedule or plan for them and attracts attention to those which do not conform to this schedule, those about which something must be done if the progress of the entire job is not to be jeopardized. It is particularly useful where large batches of fairly complex products, requiring many operations, are to be delivered or completed over a period of time.

The technique can be regarded as a slightly more sophisticated form of the Gantt chart, the objective being to study the progress of jobs at regular intervals, to compare progress on each operation with the progress necessary to satisfy the eventual delivery requirements, and to identify those operations on which progress is unsatisfactory.

We can best describe the technique by means of a simple example. Two pieces of information are required, firstly the delivery requirements and secondly an operations programme, i.e. the sequence and duration of the various operations. Four stages are involved in the use of the technique:

1. the delivery schedule
2. the operations programme
3. the programme progress chart
4. analysis of progress

The Delivery Schedule

Construction of the delivery schedule is the first step. The cumulative delivery requirements must be calculated and presented as either a table (Table 11.4) or, and this is more useful later, as a graph (Fig. 11.10), which may also be used to record actual deliveries in the manner shown.

The Operation Programme

The operation programme depicts the 'lead-time' of the various operations, i.e. the length of time prior to the completion of the final operation, by which intermediate operations must be completed.

---

[3] Line of Balance is not strictly a planning technique, nor is it entirely concerned with production control. It is however more appropriately discussed in this chapter rather than elsewhere.

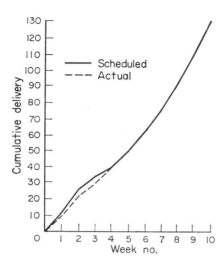

FIGURE 11.10. Cumulative deliveries

In a simple job it is possible to show such information for *all* operations in the job, but in more complex jobs we concern ourselves only with those operations which are important or critical to the progress of the job and the satisfaction of the schedule.

The operation programme is best depicted as a chart, with the final delivery date as zero. Figure 11.11 is such an operation programme. The final delivery date (completion of operation 15) is zero and the time scale runs from right to left. This programme shows that items B and C must be assembled together (operation 14) two days before delivery. Item C, prior to this final assembly, undergoes two fabrication operations, the second must be completed five days before final delivery and the first, two days before that. Purchase of the material for item C must be completed by ten days before final assembly. The item with longest lead time, seventeen days, is B.

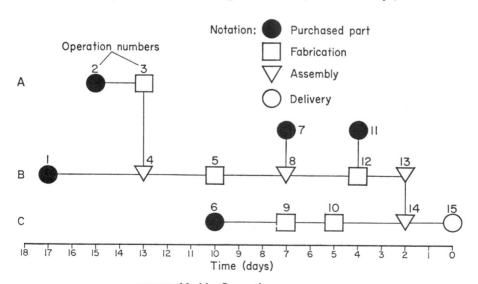

FIGURE 11.11. Operation programme

These two pieces of information—delivery schedule and operation programme—are prerequisites for use of the line of balance technique. They need to be constructed only once for any job, unlike the following documents which must be constructed each time the schedule and progress is examined.

The Programme Progress Chart

This chart shows the number of items which have been finished at each of the critical or important operations, at a given date. Suppose, for example, the review date is week no. 4, by which, according to the delivery schedule, 40 complete items should have been delivered, i.e. 40 items should have passed operation 15 of the operation programme. The number of items that have completed this and each of the other operations can be obtained simply by checking inventory levels. The results can then be depicted by means of a histogram. Figure 11.12 shows the programme performance at week No. 4.

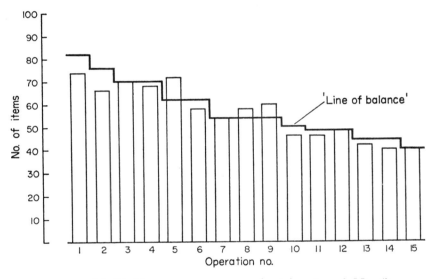

FIGURE 11.12. Programme progress chart (as at week No. 4)

Since the object of the exercise is to compare actual progress with scheduled or planned progress, the information given on Fig. 11.12 must be compared to required progress. This is done by constructing a line on the programme progress chart which shows the requisite number of items which should have been completed at each operation at the time of review. This line—the line of balance—can be constructed analytically or graphically, the latter method being perhaps the more convenient for our purposes. The line of balance shows the total number of items which should have been completed at each operation. Clearly, since a cumulative delivery of 40 items is required for week No. 4, a total of 40 items must have completed operation 15 by this date. Operation 14 has a lead time of two days, consequently at week 4 sufficient items must have completed operation 15 to ensure that delivery requirements two days later are satisfied. From the delivery schedule the delivery for week No. 4 plus 2 days is 44 units (assuming five working days per week). The longest lead time—operation 4, is seventeen days, consequently at week No. 4 sufficient items to satisfy the

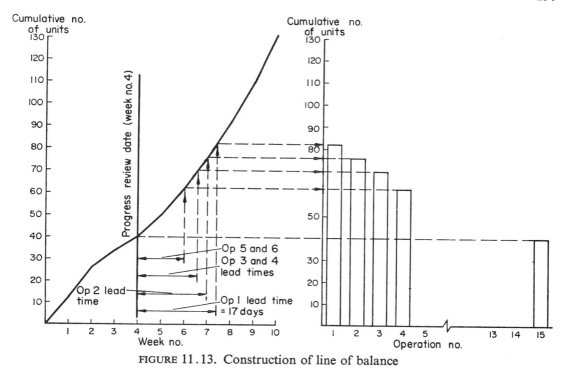

FIGURE 11.13. Construction of line of balance

delivery requirements for week No. 4 plus seventeen days, i.e. 82 units, should have been completed. The graphical procedure shown in Fig. 11.13 is a convenient way of performing these calculations.

Analysis of Progress

In comparing required with actual progress it is again convenient to work backwards, beginning with the last operation (15). From Fig. 11.12 it is clear that the requisite number of completed items have been delivered to the customer (operation 15 = 40), a fact which is reflected by the actual performance line on the delivery schedule. Clearly there is a shortage on both operations 14 and 15 and unless production can be expedited in some way, deliveries during the next week may fall short of requirements. When shortages occur we must obviously attempt to ascertain the reasons. If operations other than those considered as critical are the cause of shortages then those operations must be included in subsequent versions of the progress and line of balance chart. As an aid to control, colour codes might be used for the 'bars' on the progress chart to depict responsibility, alternatively additional charts might be constructed containing progress information on operations in various manufacturing areas. Figure 11.14 shows three additional programme progress charts each containing one type of operation—purchasing, fabrication and assembly. From these it is clear that performance on the purchasing operations may well jeopardize future deliveries. We must therefore attempt to ensure that items, particularly on operations 1 and 2, are purchased more quickly, or failing this we should alter the lead time on these operations. Charts such as these might be issued to and used by departmental managers or production controllers.

The line of balance is a simple and useful planning and control technique, its main advantage being, like network analysis, that it formalizes and enforces a planning discipline which in itself is

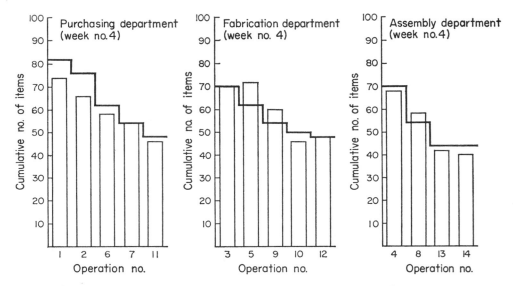

FIGURE 11.14. Additional programme progress charts

useful. It is a simple but powerful procedure, which relies on several assumptions. For example, we have assumed that the lead times shown in Fig. 11.11 are constant, and that the type and sequence of operations is independent of production quantities. Such assumptions are very often justified in practice, and consequently the technique as it has been presented here is of direct value.[4]

Line of Balance Computer Procedure

Several computer programmes have been written (see reference H. P. Levitt, Selected Readings) and use of these, particularly where many operations are involved and progress reviews are frequent, simplifies the application of line of balance.

One typical programme is that offered by International Computers Ltd., for use on their 1900 series of machines. Data, i.e. 'milestone' number (a 'milestone' for the purpose of this programme is equivalent to an 'operation' as used in the description in this chapter); lead time; quantity required; etc., are input on cards, paper tape or magnetic tape. Output is in lineprinted form.

There are three types of output, i.e.

1. Project reports—an output which shows, in tabular form, the *target* quantities for each operation.
2. Progress reports—an output which shows, in tabular form, the state of production relative to the initial plan.
3. Progress chart—an output which shows, in bar chart form, the state of production, relative to the initial plan.

Figure 11.15 shows a project report output for a simple job consisting of only fourteen operations. The data is listed vertically by order of ascending operation number. The quantity of items to be completed at a given date at each operation is listed on the output. The dates are presented in

---

[4] It is possible to use a modified version of the line of balance technique in situations where lead times are variable. See E. Turban, 'The line of balance—A management by exception tool', *J. Ind. Eng.*, Sept. 1968, 440–448.

PROJECT NO. XB/41/4   PRODUCTION OF DESKS/AO MODIFIED C/41   PROJECT REPORT

LINE OF BALANCE

DATE 07/07/56

PROJECT TARGETS   CODED DATE 43

MILESTONE NUMBER	NUMBER ACHIEVED	45	46	47	50	55	60	80	90
OA32	O	O	O	O	O	5	14	65	117
OB16	O	O	O	O	O	42	96	420	738
OB32	O	O	O	O	O	7	16	70	123
OB41	O	O	O	O	O	14	32	140	246
OCO8	O	O	O	O	36	72	120	400	632
OC21	O	O	O	O	O	72	132	510	840
OC24	O	O	O	O	54	108	180	600	948
OC27	O	O	O	O	O	72	132	510	840
OC32	O	O	O	O	9	18	30	100	158
OC40	O	O	O	O	O	72	132	510	840
OC90	O	O	O	O	18	36	60	200	316
OCA6	O	O	O	O	O	144	264	1020	1680
OD22	O	O	40	56	96	176	280	896	1352
ODA9	O	O	20	28	48	86	140	448	676

SEQUENCED BY ASC. MILESTONE NUMBER   PAGE 1/1

FIGURE 11.15. Line of balance project report

code form, i.e. week No. 45, 46, 47, etc. This particular project report was obtained after the first computer run on week No. 43. The number of items completed at each operation is zero in each case, since none are required until week No. 46.

Figure 11.16 is a project report for the same job for week No. 88. Again the output shows the target requirement for each operation for several future dates. Figure 11.17 is the progress report produced during the same computer run, the output shows the progress at each operation by

PROJECT NO. XB/41/A   PRODUCTION OF DESKS/AO MODIFIED C/41   PROJECT REPORT

LINE OF BALANCE

DATE 26/07/66

PROJECT TARGETS   CODED DATE 88

MILESTONE NUMBER	NUMBER ACHIEVED	55	70	85	88	91	94	97	100
OA32	103	5	37	90	106	123	140	158	175
OB16	700	42	240	570	672	774	876	978	1050
OB32	95	7	40	95	112	129	146	163	175
OB41	243	14	80	190	224	258	292	326	350
OCO8	629	72	220	516	584	652	700	700	700
OC21	763	72	282	672	774	876	978	1050	1050
OC24	655	108	330	774	876	978	050	1050	1050
OC27	701	72	282	672	774	876	978	1050	1050
OC32	100	18	55	129	146	163	175	175	175
OC40	1001	72	282	672	774	876	978	1050	1050
OC90	226	36	110	258	292	326	350	350	350
OCA6	1700	144	564	1344	1548	1752	1956	2100	2100
OD22	1352	176	480	1120	1264	1400	1400	1400	1400
ODA9	651	88	240	560	632	700	700	700	700

SEQUENCED BY ASC. MILESTONE NUMBER   PAGE 1/1

FIGURE 11.16. Line of balance project report

PROJECT NO. XB/41/A   PRODUCTION OF DESKS/AO MODIFIED C/41   PROGRESS REPORT

                                         LINE OF BALANCE   DATE   27/07/66

                                         PROJECT TARGETS   CODED DATE   88

MILESTONE NUMBER	NUMBER PER ITEM	LEAD TIME	NUMBER ACHIEVED	TARGET	CRITICALITY ABSOLUTE	CRITICALITY RELATIVE
OD22	8	9	1352	1264	88	11
ODA9	4	9	651	632	19	5
OCO8	4	7	629	584	45	11
OC24	6	7	655	876	-221	-37
OC90	2	7	226	292	-66	-33
OC32	1	7	100	146	-46	-46
OC27	6	4	701	774	-73	-12
OC21	6	4	763	774	-11	-2
OC40	6	4	1001	774	227	38
OCA6	12	4	1700	1548	152	13
OB16	6	1	700	672	28	5
OB32	1	1	95	112	-17	-17
OB41	2	1	243	224	19	10
OA32	1	0	93	106	-13	-13

SEQUENCED BY DSC. LEAD TIME   PAGE: 1

FIGURE 11.17. Line of balance progress report

comparing of the number of items completed with the target requirements. The final two columns give a measure of the criticality of the situation. 'Absolute criticality' is a measure of over-production at an operation, whereas 'relative criticality' is a measure of the overproduction in terms of the final operation. For example, for operation OD.22 the target for week No. 88 is 1 264, whereas 1 352 have been completed, hence the 'absolute criticality' is $1\,352 - 1\,268 = 88$. The 'relative criticality' is 88 divided by the number of items required for the final operation, i.e. $88/8 = 11$. It is therefore a measure of overproduction in terms of finished products, rather than individual components.

Underproduction is emphasized, of course, by negative criticality values, as in the case of OC.24 where a severe under-achievement has resulted for week No. 88.

This progress information may also be presented in terms of a bar chart (Fig. 11.18). Here targets are represented by I's and achievements by X's. For further information target quantities for the next report date may also be shown by extending the I's with the symbol =.

GROUP TECHNOLOGY

In Chapter 2 we discussed methods of component or workpiece coding and classification and indicated that one of the principal benefits of an effective classification system was the possibility for group technology or family machining. Although group technology has little directly in common with the topics previously discussed in this chapter, it is appropriate to consider it here, since by definition it is concerned with the manufacture of components in *larger batches* in order to obtain the benefits normally associated with large batch production and absent from unit or small batch production.

The principal pre-condition for large-scale (large batch and mass) production is a stable and high demand for products. The principal benefits of this type of production are high machine utilization, few machine set ups and low work in progress. Group technology is an attempt to obtain these benefits in situations where the necessary pre-condition does not exist and it attempts to do this by concentrating on components rather than products.

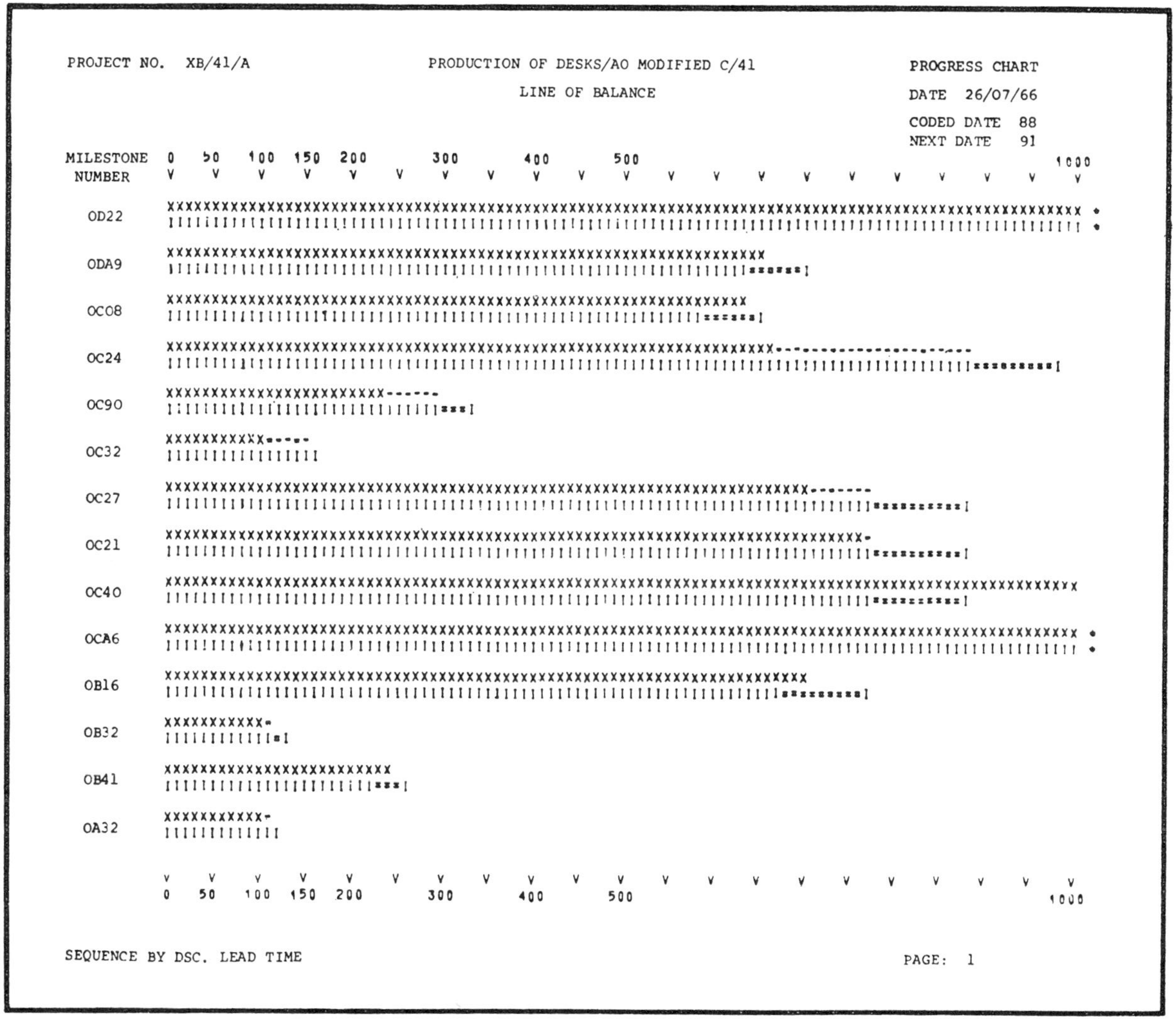
PROJECT NO. XB/41/A
PRODUCTION OF DESKS/AO MODIFIED C/41
LINE OF BALANCE
PROGRESS CHART
DATE 26/07/66
CODED DATE 88
NEXT DATE 91
MILESTONE NUMBER
0 50 100 150 200 300 400 500 1000
OD22
ODA9
OC08
OC24
OC90
OC32
OC27
OC21
OC40
OCA6
OB16
OB32
OB41
OA32
SEQUENCE BY DSC. LEAD TIME
PAGE: 1

FIGURE 11.18. Line of balance progress chart [Figs. 11.15–11.18 reproduced by permission, 'Line of balance users guide', International Computers Ltd.]

In conventional batch production work batch sizes and operations sequences are determined from the information available to the appropriate manager. Such information normally derives directly from the sales order or works order documents, consequently production batch sizes are usually directly related to customer order sizes. The net result of this type of situation is that similar *components* are often passed through widely differing sequences of operations and usually constitute different production batches. This situation leads directly to low production efficiency because of frequent machine set ups and high work-in-progress.

Adopting a group technology method, the following stages are achieved:

1. The component parts of each of the products manufactured are examined and placed into logical classes according to a previously derived coding and classification system (see Chapter 2)
2. The operations sequences for each class of components is determined and specified
3. Groups of facilities (machine tools) suitable for the manufacture of these classes of components are specified using the operations planning details (2), and forecasted demand for the products and hence the components
4. The planning of the work programme for each class of components and each group of facilities.

For purposes of implementing group technology, two types of families or groups and three methods of manufacture, can be identified (see reference J. Gombinski, Selected Readings).

The two types of family are:

Type A—consisting of parts which are similar in shape and which have all, or the majority, of manufacturing operations in common
Type B—consisting of apparently dissimilar parts which are related by having one or more manufacturing operations in common
The three methods of production utilizing group technology are therefore as follows:
Method 1—manufacture of a type A family on a group of different conventional machines
Method 2—manufacture of a type A and/or type B family on one or more similar and conventional machines
Method 3—manufacture of a type B family on a group of different machines

In conventional terms the manufacture of a large quantity of type A parts, by method 1 corresponds to flow line production, which is, of course, an efficient method of production since it maximizes machine utilization. It is the object of group technology, by identifying common features in parts, to extend this type of application and to obtain increased efficiency in production by adopting one of the three methods described above.

Clearly the most important decision influencing both the nature and the success of group technology relates in the classification of components. There are really only three useful methods of component classification in this context namely:

1. Universal (or macro) classification systems[5]
2. Specific (or micro) classification systems[5]
3. Production flow analysis.

Universal classification systems, such as the one developed by Opitz,[5] are based on the contention that the proportions of components of various types (e.g. rotational, flat etc.) are similar in different industries and different companies and consequently a method of coding and classification can be developed which is of value in any factory, irrespective of the type of product. Furthermore the code for components constructed by such methods is usually based solely on design

[5] See Chapter 2.

considerations and is therefore of limited value during production planning, when production quantities etc. are also required.

Specific or micro classification systems are tailor-made for specific situations. The design code so developed is normally called the 'monocode' whilst an additional code, the 'polycode' is usually included to specify production details for group technology purposes.

Production Flow Analysis (PFA) was originally suggested by Burbidge[6] (see Selected Readings), and is based solely on the operations routing data for components. Planning cards or operations routing documents are analysed and sorted in order to determine groups of components which require similar or identical manufacturing sequences.

The Composite Component

The idea of a composite component is important in group technology. The composite component is a design concept and hence is concerned with the first two methods of component classification described above, but not with PFA.

A composite component is one which incorporates all or the majority of the design features of a particular class of components. The composite rarely exists in practice, and is usually a 'theoretical' component for which a drawing has been prepared. It is of considerable value during production planning since it facilitates operations planning and hence the provision of a group of machine tools for the particular class of components that it represents.

The Benefits of Group Technology

The following advantages are claimed for this method of production (see reference E. K. Ivanov, Selected Readings).

1. The volume of production documentation and number of attachments are reduced.
2. A significant proportion of any new components can be allocated to existing groups for machining on the machines and with the attachments set up for that group.
3. It becomes possible to use a wide range of high-productivity equipment and unit-head machine tools, and to adapt the existing equipment specifically to the group operations allocated to them.
4. The stage is set for the adoption of group flowlines as the most advanced method of organizing production.

SUMMARY

One final point that should be made, is that the determination of machine tool groups and the general analysis of component groups, whether for production or design purposes, is considerably easier if component codes are prepared on punch cards and sorted on data processing machinery.

Before closing this brief discussion it is interesting to examine the similarity of the concepts of group technology production, and mixed-model assembly line production (Chapter 10). In both cases dissimilar items are processed through an identical or very similar sequence of facilities although in the former case the model (or component) mix may be greater and there may also be occasion for items to miss certain of the production stages. As far as we are aware the design of group technology production has never explicitly been formulated as a mixed-model assembly line design problem, however it is clear that in practice good group technology production closely approaches this latter stage.

---

[6] PFA was not described in Chapter 2 since it is not a method of classification which lends itself to design standardization.

Group technology has been slow to catch on in Western Europe and Britain but is widely adopted in Eastern Europe particularly in Russia. Considerable interest is now being shown in this technique,[7] through which higher productivity can undoubtedly be achieved in many situations. Batch production is, by definition, the production method which exists between the two extremes of mass production and jobbing production. In batch production fewer different products are produced than in jobbing production, yet the quantity required is insufficient to permit continuous production. Products are not produced to individual customer order but in anticipation of orders and for stock. The rate of production is therefore in excess of the rate of demand or consumption.

One of the main management problems associated with this type of production is the determination of optimum production batch sizes. The minimum cost batch size can be determined by use of formulae developed in this chapter providing, of course, that certain assumptions concerning both production and consumption are satisfied. Several monographs and charts have been developed for use in batch size determination during production planning, but like the formulae these should be used selectively, only when the actual situation corresponds sufficiently closely to the situation assumed for the purpose of developing the formulae.

One of the main difficulties in batch size determination is the accurate establishment of costs. Fortunately, however, quite a large tolerance exists around the optimal batch size, thus estimates of parameters are not very critical.

Scheduling is the second problem of batch production, i.e. determining when batches of each product are to be manufactured. Where more than one product is to be manufactured on the same facilities it is often inadequate to determine production batch sizes for each individually, since this may result in an unfeasible production schedule. Batch quantities and cycles must often be determined collectively to ensure both feasibility and adequate use of the facilities.

The line of balance technique is invaluable in batch production, not only as a planning aid but also to facilitate production control. It is often desirable during batch production to allow batches of items to be split, i.e. subsequent operations begun before the entire batch has completed preceding operations. The line of balance technique facilitates the planning of production, i.e. the setting of output targets for each operation and enables progress on each operation to be closely maintained. It is a management by exception tool, in that it emphasizes the important operations and highlights those on which progress has been inadequate.

Group technology is a method of manufacturing *components* in larger batches than might otherwise be the case, thus obtaining some of the benefits of large-scale production in situations where large and stable demands for products do not exist.

SELECTED READINGS

Few books relate solely or predominantly to batch production, however, the following cover most of the topics discussed in this chapter:

J. F. MAGEE and D. M. BOODMAN, *Production Planning and Inventory Control*, McGraw-Hill, London (1967).

F. HANSSMANN, *Operations Research in Production and Inventory Control*, Wiley, London (1962).

S. EILON, *Elements of Production Planning and Control*, Collier-Macmillan, London (1966).

The above books deal adequately with batch size determination. Magee (Chapter 4 and Appendix

---

[7] A £300 000 centre for group technology has recently been set up by the Ministry of Technology to develop and encourage the use of this technique.

A) deals with the multiple product case, whilst Eilon deals at length with batch size determination (Chapter 9) and batch production scheduling (Chapter 13).

Descriptions of the line of balance technique can be found in the following:

L. A. DIGMAN, 'PERT/LOB: Life cycle technique', *J. Ind. Eng.*, Feb. (1967), p. 154–158.
K. G. LOCKYER, 'Keeping the batch in balance', *Manager*, June, 37–39 (1964).
E. TURBAN, 'The line of balance—A management by exception tool', *J. Ind. Eng.*, XIX, No. 9, 440–448 (1968).
L. J. GARRETT and M. SILVER, *Production Management Analysis*, Harcourt, Brace & World Inc., New York, 1966, Chapter 18, 603–608.
H. P. LEVITT, 'Computerized line of balance technique', *J. Ind. Eng.*, Feb. 1968, 61–66.

Group technology is described in the following references and introduced in Chapter 2 of this book.

J. GOMBINSKI, 'Group technology—an introduction', *Prod. Engr.*, **46**, No. 9, 557 (1967).
E. A. HOWARTH, 'Group technology, using the Opitz system', *Prod. Engr.*, **47**, No. 1, p. 25 (1968).
E. K. IVANOV (1966), 'Group production organization and technology', Business Pub. (English translation 1968).
V. A. PETROV, 'Flowline group production planning', Business Pub. (English translation 1968).
J. L. BURBIDGE, 'Production flow analysis', *Prod. Eng.*, **42**, No. 12 (1963).

QUESTIONS

11.1. What circumstances necessitate the use of batch production methods of manufacture? What are the principal characteristics of this method of manufacture and what are the principal managerial problems involved?

11.2. (a) Calculate,
  (i) the optimum production batch quantity, and
  (ii) the production cycle time, given the following information.

Set-up cost per batch	= £17
Stock holding cost per item per month	= £0·05
Buffer stock required	= 25 items
Demand rate per year	= 12 000 (stable)
Production rate per month	= 1 500
Manufacturing cost per item	= £25

The manufacturing process is such that all items in a batch are completed at the same time.
  (b) Because of deterioration in the production facilities, the production rate per month drops from 1 500 to 900. How does this change affect production?

11.3. Experimental Brewers Ltd. are the sole manufacturers of 'Instant Beer'. Because of the market potential for this new style of beverage, an entirely new production facility has been established, the capacity of which is 5 000 gallons (equivalent) per day. At the moment demand for

'Instant Beer' is stable at 3 000 gallons (equivalent) per day. The product is manufactured inter-mittently, set-up costs for the facility being £250 and storage costs per day per 10 000 gallons (equivalent) being £100.

The company is prepared to tolerate the occasional stock-out which it estimates to cost £500 per 10 000 gallons (equivalent) per day.

In what batch quantities should 'Instant Beer' be manufactured?

11.4. Lettered rock is made at a rate of 240 sticks per hour by an automatic confectionary machine. The rock is sold through a retail shop on the same premises at a rate of 100 sticks per hour (virtually constant). The cost of setting up the machine for production of the rock is £15 (the same machine is also used to produce other items). The cost of stocking rock is £1 per 1 000 sticks per hour.

What is the optimum batch production quantity and how frequently should such batches ideally be produced? (neglecting limitations caused by the need to produce other items).

11.5. Referring to the situation faced by Experimental Brewers Ltd. (Q 11.3).

The company decide to adopt a policy of allowing a variation in production batch quantities equivalent to a variation of plus or minus 8 per cent of the cost associated with the economic batch quantities.

What is the 'production range' in such circumstances?

11.6. The assembly section of a factory uses a certain component at a rate of 40 units per day.

The machine shop within the factory can produce this component at a rate of 200 units per day. The associated set up cost is $100 \, \mu$, the manufacturing cost is $5 \, \mu$ per unit and the inventory holding is $0 \cdot 1 \, \mu$ per unit per day.

If the management is prepared to tolerate an increase of up to 1 per cent in the minimum total cost per unit what flexibility does this give in the choice of batch quantities and what is the total cost per unit of the cheapest solution if for technical reasons production batches are restricted to multiples of 50 units?

(NB μ = money units)

[Univ. of London, Imperial College, M.Sc. *Industrial Engineering*, Management Operationa Research and Studies, *Production Planning and Control*, April 1968—part of question only]

11.7. Assuming production of equal batch sizes at regular intervals and given the following, calculate the production cycle time:

(a) $C_s = £150$
$C_1 = 50$p per item per annum
$r = 5\,000$ per month

(b) $C_s = £150$
$C_1 = 50$p per item per annum
$r = 5\,000$ per month
$C_2 = £1$ per item per month

(c) $C_s = £150$
$C_1 = 50$p per item per annum
$r = 5\,000$ per month
$q = 50\,000$ per month

11.8. Discuss the advantages, disadvantages and limitations of the line of balance planning and control technique.

Compare and contrast it with any other planning and control technique, such as network analysis, with which you are familiar.

[Univ. of London, Imperial College, M.Sc. Operational Research and Management Studies, Industrial Engineering 1, Productional Planning and Control, April 1968—45 minutes]

11.9. Ornamental Doorknobs Ltd. manufacture four types of door knocker, i.e. *Elizabethan, Victorian, Georgian* and *Modern*, in batches on the same equipment. The following table gives the annual demand, the production rate and the inventory cost per item per annum for each type of knob. A change in the equipment set-up is necessary whenever there is a change in the type being manufactured. This set-up cost is £10 irrespective of the type of change. Assume a working year of 250 days.

Calculate the production batch sizes for each type of knocker and how many complete production runs of all four types should be made per year.

TABLE Q11.9

Knocker	Demand (per year)	Production rate (per day)	Inventory cost (per item p.a.)
Elizabethan	7 000	150	0·008
Victorian	10 000	250	0·006
Georgian	15 000	300	0·005
Modern	5 000	100	0·007

11.10. The delivery schedule of items and the operation programme for the manufacture of these items, are given below.

TABLE Q11.10

Week no.	Delivery required	Cumulative delivery
0	0	0
1	12	12
2	15	27
3	12	39
4	20	59
5	5	64
6	10	74
7	15	89
8	20	99
9	27	126
10	15	141
11	20	161
12	17	178

Cumulative Delivery Requirements

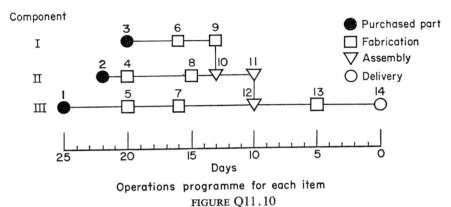

Operations programme for each item

FIGURE Q11.10

Construct the line of balance for weeks 3, 6 and 10. Indicate how you would use the line of balance to analyse production progress in the several different departments involved in the production of the items.

11.11. What is group technology, and what benefits are likely to be obtained by introducing group technology, if appropriate, into a manufacturing company?

What steps would be followed during an investigation to determine whether group technology is appropriate in a given manufacturing situation?

Describe briefly the principal methods of component classification, designed for use in group technology.

[Univ. of Bradford, Management Centre, Dip. Industrial Admin., Production Management, 1970—45 minutes]

III

The Operation of Production Systems

In this section we are concerned primarily with the problems of control, the problems associated with the execution of production plans and the maintenance of the production systems.

12

Stock or Inventory Control

The control of stocks[1] is one of the main areas of responsibility for production management. Furthermore it is an area in which company accountants usually express considerable interest and a function of considerable importance to the marketing or sales side of any business. The problems of stock control have always been a popular area of investigation for operational research workers and stock-keeping and control procedures have attracted a great deal of attention from work study and organization and methods practitioners.

All of this is a sufficient indication of the importance attached to this function and the practical difficulties experienced by those responsible for it. In this chapter we will concern ourselves mainly with the latter point, namely the problems of stock control, but firstly, by way of introduction, let us consider the importance or advantages of stocks and stock control.

The Purpose of Stock

Consider firstly stocks of *finished products*. The purposes and advantages of these stocks are:

1. To act as a *buffer against fluctuations in demand*. If the demand for a product is constant and known then it is possible to manufacture it at a compatible rate, in which case no stocks are necessary. If, however, demand fluctuates in either a known or unpredictable manner then a stock holding of finished products can be used to absorb such fluctuations.
2. To provide *quick service* to the customer. Use of stocks enables products to be offered to customers immediately upon request, or after only a short waiting time. In other words, stocks of finished products in sufficient quantities assist the marketing department by ensuring that delivery time is substantially less than the total manufacturing or procurement period.
3. *To compensate for fluctuations or stoppages in production.* Often, because of disputes, failure of equipment, and so on, production is reduced or perhaps interrupted. Stocks of sufficient finished products enable the consequences of such interruptions on supply to be avoided or delayed.
4. One further advantage which is associated with point 1. above is that even though quite severe fluctuations or seasonal changes in demand might exist, a stock-keeping policy enables production to be continued at a constant rate and therefore *stabilizes employment*.

Consider now *work in progress* stock which has the following benefits:

1. It *'decouples' the production stages*, so that failure or breakdown of any stage of the production process does not lead immediately to the stoppage of subsequent stages. Likewise, small work-in-

---

[1] In the context of this chapter 'stock' and 'inventory' are synonymous and consequently we use them interchangeably.

progress stocks enable the output rate of adjacent stages of the production process to fluctuate slightly (see System Loss—Chapter 10).

2. Work-in-progress stock in larger quantities also enables *production rates* and to a lesser extent *employment*, to be *stabilized*. For example, if two machines which are adjacent in the production process have widely differing production capacities, then the provision of work-in-progress stock between them and the double shift or overtime working of the slower machine enables constant production and employment where otherwise stoppages would have been necessary.

Consider now the stock holding of *raw materials* and *purchased items* from which the following advantages arise:

1. It enables the cost of purchased items to be reduced by permitting the company to take advantage of quantity *discounts* and also to purchase items in quantity during periods in which the price has fallen. Particularly in the basic raw material market, a great deal of attention is given to purchasing supplies at *advantageous prices*.
2. It enables companies to ensure against *disruptions in the production of suppliers*, e.g. strikes, etc., and against scarcity of supply for other reasons, such as bad crops and harvests.
3. It enables companies to *ensure against delays in the delivery* of purchases because of the supply of wrong quantities, failure of transport and so on.

The Costs of Storage

These advantages are not, of course, gained without some disadvantages. The decoupling of processes ensuring against failure of supply and accommodating fluctuations in demand are benefits which are achieved only at the cost of increased need for space, the use of more stores personnel, the tying up of capital in stock, and so on. Any stock control system must, of course, be cost effective, that is its cost benefits must outweigh its cost disadvantages. Consequently the design of a stock control system is dependent upon the identification and qualification of all the relevant costs.

With respect to *purchased items* these costs include:

1. *Quantity Discounts* Companies are often able to obtain a reduction in the unit price of purchases if they undertake to acquire these in large quantities.

To take advantage of such terms, companies must make few large purchases rather than a larger number of small purchases. This, of course, is only achieved at the cost of increased inventory levels. Figure 12.1 describes the order quantity problem. Clearly policy (a) is preferable if the saving through large quantity purchase is greater than the additional cost of stock-keeping, i.e.

$$\text{If } 3Q\,(D) > [0.5\,(3Q) - 0.5\,(Q)]\,ST$$

Where D = Discount per item (£)
S = Cost of stock holding per unit of time per item (£)
T = Time

2. *Procurement Costs* Every time a purchase is made, irrespective of the quantity of items concerned, a certain, often substantial, cost is incurred. For example, purchase requisitions must be prepared, orders placed, enquiries made and finally goods must be received, checked, passed, returned, etc. Since such costs are often constant, and not a function of the order size or value, then it is clearly beneficial to reduce the number of purchase orders made.
3. *Price Changes* Because of either long- or short-term fluctuations perhaps reflecting demand or

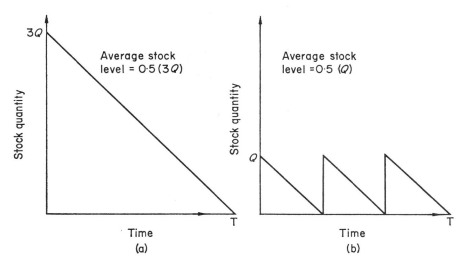

FIGURE 12.1. The order quantity problem

seasonal effects, purchased items may (at certain times) be available more cheaply. Companies will be inclined to purchase larger quantities at such times in order to take advantage of these favourable prices. Alternatively, if there are indications that prices will fall still further, then only small quantities will be purchased at the present price.

With respect to *work-in-progress and final inventory* the following costs are pertinent:

1. *Set-up Costs* Such costs are incurred every time equipment and facilities are prepared for the manufacture of an item. Such costs include the cost of new jigs or tools, the cost associated with the setting of machines, the rearrangement of equipment, provision of services, redeployment of labour and the establishment of procedures for inspection, handling, etc.

Frequently set-up costs are constant, since they do not depend upon the size of the subsequent production run. An exception occurs when different methods or equipment are required for production runs over a given size.

Since the total number of units to be produced in the year should be the same, irrespective of the size or frequency of production runs, there is possible cost benefit in having fewer yet larger runs since, at the expense of larger work-in-progress stock levels, this policy incurs fewer set-up costs.

2. *Wastage Costs* Often when production of an item begins, defective items are produced until either the production process stabilizes itself, or the correct settings can be found. Such defectives often occur in the same quantities and are unconnected with the subsequent length of the production run. The cost of such wastage can be likened to, or included in, set-up costs, since both encourage the use of fewer production runs at the expense of increased inventories.

3. *Unit Direct Labour Costs* Often, because of the 'learning effect' and the increasing competence and speed of a worker the direct labour cost associated with items may decrease as production continues. This phenomenon also encourages the use of fewer but larger production runs.

Each of the costs considered above will influence our purchasing or production policy which will in turn determine stock levels of either purchased items, work in progress, or finished goods.

The following factors which relate to the cost of stock-keeping will also influence our purchasing or production policy.

1. *Deterioration Costs* Holding large inventories of products or materials will be discouraged if the items are liable to deterioration. The value, both financial and functional, of many types of material and many products will reduce with the passage of time. Foodstuffs are a good example and clearly in such cases it is beneficial to minimize stock levels in order to maximize stock turnover.

2. *Obsolescence Costs* Fashion goods from cars to fabrics are liable to rapid obsolescence, consequently large stocks are a risky investment. Any item or material which is liable to be superseded is in danger of becoming obsolete and hence stocks should be minimized.

3. *Insurance and Storage Costs* Storage costs, such as the cost of space, heating, protection, staff, and so on, will largely depend upon stock levels. Such factors encourage the reduction of stock levels. Insurance of stored items is also often a substantial cost.

4. *Loss of Return on Capital* The capital tied up in stock might be invested by the company elsewhere and thus provide interest or additional returns. This notional loss of interest encourages minimization of stock levels.

5. *Loss of Orders and Goodwill* Whilst it is undoubtedly very difficult to assess accurately the cost of loss of present and future orders through inadequate stock levels, such a cost is important and encourages high stock levels of finished goods.

6. *Costs of Overtime, Hiring, Training, etc.* As an alternative to maintaining stocks of goods to satisfy fluctuating demand, production rates may be varied by overtime working or by changes in the size of the labour force. This latter policy incurs costs such as overtime premiums, cost of starting labour, e.g. advertising, interviewing, training cost, etc.

TABLE 12.1. Extent of stocks in selected companies

		Current Assets —Stock (£)	Turnover or External Sales (£)	Stock as percentage Turnover
Stores, Mail Order				
Empire Stores	(1968)	2 270 320	18 526 000	12·3
Gratton Warehouses	(1969)	8 305 000	55 438 000	15·0
Civil Engineering, Building				
Wimpey	(1967)	33 657 245	190 000 000	17·7
Mechanical Engineering				
Anderton – Forco	(1968)	375 618	2 020 668	18·6
A.E.I.	(1966)	98 906 000	264 778 000	37·4
Hawker Siddeley	(1968)	103 026 000	316 047 000	32·6
Textiles, Carpets				
Courtaulds	(1968)	115 930 000	394 259 000	29·4
Viyella	(1967)	18 857 000	61 772 000	30·5
Thos. Bond Worth	(1968)	2 760 117	10 075 330	27·4
Chemicals, Petroleum				
Esso	(1967)	40 834 000	502 311 000	8·1
Imperial Chemical Industries	(1968)	261 600 000	1 237 300 000	21·2
Clothing				
Aquascutum	(1968)	2 026 814	6 921 018	29·3
Montague Burton	(1968)	8 450 000	65 604 000	12·9

The Inventory Problem

It is clear from the foregoing discussion that several factors will influence inventory levels and policy. It is clearly in the interest of the marketing department to advocate large stocks of finished goods since this assists in achieving their objectives. The larger the finished stock in relation to demand, the quicker the delivery of products and consequently the more attractive they are to consumers. The production departments will prefer an adequate though not excessive work-in-progress stock level, since this adds flexibility to the production process and facilitates better utilization of resources. The purchasing department will advocate large and infrequent order quantities, since those will reduce both administrative load and purchased item unit costs. The accounts department, on the other hand, will tend to oppose each of these wishes in order to reduce investment in stock.

It is plain to see that a stock control policy must attempt to satisfy many seemingly conflicting requirements. It must seek to achieve an optimum position which provides maximum cost benefit yet it must attempt to do this knowing that much of the information required is either unavailable or of questionable accuracy.

In Table 12.1 we show the magnitude of inventories in certain public companies, the figures having been taken from recent published accounts of the companies concerned.

STOCK CONTROL SYSTEMS

The problem of how best to deal with this subject is one that has faced many authors. Two basic approaches exist, firstly a discussion of the procedures of stock control—how stock is administered, how control procedures operate, how stock is kept, replenished, and so on. Alternatively we might consider the mathematical basis of stock control systems—the decision rules involved, the data, assumptions, model and concept upon which systems are based.

Many authors concentrate either explicitly or implicitly upon stock control from a purchasing point of view, fewer consider work-in-progress stock control, whilst others are concerned with the control of finished stock.

It seems logical in our context to look firstly, but briefly, at stock control procedures to determine the nature of the decisions which must be made, then secondly to look at the mathematical basis or design of stock control systems. In doing this we shall consider, where appropriate, the stocking of purchased goods, work-in-progress and finished goods.

Stock Control Procedures

The object of a stock control procedure is to maintain records of existing stock levels, compare these levels with desirable stock levels and to repair the difference between the two. This replenishment of stock is achieved by ordering (for purchased items) or by initiating further production (finished stock). It is normal however to use the term 'ordering' irrespective of the type of stock concerned and this convention will be adopted in this chapter.

It is clear that the ordering decision forms the main part of the stock control procedure, the decision being of course, how much to order and when to order.

Two fundamental types of stock control system, and hence ordering procedure, exist—firstly the *maximum-minimum, order quantity* or *two-bin system* and secondly the *order cycle system*.

The Maximum–Minimum Ordering System

This system, which is probably the oldest type of ordering system, depends on the use of a *fixed order quantity* and *variable ordering intervals*. Under such a system, the same quantity of material,

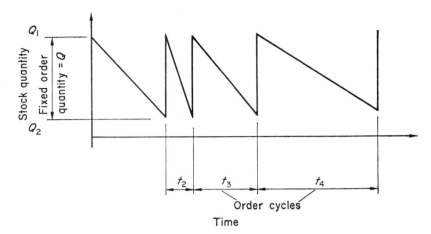

FIGURE 12.2. 'Maximum-minimum' stock ordering policy

items, etc., is always ordered, but the time at which the order is placed varies with the usage rate. The policy is depicted in Fig. 12.2.

The two-bin system is the traditional version of this policy. In this system, which is frequently used where high quantities of inexpensive items are concerned, the stock is held in two 'bins' or containers. Stock is drawn from one bin only until it is empty, at which stage a further full bin of items is ordered. Whilst this is being obtained stock is drawn from the second bin.

This is clearly a simple and effective system, which requires the minimum of clerical work and administration. The physical division of stock into two areas (bins) makes the order decision almost automatic, whereas the same system, operating without physical division, requires a clerical record of usage to be maintained, or frequent stock level checks to be made in order to 'prompt' the order decision. Nevertheless, conceptually, whether division of total stock is physical or clerical, both versions operate on the same principle.

During the design of such an ordering system, we must determine the reorder quantity (Q) and the maximum and minimum stock levels (Q_1 and Q_2)—see Fig. 12.2.

The Order Cycle System

This ordering system depends on a policy opposite to that of the maximum-minimum system, namely that of a *fixed order interval* or cycle and *variable order quantities*. Such a system is shown in Fig. 12.3. After each ordering cycle, the stock level is brought up to the desired level (Q_1).

The principal advantage of this system is administrative. Since orders are placed at regular intervals those responsible for ordering, i.e. the purchasing, the stock control, or the production planning or control departments, are better able to plan their work.

Which Items to Control?

Many companies subject all items, purchased and produced, irrespective of their value, usage or quantity, to the same type of stock control procedure. Such a policy can be a waste of time and effort.

Although a high usage rate does not necessarily mean high stock levels, fast moving items, i.e. those for which the usage rate is high, and expensive items, are likely to incur greater storage

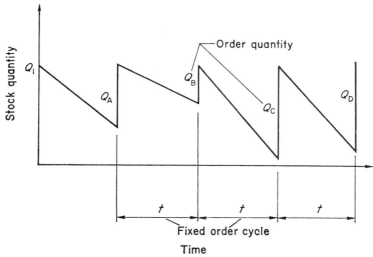

FIGURE 12.3. The order cycle system

cost than slow moving and inexpensive items. Consequently it should be our primary aim in stock control, to control the 'fast moving/expensive' items, since by so doing greater potential savings are possible than by concentrating on inexpensive items, usage of which is small.

One of the ubiquitous phenomena of business is expressed by the so-called '80/20 law'. In relation to inventory or stock, the law reads as follows: '80 per cent of the firm's total inventory cost is caused by only 20 per cent of all items'. In other words the 20 per cent cost/high usage items

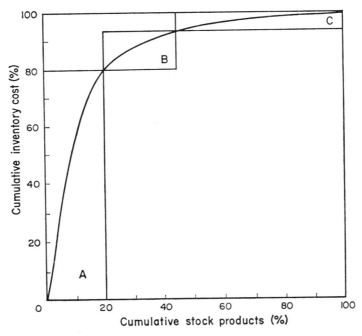

FIGURE 12.4. ABC chart for stock products

account for 80 per cent of total inventory costs. This 'law' or relationship can be expressed by the *ABC* or *Pareto* curve and often such curves are used by companies to divide stock items into three classes, A. B and C, i.e. those accounting for 80, 13 and 7 per cent of total inventory costs (Fig. 12.4). Such a classification, once achieved, enables stock control 'rules' for each type of product or item to be implemented. Thus, a comprehensive and regular stock control procedure should be designed for items of type A. Less rigorous control is necessary for type B whereas for C a simple procedure is sufficient.

THE DESIGN OF ORDERING SYSTEMS

We will now look more closely at the design of ordering systems, and will pay particular attention to the maximum–minimum system, which is perhaps more frequently adopted than the order cycle system.

If we look back to Fig. 12.2 it should be clear that two things must be considered, i.e. what is the fixed order quantity (Q) and what is the reorder level (Q_1)? We can deal with each of the questions separately.

Maximum–Minimum Systems—Order Quantity

As we have already pointed out, the act of replenishing inventories is costly. Such replenishment costs are proportionate only to the number of orders placed and not to the size of the orders. *The ordering cost* is then equivalent to the 'set-up' cost considered during our discussion of batch quantities for production in Chapter 11.

With respect to purchased items, the ordering cost consists of:

1. cost of placing order
2. cost of transport
3. cost of receiving
4. cost of clearing payment.

With respect to finished stock items, the ordering cost consists of:

1. set-up of machinery, etc.
2. defectives produced because of new tool and machine set-ups.

The fact that 'ordering cost' might refer to either purchased or manufactured items is irrelevant to the ensuing discussion.

A second group of costs that must be considered relates to stock levels and is considered proportionate to stock value. Such *holding costs* result from the cost of stores administration, depreciation, damage of items, insurance, notional loss of interest on capital, and so on.

A third group of costs is related to the occurrence of 'stock-outs' and is related to both the number of times and the durations for which stock items are not available to satisfy demand. Such costs comprise loss of orders present and future, loss of goodwill, etc.

The order quantity decision then is the determination of the most *economical order quantity*, the quantity which minimizes total variable costs. In graphical terms the problem is one of establishing the order or batch quantity corresponding to the lowest point on a total cost curve such as that shown in Fig. 12.5. Various economic order quantity (EOQ) models have been developed over the past 50 years so that now not only formulae but also tables, graphs, charts, etc., are available for calculating optimum order sizes in a variety of situations. The following are those commonly adopted and of most value.

Model 1(*a*)

1. Known constant demand
2. Complete deliveries
3. No shortages

The derivation of the economic order quantity formula for this model is unnecessary since it has previously been presented in Chapter 11.[2]

The notation adopted is:

Q = Order quantity

C_s = Ordering cost/Order

C_1 = Holding cost/Item/Unit of time

r = Usage rate

p = Direct cost per unit (price or manufacturing cost)

EOQ = $\quad Q^* = \sqrt{\dfrac{2C_s r}{C_1}}$ 1a.1

Order cycle $\quad t^* = \dfrac{Q^*}{r} = \sqrt{\dfrac{2C_s}{rC_1}}$ 1a.2

Total ordering and

holding cost per $\quad C^* = \sqrt{2C_s r C_1}$ 1a.3

unit time

Model 1(*b*)

As Model 1(a) *plus discontinuous discounts*, i.e. bulk discounts on purchase price or reductions in cost of manufacture resulting from use of different equipment for larger orders sizes.

To take advantage of such discounts we are encouraged to order a quantity larger than the economic order quantity.

Previously the total cost equation for C included only holding and ordering costs, since only these varied with order quantity. Now the price of the item, or its direct manufacturing cost, p is a function of order quantity and this must, therefore, be included in the cost equation, which is now as follows:

$$C^1 = \frac{C_s r}{Q} + C_1 \left(\frac{Q}{2}\right) + rp \qquad \text{1b.1}$$

The problem is to find the order quantity Q which leads to the minimization of this total cost C^1.

The item price p is a constant within each quantity range, e.g. let price = p_i within the quantity range:

$$q_i \leqslant q < q_{i+1}$$

---

[2] See Fig. 11.2 for the equivalent batch production model.

i.e. the price structure will be as follows:

$$p_1 \quad \text{for quantities } q_1 \leqslant q < q_2$$
$$p_2 \quad \text{for quantities } q_2 \leqslant q < q_3$$
$$p_3 \quad \text{for quantities } q_3 \leqslant q < q_4$$
$$p_{n-1} \text{ for quantities } q_{n-1} \leqslant q < q_n$$
$$p_n \quad \text{for quantities} \qquad q \geqslant q_n$$

A total cost function C^1 for a system with price breaks is shown in Fig. 12.5. Clearly our problem is to find the minimum (lowest) point on such a curve. This will occur at *either* the lower end of one of the price/quantity ranges *or* at the point at which the continuous part of the curve is minimum.

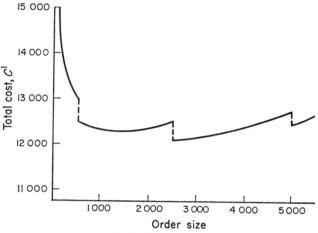

FIGURE 12.5. Total cost curve

Example

Order quantity	100–499	500–2 499	2 500–4 999	5 000 over
Price per unit	£5	£4·75	£4·6	£4·5

Find the economic order quantity given that the constant usage rate is 2 500 units per year, the holding cost, expressed as a percentage of unit price, is 10 per cent per unit per year and the ordering cost is £100.

To determine the optimum order quantity we must first calculate the total cost C associated with order quantities at the bottom of each price/quantity range, since one of these points may be the lowest on the curve, i.e.

Range 100–499 ($p = 5$)

$$C^1 = \frac{C_s r}{Q} + C_1 \left(\frac{Q}{2}\right) + rp$$

$$= \underbrace{\frac{100 \times 2\,500}{100}}_{\substack{\text{Ordering} \\ \text{cost/year}}} + \underbrace{\frac{0 \cdot 1\,(5)\,100}{2}}_{\substack{\text{Holding} \\ \text{cost/year}}} + \underbrace{2\,500\,(5)}_{\substack{\text{Item} \\ \text{cost/year}}}$$

$$\doteqdot £15\,025 \text{ per year}$$

Similarly

Range 500–2 499 $(p = 4\cdot75)$

$$C^1 = £12\ 494$$

Range 2 500–4 999 $(p = 4\cdot6)$

$$C^1 = £12\ 175$$

Range 5 000 and over $(p = 4\cdot5)$

$$C^1 = £12\ 425$$

Now we must look for the lowest point of the continuous part of the curve. This can be found by using the formula for economic order quantity.

$$Q = \sqrt{\frac{2C_s r}{C_1}}$$

but since C_1 is now a function of item cost we must calculate Q for each price/quantity range, i.e.
Range 100–499 $(p = 5)$

$$Q = \sqrt{\frac{2 \times 100 \times 2\ 500}{0\cdot1\ (5)}} = 1\ 000$$

Range 500–2 499 $(p = 4\cdot75)$

$$Q = \sqrt{\frac{2 \times 100 \times 2\ 500}{0\cdot1\ (4\cdot75)}} = 1\ 025$$

Range 2 500–4 999 $(p = 4\cdot6)$

$$Q = \sqrt{\frac{2 \times 100 \times 2\ 500}{0\cdot1\ (4\cdot6)}} = 1\ 040$$

Range over 5 000 and over $(p = 4\cdot5)$

$$Q = \sqrt{\frac{2 \times 100 \times 2\ 500}{0\cdot1\ (4\cdot5)}} = 1\ 055$$

Notice that only one of these values of Q falls on the total cost curve, since there is only one minimum point to such a curve. The point in question is $Q = 1\ 025$ which is within the quantity range 500–2 499. We must now calculate the total cost (C) for this ordering policy and compare it with the minimum previously obtained.

For $Q^* = 1\ 025$.

$$C^1 = \frac{C_s r}{Q} + C_1 \left(\frac{Q}{2}\right) + rp$$

$$= \frac{100 \times 2\ 500}{1\ 025} + 0\cdot1\ (4\cdot75)\ 1\ 025 + 4\cdot75\ (2\ 500)$$

$$= 244 + 243 + 11\ 875$$

$$= 12\ 362$$

This value is greater than the previous minimum of $C = £12\ 175$, consequently in this case it is economically beneficial to take advantage of the quantity discounts and order a quantity higher than might otherwise have been the case, i.e. $Q^* = 2\ 500$ units.

The total cost curve shown in Fig. 12.5 is plotted from the costs calculated above.

Model 1(*c*)

As model 1(a) *plus holding costs*, a proportion of which vary with the order quantity.

We have so far taken the unit holding cost C_1 as being a constant with respect to the order quantity, but there may be occasions where this relationship is untrue. For example, we have considered the holding cost (in the previous example) as being related to the price or value of the item being stored but since the price is perhaps dependent upon order quantity we ought logically to consider the case in which holding cost is a function of order quantity. Two such functions will be investigated, firstly, the case where holding cost varies continuously and secondly the discontinuous variation of holding cost.

(a) *Continuous Variation*

Let C_1 = Holding cost/unit/unit of time.

$\quad C_{11}$ = The fixed portion of C_1 which is unrelated to order quantity.

$\quad C_{12}$ = The variable portion of C_1 which is a function of order quantity.

Total cost of holding and ordering = C

$$= \quad \frac{C_s r}{Q} \quad + \quad C_{11}\left(\frac{Q}{2}\right) \quad + \quad C_{12}Q \qquad \text{1c.1}$$

Ordering   Fixed holding   Variable holding
cost/unit time   cost/unit time   cost/unit time

Differentiating with respect to Q:

$$\frac{dC}{dQ} = -\frac{C_s r}{Q^2} + \frac{C_{11}}{2} + C_{12}$$

Equating this to zero to obtain a minimum or maximum point gives:

$$Q^* = \sqrt{\frac{2\,C_s\,r}{C_{11}+2C_{12}}} \qquad \text{1c.2}$$

(b) *Discontinuous Variation of Holding Costs*

When storage space is rented it is frequently possible to obtain space only in fixed increments. For example, if a manufacturer who rents space in a warehouse finds that more space is required because of his new stock-holding policy, he may be offered the use of one further floor or department rather than the exact additional space required. In such cases the cost of holding varies discontinuously with order quantity as shown in Fig. 12.6. A similar situation may apply where a company finds it necessary to build additional storage space since again only certain increments can be added rather than the exact requirements. In the example shown in Fig. 12.6, order quantities of size Q_2 or greater necessitate an increase in holding costs to level H_2. The same increase is necessitated for each increase in order quantity (Q_0).

If this variable holding cost associated with the cost per unit of time for renting one increment of storage is C_{1A}, whilst C_{11} is the holding cost per item per unit of time which does not vary with order quantity, then the total cost of storage per unit of time, neglecting buffer stock, is:

$$C_1 = C_{1A}\left\{\frac{Q}{Q_0}\right\} + C_{11}\frac{Q}{2}$$

where $\left\{\dfrac{Q}{Q_0}\right\} = \begin{array}{l}\text{is the next integer larger} \\ \text{than } Q/Q_0\end{array}$ 1c.3

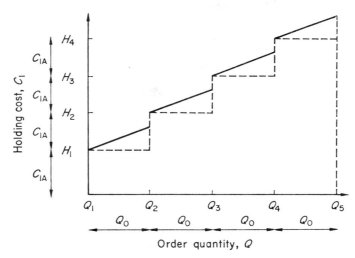

FIGURE 12.6. Holding cost—varying discontinuously with ordering quantity

Example

If storage space is available in increments each sufficient for 500 items, the cost per year for each increment being £400, and if the fixed cost of holding is £1 per item per year, what is the total annual holding cost if the order quantity is 750 items? There is no buffer stock.

$$C_1 = C_{1A}\left\{\frac{Q}{Q_o}\right\} + C_{11}\frac{Q}{2}$$

$$= 400\left\{\frac{750}{500}\right\} + 1\frac{750}{2}$$

$$= 400\,(2) \qquad \frac{750}{2} = £1\,175\,p.a.$$

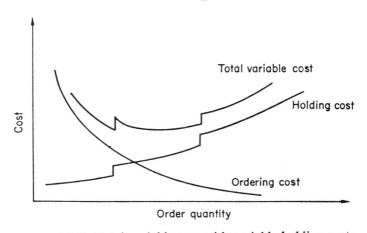

FIGURE 12.7. Total variable cost with variable holding costs.

In such cases the total cost of holding and ordering (C):

$$C = \frac{C_s r}{Q} + C_{1A}\left\{\frac{Q}{Q_0}\right\} + C_{11}\left(\frac{Q}{2}\right)$$

$$\underset{\text{Ordering}}{} \quad \underset{\text{Variable}}{} \quad \underset{\text{Fixed}}{}$$
$$\underset{\text{cost}}{} \quad \underset{\text{holding cost}}{} \quad \underset{\text{holding cost}}{}$$

The curve for total variable cost C is shown in Fig. 12.7. The economic order quantity can be determined in a similar manner as was used previously for price breaks. In this case the economic order quantity (i.e. the minimum point of the total variable cost curve) will occur *either* at the upper point of one of the holding cost increments *or* at the point at which the continuous part of the curve is at a minimum.

Model 1(d)[3]

As model 1(a) *except shortages allowed*. (See Fig. 11.5 in previous Chapter.)
    Notation—as before

plus C_2 = Shortage or stock-out cost per item per unit of time

Holding cost/unit of time $= \dfrac{C_1 S^2}{2Q}$

Shortage cost/unit of time $= \dfrac{C_2 (Q-S)^2}{2Q}$

Ordering cost/unit of time $= \dfrac{C_s r}{Q}$

Total variable cost $C \quad = \dfrac{C_1 S^2}{2Q} + \dfrac{C_2 (Q-S)^2}{2Q} + \dfrac{C_s r}{Q}$

Differentiating with respect to S and equating to zero gives:

$$S^* = \frac{QC_2}{C_1 + C_2} \qquad\qquad \text{1d.1}$$

Differentiating with respect to Q and equating to zero gives:

$$EOQ = Q^* = \sqrt{\frac{2rC_s}{C_1}}\sqrt{\frac{C_1 + C_2}{C_2}} \qquad\qquad \text{1d.2}$$

The total variable cost associated with this ordering policy is:

$$C^* = \sqrt{2rC_1 C_s}\sqrt{\frac{C_2}{C_1 + C_2}} \qquad\qquad \text{1d.3}$$

Model 1(e) Model 1(a) for multiple products (Fig. 12.8)

Our previous models have related to the ordering of a quantity of a *single* product, but in practice many occasions exist when our ordering decision and our ordering cost covers quantities of more

---

[3] The derivation of these formulae is given in Chapter 11, 'Planning for Batch Production'.

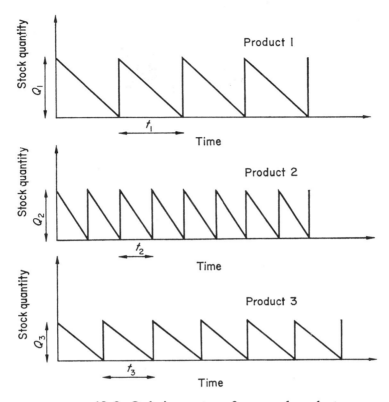

FIGURE 12.8. Ordering systems for several products

than one type of product. If, for example, the ordering cost during purchasing consists mainly of the cost of transport of items by road from the suppliers, then it is reasonable that the cost of ordering should be independent of both quantity of items and also the number of different types of products (except, of course, that larger quantities may necessitate a larger number of journeys).

Consider such a situation in which there are N different types of product to be ordered, where:

C_s = Ordering cost
Q_i = Order size for product i
　　　$(i = 1, 2, 3, \ldots N)$
r_i = Usage or consumption rate for product i
C_{1i} = Holding cost/item i/unit of time
t_i = Reorder cycle for item i

Since ordering cost is independent of the number of items ordered our objective, in order to attempt to minimize costs, must be to arrange the ordering policy so that as few orders as possible are made.

Referring to Fig. 12.8, the longest order cycle is for product 1 (t_1) and the shortest is for product 2(t_2). If the order cycle for product 1 is reduced then the average stock is also reduced from the present level $Q_1/2$. This in itself results in a reduction in the holding cost. Normally such savings would be offset to some extent by an increase in the costs of ordering due to the increase in the number of orders placed over a given period. However, in this case, if the order cycle is reduced so that it coincides with the order cycle for one of the other products, say $t_1 = t_2$, then since ordering cost is independent of order size and since no more orders are being placed than previously, ordering costs are *not* increased and total costs are decreased.

It follows then that for an optimum ordering policy, all ordering cycles should be of equal length and orders for different products should be made at the same time.

Now the order size for each product Q_i $= r_i t$

Ordering cost/unit of time $= \dfrac{C_s}{t}$

Holding cost per unit of time $= \displaystyle\sum_{i=1}^{N} \left(C_{1i} \dfrac{Q_i}{2} \right) = \sum_{i=1}^{N} \left(\dfrac{C_{1i} r_i t}{2} \right)$

∴ Total ordering and holding cost/unit of time $C = \displaystyle\sum_{i=1}^{N} \left(\dfrac{C_{1i} r_i t}{2} \right) + \dfrac{C_s}{t}$ 1e.1

Differentiating with respect to t:

$$\dfrac{\mathrm{d}C}{\mathrm{d}t} = \sum_{i=1}^{N} \left(\dfrac{C_{1i} r_i}{2} \right) - \dfrac{C_s}{t^2}$$

Equating to zero gives

$$\text{Optimum order cycle} = t^* = \sqrt{\dfrac{2C_s}{\displaystyle\sum_{i=1}^{N} C_{1i} r_i}} \qquad \text{1e.2}$$

by substituting for t in equation

$$\text{EOQ} = Q^* = r_i \sqrt{\dfrac{2C_s}{\displaystyle\sum_{i=1}^{N} C_{1i} r_i}} \qquad \text{1e.3}$$

Notice that when N (the number of different products) $= 1$ the equation for Q^* reduces to EOQ equation for the basic model–1(a).

Example

The table below gives data relating to three types of product which a company purchases for eventual use in its own products.

Purchased product	Annual usage (r_i)	Holding cost/ item/year (C_{1i})
A	5 000	£0·5
B	3 250	£1·0
C	2 900	£0·75

The cost of ordering is £125 per order irrespective of its content. Items of each product are delivered to the company by the supplier in complete orders. Neglecting buffer stock, what is the economic order size for each product and consequently the total order size.

$$Q^* = r_i \sqrt{\dfrac{2C_s}{\displaystyle\sum_{i=1}^{N} C_{1i}\, r_i}}$$

Product	$C_{1i}\, r_i$
A	2 500
B	3 250
C	2 275

$$\sum_{i=1}^{N} C_{1i}\, r_i = 8\,025$$

$$Q^*_A = 5\,000 \sqrt{\dfrac{2 \cdot 125}{8\,025}} = 878$$

$$Q^*_B = 3\,250 \sqrt{\dfrac{2 \cdot 125}{8\,025}} = 571$$

$$Q^*_C = 2\,900 \sqrt{\dfrac{2 \cdot 125}{8\,025}} = 509$$

$$\therefore Q^* = 1\,958$$

Model 2(a)[4]

1. Known constant demand
2. Delivery of order at a known and constant rate
3. No shortages
4. Buffer stock

Notation Q = Order quantity
C_s = Ordering cost
C_1 = Holding cost/item/unit of time
q = Delivery or production rate
r = Usage or consumption rate

Holding cost/unit of time $= \dfrac{C_1 Q}{2}\left(1 - \dfrac{r}{q}\right)$

Ordering cost/unit of time $= \dfrac{C_s r}{Q}$

Total variable cost $C = \dfrac{C_1 Q}{2}\left(1 - \dfrac{r}{q}\right) + \dfrac{C_s r}{Q}$

---

[4] The derivation of these formulae is given in Chapter 11, 'Planning for Batch Production'. This stock model is equivalent to the production model described by Fig. 11.1 in the previous chapter.

Differentiating with respect to Q and equating to zero gives:

$$\text{EOQ} = Q^* = \sqrt{\frac{2C_s r}{C_1\left(\frac{1-r}{q}\right)}} \qquad \qquad 2a.1$$

The total variable cost associated with this ordering policy is:

$$C^* = \sqrt{2C_s r C_1}\sqrt{1-\frac{r}{q}} \qquad \qquad 2a.2$$

Example

A company which uses a maximum-minimum stock ordering policy, orders 2 500 of purchased item A at a time. They wish to determine what annual saving might be made by ordering this item in different quantities. An examination of previous stock records indicates that the annual usage of these items is constant at 7 000. They further find that the cost of making an order, which is independent of the order size, is £10. The purchase price of the items is £0·5 and the cost of holding stock is 7 per cent of item price per item per year. The supplier undertakes to deliver the items at a constant rate of 50 per day.

q　　$= 50 \times 250/\text{year}$ (Assuming that there are 250 working days per year)
r　　$= 7\,000/\text{year}$
C_s　$= £10$
C_1　$= 0·07\,(0·5) = £0·035/\text{item/year}$

$$\text{EOQ} = Q^* = \sqrt{\frac{2 \times 10 \times 7\,000}{0·07\,(0·5) \times \left(1 - \frac{7\,000}{12\,500}\right)}}$$

Q^*　$= 3\,020$ units

Total annual variable cost associated with this policy C^*:

$$= \sqrt{2 \times 7\,000\ \ 10 \times 0·07\,(0·5)}\sqrt{1 - \frac{7\,000}{12\,500}}$$

$$= £46·5 \text{ p.a.}$$

Total annual variable cost associated with present policy:

$$= \frac{C_1 Q}{2}\left(1 - \frac{r}{q}\right) + \frac{C_s r}{Q}$$

$$= \frac{0·035 \times 2\,500}{2}\,(0·44) + 10 \times \frac{7\,000}{2\,500}$$

$$= £47·25 \text{ p.a.}$$

Potential annual saving on item A $= £0·25$.

Maximum–minimum Systems—Order Level

We decided earlier that in the *maximum-minimum, two-bin* or *order quantity* ordering system, two questions must be answered, namely—what is the fixed order quantity (Q) and what is the reorder level (Q_1)?

We have decided how, in a few typical situations, the fixed order quantity can be determined and we must now look at the problem of reorder levels.

If the usage or consumption of items is perfectly constant and accurately known and if stock replenishment time is zero, then the stock order *level* may be zero and orders for stock replenishments can be placed when stock falls to this level.

Unfortunately such an ideal situation rarely, if ever, exists. In practice two complications can arise. Firstly, usage rate may not be absolutely constant and consequently there is the risk that stock may be prematurely exhausted. Even so, if replenishment of stock is instantaneous, no problems arise because exhausted stock can immediately be replaced. The second complication concerns replenishment. If this is not immediate, then it becomes necessary to place orders some time prior to the items being needed. The occurrence of both these complications necessitates the maintenance of *buffer* or *safety stocks*.

If both of these complications arise in any magnitude then we cannot reasonably use any of the ordering models discussed in the previous section, since all of those assume a static and deterministic state. However, if these fluctuations are not excessive then these models can be used since only a slight, and usually tolerable, error is introduced.

To summarize then, the need to consider reorder levels other than zero arises because of uncertainty in demand and order or replenishment lead time. Such uncertainty is alien to the ordering models we have discussed but they can nevertheless be used, with only minor error, provided demand and lead time vary only marginally.

Figure 12.9 shows how variations in either, or both, lead time and demand might, unless buffer stock is used, result in a stock-out situation. Since we are dealing with potential variations in either usage or lead time or both, it will be convenient if we can find a way of measuring the consequences of both. This can be done by use of the term *Lead time usage* which is shown on Fig. 12.9 as U.

Lead time usage (U) for any product can be determined by an examination of stock records which should show when an order was placed, when it was received and what the usage was during this period. Lead time usage will not be constant, consequently a probability distribution such as that shown in Example 1 (Table 12.2) might be obtained.

Table 12.2 shows that usage during the lead time has varied from 32 items to 40 items, and has averaged 36. Stock-outs will have occurred on those occasions on which usage was in excess of the reorder level. For example, in this case, had the reorder level been 36 then the probability of lead time usage in excess of 36, and hence the probability of stock-outs, is 0·43.

In practice the probability distribution of lead time usage often conforms to the lognormal distribution, however the normal distribution can often be used as a close approximation and, of course, is computationally more convenient. Alternatively, and in cases where the distribution is not normal, the actual distribution obtained from stock records can be used in reorder level calculations.

To set the reorder level at a value which represents the absolute maximum lead time usage may be an unduly costly policy, since on comparatively few occasions will stock fall to zero. Setting the reorder point to a lower level will mean that stock-outs will occur, even so the cost over a given period of a few stock-outs may be less than the additional holdings costs that would be incurred if stock-outs were to be avoided. Ultimately, it is the magnitude of these costs—stock-outs and holding—that will determine the reorder level and hence the buffer stock level.

Stock-outs result in one of the following consequences:
1. The user, unable to obtain immediate satisfaction of his demands, takes his business elsewhere and hence there is a *lost sales* cost.
2 The user, unable to obtain immediate satisfaction of his demands, is *patient*, places his order

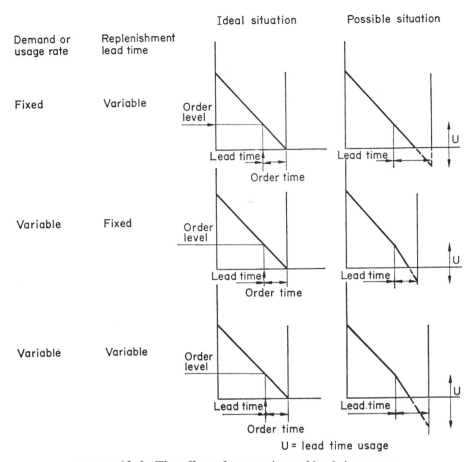

FIGURE 12.9. The effect of uncertainty of lead time usage

and awaits later delivery. This is typical of the situation where the user is another internal department of the company.

The cost of holding buffer stock will, of course, influence the choice of reorder level but increased buffer stock holding costs will be partly offset by reduction in the cost of stock-outs. In determining reorder levels these two costs must be compared. It is comparatively easy to determine the holding cost for buffer stock but more difficult to determine the cost of stock-outs. Consequently one solution is to avoid placing a cost on the incidence of stock-outs and merely to specify that a reorder level should be established which results in the occurrence of not more than a given number of stock-outs in a given period, say a year. This is known as specifying the *service level*. Alternatively, a cost figure can be placed on stock-outs, either as a fixed cost for stock-out period or as a cost per unit of the product per stock-out period.

The following three examples will illustrate how reorder levels are calculated for each of these three cases, i.e.

1. Service level
2. Fixed cost per stock-out period
3. Stock-out cost per unit per period

Example 1

The annual usage rate of a purchased product is 5 000. The cost of the product is 25p each, cost of placing the order is £1·25 and the cost of holding stock is 10 per cent of item price per year per item. Complete orders are delivered by the supplier.

An examination of the stock records indicates that lead time usage varies from 32 to 40 as shown in Table 12.2. Stock-outs are permitted, but no more than one per year should occur.

What is to be the reorder level?

TABLE 12.2

U	P(U)	P (actual usage > U)
32	0·02	0·98
33	0·07	0·91
34	0·12	0·79
35	0·16	0·63
36	0·20	0·43
37	0·17	0·26
38	0·13	0·13
39	0·10	0·03
40	0·03	0·00

Using EOQ formula 1a.1

$$Q^* = 700$$

Hence number of orders per year is $\dfrac{r}{Q}$

$$= \frac{5\ 000}{700} = 7·15$$

Now buffer stock (B) can be defined as the difference between the reorder level (R) and the average lead time usage $(\bar{U})$. Hence, if in this case the reorder level is set at 37:

$$B = R - \bar{U}$$
$$= 37 - 36$$
$$= 1$$
$$\text{etc.}$$

Now we can present all the information necessary for a solution in the form of a table (Table 12.3).

TABLE 12.3

	36	37	38	39	40
Re-order level R	36	37	38	39	40
Buffer stock B	0	1	2	3	4
Holding cost p.a. (10 per cent × B × 25p p.a.)	0	2·5p	5p	7 5p	10p
Stock-outs Probability per order	0·43	0·26	0·13	0 03	0·00
No. per year (Probability × 7·15)	3·07	1·86	0·93	0 21	0·00

Clearly from this table a reorder level of 38 must be used if no more than one stock-out per year is to occur.

Example 2

As for example 1 but instead of determining the reorder level to provide not more than one stock-out per year, determine the reorder level to minimize total cost. An analysis of past records has shown that stock-outs of this product lead to a fixed cost of 50 p per stock-out period. Alternative reorder levels are examined in Table 12.4.

TABLE 12.4

Reorder level R	36	37	38	39	40
Buffer stock B	0	1	2	3	4
Holding cost p.a. (1) (10 per cent × B × 25p p.a.)	0p	2·5p	5p	7·5 p	10p
Stock-outs No. per year		3·07	1·86	0·93	0·21	0·00
Cost per year (2) (at 50p each)	153·5p	93p	46·5p	10·5p	0p
Total cost per annum (1)+(2)	153·5p	95·5p	51·5p	18p	10p

Since the stock-out costs dominates the holding cost of buffer stock, in order to minimize total cost it is clearly beneficial in this case to adopt a reorder level of 40 which corresponds, of course, to the maximum lead time usage.

Example 3

As for example 1 but in this case it has been found that the stock-out costs depend not only on the number of times stock-outs occur but also on the number of units short or required during the stock-out periods. It has been found from records that the stock-out cost is 5p per item.

To determine the reorder level which provides minimum cost we must calculate not only the number of stock-outs per year at each reorder level but also the average number of units short during the stock-out periods, i.e.

$$\frac{\text{Average stock-out quantity}}{\text{during stock-out periods}} = \text{Average stock-out per order} \times \text{Probability of stock-outs occurring}$$

i.e. For reorder level $R = 36$

TABLE 12.5

Actual usage (U)	Stock-out quantity (U−R)	Probability P(U)	P(U)×(U−R)
37	1	0·17	0·17
38	2	0·13	0·26
39	3	0·10	0·30
40	4	0·03	0·12
		0·43	0·85

$$\therefore \text{ Average stock-out quantity during stock-out periods is } = \frac{0 \cdot 85}{0 \cdot 43} = 1 \cdot 98$$

Similarly:

For $R = 37$ Average stock-out quantity $= 1 \cdot 62$

$R = 38$ —,,— $= 1 \cdot 23$

$R = 39$ —,,— $= 1 \cdot 00$

$R = 40$ —,,— $= 0 \cdot 00$

Now all the data necessary to compare the merits of different reorder levels can be presented in tabular form, as in Table 12.6.

TABLE 12.6

Reorder level R	36	37	38	39	40
Average stock-out quantity per stock-out period	1·98	1·62	1·23	1·00	0·00
Buffer stock B	0	1	2	3	4
Holding cost per annum (1)	0p	2·5p	5p	7·5p	10p
Stock-outs Number per year	3·07	1·86	0·93	0·21	0·00
Cost (No × quantity × 5p) (2)	30·4p	15p	5·7p	1p	0p
Total cost per annum (1) + (2)	30·4p	17·5p	10·7p	8·5p	10p

These figures indicate that the minimum cost reorder level is 39, which results in an average of 0·21 stock-outs per year.

Merits of the Maximum–Minimum System

The chief advantage of this type of system is its simplicy and reliability. Where stock levels of each product can be continually monitored, either by a perpetual inventory system or by visual inspection, the system is easily, and often efficiently, adopted. It is particularly suitable where low cost items are concerned, since such items can be ordered in large quantities and obtained at comparatively short notice. However, this system may incur high ordering costs if a large variety of products are stocked.

The Order Cycle System

If, to begin with, we again assume that usage or demand is constant and known, then this system of ordering is, in both practice and theory, identical to the maximum-minimum or order quantity system. In the maximum–minimum system, when stock falls to a predetermined level (which can be zero if order delivery is instantaneous), a further predetermined quantity of items is ordered. In the order cycle system, at predetermined intervals, a quantity of goods sufficient to restore stock to a given level is ordered. In the ideal conditions we have assumed both the order quantity and the order cycle would be the same, irrespective of the system we adopt. Consequently for such cases the answers to our two basic questions—when to order and how much to order—can be found in the previous section, i.e.

$$\text{Order interval} = \frac{\text{Order quantity}}{\text{Usage rate}}$$

$$\text{Optimum order interval} = \frac{\text{EOQ}}{\text{Usage rate}}$$

$$\text{i.e. } t^* = \frac{Q^*}{r}$$

For the models we examined in the previous section the optimum order intervals are given by the following formulae:

Model 1(a)

$$t^* = \sqrt{\frac{2C_s}{rC_1}}$$

Model 1(b)

$$t^* = \frac{Q^*}{r}$$

Model 1(c)

$$t^* = \sqrt{\frac{2C_s}{r(C_{11}+2C_{12})}}$$

Model 1(d)

$$t^* = \sqrt{\frac{2C_s}{rC_1}}\sqrt{\frac{C_1+C_2}{C_2}}$$

Model 1(e)

$$t^* = \sqrt{\frac{2C_s}{\sum_{i=1}^{N}(C_{1i}\,r_i)}}$$

Model 2(a)

$$t^* = \sqrt{\frac{2C_s}{rC_1\left(1-\dfrac{r}{q}\right)}}$$

It is only during conditions of uncertainty that these two methods of ordering differ. The fundamental characteristic of the order cycle system is that the stock status of each product is examined at regular and fixed intervals, at which time the following questions are asked:
1. Should an order be placed to replenish stock now?
2. If so, how many units must be ordered?

Under conditions of uncertainty of either demand or order lead time or both, a buffer stock must be maintained. But unlike the maximum–minimum ordering system, buffer stocks in the order cycle system must protect against not only changes in lead time demand but also variations in demand at all other times. For example, consider the situation shown in Fig. 12.10. The fixed order cycle is t whilst lead time is constant at 1. Usage during lead time 1_2 conforms exactly to expectations, consequently order for quantity Q at this time eventually results in the replenishment of stock to the desired level Q_2. Usage remains constant during the following period and during the order lead time 1_3 and again stock is replenished to the desired level. However, during the next lead time usage is greater than normal and consequently some of the buffer stock is

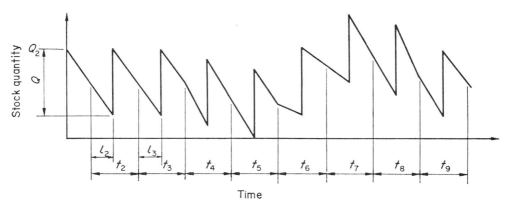

FIGURE 12.10. Order cycle stock ordering system (using a fixed order quantity)

consumed before replenishment can take place, therefore, unless a larger quantity is ordered, stock is replenished to a level less than Q_2. Usage during the entire next period is again greater than normal and further buffer stock is consumed. Again, unless a larger quantity of the product is ordered, the maximum stock level will fall since buffer stock must, as shown here, accommodate usage fluctuations throughout the entire period rather than just fluctuations during lead time, larger buffer stocks are normally required for order cycle systems than for maximum–minimum systems.

The order cycle system is clerically more convenient than the maximum–minimum system. Since stocks are reviewed and orders placed at regular intervals, the stock control department can more easily plan their activities and make better use of their time, however, the penalty for this administrative convenience is that generally the use of such a system involves the adoption of higher stock levels. The system is particularly suitable where stocks consist of a larger number of different products, since in such cases the ordering cost is often less than the equivalent cost for variable interval (maximum–minimum) ordering.

Computers in Stock Control

The use of computers in stock control occurs in three broad categories as follows:

1. *The design of decision rules*

Several companies offer programmes which can be used to develop and test different stock control systems. Simulation can be used to test the effect of various stock control policies, thus avoiding the necessity and dangers of real experiment. The ICL 'Stockplan' service is an example of this type of computer application.

Input to the 'Stockplan' programmes include:

(a) *Historical transaction data* showing the quantities of each product received into or issued from stores and the date of the transactions.

(b) *Stock bin data* showing, for each product, the order lead time, price, set-up cost, etc.

(c) *Operating costs*, including costs of holding and servicing stock, ordering costs, etc. The 'Stockplan' programmes can be used to analyse the stock transactions, apply several forecasting techniques to the data[5] and test a variety of stock ordering rules against the data in order that appropriate and effective stock control procedures can be developed and adopted.

---

[5] Moving averages, regression on past values, exponential smoothing and a probability method.

2. *The recording of stock transactions*

Pre-punched cards fed into and read by remote card readers placed in the stores might be used to record stock transactions. Alternatively stock transactions over a period might be punched on tape or cards and stock records up-dated by regular computer runs.

3. *Actual operation of stock control procedures*

Once appropriate stock control rules have been developed and tested a computer may be used to control stocks either on a continuous or periodic run basis. In addition to maintaining and using current stock records, reports and summaries such as the following might be prepared for use by management:

> Stock exception reports
> Stock status reports
> Stock analysis showing frequency of transactions,
> Stock values, usage, etc.

SUMMARY

Almost every company maintains stocks of raw materials, work-in-progress and finished products. The purpose of stock is as follows:

1. To act as a buffer against changes in demand
2. To provide quick service to customers
3. To act as a buffer against fluctuations in production
4. To stabilize employment and production
5. To 'decouple' production stages
6. To enable quantity purchasing discounts to be obtained
7. To ensure against disruptions in supply.

These benefits are to some extent off-set by the costs associated with increased inventory levels. The cost of inventory arises from:

1. Procurement or ordering costs
2. Set-up costs
3. Holding costs.

Two basic stock control systems exist, firstly the 'maximum-minimum', 'two bin' or 'order quantity' system and secondly, the 'order cycle' system. In the former fixed quantities of items are ordered and in the latter orders are placed at fixed intervals. Where demand or usage rate is perfectly constant, the practical results of both these systems are identical, since in both cases the order cycle and order quantity would be the same. Only where there is uncertainty in usage or demand does the operation of the two systems differ. Furthermore, it is only because of uncertainty in demand that it is necessary to maintain buffer stocks, the sole purpose of which is to ensure against changes of usage during the order lead time, i.e. the time between the placing of the order and its receipt.

The various formulae for determining economic order quantities depend upon the assumption of known and constant demand. Such an assumption is rarely justified in practice, nevertheless where only minor variations exist these formulae can be used in the design of ordering and stock control systems. Where major variations in demand and order lead time exist, conventional EOQ and buffer stock formulae are inadequate and probabilistic methods *not* discussed in this chapter must be used in the design of stock control systems.

Many stock control procedures, particularly those involving the control of a large number of products and a large number of stock transactions, depend upon electronic data processing or computing. Computers find use in three ways, namely for the design and testing of stock decision rules, the recording of stock transactions and the operation of stock control procedures.

SELECTED READINGS

R. G. BROWN, *Decision Rules for Inventory Management*, Holt, Rinehart and Winston, London, 1967.

R. STANSBURY STOCKTON, *Basic Inventory Concepts and Analysis*, Allyn and Bacon, Boston, Mass., 1965.

P. G. BRIGGS, etc., ICI Monograph No. 4, *Problems of Stocks and Storage*, Oliver and Boyd, London, 1967.

J. F. MAGEE and D. M. BOODMAN, *Production Planning and Inventory Control*, 2nd ed., McGraw-Hill, London, 1967.

The above books give a mathematical treatment of stock control whereas the following are more descriptive, and are primarily concerned with stock control procedures:

A. MORRISON, *Storage and Control of Stock*, 2nd ed., Pitman, London, 1969.

A. BATTERSBY, *A Guide to Stock Control*, BIM/Pitman, London, 1962.

A. B. THOMAS, *Stock Control in the Manufacturing Industries*, Gower Press, London, 1968.

The following book deals at length with forecasting for stock control:

D. A. BARRETT, *Automatic Inventory Control Techniques*, Business Publications, London, 1969.

QUESTIONS

12.1. Describe the principles of Maximum–Minimum and Order Cycle systems of stock control. In what circumstances is the use of each of these types of system appropriate?

In what circumstances would the use of either system give rise to basically the same stock control system (i.e. the same ordering decision).

12.2. In a certain situation, demand for products is both known and stable. The products are ordered from an 'outside' supplier, they are delivered in complete batches and no quantity discount arrangements apply. No buffer stock is to be maintained.

Determine (a) the economic order quantity, given:

Ordering cost per order	£20
Holding cost per item per annum	£0·05
Demand per annum	10 000
Price per item	£15

(b) the economic order quantity, given:

Ordering cost per order	£20
Holding cost per item per annum	5 per cent of item price
Demand per annum	10 000
Price per item	£15

(c) the regular economic ordering interval, given:

Ordering cost per order	£50
Holding cost per item per annum	5 per cent of item price
Demand per annum	15 000
Price per item	£25

12.3. Determine the economic order quantity for the following:

(a) C_s (ordering cost)   £20
    C_1 (holding cost per item)   £0·07
    r (demand)   12 000
    p (price)   £25

(b) C_s £20
    C_1 £0·07
    r 12 000
    Purchase discounts as follows:

Order quantity	0–500	500–999	1 000–2 500	Over 2 500
Price per item	£25	£22	£20	£19·5

(c) C_s £20
    C_1 10 per cent of price per annum
    r 10 000
    Purchase discounts as follows:

Order quantity	0–500	500–999	1 000–2 500	Over 2 500
Price per item	£25	£22	£20	£19·5

12.4. Determine the economic order quantity given the following situation:

C_s £100
r 10 000

Holding cost per item per annum, a portion of which is fixed and unrelated to the order quantity, i.e. £0·05, and a variable portion which *is* related to the order quantity, i.e. £0·07.

12.5. Determine the cost of storage and ordering per annum for order quantities of (a) 1 000, (b) 2 000 and (c) 3 000 items, given the following:

C_s £150
r 12 000

also, storage space is available in increments each sufficient for storing 1 000 items. The cost per annum for each of these increments is £500 and the fixed cost of storage irrespective of quantity is £0·5 per annum.

No buffer stock is required.

12.6. (a) Derive the formula used to determine economic order quantities in the following circumstances:

Stock-outs permitted
Delivery of complete batches of ordered items
Deterministic and stable demand

(b) What is the EOQ given the following:

  Ordering cost   £125
  Annual demand 7 500 items
  Shortage or stock-out cost per item per month £5
  Stock-holding cost per item per annum, 10 per cent of price
  Price of each item £50

12.7. A company uses 75 000 components of a certain type each year, which it purchases from an outside supplier under the following terms:

Order size units	Price per unit (£)
1 to 999	0·60
1 000 to 9 999	0·54
10 000 upwards	0·45

Each time an order is placed clerical and handling costs of £5 and transport costs of £15 are incurred.

The cost of storage, interest and deterioration is £0·08 per unit stored per year. No safety stock is held.

If the components are used at a uniform rate calculate the economic order size and the total annual cost to the company.

[Univ. of Salford, Dip. for Advanced Studies in Management 1st year, *Production Management*, July 1968—part of question only.]

12.8. (The first part of this question was also given after the previous chapter.)

(a) The assembly section of a factory uses a certain component part at a rate of 40 units per day.

The machine shop within the factory can produce the component at a rate of 200 per day. The associated set-up cost is 100 mu (money units), the manufacturing cost is 5 mu, and the inventory holding cost is 0·1 mu per unit per day.

If management is prepared to tolerate an increase of up to 1 per cent in the minimum total cost per unit, what flexibility does this give in the choice of batch quantities and what is the total cost per unit of the cheapest solution if, for technical reasons, production batches are restricted to multiples of 50 units?

(b) The component part can be purchased in any quantity from an outside source, the terms depending upon the quantity supplies as shown below:

Order quantity (no. of units)	Price per unit (mu)
0–249	5·5
250–499	5·2
500 or more	5

If the ordering costs are 15 mu per order, what is the economic order quantity in this case? Is it cheaper to manufacture the component in the factory or purchase it from the outside supplier?

[Univ. of London. Imperial College, M.Sc. Operational Research and Management Studies, Industrial Engineering 1, *Production Planning and Control*, April 1968— 45 minutes.]

12.9. Quick Start Ltd, are the 'manufacturers' of automobile batteries. They purchase three types of second-hand battery from a local company which, after rebuilding, they sell to local dealers. Sales of each type of battery are stable. The cost of storage and the annual demand for the batteries are shown in the table below.

Quick Start Ltd. like to order all three types of second-hand battery from their suppliers simultaneously. The cost of ordering is £175. They do not believe in maintaining buffer stocks of batteries.

(a) What are the economic order quantities for each type of battery?

Type of battery	Annual demand	Stock-holding cost of item per annum
Startrite	5 000	£0·5
Quickfire	7 000	£0·7
Longlife	3 500	£0·7
Highpower	2 750	£0·4

(b) What is the order interval?

12.10. A shoe shop takes delivery of Phrayle shoes once every three months. The shoes cost about £2 per pair and retail at £4.

What recommendations on stocks would you make for the various sizes and fittings?

[Univ. of Warwick, M.Sc., Management, *Quantitative Methods* 1, September 1968.]

12.11. The Universal Manufacturing Co. purchase plastic 'U' bends from a local company. They use the bends at a fairly constant rate of 2 500 per year. The cost of placing an order for the bends is £15 and the stock-holding cost per bend per year is £0·10.

Unfortunately, the supplier of the 'U' bends is a little unreliable and, consequently, the lead time on orders (which are always delivered complete) varies. In fact, a study of the purchase and production records reveals that lead time varies from two to four days and that the usage of bends during the lead time varies from 15 to 25 with the probabilities shown below.

Lead time usage of bends	Probability of usage
15	0·02
16	0·05
17	0·07
18	0·10
19	0·16
20	0·20
21	0·17
22	0·14
23	0·06
24	0·02
25	0·01

The Universal Manufacturing Co. insist that on no more than one occasion per year should there be stock-outs of 'U' bends.

(a) What should the order quantity and reorder level be?

(b) If the cost per stock-out is found to be £0·25, what reorder level provides the minimum cost?

12.12. Calculate the order quantity and the reorder level, to minimize costs, given the following information:

Annual usage	= 3 000
Ordering cost	= £150
Price per item	= £50
Stock-holding cost/item per annum	= 20 per cent of item per annum
Fixed cost of stock-out	= £1
Maximum number of stock-outs allowed per annum =	1

Lead time usage	Frequency
20	5
21	15
22	22
23	32
24	40
25	32
26	22
27	15
28	5

12.13. Referring to the previous question, it has recently been discovered that the cost of stock-outs depends not only upon the frequency of stock-outs but also upon the number of items short during stock-outs. The stock-out cost has been found to be £1 per item short during the stock-out period. Using the information provided in the previous question, determine the reorder level and order quantity which minimizes costs.

12.14. A store stocks an item for which the annual average demand is 250. The demand during the lead time is normally distributed (15, 4).

The item sells at £32·5 and is bought at:

> £20   (if up to 39 are bought)
> £18·5   (if between 40 and 99 are bought)
> £16·5   (if 100 or more are bought in any order).

Inventory cost per year is taken as 20 per cent of stock value. The goodwill loss for each item not supplied against customer demand is taken as £10 and the cost of an order to the suppliers as £1·5.

If a lot size/reorder point system is used, determine the best order quantity, reorder point, safety stock and the annual cost.

[Universities of Lancaster and Sussex, Masters degree in Operational Research *Paper 3*— 35 minutes.]

M

13

Production Control

Few processes will operate continuously and effectively without the exercise of a certain amount of external control. The government as well as planning, must also exercise control in order to maintain a healthy national economy, within the economy, managements must exercise control to maintain or improve the performance of their companies and within such companies control must be exercised over the various manufacturing and administrative processes.

The production control department is responsible not only for the use but also for the design of such control systems in the production function. Theirs will be the responsibility for diagnosis and, perhaps, also for treatment, although in many cases, particularly when applied to processes, treatment is the responsibility of other departments, such as production engineering.

Ideally, the efficiency of an individual process or an amalgam of processes is measured by comparing output to input, but not only is it in practice difficult to measure input (which might consist of materials, administration, labour, etc.) and output, but also this ratio takes no direct account of duration, i.e. the time period between input and output. Consequently some more ready and realistic measurement of efficiency must be used. Such a measure is the comparison of requisite performance with actual performance, i.e. comparison of targets with results. This is not only a responsibility of production control but also a measure of the effectiveness of production control, always assuming of course that targets, i.e. production plans, have been established realistically.

Production control is concerned with the monitoring and *regulation* of production. It is concerned with the implementation of a predetermined production plan or policy and the control of all aspects of production to ensure that planned targets and schedules are satisfied. Production control, therefore, is a function which operates after production planning. Planning is concerned exclusively with the pre-production period, while control is concerned with the immediate pre-production, and during-production stages.

The five rudimentary steps of production control are:

1. Initiating operations
2. Recording the progress of jobs
3. Analysing progress by comparison with plans or schedules
4. Control, i.e. modification of plans or rearrangement of jobs, in order to conform, as near as possible, to original targets.
5. Final analysis of completed production to provide information to improve future production planning and control.

As in production planning the precise nature, extent, complexity and importance of each of these steps is mainly a function of the type of production which, of course, is largely dependent upon the nature of the product. Before discussing production control further, it will be of value to recap briefly about the different types of production and examine some of the characteristics which influence production control.

PRODUCTION CONTROL IN DIFFERENT TYPES OF PRODUCTION

In *continuous*, large-scale, mass or large-batch production, a large volume of standardized parts are produced. Specialized equipment is invariably used, often taking the form of purpose designed assembly lines. Little flexibility is evident in such systems, semi-skilled and unskilled labour is usually employed and work is often of a repetitive, highly rationalized nature. Production in continuous manufacture is usually for stock rather than to order, i.e. a standard range of products is made in sufficient numbers to meet a known or expected demand. Individual customers are not associated with individual products during the manufacturing stage but only at a later (often retailing) stage, when products are drawn from finished stock. Production control in this type of production is known as *flow* or *serialized* control because its primary purpose is to control the flow or rate of production through the plant.

In *intermittent*, small-scale, jobbing or small-batch production, companies generally manufacture a wide range of varied products, often in small quantities. General purpose equipment, both production and service, (e.g. materials handling etc.) is normally used and a great deal of flexibility must exist in the system in order that the company might accommodate demand fluctuations, product design changes, special customer requirements, etc. Layout is normally on a 'process' basis, a high proportion of the labour used is skilled and production is often, in fact normally, to specific customer order rather than for stock. The production control procedure in this type of manufacture is known as *order* control, since the principal objective is to ensure that a particular order is delivered on or before the time required. In *process* production, which is in fact only an extension of mass production, one or more products are produced in bulk. In other words, whereas above we have been talking about discrete items, e.g. cars, pieces of engineering equipment, etc., in the *process* type of continuous manufacture we are concerned with output measured in terms of gallons, cubic feet, etc. Equipment in process production is special purpose, e.g. oil refineries, production is usually for stock, labour is skilled, flexibility is low and investment large. Production control in the process industries is normally referred to as *process* control, a term which nowadays is mainly associated with the use of digital or analogue computers.

Other, hybrid, types of production control exist which have been developed to fit the needs of specific industries, often these consist of components of the above types or embellishments on one or more of them. We will, therefore, confine our discussion to these three basic and common types.

Production Control in Continuous Production

After our fairly length discussion of assembly line design in Chapter 10, there is little else to say in this section, since once the decision to manufacture certain products in certain quantities has been made and the assembly line designed, there should be little need for external control. *The emphasis in mass or continuous production is on planning and not control.* In fact, an assembly line might be likened to one large machine (particularly so in the case of transfer lines) for which it is necessary only to adjust the output rate as one might adjust the performance of a single machine.

Strictly speaking, the same steps are involved as in any other type of production control, but in many cases they are trivial. Consider the first of our five rudimentary steps—initiate operations, i.e. load machine. In a less sophisticated continuous production system it will be the responsibility of production control to 'set up' the system to perform at the planned rate. Authorization to produce will be provided from production planning on a document such as the production programming release, which gives the requisite production of each product for a comparatively short period ahead, e.g. the next week or even the next shift. The output quoted will reflect not only the demand but also the production capacity. An assembly line designed to produce items at an average rate of 500 per 8-hour shift with not normally be required to provide quantities differing greatly from this capacity, since such requests would indicate either the need for redesign of the line to meet an adjusted demand level, or the need for a different stock-keeping policy to provide even loading of production facilities. In such cases the biggest potential problem for production control is arranging overtime, second shifts and rearrangement of labour and often the problem is one of merely ensuring continuing production at the existing level.

In elaborate and comprehensive continuous production systems, even the regular supply of materials and components to the assembly line will be automatic. The production programming release, copies of which will have been sent to other departments such as stores, will ensure the supply of materials and components at the correct frequency and the provision of services such as inspection, etc. Alternatively, this may be the job of production control. Again, the production control department should only need to arrange for their provision, since the fact that such items are required by the production plan should be sufficient to indicate their existence. (There is little benefit in calling for an output quantity which is in excess of the available material levels). Likewise, the provision of materials and components from outside suppliers will usually be geared to the requisite production rate, often being supplied daily and being transported directly to the point of use.

The second step of the production control procedure—record the progress of jobs—does not give rise to any substantial task since, once started in production, the progress of jobs will be automatic. Analysis of the progress of jobs (step 3) and the modification of production plans or rearrangement of jobs (step 4) is unnecessary in this type of production except, perhaps, where facilities, labour or work methods are being used for the first time, in which case some adjustment in production schedules, rearrangement of equipment or changes in work methods may be necessary. Similarly, retrospective analysis (step 5) will be invaluable in newly-designed continuous production systems but unnecessary once an acceptable arrangement has been obtained.

It is clear, therefore, that in continuous production, production control is neither a large or difficult tasks. It is, nevertheless, important since accuracy and timing are fundamental to efficient mass production, minor errors in quantity and timing often resulting in very expensive hold-ups and heavy losses of production.

Errors do occur. Materials and components may not be available because of the failure of outside suppliers or because of breakdowns in other departments and in such cases the production controller, in conjunction with departmental management, must make emergency provisions, arrange for temporary stocks, redeploy labour, etc. Additionally continuous manufacture may necessitate a small amount of batch manufacture, consequently the production controller may assume duties similar to those discussed in the next section. (Such a situation might arise on a multi-model assembly line when a small quantity of a certain product requiring peculiar or modified components is produced.)

Production Control in Intermittent Manufacture

The complexity of production control varies inversely with the accuracy of production planning. As we have already seen, in mass production it is possible to construct detailed and realistic production schedules because the products we are making are few and the equipment has been specifically designed for their manufacture. Consequently, production control is easy. In intermittent manufacture it is possible to construct production schedules for each order or product, but inevitably such schedlues are frequently inaccurate and often unrealistic. Consequently their use, whilst necessary, makes for difficulties in production control. Inaccuracy in production planning results from the fact that a variety of products are to be made each likely to require processing for different durations on different machines and in a different order. Often such products have not been made before and consequently the operation times, which are the basis of production planning, have only been estimated from previous experience. Allowances for contingencies, delays and queueing also features in the production schedule since a considerable amount of work in progress is a feature of this type of production.

In intermittent manufacturing, the emphasis is on control rather than on planning. The most complex situation occurs in the classic jobbing shop situation which we shall use for illustrative purposes throughout this section.

To recap briefly, the following features of jobbing production are the causes of complexity in production control:

(a) Unique or varied nature of products
(b) Variable nature of demand for parts
(c) General purpose, often expensive, equipment.

Jobbing shops generally operate with the following characteristics, all of which contribute to make production management and particularly production control in jobbing manufacture, one of the most complex and challenging aspects of industrial management.

1. Comparatively long manufacturing intervals from receipt of order to despatch of goods
2. Very high 'work-in-progress' stocks
3. Long queues of jobs between machines, yet paradoxically—
4. Underutilization of equipment
5. Frequent overtime and sub-contracting of work
6. Comparatively large number of indirect, supervisory or clerical workers
7. Great deal of 'job idle' time, i.e. the total processing time is greatly in excess of the sum of operationg times.[1]

Referring again to the five rudimentary steps in production control:

1. *Initiating operations* During production planning a schedule for the production of each item has been constructed, in the manner described in Chapter 8. The starting date or the finish date of each operation will have been defined but the interval between successive dates is composed of both operation times and contingency or queueing allowance, the latter being necessary because of the inevitable formation of queues. A machine operator, on completion of his operation on one job, is therefore able to choose one of several waiting jobs to process next. The selection is determined by the production control department whose task it is to place these waiting jobs in the requisite priority order. (Remember that they may all have the same schedule date). This is known as the *dispatching* or *sequencing* problem, a problem of fundamental importance in job shop production control, which we will deal with in detail later in this section.

In order to avoid confusion either now or at a later stage, it will be worth our while to pause

---

[1] The average ratio of total processing time (total time in shop) to the sum of the operation times for jobs in a medium machine shop in a jobbing production factory known to the author is 20 : 1.

here to sort out some of our terminology. Throughout this text we have used the term *scheduling* to correspond to the planning function of attaching dates to jobs—drawing bar charts, as it were. There is, however, considerable controversy and confusion concerning the meaning of four terms frequently used in relation to production planning and control, namely *scheduling, sequencing, loading* and *dispatching*. In this chapter we shall use only two of these terms, *sequencing* and *dispatching*. Both sequencing and dispatching will be used as terms describing the method by which the order in which jobs are to be processed on one or more machines is determined. Dispatching will be used to describe the selection of jobs from a waiting queue of jobs at one machine, i.e. the determination of priorities in the queue at a *single* facility. Sequencing will be used where the decision concerns the order of jobs on *several* machines. Our use of the term dispatching is conventional but some authors prefer to use the term scheduling to describe what we shall call sequencing. Clearly the two have something in common but we prefer to retain the term scheduling for the longer term production planning problem.

2. *Recording the progress of jobs* A close check on the progress of jobs must be maintained in order that corrective action may be taken whenever necessary. Traditionally this function is known as *Progressing* or *progress chasing* and is normally such an essential feature of production control that it is frequently mistaken for production control! With the recent advent of the use of computers in production control, progress monitoring is changing from a substantially clerical function to a semi-automatic procedure.

3. *Analysing progress* by comparison with plans or schedules. Before adjustments and modifications can be made facts must be compared to intentions, again traditionally a function of the progress chaser, who was also often responsible for taking corrective action.

4. *Control* Delays in processing will necessitate reassessment of sequencing decisions for the items concerned and also for all other dependent items, of which there may be many. Minor delays can be accommodated because of the allowances made in the production schedule but major delays may necessitate adjustment of original schedules or even of product delivery dates.

5. *Final analysis* Systems, including production planning and control, should ideally be self-improving. Such might be the case in computer-based process control but it is not normally a major feature of manual systems. The primary purpose of retrospective analysis is to ensure that mistakes, errors and delays which have occurred will not occur again. For example, it may be necessary to increase the delay or idle allowance in scheduling for certain types of items, for certain machines or certain machine shops. It may also (hopefully) be possible to reduce such allowances. Details of production performance should be accumulated so that future decisions can be made and of course opportunities should be taken to improve both planning and control procedures whenever desirable.

The Sequencing and Dispatching Problem

As mentioned previously scheduling is concerned with the timing of operations and hence with the timing of the arrival of jobs at machines. In continuous production, assembly lines for example, planning and scheduling can be performed accurately, hence unplanned queues of jobs rarely occur between machines. In jobbing production this is not the case, work-in-progress inventories do occur, queues do form before machines, and hence the decision has to be made as to which of the several available jobs will be processed next, when each machine becomes vacant. More often than not it is a question of which job to do on one machine and the selection of the job is referred to as the 'dispatching' problem. Far less frequently it is a question of what order shall available jobs be done on several machines. This we shall refer to as the 'sequencing' problem.[2]

The sequencing problem as described above is far less frequent than the dispatching problem, and therefore we will deal with this problem first.

Consider an apparently simple situation, in which five jobs must all be processed on each of six machines. Neglecting precedence constraints there are $(5!)^6$ i.e. 2·9 million million, alternative solutions! In view of such alarming combinatorial mazes, which can result from seemingly simple problems, it is hardly surprising that the sequencing problem is one of the most complex facing the production manager. Analytical investigation of the problem began only about ten years ago but a great deal of useful work has been done.

Many of the early algorithms relied on numerous assumptions and simplifications in order to achieve a solution and, consequently, were of value only in simple and abstract cases. Even now no practical rigorous solution to the problem has been found.

It is important to distinguish between two classes of problems. Firstly, the *static* case, in which all jobs to be processed are known and are available and in which no additional jobs arrive into the queue during the exercise. Secondly, the *dynamic* case which allows for the continuous arrival of jobs into the queue. Associated with these two cases are certain objectives. In the static case, the problem is merely to sequence a given queue of jobs through a given number of machines, each job passing through the machines in the requisite order and spending the necessary amount of time at each. The objective in such a case is usually to minimize the total time required to process all jobs—the *throughput* time. In the dynamic case, the objective of sequencing might be to minimize machine idle time, minimize work in progress or to achieve the requisite completion or delivery dates for each job.[3]

The first rigorous solution to a job-shop sequencing problem was given by Johnson (see Selected Readings) who, initially, dealt with the very simple case of two machines ($m = 2$) and n jobs and later produced an extension for three machines ($m = 3$).

Sequencing—Two Machines, n Jobs. Where n jobs are to be processed on each of two machines (A and B) with the same order (A, B) and no passing.

Let A_i = set up time + processing time for job i on machine A
$$A_i > 0 \cdot (i = 1 \ldots n)$$
B_i = the same for machine B

Objective: to minimize T (total throughput time)

TABLE 13.1

i	A_i	B_i
1	A_1	B_1
2	A_2	B_2
3	A_3	B_3
↓	↓	↓
n	A_n	B_n

[2] This notation is, unfortunately, not adopted by all authors and we shall have cause to cite papers which adopt several different terminologies.

[3] The description of sequencing methods and the examples used are based on the following articles by the author: 'Jobbing shop sequencing', *Chartered Mech. Engr.*, Jan. 1968.
'The sequencing problem', *Production Methods and Machines*, Part 1—Dec. 1968, Part 2—Jan. 1969, Part 3—Feb. 1969.

Solution procedure:

1. List information as shown in Table 13.1.
2. Select shortest time (or remaining time)
3. If this is A_i put that job first (or nearest first)
4. If it is B_i put that job last (or nearest last)
5. Delete this job from the table
6. Return to 1.

An example of the two machine n job sequencing problem and its solution using this procedure is shown in Table 13.2 and Fig. 13.1.

TABLE 13.2

i	A_i	B_i	Order
1	5	1————————————→6th
2	4————5————————→3rd
3	6————5————————→5th
4	7	6	4th
5	2————6————————→1st
6	3————4————————→2nd

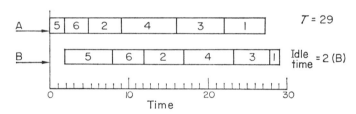

FIGURE 13.1. Programme to minimize T

Sequencing—Special Case of $m = 3$ (A, B, C). Where n jobs are to be processed on each of three machines (A, B and C) with the same order (A, B, C) and no passing.

Let A_i = set up time + processing time for job i on machine A
$\qquad A_i > 0 \cdot (i = 1 \ldots n)$
$\quad B_i$ = the same for machine B
$\quad C_i$ = the same for machine C

One of the following requirements must be satisfied:

1. min $A_i \geqslant$ max B_i
2. min $C_i \geqslant$ max B_i

Objective: to minimize T (total throughput time)

The example shown in Table 13.3 satisfies requirement (2) on page 349
Solution procedure:

1. Calculate $(A_i + B_i)$ and $(B_i + C_i)$
2. Proceed as before (Table 13.4).

TABLE 13.3

i	A_i	B_i	C_i
1	6	5	5
2	8	3	7
3	4	2	8
4	3	2	11
5	5	5	9

TABLE 13.4

i	A_i+B_i	B_i+C_i	Order
1	11	10————→5th
2	11	10	4th
3	6————10————→2nd
4	5————13————→1st
5	10————14————→3rd

Solution: 4, 3, 5, 2, 1 or 4, 3, 5, 1, 2. T = 45.

Jackson (see Selected Readings) has developed a simple generalization of the two machine problem dealt with by Johnson and gives a simple computational routine for the solution of sequencing problems of the following types:

1. Jobs which require processing by machine A only
2. Jobs which require processing by machine B only
3. Jobs which require processing by machine A then by machine B
4. Jobs which require processing by machine B then by machine A

This grouping includes all possible one and two operation jobs when the order of the latter is predetermined.

Sequencing—Two Jobs ($n = 2$) and m Machines. This graphical solution to a problem where two jobs are to be processed on each of m machines, but in different orders, was developed by Sasieni (see Selected Readings).

Consider the example shown in Table 13.5 where there are five machines A, B, C, D and E. The solution is shown in Fig. 13.2. The graph shows job 1 plotted on the x axis and job 2 plotted

TABLE 13.5

Job (i)	1		2	
	Machine order	Time (hours)	Machine order	Time (hours)
First operation	A_1	4	A_2	2
Second operation	B_1	3	D_2	2
Third operation	C_1	1	C_2	4
Fourth operation	D_1	3	B_2	2
Fifth operation	E_1	2	E_2	2

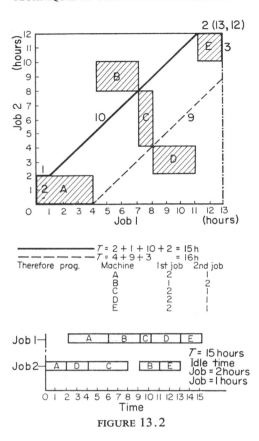

FIGURE 13.2

on the y axis. Ordinates (O, O) represent the time at which the programme begins and the ordinates $(13, 12)$ the time the programme finishes. Because each machine can only process one job at a time the shaded rectangular areas represent unfeasible areas. The problem is, therefore, to travel from (O, O) to $(13, 12)$ by the shortest route (to minimize T) using only vertical (processing job 2) or horizontal (processing job 1) or 45° lines (processing jobs 1 and 2). The graph shows two possible solutions.

With a little ingenuity the sequencing of jobs on machines can be represented by a series of linear equations or inequalities,[4] e.g. let x_i = time at which operation i must begin and
$$a_i = \text{processing time for operation } i$$
then, since each machine can only process one job at a time, one job must precede the other by an interval equal to or greater than its processing time.
Either $x_2 - x_1 \geqslant a_1$ (job 1 precedes job 2) or
$x_1 - x_2 \geqslant a_2$ (job 2 precedes job 1)
Additional requirements can be presented in a similar manner, e.g.

1. Order requirements

$x_l + a_l \leqslant x_m$ (operation l precedes operation m)
$x_m + a_m \leqslant x_n$ (operation m precedes operation n)

---

[4] A. S. Manne, 'On the job scheduling problem' *Operations Res.*, **8**, 219–223 (1960).

2. Delay in interval requirements

$x_p + a_p + \Delta_{pq} = x_q$ (There must be a given interval Δ_{pq} between the end of operation p and the start of operation q).

Linear programming is a method of solving a set of such simultaneous linear equations or inequalities. The use of this technique in the treatment of sequencing problems was undoubtedly an important development in this field of operational research, since it was the first major step towards a more general technique, capable theoretically of providing an optimal solution for a wide range of problems. One of the main reasons behind this development was the recent availability of high-speed electronic computers able to deal rapidly with the lengthy calculations involved. However, even with the aid of immensely powerful present day digital computers, the extensive computations necessary with this otherwise attractive treatment of the problem obviate its use in any but the simplest problems.

Other attractive techniques have been applied but none offer practical solutions to the general problem. For example, the branch and bound algorithm was developed for solving the classic 'travelling salesman' problem, i.e. the routing of a salesman from a 'base' once through several locations and back to base again, minimizing either the distance travelled or the travelling time. In more general terms the problem can be considered as one of determining the order of a set of locations for one salesman or of sequencing one salesman through the locations. Hence the special case of job/machine sequencing in which each job has to be processed on machines in the same order is directly analogous.

All possible sequences of n jobs can be represented as a tree, (see Fig. 13.3).

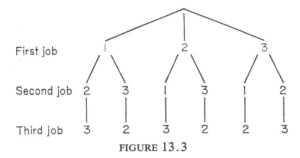

FIGURE 13.3

Branch and bound is a heuristic technique which searches the tree until the 'best' branch is found, i.e. in our case the branch which provides minimum total processing time. Committing a job to the sequence produces a *node* and *branching* from that node commits further jobs to the sequence. In practical cases, *all* of the possible paths cannot be considered and to reduce computation the concept of a *bound* is used. The 'lower bound', calculated for each node, is the minimum length of any path emanating from that node. This enables us to concentrate on the most promising paths, i.e. those with low 'lower bounds' and provisionally to discard others.[5]

Figure 13.4 shows the final solution to a 4- job, 3-machine problem. The calculations necessary to arrive at the Lower Bound figures for each node, and hence the solutions, are not shown but they can be performed by a simple iterative routine. The solution illustrates how, in this case,

---

[5] For examples of this use of this technique see: Z. A. Lomnicki, 'Branch and Bound for exact solution of the three machine scheduling problem', *Operational Res. Quart.*, 16, 89–100 (1965). A. P. G. Brown, Z. A. Lomnicki 'Some applications of the Branch and Bound algorithm to the machine scheduling problem', *Operational Res. Quart.*, 17, 173–186 (1966).

by branching from the node with the lowest 'lower bound', an optimum solution is eventually obtained (i.e. the order of jobs is 3, 1, 4, 2, for each machine). The total completion time is 26.

Problem 4 jobs (1, 2, 3, 4)
        3 machines (A, B, C)
        Minimize through-put time
        Each job to be processed on each machine in the order T, B, C.

		Processing times		
		A	B	C
Jobs	1	7	3	6
	2	6	2	2
	3	4	1	7
	4	5	4	3

Solution

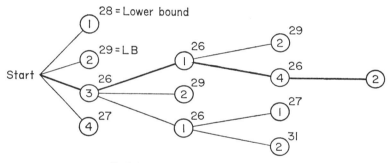

∴ Optimum sequence of jobs = 3; 1; 4; 2

FIGURE 13.4. An example of the Branch and Bound method used to solve a simple 3 machine/ 4 job sequencing problem

Many of the techniques we have described above offer optimum solutions to sequencing problems, but a question that should be asked is whether or not optimum solutions are necessary or even desirable. Clearly, if a solution to this problem can only be obtained after excessive computation (e.g. Linear Programming) or through over-simplification (e.g. the early algorithms, or even the Branch and Bound method) then there is little to recommend it.

Furthermore, all of the foregoing methods have dealt only with the static rather than the dynamic problem. When the dynamic situation arises, there is no practical and general method of ensuring an optimum solution. If this fact is accepted, then it is reasonable to consider such problems in simpler 'dispatching' terms, i.e. considering the order in which jobs will be done on one machine, rather than attempting explicitly to consider several machines at once. The dispatching problem is widespread in industry, and to a large extent it is the nucleus of the production control function. The efficiency with which dispatching is performed to a large extent determines overall production efficiency, since it can affect such crucial things as manufacturing time, work-in-progress, machine loading etc.

The principal method of job dispatching, is by means of *priority rules*.

Priority Rule Dispatching

By default, the dispatching decision is often left to shop floor personnel—usually the foreman, hence the choice as to which one of several jobs is to be processed next is usually dependent on external stimulii, i.e. whether the job is already late and by how much, its value and piecework rate, the influence wielded by the progress chaser, etc. Inevitably, decisions of this type tend to be subjective and parochial. However, if an acceptable formula can be programmed from the mass of possible functional relationships that exist, then decisions can be taken more consistently and expeditiously. Priority rule dispatching is therefore an attempt to formalize the decisions of the 'human' dispatcher. Most of the simple priority rules have that been suggested are listed below.

1. *Job slack* (S) This is the amount of contingency or free time, over and above the expected processing time, available before the job is completed at a predetermined date (t_0).[6]

$$\text{i.e. } S = t_0 - t_1 - \Sigma a_t$$

where t_1 = present date[6]

and Σa_t = sum of remaining processing times.

Where delays are associated with each operation, e.g. delays caused by inter-machine transport, this rule is not suitable, hence the following rule may be used.

2. *Job slack per operation* i.e. S/N where N = No. of remaining operations.

Therefore where S is the same for two or more jobs, the job having the most remaining operations is processed first.

3. *Job slack ratio*, or the ratio of the total remaining time to the remaining slack time, i.e.

$$\frac{S}{t_0 - t_1}$$

In all the above cases, where the priority index is negative the job cannot be completed by the requisite date. The rule will therefore be to process first those jobs having negative indices.

4. *Shortest imminent operation* (SIO) i.e. process first the job with the shortest processing times.

5. *Longest imminent operation* (LIO) This is the converse of (4).

6 *Scheduled start date.* This is perhaps the most frequently used rule. The date at which operations must be started in order that a job will meet a required completion date is calculated, usually by employing reverse scheduling from the completion date.

$$\text{e.g. } \quad x_i = t_0 - \Sigma a_i$$
$$\text{or} \quad x_i = t_0 - \Sigma(a_i = f_i)$$

where x_i = scheduled start date for an operation

and f_i = delay or contingency allowance.

Usually some other rule is also used, e.g. first come, first served to decide priorities between jobs having equal x_i values.

7. *Earliest due date*, i.e. process first the job required first.

8. *Subsequent processing times.* Process first the job that has the longest remaining process times. i.e. Σa_t or in modified form $\Sigma(a_i + f_i)$

---

[6] Again we are using a system in which dates in the future have higher numerical values than the present date, e.g.

0	1	2	3		4	5	6	7	8		9	10	11	12	13	Week No.

t_1 t_0

9. *Value*. To reduce work in progress inventory cost, process first the job which has the highest value.

10. *Minimum total float*. This rule is the one usually adopted when scheduling by network techniques.

11. *Subsequent operation*. Look ahead to see where the job will go after this operation has been completed and process first the job which goes to a 'critical' queue, that is a machine having a small queue of available work, thus minimizing the possibility of machine idle time.

12. *First come, first served* (FCFS)

13. *Random* (e.g. in order of Job No etc.) Rules 12 and 13 are random since, unlike the others, neither one depends directly on job characteristics such as length of operation, value etc.

Priority rules can be classified further, as follows:

1. *Local rules* depend solely upon data relating to jobs in the queue at any particular machine.

2. *General rules* depend upon data relating to jobs in the queue at any particular machine and/or data for jobs in queues at *other* machines.

Local rules, because of the smaller amount of information utilized, are easier and cheaper to calculate than general (sometimes called *global*) rules. All of the above rules with the exception of No. 11 are local rules.

One further classification of rules is as follows.

1. *Static rules* are those in which the priority index for a job does not change with the passage of time, during waiting in any one queue.

2. *Dynamic rules* are those in which the priority index is a function of time.

Rules 4, 5, 6, 7, 8, 9, 10, 11, 12, 13 above are all static, whereas the remainder are dynamic.

Research into Priority Rule Dispatching

Over the last ten years a great deal of research work has been conducted in an attempt to determine the merit of priority rule dispatching, and in particular to evaluate the relative merit of the numerous rules that have been suggested. This research work has normally taken the form of simulation studies. In general researchers have used digital computers, to simulate job shop conditions, and have frequently relied on many simplifying assumptions such as the following.

The operation times (including set-up times) for all jobs are known and are independent of the order in which jobs are processed on machines.

Operations once started must be completed.

No machine may process more than one job at a time.

Transport time of jobs between machines can be neglected.

Each job must be processed on machines in a given predetermined order.

Machines do not break down.

Machines and labour resources are available in known quantities.

The splitting of job 'lots' is not permitted.

Several criteria for assessing the results of the simulations have been used, the following measures of dispatching performance being adopted by many researchers.

1. *Due Date Criteria*, i.e. assessing the performance of priority rule dispatching by whether or not jobs satisfy specified 'due' or completion dates.

(a) *Mean of the completion distribution*. The completion distribution shows the relative frequency with which jobs are completed early, on time, and late. The mean of the distribution represents the average despatching efficiency. Early completion is assumed to offset late completion.

(b) *The variance of the completion distribution.* The variance is a measure of the dispersion of values or the spread of a distribution, hence the variance of the completion distribution is a measure of the consistency of despatching results.

(c) *Mean lateness.* If we consider that only the *late* completion of a job is detrimental, then the mean lateness is a measure of dispatching efficiency.

(d) *The number of jobs late*

2. Criteria related to *through-put*, or *waiting time* and the *congestion* of jobs, e.g.

 (a) Mean through-put time
 (b) Through-put time variance
 (c) Mean number of jobs in shop
 (d) Variance of number of jobs in shop

As a result of the enormous amount of research that has been conducted in this area, many researchers have suggested and tested variations to, or extensions of, many of the simple priority rules listed above. For example at least five variations of the Shortest Imminent Operation rule have been developed and tested, in attempts to overcome the main disadvantage of this rule, namely the long waiting times incurred by jobs with long processing times.

1. *Truncated SIO rule.* An upper limit is placed on waiting time, hence jobs which have waited for longer than a given time take precedence.

2. *Two class SIO rule* Operations are considered to be either short or long. A further rule such as FCFS being used to select jobs from each class.

3. *SIO with FCFS* The simple SIO rule is used, along with the FCFS rule, the purpose of which is to reduce the backlog of jobs with long operation times.

4. *SIO rule with imperfect prediction* of operation times.

5. *Two class truncated SIO rule.* The job with the shortest operation within a critical class of jobs is selected, or if this class is empty the SIO is taken.

More complex rules have been developed by Rowe[7] in particular two 'sequential' rules, the simplest of which is as follows:

$$\text{Priority index} = \frac{(t_i - x_i) - f_i}{N \pm b}$$

where t_i = present date
 x_i = scheduled start date for operation
 f_i = flow or contingency allowance
 b = empirically derived constant
 N = number of remaining operations

This priority index is a comparison of the flow allowance (f_i) with the deviation from the planned start date $(t_i - x_i)$. When $(t_i - x_i) - f_i$ is a positive value then all the flow allowance has been consumed by the late start, therefore the first jobs to be processed are those with high priority indices.

W. S. Gere has concentrated on the improvement of simple priority rules by the addition of heuristic decision rules. He tested eight such heuristic rules, but concluded that only three of

---

[8] A comprehensive list of references for this section is given at the end of this chapter.

these offered significant improvements over the results obtained by the priority rules themselves. These three heuristics were:

1. *Alternative operation.* The simple priority rule is used, but before processing the job with the highest priority according to this rule (say job 1) check to see whether or not by so doing any of the remaining jobs becomes even more critical. If so, give highest priority to this job (say job 2). Check again to see if this makes any of the remaining jobs more critical. If none of the others are more critical, process job 2, otherwise process job 1.

2. *Look Ahead.* Before processing the next job (say job 1) according to the priority rule, look ahead to see whether a more critical job (say job 2) is due to arrive at the machine before job 1 is finished. If so, leave the machine vacant and await that job.

3. *Insert.* (To be used in conjunction with 'Look Ahead'). Rather than leave a machine idle, through the 'Look Ahead' heuristic, process the longest of the available jobs that can be completed before job 2 arrives.

An important priority rule has been developed by Carroll, which has been given the mnemonic COVERT standing for c over t, $\left(\dfrac{c}{t}\right)$

where c = the expected delay cost for an operation
$\quad\ \ t$ = processing time for an operation

The purpose of this rule which has been tested with encouraging results, is to give high priority to jobs with high ratio of expected lateness to operation time.

Various *combinations* of priority rules have been suggested and tested, perhaps the best known being:
Scheduled start date + total float.

Such a rule is invariably used as a means of selecting jobs to be processed, when Network Analysis has been used during production planning. For example if we refer back to the Network Analysis computer print-out shown in Figs 9.35–36 (Chapter 9) we see that jobs are listed in order of 'Planned Start date' (firstly) and 'Total Float'.

These documents list, for the benefit of shop floor personnel, jobs in the order in which they are to be done, in otherwords, jobs are listed according to the priority index *Planned (or Scheduled) Start date + Total Float.*

Simulation research into the comparative merits of numerous priority rules under different conditions of shop loading, assuming different arrival rates, and using different performance criteria has been perhaps the most popular item of research in the whole field of Production Management. It would therefore be an extremely onerous and space consuming job to attempt to review all of the findings, consequently here we will confine ourselves to a resumé of the principal conclusions of research to date. The references at the end of this chapter contain a list of all of the important research work, should the reader wish to pursue this topic further.[8]

Gere found that the use of the three heuristics, 'Alternative operation', 'Look Ahead' and 'Insert', when used in conjunction with a simple priority rule, significantly improved shop performance. Furthermore he found that whenever one of these 'additions' were used there was little difference between the results obtained by any of the priority rules, thus suggesting that the ones simplest to calculate (i.e. local and static) should be adopted.

[8] Good reviews of the research in this field are to be found in R. L. Sisson, 'Sequencing Theory', *Progress in Operations Research*, 1, Chapter 7, Wiley London, 1961.
J. M. Moore, R. C. Wilson, 'A review of simulation research in job shop scheduling', *Prod. and Inventory Management*, Jan. 1967. 1–10.

The sequential rules suggested by Rowe, were found by him to offer significant improvements over the simple rules, but to date, such rules in common with those suggested by Gere, have not been extensively adopted in practice.

Undoubtedly the most effective rule, according to all the research conducted to date is the SIO rule, and, more particularly, the various extensions of this rule. Massive simulation studies by researchers such as Conway, Le Grande, Nelson, Nanot and others have shown that of all 'local' rules, rules based on the SIO rule are perhaps the most effective, certainly when considered against criteria such as minimizing the number of jobs in the shop, the mean of the 'completion distribution' and the throughput time. The SIO rule appears to be particularly effective in reducing throughput time, the 'truncated SIO' and the 'two class SIO' rules being perhaps the most effective derivatives, having the additional advantage of reducing throughput time variance and lateness. Several researchers have supported these general findings, the most recent (at the time of writing) being Eilon and Cotterill who tested twelve rules and found the 'two class SIO' to give good results.

The First Come First Served priority rule has been shown to be particularly beneficial in reducing average lateness, whereas the Scheduled Start Date and Total Float rule has been proved an effective rule for use where jobs are of the network type.

One of the intrigueing things about Priority Rules is the almost alarming difference between research results and conventional practice. As we shall see later, production control systems rarely utilize the SIO rule, which in view of the above summary is perhaps surprising. This inevitably leads one to ask whether or not some of this research has not been misdirected. Certainly there has been disagreement concerning performance criteria and more recently it has been shown that one of the assumptions basic to much of the research is perhaps only rarely justified.[9] We refer to the assumption that shops are machine limited—that machines are the important resource. In practice, labour is often the more scarce resource, this therefore opens up new possibilities for research in this, far from exhausted area of research.

Recording the Progress of Jobs

Even without contingencies such as machine break-downs, labour absenteeism, lack of equipment, disputes etc., we cannot reasonably expect to predict, other than tentatively, the progress of jobs throughout manufacture. We need to know the current state of jobs in order to determine dispatching priorities; in order to inform the customer, through sales department, of the progress of his jobs; in order to arrange for associated tasks, such as inspection; in order to withdraw materials, drawings, tools, etc., from stores in time for subsequent operations; and for many other reasons.

How is job progress ascertained and recorded? Clearly, the staff of the production control department will be reasonably familiar with the current state of jobs, because of direct observation and through verbal reports, but we cannot rely solely on such information systems. If our production control system is to be efficient, some routine reliable and rapid method of feedback is essential.

Consider how various types of shop documentation are used for progress reporting. Firstly, *job tickets*, which will be prepared for every operation on every item. Sufficient information will be given to identify the order, the item or part, the quantity required, material, equipment and accessories required, the work centre or machine to be used, the operation to be performed and the time allowed (A typical Job Ticket is shown in Fig. 8.3, Chapter 8). Such tickets are usually

[9] R. T. Nelson, 'Labour and machine limited production systems', *Management Sci.*, 13, No. 9, 648–71 (1967).

dated according to the production schedule by either production planning or by production control and are kept, prior to the operation being performed, in the appropriate section of a loading board or rack which shows the amount of work waiting at each machine. The job ticket is given to the operator, together with drawings etc. immediately prior to beginning the operation, and returned upon completion of the operation. For job costing, and piecework payment purposes, it will be necessary to 'clock' or 'book' the operator onto and off the job—this is often done by inserting the job ticket into a punch clock. On its return, the ticket is used to indicate job progress before being passed firstly to the wages and, finally, to the costing departments.

Move orders, might also be used to indicate the progress of jobs. Such documents are used on every occasion on which jobs must move from one machine to another. They are necessary, of course, because the pattern of movement in jobbing shop situations is extremely complex. Consequently materials handling personnel must be instructed where each job should be taken. Move orders might be made out by shop supervision, by progress men, or by inspectors. In each case they will only be completed when the job has passed any necessary inspection, and duplicate copies will often be used to indicate progress.

Finally, *inspection reports* are also used for this purpose. Inspection tickets, sheets or orders will be made out for each operation to be inspected, indicating the characteristic(s) to be examined and making provision for comments about quality or recommendations for reprocessing. Often the ordinary job ticket is used; the inspector, who may need to refer to the necessary drawings, will sign or stamp the ticket to indicate that the job might proceed to the next operation.

Often the method and documents of production planning allow for the feedback of progress information. For example, when using computer processed network analysis for planning or scheduling, the production control department will be provided regularly with documents such as that shown in Fig. 9.34 (Chapter 9) which shows the order in which all jobs in a project must be finished. The equivalent document for use either by the Shop Supervisor, or by production controllers associated with separate shops are shown in Figs 9.35 and 9.36. Notice that a blank column 'Actual Finish' is provided, into which must be written the actual finish date of the job, or the estimated actual finish date for jobs in progress. Such information can then be used in network calculations which up-date the network, e.g. Figs. 13–6(a) and (b).

A great many production control departments rely upon the use of such documents for progress information, but the problems are obvious—namely, documents may be lost, their return may be delayed or they may be filled out inaccurately. To overcome such problems it is traditional and necessary to employ progress chasers, whose principal job it is to ensure that current progress information is obtained.

Recently, there has been a welcome trend to automate (or, at least, mechanize) this feedback system. Clearly, the stage at which to retrieve information is the booking of operators on and off jobs. This information is crucial for the effective control of production as well as for the calculation of wages and labour costs for jobs. Figure 13.5 is a photograph of a typical remote data collection terminal which can be used to retrieve data from the shop floor, either for direct processing on a computer or for printing out in the production control department. Such terminals will read appropriate information from suitably prepared job tickets, and feed this information (e.g. job no., operation no.) to the production control department or into the computer, together with the following:

1. The time.

2. The operator's name and/or clock no., read from a badge or card, also inserted into the terminal.

3. Other appropriate information such as whether the operator is booking onto as off the job, in the latter case whether the job has been completed or suspended. Where *batches* of items are

FIGURE 13.5. Data collection terminal—Data are entered by inserting a punched card or badge and by adjusting the two dials [Reproduced by permission, IBM United Kingdom Ltd]

processed, whether part or the whole of the batch is complete, and the number of defective items produced. Information such as this is entered by depressing one or more coded keys or buttons.

Analysis of Progress and Control

Little remains to be said about these two steps, since their purpose and methods are readily apparent from the previous discussion. Progress information fed-back by one of the previous methods will be used to update or confirm the production programme or schedule, from which production control decisions will be taken. Where priority rule sequencing is used, such information is vital since, in several cases, the relative priority of jobs may change even though the basic schedule has not changed. For example, the job 'slack' (priority rule 1) may have been reduced without affecting the production schedule.

Where network analysis is used, periodic feedback of progress information will be used to up-date the network. Up-dating is often carried out over-night or during weekends so that new information is available on the next working day. The procedure is as follows:

1. Actual finish dates for jobs, or estimated finish dates of partially completed jobs, will be supplied

```
                              FLOATSHIP + CO. LTD
CONSTRUCTION OF A MOTOR YACHT    ACTIVITY PERT        ORDER: DEPT              PAGE 1
      RUN NUMBER:  2                                  BY PLANNED START
      REPORT DATE: 15MAR65                            BY TOTAL FLOAT


DEPT    PROJECT                                   ACT    PLANNED    PLANNED    ACTUAL    REMARKS   Estimated Finish
                        DESCRIPTION               DUR    START      FINISH     FINISH

OFFICE  MY039   DRAW PLANS FOR HULL               2.0    05APR65    21APR65    18 April
OFFICE  MY039   ORDER TIMBER FOR HULL             3.0    21APR65    12MAY65    12 May
OFFICE  MY039   DRAW PLANS FOR DECK               1.0    21APR65    28APR65    28 April
OFFICE  MY039   ORDER AND AWAIT ENGINE            6.0    21APR65    02JUN65               11 June
OFFICE  MY039   ORDER AND AWAIT JOINERY FITTINGS  6.0    28APR65    10JUN65               18 June

OFFICE  MY039   ORDER TIMBER FOR DECK             1.0    28APR65    05MAY65    5 May
OFFICE  MY039   ORDER AND AWAIT PAINT + VARNISH   4.0    28APR65    26MAY65               28 May
```

FIGURE 13.6(a). Feedback of progress information via network analysis schedules

```
                              FLOATSHIP + CO. LTD
CONSTRUCTION OF A MOTOR YACHT    ACTIVITY PERT        ORDER: DEPT              PAGE 1
      RUN NUMBER:  2                                  BY PLANNED START
      REPORT DATE: 15MAR65                            BY TOTAL FLOAT


DEPT    PROJECT                                   ACT    PLANNED    PLANNED    ACTUAL    REMARKS
                        DESCRIPTION               DUR    START      FINISH     FINISH

YARD    MY039   MAKE TEMPLATE FOR HULL            2.0    21APR65    05MAY65    5 May
YARD    MY039   MAKE JOINERY UNITS                3.0    05MAY65    26MAY65    21 May
YARD    MY039   CUT TIMBER FOR DECK               4.0    05MAY65    02JUN65    04 June
YARD    MY039   CUT TIMBER FOR HULL               4.0    12MAY65    10JUN65    11 June
YARD    MY039   PREPARE ENGINE                    2.0    02JUN65    17JUN65

YARD    MY039   CONSTRUCT HULL                    4.0    10JUN65    08JUL65
YARD    MY039   ASSEMBLE JOINERY UNITS + FITTINGS 3.0    10JUN65    01JUL65
YARD    MY039   INSTALL FITTINGS + JOINERY        2.0    08JUL65    22JUL65
YARD    MY039   INSTALL ENGINE                    1.0    08JUL65    15JUL65
YARD    MY039   CLEAN OFF HULL                    1.0    08JUL65    15JUL65

YARD    MY039   CONSTRUCT DECK + CLEAN OFF        3.0    22JUL65    12AUG65
YARD    MY039   PAINT + VARNISH                   4.0    12AUG65    23SEP65
YARD    MY039   FINAL FIT OUT                     2.0    23SEP65    07OCT65
```

FIGURE 13.6(b). Feedback of progress information via network analysis schedules

to either the production control or planning department on the departmental printout (Fig. 13.6).
2. All such information will be fed into the computer (it is usually necessary to input only amendments or additions, rather than the complete network, since the information from the previous run is normally stored on magnetic tape.
3. These dates will then be used as a basis for a complete set of calculations for the remainder of the network.
4. An up-dated set of figures will be printed out in the same format as before, and distributed prior to the beginning of the next working week or shift (Fig. 13.7).

Production Planning and Control Systems

The purpose of the final step is to assess the performance of both the production plan and the control of production during the manufacture of a product in order to:

1. Accumulate date on which production plans for future similar orders might be based.
2. Assess the planning and control procedures used.

Again, there is little of pertinance which can be said about this step, but it does present us with a good opportunity, after having discussed the components of Production Control, to discuss the systems appropriate to jobbing shop type situations. In particular we shall look at computer based systems.

```
                        FLOATSHIP + CO. LTD
CONSTRUCTION OF A MOTOR YACHT      ACTIVITY PERT          ORDER: DEPT              PAGE 1
        RUN NUMBER:   3                                          BY PLANNED START
        REPORT DATE: 14MAY65                                     BY TOTAL FLOAT

DEPT    PROJECT                              ACT    PLANNED   PLANNED   ACTUAL    REMARKS
                       DESCRIPTION           DUR    START     FINISH    FINISH

OFFICE  MYO39   ORDER AND AWAIT ENGINE       4.0              11JUN65
OFFICE  MYO39   ORDER AND AWAIT JOINERY FITTINGS  5.0         18JUN65
OFFICE  MYO39   ORDER AND AWAIT PAINT + VARNISH   2.0         28MAY65
```

FIGURE 13.7(a). Updated printouts

```
                        FLOATSHIP + CO. LTD
CONSTRUCTION OF A MOTOR YACHT      ACTIVITY PERT          ORDER: DEPT              PAGE 1
        RUN NUMBER:                                             BY PLANNED START
        REPORT DATE:                                            BY TOTAL FLOAT

DEPT    PROJECT                              ACT    PLANNED   PLANNED   ACTUAL    REMARKS
                       DESCRIPTION           DUR    START     FINISH    FINISH

YARD    MYO39   MAKE JOINERY UNITS           1.0              21MAY65
YARD    MYO39   CUT TIMBER FOR DECK          3.0              4JUN65
YARD    MYO39   CUT TIMBER FOR HULL          4.0              11JUN65

YARD    MYO39   CONSTRUCT HULL               4.0    11JUN65   9JUL65

YARD    MYO39   PREPARE ENGINE               2.0    11JUN65   25JUN65
YARD    MYO39   ASSEMBLE JOINERY UNITS + FITTINGS  3.0  18JUN65  9JUL65
YARD    MYO39   INSTALL FITTINGS + JOINERY   2.0    9JUL65    23JUL65
YARD    MYO39   INSTALL ENGINE               1.0    9JUL65    16JUL65
YARD    MYO39   CLEAN OFF HULL               1.0    9JUL65    16JUL65

YARD    MYO39   CONSTRUCT DECK + CLEAN OFF   3.0    23JUL65   3AUG65
YARD    MYO39   PAINT + VARNISH              4.0    13AUG65   10SEP65
YARD    MYO39   FINAL FIT OUT                2.0    10SEP65   24SEP65
```

FIGURE 13.7(b). Updated printouts

In practice, production control systems will rarely exist in isolation, as there is normally the need for an interchange of data between production, stock, accounting, purchasing and marketing departments. The production control system is therefore only one part of a larger information and control system.

Such larger systems may exist only because of necessary interdependence and inter-communication and may be based largely on manual or clerical operations, alternatively, as is increasingly possible with large or with time sharing computers, these systems might be integrated by design, each part being designed for total compatibility with each other. Figure 13.8 shows how information flows between various 'departments' and indicates the requirements for a truly integrated production planning and control system.

There is little point in generalizing about computerized production control or integrated systems since although many of the companies using such systems depend to some extent on the programmes developed by computer manufacturers, each system, if it is to be completely successful, must be tailored to the specific requirements of the individual firm. It will however, be beneficial at this stage to look at some of the better known and successful system, and to examine the principles upon which they are based.[10]

One of the best known systems (certainly the best documented) is operating at the El Segundo works of the Hughes Aircraft Company.[11] The Hughes Aircraft works is engaged in jobbing production, as many as 3 000 jobs being processed at any one time on machines grouped into 120 machine centres. Operations planning details for each item are placed in the computer storage

---

[10] Descriptions of many such systems have appeared in the literature. Here we consider only well established and hence successful systems rather than propositions and suggestions.
[11] References for this section are given at the end of the chapter.

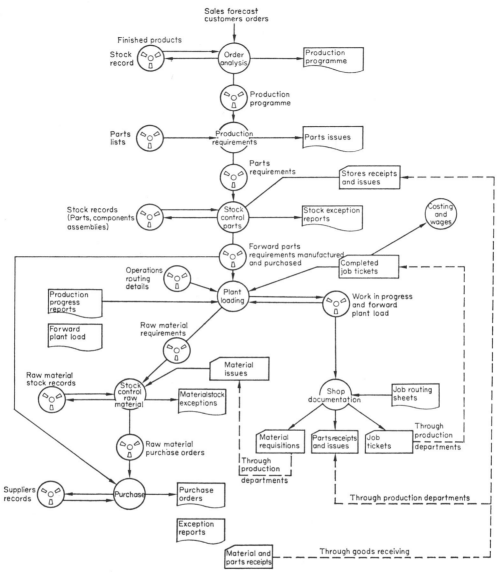

FIGURE 13.8. Flow diagram for integrated production planning and control system

after operations planning has been completed. On receipt of a fabrication order, the order and a master set of job or operation cards are despatched to the shops, ready for release. When the order has been released to the shops, the operation cards are used to feed back programme information by use of remote data collection terminals. Each day progress information is used to update the file containing the location of each item in the shops. The information is also used in the preparation, by means of a simulation programme, of a weekly shop load forecast, plus daily job schedules. The weekly shop load forecast shows the load for each machine group for 10 weeks ahead. The simulation programme determines the priority of jobs using mainly the 'slack per

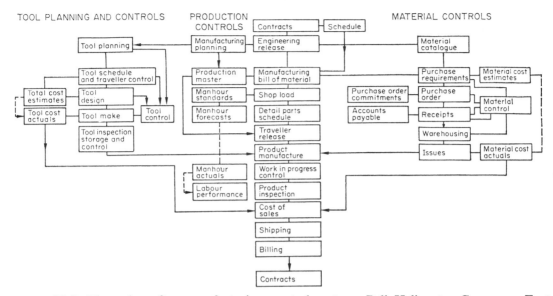

FIGURE 13.9. Flow chart for manufacturing control system—Bell Helicopter Company, Fort Worth, Texas [Reproduced by permission, R. D. Bernhard, 'Providing timely production data', *Automation*, March 1964. Copyright (1964) by Penton Publishing Co., Cleveland, Ohio 44113]

operation rule for each job. The simulation programme then allocates jobs to machine groups, arranges the queues of jobs into priority order, and simulates the dispatching and the actual processing of jobs. On completion of operations, the simulation programme calculates new priority indices for jobs and moves them to the next machine and so on for a complete shift. The whole of this simulation is recorded and printed out to form the daily job schedule for each of the machine centres.

Figure 13.9 is a flow chart for the manufacturing control system installed by the Bell Helicopter Company, Fort Worth, Texas in the early 1960's. Design of the system was begun in 1959 and it was intended to satisfy the requirements inherent in the jobbing and small batch manufacture which the company was engaged upon. The control of materials is an important part of the system, because of the large inventories of raw materials and tools necessarily held by the company. The system, on receipt of an order, establishes all manufacturing requirements and establishes a schedule for manufactured and purchased items. Progress information is obtained by means of remote data collection terminals, similar to that shown in Fig. 13.5. The system offers the Management of the company, up-to-date production data; forecasts of material requirements and basic manufacturing data on all products and items. It has greatly reduced the duplication of clerical effort, and enables the company to control accurately work in progress, labour costs etc.

Figure 13.10 illustrates diagrammatically the operation of one part of a computerized production control system installed at the General Electric Company, Phoenix, Arizona. Each work station dispatch report lists the jobs in the order in which they must be begun (a dispatching system relying on the 'Scheduled Start Date' priority rule is used). On completion of an operation progress information is fed back either manually as shown in (b), or automatically as shown in (c), by means of Friden 'Collectadata' remote data collection terminals on the shop floor.

Many other computer based systems have been described in numerous publications. One of the first systems for job shop planning and control was installed at the American Western Electric Company in 1962. In common with many of the other systems described, this installation relies

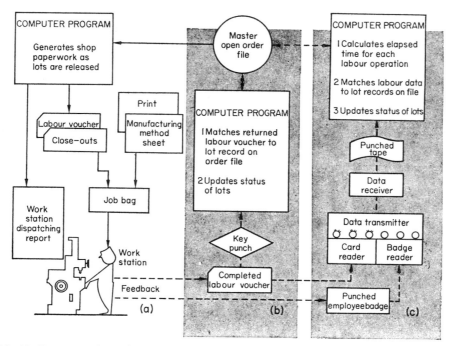

FIGURE 13.10. In processing a job lot, computer generated paper work and other necessary information are sent to the shop floor in a job bag, (a). Operator schedules job in accordance with the work station dispatching report at his position. When his portion of work is completed on the job lot, he can feed back information to the central control either manually as shown in (b) or automatically by means of a data transmitter as shown in (c). [Reproduced by permission, S. D. Beaird, 'Computerized production control for job lot manufacture', *Automation*, February 1966. Copyright (1966) by Penton Publishing Co., Cleveland, Ohio 44113]

on priority rule dispatching based on slack time, and progress reporting through remote data collection devices. A large system is in operation at the Fairfield Manufacturing Company, where a simulation procedure similar to the Hughes system is adopted and job dispatching is a function of 'slack' time.

In the United Kingdom, several computer based, integrated production planning and control systems have been developed, perhaps the most comprehensive being that used at the Rolls Royce Company aero engine works at Derby. Systems based on the network methods described previously have been adopted by companies such as English Electric, but few of the Britsh systems have been described in detail in publications, hence the main examples in this section are of American origin.

In general the following advantages are claimed for the type of systems briefly described above:

Reduction in cycle times
Increases in productivity
Reduced need for 'progress chasing'
Reduced work-in-progress
Reduced lateness of jobs
More jobs meet delivery dates
Better facility utilization.

Production Control in Process Production—Process Control

The direct control of industrial processes by means of electronic computers is now acknowledged to have begun about 1954. During this early period mainly analogue computers were used, because of their speed and reliability. In 1954[12] analogue computers were used by the Southern Company Power Pool of America to calculate continuously the most economical distribution of power loading within a generating network serving four companies. Similar applications of analogue computers existed at the Ohio Edison Company in 1956, and at the West Penn Power Company in 1957, in both cases computers being used to control power distribution in electrical generation networks.

Since that time digital computers have been developed which are sufficiently flexible and reliable for on-line control use, and consequently their application in this field has increased considerably, although, of course, analogue computers remain preferable for certain types of installation.

Early digital installations included the following:

1. Electrochemical Division of Du Pont, Niagara Falls, 1956.
A process was connected to a remote digital computer, data from several instruments being used to calculate the performance of the process.
2. Esso, Baton Rouge Refinery, 1958.
An analogue to digital conversion system was used to enable 160 variables to be scanned, the data from which were used in calculations to produce 27 operating guides to facilitate near optimum *manual* control of the system.
3. Philadelphia Electric Company (circa 1960).
A Honeywell computer was used to calculate the most economical allocation of generator capacity, this information then being transmitted automatically to the generators.
4. ICI Soda Plant, Fleetwood, England, 1962.
A Ferranti Argus 100 computer was installed to accept data from 224 inputs, and generate the required action to operate 120 control valves in response to changes in plant operating conditions.

These four examples illustrate several different types or levels of application of digital computers to the management of industrial processes. A common feature of each of these applications is the provision for the 'feed-back' of information. Also in each case, control of the process is a result of information feedback, but the nature of the feedback-control loop differs. In the first two examples an 'open loop control' system operates and in the last two cases the control loop is 'closed'.

Nowadays managers and scientists are primarily concerned with the closed loop or direct control of industrial processes by means of digital computer. (In fact recently it has been suggested that process control should begin with direct digital control rather than with data logging, as was usual previously.[13] In order to further illustrate the different levels of application and the evolution of process control, we will refer to the three basic types of application i.e. Data Logging, Supervisory Control Systems and Direct Digital Control.

Data Logging

This is the simplest application and hence is typical of the extent of early applications. Computers are used to scan very rapidly and frequently the information displayed by numerous instruments

---

[12] The 'historical' examples in this section are taken largely from 'Process Control by Computer—Part 2' R. A. Morley, M. B. Wood. Control, June 1960.
[13] T. C. Wherry, E. N. Pennington, D. E. Lupfer and E. C. Miller, 'Direct digital control'. *Chem. Eng. Progr.*, **64**, No. 4, 33–38 (1968).

connected to the process e.g. flowmeters, transducers, thermometers etc. this information being recorded, printed out and often used to calculate performance indices or guides which subsequently might be used by those concerned with the manual control of the process. Alarm systems are frequently incorporated so that the computer will signal the occurrence of faults or other unusual conditions in the process and also carry out simple diagnostic procedures, using the input data, to determine and indicate the cause of such conditions.

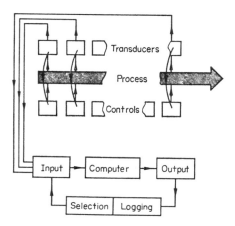

FIGURE 13.11. Data logging system

Data logging systems are finding increasing application on board large ships, but as regards industrial application they are frequently installed merely as the first stage of development of larger systems concerned with both monitoring and control. Figure 13.11 is a diagrammatic representation of a data logging and alarm system, and examples (1) and (2) above are typical installations.

Supervisory Control Systems

One of the main reasons for the emergence and development of methods of computer based process control, was that the increasing complexity of both equipment and systems was such that efficient manual control was increasingly difficult to achieve. Furthermore, in complex and expensive installations the penalties of inferior or poor performance are considerable, consequently expensive control systems are readily justifiable. Sequentially dependent processes such as are found in the chemical industries depend entirely for their efficient operation upon the near optimum control and the stable operation of their parts, since any disturbance in any part will be reflected and, perhaps, amplified in subsequent parts of the process.

Conditions such as these mitigate against manual control and necessitate some form of automatic monitoring and control system, capable of monitoring performance, compensating for changes in operation, and controlling subsequent sections according to the dynamic nature of the process.

Figure 13.12 represents such a supervisory control system. The efficiency of supervisory systems depends on their being 'fed' with the correct information, i.e. efficient data logging, and on the speed with which the control system works. Such systems must be carefully designed to accord with the characteristic of the process. The nature of the inputs must correspond to known

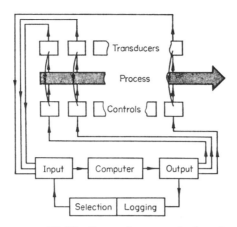

FIGURE 13.12. Supervisory control system

and foreseeable disturbances of the process and the speed of the computer to the nature of the process. There is little point in installing a control system whose reaction time is greatly in excess of the reaction time of the process it is controlling.

Direct Digital Control

Direct digital control is an extension of supervisory control and eliminates the need to place analogue controllers between process and computer (see Fig. 13.13). Direct digital control (d.d.c.) therefore is 'the control of a plant by a digital computer which replaces all the conventional analogue controllers'.[14]

The 1962 ICI Fleetwood installation is said to have been the world's first d.d.c. installation;[15] although at about the same time d.d.c. was used by Monsanto in the U.S.A. Up until these early

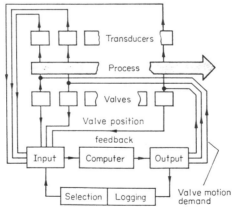

FIGURE 13.13. Direct control system [Figs 13.11, 13.12 and 13.13 reproduced by permission, 'Process control by computer', R. A. Morley and M. B. Wood, *Control*, May (1960)]

[14] M. S. Beck and N. Wainwright (1969) 'Direct digital control of chemical processes'. Seminar paper 'Use of computers in process control', Univ. of Bradford, Management Centre, Feb. 1969.
[15] P. 12 *Electronic Automation in Britain* 1966, HMSO, prepared by Ministry of Technology and Central Office for Information, London, 1966.

installations, process control computers had been used mainly to adjust analogue controllers, but in the ICI application a Ferranti Argus 200 digital process control computer was used to control *directly* 90 valves in th soda ash plant. (This particular plant having been chosen because of the relative simplicity of the control problem and because of the lack of toxic or explosive hazards).

Again, there is little point in attempting general descriptions of process control, because, perhaps even more so than in control systems for intermittent production, systems are tailor-made for specific applications. We will therefore confine ourselves to brief descriptions of one or two well known and well established examples, but before doing this let us look at the process control computer.

A general specification for d.d.c. computers was evolved during a conference held in 1964. Two types of d.d.c. computer were described, firstly a special purpose machine without data logging facilities and secondly a general purpose machine with data logging facilities and with the ability to undertake complex control calculations. A process control computer, particularly one of the general purpose type has a very similar configuration to a normal digital business or scientific computer, and consists basically of six units namely:

1. The memory unit which stores all relevant data.
2. The arithmetic unit, which performs all calculations using data from the memory, and readings from the process.
3. The control unit by which control is exercised over the actions of each of the other units.
4. The input unit by means of which readings are obtained from the process.
5. The output unit which transmits the information from the computer to the process in an appropriate form.
6. The operator unit by means of which the plant operator communicates with the computer. (The layout of an operator unit is shown in Fig. 13.14).

Wolvercote Paper Mill is a department of the Oxford University Press, and the paper making process there was placed under the control of an Elliot Automation 'Arch 1 000' computer in 1965. Figure 13.14 shows both the various stages of the paper making process and the manner in which computer control is achieved. The computer continuously, and automatically, calculates the correct setting for five variables at the 'wet end' of the process and makes whatever adjustments are necessary to maintain the correct setting. The final control, a beta-ray gauge, measures the paper's weight per unit area to assist the computer to make fine adjustments to paper quality. The computer stores information describing standard running conditions for each grade of paper, consequently, changes of grade may be made without incurring lengthy delays, and the improved control provided by the computer has enabled the machine to be run faster without loss of paper quality. The installation of the on-line control system was expected to provide an immediate increase in output of 5 per cent through time-saved in grade changes and a reduction in the output of sub-standard quality paper.

The manufacturing process at the Spencer Steel Works is both more complex and more extensive than the paper making process in the previous example. Consequently, complete process control in such a situation necessitated a different type of solution. Theoretically, it would have been possible to instal one large computer to take charge of the entire process but this would need to be a very large and expensive piece of equipment, and, furthermore, the consequences of its failure would have been considerable. The solution adopted, therefore, was a hierarchical system of computer control, involving several computers. It is interesting to note that such an arrangement is analogous to the conventional system of management control in that information and instructions are filtered, used, and controlled at several levels of the organization. Computers at the lowest level exercise physical control over the various individual processes, such as the hot strip, the slabbing and cold reduction mills. Above these there are two further computers, each controlling one end of the steel-making process (the heavy end, and the finishing end).

The first stage of the implementation of this automation or control system, involved the finishing end of the plant—Fig. 13.15—and utilized two Elliot 803 digital computers as the finishing end scheduler and the ingot-slab controller. A GE 412 computer is in direct on-line control of the hot stip mill. The finishing end scheduler plans and co-ordinates the entire finishing end

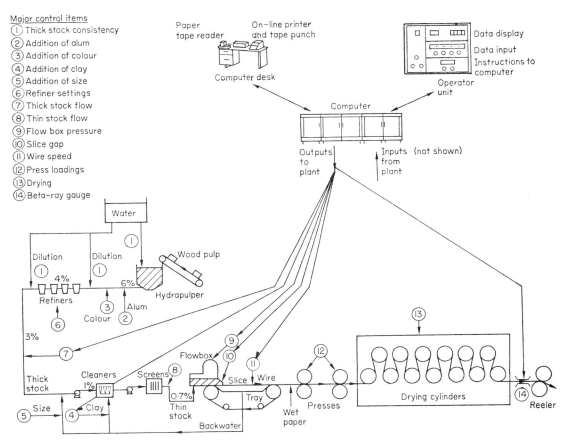

FIGURE 13.14. Computer control of paper machinery—AEI-Elliott Process Automation Ltd/ Wolvercote Paper Mill [Figure based upon Figs. 1 and 2 in *The Wolvercote Story—Automation in Action* Reproduced by permission, GEC-Elliott Automation Ltd]

process, it prepares and revises schedules, checking at each stage whether or not excess steel might be used as part of the orders. It checks on the progress of each order and orders more steel when reject levels make this necessary. The ingot-slab computer is responsible for guiding the production programme produced by the former computer, from the steel producing unit to the end of the hot strip mill. Information from each stage is collected and compared to schedules—discrepancies being reported to the finishing end scheduler. This information emanates from keyboards, and output is to line printers and visual displays. It is not, therefore, in direct control, unlike the hot strip mill controller whose task is to execute the rolling schedule produced by the ingot-slab controller.

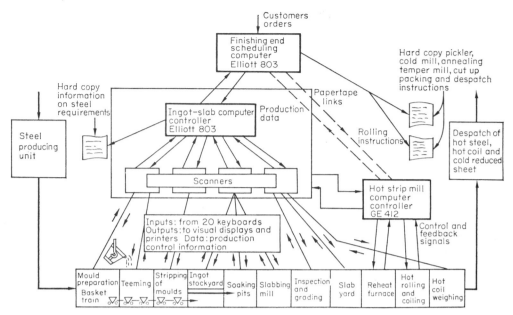

FIGURE 13.15. Computer control of finishing end operations—Spencer Steel Works [Reproduced by permission, Supplement on Spencer Steel Works, *The Times*, October 26, 1962]

SUMMARY

Production control is concerned with the monitoring and regulation of production. Its function is to ensure the implementation of a pre-determined production plan or schedule. The extent and complexity of this function is largely dependent upon the nature of the production process—production control being straight forward and quite simple in continuous production, but both elaborate and complex in intermittent production, particularly in jobbing shops.

The five rudimentary steps of production control are:

1. Initiating operations i.e. machine loading
2. Recording the progress of jobs
3. Analysing progress by comparison with schedules
4. Control: i.e. Modification of plans or rearrangement of jobs as a result of analysis
5. Final analysis of completed production to provide information to improve future Production Planning and Control.

One of the main problems of production control in intermittent manufacture is *sequencing*, i.e. deciding the order in which available jobs will be processed. Several rigorous methods of solving this problem have been suggested but they suffer from either depending on too many assumptions and simplifications or from involving and impractical amount of calculation. Consequently, heuristic methods must be adopted principally the use of Priority Rules, such as 'First come, first served' 'minimum remaining slack' etc.

The feed-back of progress information in this type of production is traditionally by clerical and 'postal' means, there is, however, a *trend* towards the use of remote electronic data collection devices, particularly where a computer based production control procedure is used.

Process control is the title applied to computer control of production in the process industries. Several levels or types of control exist. i.e.

1. Data logging in which the computer prints out readings from instruments on the process and performs simple calculations on them.
2. Supervisory control in which the computer both monitors and automatically controls the process.
3. Direct control which is an extension of supervisory control which does not rely upon analogue controllers between computer and process.

Although analogue computers were mainly used ten years ago, it is now usual for digital machine computers to be used for industrial process control. The steel industry was amongst the first to apply digital computers to process control, this industry was also the first to develop integrated process control using a hierarchy of digital computers to directly control production.

SELECTED READINGS

W. VORIS, *Production Control*, Irwin, Illinois, 1966 (3rd edition).
F. G. MOORE, *Production Control*, McGraw-Hill, London, 1959.

The above two books present comprehensive treatments of the subject from a practitioner's point of view, whereas the following presents a predominantly analytical treatment of some of the areas.

S. EILON, *Elements of Production Planning and Control*, Collier-Macmillan, London, 1966.

A recent review of simulation research in Dispatching can be found in the following:

J. M. MOORE and R. C. WILSON, 'A review of simulation research in job shop scheduling', *Prod. and Inventory Management*, Jan. (1967).

The following list contains in chronological order a selection of some of the more important simulation researches in Dispatching:

A. J. ROWE, 'Towards a theory of scheduling', *J. of Indus. Eng.*, II, March (1960).
R. W. CONWAY, 'An experimental investigation of priority dispatching', *J. of Indus. Eng.*, III, 221–230 (1960).
R. W. CONWAY and W. L. MAXWELL, 'Network dispatching by the shortest operation discipline', *Operations Res.*, 10, No. 1, 51–73 (1962).
Earl LeGRAND, 'The development of a factory simulation using actual operating data', *Management Tech.*, 3, No. 1, (1963).
Y. R. NANOT, 'An experimental investigation and comparative evaluation of priority disciplines in job shop-like queueing networks', *Ph.D. Diss.*, Univ. of Calif., Los Angeles, (1963).
W. GERE, 'Heuristics in job shop scheduling', *Management Science*, 13, No. 3, (1966).
D. TRILLING, 'Job shop simulation of orders that are networks', *J. of Indus. Eng.*, Feb. 59–71 (1966)
R. T. NELSON, 'Labour and machine limited production systems', *Management Science*, 13, No. 9, 648–671 (1967).
S. EILON and D. J. COTTERILL, 'A modified S.l. rule in job shop scheduling', *Int. J. of Prod. Res.*, 7, No. 2, (1968).

Computer based production planning and control systems are described in the following papers:

M. H. BULKIN, J. L. COLLEY and H. W. STEINHOFF, 'Load forecasting, priority sequencing and simulation in a job shop control system', *Management Science*, **13**, No. 2, (1966). (Hughes Aircraft).

S. REITER, 'A system for managing job shop production, *J. of Business*, **34**, No. 3, (1966) (Fairfield).

S. E. ELMAGHRABY and R. T. COLE, 'On the control of production in small job shops', *J. of Indus. Eng.*, No. 4, (1963) (Western Electric).

S. D. BEAIRD, 'Computerized production control for job lot manufacture', *Automation*, Feb. (1966), 76–82 (General Electric).

R. D. BERNHARD, 'Function of a total information system—providing timely production data', *Automation*, March 1964, 48–55.

Several of these systems are reviewed and compared in:

C. L. MOODIE and D. J. NOVOTNY, 'Computer scheduling and control systems for discrete part production', *J. of Indus. Eng.*, **19**, No. 7, 336–341 (1968).

The following articles relate to the sequencing procedures described in this chapter.

A. P. G. BROWN and Z. A. LOMNICKI, 'Some applications of the branch and bound algorithm to the machine scheduling problem', *Operational Res. Quart.*, **17**, 173–186 (1966).

J. R. JACKSON, 'An extension to Johnson's results on job lot scheduling', *Naval Res. Logis. Quart.*, **3**, 201–203 (1956).

S. M. JOHNSON, 'Optimal two and three stage production schedules and set up times included', *Naval Res. Logis. Quart.*, March, 61–68 (1954).

Z. A. LOMNICKI, 'Branch and Bound for exact solution of the three machine scheduling problem', *Operational Res. Quart.*, **16**, 89–100 (1965).

A. S. MANNE, 'On the job scheduling problem', *Operations Res.*, **8**, 219–223 (1960).

QUESTIONS

13.1.(a) Five jobs—1, 2, 3, 4 and 5 must be processed on each of three machines A, B and C, in that order. Process times are given below.

Use Johnson's Rule to determine the best sequence for the five jobs and use a GANTT chart to show an optimum schedule for the machines.

Table of process times (h)

		Job			
	1	2	3	4	5
Machine A	5	4	9	7	6
Machine B	3	2	4	3	1
Machine C	8	3	7	5	2

(b) Describe and comment upon a graphical method for finding the optimum programme for machines and 2 jobs when each job takes a different route through the machines.

[Univ. of Bradford, Management Centre, Post-Grad. Dip Industrial Admin., Production Management, May 1967—35 mins.]

13.2. Distinguish between the sequencing and the dispatching problems. How important is the sequencing problem in production control and how useful in practice are the various algorithms which can be used to provide optimal solutions to such problems?

13.3. Solve the following sequencing problems, the objective in each case being to minimize the throughput time of all jobs.

(a) Two machines A, B.

   Seven jobs   1, 2, 3, 4, 5, 6, 7.

Each job to be processed on each machine in order A–B. No over taking of jobs.

Table of process times (h)

		Machine A	B
Job	1	8	5
,,	2	6	7
,,	3	3	10
,,	4	7	8
,,	5	6	4
,,	6	5	10
,,	7	7	7

(b) Two machines X, Y.

   Six jobs   1, 2, 3, 4, 5, 6.

No overtaking of jobs.
Jobs to be processed on machines in order X–Y.
Job 4 process on Machine Y only.
Job 1 process on Machine X only.

Table of process times (h)

		Machine X	Y
Job	1	5	–
,,	2	7	6
,,	3	5	9
,,	4	–	8
,,	5	7	4
,,	6	9	3

(c) Three machines X, Y, Z.

   Four jobs   1, 2, 3, 4.

Each job to be processed on each machine in order X–Y–Z.
No overtaking of jobs.

N

Table of process times (h)

		Machine		
		X	Y	Z
Job	1	4	3	3
,,	2	2	4	2
,,	3	4	4	4
,,	4	6	2	4

13.4. Two jobs (1, 2) must be processed on all of 5 machines (A, B, C, D, E). The processing times and the order of the operations for each job are given below. Draw a bar chart showing the minimum throughput time programme for the processing of the two jobs.

	Job 1		Job 2	
Operations No.	Machine	Time (h)	Machine	Time (h)
1	A	4	A	5
2	D	3	C	7
3	E	5	D	4
4	B	6	B	3
5	C	4	E	5

13.5. Ten jobs are waiting to be processed on a machine.
(a) Given the information below arrange these jobs in priority order (the one with highest processing or dispatching priority first) according to the following priority rules.

1. Job slack.
2. Job slack per operation.
3. Job slack ratio.
4. Shortest imminent operation.
5. Longest imminent operation.
6. Scheduled start date.
7. Earliest due date.
8. Subsequent processing time.
9. First come, first served.

Job	Scheduled Completion date (Week No.)	Sum of remaining processing times (Weeks)	Number of remaining operations	Duration of operations on this machine	Arrival order at this machine
1	17	4	2	1	1
2	15	6	3	2	10
3	17	3	4	1	2
4	16	5	1	3	4
5	19	7	2	0·5	9
6	21	4	5	2	3
7	17	2	4	0·5	5
8	22	8	3	3·5	8
9	20	6	2	2	6
10	25	10	1	2	7

N.B. The present date is week No. 12.

(b) Use the First Come, First Served priority rule to resolve 'ties' given by the above rules.

13.6. The network diagram below is used whilst planning the production of an item. Using the earliest start dates draw up a list of all jobs to be started during the period week Nos. 10–15. Use the priority rule, 'Scheduled start date (Earliest start date)+Total float' to arrange these jobs in priority order— (the job to be started first, being placed at the top of the list).

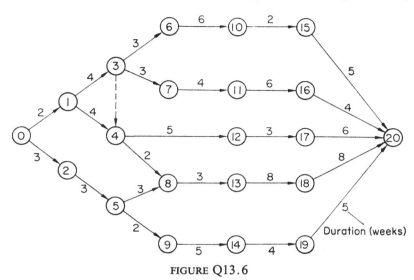

FIGURE Q13.6

13.7. 'Traditionally, the progress chaser was an essential feature of an effective production control system, since his was, amongst other things, the responsibility for *recording* the progress of jobs. By use of effective clerical and/or computer based systems, the need for progress chasing can be largely eliminated.' Discuss.

13.8. Describe, using examples, the manner in which digital electronic computers can be used to control or assist in the control of production in (a) process industries and (b) jobbing or batch manufacturing industries.

13.9. Priority Rules are frequently used to allocate available jobs to the necessary machines in jobbing shop type manufacture. Discuss this technique, describe several such rules and identify random, local and general rules. Describe also the heuristic rules suggested by Gere.

14

Quality Control

Most of us would, no doubt, regard Rolls-Royce motor cars as being high quality products, but why do we believe this and what, apart from prestige, would the ownership of a Rolls-Royce give us that ownership of any other large car would not? We perhaps consider these cars to be well designed, not necessarily in an aesthetic sense but certainly designed to function well and to last for a considerable number of years. We also regard Rolls-Royces as being well made, as consisting of good components and parts assembled in a careful and craftsman-like manner, consequently ownership of such a car would, we believe, result in trouble-free motoring. A Rolls-Royce would be reliable and would function well for many years, whereas lower quality cars would not. What then prevents us all from owning such cars—simply that for the majority of people they are too expensive. Consequently, we must undertake our motoring in lower quality, less reliable vehicles which are available at a price that we can afford.

Similar considerations no doubt apply to other items. When buying our vacuum cleaner and washing machine and even when buying the groceries, we are often aware that higher quality items exist but, nevertheless purchase items at a lower price, confident that these will meet our requirements.

Three points in the previous paragraphs are worth looking at more closely. Firstly, why do we regard items as being of high quality and what aspects of any product contribute to this intangible and indefinite characteristic? Our admiration of the design and construction of Rolls-Royces provides the answer to this question. Quality, however we care to define the term, is given to a product during the design stage and during manufacture or the execution of the design. A house which is designed to be constructed of stone and well-seasoned timber is, on paper at least, of better quality than one to be built with second hand timbers and 'breeze-blocks'. The comparison may be adjusted during actual construction, since the accuracy with which the walls are built, the care with which the timbers and the roof are erected, and so on, will also determine the quality of the finished house. The eventual quality of a manufactured product is, therefore, a function of the two stages—design and manufacture.

The second point worth considering is the consequences of quality. We have said that a high quality motor car is likely, other things being equal, to be more reliable than one of lower quality. Quality and reliability it seems are in some way related. *Design Quality* is determined by the specification of the product, for example the tolerance placed on dimensions, the composition and treatment of materials, finishes etc. *Manufacture Quality* is determined by the degree of conformity to these specifications during manufacture. *Reliability* is one consequence of quality; it is concerned with satisfaction during use and the extent to which the product fulfils its intended purpose. Reliability can be expressed mathematically as the probability that the product will operate satisfactorily for a given length of time under normal working conditions. The manufacture of products of inferior quality, because of either inferior design or manufacture, or both, will result in comparative unreliability during use. Reliability will, of course, reduce throughout usage. The contribution of each of these three stages to quality and reliability is shown diagrammatically in Fig. 14–1.

The final point concerns cost—the principal reason why we all do not own Rolls-Royces. Quality, reliability and cost are all interconnected. With sufficient expenditure, motor cars of any size can be endowed with quality equal to that of a Rolls-Royce, and with sufficient expenditure almost any proprietory product can be made to be very reliable. It follows then that a company can manufacture a product at numerous quality levels, each of which necessitates the sale of the

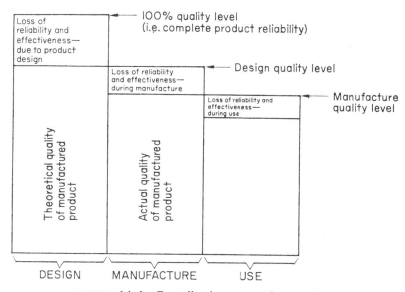

FIGURE 14.1. Contribution to product quality

product at a different price. There is no single level of quality nor is there an absolute quality level. No product will be perfect, and all products, no matter how much they cost to make, are liable to failure. Decisions relating to product specification, quality, and consequently cost will be influenced by the policy and behaviour of competitors in the market. Before launching a new product a company will investigate the quality and the reliability of equivalent products already on the market, and their objective may then be to better both the quality and or the price of these products. There are circumstances in which such a procedure for establishing quality levels is unnecessary, for example certain products must be manufactured to national or international standards, such as those produced by the British Standards Institute. Adherence to such standards is frequently mandatory. Except on such occasions, price and quality decisions are often taken empirically. Furthermore, both price and quality will often change as a result of market pressures.

MANUFACTURE QUALITY

In this chapter we are not primarily concerned with product design and hence the remainder of the chapter will be devoted to manufacture quality. We can assume, therefore, that the product specifications have been established and all that remains is to adhere to these specifications during manufacture. To achieve this objective three stages can be defined. We must first ensure that only raw materials and parts which conform to the given specifications are accepted from suppliers. Secondly, we must implement control procedures to attempt to ensure that during the conversion of these items only products which conform to the specifications are produced; and and finally, we must ensure that only those products which do conform to the specifications are offered to the customers. These procedures are outlined diagrammatically in Fig. 14.2 and are discussed below.

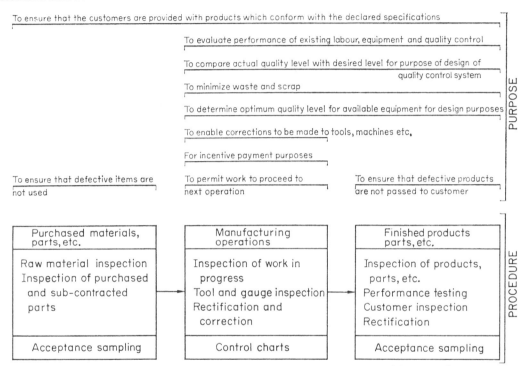

FIGURE 14.2. The procedures and purposes of quality control in manufacture

Inspection of Purchased Materials and Parts

A manufacturer may adopt one or (usually) both of the the following procedures to attempt to ensure that he uses only material and parts which fully conform to the required specifications and standards.

1. He may use some form of inspection procedure.
2. He may purchase items from only those firms which are known to be reliable suppliers.

There is little that can be said about the second but a great deal that can be said about the first procedure. The materials and parts which are supplied to the firm will doubtless have been subjected by the supplier to some form of quality control. The purchasing firm will either institute his own inspection procedure carried out in the receiving department on his own premises and/or conduct or observe the inspection processes conducted by the supplier. He may ask to be supplied with regular information concerning the quality of the parts or materials as they are manufactured. He may ask for copies of all the final inspection documents to be supplied along with the materials or parts or, finally, he may ask a third party to ensure that the items manufactured for him conform to the requisite minimum quality.[1] Inspection of purchased materials, parts etc. should be conducted on receipt and prior to placing the items in stores. One or both the following procedures will be adopted.

1. Exhaustive inspection of every item received.
2. An inspection of a sample of the items received. This procedure, which is commonly adopted, is referred to as *acceptance sampling* and is discussed in some detail later in the chapter.

The nature of the inspection procedure will, of course, depend upon the type of items concerned. There is often little that can be done about raw materials except to establish the correct quantity has been received and to conduct metallurgical or physical tests (e.g. to test composition, tensile strength, percentage elongation etc.) on sample pieces from each batch received. Parts or components may be inspected dimensionally, certain attributes such as the finish, the appearance and so on may be checked. Furthermore, sample performance tests might be made on such items as motors, pumps, etc. Defective or damaged items will, of course, be returned to the supplier for rectification or replacement.

Inspection during manufacture

Inspection of products or parts between operations during manufacture is undertaken, not only to ensure that faulty or defective items do not proceed to the subsequent operations, but also in order to predict when manufacturing processes are likely to produce defective items in order that necessary preventative adjustments might be made.

The layman might tend to think that expensive pieces of equipment, such as machine tools, will produce parts continually to the correct specification. This, unfortunately, is not so. Even in apparently simple operations like drilling holes, dimensions will vary over a period of time because of wear, temperature changes etc. Needless to say, the propensity of equipment to produce parts which vary from the required specification is increased if human operators are involved in the work cycle. Consequently, some form of inspection is necessary during almost all manufacturing operations.

In jobbing production, inspection often involves every item after most operations but in batch production it is often sufficient to inspect only the first and last items to be produced. In mass production, continuous sampling inspection is frequently undertaken and, of course, the possibility of inspection during process type manufacture is often dependent upon the 'chemistry' of the process. Quality control during manufacture frequently involves the use of *control charts* which will be discussed in some detail shortly.

Inspection during manufacture is normally the principal commitment of the quality control department and the design of such inspection schemes is an interesting and complex problem. The number and disposition of inspection 'operations' should reflect both the probability of faults or defectives occurring, the consequences of such occurrences and also the cost of conducting inspection. Frequently, technical considerations determine the position and number of inspection operations but nevertheless, within certain limitations production management is usually able to design the inspection procedure.

Well defined procedures should be established for the selection and inspection of the parts; for the recording and analysis of data; for reprocessing, rectifying or scraping of defectives;

[1] e.g. in the manufacture of diesel engines for marine propulsion purposes, customers (i.e. shipping lines) invariably specify that manufacture shall conform to a particular class of the Lloyds Insurance standards. In such case, inspection on the suppliers' premises of both raw materials and manufactured products is undertaken by Lloyds Inspectors.

and for the feedback of information to the workers, machine setters, wages, product engineering and design departments. We have tended to assume that a group of people attached to a separate department within the production function is involved on these quality control procedures but two other alternatives exist. Firstly, the use of automatic 'on line' inspection or gauging, using pneumatic, optical or electronic devices attached to machine tools. Such procedures are increasingly used for automatic inspection and checking of variables (dimensions) often the equipment involves a 'feed-back' to the tool, which is self correcting. A second alternative is for workers to be responsible for checking and inspecting their own work. In such cases appropriate time allowances must be provided.

Inspection of Finished Products and Parts

Quality inspection of finished products is essential, yet ironically—unfortunate. It is essential because unless defective products are identified by the producer they will be passed on to the consumer where they may either be identified and not accepted, or accepted and provide unsatisfactory service. Both results reflect adversely upon the producer's manufacturing and quality control systems. Final inspection is perhaps unfortunate, since the purpose of all previous inspection has been to ensure that defective or faulty products are *not* manufactured, nevertheless final inspection is not a reflection on the ineffectiveness of earlier inspection since components can be damaged at any time during the entire production process.

Final inspection, like those previously conducted may involve only a sampling procedure or involve exhaustive checks. In addition to the inspection of dimensions, appearance etc., final inspection may well involve an examination of function to establish that the product is capable of performing in the manner specified and required by the customer. In the motor industry a short duration performance test is given to all engines produced and a long duration performance and endurance test is given to a small sample of engines. Again, suitable procedures must be designed for the collection and retention of inspection data, for the correction, replacement, or further examination of faulty products and, if necessary, for the adjustment or modification of either previous inspection operations or the manufacturing operations to ensure that faulty products do not continue to be produced, at least not for the same reasons.

Inspection of finished products is normally conducted in a similar manner to the inspection of purchased parts and materials, the procedures being referred to as Acceptance Sampling.

Inspection of Inspection

Quality control and inspection procedures almost invariably involve the use of equipment such as gauges and other apparatus. If products are to be made accurately then we must ensure that the means by which they are checked is also accurate. A periodic examination and recalibration of all gauges should be undertaken, and all other apparatus used in inspection should be inspected e.g. equipment for metallurgical analysis, destructive and non-destructive testing etc.

The Economics of Quality Control

As more effort is made to control the quality of either the products leaving a firm or the parts leaving a particular production operation, then, not unreasonably, fewer defective parts pass by unnoticed. Any increase in quality control effort will, of course, cost more and there is therefore a point at which the total variable cost of quality control is minimized (see Fig. 14.3). Any increase

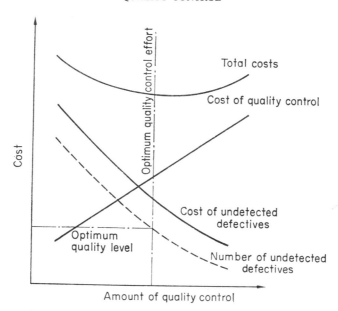

FIGURE 14.3. Optimum quality level and amount of quality control

in effort beyond this level, whilst reducing the number of defective items passing undetected, will also increase total cost and less effort will also increase cost because of the greater number of defective items allowed to pass. If we were able to construct or obtain formulae for the curves shown in Fig. 14–3 then the determination of the optimum quality level and the optimum quality control effort would be a simple matter. Unfortunately however, this type of information is usually unobtainable. Even though the curve 'cost of quality control' is reasonably easy to construct, the two curves relating to the number and cost of rejected items would be almost impossible to construct with sufficient accuracy. In practice, therefore, the amount of quality control effort made by a company, and consequently the actual quality level obtained is determined by judgement, by experiment and by experience. The actual or average quality level may be high if the subsequent cost of defective items, in terms of loss of future orders, rectification costs, cost of wasted subsequent processing, etc., is high, and vice versa. The average quality level obtained will be determined, to a large extent, by the various 'pressures for quality' or the known consequences of producing inferior items.

ACCEPTANCE SAMPLING

When material or parts are purchased, or when sub-contracted work is returned, we must establish a procedure whereby we can ensure, with reasonable certainty, that the items we are being offered conform to the requisite standards. Whether such a procedure is conducted on our own premises or on the premises of the supplier is immaterial to the following discussion. Clearly, some form of inspection or test procedure is required and it is with the design of such procedures that we shall be concerned.

Inspection of each critical feature of every item received may be a very desirable procedure in that by so doing no defective items would pass unnoticed, except by a mistake or error in the inspection procedure. There are, however, several reasons why such a procedure may be uneconomical or even impossible; i.e.

1. Inspection may cause damage or even complete destruction of the items (e.g. the testing of electrical fuses).
2. The accuracy of inspection may be diminished after frequent repetition. For example, an inspection task may take only a few seconds to complete but if this is undertaken continually over a long period, it may be excessively fatiguing and boring for the Inspector, whose accuracy and judgement might then be affected.
3. Handling of the item may result in deterioration, or alternatively, items may naturally deteriorate rapidly prior to use and lengthy inspection procedures may be undesirable.
4. Inspection may be a particularly expensive procedure involving the unpacking or dismantling of items, the use of special machines etc.
5. Inspection may be a hazardous even dangerous procedure (e.g. the test of pressure vessels).

For these reasons, some form of *sampling inspection* is often required. In acceptance sampling decisions about the quality of batches of items are made after inspection of only a portion of those items. If the sample of items conforms to the requisite quality levels then the whole batch from which it came is accepted. If the sample does not conform to the requisite quality level, then the whole batch is rejected or subjected to further inspection. Adopting this procedure decisions about the quality levels of items can be made fairly quickly, easily and cheaply. However, a certain amount of risk is involved, since there is the possibility that the sample taken will not be of the same quality as the batch from which it came. A greater proportion of defectives in the sample will lead us erroneously to attribute a lower quality level to the batch and vice versa.

Several types of acceptance sampling plans may be used. For example, some necessitate taking a *single* sample lot from a batch, upon which a quality decision is made, whilst others may necessitate the use of *multiple* samples from the same batch. Plans will also vary in the types of measurements that are involved. The most common, and simplest type of inspection decision involves classifying items as good or bad, as acceptable or unacceptable. This is referred to as

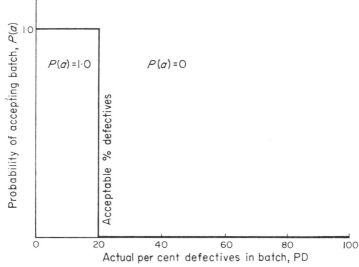

FIGURE 14.4. The probability of accepting batches, with 100 per cent inspection (Acceptable per cent defectives = 20 per cent of less)

acceptence sampling by *attributes*. Less often, acceptance sampling by *variables* is utilized in which the purpose of inspection is to obtain exact measurements for dimensions. We shall concentrate initially on the more usual procedure which is *single acceptance sampling* by *attributes*.

Acceptance sampling by attributes is suitable, not only for items whose critical features cannot easily be measured, such as the quality of finish of furniture, the power of light bulbs etc, but may also be used where inspection is concerned with dimensions since such dimensions ultimately are either acceptable or not. For example, the size of a hole in a component will either fall within the upper and lower tolerance specified, and hence be acceptable, or if it doesn't then it will be rejected. In such cases Go/No Go gauges are often used to check the acceptability of variable.

Customers would ideally like 100 per cent of the products which they purchase to be acceptable but this, as we have pointed out previously, is impractical. Therefore, some lower quality level must, of necessity, be agreed. Even so, except by 100 per cent inspection (and even then, only if there are no errors during inspection) can we be absolutely certain that a batch conforms to this agreed standard. In Fig. 14.4, 100 per cent inspection has been used—consequently we can be 100 per cent certain that batches do, or do not, conform to the agreed quality level, which is a maximum of 20 per cent defectives per batch. (Again assuming no mistakes during inspection.)

A curve such as this is known as an *operating characteristic* curve and shows the probability of accepting batches with various percentage defectives. Operating characteristic (OC) curves can be calculated and drawn for any sampling plan, if we specify:

1. The sample size
2. The acceptable quality level i.e. the allowance number of defects in the sample.

If the batches are large compared to the size of the sample, the construction of such curves is based on the use of the *binomial* probability expression, from which we can calculate the probability that a given number of defectives will be found when a sample of given size is drawn from a batch with a given proportion of defectives.

i.e.[2] $P(r) = \dfrac{n!}{r!\,(n-r)!}\, p^r q^{(n-r)}$

where r = No. of defectives found

n = Sample size

p = Proportion of defectives in batch

q = Proportion of good items in batch (i.e. $q = 1-p$)

$P(r)$ = Probability of finding r defectives

Example:

Sample size $n = 10$

Acceptable No. of defectives $c = 1$ or less ($\leqslant 1$)

If actual percentage of defectives in batch $= 10$ per cent

$$P\ (1) = \frac{10!}{1!\ \ 9!} \times 0{\cdot}1^1 \times 0{\cdot}9^9 = 0{\cdot}392$$

$$P\ (0) = \frac{10!}{0!\ \ 10!} \times 0{\cdot}1^0 \times 0{\cdot}9^{10} = 0{\cdot}352$$

$\therefore P(\leqslant 1) = P(0) + P(1) \qquad\qquad = 0{\cdot}744$

---

[2] $n! = n \times (n-1) \times (n-2) \ldots \ldots \times (n-(n-1))$

e.g. $3! = 3 \times 2 \times 1$

NB O! is taken to be 1.

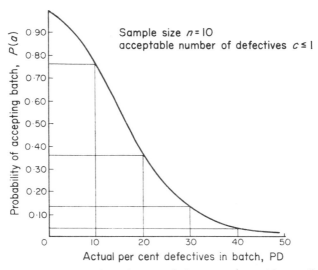

FIGURE 14.5. Operating characteristic curve ($n = 10$; $c \leqslant 1$)

Consequently by performing similar calculations for different levels of actual percentage batch defectives the curve shown in Fig. 14.5 can be constructed.

Where the value of n (sample size) is large, the use of this method of calculation becomes laborious, and it is fortunate therefore that in most cases it is possible to use an approximate yet adequate method of determining probabilities. It can be shown that when the expected number of defectives

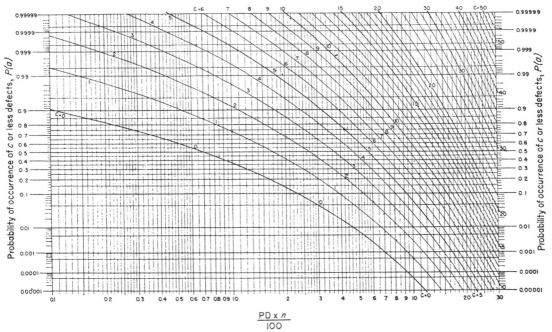

FIGURE 14.6. Thorndike chart [Adapted from H. F. Dodge and H. G. Romig, *Sampling Inspection Tables*, Wiley, London, 1959]

$(p \times n)$ is small relative to the lot size, (N) the *Poisson* distribution can be used as an adequate approximation to the Binomial.[3] To simplify matters further in such circumstances the calculations may be performed with the assistance of the *Thorndike chart*. This chart, as shown in Fig. 14.6, is in fact a set of cumulative Poisson probability curves from which the probability of c or less defectives (Pa on the vertical axis) for given values of $PD \times n/100$ (on the horizontal axis can be determined

where PD = Actual percent defectives in a batch or lot.
$\quad\quad n$ = Sample size.

Example

Use the Thorndike chart to construct an Operating Characteristic curve for

$$n = 100 \text{ sample size}$$
$$c = 3 \text{ allowable no. of defects.}$$

Answer

Actual percent defectives in batch (PD)	$\dfrac{PD \times n}{100}$	Pa
1	1	0·98
2	2	0·86
3	3	0·65
4	4	0·44
5	5	0·26
6	6	0·15
7	7	0·08
8	8	0·04
9	9	0·02
10	10	0·01

These figures can now be used to plot an OC curve of the type shown previously.

The ability of a sampling procedure to distinguish between good and bad batches is primarily a function of the sample size. If three sampling processes are designed to test the quality level of batches of components for which the acceptable quality level is 1 per cent or less of defectives, then the procedure using the largest sample will be more accurate than those using smaller samples —particularly, where the actual percentage of defectives in the batch is high. Fig. 14.7, shows three such OC curves, each of which is fairly accurate up to a percentage defective level just below the acceptable level but above that point, curve 3 is superior. As the sample size is increased, the curves become steeper and begin to approach the perfectly discriminating OC curve given in Fig. 14.4.

---

[3] It is generally accepted that the Poisson distribution may be used where N is large, where N is over 5 times the sample size n and where the proportion of defects p is less than 0·10. In cases where the batch or lot size is small neither the Poisson nor the Binomial distributions are satisfactory and use should be made of the hypergeometric distribution. Tables for this distribution are available (e.g. see G. D. SELF, 'Hypergeometrically computed LTPD sampling planner', *J. Ind. Eng.*, **XIX**, No. 12, 608–611.)

For both large N and large n and when p is greater than 0·1 the use of the normal distribution is satisfactory.

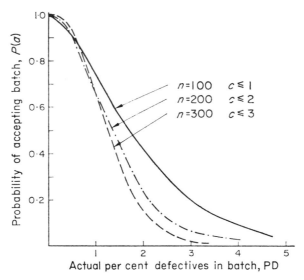

FIGURE 14.7. Operating characteristic curves

The Design of Single Acceptance Sampling Plans

The merit of any sampling plan depends on the relationship of sampling cost to risk. As the cost of inspection decreases and the cost of accepting defective items increases, then the merit of inspection increases and the more willing we are to use larger samples. The OC curve shows, for any plan, both the probability of accepting batches with more than the acceptable number of defectives, as well as the probability of rejecting batches with less than the acceptable number of defectives.

It is the consumer's desire to reduce the probability of accepting batches including too many defectives and the producer's desire to minimize the probability of rejecting batches including an acceptable number of defectives. These are called respectively, the *consumer's risk* (β) and the *producer's risk* (α). These two values are used in order to design Acceptance Sampling plans and, in addition, two further points are used:

Acceptable Quality Level (*AQL*)—the desired quality level—a level at which probability of acceptance should be high.

Lot Tolerance Percent Defective (*LTPD*)—a quality level below which batches are considered unacceptable, and a level at which probability of acceptance should be low.

These four points are shown on the OC curve in Fig. 14.8. Consumers' risk (β) is usually specified at about 10 per cent and the Producer's Risk at approximately 5 per cent. Acceptable quality level is often around 2 per cent and lot tolerance per cent defective around 10 per cent. These four figures are specified in designing the sampling plan, all that then remains is to construct an OC curve which passes through the two points (*AQL*; α) and (*LTPD* : β). This can be done by trial and error, selecting various values for sample size (n) and acceptable number of defectives (c) and substituting into the Binomial probability formula until an acceptable curve is obtained, or by use of the Thorndike chart.

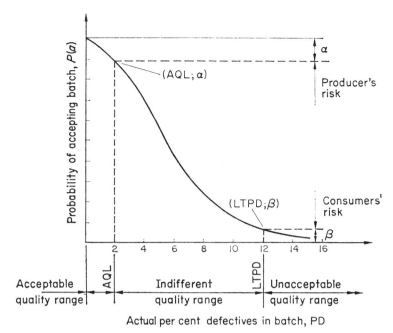

FIGURE 14.8. Operating characteristic curve and points specifying a sampling plan

Example

Use the Thorndike chart to construct an OC curve which as near as possible satisfies the following requirements

$$LTPD = 5 \text{ per cent} \qquad \beta = 10 \text{ per cent}$$
$$AQL = 2 \text{ per cent} \qquad \alpha = 5 \text{ per cent}$$

To specify the OC curve we must establish a value for n and for c. Consider first of all the point on the OC curve located by $LTPD$ (5 per cent) and β (10 per cent). Here the probability of acceptance, or Pa on the Thorndike chart, is 0·1. Reading along the $Pa = 0·1$ ordinate we can determine the value on the other axis $PD \times n/100$ for each value of c, i.e.

when $\dfrac{Pa = 0·1}{(\beta = 10 \text{ per cent})}$	c	$\dfrac{PDn}{100}$
	1	3·9
	2	5·3
	3	6·7
	4	8·0
	5	9·3
	6	10·5
	7	11·8
	8	13·0
	9	14·2
	10	15·5
	11	16·7

Now consider the point on the OC curve located by AQL (2 per cent) and α (5 per cent). Here $Pa = 0.95$, $(1-\alpha)$, hence the values of $PD \times n/100$ can be determined as follows:

when $\dfrac{Pa = 0.95}{(\alpha = 5 \text{ per cent})}$	c	$\dfrac{PD \times n}{100}$
	1	0·36
	2	0·82
	3	1·37
	4	1·97
	5	2·6
	6	3·3
	7	4·0
	8	4·6
	9	5·4
	10	6·2
	11	7·0

Now in order to determine which OC curve best fits our requirements we must use the two sets of $PD \times n/100$ values. In the first set ($Pa = 0.1$ or $\beta = 10$ per cent) we require a $PD \times n/100$ value equivalent to the AQL of 2 per cent, whilst in the last set we require a $PD \times n/100$ value equivalent to $LTPD = 5$ per cent. If we divide the pairs of $PD \times n/100$ values for each value of c we have in fact determined the value of $LTPD/AQL$, i.e.

c	$\dfrac{PD \times n}{100}$ for $\beta = 10$ per cent	$\dfrac{PD \times n}{100}$ for $\alpha = 5$ per cent	$\dfrac{PD \times n/100 \text{ for } \beta = 10}{PD \times n/100 \text{ for } \alpha = 5} = \dfrac{LTPD}{AQL}$
1	3·9	0·36	10·8
2	5·3	0·82	6·45
3	6·7	1·37	4·9
4	8·0	1·97	4·06
5	9·3	2·6	3·58
6	10·5	3·3	3·18
7	11·8	4·0	2·95
8	13·0	4·6	2·82
9	14·2	5·4	2·66
10	15·5	6·2	2·50 ←
11	16·7	7·0	2·38

In fact the ratio for $LTPD/AQL$ specified in the question is $5/2 = 2.5$ which corresponds to the ratio obtained for $c = 10$. It now remains only to determine n, which can be found as follows: where $c = 10$ for $\beta = 10$ per cent

$$\frac{PD \times n}{100} = \frac{LTPD \times n}{100} = 15.5$$

$$\therefore n = \frac{15.5 \times 100}{LTPD}$$

$$= \frac{15.5 \times 100}{5}$$

$$= 310$$

Our OC curve is therefore specified by $c = 10$ and $n = 310$.

Defective items found in the *samples* will always be either rectified or replaced. If, during inspection, samples are drawn from the batch which include more than the acceptable number of defectives, then two alternatives are available:

1. Reject and scrap the complete *batch*
2. Subject the complete *batch* to 100 per cent inspection and replace or rectify all faulty items found therein.

The choice of alternative (1) or (2) will depend upon the value of the items concerned and the cost to replace or rectify them, but often in order to obtain a high quality level for batches with a minimum of inspection, the second alternative is adopted. In such a case we can represent our Acceptance Sampling procedure diagrammatically as shown in Fig. 14.9. Referring to this diagramtic representation a random sample of n items is taken from the batch of N items. The sample is inspected and c' defectives are found, which are then replaced or rectified. Depending upon whether c' is greater than c (the acceptable number of defects) the entire batch is either accepted or rejected. If the batch is rejected ($c' > c$) the remaining $N-n$ items in the batch are all inspected, defective items being either rectified or replaced. In this case we can be certain (subject to inspec-

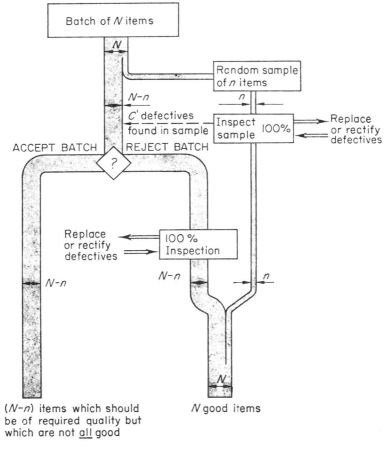

FIGURE 14.9. The operation of a sampling procedure in which batches are subject to 100 per cent inspection if necessary

tion error) that we are left with N good items. If on the other hand the batch is accepted because $c' \leqslant c$, then we can be certain that the sample contains all good items, but of course some of the remaining $N-n$ items will be defective.

The *average outgoing quality* (AOQ) is the overall proportion of items in a large number of batches, when all batches have the same actual per cent defectives (PD) and when all batches are subjected to the type of inspection procedure described above. The AOQ per cent which must be less than PD can be found as follows:

$$\text{AOQ per cent} = \frac{\text{Number of defectives remaining}}{\text{Total number of items}} \times 100$$

$$= \frac{\text{Number of defective items in accepted batches each of size } N\text{-}n}{\text{Total number of items}} \times 100$$

$$\therefore \text{AOQ per cent} = \frac{Pa(PD)(N\text{-}n)k}{Nk}$$

where Pa = Probability of accepting batch, (from OC curve)
PD = Actual per cent defectives in all batches
N = Batch sizes
n = Sample sizes
k = Large number of batches.

i.e. AOQ per cent $= \dfrac{Pa(PD)(N\text{-}n)}{N}$

Curves showing the average outgoing quality level, for any actual per cent defectives, can be calculated quite simply.

Example

Construct the AOQ curve for the sampling plan shown in Fig. 14.5 with batch sizes of $N = 200$

$$\text{AOQ per cent} = Pa\,PD\,\frac{N\text{-}n}{N}$$

$$= Pa\,PD\,0.95$$

Pa (from OC curve)[a]	PD per cent	AOQ per cent
0·90	5	4·3
0·77	10	7·3
0·55	15	7·8
0·37	20	7·0
0·22	25	5·2
0·13	30	3·7
0·08	35	2·7
0·06	40	2·4

[a] See Fig. 14.5.

This AOQ curve is shown in Fig. 14.10.

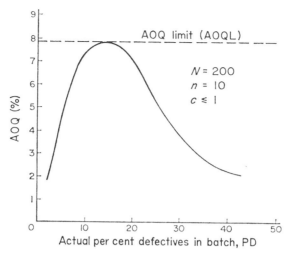

FIGURE 14.10. AOQ curve

Using such a sampling procedure, not only is the AOQ better than the specified acceptable quality level, but also a 'built-in' *limit* for the proportion of defectives—the average outgoing quality limit—exists. This limit represents the worse average quality, which over a large number of batches we may expect to pass either to the customer or to the next production stage. Acceptance sampling plans may also be designed to provide a given AOQL.

Summary of the Design of Single Acceptance Sampling Plans for Attributes

Sampling plans may be designed to provide:

1. An average outgoing quality limit (AOQL)
2. A given consumer or producer risk (LTPD and AQL)

AOQL plans are usually adopted where interest centres upon the average quality level after inspection, whereas LTPD and/or AQL plans are used where a certain given level of risk is to be satisfied.

The basic steps involved in the design and use of an Acceptance Sampling procedure are as follows:

1. Decide what features or characteristics of the items will be inspected.
   (a) If necessary treat different characteristics with separate sampling procedures.
   but
   (b) wherever possible combine all characteristics which are the subject of the same kind of inspection (e.g. all characteristics necessitating visual inspection) and treat them all with the same acceptance sampling plan.
2. Decide what, for the purpose of the sampling procedure, constitutes a batch, i.e.
   (a) A batch should as far as possible, consist of homogenous items from the same source.
   (b) Batches should be as large as possible to minimize inspection.
3. Choose the type of sampling plan to be used, i.e. AOQL or AQL/LTPD plans and determine suitable quality or risk figures to be used in the plan.
4. Select a random sample from the batch and inspect appropriate characteristics on each item.
5. As a result of quality level of the sample, accept or reject batch.

Double and Multiple Sampling

The total amount of inspection required to obtain a certain output quality level can be reduced if *double* or *multiple sampling* is used.

In single acceptance sampling as described above, the decision to accept or to reject the batch of items is dependent upon the inspection of a single random sample from that batch. In *double* sampling there exists the possibility of delaying that decision, until a second sample has been taken. A random sample of n items is drawn from the batch, each item is inspected and the number of defectives (c) is counted. If this number is less than or equal to a given acceptance number ($c1$) then the batch is accepted. Alternatively, if it is greater than a larger given acceptance number ($c2$) the batch is rejected. If, however, the number of defectives in the sample falls between these two levels, then the result is inconclusive and a second sample is drawn from the same batch. Again, the number of defectives is counted and this number is added to the number of defectives found in the first sample. If the total number is less than $c2$, the batch is accepted but if the total number is greater than $c2$, the batch is rejected.

Multiple or sequential sampling is a similar procedure but here there is the possibility of taking more than two samples from the same batch. An initial sample is drawn from the batch and, depending upon the number of defectives found, the batch is either accepted ($c \leqslant c1$), rejected ($c > c2$) or a decision is deferred ($c1 < c < c2$). The number of defectives in the second sample is added to the number found in the first and the total is compared to two further acceptance numbers—the batch being accepted, rejected or the decision deferred as before. This procedure is repeated until a decision can be made. A multiple sampling plan is depicted diagrammatically in Fig. 14.11.

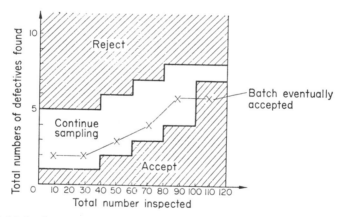

FIGURE 14.11. Multiple (sequential) sampling plan (for batch sizes of 500–799 for 3 per cent AQL)

Double or multiple sampling permits smaller sized samples to be taken. Consequently, on the occasions when the items or material inspected is well within, or well beyond acceptable quality levels, fewer items need be inspected. In such cases double or multiple sampling is more economical than single acceptance sampling.

In practice people responsible for the design and use of Acceptance Sampling rarely establish their sampling plans from first principles. More frequently one or more of the numerous sets of published charts or tables are used, the most popular of which are those developed by Dodge and Romig at the Bell Telephone laboratories.

The Dodge and Romig tables (see Selected Readings) are of four types:

1. Single Sampling Lot Tolerance tables, (e.g. see Fig. 14.12)
2. Single Sampling AOQL Tables, (e.g. see (Fig. 14.13)
3. Double Sampling Lot Tolerance tables, (e.g. see Fig. 14.14).
4. Double Sampling AOQL tables, (e.g. see Fig. 14.15).

Lot Size	Process Average 0 to 0.05%			Process Average 0.06 to 0.50%			Process Average 0.51 to 1.00%			Process Average 1.01 to 1.50%			Process Average 1.51 to 2.00%			Process Average 2.01 to 2.50%		
	n	c	AOQL %	n	c	AOQL %	n	c	AOQL %	n	c	AOQL %	n	c	AOQL %	n	c	AOQL %
1-30	All	0	0	All	0	0	All	0	0	All	0	0	All	0	0	All	0	0
31-50	30	0	0.49	30	0	0.49	30	0	0.49	30	0	0.49	30	0	0.49	30	0	0.49
51-100	37	0	0.63	37	0	0.63	37	0	0.63	37	0	0.63	37	0	0.63	37	0	0.63
101-200	40	0	0.74	40	0	0.74	40	0	0.74	40	0	0.74	40	0	0.74	40	0	0.74
201-300	43	0	0.74	43	0	0.74	70	1	0.92	70	1	0.92	95	2	0.99	95	2	0.99
301-400	44	0	0.74	44	0	0.74	70	1	0.99	100	2	1.0	120	3	1.1	145	4	1.1
401-500	45	0	0.75	75	1	0.95	100	2	1.1	100	2	1.1	125	3	1.2	150	4	1.2
501-600	45	0	0.76	75	1	0.98	100	2	1.1	125	3	1.2	150	4	1.3	175	5	1.3
601-800	45	0	0.77	75	1	1.0	100	2	1.2	130	3	1.2	175	5	1.4	200	6	1.4
801-1000	45	0	0.78	75	1	1.0	105	2	1.2	155	4	1.4	180	5	1.4	225	7	1.5
1001-2000	45	0	0.80	75	1	1.0	130	3	1.4	180	5	1.6	230	7	1.7	280	9	1.8
2001-3000	75	1	1.1	105	2	1.3	135	3	1.4	210	6	1.7	280	9	1.9	370	13	2.1
3001-4000	75	1	1.1	105	2	1.3	160	4	1.5	210	6	1.7	305	10	2.0	420	15	2.2
4001-5000	75	1	1.1	105	2	1.3	160	4	1.5	235	7	1.8	330	11	2.0	440	16	2.2
5001-7000	75	1	1.1	105	2	1.3	185	5	1.7	260	8	1.9	350	12	2.2	490	18	2.4
7001-10,000	75	1	1.1	105	2	1.3	185	5	1.7	260	8	1.9	380	13	2.2	535	20	2.5
10,001-20,000	75	1	1.1	135	3	1.4	210	6	1.8	285	9	2.0	425	15	2.3	610	23	2.6
20,001-50,000	75	1	1.1	135	3	1.4	235	7	1.9	305	10	2.1	470	17	2.4	700	27	2.7
50,001-100,000	75	1	1.1	160	4	1.6	235	7	1.9	355	12	2.2	515	19	2.5	770	30	2.8

n = sample size; c = acceptance number
"All" indicates that each piece in the lot is to be inspected
AOQL = Average Outgoing Quality Limit

FIGURE 14.12. Single sampling table for lot tolerance per cent defective (LTPD) = 5·0 per cent

The LTPD tables provide values of n and c for a consumers risk of 10 per cent and for LTPD's from 0·5 per cent to 10·0 per cent. To use the tables the batch or lot size and the actual process average percentage defective must be known. The latter will usually be obtained from a pilot study. The LTPD tables also show in each case the AOQL which would result if rejected batches are subject to 100 per cent inspection.

The AOQL tables provide values of n and c for a consumers risk of 10 per cent and for AOQL's from 0·1 to 10 per cent. Again to use these tables the batch size and process average percentage defective must be known. The tables also give the LTPD which will result from each sampling plan.

CONTROL CHARTS

Acceptance Sampling is a method of quality control which is used to ensure that defective items or parts are not accepted by the firm and to ensure that defective products are not offered to the customer. It is concerned with both ends of the quality function but not—at least not in this form—with the middle. It is not concerned with controlling the quality of parts or products during the manufacturing operations. This problem however, is particularly important, since it

Lot Size	Process Average 0 to 0.05%			Process Average 0.06 to 0.50%			Process Average 0.51 to 1.00%			Process Average 1.01 to 1.50%			Process Average 1.51 to 2.00%			Process Average 2.01 to 2.50%		
	n	c	p_t %	n	c	p_t %	n	c	p_t %	n	c	p_t %	n	c	p_t %	n	c	p_t %
1–10	All	0	--	All	0	–	All	0	--	All	0	--	All	0	--	All	0	--
11–50	11	0	17.6	11	0	17.6	11	0	17.6	11	0	17.6	11	0	17.6	11	0	17.6
51–100	13	0	15.3	13	0	15.3	13	0	15.3	13	0	15.3	13	0	15.3	13	0	15.3
101–200	14	0	14.7	14	0	14.7	14	0	14.7	29	1	12.9	29	1	12.9	29	1	12.9
201–300	14	0	14.9	14	0	14.9	30	1	12.7	30	1	12.7	30	1	12.7	30	1	12.7
301–400	14	0	15.0	14	0	15.0	31	1	12.3	31	1	12.3	31	1	12.3	48	2	10.7
401–500	14	0	15.0	14	0	15.0	32	1	12.0	32	1	12.0	49	2	10.6	49	2	10.6
501–600	14	0	15.1	32	1	12.0	32	1	12.0	50	2	10.4	50	2	10.4	70	3	9.3
601–800	14	0	15.1	32	1	12.0	32	1	12.0	50	2	10.5	50	2	10.5	70	3	9.4
801–1000	15	0	14.2	33	1	11.7	33	1	11.7	50	2	10.6	70	3	9.4	90	4	8.5
1001–2000	15	0	14.2	33	1	11.7	55	2	9.3	75	3	8.8	95	4	8.0	120	5	7.6
2001–3000	15	0	14.2	33	1	11.8	55	2	9.4	75	3	8.8	120	5	7.6	145	6	7.2
3001–4000	15	0	14.3	33	1	11.8	55	2	9.5	100	4	7.9	125	5	7.4	195	8	6.6
4001–5000	15	0	14.3	33	1	11.8	75	3	8.9	100	4	7.9	150	6	7.0	225	9	6.3
5001–7000	33	1	11.8	55	2	9.7	75	3	8.9	125	5	7.4	175	7	6.7	250	10	6.1
7001–10,000	34	1	11.4	55	2	9.7	75	3	8.9	125	5	7.4	200	8	6.4	310	12	5.8
10,001–20,000	34	1	11.4	55	2	9.7	100	4	8.0	150	6	7.0	260	10	6.0	425	16	5.3
20,001–50,000	34	1	11.4	55	2	9.7	100	4	8.0	180	7	6.7	345	13	5.5	640	23	4.8
50,001–100,000	34	1	11.4	80	3	8.4	125	5	7.4	235	9	6.1	435	16	5.2	800	28	4.5

n = sample size; c = acceptance number
"All" indicates that each piece in the lot is to be inspected
p_t = lot tolerance per cent defective with a Consumer's Risk (P_C) of 0.10

FIGURE 14.13. Single sampling table for average outgoing quality limit (AOQL) = 2·5 per cent

is during manufacture that steps may be taken to *prevent* the production of defective and sub-standard items. In fact, we can regard this as being the *quality assurance* function, as opposed to the *quality control* exercised by Acceptance Sampling.

The instrument used during quality assurance is the *control chart*, which is a special application of statistical sampling techniques. Much of the work of a quality control department in industry is dependent upon the use of control charts in one form or another and a great deal of the literature on quality control and quality assurance, deals with the design and use of such charts, all of which illustrates the importance of the technique, which we shall discuss for a large part of the remainder of this chapter.

Again, we must be grateful to the Bell Telephone Company of America, for it was in their laboratories around 1924 that Walter Skewhart developed this technique, the principles of which have remained basically unchanged to the present day.

Irrespective of how well designed or maintained, or how skilfully manufacturing equipment is used, the items produced by such equipment will inevitably be subject to some variation, e.g. the length of steel bars, cut on a cropping press will vary slightly, as will the diameter of holes drilled on a drilling machine and the diameter of shafts turned on a lathe. It is not only variables such as these (length, diameter etc.) but also attributes which will be subject to some variations. These variations might be caused by one or more of numerous factors but we can classify the variations into two categories.

1. *Usual or chance* variations, which are likely to occur in a random manner and about which comparatively little can be done.

2. *Unusual or assignable* variations which occur less frequently and can normally be traced to some 'external' causes, such as wear on tools, faulty materials, etc.

'Usual' variations are normally of a lesser magnitude than 'Unusual' variations and since they result from some inherent process variability, they occur randomly and can be described by the

Lot Size	Process Average 0 to 0.05% Trial 1 n_1	c_1	Trial 2 n_2	n_1+n_2	c_2	AOQL in %	Process Average 0.06 to 0.50% Trial 1 n_1	c_1	Trial 2 n_2	n_1+n_2	c_2	AOQL in %	Process Average 0.51 to 1.00% Trial 1 n_1	c_1	Trial 2 n_2	n_1+n_2	c_2	AOQL in %
1–30	All	0	—	—	—	0	All	0	—	—	—	0	All	0	—	—	—	0
31–50	30	0	—	—	—	0.49	30	0	—	—	—	0.49	30	0	—	—	—	0.49
51–75	38	0	—	—	—	0.59	38	0	—	—	—	0.59	38	0	—	—	—	0.59
76–100	44	0	21	65	1	0.64	44	0	21	65	1	0.64	44	0	21	65	1	0.64
101–200	49	0	26	75	1	0.84	49	0	26	75	1	0.84	49	0	26	75	1	0.84
201–300	50	0	30	80	1	0.91	50	0	30	80	1	0.91	50	0	55	105	2	1.0
301–400	55	0	30	85	1	0.92	55	0	55	110	2	1.1	55	0	55	110	2	1.1
401–500	55	0	30	85	1	0.93	55	0	55	110	2	1.1	55	0	80	135	3	1.2
501–600	55	0	30	85	1	0.94	55	0	60	115	2	1.1	55	0	85	140	3	1.2
601–800	55	0	35	90	1	0.95	55	0	65	120	2	1.1	55	0	85	140	3	1.3
801–1000	55	0	35	90	1	0.96	55	0	65	120	2	1.1	55	0	115	170	4	1.4
1001–2000	55	0	35	90	1	0.98	55	0	95	150	3	1.3	55	0	120	175	4	1.4
2001–3000	55	0	65	120	2	1.2	55	0	95	150	3	1.3	55	0	150	205	5	1.5
3001–4000	55	0	65	120	2	1.2	55	0	95	150	3	1.3	90	1	140	230	6	1.6
4001–5000	55	0	65	120	2	1.2	55	0	95	150	3	1.4	90	1	165	255	7	1.8
5001–7000	55	0	65	120	2	1.2	55	0	95	150	3	1.4	90	1	165	255	7	1.8
7001–10,000	55	0	65	120	2	1.2	55	0	120	175	4	1.5	90	1	190	280	8	1.9
10,001–20,000	55	0	65	120	2	1.2	55	0	120	175	4	1.5	90	1	190	280	8	1.9
20,001–50,000	55	0	65	120	2	1.2	55	0	150	205	5	1.7	90	1	215	305	9	2.0
50,001–100,000	55	0	65	120	2	1.2	55	0	150	205	5	1.7	90	1	240	330	10	2.1

Lot Size	Process Average 1.01 to 1.50% Trial 1 n_1	c_1	Trial 2 n_2	n_1+n_2	c_2	AOQL in %	Process Average 1.51 to 2.00% Trial 1 n_1	c_1	Trial 2 n_2	n_1+n_2	c_2	AOQL in %	Process Average 2.01 to 2.50% Trial 1 n_1	c_1	Trial 2 n_2	n_1+n_2	c_2	AOQL in %
1–30	All	0	—	—	—	0	All	0	—	—	—	0	All	0	—	—	—	0
31–50	30	0	—	—	—	0.49	30	0	—	—	—	0.49	30	0	—	—	—	0.49
51–75	38	0	—	—	—	0.59	38	0	—	—	—	0.59	38	0	—	—	—	0.59
76–100	44	0	21	65	1	0.64	44	0	21	65	1	0.64	44	0	21	65	1	0.64
101–200	49	0	51	100	2	0.91	49	0	51	100	2	0.91	49	0	51	100	2	0.91
201–300	50	0	55	105	2	1.0	50	0	80	130	3	1.1	50	0	100	150	4	1.1
301–400	55	0	80	135	3	1.1	55	0	100	155	4	1.2	85	1	105	190	6	1.3
401–500	55	0	105	160	4	1.3	85	1	120	205	6	1.4	85	1	140	225	7	1.4
501–600	55	0	110	165	4	1.3	85	1	145	230	7	1.4	85	1	165	250	8	1.5
601–800	90	1	125	215	6	1.5	90	1	170	260	8	1.5	120	2	185	305	10	1.6
801–1000	90	1	150	240	7	1.5	90	1	200	290	9	1.6	120	2	210	330	11	1.7
1001–2000	90	1	185	275	8	1.7	120	2	225	345	11	1.9	175	4	260	435	15	2.0
2001–3000	120	2	180	300	9	1.9	150	3	270	420	14	2.1	205	5	375	580	21	2.3
3001–4000	120	2	210	330	10	2.0	150	3	295	445	15	2.3	230	6	420	650	24	2.4
4001–5000	120	2	255	375	12	2.1	150	3	345	495	17	2.3	255	7	445	700	26	2.5
5001–7000	120	2	260	380	12	2.1	150	3	370	520	18	2.3	255	7	495	750	28	2.6
7001–10,000	120	2	285	405	13	2.1	175	4	370	545	19	2.4	280	8	540	820	31	2.7
10,001–20,000	120	2	310	430	14	2.2	175	4	420	595	21	2.4	280	8	660	940	36	2.8
20,001–50,000	120	2	335	455	15	2.2	205	5	485	690	25	2.5	305	9	745	1050	41	2.9
50,001–100,000	120	2	360	480	16	2.3	205	5	555	760	28	2.6	330	10	810	1140	45	3.0

Trial 1: n_1 = first sample size; c_1 = acceptance number for first sample
"All" indicates that each piece in the lot is to be inspected
Trial 2: n_2 = second sample size; c_2 = acceptance number for first and second samples combined
AOQL = Average Outgoing Quality Limit

FIGURE 14.14. Double sampling table for lot tolerance per cent defective (LTPD) = 5·0 per cent

Lot Size	Process Average 0 to 0.05% Trial 1 n_1	c_1	Trial 2 n_2	n_1+n_2	c_2	p_t %	Process Average 0.06 to 0.50% Trial 1 n_1	c_1	Trial 2 n_2	n_1+n_2	c_2	p_t %	Process Average 0.51 to 1.00% Trial 1 n_1	c_1	Trial 2 n_2	n_1+n_2	c_2	p_t %
1–10	All	0	–	–	–	–	All	0	..	–	..	–	All	0	...	..	..	
11–50	11	0	–	–	–	17.6	11	0	..	–	..	17.6	11	0	...	..	..	17.6
51–100	18	0	10	28	1	14.1	18	0	10	28	1	14.1	18	0	10	28	1	14.1
101–200	20	0	11	31	1	13.7	20	0	11	31	1	13.7	23	0	25	48	2	11.7
201–300	21	0	13	34	1	13.0	21	0	13	34	1	13.0	24	0	25	49	2	11.4
301–400	21	0	14	35	1	12.8	24	0	26	50	2	11.3	26	0	26	50	2	11.3
401–500	22	0	13	35	1	12.7	25	0	25	50	2	11.1	28	0	47	75	3	9.8
501–600	22	0	14	36	1	12.5	25	0	30	55	2	10.9	28	0	47	75	3	9.8
601–800	22	0	14	36	1	12.5	26	0	29	55	2	10.8	28	0	47	75	3	9.8
801–1000	26	0	29	55	2	10.8	26	0	29	55	2	10.8	29	0	46	75	3	9.6
1001–2000	27	0	33	60	2	10.5	27	0	33	60	2	10.5	33	0	72	105	4	8.3
2001–3000	27	0	33	60	2	10.5	30	0	50	80	3	9.3	33	0	72	105	4	8.3
3001–4000	27	0	33	60	2	10.5	31	0	49	80	3	9.1	33	0	77	110	4	8.2
4001–5000	27	0	33	60	2	10.5	31	0	49	80	3	9.1	36	0	94	130	5	7.6
5001–7000	28	0	32	60	2	10.3	31	0	49	80	3	9.1	36	0	94	130	5	7.7
7001–10,000	28	0	32	60	2	10.3	31	0	49	80	3	9.2	36	0	94	130	5	7.7
10,001–20,000	28	0	32	60	2	10.3	31	0	49	80	3	9.2	36	0	94	130	5	7.8
20,001–50,000	28	0	32	60	2	10.3	33	0	87	120	4	7.7	70	1	145	215	8	6.6
50,001–100,000	28	0	37	65	2	10.2	33	0	92	125	4	7.6	70	1	170	240	9	6.4

Lot Size	Process Average 1.01 to 1.50% Trial 1 n_1	c_1	Trial 2 n_2	n_1+n_2	c_2	p_t %	Process Average 1.51 to 2.00% Trial 1 n_1	c_1	Trial 2 n_2	n_1+n_2	c_2	p_t %	Process Average 2.01 to 2.50% Trial 1 n_1	c_1	Trial 2 n_2	n_1+n_2	c_2	p_t %
1–10	All	0	..	..	–	–	All	0	..	..	..	–	All	0	..	..		..
11–50	11	0	..	–	–	17.6	11	0	..	–	–	17.6	11	0	...	.	..	17.6
51–100	18	0	10	28	1	14.1	20	0	20	40	2	13.0	20	0	20	40	2	13.0
101–200	23	0	25	48	2	11.7	23	0	25	48	2	11.7	25	0	35	60	3	10.8
201–300	26	0	44	70	3	10.3	26	0	44	70	3	10.3	28	0	57	85	4	9.5
301–400	27	0	43	70	3	9.9	29	0	61	90	4	9.3	49	1	71	120	6	8.8
401–500	28	0	47	75	3	9.8	30	0	60	90	4	9.2	50	1	80	130	6	8.4
501–600	30	0	65	95	4	9.1	30	0	65	95	4	9.1	55	1	95	150	7	8.0
601–800	31	0	69	100	4	8.8	55	1	85	140	6	8.0	60	1	115	175	8	7.6
801–1000	32	0	68	100	4	8.7	60	1	100	160	7	7.8	85	2	120	205	9	7.2
1001–2000	60	1	90	150	6	7.6	65	1	150	215	9	7.0	95	2	210	305	13	6.5
2001–3000	65	1	115	180	7	7.2	90	2	170	260	11	6.8	125	3	265	390	16	6.0
3001–4000	65	1	140	205	8	6.8	95	2	205	300	12	6.4	185	5	350	535	21	5.5
4001–5000	70	1	160	230	9	6.5	100	2	255	355	14	6.0	220	6	410	630	24	5.2
5001–7000	75	1	190	265	10	6.2	130	3	265	395	15	5.7	255	7	495	750	28	5.0
7001–10,000	100	2	195	295	11	6.0	140	3	355	495	18	5.3	325	9	665	990	36	4.7
10,001–20,000	105	2	215	320	12	5.9	170	4	380	550	20	5.2	360	10	830	1190	43	4.6
20,001–50,000	105	2	245	350	13	5.8	205	5	485	690	25	5.0	415	11	1145	1560	54	4.3
50,001–100,000	110	2	295	405	15	5.6	245	6	610	855	30	4.7	510	14	1370	1880	65	4.2

Trial 1: n_1 = first sample size; c_1 = acceptance number for first sample
"All" indicates that each piece in the lot is to be inspected
Trial 2: n_2 = second sample size; c_2 = acceptance number for first and second samples combined
p_t = lot tolerance per cent defective with a Consumer's Risk (P_c) of 0.10

FIGURE 14.15. Double sampling table for average outgoing quality limit (AOQL) = 2·5 per cent [Figs 14.12–14.15 reproduced by permission, H. F. Dodge and H. G. Romig, *Sampling Inspection Tables*, Wiley, London, 1959]

normal probability distribution. Quality controllers define *limits* within which variations are acceptable and beyond which they are either unacceptable, or necessitate some examination. Such limits are called *control limits*. For example, using a normal probability distribution, 99·73 per cent of all chance or usual variations would be expected to occur within limits placed three standard deviations larger, and smaller than the mean value of the variable. Therefore, any variation occurring beyond such limits would, very likely, have resulted from some other unusual or assignable cause and would merit some investigation.

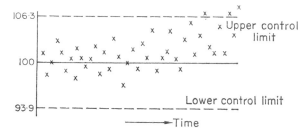

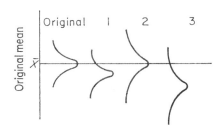

FIGURE 14.16. A simple control chart for the lengths of rods

FIGURE 14.17. Types of change which might occur in a process

For example: after a pilot investigation of the length of rods produced by our cropping press, we discover that the mean length ($\bar{x}$) is 100 inches and that after excluding the faulty rods that were produced when the setting on the press was accidentally altered, the standard deviation[4] (σ) which is a measure of the variability of the rods produced, was 2·1 inches. We could then set up a control chart with a mean of 100, and control limits of plus and minus three standard deviations. Such a chart (Fig. 14.16) might then be used to test the quality of rods produced by this press. Rather than examine every rod, we take a sample rod every hour and examine it, then plot our result on the control chart and by so doing we are able to discover that the process, whilst initially 'in control' is now running 'out of control' and often producing rods which are too long.

A process is considered to be statistically 'under' or 'in control' if it regularly produces items whose attributes or variables fall within the acceptable or tolerable range. Whereas, a process is said to be 'out of control' if items are produced whose attributes or variables are beyond the acceptable or tolerable range. In this case (Fig. 14.16) the process appears to have gone out of control because of a change in the mean value ($\bar{x}$).

This is only one of the three possible types of change which might occur in a process, i.e. in Fig. 14.17.

1. Has resulted from a change in the value of mean
2. Has resulted from a change in the standard deviation
3. Has resulted from a change in both of these characteristics

Each of these changes or disturbances in the process might lead to the production of defective items, but in each case the use of a control chart to monitor output will enable such items to be observed and action to be taken to prevent the production of defective items.

---

[4] The standard deviation (σ) for a large sample is calculated using the formula:

$$= \sqrt{\frac{\Sigma(\bar{x}-x)^2}{N}}$$

Where x = length of individual bar
$\bar{x}$ = mean length of all bars
N = No. of bars measured.

Control charts would therefore be used as follows:

Step 1. Decide which characteristics of the items are to be controlled.

Step 2. Conduct a pilot study of the process to determine the Mean and the Standard Deviation of the characteristics.

Step 3. Design the control chart(s) using this data.

Step 4. Check these control limits to ensure that they are economically feasible and realistic.

Step 5. Take samples of the process output, and plot the characteristics on the control charts.

Step 6. Whenever points fall beyond the control limits:

      (a) Investigate causes

      (b) Take corrective action

      (c) Inspect remainder of batch if necessary

Control Charts for Variables

Control charts for variables are usually based on the normal probability distribution and are most frequently designed to test the *means* of samples rather than individual measurements. The main reason why means are used is that even when the actual distribution of a variable resulting from a process does not conform to the normal distribution, sample means will tend to be distributed normally. This is known as the Central Limit Theorem of Statistics. In practice, therefore, the dimensions of individual components are not plotted separately on control charts, only the *mean*, or average value of the dimensions in the sample is plotted. Because we are now concerned with a distribution of means, the standard deviation ($\sigma_{\bar{x}}$) is calculated by a different formula as follows:

$$\sigma_{\bar{x}} = \frac{\sigma}{\sqrt{n}}$$

where $\sigma_{\bar{x}}$ = Standard deviation of sample means.

     σ = Standard deviation of individual means.

     n = Sample size.

Two upper and two lower control limits are normally used, these being referred to as the *upper and lower warning limit* and the *upper and lower action limit*. If points fall beyond the warning limits, this is taken to indicate that the process may be going out of control and that careful observation or additional sampling is required. Points falling beyond the action limits indicate the need to take immediate steps to establish and to eliminate the causes. Action limits are normally set so as to exclude only 0·2 per cent of the points through usual or random variations. Warning limits are set so as to exclude 5 per cent of the points through usual or random variation. i.e.

$$\text{Upper Action Limit} = \bar{x} + 3 \cdot 09 \, \sigma/\sqrt{n}$$

$$\text{Upper Warning Limit} = \bar{x} + 1 \cdot 96 \, \sigma/\sqrt{n}$$

$$\text{Centre} = \bar{x}$$

$$\text{Lower Warning Limit} = \bar{x} - 1 \cdot 96 \, \sigma/\sqrt{n}$$

$$\text{Lower Action Limit} = \bar{x} - 3 \cdot 09 \sigma \sqrt{n}$$

In practice it is a little tiresome to calculate standard deviations for samples, particularly under the conditions which often exist in factories and, consequently, the *range* (*w*) is usually used as a measure of variability in place of the standard deviation. The *range* is merely the difference between the largest dimension and the smallest, and for small samples it has been shown that:

$$\sigma = \frac{\bar{w}}{d_n}$$

where σ = Standard deviation of individual items produced by process

$\bar{w}$ = Mean range of several samples

d_n = A constant depending on the sample size

Consequently, our control limits are now calculated as follows:

Mean
$$\text{Upper Action Limit} = \bar{x} + \frac{3 \cdot 09\,(\bar{w}/d_n)}{\sqrt{n}}$$

$$\text{Upper Warning Limit} = \bar{x} + \frac{1 \cdot 96\,(\bar{w}/d_n)}{\sqrt{n}}$$

$$\text{Centre} = \bar{x}$$

$$\text{Lower Warning Limit} = \bar{x} - \frac{1 \cdot 96\,(\bar{w}/d_n)}{\sqrt{n}}$$

$$\text{Lower Action Limit} = \bar{x} - \frac{3 \cdot 09\,(\bar{w}/d_n)}{\sqrt{n}}$$

To simplify such calculations even further, tables for $3 \cdot 09/\sqrt{n}\, d_n$ and $1 \cdot 96/\sqrt{n}\, d_n$ can be used. (See Table 14–1).

TABLE 14.1. Factors for calculating control limits for control charts for means

Sample size n	Constant d_n	Factors (m) for warning limits $= \dfrac{1 \cdot 96}{\sqrt{n}\, d_n}$	Factors (m) for action limits $= \dfrac{3 \cdot 09}{\sqrt{n}\, d_n}$
2	1·128	1·23	1·94
3	1·693	0·67	1·05
4	2·059	0·48	0·75
5	2·326	0·38	0·59
6	2·334	0·32	0·50
7	2·704	0·27	0·43
8	2·847	0·24	0·38
9	2·970	0·22	0·35
10	3·078	0·20	0·32

N.B.   To calculate control limits multiply range $\bar{w}$ by factor (m) and add or subtract from the mean value $\bar{x}$.

Even though the mean value is constant, we have seen how the process might produce defective items by an increase in variability. (Fig. 14.17). Consequently, a process cannot be said to be fully under control, unless *both* mean and standard deviation are under control. We should, therefore, also construct a control chart on which to plot standard deviations but for the same reasons as before, it is found to be easier to use the range (w) as a measure of variability. In much the same way as for control limits for means, factors can be calculated from which control limits ranges can be established. These are shown in Table 14·2.

TABLE 14.2. Factors for calculating control limits for control charts for ranges

Sample size n	Factor (R) for warning limits		Factor (R) for action limits	
	Upper	Lower	Upper	Lower
2	2·81	0·04	4·12	0·00
3	2·17	0·18	2·98	0·04
4	1·93	0·29	2·57	0·10
5	1·81	0·37	2·34	0·16
6	1·72	0·42	2·21	0·21
7	1·66	0·46	2·11	0·26
8	1·62	0·50	2·04	0·29
9	1·58	0·52	1·99	0·32
10	1·56	0·54	1·94	0·35

N.B.   To calculate control limit multiply $\bar{w}$, the range by appropriate factor R.

Example

The construction of control charts is really a rather simple matter, as will be illustrated in this example.

Again, referring to a cropping press on which bars are to be cut continually to a length of 12″, a random sample of 5 bars is taken from each hour's production, and for each sample the Mean and Range is calculated, i.e.

Sample (Size $n = 5$)	Mean ($\bar{x}$)	Range (w)
9.00 a.m.	12.005	0.007
10.00 a.m.	12.001	0.008
11.00 a.m.	11.993	0.010
12.00	11.991	0.003
1.00 p.m.	12.001	0.006
2.00 p.m.	12.003	0.015
3.00 p.m.	11.995	0.011
4.00 p.m.	12.004	0.008
5.00 p.m.	12.003	0.009
6.00 p.m.	12.000	0.010
7.00 p.m.	11.999	0.006
8.00 p.m.	11.997	0.013
9.00 p.m.	11.999	0.011
10.00 p.m.	12.000	0.010
	167.991	0.127

From these individual sample means ($\bar{x}$) and the ranges (w), we can calculate an overall mean ($\bar{X}$) and average range ($\bar{W}$) for the process.

$$\bar{X} = \frac{167·991}{14} = 11·9994 \quad \bar{W} = \frac{0·127}{14} = 0·0091$$

Now using the factors from Table 14.1 and Table 14.2 control limits for means and ranges can be calculated.

$$\text{Mean} \begin{cases} \text{U.A.L.} = 11 \cdot 9994 + 0 \cdot 59 \ (0 \cdot 0091) = 12 \cdot 0048 \\ \text{U.W.L.} = 11 \cdot 9994 + 0 \cdot 38 \ (0 \cdot 0091) = 12 \cdot 0029 \\ \text{Centre} = 11 \cdot 9994 \\ \text{L.W.L.} = 11 \cdot 9994 - 0 \cdot 38 \ (0 \cdot 0091) = 11 \cdot 9959 \\ \text{L.A.L.} = 11 \cdot 9994 - 0 \cdot 59 \ (0 \cdot 0091) = 11 \cdot 9940 \end{cases}$$

$$\text{Range} \begin{cases} \text{U.A.L.} = 0 \cdot 0091 \times 2 \cdot 34 \qquad = 0 \cdot 0213 \\ \text{U.W.L.} = 0 \cdot 0091 \times 1 \cdot 81 \qquad = 0 \cdot 0165 \\ \text{Centre} = 0 \cdot 0091 \\ \text{L.W.L.} = 0 \cdot 0091 \times 0 \cdot 37 \qquad = 0 \cdot 0034 \\ \text{L.A.L.} = 0 \cdot 0091 \times 0 \cdot 16 \qquad = 0 \cdot 0015 \end{cases}$$

The control charts can now be constructed using these figures, and the individual sample means and ranges plotted (Fig. 14.18). The charts indicate that the process is beginning to settle down. The mean lengths from early samples were unacceptable but towards the end of the day the process was under better control.

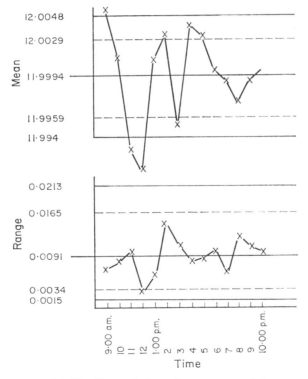

FIGURE 14.18. Control chart for means and for range

Design Limits and Control Limits

The control limits we have discussed do not necessarily bear any relationship to the design limits, since in constructing the control charts no account was taken of the dimensional tolerance specified on component drawings etc. It is possible then, using the control charts, to accept items which are *not* manufactured to design specifications. To avoid such a situation the design limits, i.e. the tolerances on a dimension must fall outside the action limits of the control chart, i.e. the dimensional tolerance should be a minimum of $6.18\,\gamma$. During design it is important, therefore, to ensure that manufacturing equipment is capable of producing parts to the required tolerance so that (say) 99·8 per cent of the items should be within such tolerances. During the design of the control charts it is essential to ensure that the limits constructed after a pilot study are within the design limits.

Control Charts for Attributes

Often, as was the case during Acceptance Sampling, it is possible after inspecting items to classify them only as 'good' or 'bad', as 'acceptable' or 'not acceptable' and it is for reasons such as these, that control charts for attributes have been devised. Such charts are developed in much the same way as were control charts for variables.

Two types of chart are most popular, i.e.

1. Control chart for proportion or per cent defective
2. Control chart for number of defects

The method of using the charts is similar to that outlined previously, except that in this case, rather than calculate the mean and range of all the items in each random sample, only the number, or the percentage of defective items in the sample is calculated.

Control charts for *proportion* or *per cent defective* are known as *p-charts*. Control limits are constructed after a pilot investigation and if, during production, the proportion of defectives in a sample falls within these limits the proces is considered to be 'under control' whereas, if the proportion of defectives in a sample falls beyond these limits, this is taken to be a good indication that the process is, for some reason, out of control and that some invesitgation and corrective action is required.

The proportion defective produced by the process ($\bar{p}$) is obtained after a pilot study consisting of several samples, i.e.

$$\bar{p} = \frac{\text{Total number of defectives in 10 to 20 samples}}{\text{Total number inspected}}$$

2 per cent (and less frequently 5 per cent) control limits are set in the usual way.

i.e. Action limits $= \bar{p} \pm 3.09\,\sigma_{\bar{p}}$

where $\bar{p} =$ Proportion of defectives produced by the process.

$\sigma_{\bar{p}} =$ Standard deviation of this distribution

The statistical theory of the Binomial probability distribution is used, by which is can be shown that:

$$\sigma_{\bar{p}} = \sqrt{\frac{\bar{p}(1-\bar{p})}{n}}$$

Consequently, the action limits are set at:

$$\text{Upper: } \bar{p} + 3.09\sqrt{\frac{\bar{p}(1-\bar{p})}{n}} \qquad \text{(where } \bar{p} > 0.1)$$

$$\text{Lower: } \bar{p} - 3.09\sqrt{\frac{\bar{p}(1-\bar{p})}{n}}$$

where $n =$ sample size.

Example

Time of sample	Sample size (n)	Numbers of defectives in sample	$\bar{p}$
9.00 a.m.	205	12	0·0585
10.00 a.m.	206	14	0·07
11.00 a.m.	195	12	0·0615
12.00	200	15	0·075
1.00 p.m.	210	14	0·0665
2.00 p.m.	195	12	0·0615
3.00 p.m.	200	15	0·075
4.00 p.m.	200	16	0·080
5.00 p.m.	205	13	0·0635
6.00 p.m.	195	14	0·0715
7.00 p.m.	200	15	0·075
8.00 p.m.	195	14	0·0715

Output for previous week = 12 100

No. of defectives included in this output = 750

The proportion defective produced by the process can in this case be established from the figures given for the previous week's production. i.e.

$$\bar{p} = \frac{750}{12\ 100} = 0·062$$

Therefore upper action limit $= \bar{p} + 3·09 \sqrt{\dfrac{\bar{p}(1-\bar{p})}{n}}$

$$= 0·062 + 3·09 \sqrt{\frac{0·062(0·938)}{200}}$$

$$= 0·079$$

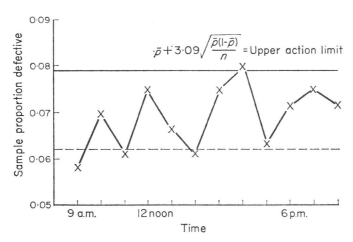

FIGURE 14.19. *p*-Chart

This action limit is shown on the *p*-chart given as Fig. 14.19. The proportion defective in each of the twelve samples are plotted on the chart from which it can be seen that compared to the previous week's production the proportion of defectives in the batches has increased, and the process is almost 'out-of-control'.

Since the control limits for a *p*-chart are a function of *n*, (the sample size), when the sample size changes the control limits must also change. (e.g. Fig. 14.20). In the above example, the sample size was nearly constant, hence a mean *n* = 200 was taken.

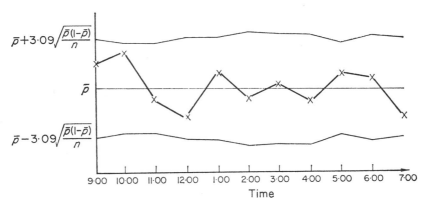

FIGURE 14.20. A proportion defective control chart (*p*-chart) in which the sample size, *n*, has changed

Control charts for *number* of defects are known as *c-charts* and are of particular value for controlling the number of defects in, or on, a particular unit: i.e. a single item, a group of items, or a part of an item. For example the *c*-chart might be used to control the quality of cloth by counting the number of defects in a roll, to control the quality of a rivetted structure by counting the number of faulty rivets etc. Conditions such as these enable the Poisson distribution to be used. The symbol, $\bar{c}$, is the average number of defects per unit obtained after a pilot investigation. The standard deviation of the Poisson distribution is given by $\sqrt{\bar{c}}$, consequently, the control limits are set at:

$$\text{Upper action: } \bar{c} + 3 \cdot 09 \sqrt{\bar{c}} \qquad \text{(where } \bar{c} > 15)$$

$$\text{Lower action: } \bar{c} - 3 \cdot 09 \sqrt{\bar{c}}$$

The manner in which *c*-charts are constructed and used is very similar to the construction and use of $\bar{p}$-charts.

CUMULATIVE SUM TECHNIQUES IN QUALITY CONTROL

The control chart is a useful and convenient method of recording successive readings, and it provides a clear presentation of historical data. The action limits are a convenient device for prompting corrective action, but unfortunately it is often difficult to detect small changes in the mean value of observations. In fact the control chart is basically a means to study observations independently, rather than a method of studying trends in a series of observations. This insensitivity is to some extent overcome by the use of warning limits, but even so it is often desirable in quality control, to use a procedure which is more sensitive to small changes in mean values.

The principal advantage of the *cumulative sum* (Cusum) *chart*[5] is its ability to show such changes, indeed the CUSUM chart actually emphasizes changes in such mean values. Cumulative sum charts can also be constructed for ranges, and number or proportion defectives. Their use, in the manner outlined above, maximizes the value of the data collected, since, unlike control charts which concentrate attention on the latest figures, CUSUM charts promote an examination of long sequences of data.

COMPUTERS IN QUALITY CONTROL

There are of course numerous computer programmes available for analysing the data obtained during quality control and for performing the calculations we have dealt with in this chapter. Whilst this is a useful service particularly where large quantities of data are obtained which must be analysed rapidly, it is of course only an indirect computer application and in no way represents any degree of automation.

We have previously mentioned the increasing use of automatic gauging in manufacture. This does represent one step towards a more automated process but it is surprising in view of the great variety of such automatic inspection and gauging devises now available, that few attempts have been made to extend the gauging or inspection to automatic analysis of data and control of process, in the manner now commonplace in direct process control.

Over seven years ago a system developed by Pratt and Whitney enabled readings taken by a number of automatic inspection devices to be converted into digital form, analysis of which enabled the average dimension of a sample, the number of accepted and rejected parts, the range of dimensions etc. to be calculated. Recently an Elliot ARCH 102 computer has been installed in a large machine shop in Raleigh Company, Nottingham.[6] The online computer is connected to eight work holding fixtures, each equipped with a number of measuring probes. Components are placed into the fixtures, from where, by means of analogue to digital converters the relevant dimensions are signalled to the computer. During this period a 'Wait' signal is displayed, followed by either an 'Accept' or 'Reject' signal. The dimensions are stored, and histograms showing dimensional scatter are automatically prepared. These may be printed out on request. The computer indicates whether the sample has passed or failed inspection, and could be programmed to forecast the need to reset or adjust machine tools.

PEOPLE AS INSPECTORS

Despite the fact that increasing use is being made of automatic gauging during manufacture, the principal method of inspection, and hence of quality control and assurance, is still the human inspector. We have taken care throughout this chapter to indicate that 100 per cent inspection does not necessarily ensure the complete absence of defects from the output, because inspectors being human are liable to make mistakes. In closing this chapter it is appropriate to look briefly at the problem of error or mistake during inspection. What sort of decisions are our inspectors asked to make? Essentially, there are two types. Firstly, those connected with the inspection of variables (i.e. measurement) and, secondly, those connected with the inspection of attributes (i.e. assessment).

---

[5] The Cumulative Sum technique is described in Appendix 2.
[6] 'Automated part control', *Financial Times*, 16th December, 1968.

In measurement an inspector compares a characteristic of the item with a defined standard. Often this involves the use of a gauge or instrument against or within which the item is placed. Greater opportunity for error or mistake exists as the ease of comparison of characteristics and standard decreases. For example, where the length of rods is to be measured by means of a steel rule, mistakes can occur because of poor positioning of the role against the item, because of mis-reading of the figures, because of inadequate interpolation of markings on the scale etc. Had a micrometer been used then fewer opportunities would have existed for inadequate positioning of standard and item, and if a 'Go'/'No Go' gauge had been used, the possibility of mistakes by faulty readings would have been eliminated.

A similar situation exists with respect to assessment. It is not too difficult to make decisions about the acceptability of certain noise levels, and of attributes such as brightness or surface roughness, because the inspector, conceptually at least, is able to compare such attributes with a known standard. In fact, these could be considered as only slightly more difficult problems of *measurement* since it is possible to use decibel meters to measure noise levels, light meters to measure light levels and interferometry to measure surface roughness. More difficult is the assessment of colour quality, since it is more difficult to define colour standards. The assessment of smell and taste is even more difficult because such characteristic standards are virtually impossible to define.

Although it has been convenient to identify two classes of decision—measurement and assessment—to correspond to the control of variables and attributes, it is clear that assessment might alternatively be considered merely as difficult measurement and that measurement could be considered as assessment simplified by the presence of well defined standards.

The more remote and ill-defined the standard the more difficult is the comparison of characteristic and standard and, consequently, the more difficult and the more equivocal the decision. It should, therefore, be clear that in order to ensure adequate and consistent inspection procedures, instruments and gauges should be used which ensure easy and accurate comparison of characteristic and standard. Furthermore, standards for which gauges or instruments cannot be used should be clearly defined: e.g. colour shade cards might be used and inspectors could be trained and retrained to recognize standard noise levels, brightness levels etc. in much the same way that time study practitioners are trained to recognize a notional concept of standard performance. Workplaces should be designed to permit and, preferably, emphasize the comparison of characteristic and standard.

The following notes will illustrate how the equipment and the situation might be designed to facilitate accurate and consistent inspection.

1. Ideally the standard itself should be used during the inspection process as, for example, in the physical comparison of dimensions whilst using 'Go'/'No Go' or snap gauges.

2. The standard, if not used during inspection, should be prominently displayed so that comparison of characteristic and standard is easy or, alternatively, so that the inspector might regularly refer to the standard in order to 'recalibrate his perception'.

3. Where possible, inspection procedures might be 'reconstructed' as pattern recognition procedures. For example, in the design of instrument displays, dials are often arranged so that when each instrument is reading correctly all pointers appear horizontal or vertical. Consequently, when one instrument shows an unusual or wrong reading the pattern is disrupted and recognition of the fact is facilitated. In such a case, the acceptable standard has been redefined, acceptability now being associated with consistancy of appearance.

4. Where-ever possible the workplace conditions should be arranged to emphasize the characteristic being measured or assessed. For example, lighting might be arranged to emphasize irregularities or roughness of surfaces.

SUMMARY

There are two stages during which the quality of products is determined. First, the design stage on which the product is specified and, secondly, the actual manufacturing stage during which the specified design physically materializes. In this chapter we have concentrated on problems of quality control and assurance during the second stage.

It was further shown that this second stage might be considered as three steps, as follows:

1. Purchasing and receipt of materials, parts, etc.
2. Actual manufacturing operations using these materials and parts.
3. Despatch of products to the customer.

Acceptance sampling is a *control* procedure undertaken to attempt to ensure that only good items are accepted by the company during the first step and also to attempt to ensure that only good products are offered to the customer during the final step.

Control charts are used during the second step in an attempt to ensure that only good items are manufactured. The use of control charts is a form of quality assurance since, to some extent, the production of defective items can be predicted and appropriate adjustments or corrections made in the manufacturing processes.

SELECTED READINGS

The following is a very simple introduction to the subject in which the emphasis is on Control Charts rather than Acceptance Sampling:

A. HUITSON and J. KEEN, *Essential of Quality Control*, Heinemann, London, 1965.

The following books gives a good, introductory, analytical treatment:

A. J. HOPPER, *Basic Statistical Quality Control*, McGraw-Hill, London, 1969.
A. J. DUNCAN, *Quality Control and Industrial Statistics*, Irwin, Illinois, 1965. (3rd edition).
R. B. FETTER, *The Quality Control System*, Irwin, Illinois, 1967.

The following two books present a great deal of data which is of value in the construction of acceptance sampling plans, and (in the case of Bowker and Leibermann) control charts:

A. H. BOWKER and G. L. LEIBERMANN, *Handbook of Industrial Statistics*, Prentice-Hall, New Jersey, 1955.
H. F. DODGE and H. G. ROMIG, *Sampling Inspection Tables*, Wiley, London, 1959.

The following books describe the use of Cumulative Sum charts in quality control:

G. R. GEDYE, *Scientific Method in Production Management*, Oxford Univ. Press, London, 1965.
R. H. WOODWARD and P. L. GOLDSMITH, *Cumulative Sum Techniques*, ICI Monograph No. 3, Oliver and Boyd, Edinburgh, 1964.

QUESTIONS

14.1. (a) What is the purpose of acceptance sampling?

(b) What is an operating characteristic curve?

(c) Use the binomial probability expression to calculate the probability of finding two or less defectives in a sample of size 12, if the actual percentage defectives in the batch from which the sample was drawn is 20 per cent.

14.2. Construct an operating characteristic curve to show the probability of accepting batches of varying percentage actual defective levels, if sample sizes of 80 items are drawn from the batches and if batches are accepted when two or fewer defectives are found in the samples.

14.3. Use the 'Thorndike' or cumulative Poisson probability chart to specify an OC curve which can be used in a single acceptance sampling plan specified as follows:

Lot tolerance percent defective	6 per cent	Producers' risk	6 per cent
Acceptable quality level	3 per cent	Consumers' risk	12 per cent

14.4. Construct an average outgoing quality curve and determine the average outgoing quality limit for the operating characteristic curve for $n = 200$, $c \leqslant 2$ shown in Fig. 14.7 and batch size of $N = 2\,500$.

14.5. A machine produces 2 000 items every working shift. From every lot produced a random sample of 100 is subjected to a visual quality check.

The defectives found in the samples are rectified or replaced and if more than one defective is found in a sample of 100 the entire lot produced is subjected to a quality inspection during which all defectives are either rectified or replaced. If only one or no defectives are found in the sample the entire lot is accepted without further inspection.

The figure shown is the OC curve for the sampling plan. It has been calculated using binomial probabilities.

(a) What is the average outgoing quality limit for this quality control procedure?

(b) Under what circumstances can the Poisson probability distribution be used to design the sampling plan?

N.B. Poisson probability $P(c) = \dfrac{e^{-pn}(pn)^c}{c!}$ where c = Number of defectives in sample

n = Sample size

p = Actual per cent defective in lot

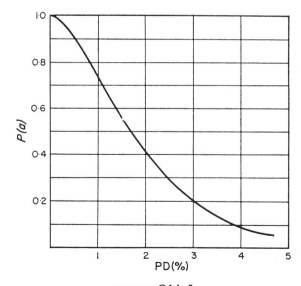

FIGURE Q14.5

(c) Using the cumulative Piosson probability chart, design a single acceptance sampling plan to satisfy the following requirements.

Producers' risk 0·050
Consumers' risk 0·100
Acceptance quality level 0·022
Lowest tolerance per cent defective 0·090

14.6. (a) Distinguish between and describe double acceptance sampling and multiple acceptance sampling.

(b) Using the tables provided in the chapter (Figs. 14.12–14.15) specify the sample size and the maximum acceptable number of defectives in the sample for:

Single acceptance sampling

Average outgoing quality limit 2·5 per cent
Batch sizes 1 500
Actual process per cent defective 0·5–1·0 per cent

Double acceptance sampling

Lot tolerance percent defective 5 per cent
Batch sizes 1 500
Actual process per cent defective 0·5–1·0 per cent

(c) Using the tables provided:
What is the average outgoing quality limit given:

Single acceptance sampling
Lot tolerance per cent defective 5 per cent
Batch sizes 2 000
Actual process per cent defective 0·5–1·0 per cent

What is the lot tolerance per cent defective given:

Single acceptance sampling
Average outgoing quality limit 2·5 per cent
Batch sizes 750
Actual process per cent defective 0·5–1·0 per cent
Consumers' risk 10 per cent

14.7. Consider two single acceptance sampling plans specified as follows:

1. Sample size 50. Acceptable number of defects 1.
2. Sample size 100. Acceptable number of defects 2.

For each plan determine:

(a) The producers' risk for an acceptable quality level of 2 per cent.
(b) The consumers risk for a lot tolerance per cent defective of 5 per cent.

Which of these two plans would be considered preferable by:

i. The producer
ii. The consumer

What is the average outgoing quality limit for each plan if in each case the batch sizes are equal to 1 000?

State the statistical assumptions you have made in arriving at your answers.

[Univ. of Bradford, Management Centre, Post-Grad. Dip. in Industrial Admin., *Production Management*—1970]

14.8. (a) Distinguish between quality assurance and quality control.

(b) Distinguish between quality control as regards the 'attributes' of items and the 'variabiles' of items.
(c) Distinguish between design limits and control limits.
(d) Distinguish between usual or chance variation and unusual or assignable variation, in respect of quality control.
(e) Distinguish between warning limits and action limits in respect to control charts.

14.9. (a) A machine produces components at a rate of 100 per hour. Every hour a random sample of five components is taken and their lengths measured. After 10 hours the data given below has been collected. Use this data to design control charts for the sample mean and range of the dimension concerned.

Sample No.	Measurements (in)				
1	9·00	9·10	9·00	9·05	8·95
2	9·10	9·10	9·00	9·05	9·05
3	9·00	9·05	9·00	9·05	9·00
4	9·00	9·00	8·95	9·00	9·05
5	9·00	9·05	9·05	9·05	9·00
6	9·00	9·10	9·10	9·05	9·00
7	9·00	9·10	9·05	9·15	9·05
8	9·00	9·10	9·10	9·00	9·05
9	9·00	9·00	8·95	9·00	9·00
10	9·00	9·05	9·00	9·10	8·95

(b) Following the construction of the charts, the same sampling procedure is followed and the data shown below is obtained. Plot this data on the control charts and comment on the quality 'performance' of the process.

Sample No.	Mean length (in)	Range	Sample No.	Mean length (in)	Range
1	9·020	0·100	11	9·040	0·150
2	9·030	0·100	12	9·040	0·125
3	9·025	0·050	13	9·035	0·100
4	9·030	0·100	14	9·040	0·055
5	9·035	0·025	15	9·030	0·100
6	9·040	0·105	16	9·025	0·050
7	9·020	0·050	17	9·030	0·125
8	9·030	0·100	18	9·025	0·100
9	9·040	0·050	19	9·025	0·150
10	9·035	0·065	20	9·030	0·150

14.10. Using the data given in the first table below, which has resulted from a study over a period of one week, construct a control chart and, on that control chart plot the data given in the second table below. Comment on the results.

Target production of Brazed Connector pieces for period	= 6 250
Output of good quality Brazed Connector pieces	= 5 620
Total number of defective Brazed Connector pieces produced =	99

Percentage performance, $\dfrac{\text{Acceptable output}}{\text{Target}} \times 100$ = 90 per cent

Sample		Output	Sample	No. defective in sample
Mon.	a.m.	575	60	1
Mon.	p.m.	600	60	2
Tues.	a.m.	550	60	2
Tues.	p.m.	550	60	1
Wed.	a.m.	600	60	2
Wed.	p.m.	650	65	2
Thurs.	a.m.	625	65	1
Thurs.	p.m.	590	70	2
Fri.	a.m.	625	75	2
Fri.	p.m.	490	60	1
Sat.	a.m.	565	60	1

14.11. Phragyle Products Ltd. manufacture imitation glass decanters. Because of the delicate nature of the manufacturing process, each decanter is expected to have some minor blemishes, most of which are completely invisible to the naked eye. These very minor blemishes may occur almost anywhere on the product and are not usually sufficient to lead to the rejection of the item. Nevertheless, the Production Manager of Phragyle Products is anxious to investigate the effects of recent efforts that have been made to improve the manufacturing process and the quality of the product.

Prior to the modifications to the process, each decanter had an average of five almost imperceptible blemishes. The table below shows the number of blemishes on every fifth decanter for a short period after the adjustment to the process. Comment on the success of the adjustments to the manufacturing process.

No. of blemishes per product. 6, 7, 6, 5, 6, 7, 7, 6, 8, 7, 7, 7, 6, 8, 9, 8, 7, 8, 9, 8, 8, 7

14.12. (a) 'Even if 100 per cent acceptance sampling is adopted it is likely that a certain number of defective items will be accepted'.   Discuss.

(b) What measures can be taken, and in what circumstances, to decrease the error of human inspectors?

14.13. Referring to Question 14.9 above, plot a cumulative-sum chart of the 'mean' values given in the second table. Comment on the resulting chart and compare the results obtained with those obtained from the control chart previously constructed.

15

Maintenance and Replacement

You will recall that in this section of the book, we are dealing with the *operation* of production systems. Our production system has been designed and installed, plans have been established to enable products to be made as and when required, and furthermore, we have established an elaborate set of control procedures to ensure that everything proceeds according to plan. Even so, the management of production is not yet complete, and our well laid plans may yet go astray if we are unable to keep our production facilities operating.

It is an unfortunate but inescapable fact that equipment of whatever type, however complex or simple, however cheap or expensive, is liable to breakdown. This fact is of considerable importance since it means that not only must facilities and a system be provided for equipment maintenance, but also the inevitability of breakdowns and disruptions in production must also be considered during production planning.

The effective operation of any production system is dependent upon the maintenance of all parts of the system, i.e., machines, buildings, services. With use, and the passage of time, such facilities tend to wear or deteriorate, a change in state which naturally affects their efficiency, which in turn affects the quality of the manufactured product.

In this chapter we shall be concerned only with the maintenance of mechanical rather than human facilities, although, in concept at least, the maintenance requirement also applies to workers. Indeed, company welfare or personnel practice may well be designed partly as a maintenance activity, e.g. training and retraining to maintain the availability of appropriate skills, medical facilities to maintain human capacity, counselling to maintain interest and motivation etc.

In many cases the responsibility for routine minor maintenance of equipment may rest with the worker or operator, who may be required to lubricate and undertake periodic adjustments or inspections of his equipment. Often, particularly in the case of complex equipment, maintenance may be the responsibility of the supplier or manufacturer, or his agent. In such cases a company will sub-contract such work when necessary, or alternatively, maintenance of equipment may form part of the purchase contract. The majority of maintenance falls between these two extremes, in that it is too large to expect individual operators to undertake, but is not the responsibility of a third party. In such cases, a specialized maintenance function within the firm will be expected to undertake the work. It is only when there is sufficient of this type of maintenance that the establishment of a Maintenance Department employing permanent specialized staff is justified.

The size of the maintenance department, the number and the types of maintenance staff, the stock of spare parts, and the amount of equipment will depend, of course, not only upon the amount of equipment that has to be maintained, but also upon the variety of this equipment, its 'maintainability' (i.e. ,the ease with which maintenance work can be conducted) and the probability of its requiring maintenance. In a small company the maintenance department may consist only of a few skilled men and a small stock of spare parts, whereas in a large machine intensive company the maintenance department may consist of a large number of people of different skills, e.g., mechanics, plumbers, electricians, etc., large stocks of spare parts and materials and a large and diverse amount of specialized and expensive equipment, such as jig borers, shapers and so on, all of which must also be maintained. In such cases the organization of maintenance is a complex task, the size of maintenance teams must be established, work scheduled, stocks controlled etc.

The Objectives of Maintenance.

The purpose of maintenance is to attempt to maximize the performance of production equipment by ensuring that such equipment performs regularly and efficiently, by attempting to prevent breakdowns or failures, and by minimizing the production loss resulting from breakdowns or failures. In fact it is the objective of the maintenance function to maintain or increase the reliability of the production system as a whole.

Many steps can be taken to ensure that such an objective is achieved, but only a few of these are normally considered the responsibility of the maintenance department. For example, each of the following will contribute to the reliability of the production system:

1. Improvement of the quality of equipment and components through improved design and/or 'tighter' manufacturing standards.
2. Improvements in the design of equipment so as to facilitate the replacement of broken items, to facilitate inspection and routine maintenance work.
3. Improvements in the layout of equipment to facilitate maintenance work, i.e. providing space around or underneath equipment.
4. Provide 'slack' in the production system, i.e., provide excess capacity so that the failure of equipment does not affect the performance of other equipment.
5. Use 'work-in-progress' to ensure that the failure of equipment is not immediately reflected in the shortage of materials or parts for a subsequent piece of equipment.
6. Establish a *repair* facility, so that through speedy replacement of broken parts, equipment down-time is reduced.
7. Undertake *preventive* maintenance, which, through regular inspection and/or replacement of critical parts, avoids the occurrence of breakdowns.

These points may be summarized in two overall objectives which are:

(a) To attempt to ensure that breakdowns or failures *do not* occur. (see 1 and 7 above).
(b) To attempt to minimize the disruption or loss of production caused by the breakdowns which do occur (see 2, 3, 4, 5 and 6 above).

Excluding the influence of improvements in equipment design and layout, discussion of which is not appropriate to this chapter, it is clear that two distinct facets of maintenance may contribute to the increased reliability of the production system, namely: *preventive maintenance* and *repair*.

We can, of course, draw the now familiar total cost curve as shown in Fig. 15·1. Clearly increased effort in preventive maintenance should reduce the cost of repair maintenance. Were we able to define both of these curves mathematically or graphically, then it would be a simple matter to determine the minimum cost maintenance policy. However, as might be expected, the problem is not as simple as this, consequently maintenance policy is substantially more difficult to determine.

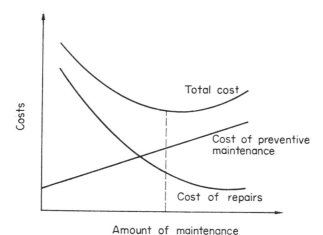

FIGURE 15.1 Maintenance costs

PREVENTIVE AND BREAKDOWN MAINTENANCE

Preventive maintenance is used to delay or prevent the breakdown of equipment, and also to reduce the severity of any breakdowns that occur. Two aspects of preventive maintenance can be identified:

1. *Inspection*. Inspection of critical parts will often indicate the need for replacement or repair well in advance of probable breakdown. (Inspection forms an important part of motor vehicle maintenance, regular inspection of tyres, radiator, battery, brakes, etc., being called for by all maintenance schedules). Regular inspection, conducted either by the equipment operator, or by the maintenance department is the most important direct means of increasing equipment reliability.

2. *Servicing*. Routine cleaning, lubrication and adjustment may significantly reduce wear and hence prevent breakdowns. Frequently such duties belong to the equipment operator rather than being the direct responsibility of the maintenance department, however, irrespective of responsibility, servicing or routine preventive maintenance must be conducted regularly according to schedules constructed from both operating experience and manufacturers recommendations.

No matter how much preventive maintenance is undertaken, failures will still occur, if only because of the use of defective of sub-standard parts, or the misuse of equipment. It will always be necessary, therefore, to provide breakdown maintenance. Repair policy may involve the use of sub-contractors, the repair of equipment immediately upon breakdown or later, the replacement of parts or sub-assemblies, or even the replacement of whole pieces of equipment. Repairs may be conducted on equipment in situ or equipment may be removed to a more appropriate situation. Standby equipment may be available for permanent or temporary replacement in cases of breakdown.

Preventive Maintenance

Whilst preventive maintenance is clearly an important means of increasing the reliability of equipment, it is not necessarily generally applicable.

We want to perform the minimum amount of preventive maintenance, since maintenance even of this type will be costly in terms of direct labour and material costs, and possible costs of disrupting production. Ideally, therefore, we would like to perform our preventive maintenance of equipment just before it would otherwise have broken down. Such a policy is only possible if either, because of the nature of the equipment, we receive some advanced warning of impending failure, or if failure of equipment is perfectly predictable. Rarely is warning of impending failure of value in practice, since either the warning is insufficiently in advance of failure (e.g. a bearing smoking before seizing up) or the warning is itself associated with some loss of efficiency or capacity

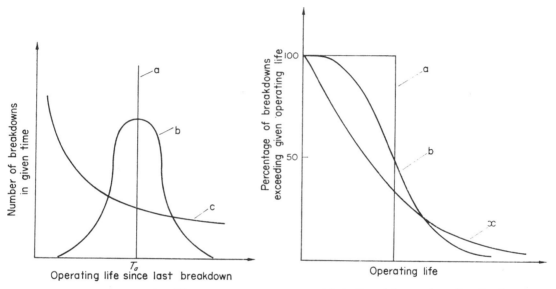

FIGURE 15.2. Operating life curves   FIGURE 15.3. Breakdown time distributions

in the equipment. Optimum preventive maintenance, therefore, depends upon a situation such as that shown by (*a*) in Fig. 15.2 in which the operating life of equipment between breakdowns, is perfectly constant. Rarely, however, will such a situation exist, indeed it is more likely that one of the other curves shown in this figure will result, i.e.

Curve *b* Random operating life, normally distributed amount, mean T_a.

    For example, equipment consisting of many parts each subject to failure will have an operating life distribution with quite large variance.

Curve *c* Large probability of failure immediately after repair.

    For example, equipment necessitating intricate and careful 'setting-up' for efficient performance, errors during setting-up causing fairly rapid failure.

    The design of maintenance programmes depends, to a large extent, upon the operating life characteristics of the equipment, a thorough investigation of which should be made either by equipment manufacturers, trade associations or users prior to the determination of maintenance procedures. For convenience, such data is normally presented in the manner shown in Fig. 15.3, such curves being referred to as *breakdown time distributions*. Obviously the nearer the actual breakdown time distribution approaches to the ideal distribution (a), the more appropriate and effective preventive maintenance will be.

    In Fig. 15.3 curve *a* corresponds to curve *a* of Fig. 15.2, i.e., a situation in which operating life between breakdown is constant. Curve *b* also corresponds to *b* in the previous figure. It is worth noting at this point that the remaining curve x corresponds closely to the exponential distribution. This is important since statistical queueing theory, which will be used shortly, depends to a large extent on the use of the exponential probability distribution.

An important function of the maintenance department is to collect and record data in order that breakdown time distribution curves can be kept for all pieces of equipment. Not only will the initial design of the maintenance policy depend upon this data, but subsequent changes in policy may be required if, over a period of time, the breakdown characteristics of equipment change.[1]

One other factor which determines the merit and hence the design of preventive maintenance is the time required to conduct preventive, compared to breakdown maintenance. If preventive maintenance takes as much time as, or more time than, breakdown maintenance, then even where

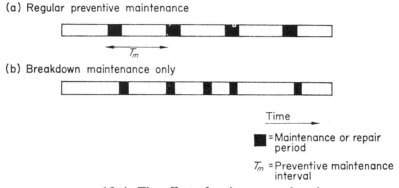

(a) Regular preventive maintenance

T_m

(b) Breakdown maintenance only

Time

■ = Maintenance or repair period

T_m = Preventive maintenance interval

FIGURE 15.4. The effect of maintenance durations

the breakdown time distribution for equipment permits the efficient adoption of preventive maintenance it will still be beneficial to rely on breakdown maintenance only. For example, Fig. 15.4 indicates that even though preventive maintenance may result in fewer 'down time' periods, the total 'down time' is greater than it would have been if breakdown maintenance alone had been used.

It is not sufficient, however, to consider only the time factor, since even though preventive maintenance operations may be comparatively time consuming, they may be scheduled to occur at convenient times, such as during holidays, weekends, or periods during which the load on equipment is low. We should, therefore, compare the costs of maintenance in order to evaluate the benefit of preventive maintenance.

Having established the conditions in which preventive maintenance is likely to be beneficial, let us now look more closely at the subject.

The scheduling of preventive maintenance for a single machine

One of the best treatments of this problem was developed by Morse.[2] If the breakdown time distribution approaches the ideal one, then if preventive maintenance is used effectively one would

---

[1] In practice since preventive maintenance will only be applied in appropriate situations, distribution can only be drawn for equipment which depends only on breakdown maintenance. Changes in breakdown characteristics of other equipment will be evident in an increase in the number of breakdowns despite preventive maintenance.

[2] P. M. Morse, *Queues, Inventories and Maintenance*, Wiley, London, 1958.

expect comparatively few breakdowns to occur. On the other hand, if the distribution is more variable, then even if preventive maintenance is used, breakdowns may still occur, i.e. a breakdown may occur before another preventive maintenance is due. If we let

T_p = fixed preventive maintenance interval, i.e. the time period between successive preventive maintenance operations on the same item of equipment

T_m = average time required to perform a preventive maintenance operation

T_s = average time required to perform a repair

T_a = average operating life without breakdowns;

and if we further assume that maintenance on a piece of equipment, whether it is preventive maintenance or repair maintenance, is equally effective in that both leave the equipment with the same probable operating life, then it has been shown by Morse that the operating efficiency of equipment, in terms of the percentage of time spent running, is a function of the ratio of the preventive maintenance interval to the average operating life, i.e. T_p/T_a.

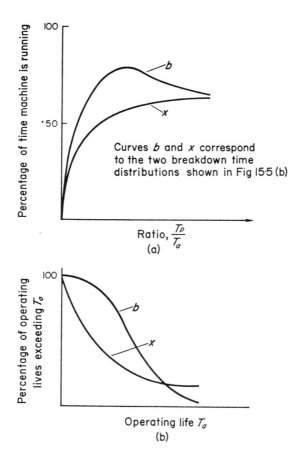

FIGURE 15.5. Breakdown time distributions

Using this relationship, curves can be drawn like those in Fig. 15.5a. Notice that where the preventive maintenance interval is short in comparison to the average operating life, the operating efficiency of the equipment is low because a large proportion of the time is spent in preventive maintenance. On the other hand, as the preventive maintenance period is increased in comparison to the average operating life, then a larger number of breakdowns will occur. Notice also that where the breakdown time distribution *does not* approach the ideal situation, operating efficiency continues to increase as the comparative length of the preventive maintenance interval increases, whereas in the situation shown by curve *b* in which the operating life has low variability, the curve reaches a peak. In other words, the use of preventive maintenance enables equipment operating efficiency to be maximized only when the variability on equipment operating life is small. We can, as a general rule, consider that preventive maintenance leads to an optimal policy for breakdown time distributions which have variability less than the exponential distribution (curve *x*).

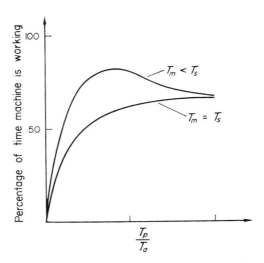

NB Both of these curves correspond to breakdown time distributions with low variability, i.e. curve *b* Fig. 15.5(a)

FIGURE 15.6

It has been mentioned previously that the merit of preventive maintenance depends also upon the relative time required for preventive maintenance operations. Fig. 15.6 shows how an increase in the size of T_m (the time required for preventive maintenance) relative to T_s (the time required for repair) reduces or eliminates the advantages previously offered by the preventive maintenance policy.

Clearly, if the breakdown time distribution for equipment is known, or can be obtained from records, then using this method developed by Morse, the merits of a preventive maintenance policy, and the optimum preventive maintenance interval, can be established.

This clearly is not an appropriate place in which to study statistical queueing theory, since this can be a somewhat complex subject. It is, however, necessary to touch briefly upon the subject in order to deal more satisfactorily with preventive maintence.

We have pointed out above that only where breakdown time distributions show comparatively little variability will preventive maintenance produce an optimal result. We should, therefore,

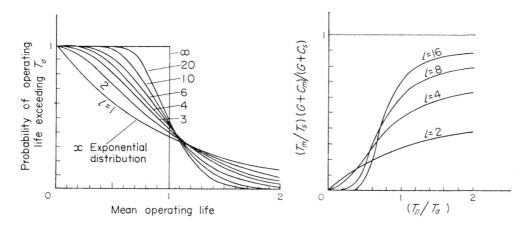

FIGURE 15.7. Erlang breakdown time distributions [Figs. 15.7 and 15.8 adapted from P. M. Morse, *Queues, Inventories and Maintenance*, Wiley, London, 1958 and reproduced by permission]

FIGURE 15.8. Curves for determining the optimum period T_p for preventive maintenance for different degrees of variability of breakdown time distribution (see Fig. 15.7) and for different values of the ratio $T_m(G + C_m)/T_s(G + C_s)$ explained in the text

discuss only those cases in which variability is less than that of the exponential distribution (curve x in Fig. 15.3). The solution of the preventive maintenance planning problem depends on the use of queueing theory, and it so happens that useful queueing theory formulae have been developed for two types of situations which frequently occur in practice. The first deals with the exponential case mentioned above, and the second deals with the case where the *Erlang* distribution applies. The precise nature of this distribution need not concern us here, and it is sufficient to say that the Erlang distribution covers those distributions which show equal or less variability than the exponential. For example, curve x in Fig. 15.7, as well as being an exponential distribution, is also one of a family of Erlang distributions, as are the remaining curves on this figure. (The parameter l is the only parameter which determines the variability of the distribution).

If we adopt the following further notation:

G = Value of the output of the machine (£/unit of time)

C_m = Cost per hour of preventive maintenance service

C_s = Cost per hour of repair

then the optimal value of T_p—the preventive maintenance interval— can be obtained from the curves shown in Fig. 15.8. To use these curves the appropriate value of l is found by comparing the breakdown time distribution to the Erlang distribution. The factor on the Y axis is calculated from known values of T_m T_s C_m C_s and G, and hence the ratio T_p/T_a is obtained. From this, since T_a is known, T_p can be calculated.

Example

From data concerning a capstan lathe, collected over a period of several years, it has been established that the average operating life between breakdowns is 4 weeks and that the breakdown time distribution corresponds approximately to an Erlang distribution with $l = 4$. Given the following information: (a) determine the optimum regular interval at which preventive maintenance should be performed on this machine:

Average time for preventive maintenance operation on lathe = 2 hours
Average time for a repair to lathe   = 4 hours
Cost hour of preventive maintenance   = £3
Cost/hour of repair work   = £6
Value of output of this lathe   = £25/hour

Answer

$$\left(\frac{Tm}{Ts}\right)\left(\frac{G+Cm}{G+Cs}\right) = \left(\frac{2}{4}\right)\left(\frac{25+3}{25+6}\right)$$

$$= 0.452$$

From Fig. 15·8 for $l = 4$

$$\frac{Tp}{Ta} = 0.9$$

Since $Ta = 4$ weeks

Preventive maintenance
interval $Tp = 3.6$ weeks

(b) what would be the effect on the optimum preventive maintenance interval if:

(i) The average time for a repair was equal to the average time for a preventive maintenance operation?

(ii) The breakdown time distribution for the lathe corresponded to an Erlang distribution with $l = 1$?

Answer   (i)

$$\left(\frac{Tm}{Ts}\right)\left(\frac{G+Cm}{G+Cs}\right) = \underline{0.901}$$

hence for $l = 4$ there is no solution for Tp/Ta. In other words in such circumstances there is no benefit in preventive maintenance.

(ii) There is also no solution for Tp/Ta for $l = 1$, i.e. because the breakdown variance is large (no better than the exponential distribution), preventive maintenance is not appropriate.

Scheduling Preventive Maintenance for several machines

The foregoing discussion has dealt only with the planning, i.e. the scheduling, of preventive maintenance for single machines.

We should, of course, also look at the scheduling of preventive maintenance for multi-machine systems, but to do so would necessitate a prior detour through rather complex statistical theory which would be inappropriate in this book. Multi-machine systems differ from single machine systems, in that machine idle time may result if a machine breaks down whilst the maintenance team are engaged on the repair of another machine. Such a situation is, therefore, similar to the multi-machine assignment problem in which interference may occur (See Chapter 8). Indeed, were we concerned only with the repair of machines rather than repair *and* preventive maintenance, the two situations would be analogous. In the present context, however, we are concerned with the possibility of using regular preventive maintenance to reduce the occurrence of breakdowns. This, of course, adds considerably to the complexity of the situation. Readers may wish to note that a good treatment of this problem, using a Markov chain approach has been presented by Bovaird.[3] In the next section we will consider the 'repair only' maintenance policy for several machines.

REPAIRS

Consider now the situation in which several machines of the same type are to be maintained. Furthermore, let us consider a policy which provides only for repair maintenance and not preventive maintenance (a policy which might have been adopted because of large variability in breakdown time distributions).

Providing appropriate assumptions are made about the nature of breakdowns and repair time, the design of a maintenance system for such a situation can be accomplished by using conventional queuing theory.

Clearly, machine idle time caused by waiting for the service of the maintenance team currently engaged on another machine, can be reduced if the time needed to repair machines is reduced. Reduction in machine repair time, T_s, can normally be achieved by devoting more resources to maintenance, i.e. by increasing the size of the maintenance team. Such action will, however, increase costs, consequently the problem is one of achieving an acceptable balance between, on the one hand the cost incurred by machine idle time due to breakdowns, and on the other hand the cost of the maintenance facility.

Let us first of all consider the case in which only *one maintenance team* looks after several identical machines. If we consider the breakdown time distribution to be exponential with average operating life $= T_a$, then it is reasonable that our maintenance policy should rely only upon repairs, since preventive maintenance is unlikely to reduce costs. Let us further consider that the repair time is also exponentially distributed with an average of T_s. Such assumptions, which often correspond quite closely with reality, enable statistical queueing theory to be adopted. Using this approach Fig. 15.9 can be calculated (see Morse—1958). This shows the average number of machines running as a function of the ratio T_a/T_s where K is the number of machines allocated to the one maintenance team.

An examination of this figure shows that for large values of T_a/T_s the number of machines running differs only slightly from the total number of machines K. For example, if $T_a/T_s = 10$, then if the system contains four machines ($K = 4$) the average number running over a period of time is approximately 3·5. If, however, the ratio of T_a/T_s falls, because of either reduced reliability of the machines or increased average repair times (T_s) then, naturally, the efficiency of the whole system falls. In fact it seems that in order to maintain a reasonably efficient system $T_a/T_s \geqslant K$.

This figure enables us to assess the cost of machine idle time, due to breakdowns and time spent waiting for repair.

To assess the cost of the maintenance team, Fig. 15.10 may be used. This shows the proportion of time that the maintenance team are busy, as a function of KT_s/T_a.

Example

A single maintenance team is to be responsible for repairs to eight identical machine tools. It has been found from experience that the breakdown time distribution for the machines corres-

[3] R. L. Bovaird. 'Characteristics of optimal maintenance policies', *Management Sci*, 7, No. 3, 238–254 (1961). Also reprinted in 'Models and analysis for production management, Ed. M. P. Hottenstein. Pub. International 1968.

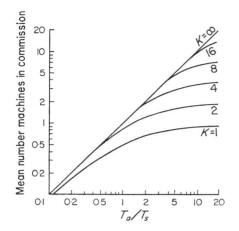

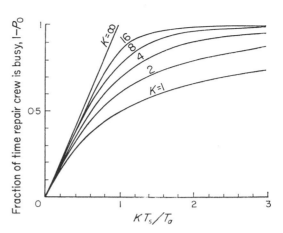

FIGURE 15.9. Mean number of machines working—for a shop containing K machines and for the exponential breakdown distribution

FIGURE 15.10. Mean fraction of time repair team is busy—for shop containing K machines and for the exponential breakdown distribution [Figs. 15.9 and 15.10 reproduced by permission, P. M. Morse, *Queues, Inventories and Maintenance*, Wiley, London, 1958]

ponds to the exponential distribution, likewise the repair times. Because of a high and stable demand from customers the production planning department has scheduled production making the assumption that the average number of machines that will be running is 6. If the average operating life of the machines is seven 5 day weeks, what average repair time should the maintenance department aim at providing, and how busy will the one team be?

From Fig. 15.9 the ratio T_a/T_s corresponding to $K = 8$, and 6 on the Y axis, is 7.

i.e.
$$\frac{T_a}{T_s} = 7.$$

$$T_s = \frac{7 \times 5}{7}$$

$$T_s = 5 \text{ days}$$

$$K\frac{T_s}{T_a} = \frac{8 \times 5}{7 \times 5} = 1 \cdot 14$$

∴ Percentage of time team is occupied = 82 per cent (from fig. 15.10).

Now let us consider a situation in which there is more than one maintenance team responsible for the repair of a set of identical machines. Let us assume again, both exponential breakdown characteristics and exponential service times for all maintenance teams. If the breakdowns are attended to on a 'First come, first served' priority basis, then curves such as those shown in Fig. 15.11 can be constructed. One interesting point is evident from these curves. It can be seen that the use of one maintenance team performing the repair work twice as quickly as each of two teams, is superior to the use of the two slower teams. For example, consider a situation in which there are four machines, where $T_a = 4$ days. Suppose that there is a choice of using one quite large maintenance team which is capable of an average repair time of $\frac{1}{2}$ day, *or* two smaller teams each

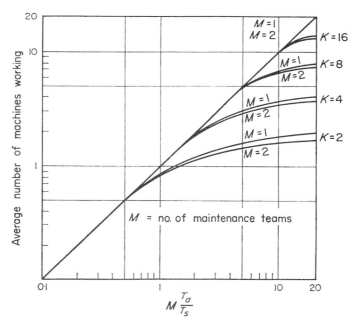

FIGURE 15.11

capable of average repair times of 1 day, then in both cases $M T_a/T_s = 8$, but it can be seen from Fig. 15.11 that the use of one team ($M = 1$) results in an average number of approx. 3.7 machines working, whereas the use of two teams results in an average of 3.5 machines working.

Clearly, if our objective is the reduction in machine idle time, then it is better, where possible, to use a single fast maintenance team rather two or more slower ones.

REPLACEMENT POLICIES

Replacement policies for items subject to sudden failure

When a machine stops, because of the failure of one component, then the maintenance team may simply go along to the machine and effect a repair by replacing the broken component. An alternative strategy is not only to replace the broken component but also all other similar components, on the assumption that since they have all been in service for some length of time, because one has already failed the others are also likely to fail in the near future. A third strategy might be adopted, namely the replacement of the broken component and *certain* of the other similar components.

As an example, consider the problem faced by an electrical maintenance man whose job it is to replace, when necessary, the bulbs in the lights of every room of a multi-storey building. His replacement strategies may be as follows:

1. Replace only those bulbs that fail—such a strategy may involve him in an excessive amount of work, since to replace a bulb he must spend an average of 30 minutes, erecting a ladder, obtaining new bulbs from stores etc. Because of the difference between the comparatively low cost of a new

bulb, and the comparatively high cost of replacement, he may prefer to adopt an alternative strategy, namely:

2. When one bulb fails, replace *all* bulbs in that room, or on that floor.

3. Alternatively, as a compromise, he may replace the bulb that has failed *and* a proportion of other bulbs, say those that have been in service for longer than 6 months, in other words those that he expects to fail fairly shortly.

The problem then is to decide which of these strategies to adopt, a decision which must, of course, be made on a basis of cost considerations. The cost involved in replacement is dependent upon the probability of component failure. In the case of strategy (1) the total cost of maintenance over, say a year, is given by the following:

$$\text{Cost of making a single replacement} \times \text{Probable number of failures during year.}$$

In the case of strategy (2), the total cost is determined by the number of components replaced each time, and the number of 'first failures' during the period. In the final strategy (3) the cost would depend upon the number of 'first failures', and the number of components at every replacement period which have been in service longer than a given time.

Although it is possible to develop formulae for the replacement problem in which items are subject to sudden failure, such formulae are often inadequate for the practical situation; consequently the choice of replacement strategy is often made with the aid of a simulation exercise, a procedure which will be adopted here.

It should be noted, that although we have spoken of the problem as being one of repair, similar considerations might apply during preventive maintenance. For example, if, during the inspection of a machine for preventive maintenance purposes, a component is seen to be likely to fail if left in service, then the decision must be made as to whether or not to replace this component only, or some or all of the similar components. The logic behind the latter strategy is that whilst some components do not yet show signs of impending failure, they are nevertheless likely to fail before the next scheduled maintenance period.

Simulation of Replacement Policies

Before using a simple example to illustrate this technique it is perhaps appropriate to consider the merits and purpose of simulation.

Very often it is impractical to contemplate actual manipulation or experiment in an industrial situation. It is inconceivable, for example, that we should determine an optimum stock control policy deliberately by trial and error, since to do so may incur the company in considerable financial loss before a satisfactory solution is achieved. In such a situation we might solve our problems by recourse to theory, i.e. by using mathematical expressions which are known to be an adequate description of the situation concerned. Often, however, this is not possible, since in complex situations, adequate formulae and equations cannot be obtained. In this type of situation simulation is invaluable since it enables us to experiment with and manipulate a situation *on paper*, and thus develop satisfactory solutions or procedures.

A type of simulation much used is the Monte Carlo method, which essentially involves the use of random sampling from distributions of variables. You will recall that on several occasions throughout this book we have made assumptions about the nature of distributions, often considering them to be normal, exponential, poisson etc., thus enabling us to develop statistical decision rules. When distributions of variables do not conform to one of these types then a simulation procedure must be adopted, often the Monte Carlo method in which use is made of the *actual* distribution of the variable rather than a convenient approximation to it.

Example

Consider the case of one machine tool which has four identical bearings, each subject to the same operating conditions.

The manufacturer is able to provide us with a probability distribution for the life of these bearings (Table 15.1) which does not, however, conform to any of the conventional types of distribution.

TABLE 15.1. Probability of failure of bearings

Bearing life (hours)	No. of failures	Cumulative No. of failures	Cumulative percentage of failures
0–49	0	0	0
50–99	1	1	1
100–149	3	4	4
150–199	5	9	9
200–249	9	18	18
250–299	16	34	34
300–349	24	58	58
350–399	20	78	78
400–449	13	91	91
450–499	6	97	97
500–549	2	99	99
500–599	1	100	100
	100		

Our own maintenance and costing department are able to tell us, from an analysis of past work sheets:

1. that the time required to replace these bearings is as follows:

To replace one bearing   = 2 man hours
To replace two bearings = 4 man hours
To replace three bearings = 5 man hours
To replace four bearings = 7 man hours

2. that the relevant maintenance costs are as follows:

(a) Cost of bearing   = £3 each
(b) Direct labour cost of maintenance = £2/man/h.
(c) Cost of idle or machine downtime = £15/h./machine

We are to decide which of the three repair strategies to adopt for this particular machine.

Firstly, we must construct a cumulative probability curve from the data given in Table 15.1. This is shown in Fig. 15.12. Now we can use this figure to simulate the failure of bearings, and to test the three repair strategies. To do this we also require the use of Random Number tables.[4]

The simulation is performed by first drawing any series of random numbers from available tables which are then used to enable us to take a random sample from the cumulative probability distribution, in order to determine the simulated bearing operating life.

---

[4] Tables of Random Numbers or Digits are available in most text books on statistics.

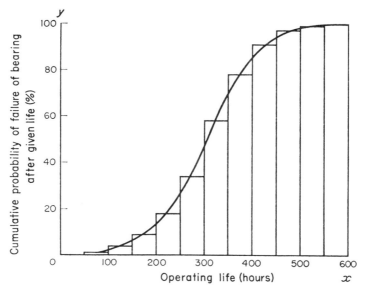

NB This distribution has been drawn using the 'discrete' data of Table 15.1. Since failure may occur at any time, probability of failure is a 'continuous' function, hence the continuous curve is used in the simulation

FIGURE 15.12. Cumulative probability of failure of bearings

For example, consider bearing No. 1. If the first random number is 2251, since we wish to sample from a scale of 0 to 100, we consider this to represent 22·5 per cent on the y axis of Fig. 15.12. A horizontal line from this point cuts the cumulative propability curve at a point corresponding to 238 on the x axis, hence the life of the first bearing No. 1 is taken to be 238 hours.

Similarly the life of the first 10, No. 1 bearings might be found to be:

Bearings No. 1.

Random No.	Operating life (h)
2251	238
7459	363
9380	450
2212	235
9237	440
3975	285
3278	270
1621	215
0413	125
3249	270

By drawing more random numbers, the probable life of several of all four bearings can be determined as shown in Table 15.2. These figures can now be used in the simulation of the three repair strategies:

1. Replace bearings individually on failure
2. Replace all bearings together whenever one of them fails

3. Replace the bearing that fails and at the same time replace those that have been in service for over 335 hours (the average operating life).

The simulation is shown by way of bar charts in Fig. 15.13. For the first strategy the simulation merely consists of the operating life figures for the bearings taken from Table 15.2 arranged sequentially on a common time scale.[5] For strategy two, each replacement is occasioned by the

TABLE 15.2. Simulated operative life for 10 of each of 4 bearings

Bearing No. 1		Bearing No. 2		Bearing No. 3		Bearing No. 4	
R. No.	Life	R. No.	Life	R. No.	Life	R. No.	Life
2251	238	3711	280	2235	240	5761	325
7459	363	0347	115	0212	100	0983	175
9380	450	5034	310	3768	280	2236	240
2212	235	7816	375	6889	350	2250	240
9237	440	1385	200	2782	255	3053	265
3975	285	7823	375	3316	275	9938	550
3278	270	9942	550	8733	410	9360	450
1621	215	9019	430	1994	230	4558	300
0413	125	6307	335	6254	340	8015	380
3249	270	1873	225	0630	150	6104	330

the failure of only one bearing (shown with a solid line) the other three beng replaced at the same time as a matter of policy (shown by dotted lines). The simulation for the third strategy is more involved. Initially bearings are replaced one at a time, because when each failure occurs, none of the others have been in service for more than the specified time (335 hours), and hence

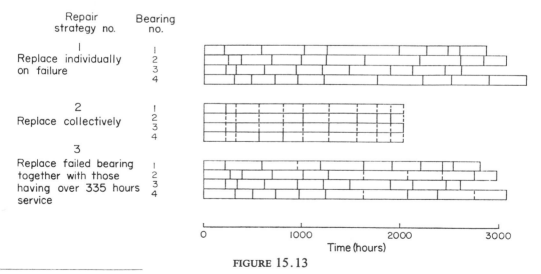

FIGURE 15.13

---

[5] Notice that for reasons of simplicity we have not attempted to include the comparatively short periods of time required for replacement on any of these charts.

do not require replacing. However, on the fourth replacement of bearing No. 4, it is found that bearing No. 1 has already been in service for a period in excess of 335 hours. Consequently it is replaced.[6] A similar situation occurs on four other occasions (shown by dotted lines).

Now let us consider the maintenance cost incurred by each of these strategies.

Let us consider a 2 000 hour period and look first at *Strategy* 1.

No. of replacements $= 24$

1. Maintenance cost $= 24 \times 2 \text{ hours} \times £2$
         $= £96$

2. Cost of machine idle time $= 24 \times 2 \text{ hours} \times £15$
         $= £720$

3. Cost of bearings $= 24 \times 3$
         $= £72$

         Total cost $= £888$

Now consider *Strategy* 2.

No. of replacements $= 9$ (each involving 4 bearings)

1. Maintenance cost $= 9 \times 7 \times 3$
         $= £189$

2. Cost of machine idle time $= 9 \times 7 \times 15$
         $= £925$

3. Cost of bearings $= 36 \times 3$
         $= £108$

         Total cost $= £1\ 222$

Now consider *Strategy* 3.

No. of replacements $= 20$ of 1 bearing
                     1 of 2 bearings
                     1 of 3 bearings

1. Maintenance cost $= \quad 20 \times 2 \times 3 \quad = \quad 120$
                   $+ \quad 1 \times 4 \times 3 \quad = \quad 12$
                   $+ \quad 1 \times 5 \times 3 \quad = \quad 15$
                       $= £147$

2. Cost of machine idle time $= \quad 20 \times 2 \times 15 \quad = \quad 600$
                   $+ \quad 1 \times 4 \times 15 \quad = \quad 60$
                   $+ \quad 1 \times 5 \times 15 \quad = \quad 75$
                       £735

3. Cost of bearings $= 25 \times 3$
         $= £75$

         Total cost $= £957$

The results of this simulation show that, considered over a 2 000 hour operating period, it is economically advisable to adopt replacement strategy 1, since this incurs less cost than strategy 3, and substantially less cost than strategy 2.

---

[6] In fact at this time bearing No. 1 has been in service for 379 hours i.e. $(325+175+240+240)-(238+363)$.

In practice, such a simulation would be conducted over a considerably longer period than the 2 000 hours used here, since it is essential to ensure that the simulated situation has stabilized itself. By using the comparatively short period adopted here, we run the risk of selecting a replacement policy which in the longer term may not be optimal. Furthermore, in practice such a simulation would be conducted with the aid of a computer, since manual simulation for a long time period would be very tedious and time consuming. (In this example, simulation of strategy 3 over a period greatly in excess of 2 000 hours would be extremely laborious).

Replacement policies for items which deteriorate

The cost of operating equipment and machinery normally increases with the increasing age of the equipment. Such increasing cost may be caused by, (1) the increasing cost of the maintenance necessary to obtain continuing reliability of the equipment and (2) the obsolescence of the equipment, making its continued operation comparatively more costly when compared to the equipment which might be used to replace it. There comes a time, therefore, when it is not only economically justifiable to replace the present ageing equipment, but economically beneficial in order to obtain equipment which has greater output, reliability etc,

Our present problem then is to decide at what time such equipment should be replaced. Such a decision must obviously be made on economic grounds, namely by a comparison of the nett economic benefit of retaining present equipment, and the nett economic benefit of replacing present equipment.

As regards *present* equipment we must consider the following:

1. Its life
2. Its salvage or sale value
3. The revenue produced throughout the rest of its life
4. The expenditure incurred throughout the rest of its life

As regards the *proposed* replacement equipment we must consider:

1. The purchase price of the equipment
2. The life.
3. The salvage or sale value at various times in its life
4. The revenue produced by the equipment
5. The expenditure incurred throughout its life

In considering the replacement of equipment it is important to remember that money has a time value. For example, £100 is of more value to us now than it would be next year. In fact, if we are able to obtain interest of say 10 per cent per annum on an investment, £100 *now* is of equal value to us as £110 next year. The evaluation of the economic worth of equipment, therefore, depends upon both its earning potential and time considerations. We must, therefore, make our replacement decisions by considering the *present value* of the nett revenue associated with its use.

If i = annual rate of interest then £100 now is worth

$$\frac{100}{(1+i)^n} \text{ in } n \text{ years' time.}$$

e.g. £100 is worth $100/1 \cdot 1^2 = $ £82·6 in two years' time.

Suppose that the investment of £10 000 in a new piece of equipment results in a nett income of £5 000 for each of the following 3 years. If we assume that the 'cost of capital' or the rate of interest which might have been achieved had the £10 000 been invested, is 10 per cent, then the *present value* of this income is £12 434, i.e.

$$\frac{5\,000}{(1\cdot1)} + \frac{2\,000}{(1\cdot1)^2} + \frac{5\,000}{(1\cdot1)^3}$$

$$= £12\,434$$

The calculation of present values in this way, by *discounting* revenues at a given rate, is the basis of the *discounted cash flow* technique for investment appraisal.

When concerned with equipment replacement, this discounting procedure can be expressed by the following equation:

$$NPV = \sum_{n=1}^{N} \frac{I_n - E_n}{(1+i)^n} + \frac{S_N}{(1+i)^N}$$

Where NPV = Nett present value
I_n = Income for year n
E_n = Expenditure for year n
i = Discount rate
N = Life of equipment
S_N = Sale or scrap value at end of life, i.e. year N

Clearly, to be economically beneficial the nett present value (NPV) must be equal to or greater than the initial investment required.

To assist discounted cash flow calculations, tables for $1/(1+i)^n$ have been prepared (see Table 15.3)

The replacement decision normally takes the following form—whether to replace existing equipment now, or at a later date, up to and including the last year in the life of the existing equipment. The problem then is one of comparing, at *present value*, the cash flows associated with the use of the present and the proposed equipment over the common period, from the present time to the end of the life of the present equipment. Naturally cash flows that have already occurred do not enter into the decision, for example, past operating costs of present equipment. We are only concerned with the cash flows that will result from the decision to retain the equipment, and the decision to replace it, i.e. the operating costs, the revenues and the changes in disposal values.

Example

The management of a company is anxious to determine whether or not to replace an existing machine with a new one of the latest type. The present machine has many years of useful service life left, but nevertheless it is thought that it may be better to obtain the new machine which is known to have lower operating costs.

The cost of the new machine is £10 000 and its anticipated life is 20 years. The present machine is known to have a current disposal value of £5 000 and an anticipated life of 16 years.

If the new machine is purchased an overhaul costing £2 000 will be necessary after it has been in service 10 years, and its disposal value after 16 and 20 years of service will be £500 and £200 respectively. If the present machine is retained, two overhauls will be required at 6 and 12 years, costing £2 500 and £1 500 respectively. Its disposal value after 16 years will be £150.

The nett income (revenue less operating costs) which is expected to result from the use of the machines is shown in Table 15.4, along with the above data.

The nett present value (using a discount rate of 10 per cent per annum) of the cash flows over the 16 years for each machine is also calculated in Table 15.4. The NPV of the cash flow associated

TABLE 15.3. Compound interest table $(1/(1+i)^n)$

n	$i = 1\%$	2	3	4	5	6	7	8	9	10
1	0·9901	0·9804	0·9709	0·9615	0·9524	0·9434	0·9346	0·9259	0·9174	0·9091
2	0·9803	0·9612	0·9426	0·9246	0·9070	0·8900	0·8734	0·8573	0·8417	0·8264
3	0·9706	0·9423	0·9151	0·8890	0·8638	0·8396	0·8163	0·7938	0·7722	0·7513
4	0·9610	0·9238	0·8885	0·8548	0·8227	0·7921	0·7629	0·7350	0·7084	0·6830
5	0·9515	0·9057	0·8626	0·8219	0·7835	0·7473	0·7130	0·6806	0·6499	0·6209
6	0·9420	0·8880	0·8375	0·7903	0·7462	0·7050	0·6663	0·6302	0·5963	0·5645
7	0·9327	0·8706	0·8131	0·7599	0·7107	0·6651	0·6227	0·5835	0·5470	0·5132
8	0·9235	0·8535	0·7894	0·7307	0·6768	0·6274	0·5820	0·5403	0·5019	0·4665
9	0·9143	0·8368	0·7664	0·7026	0·6446	0·5919	0·5439	0·5002	0·4604	0·4241
10	0·9053	0·8302	0·7441	0·6756	0·6139	0·5584	0·5083	0·4632	0·4224	0·3588
11	0·8963	0·8043	0·7224	0·6496	0·5847	0·5268	0·4751	0·4289	0·3875	0·3505
12	0·8874	0·7885	0·7014	0·6246	0·5568	0·4970	0·4440	0·3971	0·3555	0·3186
13	0·8787	0·7730	0·6810	0·6006	0·5303	0·4688	0·4150	0·3677	0·3262	0·2897
14	0·8700	0·7579	0·6611	0·5775	0·5051	0·4423	0·3878	0·3405	0·2992	0·2633
15	0·8613	0·7430	0·6419	0·5553	0·4810	0·4173	0·3624	0·3152	0·2745	0·2394
16	0·8528	0·7284	0·6232	0·5339	0·4581	0·3936	0·3387	0·2919	0·2519	0·2176
17	0·8444	0·7142	0·6050	0·5134	0·4363	0·3714	0·3166	0·2703	0·2311	0·1978
18	0·8360	0·7002	0·5874	0·4936	0·4155	0·3503	0·2959	0·2502	0·2120	0·1799
19	0·8277	0·6864	0·5703	0·4746	0·3957	0·3305	0·2765	0·2317	0·1945	0·1635
20	0·8195	0·6730	0·5537	0·4564	0·3769	0·3118	0·2584	0·2145	0·1784	0·1486
21	0·8114	0·6598	0·5375	0·4388	0·3589	0·2942	0·2415	0·1987	0·1637	0·1351
22	0·8034	0·6468	0·5219	0·4220	0·3418	0·2775	0·2257	0·1839	0·1502	0·1228
23	0·7954	0·6432	0·5067	0·4057	0·3256	0·2618	0·2109	0·1703	0·1378	0·1117
24	0·7876	0·6217	0·4919	0·3901	0·3101	0·2470	0·1971	0·1577	0·1264	0·1015
25	0·7798	0·6095	0·4776	0·3751	0·2953	0·2330	0·1842	0·1460	0·1160	0·0923
26	0·7720	0·5976	0·4637	0·3607	0·2812	0·2198	0·1722	0·1352	0·1064	0·0839
27	0·7644	0·5859	0·4502	0·3468	0·2678	0·2074	0·1096	0·1252	0·0976	0·0763
28	0·7568	0·5744	0·4371	0·3335	0·2551	0·1956	0·1504	0·1159	0·0895	0·0693
29	0·7493	0·5631	0·4243	0·3207	0·2429	0·1846	0·1406	0·1073	0·0822	0·0630
30	0·7419	0·5521	0·4120	0·3083	0·2314	0·1741	0·1314	0·0994	0·0754	0·0573

Where i = Annual interest rate
n = No. of years

with decision 1 (replace present machine) is £2 236. The NPV of the cash flow associated with decision 2 is £4 061. Clearly, therefore, it is in the company's interest to retain the present machine rather than replace it.

It should be remembered, of course, that the discounted cash flow technique takes no account of the following, all of which may influence the replacement decision:

1. Risk, i.e. the uncertainty of factors such as operating life, repair costs, disposal values etc.
2. Inflation
3. The timing of the cash flows in relation to opportunities for the use of the money elsewhere
4. The difficulty of raising money for the outlays

TABLE 15.4.

Year No.	$\dfrac{1}{(1+i)^n}$	(1) Machine is replaced				(2) Machine is *not* replaced			
		Outlays (£)	Nett income (£)	Nett cash flow	NPV	Outlays (£)	Nett income (£)	Nett cash flow	NPV
0	1·0000	10,000	5 000	−5 000	−5 000				
1	0·9091		1 500	1 500	1 365		1 000	1 000	909
2	0·8264		1 400	1 400	1 155		1 000	1 000	826
3	0·7513		1 300	1 300	980		1 000	1 000	751
4	0·6830		1 200	1 200	820		900	900	615
5	0·6209		1 100	1 100	685		800	800	498
6	0·5645		1 000	1 000	565	2 500	700	−1 800	−1 015
7	0·5132		900	900	460		700	700	360
8	0·4665		800	800	374		700	700	327
9	0·4241		700	600	255		700	700	297
10	0·3855	2 000	600	−1 400	−540		600	600	232
11	0·3505		600	600	211		500	500	175
12	0·3186		600	600	191	1 500	400	−1 100	−351
13	0·2897		600	600	174		400	400	116
14	0·2633		600	600	158		400	400	105
15	0·2394		600	600	144		400	400	96
16	0·2176		600+500	1 100	239		400+150	550	120

$$\text{NPV} = \sum_{n=1}^{16} \frac{I_n - E_n}{(1\cdot1)^n} + \frac{S_{16}}{(1\cdot1)^{16}} \qquad 2\,236 \qquad \text{NPV} = \sum_{n=1}^{16} \frac{I_n - E_n}{(1\cdot1)^n} + \frac{S_{16}}{(1\cdot1)^{16}} \qquad 4\,061$$

5. Policy after the period considered

6. Possible future development of improved equipment

Despite these omissions the DCF technique is undoubtedly of considerable value, however as regards replacement policy perhaps the major obstacle to its adoption is the difficulty of accurately predicting future cash flows. This difficulty is particularly acute in our case, since when considering capital equipment such as machine tools, anticipated life is often quite large. Estimation of cash flows ten or more years ahead is often pure speculation, indeed estimates of the life of equipment is often a hazardous procedure. Consequently it would be of considerable advantage to have available a rational decision making procedure which depends upon more immediate events, one which could be applied quickly and repeatedly if necessary, without the need for a major costing or forecasting exercise.

Such a system was developed by the Machinery and Allied Products Institute in America. Several versions of the MAPI system have existed since it was first developed in 1949,[7] however, each of these have been conceptually alike in that the objective of each version of the MAPI system has been the calculation of an *urgency rating* which is a measure of the economic benefit associated with the replacement of equipment. In other words, the urgency rating is a measure of the urgency of making an investment as compared to delaying the investment for a period of

---

[7] G. TERBORGH, *Dynamic Equipment Policy*, McGraw-Hill, New York, 1949.

time. In earlier MAPI systems the urgency rating was calculated by comparing, *for the next year only*, the relative economic merits of replacing equipment and retaining it, however, the current system permits comparisons for periods in excess of one year.

In the current system[8] the urgency rating is, in fact, a measure of the rate of return on the investment after tax, i.e.

$$\frac{\text{Operating advantage} - \text{Capital consumption}}{\text{Nett investment}} \times 100$$

The calculation of this after tax rate of return on investment is accomplished quite easily using the MAPI forms and charts shown in Fig. 15.14–15.16.

Example

Project: To evaluate the benefit of replacing an existing manual lathe by an automatic lathe.

Automatic lathe: Cost   = £9 000 (after adjustment for tax grant, etc.)
        : Service life   = 8 years
        : Disposal value after
           service   = £1 800
Existing lathe: Present disposal value   = £500

Estimated savings and costs for one year associated with replacement of existing lathe:
Savings:

(a) Increased output	£1 000
(b) on direct labour	£750
(c) on maintenance	£200
(d) on tools and jigs	£500
(e) on acceptance inspection	£150
(f) on scrap	£100

Added costs:

(a) on indirect labour	£150
(b) on power	£100
(c) for conveyers and palletts	£175
(d) increase in depreciation	£1 000

Tax rate = 40 per cent

The evaluation of this investment for a one year period is undertaken by means of the standard MAPI forms (Figs. 15.14, 15.15). Chart 1*a* (Fig 15.16) has been used to estimate the retention value of the equipment at the end of the comparison period. It has been found that the after tax return on the investment is only 5·3 per cent, thus indicating the low urgency of the project.

Perhaps the principal benefit of the MAPI system is the ease with which it can be used. The forms permit ready calculation of the 'Operating Advantage' and the capital consumption. Three methods are available for calculating the reduction in the value of the new equipment depending upon whether depreciation is: (a) of the standard straight line type; (b) accelerated towards end of life; (c) accelerated initially.

------

[8] G. TERBORGH, *Business Investment Management*, Machinery and Allied Products Institute, Washington D.C., 1967.

PROJECT NO._____

MAPI SUMMARY FORM
(AVERAGING SHORTCUT)

PROJECT _____ AUTOMATIC LATHE

ALTERNATIVE _____ RETAIN EXISTING MANUAL LATHE

COMPARISON PERIOD (YEARS)   (P) ____1____

ASSUMED OPERATING RATE OF PROJECT (HOURS PER YEAR)   1500

I. OPERATING ADVANTAGE
(NEXT-YEAR FOR A 1-YEAR COMPARISON PERIOD,* ANNUAL AVERAGES FOR LONGER PERIODS)

A. EFFECT OF PROJECT ON REVENUE

		INCREASE	DECREASE	
1	FROM CHANGE IN QUALITY OF PRODUCTS	$	$	1
2	FROM CHANGE IN VOLUME OF OUTPUT	1000		2
3	TOTAL	$ 1000 X	$ Y	3

B. EFFECT ON OPERATING COSTS

		INCREASE	DECREASE	
4	DIRECT LABOR	$	$ 750	4
5	INDIRECT LABOR	150		5
6	FRINGE BENEFITS			6
7	MAINTENANCE		200	7
8	TOOLING		500	8
9	MATERIALS AND SUPPLIES			9
10	INSPECTION		150	10
11	ASSEMBLY			11
12	SCRAP AND REWORK		100	12
13	DOWN TIME			13
14	POWER	100		14
15	FLOOR SPACE			15
16	PROPERTY TAXES AND INSURANCE			16
17	SUBCONTRACTING			17
18	INVENTORY			18
19	SAFETY			19
20	FLEXIBILITY			20
21	OTHER	175		21
22	TOTAL	$ 425 Y	$ 1700 X	22

C. COMBINED EFFECT

23	NET INCREASE IN REVENUE (3X−3Y)	$ 1000	23
24	NET DECREASE IN OPERATING COSTS (22X−22Y)	$ 1275	24
25	ANNUAL OPERATING ADVANTAGE (23+24)	$ 2275	25

* Next year means the first year of project operation. For projects with a significant break-in period, use performance after break-in.

Copyright 1967, Machinery and Allied Products Institute

FIGURE 15.4

II. INVESTMENT AND RETURN

A. INITIAL INVESTMENT

26 INSTALLED COST OF PROJECT $ _____
     MINUS INITIAL TAX BENEFIT OF $ _____   (Net Cost) $ 9000   26
27 INVESTMENT IN ALTERNATIVE
     CAPITAL ADDITIONS MINUS INITIAL TAX BENEFIT $ _____
     PLUS: DISPOSAL VALUE OF ASSETS RETIRED
        BY PROJECT * $ 500 $ 500   27
28 INITIAL NET INVESTMENT (26−27) $ 8500   28

B. TERMINAL INVESTMENT

29 RETENTION VALUE OF PROJECT AT END OF COMPARISON PERIOD
     (ESTIMATE FOR ASSETS, IF ANY, THAT CANNOT BE DEPRECIATED OR EXPENSED. FOR OTHERS, ESTIMATE
                     OR USE MAPI CHARTS.)

Item or Group	Installed Cost, Minus Initial Tax Benefit (Net Cost) A	Service Life (Years) B	Disposal Value, End of Life (Percent of Net Cost) C	MAPI Chart Number D	Chart Percentage E	Retention Value $\left(\frac{A \times E}{100}\right)$ F
Automatic Lathe	$ 9000	8	20%	1A	85%	$ 7650

        ESTIMATED FROM CHARTS (TOTAL OF COL. F) $ _____
        PLUS: OTHERWISE ESTIMATED $ _____ $ 7650   29
30 DISPOSAL VALUE OF ALTERNATIVE AT END OF PERIOD * $ 500   30
31 TERMINAL NET INVESTMENT (29−30) $ 7150   31

C. RETURN

32 AVERAGE NET CAPITAL CONSUMPTION $\left(\frac{28-31}{P}\right)$ $ 1350   32

33 AVERAGE NET INVESTMENT $\left(\frac{28+31}{2}\right)$ $ 7825   33

34 BEFORE-TAX RETURN $\left(\frac{25-32}{33} \times 100\right)$ % 11.9   34

35 INCREASE IN DEPRECIATION AND INTEREST DEDUCTIONS $ 1000   35
36 TAXABLE OPERATING ADVANTAGE (25−35) $ 1275   36
37 INCREASE IN INCOME TAX (36×TAX RATE) $ 510   37
38 AFTER-TAX OPERATING ADVANTAGE (25−37) $ 1765   38
39 AVAILABLE FOR RETURN ON INVESTMENT (38−32) $ 415   39

40 AFTER-TAX RETURN $\left(\frac{39}{33} \times 100\right)$ % 5.3   40

_____
* After terminal tax adjustments.

Copyright 1967, Machinery and Allied Products Institute

FIGURE 15.15

MAPI CHART No. 1A

(ONE-YEAR COMPARISON PERIOD AND SUM-OF-DIGITS TAX DEPRECIATION)

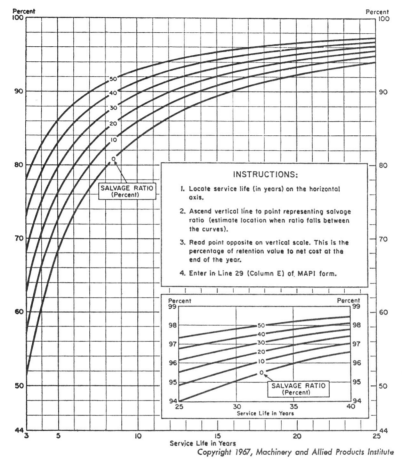

INSTRUCTIONS:

1. Locate service life (in years) on the horizontal axis.

2. Ascend vertical line to point representing salvage ratio (estimate location when ratio falls between the curves).

3. Read point opposite on vertical scale. This is the percentage of retention value to net cost at the end of the year.

4. Enter in Line 29 (Column E) of MAPI form.

Copyright 1967, Machinery and Allied Products Institute

FIGURE 15.16

Charts have been developed to enable the reduction in value to be obtained without recourse to the use of formulae. For example, the chart shown in Fig. 15.16 applies to depreciation of type (b) above. Likewise charts are available for comparison periods longer than one year.

FIGURE 15.17(a)(b)(c)

SUMMARY

Equipment of all types, irrespective of cost or complexity, is liable to failure. Such failures result in a disruption of production, and give rise, therefore, to two problems for production management. Firstly, the need to compensate for such disruptions during production planning and secondly, the need for a maintenance facility.

The objective of maintenance is to maintain or increase the reliability of a production system as a whole. All of the following will contribute to the reliability of a production system although only the latter two are considered to be the responsibility of the maintenance department.

1. Improvement in the quality of the equipment used
2. Improvements in equipment design to facilitate maintenance work.
3. Improvements in the layout of equipment to facilitate maintenance work.
4. Provide excess capacity or work in progress stock to ensure that failure of equipment does not affect production.
5. Establish a repair facility.
6. Undertake preventive maintenance.

Preventive maintenance is generally appropriate and economically beneficial where breakdown time distributions for equipment exhibit comparatively little variance, and where the cost of preventive maintenance operations is less then the cost of repair operations.

Use of statistical queueing theory enables optimum schedules for preventive maintenance to be established, and the size of repair teams to be determined.

When items are subject to possibility of sudden failure, several alternative replacement policies are available, i.e.

1. Replace item that has failed
2. Replace all items
3. Replace item that has failed plus certain of the other items.

Providing the probability of failure is known, replacement policy can be determined by means of simulation.

A replacement problem also occurs where items deteriorate, the problem being whether to replace the deteriorating equipment now, or at some future time. The discounted cash flow technique is a useful method of investigating such problems, but often difficulty is experienced in forecasting the relevant future cash flows. In such cases a technique such as the MAPI method may be of value.

SELECTED READINGS

There are no text books which fully cover the ground discussed in this chapter. However, adequate descriptions of the maintenance function, both preventive and repair, can be found in chapters in the following books:

H. L. TIMMS, *The Production Function in Business*, Irwin, Illinois, 1966. (revised ed.).

R. A. OLSEN, *Manufacturing Management—A Quantitiative Approach*, International Textbook Co., Penns., 1968.

The contributions of MORSE have been emphasized in this chapter. This work can be found in:

P. M. MORSE, *Queues, Inventories and Maintenance*, Wiley, London 1958.

Derivation of various replacement theory formulae and the Monte Carlo technique can be found in most operational research textbooks, e.g.

C. W. CHURCHMAN and R. L. ACKOFF, *Introduction to Operations Research*, Wiley, London, 1965.

M. SASIENI, A. YASPAN and L. FRIEDMAN, *Operations Research, Methods and Problems*, Wiley, London, 1959.

A description of the latest MAPI system can be found in:

G. TERBORGH, *Business Investment Management*, MAPI, Washington, D.C., 1967.

QUESTIONS

15.1. Define and differentiate between preventive maintenance and repair.
What are the objectives of maintenance?
In what circumstances is preventive maintenance particularly appropriate?

15.2. An examination of the machine operating history together with statistical information provided by the manufacturer has revealed that the breakdown time distribution of a semi-automatic capstan lathe approximates to an Erlang distribution with parameter $l = 2$. It has also been established that the average trouble-free life between breakdowns is 175 hours.

The maintenance manager estimates that the average time for repairs to this lathe is 4·6 hours, and a study of the maintenance and service instructions for the machine indicates that the average time for preventive maintenance is 2·5 hours.

It has further been estimated that the costs of maintenance and repair are as follows:

Preventive maintenance £5/h
Repair   £10/h

The average value of the output of the machine is £74·6/h.

(a) Determine the optimum preventive maintenance schedule.
(b) How would this schedule change if:

1. The cost of repairs decreased to £5/h
2. The average running life between breakdowns decreased to 75 h.

15.3. Referring to the previous question, i.e.

Breakdown time distribution	$= $ Erlang, $l = 2$
Average life between breakdowns	$= 175$ h
Time for repair	$= 4\cdot6$ h
Time per preventive maintenance	$= 2\cdot5$ h
Cost of preventive maintenance	$= £5/h$
Cost of repair	$= £10/h$

(a) Because of a change in the type of component manufactured on the lathe, the value of the hourly output changes (all other figures above remain the same). It is calculated that in the new situation the optimum preventive maintenance interval is 262 hours.
What is the value of the hourly machine output?
(b) A work study team is engaged to study work methods during preventive maintenance, with the object of reducing the average time required for such maintenance.

For the data given initially, an average trouble-free life between breakdowns of 175 hours and an output value of £74·6 per hour, what is the optimum preventive maintenance interval if:

(a) Both the cost and average duration for preventive maintenance are reduced by 25 per cent.
(b) The average duration of preventive maintenance is reduced by 50 per cent but cost is increased by 25 per cent.

15.4. If the average operating life, without breakdowns, of four similar machines is 4 weeks, and if the average time to repair a machine which has broken down is 6 weeks—what is the average number of machines working at any time?

State what statistical assumptions you have made in arriving at your answer.

If one repair team is allocated to the repair of the above machines, what proportion of the time will this team be occupied?

State what statistical assumption you have made in arriving at your answer.

15.5. (a) A single maintenance team is expected to effect repairs to several identical drilling machines as and when necessary. Because of other less important duties (which can be interrupted if necessary), the team can only devote 80 per cent of their time to the repair of the drilling machines. It is known that the breakdown distribution of the drilling machines approximates closely to the exponential distribution and that the average time between breakdowns is 75 hours.

1. How many machines can the team attend, if the repair time is exponentially distributed with mean = 15 hours.
2. What is the average number of machines in service at any time?

(b) An unlikely situation has arisen and a maintenance manager has a choice of allocating a repair team to look after one of three different groups of machines. The details of each group of machines are as follows:

Group of 'A' type machines:
- No.   = 8
- Average time between breakdowns = 50 h
- Average time to make repair   = 5 h

Group of 'B' type machines:
- No.   = 6
- Average time between breakdowns = 40 h
- Average time to make repair   = 6 h

Group of 'C' type
- No.   = 10
- Average time between breakdowns = 20 h
- Average time to make a repair   = 2 h

Assuming that the breakdown time distribution and the repair time distribution are exponential:
1. Other things being equal—which group of machines would keep the repair team busiest?
2. Which group should the repair team be allocated to if the cirteria is the maximization of the average percentage of the total number of machines in service at any time.

15.6. Describe briefly how you would collect and analyse data in order to assist in the determination of a maintenance policy for a small jobbing machine shop.

Having determined the policy, what data would you need to collect regularly in order to ensure that the maintenance procedures were adjusted to conform to changes in the characteristics of the equipment in the shop?

15.7. (a) Determine the maximum average time required to perform a repair if two maintenance teams are to attend to two identical machines and if, on average, a minimum of one machine should be in service at any time.

The repair time and the machine breakdown time are both exponentially distributed, and the average operating life of machines between breakdowns is 40 hours.

(b) What is the maximum average repair time if one maintenance team is to ensure the same performance of the machines?

15.8. A small transfer line has three identical and rather complex pneumatic clamping devices, each of which occasionally fails to operate satisfactorily because of the failure of a valve mechanism. The cumulative probability of failure of the valve mechanism is given in the graph. It has been found from experience that the replacement of one valve mechanism takes 1 hour, whilst the replacement of two together takes 1·75 hours and the replacement of all three takes 2·5 hours.

The costs associated with this operation are given below.

Direct labour cost = £8/h
Cost of replacement valve = £10
Down time cost of transfer line = £75/h

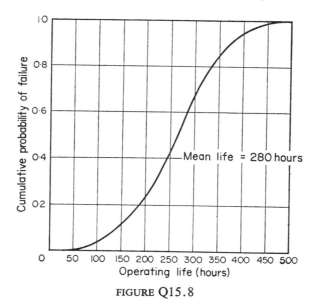

FIGURE Q15.8

Three replacement strategies are available—namely:

1. Replace each valve mechanism individually when it fails.
2. Replace all three valve mechanisms every time one mechanism fails.
3. Replace each valve mechanism when it fails and, *at the same time* replace all other valve mechanisms that have been in service for longer than the known average operating life of the mechanism.

Using a simulation approach determine the minimum cost replacement strategy.

15.9. Profit Makers Ltd. are considering the purchase of a numerically controlled machine to replace an ageing existing machine. The new machine would cost £6 000 and is expected to have a life of fifteen years during which it would earn revenue as follows:

Year	Revenue £	Year	Revenue £
This year	1 500	8	1 800
1	2 000	9	1 600
2	2 000	10	1 500
3	2 000	11	1 500
4	2 000	12	1 000
5	2 000	13	700
6	2 000	14	500
7	2 000	15	500

One major overhaul would be necessary in five years time, costing £3 750 and a second overhaul would be necessary in twelve years' time costing £2 500. It is anticipated that the realizable value on disposal of this machine would be £2 500 at any time after the twelfth year and £5 000 between the tenth and twelfth year inclusive. The existing machine is mechanically sound but technologically dated. Nevertheless, it has an expected life of a further twelve years. If it is retained it will be necessary to conduct minor maintenance work this year, at a cost of £1 500, and every fifth year thereafter at a cost of £500 each time. Its disposal value is expected to be £500 and it is expected to earn revenue as follows:

Year	Revenue £	Year	Revenue £
This year	1 500	7	1 000
1	1 500	8	750
2	1 200	9	750
3	1 200	10	600
4	1 100	11	500
5	1 100	12	400
6	1 000		

The company is in the habit of evaluating future investment, and revenues at present value, by means of a 10 per cent 'discount' rate:

(a) Should Profit Makers Ltd. replace the existing machine?
(b) What is the cost difference at present value between the two alternative strategies?

Appendices

APPENDICES

I Linear Programming

Consider the problem facing a firm making a range of different products. Each product is made in a different way, and for each product there exists a best or optimal method of manufacture. Unfortunately, there are insufficient resources to make each product in the best possible way, hence the problem is to decide which products to make, and in what proportions, in order to maximize profits, or minimize costs.

This is an *allocation* problem. Such problems arise whenever there are several activities to perform, but limitations on resources prevent the performance of each activity in *its* best way. For example, a manufacturer makes two types of product, A and B. Each product A requires one hour of machining, five hours of fabrication and three hours of assembly.

Each product B requires two hours of machining, four hours of fabrication and one hour of assembly. In a given period of time there are only 720 hours of machining, 1 800 hours of fabrication, and 900 hours of assembly time available. How should the manufacturer use this capacity in order to maximize profit, if the profit on each product A is £80 and on B, £100.

Allocation problems such as this can be solved by means of linear programming, provided:
(a) The objective to be achieved can be expressed as a linear function in terms of the various activities.
(b) The limiting constraints can also be expressed in linear form.

THE SIMPLEX ALGORITHM

The Simplex algorithm is best described by means of an example (based on the above).

Example 1—Maximizing

Two products, A and B. Manufacturing time required:

	Machining	Fabrication	Assembly	Profit on product
A	I hour	5 hours	3 hours	£80
B	2 hours	4 hours	I hour	£100
Total capacity available	720 hours	1800 hours	900 hours	

FIGURE I.1

Our *objective* in this case is to maximize profits. If W = profit obtained, we wish to maximize W

$$\text{where, } W = 80\,A + 100\,B.$$

Our *constraints* are as follows:

Machining capacity $A + 2B \leqslant 720$ (Total machining hours used cannot exceed 720)
Fabrication capacity $5A + 4B \leqslant 1\,800$
Assembly capacity $3A + B \leqslant 900$

We must express these constraints as equations rather than as the inequalities shown above. This can be done by introducing further variables (called *slack variables*) as follows:

$$A + 2B + p = 720 \tag{1}$$

$$5A + 4B + q = 1\,800 \tag{2}$$

$$3A + B + r = 900 \tag{3}$$

These slack variables (p, q, r) will, of course, represent either zero or positive figures.

The Simplex method is a procedure for solving a set of such equations simultaneously. The first step is to set down the data in a *tableau* or table form, i.e.

	A	B	p	q	r	P_0
p	1	2	1	0	0	720
q	5	4	0	1	0	1800
r	3	1	0	0	1	900
W	−80	−100	0	0	0	0

FIGURE I.2

The first three rows of figures represent equations (1) (2) and (3). P_0 is the figure on the right hand side of the equation, and p, q and r appear in the first column to indicate that they also feature in the equations. The fourth row is the objective function, but written in negative form.

The procedure by which the solution is achieved, is known as the Gauss Jordan Complete Elimination Procedure.[1]

The steps in the procedure for obtaining an optimum solution are as follows:

1. Select the largest negative figure in the W row.
   In our case this is 100 in column B.
2. Find the figure in *this column* which gives the smallest positive figure when divided into P_0.
   In our case this is 2 in the first row, since 720/2 is smaller than either 1 800/4 or 900/1.
3. Divide *this row* by *this figure*; enter the results as the equivalent row of a new tableau under

---

[1] We will use the procedure and show that an optimum answer results. The basis and development of the procedure and of the simplex alogrithm can be found in most operational research text books (see references at end of Appendix).

W, and replace the slack variable letter on the left with the variable of the column concerned, i.e.

	A	B	p	q	r	P_0
→p	1	②	1	0	0	720
q	5	4	0	1	0	1800
r	3	1	0	0	1	900
W	-80	-100	0	0	0	0
→B	$\frac{1}{2}$	1	$\frac{1}{2}$	0	0	360

FIGURE I.3

4. Eliminate this variable from each of the other rows, by multiplying the new row in turn by the negative values of the figures in the column, and adding the result to the row concerned, i.e. Consider the second row. The negative of the figure in the second column is -4. Multiply all of the new row by -4 and add the result to the original second row, i.e.

	A	B	p	q	r	P_0
p	1	②	1	0	0	720
→q	5	4	0	1	0	1800
r	3	1	0	0	1	900
W	-80	-100	0	0	0	0
B	$\frac{1}{2}$	1	$\frac{1}{2}$	0	0	360
→q	3	0	-2	1	0	360

FIGURE I.4

Consider the third row. The negative of the figure in the second column is -1. Multiply all of the first row in the new tableau by -1 and add the result to the original third row.
Do the same for the original W row, i.e. multiply first row in new tableau by 100 (the negative of -100) then adding to original W row, i.e.

	A	B	p	q	r	P_0
p	1	②	1	0	0	720
q	5	4	0	1	0	1800
→r	3	1	0	0	1	900
→W	-80	-100	0	0	0	0
B	$\frac{1}{2}$	1	$\frac{1}{2}$	0	0	360
q	3	0	-2	1	0	360
→r	$\frac{5}{2}$	0	$-\frac{1}{2}$	0	1	540
→W	-30	0	50	0	0	36 000

FIGURE I.5

5. Repeat the same procedure for the new tableau, i.e.
   Largest negative in last row is -30. Select 3 in this column. Divide this row by 3 and write the new row into the third tableau, i.e.

	A	B	p	q	r	P_o
p	1	2	1	0	0	720
q	5	4	0	1	0	1800
r	3	1	0	0	1	900
W	-80	-100	0	0	0	0
B	$\frac{1}{2}$	1	$\frac{1}{2}$	0	0	360
q	③	0	-2	1	0	360
r	$\frac{5}{2}$	0	$-\frac{1}{2}$	0	1	540
W	-30	0	50	0	0	36000
—	—	—	—	—	—	—
A	1	0	$-\frac{2}{3}$	$\frac{1}{3}$	0	120

FIGURE I.6

Eliminate this variable from each of the other rows, by multiplying in turn, the new row by the negative value of the figure in the column and adding the result to the row concerned, i.e. For first row in new tableau multiply by $-\frac{1}{2}$ and add, etc.

	A	B	p	q	r	P_o
p	1	2	1	0	0	720
q	5	4	0	1	0	1800
r	3	1	0	0	1	900
W	-80	-100	0	0	0	0
B	$\frac{1}{2}$	1	$\frac{1}{2}$	0	0	360
q	③	0	$-\frac{1}{2}$	1	0	360
r	$\frac{5}{2}$	0	$-\frac{1}{2}$	0	1	540
W	-30	0	50	0	0	36000
B	0	1	$\frac{1}{6}$	$-\frac{1}{6}$	0	300
A	1	0	$-\frac{2}{3}$	$\frac{1}{3}$	0	120
r	0	0	$\frac{4}{3}$	$-\frac{5}{2}$	1	240
W	0	0	30	10	0	39600

FIGURE I.7

6. Repeat until there are no further negative values in row W. Then optimal solution has been obtained. i.e. In this case there are no further negative values in last row. Therefore this last tableau represents optimal solution.

The solution is interpreted as follows:

The letters on the left of the tableau represent the variables which feature in the solution, i.e. in this case, variables B, A, and r. In other words p and q have been lost, hence our three equations are now as follows:

$$A + 2B \quad = \quad 720$$
$$5A + 4B \quad = \quad 1\,800$$
$$3A + B + r = \quad 900$$

From these equations the values of A and B can be found.
Alternatively they can be read straight from the final tableau, i.e.

$$B = 300 \; (P_0)$$
$$A = 120 \; (P_0)$$
$$\text{The profit } W = 80\,(120) + 100\,(300)$$
$$= £39\,600$$

Example 2.—Minimizing

It is often necessary to minimize a function such as cost. Minimization of an objective function can be achieved quite easily since the objective $Min.\ W = x + y$ is equivalent to $Max.\ (-W) = -x - y$. Consequently a Simplex solution can be obtained in exactly the same manner as previously, e.g.

Minimize the following objective function: $W = 4A - 6B$ subject to the following constraints:

$$-A + 2B \leqslant 8$$
$$-3A + 4B \leqslant 12$$

The equivalent of minimizing W is $Max\ (-W)$, i.e.

$$\text{objective} = Max\ (-W) = -4A + 6B$$

The constraints can be expressed as equalities as follows:

$$-A + 2B + p = 8$$
$$-3A + 4B + q = 12$$

The initial tableau is shown below.

	A	B	p	q	P_0
p	−1	2	1	0	8
q	−3	4	0	1	12
(−W)	4	−6	0	0	0

FIGURE I.8

A solution is obtained as follows:

1. Select largest negative figure in $(-W)$ row, i.e. −6
2. Find figure in this column which gives smallest positive figure when divided into P_0, i.e. 4

3. Divide this row by this figure, enter the result as the equivalent row of a new tableau, and replace slack variable on left, i.e.

	A	B	p	q	P_0
p	-1	2	1	0	8
→ q	-3	④	0	1	12
(-W)	4	-6	0	0	0
—	—	—	—	—	—
B	$-\frac{3}{4}$	1	0	$\frac{1}{4}$	3

FIGURE I.9

4. Eliminate this variable from each of the other rows by multiplying the new row in turn by the negative value of the figure in the column, and adding the result to the row concerned, i.e.

	A	B	p	q	P_0
p	-1	2	1	0	8
q	-3	4	0	1	12
(-W)	4	-6	0	0	0
p	$\frac{1}{2}$	0	1	$-\frac{1}{2}$	2
B	$-\frac{3}{4}$	1	0	$\frac{1}{4}$	3
(-W)	$-\frac{1}{2}$	0	0	$1\frac{1}{2}$	18

FIGURE I.10

5. Repeat this procedure for the new tableaux until there are no more negative values in the $(-W)$ row, i.e.

	A	B	p	q	P_0
p	-1	2	1	0	8
q	-3	4	0	1	12
(-W)	4	6	0	0	0
→ p	$\left(\frac{1}{2}\right)$	0	1	$-\frac{1}{2}$	2
B	$-\frac{3}{4}$	1	0	$\frac{1}{4}$	3
(-W)	$-\frac{1}{2}$	0	0	$1\frac{1}{2}$	18
A	1	0	2	-1	4
B	0	1	$1\frac{1}{2}$	$-\frac{1}{2}$	6
(-W)	0	0	1	1	20

FIGURE I.11

$$\textit{Solution Max } (-W) = \quad 20$$
$$\textit{Min } W \quad = -20$$
$$\text{when } A \quad = \quad 4$$
$$B \quad = \quad 6$$

Inequalities of the form $x+y \geqslant N$:

Suppose the constraints in a linear programming problem were as follows:

$$3x + y \geqslant 3$$
$$4x + 3y \geqslant 6$$

Then introducing slack variables gives:

$$3x + y - p = 3$$
$$4x + 3y - q = 6$$

where p and q are positive values or zero.

It is not possible, however, to use the Simplex procedure to solve equations such as these, since using this method, only slack variables with positive signs are allowed. However, a solution can be achieved by introducing a further set of variables called artificial variables, as follows:

$$3x + y - p + s = 3$$
$$4x + 3y - q + t = 6$$

Although we do not propose to describe the procedure, the Simplex method can now be used to obtain an optimum solution in a manner very similar to that described above. (A description of the procedure can be found in the references given at the end of this Appendix).

Equations

A similar situation to the above arises when constraints must be expressed as equations rather than inequalities. If, in our original example, it was essential that *all* of the machining capacity were used, our constraints would be:

$$A + 2B = \quad 720$$
$$5A + 4B = 1\ 800$$
$$3A + B = \quad 900$$

Such a situation again necessitates the use of *artificial variables*, and a solution can again be obtained using the Simplex method.

THE TRANSPORTATION ALGORITHM

The transportation algorithm is a special case of linear programming and is applicable to the special type of allocation problem in which both requirements and resources are expressed in terms of one type of unit. It can be used, for example, to minimize the total cost of distributing goods from n dispatch points to m receiving points, providing the following conditions are satisfied:

(a) The number of items to be dispatched from, and the number to be received at, each point is known.

(b) The cost of transportation between each pair of points is known.

Again the technique is best illustrated by means of a simple example.

Example 3.

Three steel mills produce steel at rate of:

$$A = 60 \text{ ton/h}$$
$$B = 100 \text{ ton/h}$$
$$C = 150 \text{ ton/h}$$

Three factories require steel at rates of:

$$1 = 140 \text{ ton/h}$$
$$2 = 120 \text{ ton/h}$$
$$3 = 50 \text{ ton/h}$$

The cost of transportation between steel mills and factories are given by the values in the cells in the following matrix.

	Factories		
	1	2	3
A	6	8	4
B	4	9	3
C	1	2	6

Steel mills = A, B, C

FIGURE I.12

Using all of this information we can construct our first transportation *tableau* for this allocation problem, where x_{ij} is the amount of steel transported or allocated from mill i to factory j

Mill (i = A,B,C) \ Factory (j=1,2,3)	1	2	3	Output per mill per hour (a_i)
A	x_{ij} 6	x_{ij} 8	x_{ij} 4	a_A =60
B	x_{ij} 4	x_{ij} 9	x_{ij} 3	a_B =100
C	x_{ij} 1	x_{ij} 2	x_{ij} 6	a_C =150
Requirements per factory per hour (b_j)	b_1 =140	b_2 =120	b_3 =50	

FIGURE I.13

The objective is to allocate steel to factories so as to minimize total transportation costs.

It is possible to obtain *a* solution to the problem by using what is known as the *North West Corner* rule which gives rise to the following procedure:

1. Start at the N.W. (i.e. top left hand) cell.
2. If $a_i < b_j$, set $x_{ij} = a_i$, and proceed vertically.
3. If $a_i > b_j$, set $x_{ij} = b_j$, and proceed horizontally.
4. If $a_i = b_j$, set $x_{ij} = a_i = b_j$ and proceed diagonally.
5. Repeat until S.E. (i.e. bottom right hand) cell is reached.

Adopting this North West rule and referring to our example, i.e.

	1	2	3	a_j
A	60 6	8	4	$a_A = 60$
B	80 → 20 4 9		3	$a_B = 100$
C		100 → 50 2 6		$a_C = 150$
b_j	$b_1 = 140$	$b_2 = 120$	$b_3 = 50$	

FIGURE I.14

The steps we would take are as follows:

(a) Start in cell A, 1 (The N.W. corner)
(b) Since $a_i < b_j$ (i.e. $60 < 140$). Set $x_{ij} = 60$ and proceed vertically to B, 1
(c) At B, 1 $a_i = 100$ and $b_j = (140 - 60) = 80$ (i.e. factory 1 required 140 but it has now been allowed 60 from steel mill A therefore still requires 80). Set B, $1 = 80$ and proceed horizontally.
(d) At B, 2 b_j now is 20 and $a_i = 120$. Set B, $2 = 20$ and proceed vertically.
(e) At C, 2 $a_i < b_j$ $(100 < 150)$. Set C, $2 = 100$ and proceed horizontally.
(f) Finally set $C, 3 = 50$.

This procedure gives us our first solution to this allocation problem, but this solution is unlikely to be the optimal solution, and we must now try to improve upon it.

In an attempt to improve upon the solution we introduce the concept of *dispatch* and *receiving* costs. *The dispatch cost plus the receiving cost will equal the transportation cost for the route in question.*

To set the dispatch and receiving costs for mills and factories respectively, let us begin with steel mill A. If the dispatch cost here is 0 then the receiving cost for factory 1 must be 6, since the transportation cost for the route is 6.

Proceeding in an identical manner and using only the cells used in the first solution we can now determine both dispatch and receiving costs for all of the routes used by the first solution.

Dispatch cost   Receiving cost

		1 6	2 11	3 (15)	
A	(0)	60 6	8	4	60
B	-2	80 4	20 9	3	100
C	-9	1	100 2	50 6	150
		140	120	50	

FIGURE I.15

After setting the two costs for route A to 1 the receiving cost at 1 can be used to set the dispatch cost for B. This must be -2 so that the total cost for the route will equal 4. This cost can now be used to set the receiving cost at 2, by considering route B2 etc.

Now let us look at the routes which were *not* used by the first solution. The 'costs' for these routes are the sum of the appropriate dispatch and receiving costs, e.g. for route A2 cost is $0+11 = 11$. Now the difference between the *actual* cost for that route (i.e. 8) and the cost just calculated (i.e. 11) represents the saving which might be obtained by introducing this route into the solution.

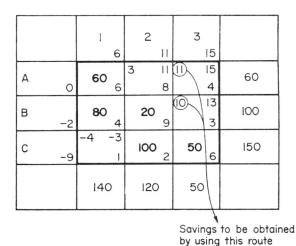

Savings to be obtained
by using this route

FIGURE I.16

In our case the maximum saving will result from the use of route A3, so let us try to introduce this route into the solution.

Let us imagine that the quantity θ is allocated to that route. The total quantity transported by the other routes must be reduced by θ in order to balance out the allocation. The problem then is merely *to place* $-\theta$ *and* $+\theta$ *on the routes in use, so that the* θ's *for both columns and rows cancel out, i.e.*

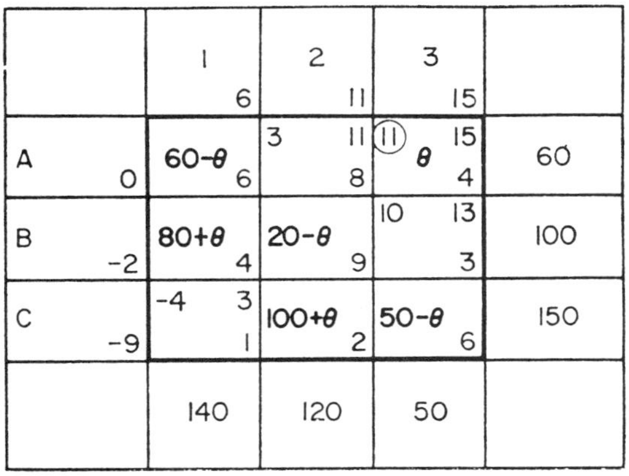

FIGURE I.17

From this tableau it can be seen that in practice the maximum value that θ can take is 20 since any quantity larger than this would result in the quantity for route B2 becoming negative, which is of course impossible. We will therefore replace θ by 20, its maximum value, to produce a new tableau which represents an improved solution.

	1 6	2 0	3 4	
A 0	40 6	-8 0 8	20 4	60
B -2	100 4	-11 -2 9	-1 2 3	100
C 2	⑦ 8 1	120 2	30 6	50
	140	120	50	

FIGURE I.18

Again we are not certain that it is the optimal solution, so we must once more attempt to improve upon it, by calculating dispatch and receiving costs, to determine if any of the other routes represent a cost saving. i.e. Route C1 would result in a cost saving of 7 we must therefore introduce this into the solution by allocating θ to that cell and then balancing out as before.

	1 6	2 0	3 4	
A 0	40-θ 6	-8 0 8	20+θ 4	60
B -2	100 4	-11 -2 9	-1 2 3	100
C 2	⑦ 8 θ 1	120 2	30-θ 6	150
	140	120	50	

FIGURE I.19

The maximum value for θ is 30, hence we can obtain a third solution. Again we can attempt to improve upon this solution, but since none of the figures in the unused cells is positive, no saving can be made, and an optimal allocation has been found, i.e.

		1		2		3		
			6		7		4	
A	0	10	6	-1	7 8	50	4	60
B	-2	100	4	-4	5 9	-1	2 3	100
C	-5	30	1	120	2	-7	-1 6	150
		140		120		50		

FIGURE I.20

The minimum total cost associatedwith this allocation is:

$$10\,(6) + 100\,(4) + 30\,(1) + 120\,(2) + 50\,(4) = 930$$

Complications

1. Maximizing

Often the objective is to maximize rather than minimize a function. In such cases basically the same procedure is adopted. The first solution is obtained using the North West Corner rule, but improvements are sought from routes not in use by selecting the cell with the largest *negative* value in the top left hand corner. For example, had we been minimizing in the previous case, an improvement to the first solution would be sought by introducing cell C1.

2. Unequal supply and demand

In the above example the output from the three steel mills was equal to the requirements of the three factories. However occasions may arise where such an equality does not arise, in which case a modified procedure is required.

(a) If total supply exceeds total demand an additional or 'dummy' column must be added to the matrix in order to accommodate this excess supply.

(b) If total demand exceeds total supply a 'dummy' row must be introduced in order to satisfy this excess demand.

In either case a solution is obtained in exactly the same manner as described previously, but in the case of (a) (supply in excess of demand) the allocations determined for the 'dummy' column (the imaginary consumer) represent the supply or production capacity not utilized, and in the case of (b) (demand in excess of supply), the allocations determined for the 'dummy' row represent the demands which are not satisfied.

3. Degeneracy

When, as in the above example, a transportation solution, either intermediate or final, utilizes at least $m+n-1$ routes or cells, it is possible to determine all 'dispatch' and 'receiving' costs, (where m = no. of rows and n = no. of columns). However, if less than this number of cells are in use it is impossible to determine these costs by the procedure outlined above. Such a situation is said to be *degenerate* and this type of problem requires a slightly different procedure, a description of which can be found in any of the books given in the references.

THE ASSIGNMENT ALGORITHM

The assignment problem is a special case of the transportation problem.[2] In terms of jobs and machines, the problem can be described as follows:

Given n jobs and n machines, and given the effectiveness of each machine for each job, the problem is to allocate each job to one machine so that a given measure of effectiveness is optimized.

In other words in the assignment problem we are concerned with the allocation of one item only from each source and the assignment of one item only to each location. The measure of effectiveness of each job for each machine can be represented as before by means of a matrix.

Jobs

		A	B	C	D	E
	1	10	5	9	18	11
	2	13	19	6	12	14
Machines	3	3	2	4	4	5
	4	18	9	12	17	15
	5	11	6	14	19	10

FIGURE I.21

For example the above matrix gives the cost associated with the manufacture of each of five jobs (A–E) on each of five machines (1–5). The problem therefore is to assign one job to each machine such that the measure of effectiveness (total cost) is optimized. The problem therefore is a *minimization* one.

The Minimization Problem

A solution to this type of problem can be obtained by means of the simple routine described below:
1. Take out the *minimum* figures from each row, i.e.

	A	B	C	D	E	*Minimums*
1	10	5	9	18	11	5
2	13	19	6	12	14	6
3	3	2	4	4	5	2
4	18	9	12	17	15	9
5	11	6	14	19	10	6

FIGURE I.22

---

[2] The assignment problem is the completely *degenerate* form of the transportation problem.

2. Deduct each minimum figure from the figures in that row, i.e.

	A	B	C	D	E
1	5	0	4	13	6
2	7	13	0	6	8
3	1	0	2	2	3
4	9	0	3	8	6
5	5	0	8	13	4

FIGURE I.23

3. Determine the least number of vertical and/or horizontal lines required to cover all zero's in the new matrix, i.e.

	A	B	C	D	E
1	5	0	4	13	6
2	7	13	0	6	8
3	1	0	2	2	3
4	9	0	3	8	6
5	5	0	8	13	4

$N=2$

FIGURE I.24

4. If the number of lines is less than the number of columns or rows proceed to next step, i.e.

since $N = 2 < 5$

5. Take out the minimum figures from each of the new columns, i.e.

	A	B	C	D	E
1	5	0	4	13	6
2	7	13	0	6	8
3	1	0	2	2	3
4	9	0	3	8	6
5	5	0	8	13	4
Minimums	1	0	0	2	3

FIGURE I.25

6. Deduct each minimum figure from the figures in that column, i.e.

	A	B	C	D	E
1	4	0	4	11	3
2	6	13	0	4	5
3	0	0	2	0	0
4	8	0	3	6	3
5	4	0	8	11	1

FIGURE I.26

7. Determine least number of vertical and/or horizontal lines required to cover all zeros in the new matrix, i.e.

	A	B	C	D	E
1	4	0	4	11	3
2	6	3	0	4	5
3	0	0	2	0	0
4	8	0	3	6	3
5	4	0	8	11	1

$N=3$

FIGURE I.27

8. If number of lines is less than number of columns or rows proceed to next step, i.e.

since $N = 3 < 5$

9. Identify *minimum uncovered element* in the new matrix, i.e.

Min $= 1$ (at 5; E)

10. (a) Subtract this number from all uncovered elements in the new matrix.
    (b) Add this number to those elements covered by two lines.
    (c) Do not change those elements covered by one line, i.e.

	A	B	C	D	E
1	3	0	3	10	2
2	6	4	0	4	5
3	0	1	2	0	0
4	7	0	2	5	2
5	3	0	7	10	0

FIGURE I.28

11. Determine least number of lines to cover all zeros, i.e.

	A	B	C	D	E
1	3	0	3	10	2
2	6	4	0	4	5
3	0	1	2	0	0
4	7	0	2	5	2
5	3	0	7	10	0

$N=4$

FIGURE I.29

12. If number of lines is less than number of columns or rows, repeat steps 9, 10 and 11 until number of lines is equal to number of columns or rows, i.e.
repeating step 9, Min = 3 (at 5; A); repeating steps 10 and 11 gives,

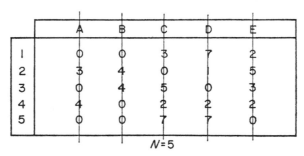

FIGURE I.30

13. The optimal assignment is obtained when the number of lines equals the number of columns or rows. The assignment of job to machine being given by the zeros in the matrix, i.e.

	A	B	C	D	E
1	⊡	0	3	7	2
2	3	4	⊡	1	5
3	0	4	5	⊡	3
4	4	⊡	2	2	2
5	0	0	7	7	⊡

FIGURE I.31

14. The cost associated with the optimal assignment may be calculated as follows:

Assignment	Cost (from initial matrix)
1–A	10
2–C	6
3–D	4
4–B	9
5–E	10
	Total = 39

The Maximization Problem

The procedure for maximizing is identical to that described for minimizing, except for:
Step 1. The maximum figures for each row are extracted.
Step 2. Each of the figures in each row are subtracted from their respective maximums, to produce the second matrix.
Hereafter the maximizing procedure follows that described above, i.e. the new matrix is modified by firstly substracting the minimum figure for each row from the figures in that row, etc.

SELECTED READINGS

An adequate treatment of the simplex and transportation and assignment methods of linear programming can be found in the following books:

W. W. THOMPSON Jr., *Operations Research Techniques*, Merrill, Ohio, 1967.

B. T. HOULDEN, (Ed.), *Some Techniques of Operations Research*, English Universities Press, London, 1969.

R. L. ACKOFF and M. W. SASIENI, *Fundamentals of Operations Research*, Wiley, London, 1968.

More advanced treatment of linear programming can be found in the following:

S. I. GASS, *Linear Programming: Methods and Applications*, McGraw-Hill, London, 1964.

G. B. DANTZIG, *Linear Programming and Extensions*, Princeton University Press, New Jersey, 1963.

QUESTIONS FOR APPENDIX I

AI.1. Given the following constraints, determine the values of x, y, and z which minimize W, where $W = x - 3y + 2z$

$$3x - y + 2z \leqslant 7$$
$$-2x + 4y \leqslant 12$$
$$-4x + 3y + 8z \leqslant 10$$

AI.2. A company is engaged in the manufacture of two types of dustbin—type X and type Y. The company is capable of making either 400 of type X or 800 of type Y per week, but because of a shortage in the supply of tin plate it is restricted to making at most 500 bins per week.

Each dustbin type X requires 4 rivets whilst each of type Y requires only half as many. There are only 500 rivets available each week. If the profit for each type X is £7 and for each type Y £5, how many of each type should be produced weekly if profit is to be maximized?

AI.3. A chemical company manufactures three types of fertilizer— *Grow*, *Quick Grow*, and *Rapid Grow*. Each fertilizer contains the same maximum number of three ingredients, i.e. potash, peat and lime, but in different proportions as shown below:

	Potash per cent	Peat per cent	Lime per cent
Grow	40	40	20
Quick Grow	60	20	20
Rapid Grow	80	0	20
	%	%	%

Each week up to 6 000 lbs of potash can be used in the manufacture of fertilizer. Up to 3 000 lbs of peat is available but there is no restriction on the lime that may be used.

The fertilizer is sold in 5 lb bags, the profit on each type being as follows:

Grow	1p
Quick Grow	1·5p
Rapid Grow	2p

How many bags of each type must be produced per week if profit is to be maximized, and the maximum total output per week is 10 000 lb.

AI.4. Solve the following minimization problem using the transportation algorithm.

		Customer A	B	C	D	E	Factory capacity
Factory	1	23	27	32	30	43	115
	2	15	15	20	16	35	65
	3	14	19	25	21	37	100
	4	35	44	47	45	60	35
Customer requirements		25	100	70	65	45	

FIGURE QI.4

AI.5. The cost shown in the cells of the matrix given below relate to the cost of transporting one product between one or three factories (A, B, C) and one of three warehourses (X, Y, Z). Warehouses X, Y and Z must receive a total of 25, 5, and 35 products respectively from the factories A, B and C which have capacities of 20, 15 and 30 products respectively.

Allocate the output of the factories to the warehouses in such a way that total transportation costs are minimized.

	X	Y	Z
A	£9	£8	£6
B	£3	£2	£5
C	£10	£7	£11

FIGURE QI.5

AI.6. A large garage wishes to pruchase four types of accessory in the following quantities:

Standard 25
De luxe 15
Super 10
Super de luxe 5

Quotations are received from three distributors who undertake to supply the garage with each of these accessories. The maximum quantities that the three distributors will supply are as follows:

A 30 of all types combined
B 30 of all types combined
C 15 of all types combined

From the quotations the Financial Manager of the garage calculates that the profit (£) on each accessory from each distributor is as follows:

	Standard	De luxe	Super	Super de luxe
A	10	11	12	15
B	9	12	15	15
C	5	7	13	20

FIGURE QI.6

The manager is confident that he can sell all accessories. How should he purchase them, i.e. how many of each type from which distributors?

AI.7. Each of five distributions depots is to supply one item to one customer. The costs involved in supplying cutomers are given in the matrix below. Find the 'assignment' of depot to customer which minimizes the total cost of supplying all fi•e customers.

		Customers				
		A	B	C	D	E
	1	2	5	4	3	7
	2	2	6	5	4	6
Depots	3	5	6	5	3	7
	4	3	4	7	2	4
	5	7	5	6	2	1

FIGURE QI.7

AI.8. A transport and general haulage company must send trucks to four cities in England. At the time in question there are six trucks vacant in different parts of the country. The matrix below indicates the costs associated with sending each of the available trucks to each of the four cities. If the company is to minimize the cost associated with redirecting these trucks, which two trucks will not be redirected, and where will the trucks presently at A and B be sent to?

		City			
		1	2	3	4
	A	3	8	2	6
	B	7	1	4	5
Present location of truck	C	3	8	5	8
	D	6	4	3	6
	E	5	2	5	3
	F	5	7	6	2

FIGURE QI.8

II Forecasting Techniques

FORECASTING BY PAST AVERAGE

If our objective is to forecast or predict the sales of an item for the next sales period, then using this method—

Forecasted sales for next period = Average sales for previous periods

Example

Period No	Sales
1	6
2	4
3	8
4	7
5	4
6	7

Forecast sales for period 7 = $(6+4+8+7+4+7) \div 6 = 6$

Using this technique we might obtain data as shown in Table II.1. Clearly our forecast for period 7 was very accurate, due to the fact that sales prior to this period had remained at much the same

TABLE II.1

Period No	Sales			Forecast Sales	Error in Forecast
1	6	8	8		
2	4	9	9	6	0
3	8	10	10	6	−2
4	7	11	12	6·25	−2·75
5	4	12	13	6·55	−3·45
6	7			6·9	−5·10
7	6			7·35	−5·65

average level. But when sales began to increase in later periods, the accuracy of our forecast reduced because it was influenced too much by the early sales figures and consequently was unable to rise quickly enough to keep up with actual sales.

FORECAST FROM LAST PERIOD'S SALES

One obvious method of overcoming this is to eliminate the influence of old data and base the forecast only upon the sales of the previous period. Had this technique been adopted our forecasts would have been as in Table II.2. Now our forecast is less accurate during the early period because of the fluctuating sales, whereas in the later period the forecast is more accurate because of the *steady* rising nature of sales.

TABLE II.2

Period No	Sales	Forecast Sales	Error in forecast
1	5		
2	4	5	+1
3	8	4	−4
4	7	8	+1
5	4	7	+3
6	7	4	−3
7	6	7	+1
8	8	6	−2
9	9	8	−1
10	10	9	−1
11	12	10	−2
12	13	12	−1

FORECASTING BY MOVING AVERAGE

This method represents a compromise between the two previous methods, in that the forecast is neither influenced by very old data, nor does it solely reflect the figure for the previous period.

Consider the historical sales figures shown in Table II.3, which are to be used to construct a sales forecast for the next year. We must use a four period moving average in this case, because it is clear from the graph Fig II.1. that sales fluctuate on an approximate four period cycle.

Seasonal variations

The moving average forecast sales for the example in Table II.3 are compared to actual sales in Fig. II.1. Clearly the effect of the moving average is to smooth the sales pattern, and it is therefore of more value in establishing trends. In this case, in order to make a useful forecast of sales, the seasonal variations must be taken into account. For example, for the four periods of 1964 the average sales were:

$$\frac{50+60+50+40}{4} = 50$$

TABLE II.3

Year	Period	Sales	Four period moving average forecast
1964	1	50	
	2	60	
	3	50	
	4	40	
1965	1	50	50
	2	55	50
	3	40	48·75
	4	30	46·25
1966	1	35	43·75
	2	45	40
	3	35	37·5
	4	25	36·25
1967	1	35	35
	2	45	35
	3	35	35
	4	30	36·25

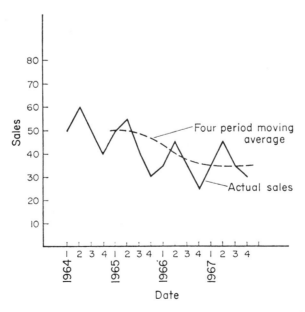

FIGURE II.1. Comparison of moving average forecast sales (Table II.3) with actual sales

The sales during periods 1 and 3 conformed to the average figure, but the sales during period 2 were high (20 per cent high) whilst those during period 4 were low (only 80 per cent of the mean for the year).

The percentage variation from the annual mean, can be calculated for each period, as shown in Table II.4.

TABLE II.4 Percentage variations calculated from annual means

	(Values in brackets indicate the mean for the year)				Average variation percentage
Period	1964 (50)	1965 (43·75)	1966 (35)	1967 (36·25)	
1	100	114·2	100	96·6	102·7
2	120	125·7	128·5	124·0	124·6
3	100	91·5	100	96·6	97·0
4	80	68·7	71·4	82·8	75·7

The average percentage variation from the mean for each period can now be used to modify the moving average forecast sales. For example the forecast for 1968 period 1 would be 36·25 (moving average) × 102·7 per cent (average percentage variation) = 37·23. Of course this method of obtaining the average percentage variation can only be justified if, as in this example, the annual figures for each period do not differ substantially.

Secular Trends

A secular trend is one which causes sales to steadily increase or decrease. The use of simple moving averages is an adequate method of forecasting, providing sales are neither subject to seasonal variation (as we have seen in Table II.4) or marked secular trends.

Consider, for example, the sales figures in Table II.5, for which a five period moving average has been calculated—(column (b)). Both actual sales and moving average forecast sales are plotted in Fig. II.2—curves (a) and (b) respectively—from which it can be seen that the forecast curve lags behind the actual curve. In fact the extent of the time-lag is given by:

$$L = \frac{\text{Time span, or number of periods of moving average} - 1}{2}$$

But since the moving average is used as the forecast for the *next* period, the time lag is increased by 1 period, i.e.

$$\text{Actual time-lag} = \left(\frac{\text{Time span} - 1}{2}\right) + 1$$

In this case the time lag of the forecast is 3 periods. In order to overcome this disadvantage it is necessary to apply a *trend correction* to the moving average forecast. The difference between pairs of moving averages is a measure of the secular trend over one period (assuming that there is no seasonal variation in the data,) hence the correction factor should equal this figure multiplied by the time-lag, which in this case is 3 periods. The corrected forecast is given in column (d) of Table II.5.

Curve (c) in Fig. II.2, shows how the corrected sales 'catch up' with actual sales after a brief lag period, then settle down to the new constant level, after a brief overshoot period.

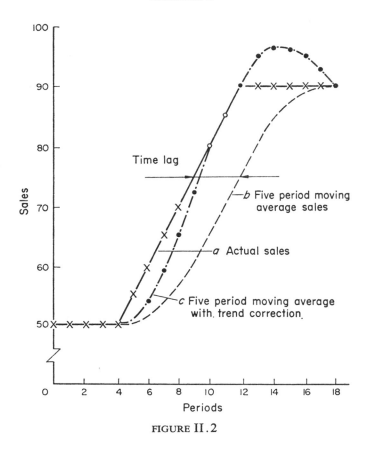

FIGURE II.2

FORECASTING BY EXPONENTIAL SMOOTHING

The main disadvantages of the moving average method are:

1. The lengthy calculations involved.
2. The need to keep quantities of historical data.
3. The fact that the normal moving average method places equal weight on each of the historical figures used (equal weight on five figures in the above case.)
4. The age of the data which increases with the number of periods used.

All of these disadvantages are overcome by the exponential smoothing technique. Using this technique it is only necessary to retain the previous forecast figure and to know the latest actual sales figure. The technique works by modifying the old forecast in the light of the new sales figure, i.e.

$$\text{New forecast} = \alpha \text{ (latest sales figure)} + (1 - \alpha) \text{ (old forecast)}$$

where α is known as the smoothing constant.

TABLE II.5

Period No	(a) Actual sales	(b) 5 period moving average	(c) Trend between successive moving averages	(d) Forecast MA + 3 (trend)
0	50			
1	50			
2	50			
3	50			
4	50			
5	55	50		
6	60	51	+ 1	54
7	65	53	+ 2	59
8	70	56	+ 3	65
9	75	60	+ 4	72
10	80	65	+ 5	80
11	85	70	+ 5	85
12	90	75	+ 5	90
13	90	80	+ 5	95
14	90	84	+ 4	96
15	90	87	+ 3	96
16	90	89	+ 2	95
17	90	90	+ 1	93
		90	0	90

Example

$$\text{Forecast sales for last period} = 22$$
$$\text{Actual sales for last period} = 20$$
$$\therefore \text{Forecast sales for next period} = \alpha(20) + (1 - \alpha)\,22$$
$$\text{let smoothing constant } \alpha = 0\cdot1$$
$$\therefore \text{Forecast sales for next period} = 0\cdot1\,(20) + (0\cdot9)\,22$$
$$= 2 + 19\cdot8$$
$$= 21\cdot8$$

The use of this technique permits the forecast to respond to recent actual events, but at the same time retain a certain amount of stability. The amount by which the new forecast responds to the latest sales figure, or the extent to which it is 'damped' by the previous forecast, is, of course, determined by the size of the smoothing constant α. The size of α should be carefully chosen in the light of the stability or variability of actual sales, and is normally from $0\cdot1$ to $0\cdot3$.

The smoothing constant (α) that gives the equivalent of an N period moving average can be calculated as follows:

$$\alpha = \frac{2}{N+1}$$

For example if we wish to adopt an exponential smoothing technique equivalent to a nine period moving average, α can be found as follows:

$$\alpha = \frac{2}{9+1} = 0\cdot2$$

R

Example

TABLE II.6

Week No	Sales	4 period moving average forecast	Error	Exponential smoothing forecast ($\alpha = 0.2$)	Error
1	10				
2	12				
3	8				
4	9				
5	10	9·75	0·25	9·8	4·20
6	14	9·75	4·25	10·63	4·37
7	15	10·25	4·75	11·50	2·50
8	14	12·00	2·00	12·00	2·00
9	10	13·25	3·25	11·60	3·60
10	8	13·25	5·25	10·90	4·90
11	6	11·75	5·75	9·92	0·08
12	10	9·50	0·50	9·94	2·06
13	12	8·50	3·50	10·36	2·36
14	8	9·00	1·00	9·90	5·10
15	15	9·00	4·00	10·92	
		11·25			

Average error in forecast = 3·14   Average error in forecast = 3·12

Secular Trends and Seasonal Variations

When a secular trend is present, the forecast sales obtained by the normal exponential smoothing method will lag behind actual sales, in just the same way as did the moving average forecast. As before, if we are able to estimate the magnitude of the trend in the data, we can apply a trend correction to the forecast, to overcome the time-lag.

Let us again estimate the trend by comparing successive pairs of forecast figures. In the example in Table II.7. any overall secular trend in the data is obscured by seasonal variations, consequently

TABLE II.7

Period	Sales	Exponential smoothing forecast	Trend in actual sales
7	15	11·08	
8	14	12·26	−1
9	10	12·78	−4
10	8	11·95	−2
11	6	10·77	−2
12	10	9·34	+4
13	12	9·54	+2
14	8	10·28	−4
15	15	9·60	+7

in such cases, rather than just taking the difference between successive sales figures as an indication of trends, we must use an estimating procedure. In fact we can use the exponential smoothing method to estimate future trend, i.e.

Forecast trend over next period $= \alpha$ (latest trend figure) $+ (1 - \alpha)$ (old trend forecast)

The forecast trend can then be used as a correction factor by adding it to the exponential smoothing forecast, in just the same way as the trend correction was added to the moving average forecast in the previous section. Hence:

Final forecast of sales = Normal exponential smoothing forecast
+ [(Time-lag) × exponential smoothing forecast of trend]

THE USE OF THE CUMULATIVE SUM TECHNIQUE

The cumulative sum method of examining data, is of comparatively recent origin. It is conceptually extremely simple and has found widespread application particularly in quality control and in forecasting. The cumulative sum chart is simply a plot of the cumulative total of a series of data, or a plot of the cumulative difference between each of the individual readings and a given constant quantity.

For example, consider the monthly sales figures shown in Fig. II.3(a). From this figure it appears that sales over the 27 periods have fluctuated about a mean of 11. If, therefore, we consider 11 to be the mean or target value for this data, and subtract this amount from each of the months sales, plotting the difference cumulatively, the CUSUM chart shown in Fig. II.3(b) is obtained.

Notice that whilst the average value of the data is near to the target value, some of the difference between actual and target value will be positive, and some negative, hence the cumulative sum (CUSUM) chart will be more or less horizontal, but if the average value of the data rises then more of the differences between actual and target values will be positive and the CUSUM graph will rise. Referring to the data in Fig. II.3(a) and (b), whilst a change in the average sales is barely perceptible in Fig. II.3(a), it is very noticeable in the CUSUM chart, which rises markedly from about period 15. Had the average sales fallen, then this would have been reflected in a noticeable negative (downward) slope of the CUSUM graph.

The great advantage of the CUSUM chart therefore, is its ability to reveal clearly changes in the average level of data. The chart is interpreted solely on a basis of its slope, a horizontal graph indicating stability in the data, a positive slope indicating an increase in the data average, and a negative slope a decrease in the data average.

Target or Reference value and Scale Sizes

If the target value chosen is less than the average value of the data, the CUSUM graph will rise steadily, and vice versa. Should this happen, then the chart can be restarted at zero, this time adopting a higher target value. Similarly it is of value to restart at zero, charts which have previously risen because of a change in the average value of the data. Unless this is done any subsequent change in average value may be less evident from the chart.

The choice of both the horizontal and vertical scale of the CUSUM chart is important since the scale factors will influence the slope of the graph and hence its ability to show up changes in

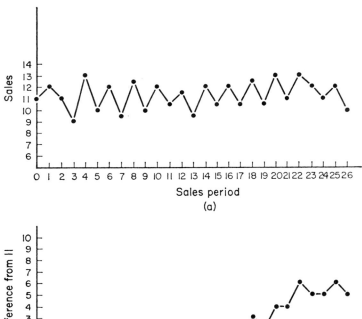

FIGURE II.3.

mean values. It has been suggested[1] that, considering the distance between successive readings on the x axis as 1 point, a similar distance on the y axis should equal 2σ units, where σ is the standard deviation about the mean of the data in the short term. This scale factor enables significant variations in the data means to be detected whilst random variations appear quite small.

Using Cumulative Sum Charts

Cumulative sum charts are not appropriate for use against data which exhibit a steady trend, or data which exhibit a marked seasonal variation. Their main value, as has already been illustrated, is in determining the nature and extent of changes in mean values. The use of CUSUM charts, therefore, centres around a study of slopes, and in particular the decision whether or not changes in slope are significant.

---

[1] R. H. Woodward and P. L. Goldsmith ICI Monograph No. 3, *Cumulative Sum Techniques*, Oliver and Boyd, Edinburgh, 1964.

There are basically two methods for examining the slope of CUSUM charts in search of significant changes, i.e.

1. *The Decision Interval Methods.* This method can be usefully adopted where the problem is one of studying either increases or decreases in slope, but not both. A significant increase in slope, necessitating corrective action is considered to have occurred if the latest point on the chart is more than a given amount (*h*) above (or below) the highest (or lowest) point which has occurred on the chart since the last decision. The amount *h* is termed the decision interval (Fig. II.4). This method is therefore analogous to the use of control limits in quality control.

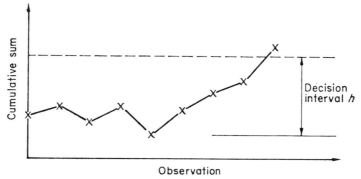

FIGURE II.4. The decision interval method

2. *The Masking Method.* This method is useful where the problem is one of examining simultaneously increases and decreases in slope. A 'V' shaped mask is made and superimposed on the CUSUM chart in such a way that if any of the points on the chart lie beyond the limits of the 'V' then it is considered that a significant change in slope has occurred. (Fig. II.5).

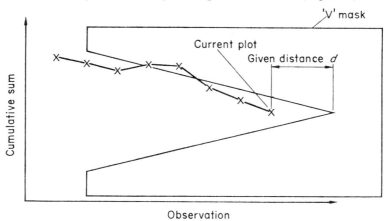

FIGURE II.5. Reduction in process mean

Methods of calculating decision internals and constructing masks are given in two of the references listed at the end of this Appendix.

The cumulative sum technique is of considerable value in both quality control and forecasting. It is invaluable as a means of detecting errors in forecasts, assessing the influence of price changes on demand and so on.

R§

ASSOCIATIVE PREDICTIONS OR ECONOMIC INDICATORS

Calculation of Correlation Coefficients

A correlation coefficient is a measure of the extent to which two variables are associated. In other words a correlation coefficient is an indication of the extent to which the knowledge of the value of one variable is useful for the prediction of the value of the other. This is the basis of a method of forecasting variously known as *associative predictions* or *economic indicators*.

For example, we may find that the sales of the product that we are making are correlated to average rainfall, then knowing the average rainfall we may be able to forecast future sales. The strength or closeness of the correlation of variables is measured by the correlation coefficient, which varies between $-1 \cdot 0$ and $+1 \cdot 0$.

Perhaps the most useful coefficient is the *Pearson Product Moment Correlation Coefficient* which is calculated as follows:

$$\text{Coefficient, } r \text{ for two variables X and Y} = \frac{\Sigma(x-\bar{x})(y-\bar{y})}{\sqrt{\Sigma(x-\bar{x})^2 \ \Sigma(y-\bar{y})^2}}$$

where $\bar{x}$ is the mean value of all the individual x values
      $\bar{y}$ is the mean value of all the individual y values.
This formula measures linear correlation, i.e.

Example 1

Observation of two variables x and y yield the following data. Calculate the linear correlation coefficient of X and Y.

$$x \ 1, \ 3, \ 5, \ 7, \ 11 \quad y \ 2, \ 4, \ 8, \ 9, \ 10$$

x	$(x-\bar{x})$	$(x-\bar{x})^2$	y	$(y-\bar{y})$	$(y-\bar{y})^2$	$(x-\bar{x})(y-\bar{y})$
1	$-4\cdot4$	$19\cdot5$	2	$-4\cdot6$	$19\cdot5$	$20\cdot0$
3	$-2\cdot4$	$5\cdot8$	4	$-2\cdot6$	$6\cdot9$	$6\cdot25$
5	$-0\cdot4$	$1\cdot6$	8	$+1\cdot4$	$1\cdot95$	$0\cdot56$
7	$+1\cdot6$	$2\cdot6$	9	$+2\cdot4$	$5\cdot8$	$3\cdot85$
11	$+5\cdot6$	$31\cdot5$	10	$+3\cdot4$	$11\cdot5$	$19\cdot6$
$\Sigma x = 27$		$61\cdot0$	$\Sigma y = 33$		$45\cdot45$	$50\cdot26$

$$\bar{x} = \frac{27}{5} \qquad \bar{y} = \frac{33}{5}$$

$$= 5\cdot4 \qquad \qquad = 6\cdot6$$

$$r = \frac{\Sigma(x-\bar{x})(y-\bar{y})}{\sqrt{\Sigma(x-\bar{x})^2 \ \Sigma(y-\bar{y})^2}}$$

$$= \frac{50\cdot26}{\sqrt{61\cdot0 \times 45\cdot5}} = 0\cdot96$$

Example 2

A comparison of the monthly sales of an expensive item, against the total number of visits made by salesmen during the previous month, yields the data shown in the table below. Is the correlation of the two variables good enough to enable the number of trade enquiries, to be adopted as an efficient indicator of future sales?

Month	Sales	Visits made					
	(x)	(y)	$(x-\bar{x})$	$(x-\bar{x})^2$	$(y-\bar{y})$	$(y-\bar{y})^2$	$(x-\bar{x})(y-\bar{y})$
1	11	605	$-1\cdot46$	$2\cdot132$	$-52\cdot5$	$2756\cdot2$	$76\cdot7$
2	13	640	$+0\cdot54$	$0\cdot292$	$-17\cdot5$	$306\cdot25$	$-9\cdot45$
3	12	625	$-0\cdot46$	$0\cdot212$	$-32\cdot5$	$1056\cdot5$	$14\cdot95$
4	12	630	$-0\cdot46$	$0\cdot212$	$-27\cdot5$	$756\cdot25$	$12\cdot75$
5	10	630	$-2\cdot46$	$6\cdot05$	$-27\cdot5$	$756\cdot25$	$67\cdot7$
6	12	645	$-0\cdot46$	$0\cdot212$	$-12\cdot5$	$156\cdot25$	$5\cdot75$
7	13	655	$+0\cdot54$	$0\cdot292$	$-2\cdot5$	$6\cdot25$	$-1\cdot35$
8	14	680	$+1\cdot54$	$2\cdot37$	$+22\cdot5$	$506\cdot25$	$34\cdot6$
9	12	660	$-0\cdot46$	$0\cdot212$	$+2\cdot5$	$6\cdot25$	$-1\cdot15$
10	14	680	$+1\cdot54$	$2\cdot37$	$+22\cdot5$	$506\cdot25$	$34\cdot6$
11	11	675	$+1\cdot46$	$2\cdot132$	$+17\cdot5$	$306\cdot25$	$-25\cdot5$
12	11	670	$-1\cdot46$	$2\cdot132$	$+12\cdot5$	$156\cdot25$	$-18\cdot25$
13	13	670	$+0\cdot54$	$0\cdot292$	$+12\cdot5$	$156\cdot25$	$6\cdot75$
14	14	690	$+1\cdot54$	$2\cdot37$	$+32\cdot5$	$1056\cdot5$	$50\cdot00$
15	15	710	$+2\cdot54$	$6\cdot45$	$+52\cdot5$	$2756\cdot3$	$133\cdot00$
	$\Sigma x = 187$	$\Sigma y = 9865$		$27\cdot730$		$11244\cdot35$	$380\cdot9$

$$r = \frac{380\cdot9}{\sqrt{(27\cdot73)(11\,244\cdot35)}} = 0\cdot681$$

The correlation between the number of salesmen's visits during the previous month, and the number of sales is $0\cdot681$, which is perhaps insufficient to justify its possible use as a method of short term sales forecasting.

Linear Regression[2]

We have seen that a linear relationship between two variables X and Y is indicated by a high value of the correlation coefficient. However this coefficient does not indicate the true relationship, hence we are unable to estimate either a value of X for a given value of Y or vice versa. To do this regression equation must be calculated, as in Fig. II.6.

The regression line for Y on X is the best line for calculating values of Y, and is obtained by minimizing the sum of the squares of the errors of estimation, i.e. the y values in Fig. II.6(a).

---

[2] We shall deal exclusively with linear regression equations, whereas in fact our data may be of a curvilinear form. A similar procedure, to the one described here may be used to derive formulas for calculating non-linear regression equations. Furthermore we shall be concerned only with the regression of two variables whereas in practice two or more variables may be involved. In such cases a similar, if somewhat lengthier, procedure to that described here can be adopted. Description of multiple and non-linear regression can be found in the last of the books mentioned in the following references.

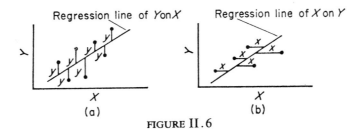

FIGURE II.6

The regression line for X on Y is the best line for calculating values of X, and is obtained by minimizing the sum of the squares of the errors of estimation, i.e. the x values in Fig. II.6(b). The general equation for the regression line of Y on X is given by:

$$Y = a + bX$$

where a and b are two constants. The values of these two constants are obtained by the following formula:

$$b = \frac{n\Sigma xy - (\Sigma x)(\Sigma y)}{n(\Sigma x^2) - (\Sigma x)^2}$$

$$a = \frac{\Sigma y + b\Sigma x}{n}$$

Similarly the general equation for the linear regression of X on Y is:

$$X = a + bY$$

where

$$b = \frac{n\Sigma xy - (\Sigma x)(\Sigma y)}{n(\Sigma y^2) - (\Sigma y)^2}$$

$$a = \frac{\Sigma x - b\Sigma y}{n}$$

Example 1

Given the following data find the regression line for predicting 'growth', and calculate the growth for a weight value of 52.

Let growth be variable Y

Let weight be variable X

Weight (x)	Growth (y)	x^2	xy
12	5·5	144	66
18	5·9	324	106·2
24	6·5	576	156
30	7·4	900	222
36	8·2	1296	295·2
42	8·9	1764	373·8
48	8·6	2306	412·8
$\Sigma x = 210$	$\Sigma y = 51$	$\Sigma x^2 = 7310$	$\Sigma xy = 1632$

$$b = \frac{7(1632) - (210)\,(51)}{7(7310) - (210)^2}$$

$$= \frac{714}{7,070}$$

$$= 0 \cdot 105$$

$$a = \frac{(51) - 0 \cdot 105\,(210)}{7}$$

$$= \frac{28 \cdot 95}{7}$$

$$= 4 \cdot 13$$

$$x = 52$$

$$\therefore y = 4 \cdot 13 + 0 \cdot 105\,(52)$$

$$= 4 \cdot 13 + 5 \cdot 460$$

$$y = 9 \cdot 59$$

The regression line provides only an estimate of the value of Y or X. The uncertainty or accuracy of the estimate can be assessed by calculating the 'standard error' of the estimate of Y on X ($S_{Y.X}$)

$$S_{Y.X} = \sqrt{\frac{\Sigma\,(y - y^1)^2}{n - 2}}$$

where y = actual value.

y^1 = value calculated from regression equation.

The standard error of the estimate, of X on Y is given similarly by:

$$S_{X.Y} = \sqrt{\frac{\Sigma\,(x - x^1)^2}{n - 2}}$$

For example in the above case:

y	y^1	$= 4 \cdot 13 + 0 \cdot 105(x)$	$(y - y^1)$	$(y - y^1)^2$
5·5	5·39		0·11	0·012
5·9	6·02		−0·12	0·014
6·5	6·65		−0·15	0·023
7·4	7·28		0·12	0·014
8·2	7·90		0·30	0·090
8·9	8·54		0·36	0·130
8·6	9·16		0·44	0·210
			$\Sigma(y - y^1)^2 =$	0·493

$$S_{Y.X} = \sqrt{\frac{0 \cdot 493}{5}}$$

$$S_{Y.X} = 0 \cdot 313$$

$S_{Y.X}$ or $S_{X.Y}$ provides a measure of the 'closeness' of the relationship between the two variables. The smaller the figure, the closer the values to the regression line and hence the more accurate the regression equation for predictive purposes.

SELECTED READINGS

The following books deal, amongst other things, with moving averages, and exponential smoothing:

R. G. BROWN, *Statistical Forecasting for Inventory Control*, McGraw-Hill, Maidenhead, 1959.

An adequate coverage of the method of moving averages is given in:

A. BATTERSBY, *Sales Forecasting*, Cassell, London, 1968.

The cumulative sum technique is described in:

R. H. WOODWARD and P. L. GOLDSMITH, *Cumulative Sum Techniques* (I.C.I. Monograph No. 3), Oliver and Boyd, Edinburgh, 1964.

W. D. EWEN, 'How and when to use CUSUM charts', *Technometrics*, **5**, 1–22 (1963).

The following book describes the use of the cumulative sum technique in quality control:

S. R. GEDYE, *Scientific Method in Production Management*, Oxford University Press, London, 1965.

Correlation methods and regression analysis are explained in the majority of textbooks on statistics and statistical methods. The following are amongst the best for our purpose:

M. J. MORONEY, *Facts from Figures*, Penguin, Harmondsworth, Middx., 1964.

B. C. BROOKES and W. F. L. DICK, *Introduction to Statistical Method*, Heinemann, London, 1951.

The following book contains a good description of multiple and non-linear regression, neither of which were discussed in this Appendix:

R. FERBER, *Statistical Techniques in Market Research*, McGraw-Hill, Maidenhead, 1949.

QUESTIONS FOR APPENDIX II

AII.1. The table below gives the monthly sales of a particular product over a 20 month period. Use (a) forecasting by previous average and (b) forecasting from last periods sales, to forecast sales for period 4 onwards. Compare the accuracy of the two forecasts and comment on the practical implications of adopting these two simple methods of forecasting.

Period	Sales
1	20
2	18
3	17
4	21
5	22
6	21
7	20
8	18
9	19
10	21
11	24
12	28
13	34
14	36
15	35
16	30
17	28
18	26
19	30
20	31

AII.2. Plot the four years' sales figures shown in the table below, along with the appropriate moving average sales figure.

Year	Sales	Year	Sales
1966	250	1968	260
	275		295
	300		320
	230		245
1967	260	1969	245
	280		290
	300		315
	240		230

How does the moving average sales graph compare with the actual sales, and what refinements are necessary before the moving average method can be used as an accurate technique for forecasting sales of this type?

AII.3. Calculate the seasonally adjusted four-period moving average sales for the data given below:

Year	Period	Sales ('000)	Year	Period	Sales ('000)
1966	1	50	1968	1	54
	2	60		2	70
	3	50		3	56
	4	44		4	50
1967	1	50	1969	1	54
	2	64		2	60
	3	56		3	52
	4	50		4	50

AII.4. Use the moving average technique with secular trend correction and seasonal adjustment to forecast quarterly sales of product X. The actual sales of product X over a five-year period are shown below. Calculate the forecasted sales over as much of this period as possible, and compare the forecasted sales with the actual.

Year	Quarter	Actual sales ('000)	Year	Quarter	Actual sales ('000)
1965	S	20		A	40
	S	15		W	35
	A	30	1968	S	30
	W	25		S	25
1966	S	20		A	45
	S	20		W	35
	A	35	1969	S	30
	W	30		S	25
1967	S	25		A	50
	S	20		W	40

AII.5. The figures below show the actual sales of product Y which have occurred on each of 20 successive periods. Calculate the appropriate simple moving average sales (without seasonal

Period No	Actual sales	Period No	Actual sales
1	10	11	10
2	12	12	13
3	12	13	14
4	10	14	12
5	8	15	9
6	10	16	10
7	13	17	13
8	12	18	14
9	9	19	11
10	8	20	10

adjustment) for as much of this period as possible, and compare the difference between actual and moving average with the difference between actual and an exponentially smoothed demand equivalent to the moving average. Comment on the nature of your results.

AII.6. Historical data for product Z indicates that there are both seasonal variations and a continuously increasing trend in sales. How can the simple exponential smoothing technique be modified to provide acceptable forecasts in such a situation?

Illustrate your answer by means of simple numerical examples of your own construction.

AII.7. (a) Use the cumulative sum technique to examine the following sales data for any changes in average monthly sales.

Year	1967	1968	1969
Month 1	10	10	9
2	11	9	12
3	10	10	11
4	12	11	13
5	8	10	12
6	10	12	11
7	12	13	10
8	9	12	11
9	12	10	10
10	7	9	9
11	9	11	10
12	10	12	11

(b) Comment on the value of this technique. How is its value affected by the choice of (a) the reference value and (b) the scale factor?

AII.8. Explain the meaning of (a) the decision interval and (b) the 'masking' method in the context of the cumulative sum technique.

AII.9. Calculate the Pearson Product Moment Correlation Coefficient:

(a) of variables X and Y   (b) of a setting x and a reading y

X	Y
15	0
16	2
17	4
18	6
19	8
20	10
21	12
22	14
23	16
24	18

x	y
1	5
2	6
3	—
4	12
5	11
6	13
7	16
8	16
9	—
10	19
11	23
12	22

AII.10. Calculate the linear regression of Y on X and using the equation calculate Y for the following values of X.
(a) 137 (b) 95.

Y	X
2	20
5	45
4	30
3	30
5	45
6	65

Y	X
7	65
6	60
8	70
9	85
10	105
12	115
13	120

AII.11. (a) Calculate the linear regression line for determining consumption from Gross National Product.

GNP (£)	Consumption
20 200	13 900
20 800	14 500
21 200	14 600
21 600	14 900
21 700	15 300
22 500	16 000
23 600	16 600
24 400	17 000
24 600	17 300
25 500	18 000

(b) It is estimated that the GNP three years hence will equal £30 000. What is consumption likely to be three years hence?

III Answers to Odd Numbered Analytical Questions

Chapter 2

2.5. (a)

Part no.	Opitz code
10/233	02500
12/2149	02600
12/528	03630
12/1954	03204
12/2380	15235
12/2372	15235

[These examples are reproduced by permission, E. A. Howarth, Group technology—using the Opitz system, *Production Eng.*, **47** No. 1, (1968).]

Chapter 3

3.3. About 60 miles north east of Birmingham.

3.5. Sunderland.

3.7 Additional factory should be established at location D.

Total cost for ABD = £16 990/month

Total cost for ABC = £17 240/month (assuming cost of excess capacity is zero).

3.9. (a) Rent D

(b) Store at B

Chapter 4

4.1.

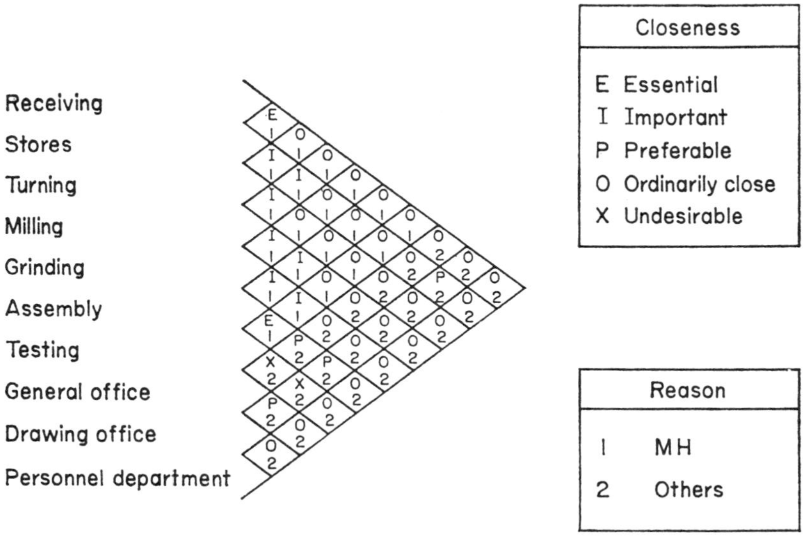

Receiving

Stores

Turning

Milling

Grinding

Assembly

Testing

General office

Drawing office

Personnel department

Closeness	
E	Essential
I	Important
P	Preferable
O	Ordinarily close
X	Undesirable

Reason	
1	M H
2	Others

4.3.

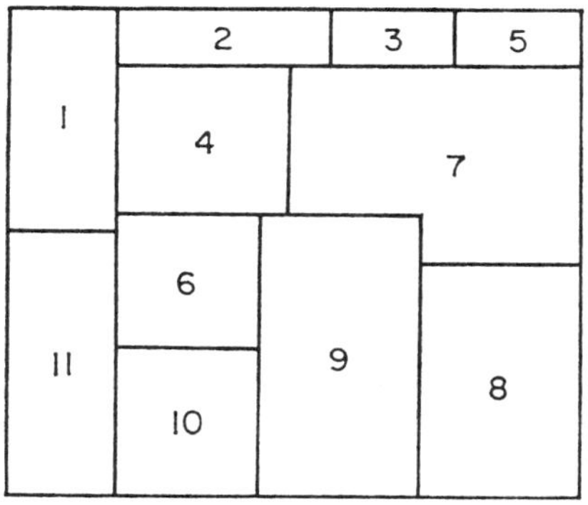

[This example is based on the example used by *Buffa* in 'Sequence analysis for functional layouts', *J. Ind. Eng.*, March/April, 12–25 (1955).]

4.7.

L value for point no.	Assumptions (a)	Assumptions (b)
1	40	31·2
2	35	40
3	40	35
4	45	43·1
5	35	32·4

Chapter 5

5.3.

(a)

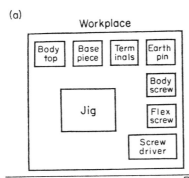

Workplace

Body top	Base piece	Term inals	Earth pin

Body screw

Flex screw

Screw driver

Jig

(b)

Left hand		Right hand	
Reach for base piece	⇨	Reach for earth pin	⇨
Grasp base	O	Grasp /orient in fingers	O
Carry to jig	⇨	Carry to jig /orient in fingers	⇨
Place in jig	O	Position in base	O
Reach to terminal	⇨	Reach to terminal	⇨
Grasp /orient	O	Grasp /orient	O
Carry to base	⇨	Carry to jig /orient	⇨
Place in base	O	Place in base	O
Reach to body top	⇨	Delay	D
Grasp	O	Delay	D
Carry to jig	⇨	Delay	D
Place in jig	O	Reach to body screw	⇨
Grasp assembly	O	Grasp /orient	O
Remove from jig	O	Carry to assembly /orient	⇨
Place inverted on bench	O	Place screw in hole	O
Hold	O	Reach to two screws	⇨
I		Grasp	O
I		Carry /orient	⇨
I		Place one screw in hole	O
I		Place second screw in hole	O
I		Reach for screw driver	⇨
I		Grasp	O
I		Carry to assembly	O
I	O	Tighten body screw	O
I	O	Tighten one flex screw	O
Grasp plug	O	Tighten second flex screw	O
Carry to bin	⇨	Return screw driver	⇨
Release	O	Release screw driver	O

5.5.

Left hand	Therblig	Therblig	Right hand
Reach for bolt	TE	TE	Reach for nut
Select and grasp a bolt head	S,G	S,G	Select and grasp nut
Carry bolt to central position	TL	TL	Carry to central position
Position bolt	P	P	Position nut
Hold head	H	A	Assemble nut onto bolt
Release assembly	RL	G	Grasp assembly
Idle		TL	Carry assembly to box
Idle		RL	Release assembly into box

Chapter 6

6.1. $N^1 = 9$ therefore sufficient observations have been made.

6.3. (a) 2 262 pieces
(b) 253 p.

6.5. Output per shift at standard performance = 200

Production cost per piece = 9 p.

6.7. 10·2 SM

6.9. (a) 1 350 p.
(b) 1 800 p.
(c) 1 215 p.
(d) 1 440 p.

Piece-rate = 27·0 p.

6.11.

Worker 1 E1 1 BM = 0·09 ⎫ 0·23/item
       E1 2 BM = 0·14 ⎭
Worker 2 E1 3 BM = 0·15 ⎫ 0·20/item
       E1 4 BM = 0·05 ⎭
Worker 3 E1 5 BM = 0·20 ⎬ 0·20/item

(This question is based on an example given in chapter 6 of C. F. GRAHAM *Work Measurement and Cost Control*, Pergamon, Oxford, 1965. This excellent little book gives a good description of the uses of Rated Systematic Sampling.)

Chapter 8

8.1. The production plan is given by the following matrix

Week no.		26	27	28	29
26	Stock	31	4		
27	⎰ Normal shift		35		
	⎱ Night shift		4	11	
28	⎰ Normal Shift			35	
	⎱ Night Shift			9	6
29	⎰ Normal Shift				33
	⎱ Night Shift				

Total cost associated with this plan = £1 743

8.3. The production plan is shown below, assuming production during one month may be used to satisfy demand in the same month.

			May A units	May B units	June A units	June B units
May	Factory 1	Normal	100	50		
		Overtime		20		
	Factory 2	Normal		80	90	
		Overtime			20	20
June	Factory 1	Normal				100
		Overtime				5
	Factory 2	Normal				65
		Overtime				

Total Cost = 2 770 mu (assuming excess capacity has zero cost)

8.5.

Month	Shift	May I II III	June I II III	July I II III	August I II III	Stock I II III	Available capacity (man hours)
May	1	5 6 4	5·5 6·6 4·5	6·0 7·2 5·0	6·5 7·8 5·5	7·0 8·6 6·0	150
	2	7 8 6	7·5 8·6 6·5	8·0 9·2 7·0	8·5 9·8 7·5	9·0 10·6 8·0	200
	3	7 8 6	7·5 8·6 6·5	8·0 9·2 7·0	8·5 9·8 7·5	9·0 10·6 8·0	200
June	1		5 6 4	5·5 6·6 4·5	6·0 7·2 5·0	6·5 7·8 5·5	200
	2		7 8 6	7·5 8·6 6·5	8·0 9·2 7·0	8·5 9·8 7·5	300
	3		7 8 6	7·5 8·6 6·5	8·0 9·2 7·0	8·5 9·8 7·5	350
July	1			5 6 4	5·5 6·6 4·5	6·0 7·2 5·0	250
	2			7 8 6	7·5 8·6 6·5	8·0 9·2 7·0	300
	3			7 8 6	7·5 8·6 6·5	8·0 9·2 7·0	300
August	1				6 7 5	6·5 7·6 5·5	300
	2				8 9 7	8·5 9·6 7·5	350
	3				8 9 7	8·5 9·6 7·5	350
Total demand numbers		20 50 30	40 65 25	25 75 50	40 72 32		3 250
man hours		100 350 150	200 455 125	125 525 250	200 504 106	3 633	

Since total demand in man hours exceeds total capacity, work will have to be sub-contracted. For example, unless work is sub-contracted insufficient sub-assembly II's will be available in May.

8.7.

Order number	Number of products	A		B		C	
		I	Hours	I	Hours	I	Hours
1	50	0·33		0·67		0	150
2	70	0·5		0	150	1·0	
3	25	0·67		0·33	100	0	
4	80	0	160	1·5		1·0	
			175 (91%)		275 (91%)		160 (94%)

8.9.

$$\text{Minimize } C = \; 2(4Q_{1A}+3Q_{2A}+5Q_{3A}+2Q_{4A})$$
$$+3(5Q_{1B}+2Q_{2B}+4Q_{3B}+5Q_{4B})$$
$$+2{\cdot}5(3Q_{1C}+4Q_{2C}+3Q_{3C}+4Q_{4C})$$

Subject to the following constraints:

$$Q_{1A}+Q_{1B}+Q_{1C}=50$$
$$Q_{2A}+Q_{2B}+Q_{2C}=75$$
$$Q_{3A}+Q_{3B}+Q_{3C}=25$$
$$Q_{4B}+Q_{4C}=80$$
$$Q_{ij}\geqslant 0 \quad \text{where } i=1,2,3,4$$
$$j=A,B,C$$

where Q_{ij} = Quantity of order i
allocated to machine j

8.11. (a) 67 per cent
(b) 2 machines
(c) i The probability of a machine requiring service by the operator is independent of the time it has been running hitherto.
ii All service times are constant.
iii There is no priority system for servicing machines
iv All machines have similar operational characteristics

Chapter 9
9.1.

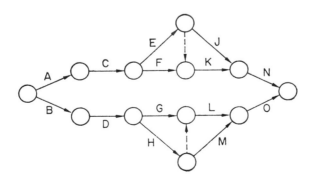

9.3.

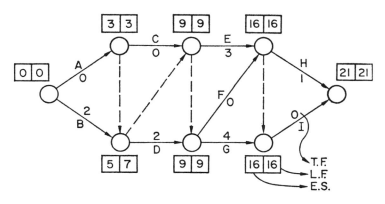

Critical path = A, C, F, I

9.5.　　　　　　　　　　Critical path = A, B, F, H
　　　　　　　　　　for which t = 28
　　　　　　　　　　　　σ^2 = 6·8
　　　　　　　　　　from tables p = 2 per cent

i.e. Considering critical path only, probability of finishing on or before 22·5 days = 2 per cent
but Minimum duration for path

　　　　　　A, C, D, G　　　= 2+9+6+7
　　　　　　　　　　　　= 24
　　∴Actual probability = 0

9.7. (a)

	TF		TF
0–1	0	5–8	7
1–2	0	5–9	0
1–3	1	6–10	3
2–4	0	7–10	8
3–5	1	8–10	3
4–5	0	9–10	0
4–6	3	10–11	0
5–7	9		

Critical path = 0, 1, 2, 4, 5, 9, 10, 11

(b)　(i) Delay project by 5 days.

　　(ii) The new critical path is 6, 10, 11 since these are the only activities whose delay will delay the project.

　　(iii) Day 5.

9.11. (a) 31 days

(b)

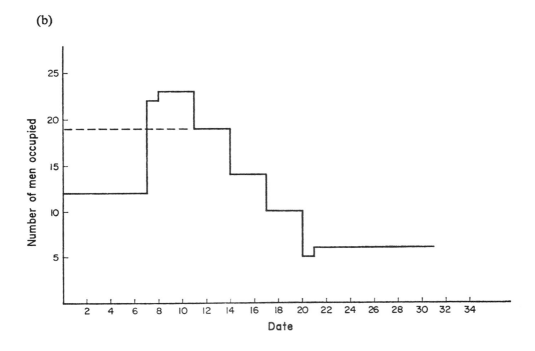

(c)

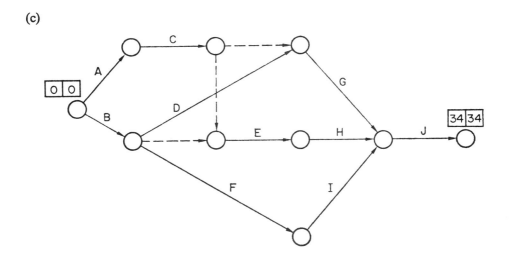

(d) 3 days

9.13.

(a) Earliest completion = 27 days
   Critical path   = A, B, E, H, J
   Total float: A = 0   G = 4
                      B = 0   H = 0
                      C = 5   I = 4
                      D = 4   J = 0
                      E = 0   K = 8
                      F = 4

(b)

Days	Manpower required
0–2	4
2–5	9
5–6	3
6–9	16
9–11	15
11–12	16
12–15	17
15–19	18
19–27	7

Chapter 10

10.1.
$$n_{min} = 28$$
$$C = 0.4 \text{ minutes}$$

10.3. Cycle time = 20 minutes

Station	Work elements	Station time
1	0, 1, 2, 4,	20 min
2	3, 5, 7, 8	20 min
3	6, 9, 10, 11	20 min

Balancing loss = zero

10.5.

	Station					
	1	2	3	4	5	6
4·61 per hour $C = 13$ minutes	0, 1, 2,	3, 4	5, 6	7	8, 10	9
Balancing loss = 25·7 per cent						
5 per hour $C = 12$ minutes						
Balancing loss = 19·6 per cent	0, 1, 2	3, 4	5, 6,	7	8, 10	9

10.7. (a) 1   (b) 2

10.11 A, E, D, B, C

£320

10.13. Using the method described at the end of the chapter:

Fixed launching interval $\gamma = 0\cdot47$ minutes
Models must be launched in cycles as follows: A C A BA CC A CC

In other words proportions of each model produced are as follows:

$$A = 0\cdot40$$
$$B = 0\cdot10$$
$$C = 0\cdot50$$
$$D = 0\cdot00$$

Except in special circumstances this method will not provide a complete solution to the problem.

10.15. Cost of present arrangement $\quad= £324$
Cost of alternative 1 (mixed-model) $= £224$
Cost of alternative 2 (multi-model) $= £270$
Use alternative 1

Chapter 11

11.3. 21 000 gal. (equivalent)

11.5. 14 100—31 200 gal. (equivalent)

11.7. (a) $1\cdot2$ months
(b) $1\cdot22$ months
(c) $1\cdot26$ months

11.9. $Q_E = 4\,670$
$Q_V = 6\,670$
$Q_G = 10\,000$
$Q_M = 3\,330$
$N = 1\cdot5$

Chapter 12

12.3. (a) 2 620
(b) 2 620
(c) 2 500

12.5. (a) £2 550
(b) £2 400
(c) £2 850
$Q = 10\,000$
$C = £34\,300$

12.9. (a) Startrite $\quad= \quad890$
Quickfire $\quad= 1\,246$
Longlife $\quad= \quad622$
Highpower $= \quad490$

(b) $2\cdot14$ months

12.11. (a) Q^* $\quad\quad\quad = 862$
$\quad\quad$ Re-order level $\quad = 21$ items

$\quad$ (b) Re-order level $\quad = 21$

12.13. $\quad$ Re-order level $\quad = 24$ items
$\quad\quad$ Re-order quantity $= 300$ items

Chapter 13

13.1.

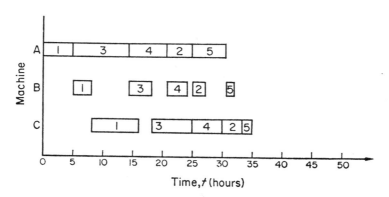

Time, t (hours)

13.3. (a) Sequence $= 3, 6, 2, 4, 7, 1, 5$
$\quad\quad\quad$ or $3, 6, 2, 7, 4, 1, 5$

$\quad$ (b) Sequence X $= 3, 2, 5, 6, 1$
$\quad\quad\quad\quad\quad$ Y $= 4, 3, 2, 5, 6$

$\quad$ (c) Several sequences give $T = 21$
$\quad\quad$ e.g. 3, 1, 4, 2; 2, 3, 4, 1; 1, 3, 2, 4; 2, 1, 3, 4; 3, 2, 4, 1; 2, 3, 4, 1.

$\quad\quad$ (obtained empirically since the special case of Johnson's rule does *not* apply).

13.5. (a)

Priority Rule

Job	1	2	3	4	5	6	7	8	9
1	4	4	4	3	7	4	3	7	1
2	1	1	1	5	3	1	1	4	10
3	5	4	8	3	7	5	3	9	2
4	2	1	2	9	2	2	2	6	4
5	3	3	3	1	9	3	6	3	9
6	10	8	9	5	3	10	8	7	3
7	8	7	10	1	9	8	3	10	5
8	5	6	4	10	1	5	9	2	8
9	5	8	7	5	3	5	7	4	6
10	8	10	6	5	3	8	10	1	7

(b)

Priority Rule ($+$ FCFS)

Job	1	2	3	4	5	6	7	8	9
1	4	4	4	3	7	4	3	7	1
2	1	2	1	8	6	1	1	4	10
3	5	5	8	4	8	5	4	9	2
4	2	1	2	9	2	2	2	6	4
5	3	3	3	2	10	3	6	3	9
6	10	8	9	5	3	10	8	8	3
7	8	7	10	1	9	8	5	10	5
8	7	6	5	10	1	7	9	2	8
9	6	9	7	6	4	6	7	5	6
10	9	10	6	7	5	9	10	1	7

Chapter 14

14.1.

(c) 0·56

14.3.

$C = 14$
$n = 317$

14.5.

(a) Approximately 0·82
(c) $n = 89$
    $c = 4$

14.7.

(a) 1. $\alpha = 26$ per cent   2. $\alpha = 32$ per cent
(b) 1. $\beta = 30$ per cent   2. $\beta = 14$ per cent

(i) Plan 1.
(ii) Plan 2.

Average outgoing quality limit:

Plan 1 = 1·65 approximately
Plan 2 = 1·25 approximately

14.9.

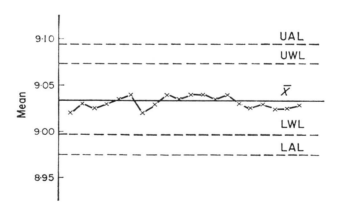

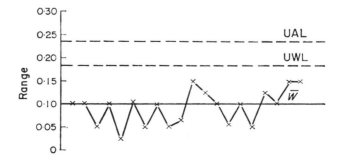

14.11.

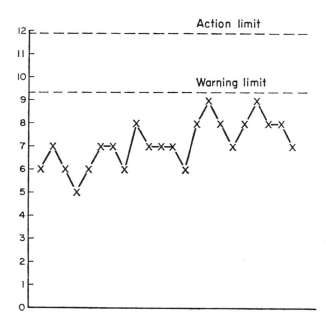

14.13.

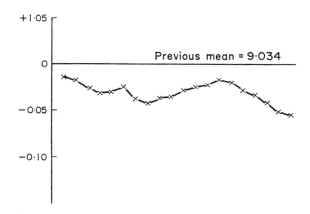

Chapter 15

15.3. (a) £2·20/hour

    (b) 1. 280 hours
       2. 157 hours

15.5. (a) 1. 6
       2. 3·5

    (b) 1. Group C
       2. Group A

15.7. (a) 47 hours
(b) 29 hours

15.9. (a) Replace original machine
(b) £18

Appendix I

I.1.
$$x = 4$$
$$y = 5$$
$$z = 10$$
$$\text{Min. } W = -11$$

I.3.
Constraints:
$$2G + Q \qquad + p = 3\,000$$
$$2G + 3Q + 4R + q = 6\,000$$
$$G + Q + R + r = 10\,000$$
$$\text{Max } W = G + 3/2Q + 2R$$

Solution
$$R = 1\,500$$
Profit $W = 3\,000$ p

I.5.

	X	Y	Z
A			20
B	15		
C	10	5	15

Minimum transportation cost = £465

I.6.

	Standard	De luxe	Super	Super deluxe
A	25			
B		15	10	
C				5

Profit = £633

I.7.

	A	B	C	D	E
1			1		
2	1				
3				1	
4		1			
5					1

Minimum cost = 14

Appendix II

II.1.

Period	Actual sales	Forecast (a)	Error	Forecast (b)	Error
1	20				
2	18				
3	17				
4	21	18·3	−2·7	17	−4·0
5	22	19·0	−3·0	21	−1·0
6	21	19·6	−1·4	22	+1·0
7	20	19·8	−0·2	21	+1·0
8	18	19·9	+1·9	20	+2·0
9	19	19·6	+0·6	18	−1·0
10	21	19·6	−1·4	19	−2·0
11	24	19·7	−4·3	21	−3·0
12	28	20·0	−8·0	24	−4·0
13	34	20·7	−13·3	28	−6·0
14	36	21·7	−14·3	34	−2·0
15	35	22·8	−13·2	36	+1·0
16	30	23·6	−6·4	35	+5·0
17	28	24·0	−4·0	30	+2·0
18	26	24·3	−1·7	28	+2·0
19	30	24·4	−5·6	26	−4·0
20	31	24·6	−6·4	30	−1·0
		25·0		31	

	Error	Error
Average error (neglecting sign) periods 4–20	5·20	2·47
Average error (neglecting sign) periods 4–10	1·6	1·71
Average error (neglecting sign) periods 11–20	7·72	3·00

II.3.
(a)

Year	Period	Sales ('000)	4 Period moving average	Seasonally adjusted 4 period moving average
1966	1	50		
	2	60		
	3	50		
	4	44		
1967	1	50	51·0	48·5
	2	64	51·0	60·8
	3	56	52·0	51·0
	4	50	53·5	47·0
1968	1	54	55·0	52·5
	2	70	56·0	66·7
	3	56	57·5	56·2
	4	50	57·5	50·8
1969	1	54	57·5	54·7
	2	66	57·5	68·2
	3	52	56·5	55·3
	4	50	55·5	49·0
			55·5	52·8

(b)

Period	1966 (Mean 51)	1967 (Mean 55)	1968 (Mean 57·5)	1969 (Mean 55·5)	Average percentage variation
1	98	91	94	97·5	95
2	118	116·5	122	119	119
3	98	102	97·5	94	98
4	86·5	91	87	90	88
				Total	400%

II.5.

Period no.	Actual	5 period moving average	Error	Exponential smoothing $\alpha = 0.33$	Error
1	10				
2	12				
3	12				
4	10				
5	8				
6	10	10·4	+0·4	10·4	+0·4
7	13	10·4	−2·6	10·3	−2·7
8	12	10·6	−1·4	11·2	−0·8
9	9	10·6	+1·6	11·4	+2·4
10	8	10·4	+2·4	10·7	+2·7
11	10	10·4	+0·4	9·8	+0·2
12	13	10·4	−2·6	9·9	−3·1
13	14	10·4	−3·6	10·9	−3·1
14	12	10·6	−1·4	11·9	−0·1
15	9	11·4	+2·4	12·0	+3·0
16	10	11·6	+1·6	11·0	+1·0
17	13	11·6	−1·4	10·8	−2·2
18	14	11·6	−2·4	11·5	−2·5
19	11	11·6	+0·6	12·3	+1·3
20	10	11·4	+1·4	11·9	+1·9
		11·6		11·3	
Average error (neglecting sign)			1·75		1·83

II.7.

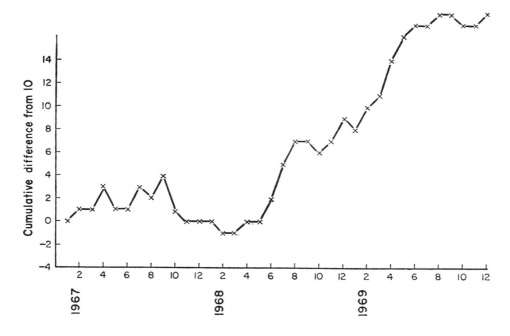

II.9.

(a) $r = 1 \cdot 0$

(b) $r = 0 \cdot 97$

II.11.

(a) $y = -1\,330 + 0 \cdot 757x$
    where Y = consumption
          X = GNP

(b) 20 670

Name Index

Subject Index

f indicates footnote reference